D1301150

Windows® 2000
Professional Bible

Windows® 2000 Professional Bible

**Michael Desmond with Michael Meadhra,
Blair Rampling, and Bob Correll**

IDG Books Worldwide, Inc.
An International Data Group Company

Foster City, CA ✦ Chicago, IL ✦ Indianapolis, IN ✦ New York, NY

Windows® 2000 Professional Bible

Published by
IDG Books Worldwide, Inc.
An International Data Group Company
919 E. Hillsdale Blvd., Suite 400
Foster City, CA 94404
www.idgbooks.com (IDG Books Worldwide Web site)

Copyright © 2000 IDG Books Worldwide, Inc. All rights reserved. No part of this book, including interior design, cover design, and icons, may be reproduced or transmitted in any form, by any means (electronic, photocopying, recording, or otherwise) without the prior written permission of the publisher.

ISBN: 0-7645-3424-6

Printed in the United States of America

10 9 8 7 6 5 4 3 2 1

1B/SY/QR/QQ/FC

Distributed in the United States by IDG Books Worldwide, Inc.

Distributed by CDG Books Canada Inc. for Canada; by Transworld Publishers Limited in the United Kingdom; by IDG Norge Books for Norway; by IDG Sweden Books for Sweden; by IDG Books Australia Publishing Corporation Pty. Ltd. for Australia and New Zealand; by TransQuest Publishers Pte Ltd. for Singapore, Malaysia, Thailand, Indonesia, and Hong Kong; by Gotop Information Inc. for Taiwan; by ICG Muse, Inc. for Japan; by Intersoft for South Africa; by Eyrolles for France; by International Thomson Publishing for Germany, Austria and Switzerland; by Distribuidora Cuspide for Argentina; by LR International for Brazil; by Galileo Libros for Chile; by Ediciones ZETA S.C.R. Ltda. for Peru; by WS Computer Publishing Corporation, Inc., for the Philippines; by Contemporanea de Ediciones for Venezuela; by Express Computer Distributors for the Caribbean and West Indies; by Micronesia Media Distributor, Inc. for Micronesia; by Chips Computadoras S.A. de C.V. for Mexico; by Editorial Norma de Panama S.A. for Panama; by American Bookshops for Finland.

For general information on IDG Books Worldwide's books in the U.S., please call our Consumer Customer Service department at 800-762-2974. For reseller information, including discounts and premium sales, please call our Reseller Customer Service department at 800-434-3422.

For information on where to purchase IDG Books Worldwide's books outside the U.S., please contact our International Sales department at 317-596-5530 or fax 317-596-5692.

For consumer information on foreign language translations, please contact our Customer Service department at 800-434-3422, fax 317-596-5692, or e-mail rights@idgbooks.com.

For information on licensing foreign or domestic rights, please phone +1-650-655-3109.

For sales inquiries and special prices for bulk quantities, please contact our Sales department at 650-655-3200 or write to the address above.

For information on using IDG Books Worldwide's books in the classroom or for ordering examination copies, please contact our Educational Sales department at 800-434-2086 or fax 317-596-5499.

For press review copies, author interviews, or other publicity information, please contact our Public Relations department at 650-655-3000 or fax 650-655-3299.

For authorization to photocopy items for corporate, personal, or educational use, please contact Copyright Clearance Center, 222 Rosewood Drive, Danvers, MA 01923, or fax 978-750-4470.

Library of Congress Cataloging-in-Publication Data

Windows 2000 professional bible Michael Desmond ... [et al.]

     p. cm.

  ISBN 0-7645-3424-6 (alk. paper)

   1. Microsoft Windows (Computer file)
2. Operating systems (Computers) I. Desmond, Michael.

QA76.76.O63 W56466 1999

005.4'4769–dc21

99-046678

LIMIT OF LIABILITY/DISCLAIMER OF WARRANTY: THE PUBLISHER AND AUTHOR HAVE USED THEIR BEST EFFORTS IN PREPARING THIS BOOK. THE PUBLISHER AND AUTHOR MAKE NO REPRESENTATIONS OR WARRANTIES WITH RESPECT TO THE ACCURACY OR COMPLETENESS OF THE CONTENTS OF THIS BOOK AND SPECIFICALLY DISCLAIM ANY IMPLIED WARRANTIES OF MERCHANTABILITY OR FITNESS FOR A PARTICULAR PURPOSE. THERE ARE NO WARRANTIES WHICH EXTEND BEYOND THE DESCRIPTIONS CONTAINED IN THIS PARAGRAPH. NO WARRANTY MAY BE CREATED OR EXTENDED BY SALES REPRESENTATIVES OR WRITTEN SALES MATERIALS. THE ACCURACY AND COMPLETENESS OF THE INFORMATION PROVIDED HEREIN AND THE OPINIONS STATED HEREIN ARE NOT GUARANTEED OR WARRANTED TO PRODUCE ANY PARTICULAR RESULTS, AND THE ADVICE AND STRATEGIES CONTAINED HEREIN MAY NOT BE SUITABLE FOR EVERY INDIVIDUAL. NEITHER THE PUBLISHER NOR AUTHOR SHALL BE LIABLE FOR ANY LOSS OF PROFIT OR ANY OTHER COMMERCIAL DAMAGES, INCLUDING BUT NOT LIMITED TO SPECIAL, INCIDENTAL, CONSEQUENTIAL, OR OTHER DAMAGES.

Trademarks: All brand names and product names used in this book are trade names, service marks, trademarks, or registered trademarks of their respective owners. IDG Books Worldwide is not associated with any product or vendor mentioned in this book.

is a registered trademark or trademark under exclusive license to IDG Books Worldwide, Inc. from International Data Group, Inc. in the United States and/or other countries.

ABOUT IDG BOOKS WORLDWIDE

Welcome to the world of IDG Books Worldwide.

IDG Books Worldwide, Inc., is a subsidiary of International Data Group, the world's largest publisher of computer-related information and the leading global provider of information services on information technology. IDG was founded more than 30 years ago by Patrick J. McGovern and now employs more than 9,000 people worldwide. IDG publishes more than 290 computer publications in over 75 countries. More than 90 million people read one or more IDG publications each month.

Launched in 1990, IDG Books Worldwide is today the #1 publisher of best-selling computer books in the United States. We are proud to have received eight awards from the Computer Press Association in recognition of editorial excellence and three from Computer Currents' First Annual Readers' Choice Awards. Our best-selling ...For Dummies® series has more than 50 million copies in print with translations in 31 languages. IDG Books Worldwide, through a joint venture with IDG's Hi-Tech Beijing, became the first U.S. publisher to publish a computer book in the People's Republic of China. In record time, IDG Books Worldwide has become the first choice for millions of readers around the world who want to learn how to better manage their businesses.

Our mission is simple: Every one of our books is designed to bring extra value and skill-building instructions to the reader. Our books are written by experts who understand and care about our readers. The knowledge base of our editorial staff comes from years of experience in publishing, education, and journalism — experience we use to produce books to carry us into the new millennium. In short, we care about books, so we attract the best people. We devote special attention to details such as audience, interior design, use of icons, and illustrations. And because we use an efficient process of authoring, editing, and desktop publishing our books electronically, we can spend more time ensuring superior content and less time on the technicalities of making books.

You can count on our commitment to deliver high-quality books at competitive prices on topics you want to read about. At IDG Books Worldwide, we continue in the IDG tradition of delivering quality for more than 30 years. You'll find no better book on a subject than one from IDG Books Worldwide.

IDG BOOKS WORLDWIDE

John Kilcullen
Chairman and CEO
IDG Books Worldwide, Inc.

Steven Berkowitz
President and Publisher
IDG Books Worldwide, Inc.

Eighth Annual Computer Press Awards ≥1992

Ninth Annual Computer Press Awards ≥1993

Tenth Annual Computer Press Awards ≥1994

Eleventh Annual Computer Press Awards ≥1995

IDG is the world's leading IT media, research and exposition company. Founded in 1964, IDG had 1997 revenues of $2.05 billion and has more than 9,000 employees worldwide. IDG offers the widest range of media options that reach IT buyers in 75 countries representing 95% of worldwide IT spending. IDG's diverse product and services portfolio spans six key areas including print publishing, online publishing, expositions and conferences, market research, education and training, and global marketing services. More than 90 million people read one or more of IDG's 290 magazines and newspapers, including IDG's leading global brands — Computerworld, PC World, Network World, Macworld and the Channel World family of publications. IDG Books Worldwide is one of the fastest-growing computer book publishers in the world, with more than 700 titles in 36 languages. The "...For Dummies®" series alone has more than 50 million copies in print. IDG offers online users the largest network of technology-specific Web sites around the world through IDG.net (http://www.idg.net), which comprises more than 225 targeted Web sites in 55 countries worldwide. International Data Corporation (IDC) is the world's largest provider of information technology data, analysis and consulting, with research centers in over 41 countries and more than 400 research analysts worldwide. IDG World Expo is a leading producer of more than 168 globally branded conferences and expositions in 35 countries including E3 (Electronic Entertainment Expo), Macworld Expo, ComNet, Windows World Expo, ICE (Internet Commerce Expo), Agenda, DEMO, and Spotlight. IDG's training subsidiary, ExecuTrain, is the world's largest computer training company, with more than 230 locations worldwide and 785 training courses. IDG Marketing Services helps industry-leading IT companies build international brand recognition by developing global integrated marketing programs via IDG's print, online and exposition products worldwide. Further information about the company can be found at www.idg.com.   1/24/99

Credits

Acquisitions Editor
David Mayhew

Development Editors
Kathleen McFadden
Paul Winters

Technical Editors
Dung Le, CCNP, CCSI, CNE, MCSE, MCT
Don Murdoch, MCSE, MCT

Copy Editors
Nancy Crumpton
Ami Knox

Book Designer
Drew R. Moore

Illustrator
Donna Reynolds

Production Coordinator
Linda Marousek

Quality Control Specialist
Chris Weisbart

Graphics and Page Layout Specialists
Mario Amador
Stephanie Hollier
Jude Levinson
Ramses Ramirez
Dina F Quan

Proofreading and Indexing
York Production Services

Cover Design
Peter Kowaleszyn
Murder By Design/Image Poetry

About the Authors

Michael Desmond is an award-winning computer industry journalist, author, and editorial consultant. He is the author of *Peter Norton's Complete Guide to PC Upgrades, 2nd Edition*, coauthor of *Platinum Edition: Using Windows 95*, and a contributor to numerous other computing books. Previously senior editor of news at *PC World* magazine and president of the Computer Press Association, Michael now runs an editorial consulting business for high-tech companies and publishers. His Web site can be found at `http://www.MichaelDesmond.com`. Michael is also an adjunct professor of journalist at St. Michael's College.

Michael earned an M.S. in Journalism from Northwestern University's Medill School of Journalism, and a B.A. in Soviet Studies from Middlebury College in Vermont. A native of Cleveland, Ohio, Michael now lives in Burlington, Vermont, with his wife Anne and sons Kevin and Patrick.

Michael Meadhra is an author and consultant who writes about a variety of computer-related topics. After several years experience in the corporate world, he began writing monthly software journals and now writes books such as this one. To date, he has coauthored or contributed to more than 30 titles on topics such as DOS, Windows, various application programs, the Internet, and online banking. Meadhra's other recent books include *Lotus SmartSuite Millennium Edition For Dummies*, *Banking Online For Dummies*, and *StarOffice For Linux For Dummies*, all published by IDG Books Worldwide.

Blair Rampling is an information technology consultant from Delta, British Columbia. He specializes in bringing large, unruly networks into neat running order. Optimizing servers and reducing administrative overhead are his main focii, along with Microsoft Exchange administration. In the off hours, he enjoys mountain biking in the incredible trails around Southern BC and building cars for drag racing.

Bob Correll received a B.S. in History at the United States Air Force Academy. He served as an Intelligence Officer in the US Air Force for seven and a half years, working in several disciplines. After leaving the Air Force he was hired by Macmillan Computer Publishing as a Software Specialist and after a year was promoted to Development Editor. He left Macmillan to work for a school corporation in Indiana and was responsible for training and professional development. He is now pursuing a full-time writing and technical editing career.

For my sons, Kevin and Patrick.
—Michael Desmond

To Corrine
—Blair Rampling

To Anne, with hugs and kisses!
—Bob Correll

Acknowledgments

A lot of talented people put a lot of hard work into *Windows 2000 Professional Bible*. I'd like to thank fellow authors Bob Correll, Michael Meadhra, and Blair Rampling for their stellar contributions, as well as network maven Jim Desmond for his help with the chapters on installing and troubleshooting Windows 2000 Professional. I'd also like to thank acquisitions editor David Mayhew, who so quickly assembled a fine team for the project, and development editor Kathleen McFadden, who poured through all those rocky first drafts and helped make sure everything fit together.

The list of key contributors goes on and on. Nancy Crumpton gets a nod for churning through all those chapter edits, while technical editors Dung Le and Don Murdoch deserves praise for keeping the entire team of authors and editors honest. Finally, I want to single out Paul Winters at IDG Books, who personally got out and helped push this project over the hump when deadlines loomed.

I also got plenty of assistance from outside IDG Books. Both Microsoft and its talented PR team at Waggner-Edstrom played a big role, responding to our furious last-minute inquiries and ensuring that we were always working with the latest versions of their software. I'd also like to thank the folks at Leadtek, the graphics board vendor, for their help in our coverage of the multimedia and display capabilities of Windows 2000.

Of course, no book project can go by without a note of thanks to my agent, David Fugate at Waterside Productions, who keeps roping me into these massive undertakings. Thanks Dave — another summer has been lost because of you!

Last, but most certainly not least, I want to thank my wife Anne for all her help, patience, and understanding. She covered the kids for countless weekends and put up with my ridiculously long work hours as I raced to finish this book. Without her, *Windows 2000 Professional Bible* would not have seen the light of day.

— Michael Desmond

Thanks to David Fugate for initiating my involvement with this project, and Michael Desmond for allowing me the opportunity to help. I would also like to thank David Mayhew for his coordination of the project from the beginning. Without the assistance of Kathleen McFadden and Don Murdoch and their technical edits, I would never have brought my part of the project to the point it is today. Thanks also to Paul Winters for bringing everything together to create the finished product. Final thanks go to Corrine for her support throughout my ups and downs while working on the project.

—Blair Rampling

First and foremost I would like to thank God who I have come to know much more as my Provider the last few years. Special thanks go to Anne who is my wife, companion, and friend. Thank you for putting up with me, supporting me, helping me with the mail (inside joke), and sharing my excitement and faith that this is the right thing to do. I also want to thank both our families for their encouragement and support.

I would like to thank fellow author and friend Molly E. Holzschlag who encouraged me as I took this leap and introduced me to David Fugate at Waterside Productions. Thank you David for giving me this opportunity! I am truly appreciative of being able to work with an author of the caliber of Michael Desmond, the lead author on this project, and want to thank him for letting me take a larger role as time went on.

Finally, I want to express my warm thanks and appreciation to David Mayhew at IDG for our friendship and now this new relationship between author and Acquisitions Editor. Thanks also to Kathleen McFadden and Paul Winters for their work developing this book and many thanks to the entire team at IDG.

—Bob Correll

Contents at a Glance

Contents

Get to Know Windows 2000

Welcome to Windows 2000

Windows 2000 Professional is perhaps the most complete, versatile, and powerful operating system (OS) ever to visit the desktop. Built atop the solid foundation of Windows NT and graced with the advanced interface technologies of Windows 98, Windows 2000 offers a truly stunning blend of stability, security, ease of use, and compatibility.

Am I overstating the point? After all, what Microsoft desktop operating system has delivered on the expectations built up for it in the market? Windows 3.0, while popular, was a mess, and the first inglorious releases of Windows NT were difficult to use and entirely too resource hungry. Even Windows 95 and Windows 98, for all their market dominance, lack the day-to-day stability to serve as the rock upon which ubiquitous, always-on computing can be established.

Which leads to Windows 2000. Here is an operating system that combines two visions of computing on the desktop. Built into the new operating system is the consumer mandate of Windows 98 — easy to use and highly compatible — and the hard-edged technical demand of Windows NT — always on, always secure, all the time. The result is a truly compelling mix of features and capabilities that make Windows 2000 appropriate for an impressively broad audience.

Who Should Read This Book?

The *Windows 2000 Professional Bible* is a comprehensive guide and reference to Microsoft's latest desktop operating system. The book appeals to a wide range of audiences, covering basic topics such as navigation and file management, and advanced issues such as networking and scripting. Whether you are brand new to the Windows family of operating systems or have been using different versions of Windows for years, the *Windows 2000 Professional Bible* will appeal to you.

So who should read this book? Here's a short list:

✦ Business and consumer users upgrading from earlier versions of Windows

✦ Business owners and managers who need to understand the capabilities of their systems and how to manage issues with the new operating system

✦ Windows newcomers, such as those transitioning from the Macintosh, Unix, Linux, or other operating systems

✦ Beginners with at least some introduction to computing concepts

✦ IT managers and network administrators who must troubleshoot or manage individual client PCs, including their own

The question, then, is who shouldn't read this book? Rank novices — those who wouldn't know Windows from a walnut — may want to get up to speed before diving into this tome. And IT managers who need to deploy Active Directory in the enterprise won't find in-depth discussions of that here. Windows 2000 Professional is a desktop operating system, and the *Windows 2000 Professional Bible* focuses on activities and features that address desktop users.

The Windows 2000 Family

It's worth noting right up front that this is a book about Windows 2000 Professional, the desktop-oriented flavor of Windows 2000. Microsoft is launching no fewer than four different Windows 2000 versions, each tailored to a separate market segment, so you should make sure that the Professional version is the one that applies to you. The quick take on the Windows 2000 flavors looks like this:

✦ **Windows 2000 Professional:** Desktop consumer and business users, developers, workstations, and mobile systems

✦ **Windows 2000 Server:** Departmental file and print servers, intranet servers, limited Web hosting

✦ **Windows 2000 Advanced Server:** Web hosting, large departmental servers

✦ **Windows 2000 Data Center:** Enterprise-class applications servers, online transaction processing, heavy-duty backend database servers, and Web hosting

Windows 2000 Professional may be the little guy on this block, but that doesn't mean it's a lightweight operating system. On the contrary, users find that Windows 2000 Professional is an impressively robust, stable, and scalable operating system. It can handle everything from business and consumer desktop high-end workstations to low-end servers. It even runs well on notebook systems, provided you've got a model that can meet Windows 2000's demanding resource requirements.

The Many Faces of Microsoft Windows

Unless you spend your days specifically following the PC software market, the proliferation of Windows versions probably has you confused. Over the years, Microsoft has broadened its Windows franchise, addressing everything from entry-level home PCs to high-end, multiprocessing servers.

A quick look at the list of Windows versions currently either on store shelves or actively in use makes the point:

✦ Windows 3.11

✦ Windows 95

✦ Windows 98 and Windows 98 Second Edition

✦ Windows NT 4.0 Workstation

✦ Windows NT 4.0 Server

✦ Windows NT 4.0 Enterprise Server

✦ Windows 2000 Professional

✦ Windows 2000 Server

✦ Windows 2000 Advanced Server

✦ Windows 2000 Data Center Server

✦ Windows CE 2.2

I think you get the idea. I just have to wonder if this is what Bill Gates was trying to achieve with his "Windows Everywhere" slogan. One thing is certain: With so many versions flying around, it can be difficult to make sense of where Windows 2000 came from. After all, it didn't spring up from the ground code complete and ready to run.

The simple answer is that Windows 2000 is the direct successor to Windows NT 4.0. The operating system was actually known as NT 5.0 until mid-1998, when Microsoft elected to change the product name.

Table 1-1 should help clear up matters.

Table 1-1
Windows 2000 Product Evolution

Old	New	Released
Windows NT 4.0 Workstation	Windows 2000 Professional	Fall 1999/ Winter 2000
Windows NT 4.0 Server	Windows 2000 Server	Fall 1999/ Winter 2000
Windows NT 4.0 Enterprise Server	Windows 2000 Advanced Server	Fall 1999/ Winter 2000
Windows NT 4.0 Enterprise Server	Windows 2000 Data Center Server	Spring/ Summer 2000
Windows 95/98	Windows 2000 Consumer	Spring 2001

Notice that Windows 2000 Consumer — the follow-up to Windows 98 — isn't scheduled to ship until 2001. What's the hold-up? Well, Windows 98 uses an entirely different code base from Windows NT. Microsoft had high hopes of merging Windows 98 into the Windows NT/2000 product family in line with the other versions, but these plans failed to pan out. The result is that Windows 98 lives on today as Windows 98 Second Edition and will continue to soldier on at least until 2001, according to Microsoft's latest statements.

For the time being, then, Windows 2000 Professional is the preeminent version of this advanced operating system family for single-user desktops. And while Microsoft markets Windows 2000 Professional primarily to businesses, the OS includes a lot of powerful ease-of-use features that make it an outstanding consumer computing platform as well. In fact, in many ways, Windows 2000 Professional is easier to use than Windows 98, thanks to some smart user interface (UI) tweaks.

Windows 2000 is a new entry on the market, so it will often be running alongside PCs running more established operating systems. Even home users are more likely than not to have a second PC in the home. So you may be wondering how Windows 2000 Professional stacks up. Table 1-2 gives you a quick rundown of the various flavors of Windows, as well as my take on the type of system you need to make them run.

Before delving into Windows 2000 Professional, it might be useful to take a stroll around the Windows neighborhood.

Table 1-2
Comparison of Key Features

Feature	Windows 2000 Professional	Windows 98 Second Edition	Windows 2000 Server	Windows 2000 Advanced Server	Windows 2000 Data Center Server
Number of processors	2	1	4	8	32
Type of system	Home or business PC	Home PC	Small server	Departmental server	Enterprise-class server
Code base	NT	Win9x	NT	NT	NT
Recommended system requirements	300-MHz CPU, 64MB RAM, 4GB hard disk	166-MHz CPU, 32MB RAM, 2GB hard disk	Single or dual 400-MHz CPU, 128MB RAM, 13GB hard disk	4-way or 8-way 500-MHz CPU, 1GB RAM, 13GB hard disk	Up to 32-way 500-MHz CPU, 16GB RAM, RAID disk array

Windows 98

Microsoft's consumer-oriented operating system is also its best-selling OS. Home users have flocked to Windows 98, thanks to its broad compatibility and useful features such as Plug-and-Play hardware detection and a simplified interface. Windows 98 is also the least expensive and least resource-intensive desktop OS from Microsoft, furthering its appeal.

Most users may think of Windows 98 as the first popular 32-bit operating system, but in fact, its core code consists of a hybrid of 16-bit DOS and 32-bit Windows code. The 16-bit code helped Microsoft establish compatibility with older software and hardware but also made Windows 98 vulnerable to system crashes. Misbehaving applications and drivers can destabilize the entire operating system, something that the rigorous memory and resource protection schemes of Windows 2000 and NT simply avoid.

Of course, the hallmark of Windows 98 (and its predecessor, Windows 95) was ease of use. From the intuitive Start button to the incorporation of Plug-and-Play technology, Windows 9x has made it easier than ever to use and maintain a PC. The latest of version of Windows 98 — dubbed Windows 98 Second Edition — continues to advance this trend. Microsoft has extended device support, added a few welcome feature tweaks (such as shared Internet access for home networks), and fixed a slew of bugs.

So who should run Windows 98? Well, economics plays a role here. Windows 98 typically costs about $89 on the street, while Windows 2000 Professional sets you back a bit more. Windows 98 also appeals to those with less than cutting-edge hardware. Anyone running a Pentium MMX-based system should stick with the Windows 98 franchise. Windows 98 also runs acceptably in a system with 32MB of RAM. Windows 2000 needs 64MB to run smoothly and 128MB to really run wild.

Compatibility is the other driving factor. If you use your PC to play a lot of games and multimedia titles — particularly older software — Windows 98 is your ticket. Yes, Windows 2000 incorporates Microsoft's DirectX multimedia technologies, and yes, it can run a lot of (particularly newer) games. But not every 3D graphics card, sound card, and joystick has Windows 2000 drivers available. And older titles may not run at all. Figure 1-1 shows the kinds of advanced graphics that Windows 98-based games can provide.

Figure 1-1: Want to play rip-roaring games such as Falcon 4.0? Windows 2000 Professional may be able to handle them, but Windows 98 remains your best bet.

It's worth noting, however, that Windows 98 is no longer Microsoft's most intuitive OS. Windows 2000 Professional has actually leapfrogged Windows 98 in terms of features and ease of use. If price, compatibility, and system resources are not obstacles, even home PC users should consider Windows 2000 Professional.

Windows 2000 Professional

The old adage goes: If it looks like a duck, walks like a duck, and quacks like a duck, it must be a duck. Well, Windows 2000 Professional may look and act a lot like Windows 98, but if Windows 98 is a duck, Windows 2000 is an armored tank masquerading as a duck—all hard steel and armor plating beneath an easy-on-the-eyes interface and intelligent features.

Touted by Microsoft as the operating system for business desktop and mobile PCs, Windows 2000 Professional is the direct descendant of Windows NT 4.0 Workstation. But the improvement over NT 4.0 is, quite honestly, almost shocking. Windows 2000 Professional includes a slew of important improvements that make it faster, more reliable, and easier to use than NT.

For example, users of Windows 98 and Internet Explorer 4.0 immediately recognize user interface tweaks such as Webified folders and icons, taskbar mini-icons, and the Web-centric Active Desktop. Figure 1-2 shows a typical Windows 2000 Professional desktop. More important, Windows 2000 embraces technologies long absent from NT, such as Plug and Play and support for such device types as USB, DVD, and IEEE 1394.

Figure 1-2: Look familiar? At first glance, there's almost no way to tell Windows 2000 Professional from Windows 98.

Alphabet Soup

Confused by terms like USB and IEEE 1394? You're not alone. The PC industry is awash in three- and four-letter acronyms that frequently change. USB, for example, stands for Universal Serial Bus, and is a technology that allows external devices like video cameras, scanners, and keyboards to easily plug into a universal connector on PCs. What's more, USB automatically senses and activates devices, making the task of adding new hardware easier—a big relief for users.

Other names can be even more confusing. DVD used to stand for Digital Versatile Disc, but the marketers have since decided that DVD is what it is—three letters that define an optical disc format. DVD discs are like CD-ROMs, except that they can hold massive amounts of data (up to 17GB) for things like high-fidelity feature films. Finally, IEEE 1394 is a universal connector—similar to USB—that enables high-speed links between external devices and PCs. IEEE stands for the Institute of Electrical and Electronics Engineers and is the standards body that cooked up the IEEE 1394 specification.

Windows 2000 Professional springs from the same architecture that drives NT, and that means Windows 2000 crashes much less frequently than Windows 98. This benefit alone is enough to make Windows 2000 a compelling upgrade in the business world. But compatibility with older 16-bit DOS and Windows 3.x applications is not perfect. Some programs that ran under Windows 98 may not run with Windows 2000 or may require reinstallation following an upgrade. The selection of available devices is also more limited than that available with Windows 98. You need to carefully consider your own compatibility situation before making the leap to Windows 2000 Professional.

So who should consider Windows 2000 Professional? Actually, the operating system appeals to anyone from the home PC user to corporate IT managers deploying 10,000 end user desktops. The inclusion of advanced power management (even better than Windows 98) makes it an outstanding platform for notebook PCs, provided you have a high-end notebook with a 300-MHz CPU and 64MB of RAM. Even game players find Windows 2000 attractive, thanks to the integration of advanced DirectX multimedia technologies.

Windows 2000 Server, Advanced Server, and Data Center Server

Just like Windows NT before it, the Windows 2000 franchise comes in a variety of flavors. Just upstream from Windows 2000 Professional is Windows 2000 Server. This lightweight server operating system employs the same code that drives Windows 2000 Professional. Naturally, Server offers the same features, usability enhancements, and device support improvements that make Professional so compelling. Windows 2000 Server essentially differs in three major directions: scalability, functionality, and price.

Scalability defines the capability of an operating system to support a large number of systems and to support the hardware needed to drive a large network. Most telling, Windows 2000 Server recognizes up to four CPUs — Professional can see two — enabling IT managers to bring plenty of processing power to bear on demanding file and print serving, Web hosting, application serving, and other network tasks. The Server edition also accommodates broader connectivity, enabling up to XX systems to connect to the server via TCP/IP.

Where Windows 2000 Server really excels is in functionality; it is packed with tools for IT managers. While Windows 2000 Professional enables you to perform some monitoring and management functions, Server extends these facilities. Network managers can establish network domains, identify and tailor user permissions, and set security parameters for client systems on the network. Windows 2000 Server also plays host to two intriguing technologies for large corporate networks: Active Directory and IntelliMirror.

Active Directory is a technology that enables IT managers to identify, track, and manage a wide variety of network resources. Active Directory provides a single repository and point of access for resource data such as user and group profiles, domain structures, network hardware configurations, system configurations, and security settings. Like Novell's Netware Directory Services (NDS) directory technology, Active Directory promises to make it possible to scale network management while reducing management overhead. IntelliMirror, meanwhile, enables network administrators to store individual system profiles on a central server. If an employee's hard disk goes south, IntelliMirror makes it easy to rebuild all the information on a new PC over a network connection.

Windows 2000 Advanced Server and Data Center Server are supersets of Windows 2000 Server, addressing ever greater network loads. Advanced Server can host 8 CPUs, double the number recognized under Server, while Windows 2000 Data Center Server can recognize a whopping 32 CPUs. These advanced versions also provide support for clustering, a technology that enables IT managers to lash server systems together so that they act like a single, powerful system.

You can expect to pay a lot more for the various server versions of Windows 2000 than for the Professional version. Of course, if you need to run a Web site, manage file and print services, or expand a database server, the price difference between Windows 2000 Professional and Server is hardly the issue. Rather, the capability of the various server packages to scale to your task will drive the decision.

Needless to say, the advanced flavors of Windows 2000 Server won't be showing up on most individual desktops or home offices. Windows 2000 Server, Advanced Server, and Data Center Server are operating systems for network professionals. If you happen to have a small home or office network, you can use Windows 2000 Professional quite comfortably as a network server OS.

Windows CE

The last stop on this Windows world tour is Windows CE, the compact operating system for handheld personal digital assistants (PDAs), smart appliances, TV set top boxes, and the like. Today, Windows CE is most often found on the many 3Com Palm-style handheld products, such as the Casio Cassiopeia, shown in Figure 1-3.

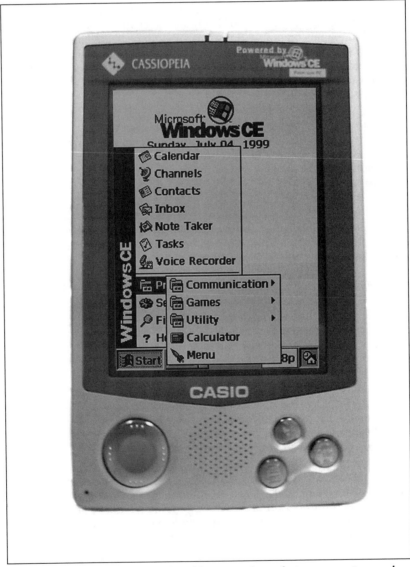

Figure 1-3: Windows CE is used to drive emerging palmtop computers such as the Casio Cassiopeia.

Of course, you won't be considering Windows CE for your desktop PC, but I wanted to bring it up because CE is a very active member of the Windows franchise. In addition, more and more users are using Windows CE–based devices as companions to their desktop PCs. You may find yourself connecting a WinCE device to your PC someday soon.

It's tempting to say that Windows CE is simply a slimmed down Windows 98 or Windows NT/2000, but the fact is that WinCE was built from the ground up to support electronic devices. So where's the connection? For one thing, Windows CE uses the same Windows interface (subject to screen size limitations) found in Windows 98. Perhaps even more important, Windows CE makes use of a modified version of the application programming interface (API) used to write software for Windows 98 and Windows 2000. The goal was to make it easy for programmers familiar with Windows to move their software to the Windows CE platform.

Unlike the other operating systems outlined here, Windows CE is an embedded operating system. That is to say, it has actually been burned into the read-only memory (ROM) of consumer electronics devices. You won't generally buy Windows CE and install it on anything; rather you select Windows CE as part of your hardware purchase decision.

Windows 2000 Professional: The Nickel Tour

In the next few chapters, you dive right into such topics as exploring the revamped user interface. But for now, I'd like to give you a walk-through of the Windows 2000 Professional operating system. This tour gives you a quick bead on what Professional is, how it differs from Windows 98 and NT 4.0, and whether or not it is appropriate for you.

Like any Microsoft Windows family operating system, Windows 2000 Professional is just jam-packed with stuff. In fact, the operating system weighs in with some 35 million lines of code! This very fact alone had a lot of pundits predicting disaster for Windows 2000, claiming the new OS was simply too unwieldy to ever make it out the door. As it turns out, Microsoft turned the corner nicely on this project, but it is clear that Windows 2000 took a lot longer to develop than the company initially planned.

So what do you get for those 35 million lines of code? Well, you get more than just an operating system, that's for sure. Consider this: The core task of an OS is to boot the system, manage the file system, act as a middleman between software and system hardware, and generally make the trains run on time. But Windows 2000 — like its predecessors — comes packed with a slew of features, utilities, applets, full-fledged applications, and even games.

Here's a quick look at what you get when you install Windows 2000 Professional:

✦ The operating system

✦ Internet Explorer 5.0 and Outlook Express

✦ FrontPage Express

✦ Many, many applets

✦ Utilities and tools

✦ Help

The operating system

The Windows 2000 Professional operating system includes everything from the lowest level boot code to the high-level user interface. Of course, Microsoft argues that Internet Explorer, Outlook Express, FrontPage Express, and other bundled applications are as much a part of the OS as the boot code. I personally don't buy that argument, but these programs are definitely a compelling part of the Windows 2000 package.

The operating system code itself has been improved in several ways. For example, the file system has been improved so that Windows 2000 recognizes disks formatted using the FAT-32 file system, which made its debut with Windows 95 and 98. Microsoft's engineers also locked down the OS kernel, offering even greater stability and system security by making it more difficult for bumbling or malevolent programs to harm the system.

But the real theme of Windows 2000 Professional can be summed up with the phrase "More like Windows 98 than Windows 98." For example, Plug and Play is part of the Windows 2000 arsenal. That's right: Pop in a new graphics card or sound board, and Windows 2000 interacts with your system BIOS and the new device to detect, configure, and initialize the hardware. There's even an honest-to-gosh Device Manager that provides a central repository of system configuration data. These are features that Windows NT users will absolutely rave over.

Windows 2000 has also gained a consumer edge. DirectX technology means that PCs using Windows 2000 can run the latest 3D games using powerful graphics accelerators, provided, of course, you have the proper drivers. There's also support for devices that connect over the USB and fast IEEE 1394 interfaces, as well as for DVD drives.

The interface also includes a slew of enhancements (all of which you learn about later) aimed at boosting ease of use. In fact, Microsoft has drastically decluttered the interface, making navigation easier. A lot of the changes take place in the Control Panel, shown in Figure 1-4, where Windows 2000 now focuses all configuration activity.

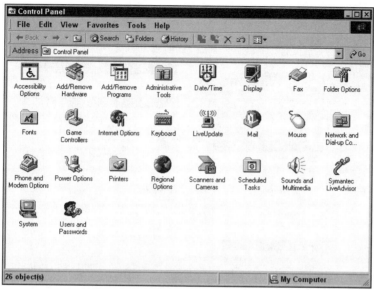

Figure 1-4: Microsoft has unified system management under the familiar guise of the Windows Control Panel.

Internet Explorer 5.0 and Outlook Express

Of course, every new version of Windows is going to come complete with Microsoft's latest iteration of Internet Explorer. Now in version 5.0, this Web browser offers significant improvements over Internet Explorer 4.0, including fixed security holes, better stability, and neat customization features. It's also the first version of Internet Explorer to provide support for the extensible markup language (XML), a powerful description language that can vastly enhance access to database, e-commerce services, and the like.

Microsoft has tweaked the usability of Internet Explorer. There are old favorites like the Search button and its handy vertical results frame — shown in Figure 1-5 — as well as the ever-useful Autocomplete feature, which prompts you with finished URL addresses as you type. A new addition is Windows Radio, for listening to radio stations over the Internet.

Microsoft has cleaned up the desktop interface with Windows 2000 Professional, but the Internet Explorer icon is still front and center when you boot up. You can't miss it.

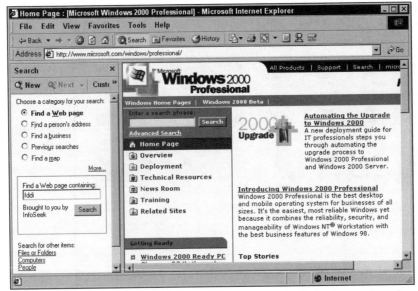

Figure 1-5: The nifty inline Search pane make it easy to find what you need on the Web without schlepping to search sites.

Also included is Outlook Express 5.0, the latest version of the integrated e-mail client. Like the browser, this version of Outlook Express incorporates all the necessary and welcome tweaks, bug fixes, and security patches that have accrued over the past year. Accessible from the Tools menu of Internet Explorer, Outlook Express is a full-fledged e-mail client that supports a number of key features:

✦ Multiple e-mail accounts and identities

✦ Multiple access modes

✦ Rules and folders

✦ Personalized signatures, formatting, and other settings

✦ Newsreader interface

An embarrassment of applets

Windows 2000 Professional is loaded with applets and utilities, most of which are quickly accessible from the Start menu. Software such as WordPad and Paint, for example, make Windows 2000 a functional computing tool right out of the box, even before you install an Office suite or other software. Of course, few users want to stick with these rudimentary tools, but they are available for spot duty. Perhaps most welcome is the Kodak Imaging application (shown in Figure 1-6), which is used for viewing and editing images as well as displaying faxes.

Figure 1-6: Kodak Imaging for Windows is a nice photo-editing application that doubles as a fax viewer under Windows 2000.

Microsoft makes it extremely difficult to dispense with unwanted utilities and software. The Windows 2000 Professional installation lacks the custom options of earlier versions, which enabled you to pick and choose the applets to be installed. What's more, the Remove Software facility in the Control Panel doesn't even show you these applets. There is a way to remove these little guys, which I discuss in Chapter 5.

You can find most of the applets by clicking Start ➪ Programs ➪ Accessories. Table 1-3 provides a quick overview of the installed applets.

A wealth of applets provide communications services, enhanced accessibility for the disabled, as well as games and entertainment. I delve into the various productivity applications in Windows 2000 in Chapter 5, while games get their due in Chapter 18. Accessibility features of Windows 2000 are covered in Chapter 9.

Table 1-3
Windows 2000 Professional Applets

Applet	Description
Calculator	An onscreen calculator
Imaging	View faxes, capture scanned images, and edit images
Notepad	No-frills text editor; useful for editing text-based configuration files
Paint	Very basic painting program
WordPad	A functional, if feature-light word processor that even reads Word 97 .DOC files

Utilities and tools

If you're coming from the Windows 98 side of the fence, you'll definitely notice that Windows 2000 comes with a lot of tools: diagnostic and performance-monitoring software, disk and partition management software, plus a slew of tools for managing and monitoring computers, users, and events. For those not used to NT 4.0, it can seem a bit overwhelming.

Unlike applets, many of these tools are not available from the Start menu (at least, not by default). A quick jaunt over to the Windows 2000 Control Panel (click Start ➪ Settings ➪ Control Panel) reveals the enormously useful Administrative Tools icon. Double-click the icon to see the items described in Table 1-4.

A Few Timely Definitions

There are so many new terms in Table 1-4 that it seems a good idea to define them here:

Component Object Model Plus (COM+): The second-generation of a Microsoft developed model for developing program code. Programmers can write COM+ objects, confident that any COM+-compliant application can access it. ActiveX is based on COM+ technology.

Open Database Connectivity (ODBC): A standard method for accessing information in databases. Applications that are ODBC-compliant are able to access information from databases that also comply with the standard.

SQL database: SQL stands for Structured Query Language, a standardized query language used to request information from a database.

Packets: A unit of data transmission used for packet-based networks such as the Internet. A packet typically consists of two parts: The payload, which contains all the data being sent between two points on the network; and the header, which includes destination address, source address, and other identifying information about the payload.

Table 1-4
Useful Resources in the Administrative Tools Folder

Tool	Description
Component Services	Manage Component Object Module Plus (COM+) programs and automate key management functions.
Computer Management	Manage local or remote PCs; review and edit system configuration, alter disk structures, manage shared resources, and more.
Data Sources (ODBC)	Set up Open Database Connectivity (ODBC) drivers to enable applications to draw information from SQL databases, both locally or over a network.
Event Viewer	Stay informed about software failures, security violations, and configuration changes using this useful logging tool.
Performance	Track a wide range of workload metrics, including processor time, network data transfers, lost packets, and more as shown in Figure 1-7.

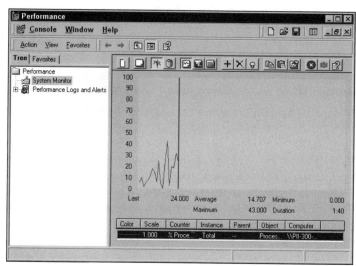

Figure 1-7: Track all areas of system performance, including processor activity, network transactions, disk throughput, and system memory transactions.

In addition to these tools, you can find a number of useful items under the Start menu. Click Start ⇨ Programs ⇨ Accessories ⇨ System Tools to find the items listed in Table 1-5.

| | Table 1-5 |
| | **More Resources in the Start Menu** |

Tool	Description
Backup	Create and perform important data backups. Also used to restore backed up data, such as after a disk crash.
Disk Cleaner	Clear unneeded files to conserve disk space.
Disk Defragmenter	Improve performance by streamlining fragmented files on the hard disk.
Scheduled Tasks	Work while you sleep! Schedule applications to run based on criteria you set. Great for overnight disk defragmentation sessions.

Help system

Finally, Windows 2000 Professional has a rather voluminous online Help system that includes everything from high-level descriptions of what applications or components do to step-by-step interactive guides — called *wizards* — that lead you through installations and troubleshooting.

You can access the Windows 2000 Help system in a variety of ways:

✦ Click Start ➪ Help to enter the general Windows 2000 Help system at the top level.

✦ Click the displayed Help button from within a Windows 2000 dialog box.

✦ Click the Help menu item on the menu bar of an application or window and click the appropriate submenu.

✦ Press F1.

Windows 2000's Help system is context sensitive, which means that the Help window you see relates specifically to what you are actively working on. Click the Help button while working in the Disk Cleanup applet, for example, and you see help material specific to using Disk Cleanup. The one exception is the Help command in the Start menu. This command always brings up a generic Help window.

The Help system interface has also been tweaked. Instead of the old one-pane window, the Windows 2000 Help system uses an embedded HTML format. Help content is displayed in a two-pane window, as shown in Figure 1-8. Users select topics in the left pane, working from within any of four tabbed pages: Contents, Index, Search, and Favorites. The larger right pane displays the selected content.

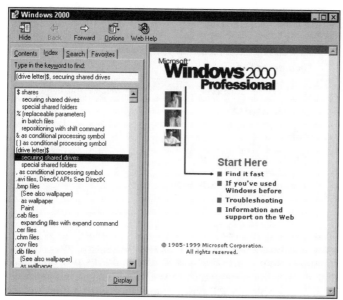

Figure 1-8: The improved Help system makes navigating topics more convenient.

I personally find the new format much more usable because I am able to maintain my overarching context even as I read about a specific topic.

System Requirements

So what does it take to join the Windows 2000 world? Unfortunately, quite a lot. Microsoft gives you the usual business about how its new operating system runs on a very lightweight system, but the truth is you won't want to use Windows 2000 Professional on anything less than a 300-MHz PC loaded with 64MB of RAM.

Perhaps most telling, Microsoft requires that any PC hoping to be anointed Windows 2000–ready must have a 300-MHz processor and come with 64MB of RAM. Table 1-6 provides the minimum and recommended system specifications.

Note   What are ACPI and APM? ACPI stands for Advanced Configuration and Power Interface, a specification that allows Windows 2000 to control power settings for each device in the system. With an ACPI-capable PC, Windows 2000 can shut down inactive peripherals such as CD-ROM drives to help prolong battery life, or enable instant power-on when a keyboard key is pressed. APM, or Advanced Power Management, is an older industry-standard application programming interface (API) that enables power management capability in the system BIOS.

	Table 1-6	
	System Configurations	
Component	*Recommended*	*Minimum*
Processor	300-MHz Pentium class	166-MHz Pentium class
System RAM	64MB to 128MB	32MB
Hard disk	4GB	2GB
Power management	Compliant with Advanced Configuration and Power Interface (ACPI) specification	Advanced Power Management (APM)

Perhaps the biggest conundrum is the one mobile PC users face. You see, Windows 2000 Professional is an absolutely fantastic mobile operating system. It features more robust power management than Windows 98 and includes powerful data-synching features that are worlds removed from Win98's hoary Briefcase facility. The problem is, how many people actually own a notebook with a Pentium II-300 CPU and 64MB of RAM? Not a lot — at least, not yet.

One claim you hear Microsoft make is that Windows 2000 Professional is actually faster than Windows 98. And in fact, that's true — if your system comes to the party with enough resources. On a Pentium II-300 or better PC with at least 64MB of RAM, you see performance about on par with Windows 98. Boost RAM to 128MB, however, and performance jumps significantly. If you want a responsive Windows 2000 PC, you may need to bite the bullet and upgrade your memory.

Compatibility

No discussion of a new operating system can happen without a nod to the issue of compatibility. Windows 2000 Professional is no exception. The fact is, people who upgrade from Windows 98 may find applications that fail to work or may not be able to gather Windows 2000 drivers for a peripheral.

No matter how rock solid you feel your compatibility situation to be, you must back up your data before you upgrade a PC to Windows 2000. Microsoft has done a fine job with the installation routine of Windows 2000 Professional, but upgrading an operating system is a drastic activity. If something goes wrong during the process — say the power gets disrupted — you could be looking at a PC and hard disk that are simply inaccessible. By backing up your data, you can avoid a lot of grief.

So what can you do to make sure you have verified compatibility?

Check the List

Before you upgrade, make note of your system configuration and software. Write down product names, version numbers, driver dates, the works. Then pay a visit to the Windows Hardware Compatibility List (HCL) Web site to check to see if your PC hardware is up to snuff. Find this up-to-the-minute resource at `http://www. microsoft.com/hcl/`. Many product entries even include links to the latest compatible driver files. Figure 1-9 shows a typical search.

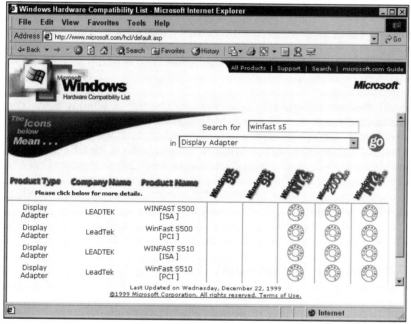

Figure 1-9: Enter a search for the device type and product name to find out the level of compatibility with all of Microsoft's active operating systems.

Tip Remember, your system is hardware too! If your PC has old BIOS code, you may be headed for an upgrade disaster. Make sure you check the HCL for your system model. And if your PC doesn't make it on the list, check with your vendor about a possible BIOS upgrade or other tweak that can bring you into compliance.

You can also find a version of the HCL on the Windows 2000 CD-ROM. Browse the disk and open the Support folder. Double-click the file HCL.TXT to view the list. Of course, this list can age rapidly, and the version you have on disc may be weeks or months old. Personally, I always go with the real-time, Web-based HCL.

Software can be a bit more tricky. But as with hardware, you can check Microsoft's list of credentialed Windows 2000–compliant applications. The Web site is `http://www.microsoft.com/windows/professional/deploy/compatible/default.asp`.

Before you start throwing away software, be aware that many applications that don't have a Windows 2000 logo in fact can work with the operating system. Your best bet, if the application isn't listed on the Microsoft site, is to contact the software vendor.

Beware

When it does come to anticipating compatibility, users are well advised to look to Windows NT 4.0 as a guide. If you have software or hardware that won't work under NT 4.0, you should assume — unless proven otherwise — that it won't work with Windows 2000 Professional.

Admittedly, this approach is a bit conservative. The fact is, Windows 2000 *can* run software and hardware that NT won't. Microsoft has upped the multimedia ante in Windows 2000 by incorporating the latest DirectX technologies, for example. That means a lot of 3D games, graphics cards, and multimedia software run perfectly well under Windows 2000. The new operating system also recognizes USB and IEEE 1394 devices, something NT does not. But when it comes to upgrading, it's better to be safe than sorry. When in doubt, verify the compatibility of suspect products directly with the vendors.

Here are the types of things that should raise your compatibility hackles:

 ✦ DOS-based software, particularly DOS games

 ✦ Windows 3.x software

 ✦ Antivirus or disk utilities not specifically designed for Windows 2000

 ✦ Any hardware or software that is more than three years old

 ✦ BIOS with a date prior to 1998

 ✦ 3D graphics cards

 ✦ Specialized devices, such as TV tuner cards, data capture cards, and the like

By exercising a little caution, you can easily sidestep most Windows 2000 upgrade gotchas. All it takes is a little common sense.

Summary

Windows 2000 Professional is as comprehensive an operating system as Microsoft has ever shipped. In fact, it is tailored to serve a broader selection of users, applications, and markets than any other Windows-based operating system. From business desktops to low-end servers, home computers to notebooks, Windows 2000 Professional comes with the features and support to handle the task.

Does this mean you should run out and upgrade to this OS right now? Well, probably not. Any operating system upgrade is a major undertaking, and moving to Windows 2000 Professional is a good deal more challenging than, say, going from Windows 95 to Windows 98. Users need to bide their time a bit, assess whether or not Windows 2000 meets their needs, and assure themselves that their existing hardware can indeed work under the new operating system. Once you've done a little planning and preparation (such as backing up your data, for starters), you can seriously consider making the move.

Among the concepts we reviewed here:

✦ A introduction to Windows 2000 Professional and a comparison with other versions of Windows, including Windows 3.x, Windows 95/98, and Windows NT.

✦ A discussion of what's included in Windows 2000, such as productivity applets, utilities, and Web browsers and e-mail programs.

✦ An important heads up on system requirements and compatibility issues with Windows 2000 Professional.

There's a lot to cover in the pages ahead. I hope this chapter gets you started off on the right foot. We'll continue our exploration of Windows 2000 with a look at the slick interface. Not only will you learn how to get around Windows 2000, but you'll find out how to do useful things like automate tasks, find troubleshooting facilities, and customize your system's look and feel.

✦   ✦   ✦

Navigation Basics

Not so long ago, I traveled to Ireland on vacation with my wife and two sons. Ireland is a family friendly country with citizens who (with rare exceptions) speak English. But even with these advantages, our biggest challenge was getting around. Street signs are often few and far between, and we struggled to adapt to driving on the left side of the road — particularly when roads got so narrow that the concept of left and right became moot. (Tip for drivers: Forget about staying on the left side and just think about keeping your body toward the center.)

Moving to Windows 2000 Professional can be a little like driving in Ireland. There's the comforting familiarity of the Windows interface but enough new features, tweaks, and gotchas to steer veteran users off course. This chapter introduces you to the ways of Windows 2000 and helps you quickly adapt to native customs.

Welcome to the Desktop

When Windows 2000 first boots up, users of Windows 95/98 and NT 4.0 alike will notice that little has changed. There's the comforting gray taskbar stretched across the bottom of the screen, a pared-down selection of icons running down the left and a stately blue background behind.

But even from the desktop, changes are evident. For example, users of Windows 95 and NT 4.0 will notice three teeny little icons next to the Start button. These form the new Quick Launch toolbar, which is familiar to users of Windows 98. And kudos go to Microsoft for cleaning up the desktop. Gone are many of the annoying extra icons for various dial-up services. Let's go find out what else Microsoft engineers have tweaked.

Logging on

Actually, you'll notice changes before you even get to the desktop. Booting into Windows 2000 looks different from NT 4.0. Under NT 4.0, the boot process puts you first into a blue, text-based screen before displaying the Microsoft splash screen. Windows 2000 does away with the DOS lookalike stuff, displaying a graphical status/splash screen instead. A horizontal bar along the bottom of the screen tells you how far along the startup process is.

Like NT 4.0, Windows 2000 challenges users to provide a user name and password at every startup. This important security feature helps ensure that only authorized users can start up and access systems. Windows 2000 updates the logon entry dialog box, but otherwise little has changed.

To increase security, set Windows 2000 to require the user to press Ctrl+Alt+Delete in order to bring up the logon dialog box. This helps prevents Trojan Horse programs, for example, from gaining access to your system. To enable this setting, click Control ➪ Settings ➪ Control Panel and double-click the Users and Passwords icon. Click the Advanced tab, and check the checkbox control labeled Require users to press Ctrl+Alt+Delete before logging on. Click OK.

To gain access to the PC, simply type your user name (which you or a network administrator provided during setup) in the User name text box. Then type your password in the Password text box and click OK. By default, the user name of the last person to log onto the Windows 2000 PC is displayed in the User name text box.

Tip   Take your passwords seriously! Any administrator will tell you that most security breaches are caused by haphazard password management. One common mistake is that people write their passwords on a Post-It note and — I am not making this up — stick it on their monitor.

Note   Remember that your Windows 2000 system password is case sensitive. If you have trouble logging on, check to make sure that you haven't inadvertently toggled the Caps Lock key on your keyboard.

Once you've entered your authentication information, Windows 2000 goes about building the desktop and loading any startup applications. Within a few moments, you find yourself staring at the trimmed down Windows 2000 desktop interface.

Where things are

Before moving on to actually working with windows, folders, and other navigational elements of Windows 2000, take a look around. Figure 2-1 shows the basic Windows 2000 desktop.

Figure 2-1: Windows 95/98 and NT 4.0 users will be quite familiar with the Windows 2000 desktop, including the ubiquitous Start button on the taskbar.

Desktop icons

The first thing you may notice is that a few icons have been renamed or shuffled around. The My Documents folder—the default file location for many Windows applications—now sits at the top-left corner of the desktop. Just beneath it is the familiar My Computer icon, which gives you access to local disk drives and the Windows 2000 Control Panel (see Figure 2-2).

Just underneath the My Computer icon is the icon formerly known as Network Neighborhood. I'm not sure what the new name "My Network Places" is supposed to do for end users, but its role is the same. Double-clicking this icon brings up a view of systems connected to the local PC over a local area or wide area network. This is the first place you can go to look for additional network resources set up on your PC.

Next in line is the Recycle Bin. No stranger to anyone who has used a PC running Windows 95/98 or NT 4.0, the Recycle Bin provides a safe place for all your deleted files. Should you mistakenly delete an item, you can recover it by double-clicking the Recycle Bin, selecting the deleted file, and clicking File ➪ Restore.

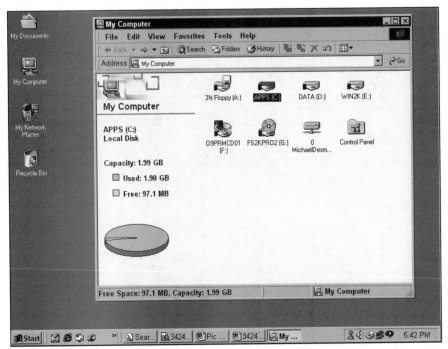

Figure 2-2: Double-click the My Computer icon to get a Windows browser view of your local disk drives and the Windows Control Panel.

 Caution   Watch out. The Recycle Bin won't keep your deleted files in cold storage forever. By default, it only sets aside 10 percent of your total disk space. Beyond that point, the Recycle Bin permanently disposes of files, starting with the oldest ones first.

The last two icons in this little vertical parade address the Internet. The Internet Explorer icon—with its trademark -e shape—launches the bundled Internet Explorer 5.0 Web browser. Finally, the Connect to Internet icon launches a step-by-step setup application—called a *wizard*—that guides users through the process of setting up an Internet account and connection.

Notably absent from this desktop are icons for MSN, the Microsoft Network online service, as well icons for AOL and CompuServe.

The Start button

Drop straight down from the Connect to the Internet icon and run smack into the Start button. Tucked into the left corner of the Windows 2000 taskbar, the Start button serves as a central point to launch programs, open documents, adjust system settings, and otherwise get stuff done.

Click the Start button to see a vertical menu that offers fly-out menus for Programs, Documents, Settings, and other entries. Installed applications typically appear in their own subfolders under the Programs folder, but you can also drag and drop items onto the Start menu. The result is a customized point-and-click starting point for Windows 2000, as shown in Figure 2-3.

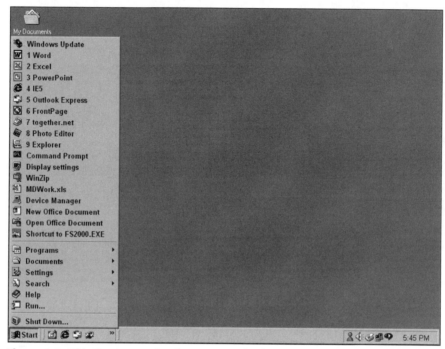

Figure 2-3: This Start menu has been customized with a number of frequently used programs.

The taskbar

The Start button itself actually resides inside the taskbar, the gray-colored bar that runs along the bottom of the screen. This bar is always visible and provides valuable information when running Windows 2000 applications. You can easily move the taskbar by clicking and dragging it to any of the four edges of the screen.

At each end of the taskbar are a number of tiny icons. The icons near the Start button are Quick Launch icons used to run programs directly from the desktop. The micro-icons on the right represent services or background applications. Double- or right-click these little guys, and you can access settings for the related program or service.

Note   It hasn't taken long for these micro-icons, first introduced in Windows 95, to catch on. In fact, they can propagate so quickly as you install new software that users have taken to calling them "taskbar lint."

The most useful function of the taskbar is to provide context when running multiple applications. Each running program is represented with a rectangular button. Clicking a button brings that program window to the front, making it easy to switch among multiple applications. Figure 2-4 shows how the taskbar can help take the confusion out of multitasking applications.

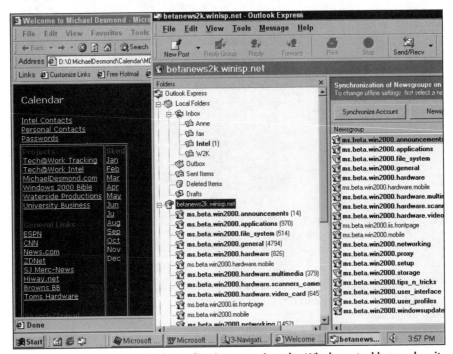

Figure 2-4: Even with multiple applications running, the Windows taskbar makes it easy to keep things in order.

The Windows Control Panel

Okay, it's time to dive in below the desktop to find a few key resources. Once again, those who have used Windows 95/98 and NT 4.0 will recognize some familiar landmarks. The first stop is the Windows Control Panel, which serves as a one-stop shop for system configuration, updates, and troubleshooting. There are two ways to get to the Control Panel window:

✦ Click Start ⇨ Settings ⇨ Control Panel.

✦ Double-click My Computer and then double-click the Control Panel icon.

Once the Control Panel is open, you see 20 or so icons, each of which corresponds to a particular system device type, Windows 2000 function, or other resource. Figure 2-5 shows what the Control Panel looks like.

Figure 2-5: From the Control Panel, you can interact with virtually every aspect of your system configuration.

Most Windows 2000 Professional configurations come with the following Control Panel items:

✦ **Accessibility Options:** Tailor your PC for those with disabilities.

✦ **Add/Remove Hardware:** The name says it all.

✦ **Add/Remove Programs:** Ditto here.

✦ **Administrative Tools:** Monitor performance, view event logs , and handle other important management tasks.

✦ **Date/Time:** Set your PC's clock.

✦ **Display:** Powerful catch-all tool that addresses graphics board and monitor drivers, display resolutions, desktop background, screen savers, and more.

✦ **Fax:** Tailor your Windows fax applet information. Windows 2000 should automatically install the fax module if you have a fax-capable modem set up.

✦ **Folder Options:** Finally, a sensible place to manage the behavior of folders and windows.

✦ **Fonts:** View, install, and delete typefaces.

✦ **Game Controllers:** Set up joysticks, gamepads, and other fun devices.

✦ **Internet Options:** Another improvement that enables you to tell Internet Explorer how to behave, update dial-up settings, and set helper applications.

✦ **Keyboard:** Customize repeat rate, cursor blink rate, and other properties.

✦ **Mouse:** Change cursor graphics, set movement speed, assign button behaviors, and more.

✦ **Network and Dial-up Connections:** Create and manage connections over both the local area network and phone-based dial-up.

✦ **Phone & Modem Options:** Beefed up modem properties interface now includes telephony hooks.

✦ **Power Options:** Take advantage of the power-saving features that NT 4.0 lacked. Great for mobile users.

✦ **Printers:** Set up and configure printers. If the Windows 2000 fax module is installed, an entry labeled Fax will appear here as well.

✦ **Regional Options:** Go local by assigning language, number formatting, currency, and date/time formatting based on country and personal preference.

✦ **Scanners and Cameras:** Configure, test, and troubleshoot imaging devices connected to your PC.

✦ **Scheduled Tasks:** Work while you sleep! Run applications and other services at specified intervals.

✦ **Sounds and Multimedia:** Catch-all place to set audio hardware, set audio and video codecs, and even assign speech input and output.

✦ **System:** The granddaddy of them all. Access the Device Manager (more on that next), tweak performance and environment settings, create hardware and user profiles, and even change your network identity.

✦ **Users and Passwords:** Administrators can add and remove users and provide passwords.

In order to access a particular resource, simply double-click the desired icon. Windows 2000 launches the appropriate wizard, property dialog box, or other service. More detail about using the various Control Panel resources is in later chapters.

The Device Manager

As noted previously, the Device Manager is accessed from the System icon in the Control Panel. To open the Device Manager, double-click the System icon, click the Hardware tab, and click the Device Manager button. Why call out this resource and not all the others? Simple. Veteran Windows 95/98 users know that the Device Manager is *the* place to assess system configuration and chase down hardware and driver conflicts.

And Windows NT migrants, take note. The addition of Plug and Play to Windows 2000 means that the Device Manager actually stores useful, dynamic information about system hardware and drivers. What both Windows 95/98 and NT users will notice is that Device Manager has a new face. Gone is the old embedded scroll-down list box and radio buttons; they've been replaced by an interface, shown in Figure 2-6, that uses a standard layout for administrative resources under Windows 2000. Called the Microsoft Management Console (MMC) interface, this layout makes use of administrative tools easier by employing a consistent format.

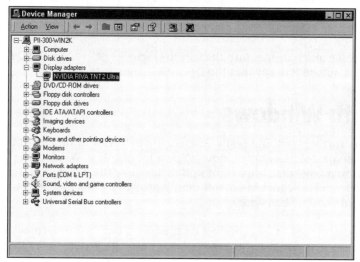

Figure 2-6: The Device Manager interface has been tweaked to work within the Microsoft Management Console scheme, but the functionality is unchanged.

The process of interacting with device entries is unchanged, however. Dig down by clicking the + sign next to the hardware type you want to investigate to see an entry for an installed device. Double-click that, and you get a powerful device properties dialog box. From here, you can troubleshoot conflicts, change resource settings, update drivers, and access device-specific features. This is powerful stuff, and it's a shame that Microsoft has buried it.

Like so many Windows resources, there are many ways to get to the Device Manager. Here are three:

1. Click Start ⇨ Settings Programs ⇨ Control Panel, double-click System, click the Hardware tab, and finally click the Device Manager button.

2. Right-click the My Computer icon and click Properties, click the Hardware tab, and click the Device Manager button.

3. Click Start ➪ Programs ➪ Administrative Tools ➪ Computer Management. In the compmgmt dialog box, click the + sign next to System Tools and click Device Manager.

Tip If you're like me, you'll need to visit the Device Manager early and often. Create a desktop shortcut directly to this resource by doing the following: Right-click the Windows 2000 desktop, and then click New ➪ Shortcut. In the Create Shortcut dialog box, enter *drive*:*root*\system32\devmgmt.msc — where *drive* and *root* are the drive letter and directory name, respectively, that contain the Windows 2000 operating system. Click Next. Now enter Device Manager or other easily remembered name in the next text box and click Finish. A new icon appears on the desktop. Double-click it, and Device Manager immediately launches.

Later chapters delve much deeper into the various facilities offered by the Device Manager. For now, suffice it to say that the Device Manager is your friend.

Working with Windows

Before going any further, I should really discuss the behavior of that most basic of interface elements: folders and windows. Yes, a lot of this is Windows 101, but Microsoft has also made some important updates to how the basic interface acts. For example, did you know that Microsoft finally provides a sensible way to modify folder and window behavior?

Windows 2000 may be the hot new product on the block, but its interface owes an awful lot to work done in the 1970s at Xerox PARC (Palo Alto Research Campus). Anyone who has used a Mac or a Windows 3.x, 95, or NT-based PC is very familiar with the point-and-click interface.

What is a window anyway?

Windows may be Microsoft's brand name for its family of operating systems, but the concept of a window in computing is important to understand. In fact, Microsoft chose the Windows name for its operating systems because all of them employ a *windowing* interface. That is, users view information, navigate the OS, and run applications in a series of overlapping windows. The advantage of windowing is that the user can easily move among many open applications and views, rather than having to toggle between full-screen instances of each app or folder view.

Think of it as shuffling papers on your office desk. No one I know keeps a single piece of paper on the desktop at a time. Rather, a slew of documents and papers may be spread across the desk — some piled up, others spread out. This arrangement makes it easy to quickly grab the document you need without having to take time to go back to a file cabinet.

A windowing interface is similar to the desktop analogy. Each window, in essence, represents a piece of paper on your office desktop. You can quickly grab what you need without losing track of the other papers in front of you.

The downside is that too much paper on your desktop creates a chaotic mess. And the same can happen in Windows. The Windows taskbar helps by displaying a rectangular box for each running application or open folder. By clicking a box, the user immediately moves that window to the foreground. This kind of always-on context really makes navigation a lot easier to handle.

Note

One of the drawbacks to a windowing interface is that it needs a lot of screen space, particularly if you tend to run multiple applications. Context-building elements such as the taskbar also grab screen space. The upshot: You get best results on Windows 2000 if you have at least a 17-inch CRT (or 15-inch flat panel) monitor running at 1024 by 768 resolution.

Using windows

One of the things that makes Windows easy to use is that behaviors are consistent. If you've seen one window, you've just about seen them all. These windows open, close, move, and generally react to input in familiar and repetitive ways — despite the fact that there are many different types of windows, including application windows, file browser windows, and child windows.

Windows may do different things, but they all have key characteristics in common. Figure 2-7 shows a Windows Explorer window that is typical of most you'll encounter.

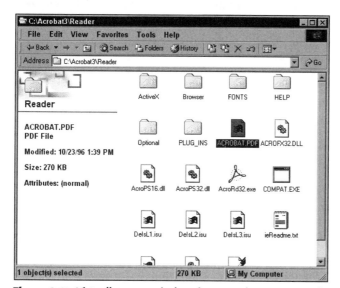

Figure 2-7: Virtually every window features the same set of interface items, including a menu across the top and a status bar at the bottom.

Figure 2-7 points out some of the common window elements. Among them:

1. The title bar identifies the window by its application or resource name.

2. The small icon in the upper-left corner opens a common window control.

3. Three icons in the upper-left corner serve to (from left to right) minimize, maximize, and close the window.

4. The menu bar enables you to access commands from menus that roll down when you click each word. Most windows include the File, Windows, and Help menu items.

Tip   You may notice a subtle change between Windows 2000 and its predecessors. Command menu items no longer include an underline indicating the Alt+hot key combination that invokes that command from the keyboard. Now, this prompt only appears after you press Alt. To access a menu item using the keyboard, press and hold the Alt key to see the appropriate hot key, and then press the appropriate hot key. For example, pressing Alt+F invokes the File menu.

5. Most windows include a status bar along the bottom edge. Information such as file sizes, application status, and interface prompts may be displayed here.

6. The corner tab in the bottom right offers an exaggerated resize space. This tab is useful for resizing windows when the bottom of the window is tucked beneath the taskbar.

7. Vertical and horizontal scroll bars may be displayed, especially if more information is present than can be displayed in a single window.

8. The main window displays the application or resource interface.

Be aware that windows come in many varieties. Some windows may display a status bar, and others may not. The user often can elect not to display the status bar, leaving more room for displaying more information inside the window itself. Other windows may not be resizable or may lack menu items altogether. Despite these quirks, windows act in predictable and familiar ways, making navigation much easier.

Tip   Close an open window by pressing Alt+F4. But remember, this key combination closes the selected application. Save any documents before shutting down an application window.

Managing windows

Any veteran computer user will tell you that using windows is easy; keeping track of them is the hard part. Windows 2000 and earlier Windows versions all encourage you to run several applications and multiple windows at the same time, but there's a problem. You often simply don't have enough screen space to display all the open windows, applications, and resources at the same time. The result: Just like my messy office desk, you end up with windows piled on top of each other. Figure 2-8 shows how quickly your screen can get overrun by competing windows.

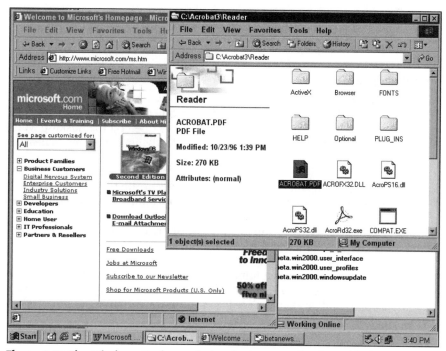

Figure 2-8: The Windows Explorer window is on top and active, with the Internet Explorer and Outlook Express applications visible. But you can't see the Microsoft Word window at all.

Get in focus with the taskbar

Look closely at the figure to notice some important distinctions. For example, the foreground window (Explorer) has a dark title bar while background windows have a lighter title bar. The different color helps you tell at a glance which window is active ("has focus" in Windows parlance).

Why is focus important? For one thing, the window with focus is the one that registers all your input. So if you press Alt+F4, the active window is the one that closes. Because the active window has a unique title bar color, you can quickly tell which window you are working in (and avoid such mishaps as closing Microsoft Word by accident).

To switch among open windows, go to the ever-present Windows taskbar where you see a rectangular, raised button for each window you have open. Useful information such as the application name and icon and the active filename are displayed. Click the desired item to bring that window to the top.

Tip   Press Alt+Tab to bring up a display of open programs, then keep holding Alt while pressing Tab to advance through each icon. Release the Alt and Tab keys to bring up the selected window.

Find the desktop

Working in Windows 2000 sometimes can be like trying to get people's attention in a crowded room. You finally have to quiet everyone down so you can get your point across. When you have half a dozen or so windows open on the desktop, you face a similar challenge. How do you find that application when it's buried beneath five other windows?

You could click the minimize or close buttons at the top-right of each interfering window, but going through each window like that could take tens of seconds — totally unacceptable for veteran channel surfers. There is a solution: Minimize all the open windows in one fell swoop by clicking the Show Desktop mini-icon on the taskbar's Quick Launch panel.

Just like that, every window is minimized, exposing a clear desktop. Now you can quickly double-click desktop elements such as My Computer or My Network without having to nudge aside half a dozen windows. Now, isn't that better?

Taskbar tricks

Did you know you can select taskbar items without the mouse? Here's how:

1. Bring focus to the taskbar by clicking the Windows command key found on many newer keyboards or by pressing Ctrl+Esc.

2. Press Tab to close the Start menu. Focus remains on the Start button, as shown by the dotted border around the inside of the button.

3. Press Tab once to move focus to the first Quick Launch mini-icon; twice to bring focus to the main windows button section, or three times to bring focus to the first taskbar tray item (on the far right).

4. Use the right and left cursor keys to move focus among the icons or items within the selected section. You usually see a faint border to identify the selected item.

5. Press spacebar or Enter to open the selected item.

Fiddling with Folders

One type of window that you work with frequently in Windows 2000 is the folder. A folder is Windows' graphical representation of a disk, partition, subdirectory, or other data storage resource.

By default, Windows 2000's folders are Web enabled. That is, they set aside space on the left side to display information about selected files, drives, and folders. As Figure 2-2 earlier in this chapter shows, you even get a useful pie chart display of free and used space on the selected C:\ drive. The blue underlined text is a hyperlink that moves you to a view of the C:\ folder. Never mind that the hyperlink is redundant, because double-clicking the selected icon does the same thing.

Note   The Web-enabled capability of Windows 2000 means that the operating system can display as part of the interface files formatted using Hypertext Markup Language (HTML), as well as Web-standard graphics such as .GIF and .JPG files. HTML uses tags — special characters embedded in the text of an HTML document — to tell Web browsers and other programs how text and graphics should be formatted. HTML support is valuable because the Web has made these text-based documents universally available.

Starting with the release of Internet Explorer 4.0 under Windows 95, Microsoft began piling a lot of options into the folder viewing experience. The idea was to make navigating Windows similar to browsing the Web. Single-clicks replaced double-clicks for icons, files were displayed as text links, and even the desktop turned into a container for dynamic Web content.

Today, Microsoft has backed off the Web-ization of its interface — as it turns out, users *like* double-clicking icons and single-clicking Web links. But the Web-ified options still remain. In addition, there are countless tweaks (many of them quite critical) to help enhance your folders.

Using folders

Like Windows 95, Windows 2000 Professional features an interface that can best be described as Macintosh-like. Directories on your hard disk are displayed as iconic folders. Double-click a folder to see its contents, including additional subfolders and files.

Navigating the folders is very much a point-and-click experience. Here are a few basics:

✦ Click an icon to select an item.

✦ Double-click an icon to open a file or launch a program.

✦ Right-click an icon to access a useful shortcut menu that presents commands such as Open, Cut, Copy, Delete, Rename, and Properties. See Figure 2-9.

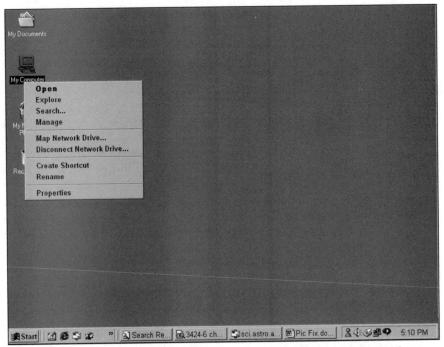

Figure 2-9: After a little practice, you'll learn to right-click first and ask questions later. Everything you need to do with a file or onscreen object often is directly available from shortcut menus.

✦ Click an open area of the window and drag the mouse over icons to select a group of icons.

✦ Click an open area of the window and release the mouse button to deselect all items in the folder.

Moving among folders is easy as well. Just double-click the desired folder icon to move into the folder. By default, Windows displays the newly opened folder in the existing window. This eliminates the ugly problem of having dozens of file folder windows open. To move back up to the original folder, click the Up icon. You'll also find familiar Forward and Back icons — similar to those used in the Internet Explorer and Netscape Navigator browsers — to help you retrace your steps.

From here, you can use the menu commands, toolbar, and right mouse clicks to access a variety of functions. Let's take a look at some of the basics.

The left pane

New to Windows 2000 is the left pane in folder windows. This section presents useful information about selected file and folder properties, including file sizes, names, important dates, and edit privileges. When you select multiple files in the right pane, the left pane displays a tally of the number of items selected, the total bytes selected, and a list of filenames.

One of the most useful features of the left pane is the ability to preview certain file types. When you select HTML files and supported image types (GIF, JPEG), you see a thumbnail preview of the selected file (as shown in Figure 2-10). This feature makes sifting through lots of images much easier.

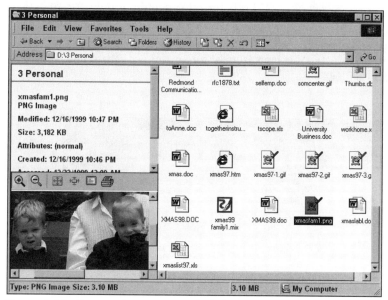

Figure 2-10: Easy on the eyes: Use the left pane to see thumbnail views of supported file types, including GIF, JPEG, and HTML.

The drawback to the left pane is that it consumes space. If you use the Detail file view in the right pane to see information such as date and file size in columnar format, you may find that the right pane forces you to scroll to see this detailed information. You can use the folder customization wizard (described in the section "Using the Customize This Folder Wizard," later in this chapter) to remove this pane.

Arranging folder views

You may want to jigger the way Windows presents information in folders. Hard disks and directories can get positively stuffed with files, making it difficult to find anything. Fortunately, Windows folders make it easy to sift through information.

The place to start is the View command menu item. From here you can order icons, change their appearance, and generally clean up. Here's a rundown of commands that can help organize your folders:

Tip

You can also access these same commands by right-clicking an open space inside the folder, clicking View on the context menu, and then selecting the desired option in the fly out menu.

✦ **View ➪ Large icons:** Get that Mac look with large icons and text underneath.

✦ **View ➪ Small icons:** Displays files in a single vertical column, with tiny icons on the left and the associated names to the right.

✦ **View ➪ List:** Another way to maximize what you see, with files ordered in multiple vertical columns. This is the most economical display of filenames.

✦ **View ➪ Details:** My personal favorite. As shown in Figure 2-11, tiny icons are displayed vertically, with helpful data regarding file size, type, and latest modification date. This view is great for sorting by date, name, and other properties.

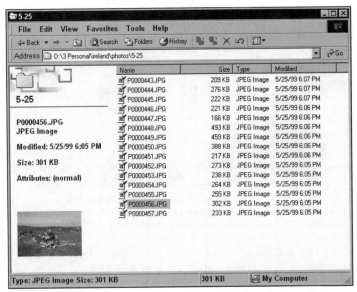

Figure 2-11: See a lot more information by using the Detail view option. If you have more than a dozen or so icons in a folder, this compact and information-filled view can help speed navigation.

✦ **View ➪ Thumbnail:** Helps you seek out graphics and HTML files by displaying thumbnail views as shown in Figure 2-12 — but response can be sloooow.

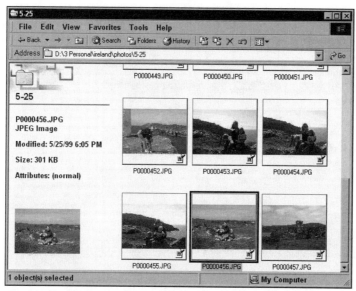

Figure 2-12: This new view proved to be helpful when it came time to cull through the digital photos I took during our summer vacation to Ireland.

As I've said, the Details view is my favorite. It fits plenty of information into a small space, while presenting useful information to help you order, browse, and manage files. What's more, you can customize this view by clicking View ⇨ Choose Columns when in the Detail view. In the Column Settings dialog box (shown in Figure 2-13), you can select what details to see and the order in which they appear. Simply activate the checkbox next to the desired item to add a column to the view (or deactivate the box to remove existing items).

Next, click the Move Up and Move Down buttons to determine the order of columns, then enter the desired width of each selected column by entering a number in the text box near the bottom of the screen. As I mentioned, I'm a date guy, so I've nudged the Modified column next to the Name column at the far left. Now I can immediately tell which files are the most recent — great for muddling through versions of similar files.

Once you've selected how you want icons displayed, you can also arrange and sort them. To do this, click View ⇨ Arrange Icons. A fly out menu presents the following options:

✦ **by Name:** Alphabetical order is best for finding files by name.

✦ **by Type:** Great if you want to separate your word processing files from your image and spreadsheet files.

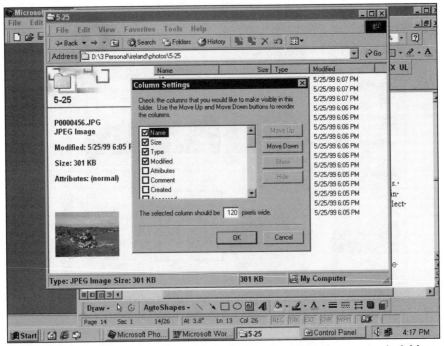

Figure 2-13: Add, remove, and reorder the column headings that appear in folders using the Detail option.

✦ **by Size:** I use this when looking to free up disk space because I can quickly browse through the largest files.

✦ **by Date:** My favorite view because I tend to use the same files over and over. Stuff I'm currently working on usually bubbles right to the top.

✦ **Auto Arrange:** This option is applicable only when large icons are being used; clicking this command snaps icons into an orderly arrangement, which is useful for cleaning up overlapping icons.

Tip   If you're in Detail view, you can quickly sort items by clicking the desired gray column header. Want to see the newest files? Just click the Modified header and scroll to the top of the list. Click the header again, and the listing sorts in the opposite direction with the newest files at the bottom.

Using the Customize This Folder Wizard

Click View ➪ Customize this Folder to launch the Customize this Folder Wizard. The wizard walks you through the process of adding tweaks to the folder you've selected. The first screen prompts you to activate checkbox controls to perform customizations, as shown in Figure 2-14.

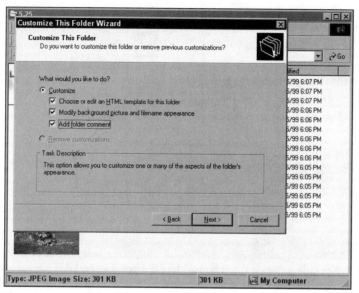

Figure 2-14: Tell the Customize this Folder Wizard what you want to do, and it guides you through the process of creating your own folder settings.

✦ **Choose or edit an HTML template for this folder:** Select from among folder templates. Switch to a Web-free Classic view, add an image preview window, or add other tweaks.

✦ **Modify background picture and filename appearance:** Add or change background patterns, graphics, or color; you can also change the appearance of text.

✦ **Add folder comment:** Adds text you input to the left pane of the folder window.

To customize a particular folder view, follow these steps. In this case, I'm assuming you want to customize all portions of the folder. Of course, you can select only the items you wish.

1. Select View ⇨ Customize This Folder, then click Next at the Customize. This action opens the Customize This Folder Wizard dialog box.

2. Make sure the Customize radio button is activated.

3. Check the desired checkboxes and then click Next.

4. First up is the Change Folder Template dialog box. Select from the four template styles in the Choose a template box, using the Preview image and Template description text to guide your choice, as shown in Figure 2-15.

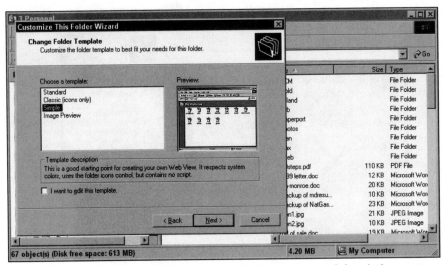

Figure 2-15: Not sure what view to choose? Use the preview and descriptive text to guide you. You can also edit your selected template by checking the checkbox control.

Note

If you clicked the checkbox labeled I want to edit this template, Notepad launches with the HTML code representing your customizations when you click the Next button. You can edit this code in Notepad and save it to tweak your template. Close Notepad to move onto the next screen.

5. Next up is the Modify Background and Filename Appearance dialog box. In the scrolling list box, select an image if you wish to alter the folder background. The Preview window lets you see the results.

6. Change icon text by clicking the button labeled Text and selecting a color from the Color window. Click OK.

7. If you want background highlighting for the text, activate the Background checkbox, and then click the button next to it. Again select a color and click OK.

8. Click Next to go to the Add folder comment dialog box.

9. Enter any text you want to appear in the left-hand pane of the folder.

10. Click Next to view a quick summary of your changes and then click Finish.

Now whenever you open this folder, you see your customized view. All other folders remain unchanged. Compare Figures 2-16 and 2-17 to see how your fiddling has changed the folder view.

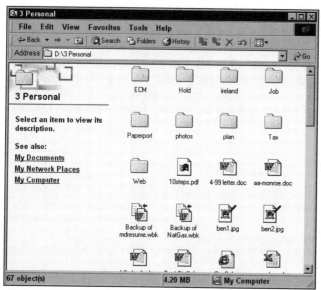

Figure 2-16: The folder before customization

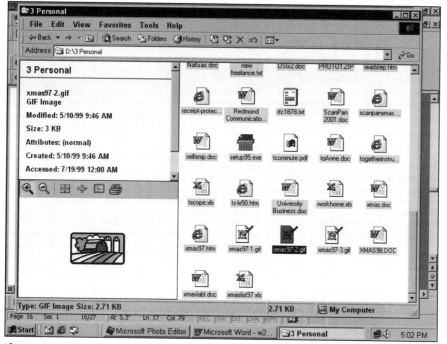

Figure 2-17: Among other changes, the new folder includes a built-in image preview window, icon text highlighting, and detailed file information in the upper-right pane.

Tip

To return your folder to normal, just click View ➪ Customize this Folder, and click the Remove customizations radio button. Click Next, and the folder returns to its default state.

When you customize an individual folder, Windows 2000 stores the settings in a hidden subfolder (called "Folder Settings") inside the one you just customized. If you set Windows to show hidden files and folders, you can see this hidden item from the Windows Explorer or Browser window. Delete the hidden folder, and your settings are lost, returning the folder to a default state.

Optimizing folder settings

Windows 2000 enables you to customize individual folders, but what about changes you want to occur for all folder views? After all, more often than not, you'll want a consistent interface among all the folders you use. Fortunately, Windows 2000 presents a one-stop shop for folder settings in the Control Panel. Click Start ➪ Settings ➪ Control Panel, and then double-click the Folder Options icon.

The Folder Options dialog box presents four tabs: General, View, File Types, and Offline Files. I address only the first two of these here. File Types and Offline Files concern specific features that I cover later in the book .

Tweaking general folder settings

The General page presents options for tailoring the appearance of all Windows 2000 folders. To access these settings, simply select the desired radio button and click OK.

The Active Desktop area presents two options. By default, the Use Windows classic desktop radio button is selected. But if you want the Windows 2000 desktop to act as a container for Web content — displaying HTML pages from your favorite news service, for example — select Enable Web content on my desktop. Just be aware that enabling Active Desktop can put a drag on performance.

The Web View area enables you to decide whether Windows folders incorporate Web functionality. The right pane, for example, is enabled with the Web view but disabled if you select the classic view.

Next is the Browse Folders area. By default Windows is set to open each folder in the same window, easing the inevitable clutter of open windows. If you like, you can have folders open in their own windows by selecting the lower radio button. This can make it easier, for example, to drag files between a folder and its subfolder.

Finally, the Click items as follows area enables you to choose the number of clicks it takes to open an icon. By default, Windows 2000 recognizes double clicks for opening icons (a single click selects an icon). To change this, select Single-click to open an item. Then decide whether to have icon titles underlined only when you float the mouse over an item, or have underlining behave the same way as in your Web browser. In either case, merely floating the cursor over an icon selects the item. Click the icon once, and it opens — just like a Web link.

Changing folder views

Click the View tab to find a bevy of options for changing the way folders look when you use them (as shown in Figure 2-18). To activate options, just check the box next to each option. Then click OK or Apply to make the changes take effect. I'll step through each option now.

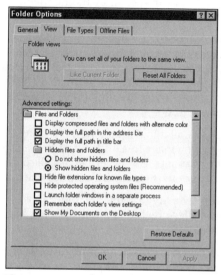

Figure 2-18: Make Windows work the way you want by changing folder behaviors provided in the Advanced settings list.

✦ **Display compressed files and folders with alternate colors:** If you use file and folder compression, this option ensures you know which items are compressed and which are not. In order for this option to have any effect, you must have your disk formatted using the NT File System (NTFS), which offers advanced security, file logging, and other features over the standard File Allocation Table file system. For more on file systems, see Chapter 7.

✦ **Display the full path in the address bar:** Helps ensure you don't get lost when moving among folders. It's also a useful tweak because you can select the contents of the Address bar and copy it elsewhere.

✦ **Display the full path in the title bar:** You can't copy the title bar text, but it does provide great context again when navigating.

✦ **Hidden files and folders:** By default, Windows 2000 won't show hidden files and folders. Intended to protect users who might accidentally delete system files, this setting really makes file management difficult. I invariably change this setting to Show hidden files and folders.

✦ **Hide extensions for known file types:** It's a Mac envy thing—by default, Windows omits the three-letter extension (.DOC, .XLS, and others) when displaying filenames. This assumes that icon graphics clearly identify the associated program for each file. I always deselect this one.

✦ **Hide protected operating system files (Recommended):** Another safety feature. In this case, Windows 2000 hopes to keep you from nuking vital .INI, .SYS, .DLL, .EXE, and other files crucial to your system by hiding them. As a power user, I always turn this option off, but you may want to leave it on.

✦ **Launch folder windows in a separate process:** By default, when folders are launched, they are treated as instances of the same program. If for some reason the browser application trips over itself, all your open folders close. By checking this item, you have Windows place each folder in its own memory space. If one window crashes, none of the others are impacted. This enhances stability but poses a slight performance drain.

✦ **Remember each folder's view settings:** Call it folder memory. Checking this option means that any format changes you make to a folder stay in effect the next time you open it. Sort orders, icon layouts, and other tweaks all remain. Uncheck this option to have folders return to their default settings when closed.

✦ **Show My Documents on the Desktop:** The My Documents folder is Windows 2000's preferred place for storing user files created in applications. Checking this icon makes it easy to open this folder.

✦ **Show pop-up description for folder and desktop items:** Activates little balloon help-like prompts that appear when you hover your mouse over an icon. Information such as user name, date, and file size appear in the balloon.

If after all your tweaking you are totally lost, you can get back to the way it was—and fast. Just click the Reset All Folders button at the top of the View sheet.

Finally, what's up with the faded button next to the Reset All Folders button? The Like Current Folder button is activated only if you access the Folder Options facility from within a folder window. From a folder, just click Tools ➪ Folder Options, and the button becomes live. Click it to make all folders conform to the settings established for the open folder. It's a quick way to make your impromptu work in a single folder pay off across your system.

Webify Windows 2000

As I mentioned before, Microsoft has added a lot of Web-centric features to its user interface over the past several years. Starting with the OSR 2 version of Windows 95, Internet Explorer 4.0, and later Windows 98, the operating system became very Web aware. HTML files and Web sites could be integrated into the desktop—sometimes with less-than-desired results—and file icons adopted a single-click look and feel reminiscent of a Web browser. In fact, to this day, Microsoft argues that the browser is part of the operating system.

Internet Explorer may or may not be an integral part of Windows 2000 — the U.S. Justice Department can decide that — but its features are there to play with. If you want to make Windows 2000 resemble a Web experience as much as possible, I'll show you how to do so. Among the Web talents you can add to Windows 2000's interface are the following:

✦ **Active Desktop:** Enables the Windows desktop to play host to HTML Web pages, ActiveX controls, and other Web services and documents.

✦ **Web-style navigation:** Causes icons to behave like HTML links — a single click launches the underlying item.

✦ **Added information display:** Folders offer thumbnail previews of Web-centric file types, including HTML, GIF, and JPEG.

✦ **Integrated browsing:** The line between Windows Explorer and Internet Explorer blurs. The same application window is used to display both types of browsing sessions.

Setting up Active Desktop

I'll start at the top, with Active Desktop as shown in Figure 2-19. To turn your Windows 2000 desktop into a container for living Web pages, do the following.

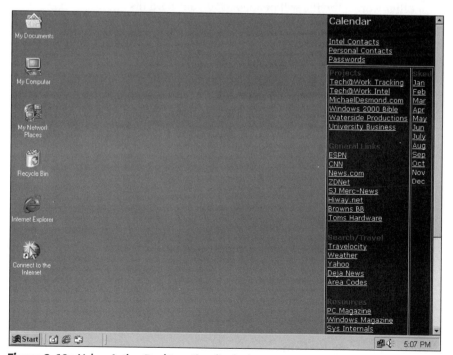

Figure 2-19: Using Active Desktop, I'm displaying a custom Web page that always provides access to frequently used Web sites and links.

1. Right-click anywhere on the desktop and click Properties.

2. Click the Web tab and then activate the checkbox labeled Show Web content on my Active Desktop.

3. By default, the My Current Home Page entry in the box below the checkbox is checked. To assign a different page, uncheck this item.

4. Click the New button.

5. In the New Active Desktop Item, enter the Web address (called a uniform resource locator, or URL) to display in the Location text box. For example, the address www.cnn.com would display the home page of CNN Online. Alternatively, you can use the Browse button to load an image or HTML file from your hard disk or network.

Note

> You can also select from an assortment of Active Desktop services from the Active Desktop Gallery on the Microsoft Web site. Click the Visit Gallery button to open a browser window to the site. You can select from services that offer news, sports, weather, and travel information, including sites such as ESPN SportsZone, CBS SportsCenter, and NEWS.COM.

6. Click OK. A dialog box prompts you for a password—if needed—and tells you that Windows will make the selected site available for offline viewing. In other words, the file will be loaded to your hard disk.

7. Next, tell Windows how often to grab new information from your site. Click the Customize button and then click the Next button on the dialog box that appears.

8. To update Active Desktop content manually, click the top radio button and click the Next button. Go to step 11.

9. To update automatically, click the lower radio button and click the Next button.

10. In the next dialog box, enter the frequency to update your content. The Every spinner control dictates how many days between updates, while the at spinner tells Windows what time to conduct the download. If you are on a modem, you might want to check the checkbox so that Windows can automatically dial up to download content.

11. If your site requires a password, click the Yes radio button and enter your user name and password in the indicated boxes. Otherwise, leave the default No radio button selected and click the Next button.

12. Now click OK to finish the task and kick off the synchronization process. The content downloads and then appears on your Active Desktop. You also see the new site indicated in the Web page of the Display Properties dialog box.

Webify folder navigation

The next step in the Windows Webification effort is to change the way folders work. By replacing double-clicks with link-like single-clicks and adding support for Web file type previews, you can inch your system closer to the Web. Here's how to bring a little more of the Web to your corner of the world.

1. Click Start ⇨ Settings ⇨ Control Panel ⇨ Folder Options.

2. In the General page of the Folder Options dialog box, make sure the top radio button (Enable Web content on my desktop) is selected.

3. In the Web View area, select Enable Web content in folders.

4. In the bottom area, click the radio button labeled Single-click to open an item (point to select).

5. The two radio buttons beneath the selected radio button now go from grayed-out to active. Click the upper of the two to have Windows display underlines for links the same way they are displayed for your Web browser.

6. Click OK or Apply to make your settings take effect.

Congratulations! Your Windows folder windows now displays files and programs that act like HTML links as shown in Figure 2-20. Hover your mouse over an icon to highlight it. Click the item once to activate the icon.

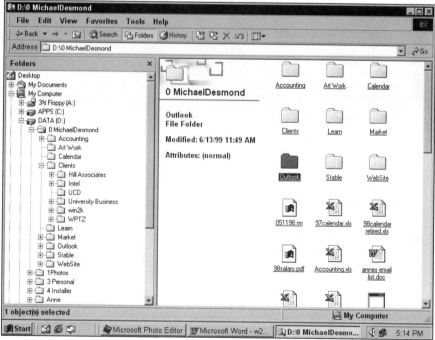

Figure 2-20: Notice anything new? Icons now feature underlining beneath the text, while the cursor turns into the familiar pointing finger when hovered above an active link.

Tip   Don't like your new look? You can jump right back to the way it was by clicking the Restore Defaults button in the General page.

Welcome to tile types

Here's a simple question. How does Windows 2000 know that INVOICE.DOC is a Microsoft Word document and that INVOICE.PDF is an Adobe Acrobat document? Unlike Macintosh files, no information is inside the data files themselves to associate them with an application. Rather, Windows 2000 relies on the three-letter extension (.DOC, .PDF, and the like) to tell the difference between file types.

Windows 2000 keeps an exhaustive list of file extensions in the File Types page of the Folder Options dialog box. To view the files in Windows' list, click Start ⇨ Settings ⇨ Control Panel ⇨ Folder Options, and then click the File Types tab. Scroll down the Registered files types window (shown in Figure 2-21) to see exactly what your operating system is keeping track of.

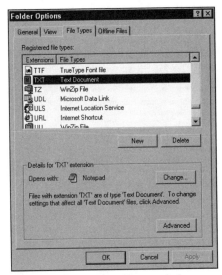

Figure 2-21: You can view and change each file association used by Windows 2000 from the File Types page of the Folder Options dialog box.

How do these files end up in this neat little list? When you install a new application, the setup routine writes information into the Windows 2000 Registry that associates one or more three-letter extensions with the program. So when you install, say, CorelDraw, the program places an entry in the Registry that equates the .CDR extension with the CorelDraw application. That's also why files that you give arbitrary extensions — such as your initials — often end up with generic icons and don't launch when you double-click them. Lacking a Registry entry, Windows simply can't tell what kind of file it's looking at.

You can change file type associations in the File Types page of the Folder Options dialog box. For example, let's say you get lots of really long text (.TXT) files. By default, Notepad is used to open these. But files larger than 32K won't open in Notepad, and Windows bugs you with an error message asking to use the WordPad applet instead. Well, why not simply open all text files in Microsoft Word? That way you reduce the number of applications you are opening.

Here's how:

1. Click the File Types tab and scroll down to the TXT entry in the Extensions column.

2. Click the Change button.

3. In the Open With dialog box, scroll down to Microsoft Word (or other desired program) and click OK.

4. You now see the Word logo displayed next to the TXT extension. Click OK to make the setting take effect.

Tip   The file type list can get very, very long, but you can speed things by clicking the Extensions header to sort the entries alphabetically. Then click on any entry and press T. You'll land on the first entry starting with the letter *T*, within spitting distance of TXT.

Now, when you double-click a .TXT file, Microsoft Word, rather than Notepad, launches to open it.

The Advanced button in the File types page enables you to further tweak Windows' associations. Click the Advanced button, and you see the Edit File Type dialog box. Here you can enter a custom description for the file type in the text box, or click the Change Icon button to select a new icon graphic for this file type.

More important, you can change what you see when you right-click the selected file type. The Actions list box contains the existing commands that you see when you right-click the file. Open is typically the default command — the one that occurs when you double-click — and appears in bold type. You can assign a different default by selecting a different command and clicking the Set Default button.

You can also add new right-click commands by clicking the New button and typing in the appropriate text and command-line information as shown in Figure 2-22. For example, you could have .TXT files open in Notepad by default, but use Word for editing so you can make use of the spell checker and other features. To do this, type the path and filename for Microsoft Word into the Application used to perform action text box. Of course, it's usually easier to use the Browse button to navigate to the executable file.

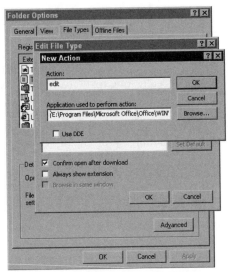

Figure 2-22: From the File Types page, you can add new functionality to the shortcut menu that appears when you click a specific file type.

Tip   Did you know Windows 2000 enables you to access the File Types facility directly from a file's properties window? Just right-click a file, click Properties, and click the Change button. In the Open With dialog box, select the new application to use and then click OK. All files that share the extension now open using the program you selected.

Using the New Search Feature

Today's cavernous hard disks give people a lot of incentive to keep old files around. The result: Your hard disk can start to resemble the overstuffed junk drawer in the utility room. Fortunately, the Windows Search feature gives you a way to cut through the clutter and zero in on a single file, no matter where it is.

Of course, searching is hardly new to Windows. Windows 95, 98, and NT 4.0 all included the full-featured Find application. With Windows 2000, however, this venerable tool gets a Web-savvy facelift (gone is the clumsy three-tab interface) and winds up tightly integrated with Windows' file folders.

There are three ways to launch Search:

✦ Click Start ➪ Search and then click For Files or Folders in the fly-out menu.

✦ Click a blank portion of the Desktop or open a Windows Explorer or browser window and press F3.

✦ From Windows Explorer or browser, click the Search icon on the Standard Buttons toolbar.

Note

One annoying change to the Search facility is that pressing F3 no longer provides a context-sensitive search. Under Windows NT and Windows 95/98, clicking a folder and pressing F3 brought up the Find window with the selected folder set as the search area. With Windows 2000, the Search facility defaults to all fixed drives, regardless of whether or not you've clicked a specific folder or drive. The only way to get a context-sensitive search is to right-click the desired folder or drive and click Search from the context menu.

In all cases, you wind up looking at a modified Windows Explorer window that features the Search facility in the left pane. Figure 2-23 shows how you can quickly enter search parameters such as filenames, text, and file locations in the text boxes. To gain access to additional search filters, click the Search Options link. Four checkboxes appear that enable you to hone your search by date, file type, file size, and other options.

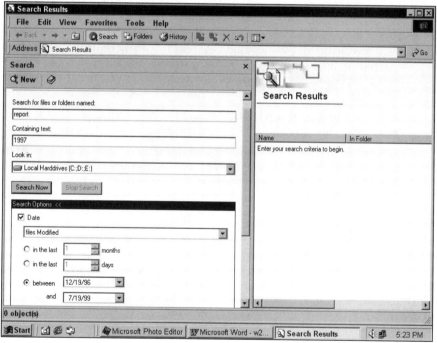

Figure 2-23: Find your files by entering values into the expandable Search Options checkbox items.

I'll walk you through a comprehensive sample search. First, I show you how to whip off a quick-and-dirty file search and then get a bit more detailed. The second scenario can prove valuable for discovering long-lost files because you can whittle down the results even if you can't remember the filename.

Quick searching

Need to find a file fast? The quickest way to do it — provided you know which drive to look in — is to select the drive icon from Windows Explorer and press F3. The window spawns the Search pane. Here's how to pick things up from there.

1. In the top text box, enter the filename or partial filename that you want to search for. By default, Search finds all filenames that include a match in their name to the entry string. So TEST.DOC turns up hits for files with names such as TEST.DOC and PERFTEST.DOC.

Tip   You can tighten the search by using quotation marks around the search string. Entering TEST.DOC finds both TEST.DOC and PERFTEST.DOC, but entering "TEST.DOC" finds only files specifically named "TEST.DOC".

2. If you are unsure of the filename — or fear too many returns — winnow the list by typing in unique text that you know to be in the target file. For example, typing "McDonnell" in this text box now only retrieves files that includes this string.

3. In the Look in drop down list box, select the drive, area, or other location for the search. This may already be set depending on how you entered Search.

4. Click the Search Now button to kick off the search. The results appear in the right pane and include useful folder location (to resolve multiple hits of the same filename), file size, and the like.

Conducting an advanced search

Okay, so maybe the quick-and-dirty search isn't enough. Perhaps you need to dredge up some obscure document — a report you produced years ago or maybe your resume — but you don't recall exactly where you left it or what it is named. Enter the Search Options section of the Search program. These four innocent-looking checkbox items — Date, Type, Size, and Advanced Options — hide some neat drill-down tools. Try them out.

1. First, enter your basic search parameters in the text boxes in the Search pane.

2. Click the Date checkbox. Several controls expand below it.

Tip   Again, in order to see the useful checkbox filters in Search, click the Search Options link just below the Search Now button.

3. In the top drop-down list box, select from files Modified, files Created, and files Last Accessed to peg the date you last changed, originally created, or last opened the file.

4. Next, enter some date parameters for your activity filter. Select the top radio button to filter by the number of months; the middle radio button to filter by the number days, and the bottom radio button to set a date range within which a file was last accessed, created, or changed.

5. Click Search Now if this is all you need; otherwise, move on by checking the Type checkbox. A drop-down list control that displays registered applications appears.

6. Click the drop-down list control and scroll through it. Click an application to filter out any files that are not registered for the selected application. Unfortunately, you can select only one application file type at a time.

7. Either click Search Now or continue digging by clicking the Size checkbox.

8. In the drop-down list item that appears, select either at least or at most. Then enter the file size you wish to filter against. Entering "at least" and 100 returns only files that are 100K or larger in size.

9. Enough for ya? Click Search Now. Otherwise, click the Advanced Options checkbox to bring up three new checkbox items: Search Subfolders, Case sensitive, and Search slow files.

10. By default, Search Subfolders is checked. If you want to search only the current folder, uncheck this option. The Case sensitive checkbox makes sure that only files with matching capitalization are returned. Finally, click Slow search files.

11. Done? Good. Click Search Now to find your results.

Saving searches

As you can tell, creating a detailed search can actually take some time and effort. Fortunately, Windows 2000 enables you to save your searches, so you can quickly reapply them to your hard disk or network area. To save a search, make sure you have set all your parameters as you want them and then click File ⇨ Save Search. Give the saved search a name in the Save Search dialog box (the .FND extension is used by Windows 2000 for these files) and click Save.

To open a saved search, find the file you saved (by default in the Windows 2000 My Documents folder, but it can be anywhere) and double-click it. The Search application window comes up with all your set parameters. Click the Search Now button to rerun the search, or tweak the saved entries to tailor the search to your immediate needs. Of course, search files can be shared and copied like any other file, which makes them useful for network searches and workgroups.

Beyond file searches

In addition to finding files and folders, the Windows 2000 Search facility reaches out to include your address book (people) your network (computers) and the Internet. By clicking any one of these links at the bottom of the Search pane, you can invoke a specific type of search.

Finding computers

To find a computer on your network, do the following:

1. Click the Computers link at the bottom of the Search pane.

2. In the Computer Name text box, type in the name that your network administrator has given to the target computer. Returns on this search include systems with the entered name as part of their complete name. So TEST returns TEST, TEST1, and TESTLAB, for example.

Keep in mind that your network must provide some form of naming service in order for this type of search to work.

Finding people

The Search application also lets you conduct searches for contacts in your Windows Address Book or from an external directory. To kick off a people search, click the People link at the bottom of the left pane of the Search window. The Find People dialog box, shown in Figure 2-24, shows how you can enter search parameters for contact name, e-mail, address, phone, and other information.

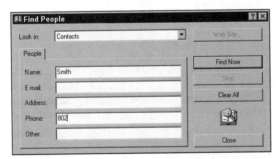

Figure 2-24: Search through your Windows 2000 Address Book or Internet-based directories using the straightforward Find People facility.

You can search in the Windows 2000 address book or Internet-based directories by selecting from choices in the Look in drop-down control at the top of the dialog box. Windows 2000 interacts with directory services based on the popular Lightweight Directory Access Protocol, or LDAP. To add a new directory service, do the following:

1. Right-click Look in drop-down control and click Directory Services.

2. In the Internet Accounts dialog box, click the Add button.

3. Enter the address of the directory server in the dialog box. (This address should have been given to you by your network administrator or Internet service provider.) Click Next.

   If you need to log on to your directory server, click the checkbox labeled My LDAP server requires me to log on. When you click Next, you will need to enter your account name and password in the text boxes shown in Figure 2-25. Click Next to continue from Step 4.

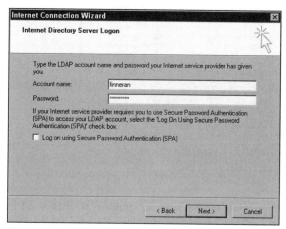

Figure 2-25: This dialog box is the same used by Internet Explorer to add new directory servers.

4. Unless otherwise instructed, click the No radio button in the Check Email Addresses dialog box.

5. Click the Finish button. The account is now set up.

Searching the Internet

Finally, the Search feature lets you hop right onto the Internet to conduct powerful Web page and other searches. Click the Internet link at the bottom of the left pane, and a new Internet-specific Search pane comes up, as shown in Figure 2-26. Of course, you will need an active connection to the Internet for this search to work.

Enter the term you wish to seek and then click the Search Now button. A list of links appears in the left pane. Click the desired link, and the right pane turns into a Web browser window—the contents of the HTML page appears where your file folders used to be. To view additional found pages, simply click the links in the left pane.

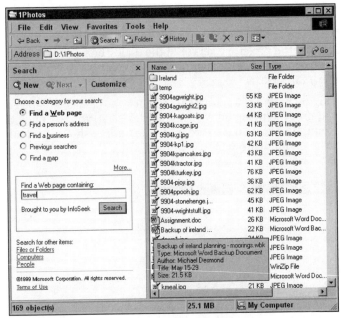

Figure 2-26: Quickly seek out Web pages, individual addresses, and other information on the World Wide Web.

Note   The Internet search facility accessed here is identical to that used by Internet Explorer 5.0. The IE5 search facility is explained in detail in Chapter 13.

Of course, switching between the Windows Explorer and Internet Explorer can get a bit confusing. After all, you may be wondering where your file listing went if you start digging around through multiple Web pages. Personally, I prefer to do my Internet searching from Internet Explorer and my file searching from Windows Explorer. This helps keep me from losing tracking of my work.

Summary

The first thing you notice about Windows 2000 is the improved interface. Users of both Windows NT and Windows 95/98 immediately notice improvements to the look, feel, and behavior of the interface. From cosmetic touches such as fading menus and shadowed cursors, to useful additions such as a Plug and Play–aware Device Manager, Windows 2000 offers superior navigation and interaction to the operating systems that preceded it.

That said, veteran Windows users will need some time to get acclimated. Microsoft did well to slim down the desktop and Control Panel icon offerings, but some useful resources have been made harder to find, most notably the Device Manager. This chapter helps novices quickly master the ways of Windows, while giving veterans insights into its changing face. Among the things we reviewed here:

✦ Windows 2000's tweaked interface and navigation quirks

✦ Powerful customization options, such as tailored folder views, Web-enabled navigation, and advanced interface options.

✦ Helpful management resources, including the ever-useful Device Manager and Windows Control Panel

✦ Strategies for searching for everything from files on the local hard disk to people on the Internet

✦   ✦   ✦

Installing and Removing Software

The Windows 2000 operating system installed on
your computer is just the beginning — the operating
system alone rarely does the work you want to do with
your computer. Instead, the operating system provides
the necessary foundation and framework for the software
programs you run within the operating system. You use
word processing programs to write letters, spreadsheet
programs to develop budgets, database programs to track
your inventory, personal finance management programs to
balance your checkbook, and so on. Installing additional
software programs on your Windows 2000 system enables
you to build a set of tools that you can use to get your day-
to-day work done.

Windows-based software is, by necessity, tightly integrated
with the operating system and requires careful installation.
Fortunately, installation programs automate the actual
installation process, and Windows 2000, like previous
versions of Windows, enables you to conveniently manage
those installation utilities from a Control Panel applet. This
chapter shows you how to do that and more.

Installing Software

You may wonder why installing software is such a big deal.
Isn't it just a matter of creating a folder on your hard drive,
copying a bunch of files to that folder, and then clicking an
icon to run the new program? In fact, if you worked with older
DOS-based computers, you might remember when installing
software was often just a matter of following instructions to

manually copy the program's files to your computer. Alas, installing Windows software programs is rarely so straightforward. Even installing simple programs involves attending to numerous details.

Windows software programs are tightly integrated with the operating system, relying on the operating system to provide major parts of the program's user interface and to furnish and control access to the computer's hardware. Also, every Windows program must be able to cooperate with Windows and with other Windows programs. Hence, installing a Windows program usually involves copying files to shared directories, adding entries to the Windows Registry, and taking other steps to integrate and incorporate the new program into your system — that's in addition to the obvious steps of creating folders, copying files, and adding the program to your Start menu.

Because there are so many behind-the-scenes steps to go through to install a Windows program, virtually all Windows programs employ a separate utility to handle the installation chores automatically. In fact, automated install and uninstall features are requirements for programs to earn any of the Windows compatibility logos that manufacturers display on the product packaging. As a result of the automation provided by the setup utilities, software installation becomes a relatively simple process from the user's perspective. You just run the application's installation program, follow the onscreen instructions to make or confirm some options, and then play the role of spectator as the installation program copies files and does all the work of installing your new software on your Windows 2000 system. When the installation program finishes its job, your new application is installed and ready to use.

So, the question of how to install new software on your system usually comes down to a question of how to start the application's installation program.

Installing programs that install automatically

By far the most common software installation scenario is a new software program distributed on a CD-ROM disc. Furthermore, most software manufacturers nowadays take advantage of Windows' AutoRun feature to automatically run the application's installation program when you insert the CD into the drive in your computer. As a result, the installation process for most new software goes something like this:

 Tip   It's always a good idea to quit any Windows programs before you start to install new software. The installation program might be unable to properly update shared files that are currently in use by another program. Obviously, you want to exit open programs, such as a word processing program, but don't forget about the assortment of utility programs represented by system tray icons. You might need to quit some of those programs as well.

1. Insert the application's installation CD into your computer's CD-ROM drive.

   Wait a moment or so for the CD to spin up to speed and for the AutoRun feature to locate and run the installation program.

2. When the installation program appears (see Figure 3-1), follow the onscreen instructions to select and confirm options and install the software.

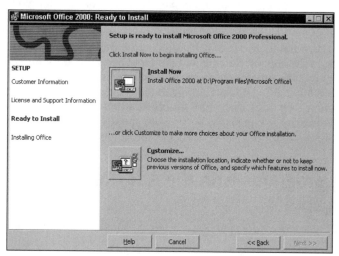

Figure 3-1: A typical software installation program provides onscreen instructions that lead you through the installation process.

Depending on the size of the software application you're installing, the process of selecting options and then waiting for the installation program to copy files and do its other work might take only a minute or so, or it might take nearly an hour.

3. Remove the installation CD from the CD-ROM drive and begin using your new software.

You might need to reboot your system in order for some of the changes made by the installation program to take effect.

That's all there is to it. The installation program leads you through the process of selecting any options and parameters you need to enter. Frequently, the installation program also elicits registration information from you at the same time — often refusing to proceed to the next step until you fill in the requisite blanks. After the installation program gathers the required information, the rest of the process is automatic.

Note

In order to install software on your system, you need to have the appropriate access permissions. If you are logged on as Administrator, you've got carte blanche to change the system. A member of the Power User group can also install software. However, members of the Guest or Restricted User groups usually can't make system configuration changes such as installing software. If you don't have the necessary system security access, contact your system administrator for assistance.

Almost all software installation programs not only install the software, they also add entries to the Start menu and/or shortcuts to the desktop to enable you to launch the new software conveniently. However, these changes normally affect only the Start menu and desktop linked to the user name you used when you installed the software, assuming, of course, that your system is configured for multiple users and that all users don't share the same Start menu and desktop. Later, if you log on with a different user name, the newly installed software won't appear on the Start menu or desktop. The software is still installed and available on your computer; all that's missing is the Start menu shortcut to launch it. You can easily remedy this problem by manually adding a shortcut for the new software to the Start menu or desktop of the new user. (See Chapter 6 for information on editing the Start menu.) The system administrator can also edit the Start menus and desktops for all users of a computer. (See Chapters 20 and 27 for details of user management.)

Installing programs with the Add/Remove Programs applet

Okay, so what if your new program doesn't begin to install itself automatically? What then?

Perhaps you or your system administrator disabled the AutoRun feature so the installation program on the CD doesn't start automatically. Perhaps the software manufacturer chose not to use the AutoRun feature to start the installation program in the first place. (That's common when different versions of the software for different operating systems are distributed on the same CD.) Perhaps your new software arrived on floppy disks or some other distribution medium that doesn't use AutoRun. If your new software's installation program doesn't start automatically, your next option is the Add/Remove Programs applet in the Control Panel.

To use the Add/Remove Programs applet to install new software, follow these steps:

1. Click Start ➪ Settings ➪ Control Panel.

2. When the Control Panel window appears, double-click the Add/Remove Programs icon to open the Add/Remove Programs dialog box as shown in Figure 3-2. Notice that the dialog box already includes a list of previously installed software.

3. Click Add New Programs. The list of installed programs is replaced by two ways to add programs (see Figure 3-3).

   One choice enables you to install a program from a distribution disk in your floppy disk or CD-ROM drive. The alternative is Windows Update, which enables you to download and install updates and supplemental Windows programs from Microsoft's Web site. Windows Update, which requires that you have TCP/IP networking installed and configured, is covered in Chapter 8.

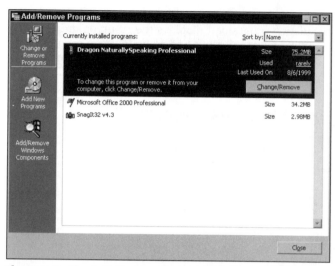

Figure 3-2: The Add/Remove Programs dialog box.

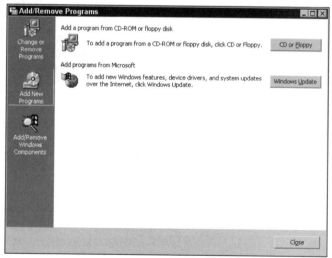

Figure 3-3: Select the source of your new program.

4. Click the CD or Floppy button. The first page of the Install Program From Floppy Disk or CD-ROM Wizard appears.

5. Make sure the software distribution disk is inserted in the CD-ROM drive or floppy disk drive and then click Next. The wizard searches your floppy disk drives and CD-ROM drives for a program file with one of the standard names

for installation programs (such as SETUP.EXE or INSTALL.EXE). If the wizard finds an installation program, it displays the result on the next page as shown in Figure 3-4. If the wizard doesn't find an installation program or finds the wrong one, you can use the text box and browse button to specify the location of the installation program.

Figure 3-4: Normally, the wizard finds the setup program for you.

Note   The Add/Remove Programs applet automatically searches the root directory of each floppy disk and CD-ROM drive looking for an installation program. If the installation program is located in a subfolder or has an unusual name, you need to enter the path name and filename of the installation program manually.

6. Click Finish. Windows closes the Run Installation Program dialog box and launches the specified installation program.

7. When the installation program's screen or dialog box appears, follow the onscreen instructions to select options and install the new software. The installation program does its thing, installing the new software. This part of the process is essentially the same, no matter how you start the installation program.

8. If the Add/Remove Programs dialog box is still open after the installation program finishes installing the new software, click Close to close the dialog box.

After the installation program finishes its work, you can begin using your new software. Remember, it's the installation program that comes with the software that does the job of installing the application. The Add/Remove Programs applet just provides a convenient way to launch that installation program.

Installing programs manually

If your new software's installation program doesn't start automatically when you insert a CD into the CD-ROM drive and the Add/Remove Programs applet doesn't find the installation program, the final alternative is to start the installation program manually. It's not hard to do. You just follow these steps:

1. Open Windows Explorer (click Start ➪ Programs ➪ Accessories ➪ Windows Explorer).

2. Navigate to the drive and folder where the setup program resides. That might be a network drive, a Zip drive or other removable media, or a folder on your hard drive where you saved files you downloaded from the Internet or expanded from an archive file.

3. Locate the installation program file (usually SETUP.EXE or INSTALL.EXE) and double-click the file's icon. This action starts the installation program.

4. When the installation program appears, follow the onscreen instructions to select options and install the software.

   As with the other options, the procedure is the same after you start the installation program. The installation process might be quick and simple or long and involved, depending on the software you're installing. Either way, the installation program leads you through the process with onscreen prompts for anything you must do and completes the installation automatically.

Note   When you download software from the Internet or other sources, it often arrives in a single compressed archive file that contains a multitude of other embedded files. If the file has a .ZIP extension, you need to use a special utility such as WinZIP to extract the component files from the archive file before you can use those files to install the software. Files with an .EXE extension are self-extracting archive files, which means you don't need a separate utility to extract the files from the archive. Instead, you can just double-click the file's icon to run a built-in extraction program. The self-extracting archive often launches the installation program automatically after it finishes extracting files to a temporary directory. If the installation program doesn't start automatically, you need to locate and start it yourself.

Removing Software

What goes up must come down — and what gets added to a computer must sometimes be removed. You might need to remove software to update or replace it with another software product to dispose of a program you no longer use or to repair corrupted files.

Whatever the reason, when you remove or change a Windows application, you need to use an uninstall program. It's nearly impossible to manually remove all the files and settings for a Windows program without leaving remnants of the program on your system or damaging other applications by inadvertently removing shared files.

What Is the Windows Installer Service?

The Windows Installer service is a new feature of Windows 2000 that offers software developers the opportunity to add robustness and versatility to software installations. When coupled with software installation programs designed to take advantage of its capabilities, Windows Installer ensures recovery from failed installations, helps prevent conflicts between applications, and improves the reliability of application removal. Windows Installer also offers the capability to diagnose and repair corrupted program files. It supports on-demand installation of program features and unattended installations that don't require user input. Windows Installer can manage program installation and uninstallation — provided the service is activated and the software being installed conforms to the new MSI package file format.

The Windows Installer service is included as part of the standard Windows 2000 Professional installation. However, by default, it isn't turned on. You can enable Windows Installer service just like any other Windows 2000 service. (See Chapter 27 for information on starting and stopping Windows 2000 services.)

The Windows Installer service, when combined with software that supports the new file format, adds some useful capabilities to a standalone system, such as the ability to dynamically install program features when they are needed. But Windows Installer really comes into its own in a managed environment where it works in conjunction with Active Directory, IntelliMirror, and Group Policy-based configuration management to make the system administrator's job easier by facilitating remote network installations and other advanced software management features.

Just as the installation process is automated to handle all the files and registration settings a modern Windows program requires, the software removal process requires the same kind of automation to reverse the process. In fact, an uninstall program is a requirement for Windows programs seeking certification as Windows 2000 compatible. So, every Windows program should include an uninstall program that will automatically remove the software from your computer.

Many uninstall programs give you just one option — completely removing the application from your computer system, but some install/uninstall programs enable you to maintain your software by adding and removing features, repairing corrupted files, and reinstalling the software to replace accidentally deleted files and reinstate default settings.

Removing programs with the Add/Remove Programs applet

Although some programs have a separate uninstall program that is accessible from the Start menu, the central clearinghouse for removing software is the Add/Remove Programs applet in the Control Panel. To use the Add/Remove Programs applet to repair or remove a program, follow these steps:

1. Click Start ⇨ Settings ⇨ Control Panel to open the Control Panel window.

2. Double-click the Add/Remove Programs icon. The Add/Remove Programs dialog box appears showing a list of currently installed programs (refer to Figure 3-2).

3. (Optional) Select a sorting option from the Sort By drop-down list box in the upper-right corner of the dialog box. Windows sorts the list of installed applications according to your selection. The default sorting order is alphabetical by name. However, you can also sort by Size, Frequency of Use, or Date Last Used. This date feature is particularly handy if you're looking for unused applications that you can delete to free up disk space and reduce clutter on your system.

4. Scroll through the list and select the program you want to remove or change.

5. Click Change/Remove. Windows starts the selected application's install/uninstall program. The options you have at this point depend on what the software manufacturer incorporated into the uninstall program.

6. Follow the onscreen instructions to confirm deletion of the software or select the software maintenance procedure you want to perform.

Tip

When an uninstall program asks if you want to delete some shared files, the safest answer is No. There is always a possibility that some other program will need access to the shared file for proper operation—even when the uninstall program finds no such links. If the shared file is located in the program folder of the application you're removing, the chances of another program needing the file are slim, and you can probably delete the file safely. If the shared file is in the Windows or System directories, the odds of another program needing the file are higher. It's best not to delete those files.

7. After the uninstall program finishes its job, click Close to close the Add/Remove Programs dialog box.

Using a program's uninstall feature

The uninstall programs for most applications should be listed in the Add/Remove Programs dialog box, but a few are not. Also, many applications have separate uninstall programs that you can run without going through the Add/Remove Programs dialog box. To find these uninstall programs, look in the application's submenu on the Start menu for an item named Uninstall or something similar. Choose that menu item to start the uninstall program. You can also use Windows Explorer to look in the application's program folder for a file named UNINSTALL.EXE, SETUP.EXE, INSTALL.EXE, or something along those lines. Double-click the install/uninstall program icon to launch the program. When the uninstall program screen or dialog box appears, follow the onscreen instructions to remove or repair the application.

Installing and Removing Windows Components

When you install Windows 2000 Professional, the installation includes all the basic operating system components and a standard set of accessories. It's a package deal, and you don't have much opportunity to pick and choose what parts of the operating system you install. However, some optional components of Windows 2000 are not included in the base installation. They include the following:

- ✦ Indexing service (enables full-text searches of files)
- ✦ Internet Information services (Web and FTP servers, and so on)
- ✦ Management and Monitoring tools (Simple Network Management Protocol)
- ✦ Message Queuing service (special network communication services)
- ✦ Network services (RIP Listener and Simple TCP/IP services)
- ✦ Other Network File and Print services (print services for Unix)
- ✦ Script Debugger (debugging tool for ActiveX script engines)

The process of adding and removing components of the Windows 2000 Professional operating system is a little different from adding and removing regular software applications. The Windows components are even more tightly integrated into the operating system and thus require different handling. To add or remove a Windows component, follow these steps:

1. Click Start ⇨ Settings ⇨ Control Panel to open the Control Panel window.

2. Double-click the Add/Remove Programs icon. The Add/Remove Programs dialog box appears, showing a list of currently installed programs (refer to Figure 3-2).

3. Click Add/Remove Windows Components. Windows starts the Windows Components Wizard in a separate dialog box as shown in Figure 3-5.

4. Scroll through the Components list box and select the components you want to install or remove. A checkmark in a component's checkbox indicates a component that is, or will be, installed. Click a checkbox to add or remove the checkmark, thus instructing Windows to install or remove the component.

Some components are composed of one or more subcomponents. You might want to install some of those subcomponents and not others. When you select a component from the list that includes subcomponents, the Details button becomes active. Click Details to display a list of subcomponents in a separate dialog box. For example, if you select Internet Information Services and then click the Details button, a dialog box appears that lists subcomponents such as File Transfer Protocol, FrontPage 2000 Server Extensions, Personal Web Manager, and World Wide Web Server. Select the subcomponents you want to install and then click OK to close the component dialog box and return to the Windows Components Wizard dialog box.

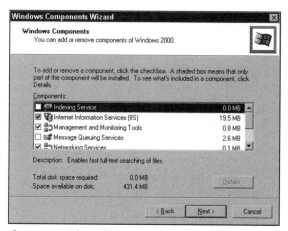

Figure 3-5: The Windows Components Wizard.

5. After selecting the components to install or remove, make sure the Windows 2000 Professional CD is available in the CD-ROM drive and click Next. The Windows Components Wizard builds a list of components to install and begins copying files and changing system settings.

6. Click Finish to close the Windows Components Wizard dialog box and return to the Add/Remove Programs dialog box.

7. Click Close to close the Add/Remove Programs dialog box.

The newly installed Windows components are available for your use. But don't expect to find them listed on the Start menu. These Windows components are deeply embedded into the operating system. See Chapter 22 for information about working with Internet Information services. See Chapter 27 for more details of some of the other component services.

Understanding Compatibility

Software compatibility with Windows 2000 is a bona fide concern. You can't run just any program in Windows 2000 and expect it to work properly. For best results, your software must be designed specifically for Windows 2000. Many other Windows programs will probably work as well. However, some programs designed for previous versions of Windows will exhibit problems ranging from minor inconsistencies and glitches to total failure and conflicts and incompatibility with other programs when run on Windows 2000.

Windows 2000 programs

Only programs that are certified to be compatible with Windows 2000 are guaranteed to run and run properly. As with previous releases of new Windows versions, Microsoft has initiated a logo program that allows software manufacturers who meet certain requirements to display a Windows 2000 compatibility logo on the packaging for qualifying products. When you see the Windows 2000 logo on a software box, you can be assured that it will install and run successfully on your Windows 2000 system.

Of course, only the latest versions and newest software are designed for Windows 2000 compatibility and carry the logo. If you had to rely on that software alone, the pickings would be very slim, and many of the programs you have depended on in the past may not be available in Windows 2000-compatible versions (at least not for many months after Windows 2000 arrives). Fortunately, many programs that don't carry the Windows 2000 logo will still work just fine.

Windows NT programs

Because Windows 2000 is the successor to Windows NT 4.0, it shares many of the same characteristics. As a result, the vast majority of Windows NT programs continue to function properly when running on Windows 2000. There are some exceptions, but the chances are good that you can continue to use your Windows NT programs after upgrading to Windows 2000. Plan on using most of your existing Windows NT programs; just be alert for the occasional program that crashes or behaves erratically. If you do encounter a problem program, check with the software developer for patches or upgrades that will enable the program to run successfully in Windows 2000.

Windows 95/98 programs

Like Windows NT and Windows 2000, Windows 95/98 is a 32-bit operating system. However, despite the superficial similarities, the internal programming of Windows 95/98 is vastly different from the Windows NT operating system family. As a result, software compatibility with Windows 95/98 is no indication of compatibility with Windows 2000. Many programs are compatible with both Windows 95/98 and Windows NT (and carry logos for both those operating systems), and many of those are compatible with Windows 2000 as well. Programs that are designed specifically for Windows 95/98 are less likely to work in Windows 2000. In particular, system utilities such as disk maintenance utilities and backup programs that are designed for Windows 95/98 often don't work with Windows NT — or Windows 2000.

Trial and error is the only reliable way to test Windows 95/98 programs for compatibility with Windows 2000. Fortunately, there's relatively little risk involved in testing a typical Windows 95/98 productivity application or similar program. You can simply install the program and then try it to see if it works. Windows 2000 warns you if the installation program attempts to overwrite your system files with an older version — you can just click No to prevent the files from being replaced. If the program doesn't run properly, you can usually uninstall it without doing permanent damage to your Windows 2000 system. You should approach installing system utilities with considerably more caution. The deeper a program must delve into your system, the more likely it is to cause problems if it isn't designed specifically for Windows 2000. The odds of corrupting your system by installing a program are small. However, unless you're prepared to reinstall Windows 2000 in the event that a serious problem does occur, you should avoid trial-and-error testing of system utilities that aren't certified Windows 2000 compatible.

Windows 3.x programs

Their numbers are getting fewer and fewer all the time, but some old 16-bit Windows 3.x programs are still around. Surprisingly, Windows 2000 can run many (but not all) of them. These old programs don't take advantage of your modern operating system's features and speed, but they might run adequately. It's hard to predict which programs will run and which ones won't. The best solution is to just give that old program a try if you really need it. (See the section "Windows 95/98 programs" later in this chapter for notes on testing old programs.) Of course, if you can locate a newer version of the software, that's even better.

MS-DOS programs

Other versions of Windows explicitly supported MS-DOS programs. Icons on the desktop and on the Start menu opened a window with a DOS prompt or restarted the computer in MS-DOS mode. Earlier versions of Windows even included a shutdown option for restarting the computer in MS-DOS mode. The operating system actually generates a virtual computer in memory in which to run MS-DOS and your DOS-based programs.

The MS-DOS icons and Start menu items are gone from Windows 2000, but the capability to run MS-DOS in a virtual machine is still present, if somewhat hidden. Windows 2000 even includes a fairly complete set of DOS commands buried in the depths of the operating system's directories on your hard drive.

You can run most MS-DOS programs and commands by clicking Start ⇨ Programs ⇨ Accessories ⇨ Command Prompt. Windows opens an MS-DOS window as shown in Figure 3-6 and displays the DOS prompt. You can run DOS commands and interact with your DOS programs in that window. Alternatively, you can start an MS-DOS program by clicking Start ⇨ Run, typing the command that starts the program in the Run dialog box, and then clicking OK.

Figure 3-6: An MS-DOS window.

Remember that your DOS-based program is running in a virtual machine with simulated links to generic hardware. If your DOS-based program follows established conventions for interacting with the machine, it might run successfully. If the program attempts to circumvent normal procedures and access your computer's hardware directly, you can expect problems. As a result, DOS commands and simple programs often run successfully while high-performance games and complex programs fail.

After running a DOS-based program in an MS-DOS window, exit the program to return to the DOS prompt. Then type EXIT and press Enter to shut down the virtual machine and close the MS-DOS window.

Summary

Adding software applications to Windows 2000 requires more than simply copying a few files to your hard disk. Fortunately, installation programs handle all the nitty-gritty details of installing, configuring, and removing programs on your Windows 2000 system.

Among the topics covered in this chapter are

✦ Installing software in Windows 2000 involves more than just copying files to your hard disk, but automated installation utilities handle all the details.

✦ The Windows Installer service makes it possible for software developers to create more robust software installation utilities.

✦ Removing installed software from Windows 2000 relies on automated utilities just as the installation does.

✦ The Add/Remove Programs applet in the Control Panel enables you to install and remove Windows 2000 components.

✦ Not every Windows program is compatible with Windows 2000, but most of your software inventory will probably work — even if it doesn't carry the Windows 2000 logo.

In the next chapter, I cover the assortment of mini-programs and productivity tools that come with Windows 2000.

✦   ✦   ✦

Installing and Removing Hardware

I have to admit that I have a love-hate relationship with computer hardware. I love it when it works, but when it doesn't, I want to throw it out a window of the tallest building I can find!

That said, I have found that knowledge is power, and installing, removing, and managing the hardware on your system takes a lot of knowledge despite everyone's best efforts to reduce the workload of the user. Whether you are installing another keyboard, a mouse, a printer, or a video adapter, you need to know some basic information to get you started and keep you out of trouble. When the trouble starts, you need to augment your basic knowledge with more advanced skills.

I hope I haven't scared you off yet because if you can install and remove hardware, you will be able to customize a system to meet your needs and significantly increase the life expectancy of your computer. My own experience is a case in point. I bought my first PC in 1992. It was a 486/33 with a 128MB hard drive, no CD, no audio card, no printer, and only 4MB of RAM. Over the years I replaced the CPU, added more RAM, added another hard drive, installed a CD-ROM drive and sound card, went through a couple of video cards, changed monitors, mice, and even printers. Building this configuration took several years because I didn't need to do everything at once, and the benefit of adding and removing all that hardware was that I had a reasonably up-to-date computer that met my needs for several years.

I have already performed significant upgrades to my current computer, built last year. I've added two hard drives, increased the RAM, added peripherals such as a scanner and printer, changed keyboards, added an external storage device, and more.

In this chapter I hope to give you enough knowledge and encouragement to enable you to be just as obsessed with hardware as I am and tell you how to do it all with Windows 2000 Professional.

Be One with Your Hardware

The first law of tinkering is to "Be one with your hardware." You need to know the different types of hardware and how each type of device connects to your computer before you can comfortably and safely purchase and install new hardware.

Types of hardware

Think of hardware as being in two distinct categories: internal and external. Internal hardware is physically inside the case of your computer, and to add or remove it, you must turn off your computer, open the case, and install or remove it. Internal hardware typically includes devices such as video adapters, internal hard drives, floppy drives, sound cards, network adapters, CD-ROM drives, and game adapters.

External hardware is obviously the opposite of internal. These devices normally connect to the back of the computer but are physically located outside the computer case. Installation and removal are much easier as a result, but space sometimes becomes a problem if you have a multitude of external hardware devices. Examples of external hardware include monitors, printers, speakers, keyboards, mice, and scanners.

Obviously some devices can be either internal or external, depending on the model you purchase based on your preference or needs. When purchasing these types of components, always make sure you are buying the appropriate version. Common instances of devices that have internal and external versions available are modems, tape drives, CD-ROM recorders, large-capacity external hard drive, and removable drives such as Iomega's Zip and Jaz drives.

Mobile computers are a different type of animal. Laptops, notebooks, and palmtops are optimized so that everything is contained inside a small, densely packed case with the option of connecting external resources at the office or while you're on the go. Today's full-featured laptops have a color monitor, mouse or other pointing device, keyboard, hard drive, modem and/or network adapter, and CD-ROM drive all in one case. They have yet to design a laptop that has an internal printer or scanner, so not all functionality is present.

Caution   It is generally not wise to open the case of a laptop computer and attempt to perform maintenance or upgrades yourself. Let a trained professional handle these tasks.

Connecting the dots

All hardware, whether internal or external, has to be connected to the motherboard of your computer in order to work. The types of connections are about as important as the type of device. You can classify the connections into the same two broad categories as the types of hardware: semipermanent (internal) and temporary (external).

Caution No two types of connections are compatible. For example, if you purchase an AGP graphics adapter you must have an AGP port on your motherboard. Similarly, purchasing a USB printer will do you no good if you do not have a USB port. If all your PCI slots are taken, you have to remove something if you buy another PCI-based expansion card. This is perhaps the most important lesson to learn in buying hardware! Know what types of connections you have available.

Typical internal connections include the following:

IDE   Integrated Drive (sometimes Device) Electronics. This connection is used for hard drives and CD-ROMs and is the most common type in use today for IBM-compatible PCs. The connection is normally located on the motherboard, but internal expansion cards may be added.

Note IDE is technically an ATA or AT connection.

SCSI   Small Computer Systems Interface. SCSI is a high-speed parallel connection used for hard drives and other peripherals such as printers, removable storage devices, and scanners. A SCSI adapter may be built into the computer, but you will typically require a SCSI adapter card. SCSI is generally faster than IDE but may be more difficult to configure and tends to be more expensive than a comparable IDE hard drive or CD-ROM drive. Up to seven SCSI devices may be "daisy-chained" together, forming a string of devices using a single connection on the computer.

PCI   Peripheral Component Interconnect. PCI expansion slots provide an interface between add-on cards and the computer. They are newer and more capable than ISA expansion slots, and they are also Plug and Play capable.

AGP   Accelerated Graphics Port. An AGP port is used solely for display adapters and provides a high-speed memory pipeline for memory-intensive graphics routines. An AGP-based video card is more capable than PCI-based graphics cards. In addition to their being more capable, buying an AGP display adapter frees a PCI slot.

ISA	Industry Standard Architecture. Today's ISA slots are almost all 16-bit. ISA slots are the most widely used, but their importance is diminishing due to PCI, AGP, and USB.

The most common external connections are these:

Parallel ports	Parallel ports are sometimes called *printer ports* or *LPT ports*. These ports transmit data in parallel and are showing their age. The high volume of data for printing and other functions can cause system slow downs. Printers, scanners, and removable storage devices commonly use this connection. Many devices have a parallel pass-through port to pass data from the computer to a device down the chain, enabling devices to share a single parallel port.
Serial ports	Serial ports are also called *COM ports*. These ports transmit data in serial fashion, at higher speeds than parallel ports. Typical devices that use this connection are modems, some mice, and serial printers.
USB	Universal Serial Bus. The new rage in computing is an external bus that features a high bandwidth, Plug-and-Play compatibility, and the ability to connect and disconnect devices without having to power down your computer. USB devices can be connected, and a single USB port can handle up to 127 devices through one connection. Most external devices are coming out with USB versions, including printers, keyboards, scanners, cameras, mice, monitors, and more. USB ports are small and rectangular.
PS/2	Most computers have two of these connections, one dedicated for a mouse and the other for your keyboard. They are small and round.

Note   FireWire, also known as the *IEEE 1394 multimedia connection*, is making waves. Currently available only for Macintosh computers, FireWire is a high-speed Plug-and-Play connection that is faster than USB or PCI and capable of supporting 63 devices on one connection. The connection used in mobile computers is unique:

PCMCIA	Personal Computer Memory Card International Association. This type of socket is used in portable computers for connecting PC cards, which are removable devices. PC cards can be modems, network adapters, and hard drives. There are three types of PCMCIA sockets.

Hardware resources

All hardware needs resources of some form or another to operate. With the advent of Plug and Play, the importance of understanding the finer points of hardware resource management is diminishing, but you should still be able to identify them if you need to perform serious troubleshooting. You should be familiar with these five types of resources: device drivers, hardware interrupts (IRQs), direct memory access (DMA), input/output port addresses (I/O ports), and memory space.

Note   USB connections do not require IRQs, memory addresses, or DMA channels.

Device drivers are software components that provide an interface between the device and your system, as well as other hardware components. Typically, the manufacturer of a hardware device creates a driver that runs it and distributes it with the device. In some cases, Windows 2000 Professional already has a device driver for a hardware component, and you won't have to do a thing. In other cases, the drivers are embedded so far into the system that if you tinker with them you're treading on dangerous ground!

Devices use an IRQ to signal the central processor that they need attention. For example, as I type this sentence, the keyboard is sending interrupts to the CPU asking it to stop whatever else it is doing and respond to the keyboard. The end result is that each letter appears promptly on my monitor. The problem with IRQs is that there are only 16 of them due to the early design of personal computers, and two of those are reserved. Normally only one device can be assigned to an IRQ, but with Plug and Play, IRQs can be shared.

DMA controllers relieve the central processor of some of the tasks associated with moving data between memory and a device, but as with IRQs, there is a limit to the total number of DMA channels.

I/O ports, or port addresses, are assigned to each device as a communications channel devoted solely to that device.

Memory addresses are allocated to each device and reserved for that device's use.

The important point to remember about all of these resource is that when a conflict occurs, it generally involves one or more of the resource types. There may be an IRQ conflict, overlapping memory addresses, an unassigned I/O port, or a bad device driver.

Plug and Play

Plug and Play was developed after the agonizing screams of users everywhere reached computer manufacturers and software developers. In the dark days before Plug and Play, each device had to be configured by the user, and all resources had to be assigned manually. Plug and Play attempts to create an environment where the computer and attached devices do all the work for you. The computer detects and identifies each Plug and Play–compatible hardware device and automatically assigns the appropriate and available resources to it. Nowadays, your computer BIOS, operating system, and devices are generally all Plug and Play, alleviating much hair-pulling and frustration. Theoretically, you plug a device into your machine, boot the computer, and the operating system identifies it and installs the device drivers needed to operate it with little or no user intervention — in theory, at least. With the advent of USB ports and devices, you don't even have to turn off your computer and reboot!

Are You Compatible?

Microsoft, in an attempt to identify hardware components that work with Windows 2000 Professional, has tested and certified a number of devices and lists them in a document called the *Windows 2000 Hardware Compatibility List (HCL)*. This list is the bible of approved hardware for use with Windows 2000 Professional. Using this list as a guideline for purchasing new hardware can save you a lot of time and money!

 Caution   Even though Microsoft has gone to great lengths to document compatible devices, they do caution you that they have not tested every device in all possible configurations. Despite this caution, if a particular device is not listed in the HCL, it may still work fine (as is the case with my video card), it's just that Microsoft has not tested it yet.

I won't bore you with the entire list of hardware types here, but some of the types that are included in the HCL are display adapters, monitors, modems, network cards, SCSI controllers, game devices, printers, sound cards, keyboards, and hard drives.

Microsoft has included the HCL on the Windows 2000 Professional CD-ROM. The file is HCL.TXT, it is located in the \Support directory, and it contains only information pertinent to Windows 2000 Professional.

For a completely up-to-date listing, visit Microsoft's Web site at `http://www.microsoft.com/hcl/default.asp`. You can browse hardware by type or search for manufacturer-specific devices. The online HCL contains information on Windows 95/98, NT 4.0 (for Intel's line of x86 and Alpha processors), and Windows 2000 (x86 and Alpha).

Note

In an attempt to make Windows NT (and now Windows 2000) an open and portable computer operating system, Microsoft has released versions compatible with Intel's x86 processors (such as the 486 and Pentium) and Digital Equipment Corporation's Alpha family of processors. As you read through the HCL, it is important that you make sure you are reading information pertaining to your processor and not another.

When you find the device you are looking for, select it, and a new browser window pops up that gives you the details of whether or not the device is compatible with your system. You may even find Microsoft-certified drivers available. The three levels of compatibility are

Logo	The product meets all the requirements of the Microsoft Logo Program.
Logo with drivers	The product meets all the requirements of the Microsoft Logo Program, and drivers are available for download.
No Logo but compatible	The product has not yet met the requirements of the Microsoft Logo Program but is compatible with a system.

Note

The Microsoft Logo Program is a process by which Microsoft tests products (hardware and software) and verifies they have been designed and actually meet compatibility standards for the Windows family of operating systems. Although I wouldn't recommend eschewing all products that don't have the logo, you should research any products that do not and verify whether they will be compatible with your system or not. It just might save you some money!

If your device meets none of these compatibility levels, it still may work, but it definitely has not yet been certified.

Managing Hardware

Before I get into actually describing how you add and remove hardware, I want to walk you through the Windows 2000 Professional components that enable you to inspect and manage your existing hardware.

Device Manager

The Device Manager is the central management point for hardware in Windows 2000 Professional. You can view all the devices attached to your system, inspect the properties of each device, disable and uninstall them, and scan for hardware changes.

Launching the Device Manager

1. Right-click My Computer and select Properties as shown in Figure 4-1.

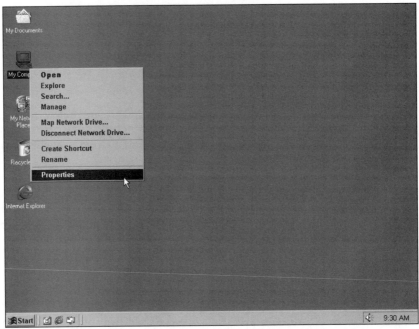

Figure 4-1: Access your computer's properties by right-clicking My Computer.

2. Choose the Hardware tab, shown in Figure 4-2.

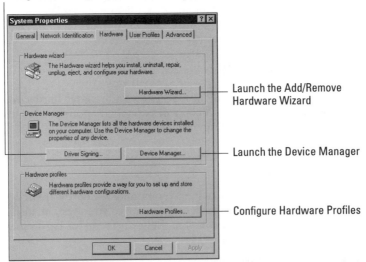

Figure 4-2: The Hardware tab enables you to add or remove hardware, launch the Device Manager, implement driver signing, and configure hardware profiles.

3. Click Device Manager to launch the Device Manager as shown in Figure 4-3.

Select to expand branch

Figure 4-3: The Device Manager, showing a computer's devices.

Note

You can also access the Device Manager by selecting Start ⇨ Settings ⇨ Control Panel. Choose System, then the Hardware tab, and select Device Manager.

Displaying device properties

1. Launch the Device Manager.

2. Expand the device tree to find a device as shown in Figure 4-4.

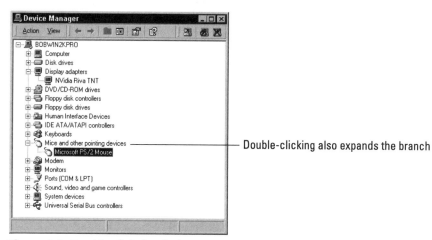

Double-clicking also expands the branch

Figure 4-4: Double-click the device type or click the plus sign to expand the tree and see the devices within.

3. Right-click the device and choose Properties.

Note You can also access a device's properties by double-clicking it.

You may see anywhere from one to five tabs. The reason for this is that different hardware types (such as a mouse and monitor) have unique properties and settings, and may offer different information or options to configure. The most common are the General tab (Figure 4-5), the Driver tab (Figure 4-6), and the Resources tab (Figure 4-7).

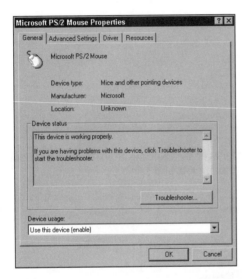

Figure 4-5: The General tab tells you basic information about your device and if it is working properly, includes a Troubleshooter, and allows you to enable or disable the device.

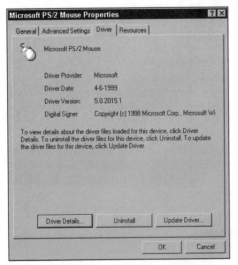

Figure 4-6: The Driver tab enables you to access driver information and to uninstall or update the driver.

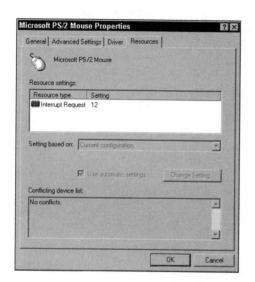

Figure 4-7: The Resources tab shows you the resources assigned to the device.

Scanning for new hardware changes

This just happened to me as I began to write this chapter. I booted Windows 2000 Professional and everything was going fine, but when I tried to access my CD-ROM, it wasn't there! At first I consigned myself to rebooting and seeing if Windows 2000 would detect it this time around, but as I was looking at the Device Manager, I realized I could select Scan for Hardware Changes. It worked!

In other words, when Windows 2000 booted, it did not successfully detect my CD-ROM drive. That could be a sign of a bad connection or driver trouble, or the signal between the CD-ROM and processor just got lost (sometimes that happens!). When you scan for hardware changes, Windows 2000 rescans all ports and hardware connections to verify the existence of known hardware and detect any changes.

1. Launch the Device Manager.

2. Select Action ⇨ Scan for hardware changes.

Showing hidden devices

The standard view shown by the Device Manager does not include all the devices that may be present on your system. Yes, that's true. Normally a device is hidden if it is not a Plug-and-Play device or if it has been removed from your system but its drivers have not been uninstalled. You may want to view hidden devices if you are compulsive, like me, and tend to peek in every corner of your computer. More practical reasons include troubleshooting and configuring non Plug-and-Play devices. Here's how to show hidden devices:

1. Launch the Device Manager.

2. Select View ⇨ Show hidden devices. Figures 4-8 and 4-9 show before-and-after looks at my hidden devices. Notice any differences?

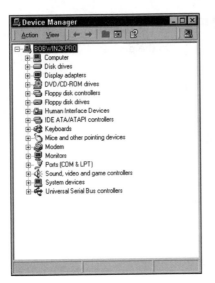

Figure 4-8: The default view before seeing the hidden devices.

Previously hidden

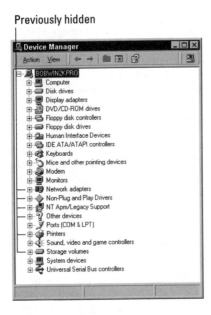

Figure 4-9: The view after showing hidden devices.

The hidden devices appear as if by magic.

Changing your view of devices and resources

The default view of the Device Manager is to display your devices by type. Each disk drive is displayed in the Disk Drive portion of the tree; each port is located in the Ports (COM & LPT) subtree. Most of the time, this is the most convenient way to view your devices but not always. The prime example of why you would want to change views is to troubleshoot hardware conflicts. Viewing hardware by the type of connection or sorting by resources is the best way to quickly determine if two devices have a conflict because the conflict will occur in one of the areas that you are viewing. To change your view, follow these steps:

1. Launch the Device Manager.

2. Select the View menu and choose a type of view.

3. Choose from four available views:

   Devices by type is the default view.

   Devices by connection, shown in Figure 4-10, displays each device according to the connection it uses, such as your system board, COM and LPT ports, USP ports, and so on.

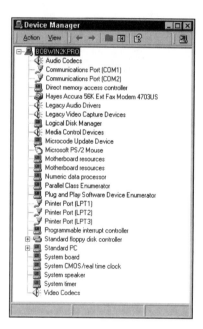

Figure 4-10: Viewing devices by connection.

Resources by type, as shown in Figure 4-11, displays the resources allocated to your hardware devices by resource type and then displays the devices according to the resources they use. Because most devices use more than one type of resource, they are listed multiple times. This is the view you want if you are having resource conflicts and want to see quickly what each device is using.

Note

It is a good idea to view your hardware by resource type and print your settings.

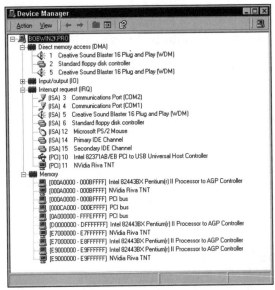

Figure 4-11: Viewing by resources instead of devices, sorted by type of resource.

Resources by connection, shown in Figure 4-12, displays the status of your resources arranged by connection type.

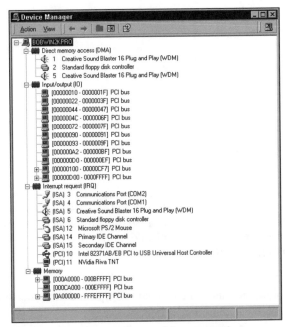

Figure 4-12: Resources sorted by connection.

Hardware profiles

Because it is often helpful to have different hardware settings for different users of the same computer, Microsoft created hardware profiles. Hardware profiles enable you to customize your hardware setup with different settings than those set up for another person who uses the same machine. Most of the time, these profiles are defined for mobile computers that have access to a variety of hardware devices at different locations. You might be set up with a docking station and network card at work but want to take the laptop home and use a modem and your personal printer. Creating different hardware profiles solves the problem of having to reconfigure your computer every time you boot in a different location. You can even have a profile for use on the road!

When you first install Windows 2000 Professional, the system creates an initial profile called "Profile 1." Every device on your system at that time is enabled by default. To create new profiles or modify existing ones, you have to do some work.

Accessing hardware profiles

The first step in configuring hardware profiles is finding it! From here, you can perform the other activities listed in this section.

1. Right-click My Computer and select Properties.
2. Select the Hardware tab.
3. Select Hardware Profiles.

Identifying a portable computer

If you have a laptop computer it should be identified as such in your hardware profile. Windows 2000 Professional should automatically detect this and create an Undocked profile as your default profile. You can verify this by viewing your hardware profile. You can even create multiple profiles, such as docked, undocked, road, or home.

1. Access Hardware Profiles.
2. Select a profile and choose Properties.
3. Figure 4-13 shows the properties of my Undocked hardware profile. Notice that the middle portion of the dialog box is greyed out. Windows 2000 Professional will not allow you to change the docking settings if it can detect the docking state by itself.

Figure 4-13: Windows 2000 Professional has successfully detected the docking state of my laptop.

Copying, renaming, and deleting profiles

The capability to copy, rename, and delete profiles enables you to manage them more easily. If you have a profile that you want to use as the basis of another profile, you can copy it, rename the new profile, and then modify it to suit your needs.

1. Access Hardware Profiles.

2. Select a profile to copy, rename, or delete.

3. Choose the appropriate button to carry out the task.

Note   It's pretty easy to copy the default profile created when Windows 2000 Professional was installed as a backup for future use and also use a copy as a template for modification.

Setting a default profile

Set a default profile to make it easy to find and select when you boot your computer. You can also have Windows 2000 automatically select the default profile.

1. Access Hardware Profiles.

2. Select the profile you want as the default and move it to the top of the list using the up and down arrows shown in Figure 4-14.

3. If you want Windows to choose the default profile automatically at startup after a given amount of time, choose Select the first profile listed if I don't select a profile in and modify the time delay to suit your taste.

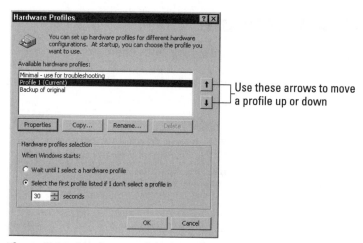

Figure 4-14: Moving an original profile
back to the top.

Force profile selection at startup

Sometimes you don't want Windows 2000 automatically selecting a profile
when it boots up. To prevent this from happening, follow these steps:

1. Access Hardware Profiles.

2. Choose Wait until I select a hardware profile as shown in Figure 4-15.

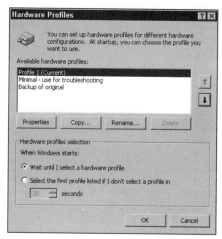

Figure 4-15: This option forces you to
make a profile decision at startup.

Adding New Hardware

Okay, are you ready to add new hardware to your computer?

For information on installing and configuring modems and display adapters, see Chapter 11 and Chapter 16.

The best method for installing hardware is to use the Add/Remove Hardware Wizard. Before you launch the wizard, power down your computer, physically install the device, and log back into the computer. For true Plug-and-Play devices, that's all you have to do. When Windows 2000 Professional reboots, it detects the device and installs the necessary drivers. You might need to have your system CD handy to install drivers, however.

USB devices are generally "hot swappable," enabling you to install them while your computer is on.

Using the Add/Remove Hardware Wizard

1. Click Start ➪ Settings ➪ Control Panel.

You can also add or remove hardware by launching the Add/Remove Hardware Wizard from the Hardware tab in the System applet (see Figure 4-2).

2. Choose Add/Remove Hardware. This action launches the Add/Remove Hardware Wizard shown in Figure 4-16.

Figure 4-16: The Add/Remove Hardware Wizard.

3. Click Next.

4. Select Add/Troubleshoot a device as shown in Figure 4-17.

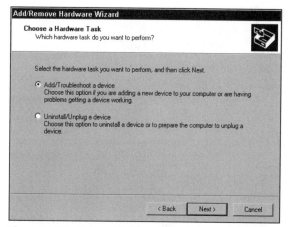

Figure 4-17: Select Add/Troubleshoot to add a device.

5. If Windows 2000 Professional does not recognize your new device, select Add a new device and choose Next as shown in Figure 4-18.

6. Windows then asks if you would like Windows 2000 Professional to search for the device or whether you will select it from a list, such as the one shown in Figure 4-18. It is my experience that if you've gotten this far and Windows hasn't recognized the hardware, you won't achieve anything by opting for Windows to search again. Select No and then choose Next.

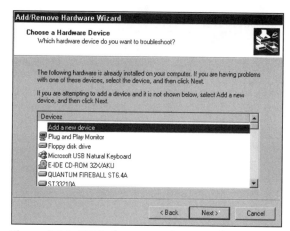

Figure 4-18: If Windows 2000 has not identified the hardware at this point, you will have to identify the device yourself.

7. Scroll down and find the type of device you are installing, select it, and choose Next, as shown in Figure 4-19.

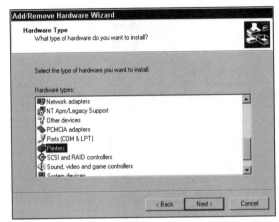

Figure 4-19: Select a device type to install.

8. You may then be prompted for information about your specific device and asked to locate the drivers. Figure 4-20 shows that I have selected the manufacturer of my printer, but alas, my model is not listed. If this is the case, Windows 2000 Professional does not have the correct drivers for your device, and you must select Have Disk and locate the .INF file yourself.

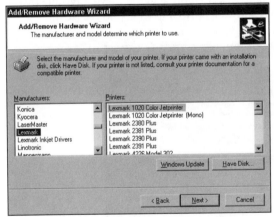

Figure 4-20: Select the manufacturer and device model.

Note   Windows .INF files contain important device and driver installation information. Some .INF files contain information about multiple devices from the same manufacturer.

9. Select a location to copy the manufacturer's files, as shown in Figure 4-21. Of course, you have to have the files to perform this step. These files should be included with the distribution disks that came with your device or that you have downloaded off the Web.

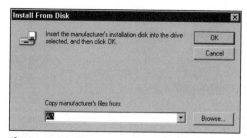

Figure 4-21: Enter a path or choose Browse to find the .INF file.

If all goes well, your device drivers will be installed, and you may be asked to configure your device. Configuring a device is highly dependent on the type of hardware you have installed. For example, if you installed a printer, you might have to install ink cartridges, align the printer heads, set up the paper type and quality, and so on.

Removing Hardware

Removing hardware is much easier that adding it! Three levels of removal are available:

✦ Disabling a device

✦ Ejecting or unplugging a device

✦ Uninstalling a device

Disabling enables you to temporarily (if desired) disable a hardware device but keep its drivers. Windows 2000 Professional simply ignores the device the next time it boots and pretends it isn't there.

For devices that can easily be unplugged and moved around, you have the option of ejecting or unplugging. It's nice to tell Windows 2000 Professional what's going on with your system before you do it, so you should always eject or unplug a device before temporarily removing it.

Note   There isn't any real harm done by just ejecting or unplugging a device and not telling Windows 2000, but if the system attempts to communicate with the missing device, it will assume there is a hardware problem and may disable the drivers. By following the steps to ensure Windows knows what you have unplugged, you prevent this from happening.

Uninstalling a device is the real meal deal. You are telling your system that you no longer want to use the device and it should remove all device drivers and reallocate system resources, and following this you promise to physically remove the device from your system.

Disabling a device

The quickest way to disable a device is through the Device Manager.

1. Launch the Device Manager.
2. Right-click a device in the Device Manager.
3. Select Disable.

Note   Not all devices can be disabled, such as internal hard drives, monitors, CPU, and other relatively permanent devices.

Unplugging, ejecting, or uninstalling a device

To perform these actions, use the Add/Remove Hardware Wizard.

Note   You normally don't have to go through these steps to uninstall a Plug-and-Play device. Simply remove it from your system, and the next time you reboot, you'll never know it was there. You can also use the Device Manager to uninstall some devices by right-clicking a device and selecting Uninstall.

1. Click Start ⇨ Settings ⇨ Control Panel.
2. Select Add/Remove Hardware and choose Next at the opening dialog box.
3. Select Uninstall/Unplug a device at the next screen, shown in Figure 4-22.

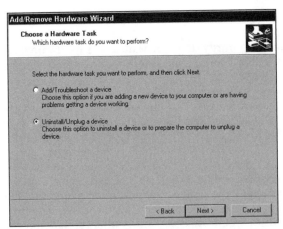

Figure 4-22: Choose Uninstall/Unplug a device to continue down that path.

4. Narrow your choice to either uninstalling or unplugging, as shown in Figure 4-23.
5. Select a device to uninstall or unplug and follow any further instructions.

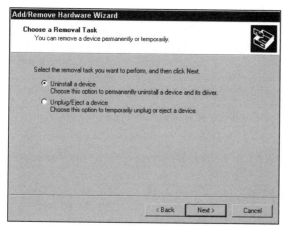

Figure 4-23: Choose uninstall to permanently remove a device or unplug if a device can be unplugged from your system.

The Eternal Search for Device Drivers

Drivers are the software components that facilitate communications between a hardware device, the operating system, and other necessary hardware. Having the correct driver is critical in ensuring your hardware works correctly.

The best place to search for the newest (or perhaps least buggy) device drivers is the Web site of the device's manufacturer. Most manufacturer Web sites have clearly identifiable driver sections where you can download the drivers for your hardware.

Note
If your hardware works fine, you may not need new drivers. If you are having problems with your device, however, the driver may be the reason. Aside from correcting bugs, manufacturers release new drivers to improve performance or provide additional capabilities. The best rule of thumb for non-bug-related driver updating is as follows: When you upgrade your operating system, major applications, or add hardware devices that interact with an existing device, that is the time to check for new drivers.

If you don't need the newest drivers and just need to reinstall, check the documentation that came with your hardware for driver information and reinstall from the distribution media.

As mentioned earlier, Microsoft may have certified drivers on its Hardware Compatibility List Web site. Go there and search for your hardware to see if the site has any drivers you can download.

Viewing driver details

Viewing the driver details enables you to see the actual files that make up your driver, the provider, and version information. This is useful information to have when troubleshooting.

1. Launch the Device Manager.

2. Select a device and open its properties page.

3. Select the Driver tab.

4. Select Driver Details. Figure 4-24 shows the drivers for my display adapter.

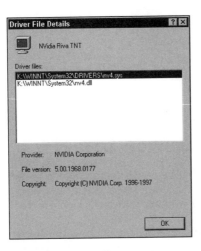

Figure 4-24: In the Driver File Details window, you can see the actual files and locations of the drivers.

Uninstalling drivers

You may be asking yourself, "Why would I want to uninstall drivers?" That's a good question! You should uninstall your existing driver prior to installing a newer version or reinstalling the same driver to resolve problems. This way you can be certain there are no holdovers from the old or possibly corrupt driver that might interfere with the new installation.

1. Access the Drivers tab for a device.

2. Choose Uninstall.

3. Windows displays a warning asking you if you really want to do this. If you do, select OK to continue.

Caution   You should only uninstall drivers if you have a newer driver ready to install, unless, of course, you want to disable the device entirely.

Updating drivers

As explained earlier, you should update your drivers if you are experiencing trouble with a device and a newer driver exists. The problems you are having could be the result of a bad or outdated driver. You should also update whenever you make significant changes to your system's hardware or software.

1. Access the Drivers tab for a device.

2. Choose Upgrade Driver, which launches the Upgrade Device Driver Wizard shown in Figure 4-25. Choose Next to continue.

Figure 4-25: The Upgrade Device Driver Wizard.

3. The wizard asks you whether it should search for a suitable device or list devices for you to choose from. Figure 4-26 shows this dialog box. If Windows is having trouble identifying the device, you should select it from a list or have a new driver waiting for you to select; otherwise, accept the recommended course of action.

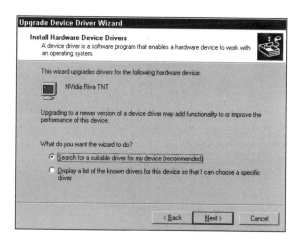

Figure 4-26: In most cases, accept the recommended course of action.

If you choose to let Windows search for a new driver, you are prompted to recommend search locations, as shown in Figure 4-27.

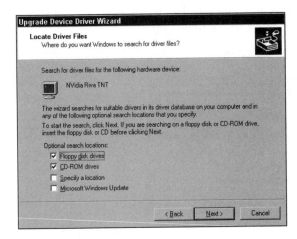

Figure 4-27: Select a location or locations for Windows to search for a new driver.

If you choose to select your device from a list, Windows shows you the compatible hardware and enables you to identify a disk (or folder) for the driver as shown in Figure 4-28.

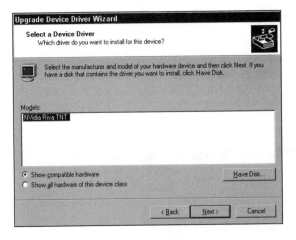

Figure 4-28: Select your device and choose Next. If you have a disk with new drivers, select Have Disk.

At this point, Windows 2000 Professional searches for the driver in the locations you have chosen and installs the required driver.

Driver signing

Driver signing is a method of ensuring you install only those device drivers that have been digitally signed by Microsoft. When you install Windows 2000, the system uses drivers from the distribution CD that are presigned and certified. This ensures the drivers are compatible, both with your hardware devices and Windows 2000. However, when you begin to install new devices and drivers afterwards, you will probably not be using the Windows 2000 CD. If that is the case and you want a level of protection against bad drivers, enable driver signing.

Driver signing offers three levels of protection, called *file signature verification*:

Ignore   Installs all files regardless of the signature. This option effectively turns off driver signing. Proceed at your own risk!

Warn   If an unsigned driver is about to be installed, Windows 2000 warns you.

Block   This option prevents any unsigned driver from being installed and is the highest level of security.

To enable driver signing or change the properties, follow these steps:

1. Right-click My Computer and select Properties.
2. Select the Hardware tab.
3. Select Driver Signing.
4. Select a file signature verification as shown in Figure 4-29.

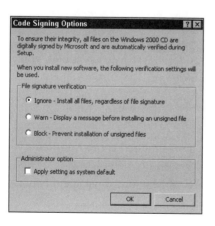

Figure 4-29: Select a file signature verification level that corresponds with the level of security you desire.

5. If you are logged on as an Administrator, you can set the system default setting for all users who log into the machine.

Trouble, Trouble, Toil, and Bubble

It's almost a given that you will eventually run into trouble adding or removing hardware. The only real questions are what you are going to do about it and when. It helps to have a logical thought process and be able to analyze problems using the scientific method, but because these aspects are beyond the scope of this chapter, I'll stick with general advice and show you the tools in Windows 2000 Professional that help you resolve problems.

Here are several good questions to ask yourself when hardware troubleshooting:

✦ Is it plugged in?

✦ Does it have power?

✦ What did you do just before it stopped working?

✦ Have you spilled anything on it?

Another good habit to get into is going to the Device Manager and seeing if the device you are having trouble with is listed, checking it's properties, and seeing if there are any conflicts. Armed with this information, you can either solve the problem yourself or pass the information along to your IT department or help desk.

The other methods that enable you to troubleshoot hardware problems involve launching the Hardware Wizard or using the Help system. There really isn't a right way or approved method—it's up to you to decide which approach suits you the best.

Using the Hardware Wizard

One of the great features of Windows 2000 is being able to perform a task multiple ways. If you are working in the Hardware tab of the System applet, you can launch the Hardware Wizard to troubleshoot problems.

1. Right-click My Computer and select Properties.

2. Select the Hardware tab.

3. Select Hardware Wizard, which when launched is the Add/Remove Hardware Wizard. Don't let the name fool you; you can troubleshoot from here as well.

4. After selecting Next, choose Add/Troubleshoot a device and choose Next again.

5. Select a device as shown in Figure 4-30 and choose Next.

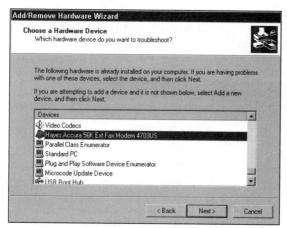

Figure 4-30: I think I've got a problem with my modem, so I've selected it.

6. The Wizard then displays information about the device as shown in Figure 4-31 and whether it thinks it is working correctly. When you select Finish, another troubleshooter starts.

Figure 4-31: Click Finish to continue troubleshooting.

The Hardware Troubleshooter then launches (see Figure 4-32) and prompts you to answer questions pertaining to your device. Answer the questions as best you can and follow any instructions carefully.

Figure 4-32: The Hardware Troubleshooter presents a series of questions that attempt to narrow down the possible causes of your problem.

Troubleshooting with the Hardware Troubleshooter

The Hardware Troubleshooter can be launched from the General tab of a device's properties display, found through the Device Manager. In other words, if you are working in the Device Manager, you can easily start troubleshooting from there.

1. Right-click My Computer and select Properties.

2. Select the Hardware tab.

3. Select Device Manager.

4. Double-click the device you are having trouble with to open the properties page, shown in Figure 4-33.

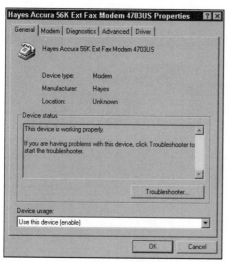

Figure 4-33: Click Troubleshooter if you think you are having problems.

5. Click Troubleshooter, which will launch the Hardware Troubleshooter.

Seek help through the interactive troubleshooter

Troubleshooters are a part of the Windows 2000 Help system and involve asking you a series of questions about your hardware and what it is doing (or not doing!) in order to determine the exact problem and suggested course of action to resolve it. This way you don't have to be working with the Hardware tab of the System applet or the Device Manager to start troubleshooting.

1. Click Start ➪ Help.

2. On the Contents tab, select Troubleshooting and Maintenance as shown in Figure 4-34.

3. Select Windows 2000 troubleshooters, which will change the display as shown in Figure 4-35.

4. Select a troubleshooter from the list in the right pane of the help window and follow all the instructions.

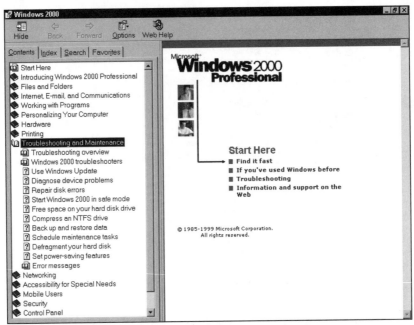

Figure 4-34: Select Troubleshooting and Maintenance from the Windows Help system to find the interactive troubleshooters.

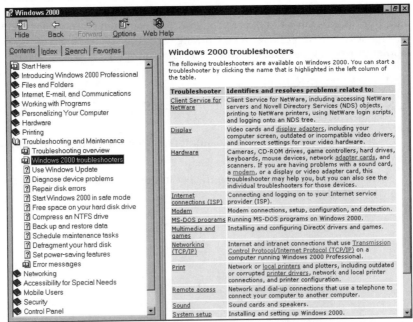

Figure 4-35: The Windows 2000 troubleshooters enable you to define a general area of problems and work from there.

Summary

You obviously can't learn everything there is to know about hardware in one chapter, but you should be able to install or remove the most common hardware components you'll use with Windows 2000 Professional. The most effective method of learning about this aspect of computing is hard-earned experience. Rip the case off that computer and go for it!

Caution   Don't rip the case off if you're installing a monitor, mouse, keyboard, or other external device! That was just a figure of speech.

✦ There are internal and external hardware types, each connected to your computer through different ports, slots, or other connectors.

✦ Study your computer and know its capabilities before you buy hardware, and be very careful to get the type of device (internal or external) you need to operate with a connection you have available.

✦ To be safe, consult the *Microsoft Windows Hardware Compatibility List* to ensure you have hardware that has been tested and certified for use with Windows 2000 Professional.

✦ Manage your hardware through the Device Manager.

✦ Set up different hardware profiles for multiple configurations or locations.

✦ Add and remove hardware with the help of the Add/Remove Hardware Wizard.

✦ Make sure you have updated device drivers.

✦ Troubleshoot with the Hardware Troubleshooter.

✦ If all else fails, visit the manufacturer's Web site (or give the manufacturer a call) for detailed product information!

And now for something completely different! Chapter 5 will walk you through several of the applications that come with Windows 2000 Professional, such as WordPad and Imaging, and provide tips on how to use them and be productive.

✦   ✦   ✦

Using the Windows 2000 Accessories

CHAPTER

5

◆ ◆ ◆ ◆

In This Chapter

Using Calculator

Using Notepad

Using WordPad

Using Paint

Using Imaging

Using Address Book

Using HyperTerminal

Using Fax

◆ ◆ ◆ ◆

Windows 2000 Professional includes an assortment of starter applications that enable you to get some real work done. These aren't just diagnostic utilities and file management tools that you might expect to be included with an operating system. The bundled applications are real productivity tools. There's a little of everything, from a word processing program to communications tools. Most of the accessory programs will be familiar to users of previous versions of Windows. However, you may not have taken full advantage of these tools in the past. It's time to take a fresh look at the accessory programs that come bundled with Windows 2000 and consider the useful features they offer.

Although none of the accessory programs can be described as full-featured applications, they are more than just demos or sample programs. Each accessory program performs a useful task, and it might be adequate to meet your needs if you don't require all the bells and whistles that come with a major commercial application. This chapter gives you a get-acquainted tour of the Windows 2000 accessories.

Using Calculator

In many ways, a computer is just a big fancy calculator. The trouble is that you normally need programming skills to access the computer's calculation power. But you don't need to be a programmer to use Windows' Calculator accessory — it's a convenient, onscreen version of your familiar pocket or desktop calculator. The Windows 2000 Calculator accessory is essentially unchanged from the Calculator included in the last several versions of Windows. But that's not a bad thing — after all, how can you improve on a simple calculator? To use Calculator, follow these steps.

1. To launch Calculator, click Start ➪ Programs ➪ Accessories ➪ Calculator. The Calculator window (see Figure 5-1) looks like a common desktop or pocket calculator.

2. To use the Calculator, simply click the buttons with your mouse just like you would press the buttons on the pocket calculator with your finger. You can also enter numbers using the numeric keypad on your keyboard. The result of your calculation appears in the text box near the top of the calculator window.

Figure 5-1: Calculator in standard view.

3. To copy the results of your calculation to another program via the Windows clipboard, choose Edit ➪ Copy (or press Ctrl+C). Then open or switch to the Windows application and choose Edit ➪ Paste (or press Ctrl+V) to paste the number from the clipboard into your application.

If you need more than a simple, standard calculator, choose View ➪ Scientific to expand the Calculator window to show Calculator's full set of scientific function keys (see Figure 5-2). In scientific mode, the Calculator accessory can go beyond simple arithmetic to handle advanced mathematical operations. If you're accustomed to using a typical desktop scientific calculator, you'll feel right at home with Calculator in scientific mode. Otherwise, you may need to refer to your trusty math textbook for a refresher on how to use some of the many buttons available in Calculator's scientific mode.

Figure 5-2: Calculator in scientific view.

Using Notepad

Notepad is Windows' venerable text editor accessory. Anyone who has used a previous version of Windows will recognize Notepad as an old friend. It's been part of the Windows scene for ages and has hardly changed a bit. Notepad reads and creates plain ASCII (or ANSI) text files with no fancy formatting options or other word processing features—just plain text. This apparent limitation is really Notepad's strength. You know that the text files you create with Notepad are clean, devoid of any extraneous data introduced by a word processing program, thus ensuring compatibility with just about every text editor and word processing program around. Because of this feature, Notepad is a favorite tool of programmers for quick work with batch files, scripts, HTML-coded Web pages, and the like. Notepad is also a handy tool for viewing plain text files such as the Readme documents that accompany just about every program disk and downloaded program.

1. To open Notepad, click Start ➪ Programs ➪ Accessories ➪ Notepad. When you launch the program, the Notepad window appears, displaying a blank, untitled document. Figure 5-3 shows the Notepad window containing a text file.

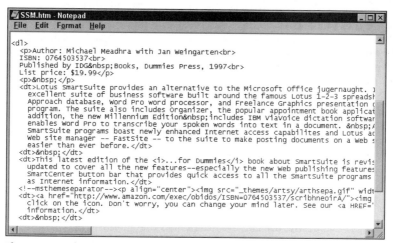

Figure 5-3: The Notepad accessory.

2. Notepad is a simple program to use. To enter text, just begin typing. After entering some text, you can use the standard mouse and keyboard techniques to move the cursor and to select and edit text. Notepad's menus are also simple. The File menu contains the customary commands to open, save, and print files, and to exit the program. The Edit menu contains the usual assortment of Cut, Copy, Paste, and Delete commands, plus commands to access the Find and Replace features. The only unexpected element is the Edit ➪ Time/Date command that automatically inserts the current time and

date into your text document. The Format menu contains just two commands: Word Wrap, which determines whether or not Notepad should wrap lines of text to fit within the window; and Font, which selects the font Notepad uses for onscreen display. The font selection affects the display only, not the text file you create with Notepad.

Tip   To create a new text file while editing an existing file in Notepad, choose File ⇨ New. Notepad will prompt you to save the current file and then display a new, blank text file in Notepad.

3. To save your text document, choose File ⇨ Save to open the Save As dialog box. Select the folder where you want to save the file and enter a name for the file. (Notepad automatically adds the .TXT extension to the filename when you save the file, unless you put double quotes around the filename.) Click Save to close the dialog box and save the file.

Tip   Notepad is the default program associated with text files (those identified by the .TXT extension). Consequently, you can simply double-click the icon for a text file in any folder window to open that file for viewing and editing in Notepad.

Using WordPad

Notepad isn't the only Windows accessory program designed for editing text. If you're looking for text editing combined with the formatting capabilities of a word processing program, check out WordPad. WordPad is another accessory that has been around for a while. The Windows 2000 version of WordPad is essentially unchanged from the accessory that has been included in all the recent versions of Windows.

This successor to the old Windows Write program offers the features you'd expect to find in a basic word processing application. You can enter and edit text and format your document with fonts, paragraph spacing and alignment, tabs and indents, bullets, and so on. You can even add pictures and similar objects to a WordPad document and print the formatted document or save it using the RTF (Rich Text Format) file format. WordPad also reads and writes plain text files and Microsoft Word 6 document files although WordPad doesn't support all of Word's features.

Tip   WordPad has the capacity to handle larger files than Notepad, so you can use WordPad as a text editor for viewing and editing text files that are too big for Notepad to handle.

What you won't find in WordPad is advanced word processing features such as tables, outlining and automatic numbering, mail merge facilities, and revision tracking. One surprising omission is the lack of a spell check feature or thesaurus in WordPad. Still, WordPad is more than adequate for preparing letters and memos and performing many other routine word processing chores.

1. To launch WordPad, click Start ➪ Programs ➪ Accessories ➪ WordPad. The WordPad window (shown in Figure 5-4) has the look of a typical word processing program.

2. Enter and format text to create a document. Routine operations in WordPad are typical of most Windows word processing programs. The menus are straightforward and hold no surprises. The buttons and drop-down list boxes on the toolbars give you easy access to most of the common formatting options, so you rarely need to explore the WordPad menus. Text entry and editing follow the conventions you expect from any Windows-based program.

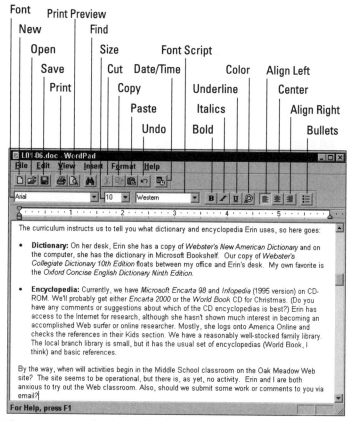

Figure 5-4: WordPad provides basic word processing functions.

3. Choose File ➪ Save As to open the Save As dialog box. Enter a name for your document, select the file type and location, and then click Save to save the file.

Using Paint

The Paint accessory program is a simple image editor for creating and editing BMP (Windows bitmap) files. Like Notepad and some of the other accessory programs, Paint has been a part of previous versions of Windows, and the Windows 2000 version of Paint is essentially unchanged from the earlier incarnations.

In the hands of a skilled artist, the Paint accessory is theoretically capable of producing impressive original images—the basic drawing and painting tools are there. However, a skilled artist is likely to want to use a more powerful program with a richer assortment of specialized tools, filters, special effects, and image manipulation features. The average computer user rarely needs to undertake anything so ambitious though, and the basic tools available in Paint are adequate for editing an icon or screen shot, cropping a picture, and even some simple retouching chores. Paint is also a favorite of kids of all ages—it makes a great onscreen doodle pad or coloring book.

1. To open the Paint accessory program, choose Start ➪ Programs ➪ Accessories ➪ Paint. When the Paint window first appears, it displays a blank, untitled image. Figure 5-5 shows an image created by using the tools from the toolbox (the toolbar of buttons on the left side of the window) to draw some simple shapes and lines.

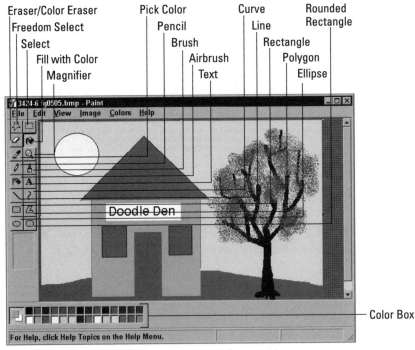

Figure 5-5: The Paint accessory brings out the artist in you.

2. Use the tools (buttons) in the Toolbox to draw an image in the Paint window. Most of the tools in the toolbox follow the same basic pattern of use. First, you click a tool button in the toolbox to select it, then click a color in the color box, and then draw on the image by dragging the mouse pointer. Some of the drawing tools have additional characteristics (such as the width of a line or the shape of a brush) that you can select by clicking options in a box that appears below the toolbox. The following list gives you a brief rundown on the tools in the Paint Tool box and what they do:

- **Freeform Select.** Drag the pointer to define an irregularly shaped selection for use in cut, copy, paste, and move operations.

- **Select.** Select a rectangular area of your image for use in cut, copy, paste, and move operations. To define the rectangle, drag the pointer in a diagonal line from one corner of the rectangle to the opposite corner.

- **Eraser/Color Eraser.** Click the main (left) mouse button and drag the pointer to erase the image under the cursor. Click the secondary (right) mouse button and drag the pointer to erase only the selected color from the image under the cursor.

- **Fill with Color.** Click an enclosed area of your image to fill that area with the selected color.

- **Pick Color.** Click a sample color in your image to make that the selected drawing color.

- **Magnifier.** Zoom in or magnify the image, centered on the spot you click with this tool. Click to magnify; right-click to reduce the image size.

- **Pencil.** Draws a single-pixel-wide freeform line that traces the path of the cursor when you click and drag.

- **Brush.** Draws a freeform line like the Pencil tool, but you can change the character of the line by selecting different brush tips.

- **Airbrush.** A drawing tool similar to the Pencil or Brush, but this one simulates the broad pattern of dots characteristic of spraying a can of spray paint.

- **Text.** Click and drag inside your image to define a rectangular area for inserting text. A text formatting toolbar appears where you can select the font, size, and other text attributes. After selecting the attributes, type the text.

- **Line.** Draws a straight line.

- **Curve.** Draws a curved line, but the tool is not intuitive. First you click and drag to draw a straight line. Then you click the middle of the line and drag it to one side to distort the straight line into a curve.

- **Rectangle.** Click and drag a diagonal line to define opposite corners of a rectangle.

- **Polygon.** Click and drag to define a line that becomes the first side of a multisided shape. Click to add another side to the shape. Continue to add sides to the shape. Double-click to add the final side and close the shape.

- **Ellipse.** Click and drag to define the size and proportions of an ellipse.

- **Rounded Rectangle.** Similar to the Rectangle tool, but the corners of the rectangle are rounded instead of sharp.

Tip To draw a solid shape instead of an outline, first draw any enclosed shape (rectangle, polygon, ellipse, rounded rectangle, or a freeform shape you draw with the Pencil or Brush tools) and then use the Fill with Color tool to make the interior of the shape a solid color.

3. If you have a compatible scanner and scanner software installed, you can use the File ➪ Select Source and File ➪ Scan New commands to bring a scanned image into Paint for editing. You can also use the Image ➪ Flip/Rotate and Image ➪ Stretch/Skew commands to distort and manipulate Paint images.

4. After creating or editing your image, use the File ➪ Save As command to save your file.

Using Imaging

The Imaging accessory is a new member of the Windows family of bundled accessory programs. It's not entirely new though — the Imaging accessory was previously available bundled with other software. It's just new to the list of accessories that are part of the default Windows installation.

At first glance, the Imaging accessory seems to be the same kind of program as Paint — after all, both programs enable you to view and manipulate digital images (the kind that are produced by scanners and digital cameras). However, there are some significant differences between Imaging and Paint. The drawing tools in Paint are designed for creating an image from scratch or editing an existing image. The Imaging accessory, on the other hand, is designed for viewing and printing existing images, such as scanned photographs and other digital images, that are stored in a variety of file formats. You can use Imaging to add annotations to an image, but you can't edit the pixels that make up the image. Perhaps the most common use of the Imaging accessory is as a viewer for the fax images that you receive with Windows' Fax service. However, you can also use it to view and print scanned pictures, clip art, snapshots downloaded from a digital camera, and other images.

1. To open the Imaging accessory, choose Start ➪ Programs ➪ Accessories ➪ Imaging. Because the Imaging program is associated with several popular image file formats, you can also open Imaging by right-clicking an image file in a folder window and choosing Open With ➪ Imaging from the pop-up menu that appears. Figure 5-6 shows the Imaging window displaying a digital image.

Figure 5-6: View images with the Imaging accessory.

2. Use the buttons on the Standard toolbar to open, save, and print images. The buttons include the typical New, Open, Save, and Print buttons, plus buttons for Cut, Copy, Paste, Undo, and Redo. In addition are a set of five buttons and a drop-down list box for manipulating the size of the image you are viewing.

3. Use the Scanning toolbar buttons to scan images into the Imaging accessory program. Imaging can handle multipage image files, so the Scanner toolbar includes buttons that enable you to insert and append pages to an existing image file, as well as scan an individual image.

4. Select and manipulate images using the buttons on the Imaging toolbar. The hand button enables you to drag the image, then there's a button you can use to select a portion of your image, and another to select an annotation. The next button toggles the Annotation toolbar (located in the lower-left corner of the Imaging window) on and off. A pair of buttons enables you to rotate the image. Another pair of buttons and a text box enable you to page through the pages of a multipage image file. The last three buttons on the Imaging toolbar enable you to select from three view options: one-page view, thumbnail view, or page and thumbnail view.

5. Use the Annotation toolbar buttons to add annotations to the images you view with the Imaging accessory. You can draw freeform lines, highlight areas with a transparent color, draw lines and boxes, add text, add notes, import text from a file, and even add large text labels with the Rubber Stamp tool. All the annotations float on top of the image, enabling you to select and manipulate the annotations separately from the image until you save the image or incorporate the annotations into the image by choosing Annotation ⇨ Make Annotations Permanent.

Using Address Book

Windows can help you keep track of all your business and personal contacts in the Address Book accessory. The Windows 2000 version of Address Book is more robust than its predecessors. The Address Book database is preconfigured with space to store all the information you would normally want to keep about your contacts. Plus, you can now organize your contacts into folders and groups. Address Book can use your modem to dial phone numbers for you and can interface with Outlook Express to automatically create e-mail messages to your Address Book contacts. You can even search for names in some of the popular Internet directory services right from within Address Book.

1. To open Address Book, click Start ➪ Programs ➪ Accessories ➪ Address Book. Address Book is also available from within Outlook Express and some other programs, such as Windows Fax service and Microsoft Outlook. The Address Book window, shown in Figure 5-7, is divided into two panes. The left pane lists the folders in your address book, displayed in a tree structure. The right pane shows the list contacts available in the selected folder.

2. To sort the list of contacts in the right pane of the Address Book window, click the column heading button at the top of a column to sort the list by the contents of that column. For example, to sort by e-mail address, click the E-Mail Address button. Clicking a column header button once sorts the column in ascending order. Clicking it again sorts the column in descending order.

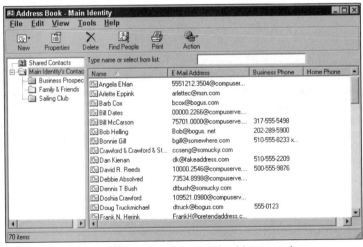

Figure 5-7: Keeping track of contacts with Address Book.

3. To create a new contact, click the New button and choose New Contact to open the Properties dialog box as shown in Figure 5-8. Enter information in the dialog box to define the contact. The various tabs of the Properties dialog box contain fields for just about any kind of information you might want to record about your contact. After entering the information, click OK to close the Properties dialog box and add the contact to the Address Book database.

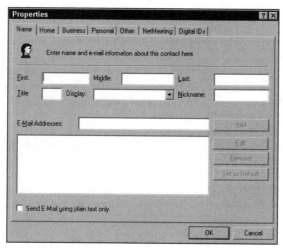

Figure 5-8: You can enter information about a contact in the Properties dialog box.

4. After entering all your contacts, you'll probably want to organize them into folders. To create a folder, click the New button and choose New Folder. Enter a name for the folder in the Properties dialog box and then click OK. The new folder appears in the left pane of the Address Book window. If you want to move an existing contact to a different folder, just drag the contact's icon from the right pane and drop it on the target folder's icon in the left pane. Click a folder icon to display the contacts of that folder in the right pane of the Address Book window.

Tip

To quickly locate a name in a long list of contacts, enter the name you want to search for in the Type name or select from list text box and then press Enter. Address Book jumps to the first matching entry in the current folder.

5. Select a contact from the list in the Address Book window and then click the Properties button (or simply double-click a contact) to open a dialog box showing all the detailed information about the selected contact.

6. You can have Address Book create a blank e-mail message addressed to a contact, dial a contact's phone number, or initiate a NetMeeting call to a contact by selecting the contact from the Address Book list, clicking the Action button, and then choosing the action you want from the menu that appears.

Using HyperTerminal

The HyperTerminal accessory is a terminal emulation program that you can use to connect to another computer (usually via a modem and phone line) and then operate as a remote terminal linked to the other computer. It used to be that using a terminal emulation program such as HyperTerminal was the standard way to connect to a computer bulletin board or corporate computer system. Now that most computer-to-computer connections are made over the Internet with Web-based interfaces, terminal emulations are rarely needed. Still, occasions do crop up from time to time when terminal emulation comes in handy. HyperTerminal stands ready to handle those occasions, just as it has in several previous versions of Windows.

Tip   You can use HyperTerminal and a direct connection through your system's serial (COM) port to connect to the console port of devices such as routers. It's a handy way for network administrators to configure routers before placing them on the network.

1. To open HyperTerminal the first time, click Start ➪ Programs ➪ Accessories ➪ Communications ➪ HyperTerminal. The HyperTerminal window appears with the Connection Description dialog box (see Figure 5-9) for defining a new connection open in front of it.

2. Define a new connection by entering information about the computer to which you want to connect. The Connection Description dialog box is the first of a wizard-like series of dialog boxes that you encounter when you define a new HyperTerminal connection. By entering and editing the information requested in the dialog boxes, you give the connection a name, enter the telephone number to call, select a modem connection to use, select or configure a dialing location, and then dial the connection.

Figure 5-9: You define a new HyperTerminal connection in the Connection Description dialog box.

3. After your modem establishes a connection with the host computer modem, the prompts from the host computer appear in the HyperTerminal window as shown in Figure 5-10. At this point, your computer is acting as a remote terminal connected to the host computer. The HyperTerminal window displays the text that would appear on the screen of a terminal attached directly to the host computer. Type your responses to the prompts to log onto the host system and conduct your remote terminal session.

4. Don't forget to log off of the host computer system when you complete your session. Then click the Disconnect button to have your modem hang up and thus terminate the online session.

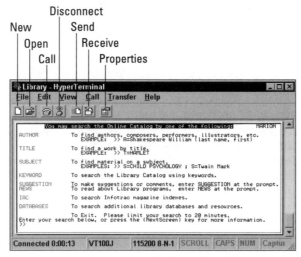

Figure 5-10: The HyperTerminal window displays your dialog with the host computer.

5. If you plan to use the same terminal connection again, choose File ➪ Save from the HyperTerminal menu before you close the HyperTerminal window.

The next time you want to connect to the host computer, you won't have to go through all the previous steps to redefine all the connection settings. Saving even one HyperTerminal session file adds a HyperTerminal folder to the Start menu so you can select a connection directly from the menu. To connect to a host computer again, just follow these steps:

1. Click Start ➪ Programs ➪ Accessories ➪ HyperTerminal ➪ SessionName, where *SessionName* is the name you assigned to the connection settings in the Connection Description dialog box. HyperTerminal launches with the specified connection settings loaded.

2. Click Dial in the Connect dialog box that appears to dial the host connection and start your online session. (To open the Connect dialog box for subsequent online sessions, click the Call button on the HyperTerminal toolbar.)

3. Log on to the host computer and conduct your online session in the HyperTerminal window.

4. Click the Disconnect button to hang up the modem and terminate the connection.

Tip

To avoid having to navigate the numerous nested menus required to launch the bundled accessory programs from the Start menu, you can use an alternative technique to start them. Click Start ⇨ Run to open the Run dialog box, and then type the accessory's filename and click OK to run the program. Type **calc** for Calculator, **notepad** for Notepad, **wordpad** for WordPad, **pbrush** for Paint, **kodakimg** for Imaging, **wab** for Address Book, and **hypertrm** for HyperTerminal.

Using Fax

Over the years, fax support has been an on again, off again thing in Windows. Fax support is on again in Windows 2000 Professional — and it looks like a permanent fixture this time. Fax support is now a service installed in the operating system instead of an application or a component of some added messaging program (such as the old Windows Messaging feature). If you have a fax modem installed in your system, you can configure Windows to send fax transmissions from just about any Windows application as easily as you send documents to a printer. In fact, Windows treats your fax modem as a printer, complete with an icon in the Printers folder. In addition, you can create cover page faxes using a simple accessory program, and you can set up your fax modem to automatically answer the phone line to receive incoming faxes.

Note

If you've not already done so, you must install your fax modem and make sure that the hardware is configured and operating properly before attempting any other fax setup. You may need to be logged on as Administrator in order to make hardware changes such as configuring your fax modem.

Before you can use your fax modem to send fax transmissions, you need to configure the device. To start the process, follow these steps:

1. Click Start ⇨ Programs ⇨ Accessories ⇨ Communications ⇨ Fax ⇨ Fax Service Management. Windows opens the Fax Service Management window as shown in Figure 5-11. This window is your master control center for configuring both device settings and logging options for Windows fax services.

2. Click Devices in the tree panel on the left side of the dialog box, and then double-click the device name of your fax modem on the right side of the dialog box to open the Properties dialog box for the device (see Figure 5-12).

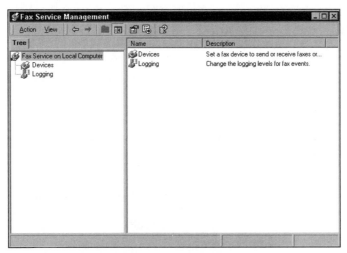

Figure 5-11: The Fax Service Management window.

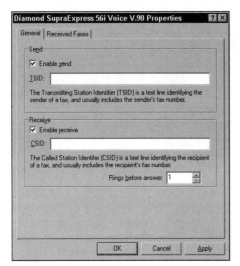

Figure 5-12: The General tab of the fax device Properties dialog box.

3. Enter or adjust the configuration settings for your fax on the General tab of the Properties dialog box. In the Send area, check the Enable Send option if you want to use your fax modem to send faxes. In the TSID text box, enter the phone number of your fax line or other identifying information. In the Receive area, check the Enable receive option to configure the modem to receive fax transmissions. Enter the phone number of your fax line or other identifying information in the CSID text box. In the Rings before answer box, set the number of times you want the telephone to ring before the fax modem answers the line. Use the up and down arrow buttons to increase or decrease the number.

4. Click the Received Faxes tab and adjust the settings there. This tab of the Properties dialog box (shown in Figure 5-13) is where you specify how you want Windows to handle incoming fax transmissions. If you have a printer already set up and want to print the fax immediately upon receipt, click the checkbox beside the Print on option and select the printer from the drop-down list box. You can also save an incoming fax as a file on your hard drive. To do so, check the Save in folder option and enter the path name for the folder where you want to save the file in the adjacent text box. If you have established e-mail accounts and messaging profiles on your machine, you can check the Send to local e-mail Inbox option and then select a profile from the Profile name drop-down list box. You can select any combination of these options for handling incoming fax transmissions.

5. After you adjust the settings, click OK to record your options, close the Properties dialog box, and return to the Fax Service Management window.

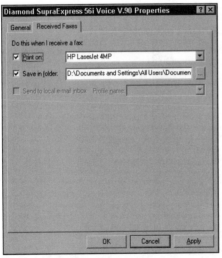

Figure 5-13: The Received Faxes tab of the fax device Properties dialog box.

After you set up fax support in Windows 2000, you can fax a document by simply using the originating program's print command to print the document and selecting Fax as the printer; then fill in the fax number and other information when prompted to do so. You can send a fax transmission immediately or store faxes in a queue for transmission at a later time.

To send a simple cover page fax, follow these steps:

1. Choose Start ➪ Programs ➪ Accessories ➪ Communications ➪ Fax ➪ Send Cover Page Fax to open the Send Fax Wizard.

2. Follow the instructions in the wizard to enter the phone number and other information about the fax number you are calling and the text you want on the cover page. Click Next to move from page to page through the wizard.

3. Click Finish to close the Send Fax Wizard and send the fax transmission.

Incoming faxes are stored in a folder on your hard disk. The simplest way to access that folder is to follow these steps:

1. Choose Start ➪ Programs ➪ Accessories ➪ Communications ➪ Fax ➪ My Faxes. Windows opens the My Faxes folder window.

2. Double-click the Received Faxes folder icon to display the list of incoming faxes.

3. To view a fax, simply double-click its icon. Windows launches the Imaging accessory program to display the fax image.

Summary

In addition to the Windows operating system, the Windows 2000 Professional package includes an assortment of accessory programs. Although none of the accessory programs is a full-featured commercial application, they may be all you need to handle some tasks.

Topics covered in this chapter include the following:

✦ Using the Calculator accessory for simple calculations

✦ Creating text files with the Notepad accessory

✦ Using Windows' bundled word processing program: WordPad

✦ Drawing pictures with the Paint accessory

✦ Viewing image files with the Imaging accessory

✦ Using Address Book to keep track of information about your contacts

✦ Using the HyperTerminal accessory as a terminal emulator

✦ Setting up Windows' Fax service

This chapter concludes the first part of the book. The next part explores the many options for tuning and customizing your copy of Windows 2000 Professional, starting with your desktop and folder options.

✦　　　✦　　　✦

Tuning Windows 2000 Professional

◆ ◆ ◆ ◆

Getting Organized

Windows 2000 is extremely flexible. As you use Windows 2000, you quickly discover that you can easily adjust many different settings to make things work the way you want. In this chapter, you learn how you can use those options to make using Windows 2000 adapt to your style of working.

In addition to the options that adjust how Windows 2000 operates, you can also adjust the appearance of Windows 2000. In many cases these changes are purely cosmetic, but some appearance changes can actually make Windows 2000 easier to use. For example, choosing a different color scheme can be one of the most effective ways to make your screen far easier to read — especially if you work in poor lighting or suffer from vision problems.

Managing Data with Windows Explorer

In Windows 2000, as in previous versions of Windows, you use Windows Explorer to view the contents of the folders that are available on your system. As you learned in Chapter 2, whether these folders are on your local hard drive, on a removable drive, or even located somewhere on your network, Windows Explorer enables you to explore that folder structure.

In Chapter 2 you learned how to customize folders to your preferences. Here you learn how to organize your data.

Windows 2000 is focused on the idea that users work with documents rather than with programs. For most people, it is more important to open a specific document or work with a certain type of document than to be concerned about which program opens that document. As a result, Windows 2000 automatically *associates* specific document types with the appropriate application programs.

This focus on the document is further reinforced when you open Windows Explorer. When you click the Start button and select Programs ➪ Accessories ➪ Windows Explorer, you open your My Documents folder in Windows Explorer.

Note   Although most Windows 2000 application programs default to saving your document files in the My Documents folder, it's a good idea to create subfolders within My Documents to organize your work. You may, for example, wish to create new folders for each new project and then save all document files relating to that project in the individual project folders. That way it's easy to locate every document for each of your projects without hunting through hundreds of files in the My Documents folder.

The Windows Explorer window has two panes. The right pane — the *contents pane* — shows the folders and files that are contained within the selected folder. The left pane typically shows the Folders Explorer Bar as shown in Figure 6-1. You use this bar to open and select specific folders.

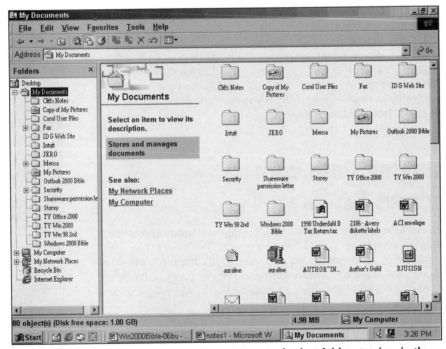

Figure 6-1: Use the Folders Explorer Bar to open and select folders to view in the contents pane.

You select a folder by clicking a folder icon in the Folders Explorer Bar. The currently selected folder appears with an open folder icon.

Notice that the Folders Explorer Bar uses a combination of vertical and horizontal lines to indicate the relationships between folders. When a folder contains subfolders, a vertical line extends from the bottom of the folder. A horizontal line then joins that vertical line to each of the subfolders.

Some folders are joined to the vertical line with a box. The box may contain a plus sign (+) to indicate that the folder contains subfolders that are currently hidden. Or it may contain a minus sign (-) to indicate that the subfolders are visible. You can click either type of box to expand or collapse the display — depending on the current state of the display. Keep in mind, however, that even when you view a folder's subfolders, some of those subfolders may contain additional subfolders that are currently hidden.

To view folders that are not contained within your My Documents folder, you must navigate through the folder tree by expanding and selecting the appropriate folders. To view folders on your local hard drives or on your CD-ROM drive, open the My Computer icon and then choose the drive and finally the folder you wish to view. Viewing shared folders on your network works pretty much the same way except that you must start by opening the My Network Places icon. You can then choose the computer, drive, and folder you wish to view.

Tip   The Windows Explorer Recycle Bin folder shows all of the files you sent to the Recycle Bin regardless of where those files originally resided. This enables you to restore accidentally deleted files without first determining their origin.

Although the default Windows Explorer view shows the My Documents folder, you can easily create custom Windows Explorer views that show any folder you prefer. To do so, first open the target folder in Windows Explorer. Next, click the Windows Explorer Restore button — the second button from the right on the Windows Explorer title bar — to view Windows Explorer in a window rather than full screen. Next, point to the folder you wish to use as the base folder for your new Windows Explorer view, hold down the right mouse button, and drag the icon onto your desktop. Choose Create Shortcut(s) Here from the pop-up menu to place the shortcut on your desktop. You can then double-click the new shortcut icon to quickly open Windows Explorer with your desired folder showing. You may wish to rename the shortcut (press F2 while the shortcut is selected) to differentiate it from the standard Windows Explorer view.

Tackling the Taskbar

You can have quite a few different things happening on your PC at the same time. As you learned in Chapter 2, the Windows taskbar makes it easier for you to see what programs are running, to switch between programs, and to access functions and programs.

Tip If the taskbar is hidden, you can usually display it by moving the mouse pointer just past the bottom edge of the screen. If the taskbar does not appear, try moving the mouse pointer just past the other edges of the screen until the taskbar appears.

In the following sections, you learn how to use and control the taskbar elements.

Tame the Start button

The Start button, located on the left edge of the taskbar, displays your Start menu. The Start menu is probably the one part of Windows 2000 that you use most often, so making it work the way you want can be important.

Tip Right-click the Start button to view its pop-up menu. The menu provides several options that you can use to view or modify your Start menu.

In Windows 2000, the Start menu is quite customizable. You can add items to the menu or rearrange existing items. You can also choose to display certain items—such as the Printers folder—as Start menu selections so that you can save a few steps in accessing those items. This latter capability is new in Windows 2000.

Adding programs to the Start menu

When you install new programs on your PC as discussed in Chapter 3, those programs are generally automatically added to your Start menu. In most cases, those programs are added to the Programs item, but they may also appear above the Programs item on the main Start menu or in one of the submenus of the Programs item.

If you add a program to your system and that program does not appear somewhere on the Start menu, Windows gives you several ways to add the item to the menu yourself. The easiest method is to use drag and drop to place the item where you want it. The process is simple:

1. Open Windows Explorer and navigate to the folder that contains the item you wish to add to the Start menu. Generally you want to select items that are listed as *Applications* in the Windows Explorer Details view.

2. Point to the item, hold down the left mouse button, and drag the item onto the Start button. Continue holding down the mouse button.

3. When the Start menu opens, drag the item to the location on the menu where you want it to appear and release the mouse button. Figure 6-2 shows the item Shortcut to HWORKS32 that has just been dropped onto the Programs ⇨ Accessories menu.

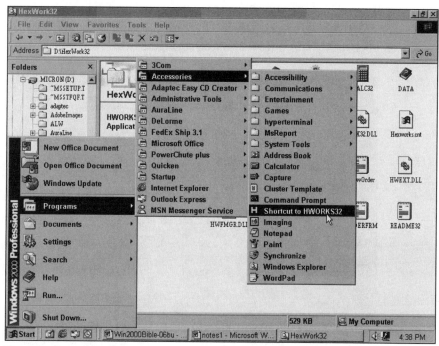

Figure 6-2: Drag and drop items onto the Start menu.

Note

You can add items above the Programs item on the main Start menu or anywhere in the Programs menu. You cannot, however, add items below Programs on the main Start menu.

Rearranging the Start menu

When you add items to the Start menu using the drag-and-drop method, Windows 2000 assumes that you are intentionally reorganizing the menus and stops alphabetically sorting the program and folder shortcuts that appear on the menus. This randomness may be fine for awhile, but when you install additional programs and the list gets longer, you most likely want to bring some order to the menu. You can rearrange the Start menu items using the same drag-and-drop techniques you used to add new items, but this process can get tedious quickly. Fortunately, Windows 2000 provides a simple method for reordering your Start menu items in alphabetical order. Here's how to quickly rearrange your Start menu:

1. Right-click the taskbar.

2. Select Properties from the pop-up menu.

3. When the taskbar and Start Menu Properties dialog box appears, click the Advanced tab.

4. Click the Re-sort button as shown in Figure 6-3.

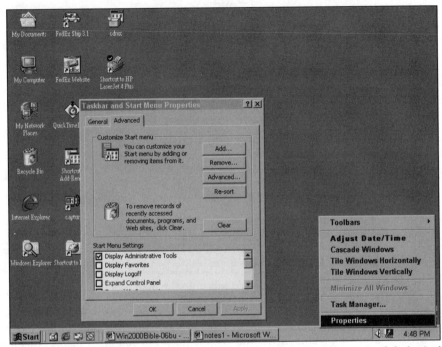

Figure 6-3: Use the Re-sort button to reorder your Start menu items in alphabetical order.

5. Click OK to close the dialog box.

You may need to repeat this process from time to time as you add new items to your Start menu. If you want certain items to appear closer to the top of the newly sorted menu, rename those items before you sort the menu. Windows 2000 sorts the Start menu items alphabetically, but you force a position on the menu by adding a numeric character at the beginning of the menu item name. Numbers sort above alpha characters.

Expanding Start menu items

You can expand the display of the Control Panel, My Documents, Network and Dial-Up Connections, and Printers items on the Start menu. Normally selecting one of these items displays the associated folder. If you choose to expand these options, you can view the contents of these folders as Start menu selections rather than first opening the folders. This enables you to choose an item that is contained in the Control Panel, for example, without first opening the Control Panel and then double-clicking the item you want. Note that the Control Panel, Network and Dial-Up Connections, and Printers items appear in the Settings selection on the Start menu.

To expand any of these items, follow these steps:

1. Right-click the taskbar.

2. Select Properties from the pop-up menu.

3. When the taskbar and Start Menu Properties dialog box appears, click the Advanced tab.

4. Select the checkboxes for any of the items that you wish to expand.

5. Click OK to close the dialog box.

Note

As you use your PC, Windows 2000 keeps track of the items that you access on the Start menu. Eventually Windows 2000 shrinks the menus by hiding items you haven't used. You can still access these items by waiting until the full menu displays or by clicking the arrows at the bottom of the menu, but if you don't care to have menu items hidden, it is easy to make Windows 2000 display full menus. Simply deselect the Use Personalized Menus checkbox on the Taskbar and Start Menu Properties dialog box.

Taskbar tricks

You can change the Windows 2000 taskbar in several ways. You can make the taskbar disappear when you don't need it, add new toolbars, and resize or move the taskbar.

Hiding the taskbar

You can make the taskbar disappear when you aren't actively using it. This feature is handy when you need the maximum available workspace on your Windows 2000 desktop.

You can use two settings to hide the taskbar, and both appear on the General tab of the Taskbar and Start Menu Properties dialog box:

✦ The Always on top setting makes the taskbar appear on top of whatever space it is using on your Windows 2000 desktop. In effect, this setting reduces the amount of desktop space that is available to your applications because most applications automatically resize their full screen size to be equal to the display resolution less the taskbar size. By removing the check for this setting, the taskbar is hidden underneath any open windows, and your applications can use the entire screen without considering the taskbar.

✦ The Auto hide setting makes the taskbar disappear when you aren't using it. When this setting is enabled, you can generally display the taskbar by moving the mouse just off the bottom of your screen (or whichever edge where the taskbar is currently docked). If you cannot make the taskbar appear using your mouse, press the Windows key or Ctrl+Esc to open the Start menu. Whenever the Start menu is displayed, the taskbar also appears.

The Always on top setting may interact with the Auto hide setting. If Always on top is not selected and if any program is running maximized, you likely find that you cannot display a hidden taskbar by sliding the mouse off the edge of the screen. If you reduce the maximized program to run in a window rather than full screen, you can display the taskbar using the mouse.

Tip   If a program — such as a software installation program — hides the taskbar, press the Windows key or Ctrl+Esc. This works no matter where the taskbar is hiding.

Adding toolbars to the taskbar

Although most people primarily use the taskbar for switching between programs, it's possible to make the taskbar far more useful by adding toolbars.

Several standard toolbars can appear on your taskbar. To choose one of these standard toolbars, right-click the taskbar and make your selection from the Toolbars menu on the pop-up menu. The standard toolbars include the following:

✦ The Quick Launch toolbar contains icons that you can click to quickly view your desktop, browse the Internet, or check your e-mail. You can even add some of your own shortcuts to the Quick Launch toolbar (I tell you how later in this chapter).

✦ The Address toolbar is one of the most useful toolbars you can add to the taskbar because it gives you quick access to Web sites. All you have to do is enter the URL into the Address bar and press Enter. Internet Explorer opens and takes you directly to the Web site, bypassing any start pages that Internet Explorer normally opens first.

✦ The Links toolbar gives you one-click access to the links on the Internet Explorer Links bar. Click one of the links to visit the associated Web site.

✦ The Desktop toolbar gives you access to anything that appears on your Windows 2000 desktop. You don't have to minimize the open windows to click a desktop icon because all of those icons appear in the Desktop toolbar.

You can also create a custom toolbar and add it to the taskbar. Select Toolbars ➪ New Toolbar from the pop-up taskbar context menu and specify any folder as the source of the toolbar shortcuts. The folder could contain documents that you access often, or you might want to create a new folder containing important shortcuts. You could even create several different folders with shortcuts to programs and documents that relate to specific projects, and then create several custom toolbars for different projects. All of the items in the selected folder appear as icons on the new toolbar, thus providing quick access to the items.

Remove toolbars by simply clearing the check from the pop-up taskbar context menu.

Rearranging the taskbar

The taskbar area can become crowded very quickly — especially if you have a number of programs open at the same time or have added additional toolbars. As you open additional programs, the program buttons on the taskbar become smaller as they are squeezed into the available space. If the buttons become too small, it's hard to read the button titles and choose the right one.

Windows 2000 gives you a couple of ways to deal with the problem of an overcrowded taskbar. You can resize the taskbar by dragging the top edge up to accommodate two or more rows of buttons. When you drag the edge, the taskbar resizes itself in full-row increments. Your second option is to dock the taskbar along one of the sides of the screen, opening up considerably more room for program buttons and toolbars as shown in Figure 6-4. The figure shows three different toolbars on the taskbar, as well as plenty of room for buttons for open programs.

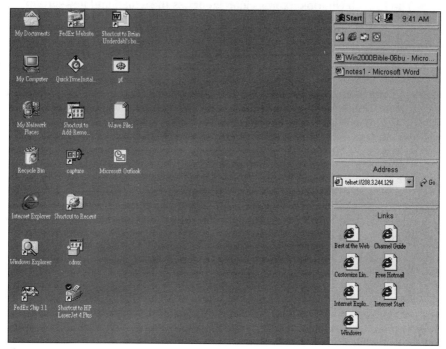

Figure 6-4: Move the taskbar to one side of the screen to create more space for program buttons and toolbars.

Tip   You can also drag the edge of the taskbar when it is docked along the side of the screen to adjust its size.

The Quick Launch toolbar

The Quick Launch toolbar normally appears just to the right of the Start button on your taskbar. This toolbar provides quick access to the programs that you use most often. You can even add your own shortcuts to the Quick Launch toolbar to complement or even to replace the existing Quick Launch toolbar icons.

Using the Quick Launch toolbar

The icons on the Quick Launch toolbar are shortcuts to programs. Clicking one of the icons quickly launches the associated program. By default, the Quick Launch toolbar has three icons:

✦ The Show Desktop icon minimizes all open windows so that you can view the desktop.

✦ The Launch Internet Explorer Browser icon launches the browser, just like the Internet Explorer icon on the desktop does.

✦ The Launch Outlook Express icon launches the e-mail and newsgroup services program.

If you move the mouse cursor over an icon for a few seconds, the icon's description appears.

Although you can easily start your programs by clicking their desktop icons or by choosing them from the Start menu, the Quick Launch toolbar offers one big advantage: it's visible whenever the Windows 2000 taskbar is visible. An open window might cover your desktop icons, and finding your favorite programs via the Start may require wading through several layers of menus.

Adding and removing Quick Launch icons

Another key advantage of the Quick Launch toolbar is the capability to add your own programs and remove the defaults. This capability enables you to customize the Quick Launch toolbar any way you want.

To add a program to the Quick Launch toolbar, follow these steps:

1. Point to the item that you wish to add. This can be an item on your desktop or in a folder you have opened in Windows Explorer.

2. Hold down the right mouse button and drag the item onto the Quick Launch toolbar.

3. Release the mouse button when the item is in the desired location on the Quick Launch toolbar. A pop-up menu displays.

4. Select Create Shortcut(s) Here from the pop-up menu.

5. If necessary, drag the right edge of the Quick Launch toolbar to resize it so that you can see all of the icons.

One practical addition to the Quick Launch toolbar is a shortcut to Windows Explorer that enables you to quickly open Windows Explorer whenever the taskbar is visible. You may find this option especially useful if you have created a Windows Explorer shortcut that displays a folder other than the default My Documents folder.

To remove icons from the Quick Launch toolbar, simply drag them to the Recycle Bin.

Customizing the Desktop

So far you've learned how to make a few changes that have a relatively minor visual impact on your Windows 2000 desktop. Now it's time to examine some changes that can pack a major visual wallop and make your PC look considerably different from anyone else's system. In the following sections, you learn how to use images on your desktop, how to make your system look more interesting when you aren't using it, how to adjust the colors, and how to change some other visual features of Windows 2000.

Wallpaper images

Adding a background — or wallpaper — image to your Windows 2000 desktop instantly adds a unique touch that can change your desktop from boring to splashy. This is one of the easiest appearance changes you can make to Windows 2000 and is also one that can have the most immediate visual impact.

Note

The background images you add to your Windows 2000 desktop are called wallpaper for a very good reason. Wallpaper appears behind the other items on your desktop rather than covering them up. This makes it possible to see all of your desktop icons even though you've added a background image. Some wallpaper images can, however, make it difficult to see the desktop icons, especially if the wallpaper is loaded with dark colors. If you encounter this type of problem with your favorite wallpaper, you may want to try centering the image rather than tiling or stretching it. Another possibility is to use your favorite graphics editing program to lighten the image somewhat or perhaps to crop the image so that it uses less space on your desktop.

Windows 2000 enables you to use several different types of graphics files as background images. The Windows Bitmap (BMP) format is the easiest to use because it is automatically supported by Windows 2000. You can use a JPEG image, but only if you activate the Active Desktop.

To add wallpaper to your desktop, follow these steps:

1. Right-click a blank spot on the desktop to display the pop-up menu.

2. Select Properties to display the Display Properties dialog box.

3. On the Background tab, select an image as shown in Figure 6-5.

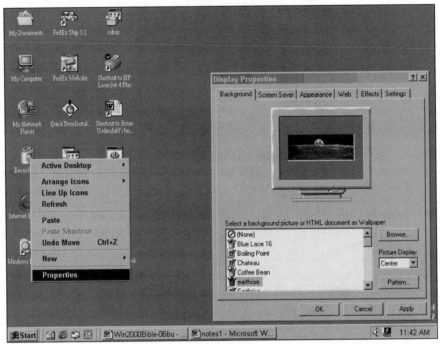

Figure 6-5: Choose a wallpaper to add an image to the background of your desktop.

4. To locate an image that does not appear in the list, use the Browse button.

5. Once you have selected an image, choose an option from the Picture Display list box:

Choose Center to display the image in its original size and centered in the middle of your desktop.

Choose Tile to display multiple copies of the image that cover your entire desktop.

Choose Stretch to expand the image both horizontally and vertically to cover the entire desktop.

6. Click OK to close the dialog box and add the wallpaper to your desktop.

Caution

If you choose a digital image that has the same dimensions as your Windows 2000 desktop, you may end up with blank space around the image, or it may extend beyond the edges of the screen. Although Windows 2000 offers you the option to stretch the image to fit the desktop, this produces distorted images unless the original image uses the same 4 wide by 3 high ratio as your screen. Divide the image width by the image height to determine if the image has the correct ratio. You may want to crop incorrectly sized images as completely explained in Chapter 17 to adjust for the correct ratio.

There are many good sources for image files that you can use as desktop wallpaper. If you have a digital camera or a scanner, you can create your own digital images. You can also find images on many CD-ROMs or on the Internet. Most of the images you find on the Internet are JPEG images. Most digital cameras also produce JPEG images. JPEG images are easier to find and use far less disk space than Windows Bitmap images.

To use an image that you find on a Web page as your Windows 2000 desktop wallpaper, right-click the image and choose Set as Wallpaper from the pop-up menu. To save multiple images so you can choose one later, right-click each image and choose Save Picture As from the context menu. You may even wish to create a new folder for saving the images you download for use as wallpaper.

To remove wallpaper, simply select None from the list.

Screen savers 101

In the early days of computing, monitors were susceptible to having an image burned into the display if the same image appeared for a long time without changing. That's why screen savers were originally introduced. If a system sat idle for a long time, the screen saver kicked in and prevented a static image from burning the display phosphors. The monitors on modern day PCs don't need screen savers because they are immune to the type of damage that could burn a permanent image into early computer screens.

Today's screen savers serve two real purposes on a Windows 2000-based PC, and neither of them has anything to do with protecting your monitor from damage. Those two purposes are entertainment and security. Having a moving image on your screen when you aren't using your PC may not be high art, but it's probably more entertaining than seeing that report that you've been working on staring back at you. Keeping prying eyes from seeing confidential information is another valid reason for using a screen saver, too.

Windows 2000 includes a number of different screen savers that you can choose on the Screen Saver tab of the Display Properties dialog box as shown in Figure 6-6.

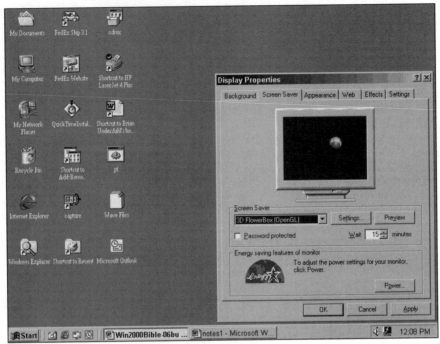

Figure 6-6: Choose a screen saver to appear on your screen when your system is idle.

To choose a screen saver, follow these steps:

1. Right-click a blank spot on the desktop to display the pop-up menu.

2. Select Properties to display the Display Properties dialog box.

3. Click the Screen Saver tab.

4. Click the down arrow next to the list box.

5. Choose a screen saver from the list.

6. Once you have selected a screen saver, you can click the Settings button to choose the options for the screen saver.

   Purely graphical screen savers generally have settings that you can use to change the shapes, textures, and resolution. Screen savers that display text enable you to specify the text that is displayed, the format of the text, the speed that the text moves across your screen, and the motion. Depending on the screen saver you choose, you may have even more customization options.

7. To use a password, click the Password protected checkbox.

If you select the Password protected checkbox, you must enter the correct password to restore your screen after the screen saver has been displayed. This password is your logon password that you enter when you log on to Windows 2000. If you have not established a logon password, anyone can simply turn off the power to your system and then restart to bypass your screen saver password.

8. Click OK.

Pressing any key on the keyboard or moving your mouse closes the screen saver. If you are using password protection, you need to enter the password to resume using your system.

Tip   Screen savers are programs, so you can create a shortcut to your screen saver on your desktop. If you plan to be away from your desk for a few moments, you can start the screen saver immediately. Screen savers are stored in your \Windows\System32 folder. To find them, change to details view and look in the Type column for screen savers. Use your right mouse button to drag the screen saver to your desktop and choose Create shortcut(s) here from the pop-up menu.

Changing the color scheme

If you don't like the colors on your Windows 2000 desktop, you can change them. Almost every element on the Windows 2000 screen can be modified to use a different set of colors. You can choose your own scheme or one of the predefined ones.

Choosing a Color Scheme

As Figure 6-7 shows, you use the options on the Appearance tab of the Display Properties dialog box to choose new colors.

Tip   Before you begin making changes to the Windows 2000 screen colors, be sure to use the Save As button to save your current selections. Then you can return to your saved selections if you find that a new color scheme is not to your liking. Once you've created a new color scheme that you like, save the new scheme, too. Then you can return quickly to your scheme if someone else uses your PC and changes the color selections.

To choose a color scheme, follow these steps:

1. Right-click a blank spot on the desktop to display the pop-up menu.

2. Select Properties to display the Display Properties dialog box.

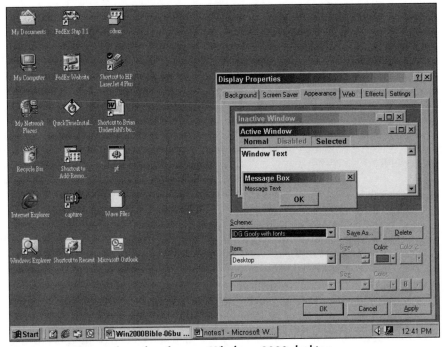

Figure 6-7: Choose the colors for your Windows 2000 desktop.

3. Click the Appearance tab.

4. To try out some of the optional color schemes rather than choosing your own color set, choose an option from the Scheme list box. For example, if you have difficulty viewing the screen, you may want to try using one of the high-contrast color schemes. These color schemes are designed to help make the screen much easier to view, especially in poor lighting conditions or for visually impaired users. You may need to experiment with the color schemes to see which one works best for you.

5. To select your own colors and other properties for screen elements, either click the element—such as the Active Window title bar or the desktop background—in the sample window near the top of the Appearance tab or select the element in the drop-down Item list box.

   A few items can be selected only by choosing them from the list box. The colors and fonts that you select in the Display Properties dialog box won't have much effect on some of your applications, however, because certain programs have their own settings that are not controlled by Windows 2000. You may wish to avoid making font changes. Selecting alternate fonts may result in a drastic adverse affect on overall system performance. Stick with the default font selections to avoid this potential problem.

6. Click OK to apply your selections and close the dialog box.

Caution Be sure to choose contrasting colors for the text and background in any elements that include text. If you pick text colors that are the same as the background colors, you won't be able to see the text. If you accidentally set your text colors this way, choose another one of the Windows 2000 color schemes to reset the colors so that you can see message text.

Adding Web content to the desktop

You can also add Web content, such as regularly updated weather maps, stock tickers, news wires, and sports scores, to your Windows 2000 desktop.

For Web content to be truly useful, you need an Internet connection that is either constantly active or at least fairly frequently connected. A stock ticker that is updated only once a day is little use to a day trader!

To add Web content, follow these steps:

1. Right-click a blank spot on the desktop to display the pop-up menu.
2. Select Properties to display the Display Properties dialog box.
3. Click the Web tab.
4. Select the Show Web content on my Active Desktop checkbox.
5. Select any of the existing elements shown in the list box.
6. Alternatively, click the New button to go to the Internet to choose new content.

   Follow the onscreen directions for selecting items from the active content Web site. Generally you have to select the category and then the specific type of content you wish to add — such as a weather map. You may also need to adjust the subscription settings — the content update interval.
7. Click OK to close the dialog box.

The Web content you can add to your desktop tends to change often. Most content providers are still experimenting with their offerings, so you may discover that content disappears and reappears in a new format fairly quickly.

Controlling the effects

The Effects tab of the Display Properties dialog box includes a real grab bag of visual options. Figure 6-8 shows the options that appear on this tab. These options include items such as alternative icons for certain desktop items, menus that fade into place, and contents of windows that can be displayed while you drag them. Menu effects are new in Windows 2000.

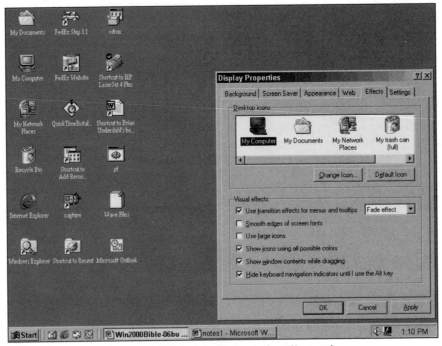

Figure 6-8: Choose the optional visual effects on the Effects tab.

To choose special effects, follow these steps:

1. Open the Display Properties dialog box.

2. Click the Effect tab.

3. In the list box near the top of the Effects tab, select the icon that is used to display one of the desktop elements.

4. Click the Change Icon button. In each case, you can then choose one of the icons that is offered as an alternative, or you can click the Browse button and choose an icon from a different file.

5. Alternatively, click Default icon to return to the original icon.

6. Select Use transition effect for menus and tooltips and choose an effect if you want to have menus and tooltips appear using special visual effects.

7. Select Smooth edges of screen fonts if you want large text to appear less jagged on your screen.

8. Select Use large icons if you want large rather than small icons on your desktop.

9. Select Show icons using all possible colors if you want the maximum number of colors used to display icons.

10. Select Show window contents while dragging to show the complete window rather than just an outline while you drag a window.

11. Select Hide keyboard navigation indicators until I use the Alt key to prevent menus from showing the underlined hot key until you press the Alt key indicating you want to use the keyboard rather than the mouse.

12. Click OK.

The options in the Visual effects area of the Effects tab are all cosmetic items. You can experiment with these options to see which settings you prefer. Although choosing some of these options may have a minor effect on performance, the changes will be so small that it is unlikely that you will notice any real difference.

The Display Properties dialog box has one additional tab that I have not covered here: the Settings tab. To learn how to use the Settings tab, refer to Chapter 16.

Setting Time, Place, and Identity

Computing has truly become a worldwide activity. People everywhere use computers, and Windows 2000 recognizes that fact by providing support for users no matter where they may be located.

In the following sections, you learn about some of the options that you can use to personalize your Windows 2000-based PC to fit your locale.

Multiple user setup

You may like a relatively clean and sparse desktop that is all business, but someone else may want a bright and lively color scheme that you find completely distracting. These differences can become a serious point of contention if several people must share a machine.

Windows 2000 provides a simple solution. All of the personalized settings that you create on a Windows 2000-based PC are saved specifically for your use. This means that each individual user can have whatever bizarre color schemes, Start menu arrangements, or rude sounds attached to system events that he or she prefers, and still not affect other people who use the same system.

The key to this personalization is simple—users must log on using their own user names. Windows 2000 then saves any changes made by that user so that they are automatically restored the next time the user logs on.

Windows 2000 stores many of the individual settings for each user in folders under the \Documents and Settings folder. To see the settings that have been saved for your user account, right-click the Start button and choose Explore from the pop-up menu. Many additional user settings are stored in the Registry, which you learn about in Chapter 25.

Setting the time

Time is important to both people and to their computers. The time and date recorded with a file is one of the most reliable methods of determining the most recent versions of files.

The system tray on your taskbar contains a time display that you can use to set the date and time on your system's clock.

The time is always displayed, and you can view the date by moving the mouse cursor to the time display and waiting a few seconds. You can modify the current settings by double-clicking the clock as shown in Figure 6-9.

To set the clock, follow these steps:

1. Double-click the clock on the taskbar.
2. Click the up or down arrow to adjust the time.
3. Click the date on the calendar to change the date.
4. Click OK.

Although most PCs have fairly accurate system clocks, many factors can affect the overall accuracy. You may need to reset the clock from time to time to maintain the correct time setting.

If you use a laptop PC, move to a different location, or are in an area that does not use daylight savings time, you may need to use the settings on the Time Zone tab of the Date/Time Properties dialog box. You may also wish to deselect the Automatically adjust clock for daylight saving changes checkbox if you operate your system in a dual-boot arrangement with another operating system. Otherwise, you may find that both Windows 2000 and the other operating system adjust the time, and you have to reverse the double correction manually.

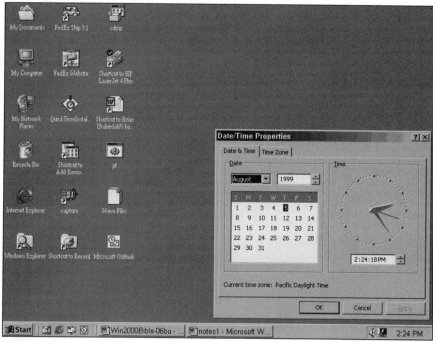

Figure 6-9: You can adjust the date and time to correct for system clock errors.

Setting regional options

If you need to make more extensive changes to the way your system operates, you may need to use the Regional Options dialog box as shown in Figure 6-10. This dialog box enables you to select and customize such items as the system language and the format of numbers, currency, time, and dates. You also can choose the proper keyboard layout for your selected language.

To open the Regional Options dialog box, follow these steps:

1. Double-click the Regional Options icon in the Control Panel.

2. Then select the settings that best suit your needs. You must be logged in as the system administrator — or as someone with equivalent rights — to make some changes such as selecting the language settings.

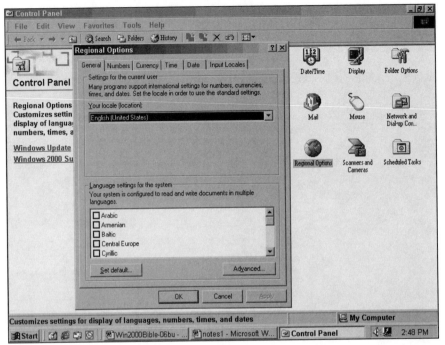

Figure 6-10: Use the Regional Options dialog box to select international settings.

3. Click OK.

Because Windows 2000 is fully year 2000 compliant, you can use a setting on the Date tab to select the 100-year range for years entered using only two digits. When you adjust the upper calendar setting, the lower-year setting is automatically adjusted to maintain a 100-year range.

Pointing Out the Input Options

Making certain that your keyboard and mouse work the way you do is an important part of configuring your system to meet your needs. You can make several adjustments to the operation of these two components in Windows 2000, and they are covered in the following sections.

Keying in on keyboard options

Different people type at different rates. Some people want their keyboard to react quickly so they can type rapidly. Other people prefer a more forgiving keyboard that enables a slower typist to be productive rather than having to constantly correct typing errors.

Figure 6-11 shows the Keyboard Properties dialog box, which you can access using the Keyboard icon in the Control Panel. This dialog box has two keyboard speed adjustments as well as an adjustment for the cursor blink rate.

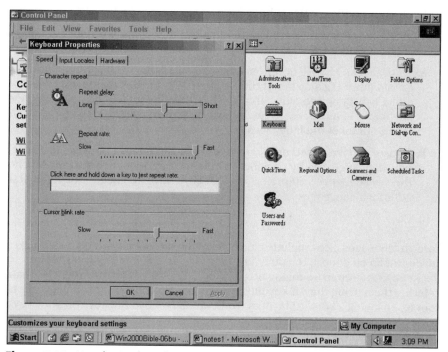

Figure 6-11: Use the Keyboard Properties dialog box to select your preferred keyboard settings.

To adjust the keyboard, follow these steps:

1. Open the Control Panel.

2. Double-click the Keyboard icon.

3. Select the repeat delay.

   The repeat delay is the measure of how long you must hold down a key before that character is repeated. Adjust this setting to the shortest delay that is compatible with your typing style.

4. Select the repeat rate. The repeat rate is a measure of how many times per second characters are repeated once you've held the key down long enough to begin repeating characters. Here too, experiment as you adjust this setting to a rate that feels most comfortable.

5. Select the cursor blink rate. The cursor blink rate setting controls how quickly the cursor blinks on and off. The rate you select is a matter of personal preference, but a slower blink rate may give the false impression that your system is running more slowly.

6. Click the Input Locales tab.

7. If you like, you can use the Input Locales tab settings to choose an alternative keyboard layout, such as one of the Dvorak keyboard layouts.

8. You can also choose additional language layouts by clicking the Add button on the Input Locales tab of the Keyboard Properties dialog box. When you add a new language, you can also select the layout for the new language keyboard. In most cases, you probably want to use the same type of layout for all of the languages.

9. Once you have added new languages, you can choose hot keys for switching between languages by clicking the Change Key Sequence button and choosing the key sequence you prefer. The hot keys have no effect until you install additional languages.

10. Click OK.

Foreign languages often include characters that are not shown on a standard keyboard. If you choose to add a new language on the Input Locales tab of the Keyboard Properties dialog box, typing those characters is far easier than entering them using the Alt key plus a sequence of keys on the number pad. Of course, changing keyboard layouts won't actually move the keys on your keyboard. If you choose to use an alternative keyboard layout, remember that what is shown on the keys won't be the same characters that appear when you type.

The Hardware tab of the Keyboard Properties dialog box is for troubleshooting keyboard problems. You might need to use the options on this tab if you add a special keyboard that requires nonstandard drivers to function correctly.

Manipulating the mouse options

Making sure your mouse feels both natural and responsive can be a big factor in how comfortable you are in using it.

You access the mouse options through the Mouse Properties dialog box as shown in Figure 6-12.

To open adjust your mouse, follow these steps:

1. Double-click the Mouse icon in Control Panel.

2. Choose the mouse button arrangement you prefer.

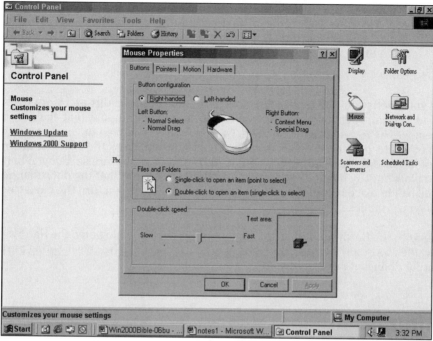

Figure 6-12: Use the Mouse Properties dialog box to adjust your mouse settings.

3. Choose the single- or double-click arrangement you prefer.

4. Drag the Double-click speed slider. This adjusts the amount of time that can pass between clicks and still have the clicks recognized as double clicks rather than as two individual clicks. If your system seems to ignore double clicks, drag the slider to adjust the interval. When you have adjusted the settings properly, the jack-in-the-box responds to your double-clicks in the Test area.

5. Click the Pointers tab. You can use the options on the Pointers tab to have a little fun with your mouse by selecting different pointers to replace the standard ones that Windows 2000 uses by default. Choose an item to customize.

6. Click Browse and select a new pointer.

7. Click OK.

8. Click the Motion tab.

9. Drag the speed slider to control the basic rate at which the pointer moves.

10. Select the acceleration option you prefer to adjust the amount the pointer accelerates as you move your mouse.

11. If you want the mouse pointer to automatically jump to the highlighted button in a dialog box, select the Move pointer to the default button in dialog boxes checkbox. You may find this option is a little disconcerting until you become used to it.

12. Click OK.

If your mouse pointer moves erratically, the cause may be dirt or a worn-out mouse pad. A small opening is probably on the bottom of your mouse that enables you to remove the mouse ball for cleaning. Once you have removed the ball, you can rinse it off in clean water and then dry it thoroughly. Then check the inside of the mouse for lint or dirt. Don't apply any liquids to the inside of the mouse, but you may want to blow out any dust before you replace the ball. Be sure that the door that holds the ball in place is turned to the proper position before you turn the mouse upright so you don't lose the ball.

As with the Hardware tab on the Keyboard Properties dialog box, the Hardware tab on the Mouse Properties dialog box is primarily used for troubleshooting purposes or for changing driver software.

Summary

This chapter has shown you how to use a number of configuration options on your Windows 2000 system to make your PC more comfortable and easier to use. You learned how you can use those options to make using Windows 2000 adapt to your style of working. You also learned how to personalize the appearance of Windows 2000 so your system doesn't look just like everyone else's.

In the next chapter, you learn how to maintain your disk drives to keep your PC running properly and to prevent loss of your important data files.

✦   ✦   ✦

Disk Maintenance

In case you haven't noticed already, Windows 2000 is big—really big. In fact, with a typical installation likely to consume about 500MB of disk space, Windows 2000 is the biggest desktop operating system from Microsoft yet. That means that a lot of PCs will be hard put to find a place for all those bits. Fortunately, Windows 2000 comes packed with utilities, resources, and automated features to help ease disk woes. From disk-scanning and repair facilities, to dynamic disk partitioning, Windows 2000 offers a host of disk-fixing solutions.

At the same time, the growing reliance on PCs has made data more critical and valuable than ever before. Any business user and even home PC user will tell you that a hard disk crash is a certified calamity. After all, so much critical data resides on these sometimes-forgotten peripherals that recovering from the loss of a hard disk can be a gargantuan task. From crucial business presentations to personal Quicken files, the PC hard disk has become the central place to store important information.

Fortunately, you can reinstall most of the applications installed on your PC. But even that task is time consuming and fraught with difficulty. Even if you have all your CD-ROM discs handy, you have to download and install all those utilities, software patches, driver files, and other programs before your system can be returned to its initial state. And even after that is done, you must restore all those personalized application tweaks—you know, custom AutoCorrect settings in Microsoft Word, tailored templates, even programmed joystick settings for your games. No doubt about it, a hard disk crash can ruin your whole day.

Of course, the best defense is prevention. There are two key ways to avoid a disk disaster.

✦ Maintain the health of your media.

✦ Perform backups.

Perhaps best of all, Microsoft put some very useful disk utilities front and center in the operating system. Figure 7-1 shows the Tools page of the Disk Properties dialog box. To get there, right-click a drive icon from the Windows Explorer or browser window, click Properties. Click the Tools tab to gain access to disk-checking, backup, and defragmentation facilities.

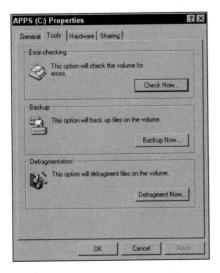

Figure 7-1: Useful disk management and data-saving features are just a mouse click away when you open the Disk Properties dialog box.

I talk about the Windows 2000 built-in Backup utility a little later in this chapter. For now, I'd like to show you how Windows 2000 can help you catch problems early, and even predict when a disk drive is starting to go south.

Using the new Check Disk tool

Windows 2000 features a handy way to quickly check the health of your hard disk and floppy disk drives. The Check Disk utility performs a scan of a specific disk or partition and returns information about any errors on the drive. You can also tell Check Disk to repair any flaws.

To access Check Disk, do the following:

1. Right-click the desired drive icon from the Windows Explorer or a file browser window.

2. Click Properties on the pop-up menu and then click the Tools tab at the top of the Drive Properties dialog box.

3. Click the Check Now button in the Error checking area of the Tools tab. The Check Disk dialog box appears, as shown in Figure 7-2.

Figure 7-2: Simple and effective, Check Disk enables you to fix file system errors and recover lost areas of the disk.

4. In the Check Disk dialog box, click the top checkbox to have Check Disk automatically fix any file system errors it discovers.

5. Next, click the lower checkbox if you want Check Disk to attempt to recover any sectors on the disk drive that are marked as bad. This can help recover disk space and data.

6. Click the Start button. The update bar increments as the drive is accessed. When the process is done, you see a dialog box that says Disk Check Complete. Click OK to finish.

Check Disk is easy to use, but you have to be aware of some conditions. For example, Check Disk won't be able to do its thing on a drive that is currently being accessed. Also, you must have rights to the drives in question. Try to run Check Disk on a company network drive, and you'll probably get a dialog box denying your request.

Note   It's worth noting that Check Disk can take a while to run on very large disks or partitions. During that time, users cannot access files or programs on the disk being checked. While Check Disk runs, the user will usually hear the disk spinning and see the drive activity blinking. Note that this utility only works on local drives and partitions, not network drives.

In addition, if you want to perform repairs as part of your Check Disk routine, the program must be able to gain exclusive rights to the disk. That means the disk cannot be in use or have any files from the disk open in memory. If Check Disk can't establish exclusive rights — quite likely for the C:\ drive that typically contains the Windows page file — it asks you if you want to perform the check at the next system startup — before pesky applications and files have been loaded. Click Yes to check the disk the next time you restart or No to cancel the checkup.

Tip   While you can't use Check Disk on CD-ROM drives, you can use the utility to check the health of floppy diskettes. This is particularly important because floppy diskettes are notoriously prone to failure. If you need to carry important data with you, it's a good idea to use Check Disk on the floppy first. That way, you know there's a good chance you won't get stonewalled by a bad disk later.

Using the old ChkDsk command

Anyone who has used MS-DOS and even many flavors of Windows is probably well versed in the command-line CHKDSK utility. This program, which started shipping as part of Microsoft DOS 5.0, performs many of the same tasks that the graphical Check Disk utility does. It simply does its work from the command line.

That said, CHKDSK offers a greater level of control than its graphical cousin, particularly if you are working with multiple file systems or want to check individual files (rather than whole drives or partitions). To run CHKDSK, do the following:

1. Click Start ➪ Programs ➪ Accessories ➪ Command Prompt; or, click Start ➪ Run, type **cmd** in the text box, and press Enter.

2. A text-only window appears on the desktop. At the prompt (C:\> in most cases), type **chkdsk c**, where c is the letter of the drive or partition you wish to check.

The program reads through the disk and displays a text report that includes the number of bytes used and free, errors detected, and other information. Figure 7-3 shows the display from a CHKDSK run.

```
Command Prompt                                            _ □ ✕

C:\>chkdsk
The type of the file system is FAT.
Volume APPS created 10/1/98 10:56 AM
Volume Serial Number is 2722-0F07
Windows is verifying files and folders...
File and folder verification is complete.

2,146,467,840 bytes total disk space.
   34,471,936 bytes in 370 hidden files.
   36,274,176 bytes in 1,103 folders.
1,910,833,152 bytes in 15,517 files.
  164,888,576 bytes available on disk.

       32,768 bytes in each allocation unit.
       65,505 total allocation units on disk.
        5,032 allocation units available on disk.

C:\>
```

Figure 7-3: With CHKDSK, you can glean useful information about your disk volumes and use switch options to tailor your diagnostic and repair activities.

Like the graphical Check Disk utility, CHKDSK can't fix a disk that has programs running or files open. In fact, the utility may return false error flags on a clean drive if that drive has not been locked.

Note

When you're checking drives for errors, close all files and programs that reside on the drive to help avoid false error messages.

CHKDSK is a command-line utility—you won't find any point-and-click help windows here. But you can tailor the program's output by using a series of *switches*, symbols and letters that tell CHKDSK exactly what to do and how to do it. To use these switch options, simply type the CHKDSK command and drive target, add a space, and type /**x**, where x is the switch letter. If you don't use any switches, the program assesses the current drive—that is, the drive letter displayed at the command prompt.

In command-line parlance, the CHKDSK command options look like this:

```
chkdsk [drive:][[path] filename] [/f] [/v] [/r] [/l[:size]]
[/x]
```

The first three items are parameters that tell CHKDSK where to look. There are no mysteries here. The drive, path, and filename options enable you to point CHKDSK at anything from an entire disk or partition to a single file. You can also have CHKDSK check a collection of files by using wildcard characters (* and ?). Using *.doc as the filename, for instance, prompts CHKDSK to look at all the .DOC files in the specified drive or directory.

After these parameters, you can enter the optional switch commands shown in Table 7-1.

Table 7-1 CHKDSK Switches	
Switch	**Description**
/f	Use the /f switch if you want CHKDSK to fix any errors it finds on the disk. Remember, the disk must be locked—all files closed—in order for the fixes to occur. This is the equivalent of the Automatically fix file system errors checkbox in the Check Disk dialog box.
/v	The /v switch is the equivalent of the Scan for and attempt recovery of bad sectors checkbox in the Check Disk dialog box. CHKDSK displays information about each stage of the check (for file verification, index verification, and so on) as well as summary information.

Continued

	Table 7-1 *(continued)*
Switch	**Description**
/r	Use the /r switch to hunt for bad sectors and recover any readable data that resides there. As with the /f option, the disk must be locked.
/l[:size]	This switch applies only to partitions and drives formatted to the NT file system (NTFS). CHKDSK /l displays the size of the NTFS log file. Enter a size (in kilobytes) after the /l switch, and CHKDSK sets the log file to the new size.
/x	Another NTFS-only switch, /x forces the scanned volume to dismount before the scan. All open handles to the volume are then invalid. This switch also includes the functionality of the /f switch.

Caution   You should be careful before using the /x switch with CHKDSK. Forcing the volume to dismount can result in lost data.

Disk-checking tactics

Whether I use the graphical Check Disk or the command-line CHKDSK utilities, I usually approach disk assessment as a four-step process.

1. Close all applications, documents, and other files.

2. Launch the application and run a check without fixing errors.

3. Review the results of the scan.

4. Run the application again, this time setting the utility to fix errors (using the /f switch in CHKDSK or clicking the appropriate radio buttons in Check Disk).

I prefer this stepped approach because it gives me a chance to decide if errors merit further exploration before trying to fix them. I might copy the contents of a floppy diskette over to my hard disk before trying to recover lost sectors, for example. Of course, you need to remember that scanning large drive volumes can take a looong time. Make sure you have enough time to wait out the diagnostic, because you may not be able to do anything else with your system during the operation.

Optimizing Disk Performance

Okay, so your hard disk is doing just fine, thank you very much. It's Windows' lackadaisical file and program load performance and interminable disk swapping that has you steamed. In fact, disk performance is one of the biggest performance bottlenecks under Windows 2000. Why? Well, everything from your applications and data files to the operating system itself need to read from and (often) write to the hard disk. Your processor may churn away at 500 million clock ticks per second, but that doesn't mean much if the chip is waiting for the hard disk to spin bits off the platter.

There are a couple ways to solve disk-bound performance bottlenecks. Buy a fast hard disk with a big memory buffer and a rotation rate of at least 7,500 rpm (effective but expensive), or use Windows 2000's built-in tools to wring more speed out of your current disk (effective and inexpensive). You can learn more about installing a fast, new hard disk into your Windows 2000 system in Chapter 4. Here I talk about how you can get more performance out of your disk using the Windows 2000 tools.

Tip

Hard disk performance really comes into play when Windows 2000 goes to *virtual memory*. Virtual memory is space on your disk that Windows uses to supplement its system RAM. When more programs and files are open than RAM can store, Windows uses the disk as an extension to RAM, swapping data in and out as needed. The problem is that even the fastest hard disk is orders of magnitude slower than RAM. So if virtual memory swapping is bogging down your Windows 2000 system, the answer isn't a faster disk, it's more RAM. I recommend 128MB of RAM to ensure smooth performance when multitasking applications.

Assessing disk performance

Before you go buying disks or noodling with utilities, you need to assess disk performance. Here are some telltale signs of a disk-bound system:

✦ Long pauses when you open programs, start Windows, or access large files

✦ Skipped or lost frames when you're playing demanding digital video or animation files

✦ Long pauses when Windows is forced to go to virtual memory, such as when you're switching among several multitasked applications You'll know your PC is going to virtual memory when you see the drive activity light blinking constantly and hear the disk spinning.

Windows 2000 makes it easy to keep tabs on disk activity by way of the ever-handy Windows 2000 Performance tool. This utility, part of the Computer Management facility, enables you to track the performance of a variety of subsystems, from CPU and memory to disk drives and network connections. Microsoft has moved this facility from its familiar place under Windows NT. To track disk performance, do the following:

1. Open the Performance tool by clicking Start ➪ Programs ➪ Administrative Tools ➪ Performance. Users can also launch the Performance monitor tool by clicking Start ➪ Run, typing **perfmon** in the Open text box, and pressing Enter.

2. To track a disk-specific item on the chart, click the plus (+) icon in the toolbar or right-click the chart area and select Add Counters from the shortcut menu.

3. In the Add Counters dialog box, from the Performance object drop-down list box, select the entry Physical Disk. You see a number of listings in the Performance counters scrolling list box.

Tip   Be sure to click the Explain button in the Add Counters dialog box to display a window that provides a description of each item you select in the Performance counters list. There are so many objects and counters that this text is very helpful for figuring out what to track.

4. Select the entry Disk Bytes/sec to track the total bytes transferred to and from the disk.

Now you can visually track the raw data transfer rate of your hard disk. By keeping tabs of this metric over time, you can assess whether or not the average transfer rate per second is falling off — a possible indicator of a badly fragmented disk drive.

What is disk fragmentation? When Windows 2000 writes data to disk, it doesn't always place entire files in one spot. Instead, the operating system seeks to maximize disk space by sometimes fragmenting files and writing them in the available nooks and crannies on the disk. That way, your hard disk doesn't need a big block of contiguous free space to find room for a 27MB AVI digital video file, for example. Windows accesses these cut up files by placing markers to all the file fragments in the disk file system. So even though your 27MB file may be broken into four fragments, your system can quickly reassemble the parts into a single whole by following the markers.

The problem with this approach is that as time passes, the data on your disk drive can grow increasingly fragmented. As your disk gets filled up with data, the trend toward file fragmentation grows acute — an ever growing percentage of your files must be split up in order to fit into scarce open space. And as Windows must spend more and more time scurrying around the disk to find and assemble files, system performance plummets.

The good news: Windows 2000 (unlike its predecessor NT 4.0) includes a disk defragmenter utility. By periodically using Disk Defragmenter to streamline your disk drive, you can maintain optimal system performance and avoid the truly lengthy defragmentation sessions that occur when drives get badly fragmented. The next section shows you how to defragment your hard disk under Windows 2000.

Defragmenting your hard disk

You've seen the symptoms and even tracked the results on the Performance tool. But the best way to see if file fragmentation is hurting disk performance is to measure the thing itself. Here's where the useful Disk Defragmenter utility comes in. This applet provides all the tools you need to keep your files and programs in perfect marching order. To open the utility, click Start ➪ Programs ➪ Accessories ➪ System Tools ➪ Disk Defragmenter. Figure 7-4 shows you the basic Disk Defragmenter interface.

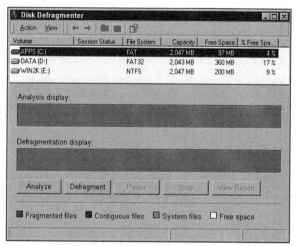

Figure 7-4: Disk Defragmenter gives you a handy bird's-eye view of your drive's fragmentation status.

Note You can also get to the Disk Defragmenter directly from Windows Explorer. Right-click the desired drive, click Properties, and then click the Tools tab on the Drive Properties dialog box. Click the Defragment Now button to launch the utility.

Disk Defragmenter gives you two options: Analyze or Defragment the drive. I usually start by analyzing each drive because that way I can decide whether or not to defragment based on what the program tells me. Click the Defragment button, and the program immediately begins working on files as soon as its analysis is done.

Before you do anything, notice the drive status window at the top of the dialog box in Figure 7-4. Just by glancing at the three displayed drive entries, you can tell that at least one of the drives (C:\) could be headed for fragmentation trouble. How can I tell? The far rightmost column shows that only 22 percent of C:\ is free. Anytime you have a drive volume with less than 30 percent of its capacity unused, Windows is going to have to start chopping up larger files to make them fit.

To get things moving, select the drive volume you wish to analyze/defragment and then click the Analyze button. You hear a lot of disk activity as the software starts reading your drive. Watch for progress in the Analysis display progress bar. This bar gives you a great end-to-end look at your disk's file structure, using colored vertical lines to represent the disk. Here's what those colors mean:

✦ **Red:** Fragmented files. If you see a lot of red, you definitely want to defragment.

✦ **Blue:** Contiguous files. The more of this, the better off you are.

✦ **Green:** System files. These usually cannot be moved by Disk Defragmenter.

✦ **White:** Free space. Take a close look here. If free space is below 20 percent of total drive capacity, file fragmentation becomes a fact of life. You might consider paring down the number of files on the drive or adding a new drive.

Once the analysis is complete, Disk Defragmenter recommends whether or not you should defragment the drive. But first, click the View Report button. This brings up the Analysis Report dialog box, which displays a detailed, text-based assessment of your drive, as shown in Figure 7-5. Here you can see the percentage of all files that are fragmented and the percent of total disk capacity that is unused. You even get a file-by-file rundown of the most fragmented files on your drive. For example, the Windows swap file on the C:\ drive (used by Windows 98 on my dual-boot machine, by the way) has been cracked into an astounding 224 pieces. You can see this data in the Most fragmented files window of the Analysis Report dialog box.

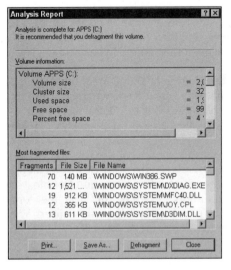

Figure 7-5: Use the Analysis Report dialog box to view a detailed record of disk fragmentation. You can even tell which specific files are most fragmented, helping you track down performance bottlenecks.

If you want to keep a record of your drive status, you can click Print to send the report to your printer or click Save As to write a text file to your disk. Or, to get right down to business, click the Defragment button to start cleaning things up. Keep in mind that disk defragmentation is often a very time-consuming process. Don't start the operation five minutes before you have to use your PC for a presentation or other task—chances are, Disk Defragmenter will still be grinding away.

Tip   I let Windows do this kind of housekeeping at night. Your PC doesn't need sleep, so why not enable it to get things done while you rest? Just before you leave the office, kick off a defragmentation session. That way, your drive will be streamlined when you return in the morning, and you won't lose any productive time.

Once you click the Defragment button, the program once again starts analyzing the selected drive volume. The lower bar, called Defragmentation display (refer to Figure 7-4), shows the same colored lines as the top bar. As Disk Defragmenter goes about its business—and it can be awhile—the red lines in the lower display disappear and are replaced by blue lines. The program also keeps you updated on its progress by showing a progress bar in the status area on the lower edge of the Disk Defragmenter window. This bar fills up from left to right as the disk is cleaned up.

Once you've successfully defragmented the volume, you can expect to see snappier performance in some applications. Of course a lot depends on the relative speed of your system and disk drive and the types of applications you run. In order to maintain the benefits of a streamlined drive, be sure to periodically defragment your drive volumes.

Making Space on Cramped Disks

Whenever Microsoft introduces a new operating system, two things are certain. One, the new product gets a ton of coverage in the press, and two, PC users and IT professionals worldwide find themselves in a mad scramble to free up disk space. True to form, Windows 2000 Professional puts a premium on disk capacity, consuming about 500MB in a typical installation.

In an era of 13GB hard disks, a lot of readers might be asking themselves, who cares? But the fact is, Windows 2000 is going to run on a lot of systems without tremendous amounts of disk space. Corporate PCs often come configured with surprisingly small hard disks, and many laptop PCs feature disks that are 3GB or smaller. Power users may find themselves particularly constrained if they run multiple operating systems (see Chapter 23 for more on this) or use demanding applications and development tools. Believe me, because I am a living example of this problem. My Dell Dimension XPS D300 has a 6GB hard disk partitioned into three 2GB volumes. The C:\ drive holds Windows 98, the D:\ drive holds all my data files, and the E:\ drive holds Windows 2000. This arrangement enables me to dual-boot operating systems and perform OS upgrades without impacting my crucial data, but it does put a squeeze on space. My C:\ drive, for example, has only 200MB free, and even with minimal applications installed on the Windows 2000 partition, only 500MB is available on E:\.

The good news is that Windows 2000 comes equipped with several tools for fighting bit bloat. Gone are the days when you spent hours sifting through long-forgotten folders, trying to assess which files you could afford to blow away and which you should keep. Instead, Windows 2000 keeps tabs on the programs and files you use and don't use, dispensing helpful insight into which bits you can afford to let go. There's also built-in file compression and automated backup facilities to help make offloading bits easier than ever.

The Disk Cleanup utility

Windows is funny in that it tends to accrue old and forgotten files the way dust gathers in the corners of a large apartment. You may never see them, but files are gathering like lint in an odd assortment of places such as Temp directories, the Recycle Bin, and Internet browser cache stores. Sure you can go peering into every corner to keep files from piling up, but who has time? Now Windows 2000 features a utility, called Disk Cleanup, to sweep up after itself. (By the way, if you use Windows 98, you probably recognize this applet.)

To run Disk Cleanup, click Start ➪ Programs ➪ Accessories ➪ System Tools ➪ Disk Cleanup. On the Select Drive dialog box that appears, pick the desired drive from the drop-down list box and click OK. Unfortunately, Disk Cleanup won't go through all your drive volumes in a single pass.

After taking a moment to analyze your drive, the system displays the dialog box shown in Figure 7-6. The Files to delete scrolling list box displays a list of file locations and Disk Cleanup's findings for each. If a check appears to the left of an item, it means Disk Cleanup found some lint that it can sweep away. For these entries, it also notes how much disk capacity can be recovered by removing the files. To deselect one of these items, just click the checked box so that it becomes blank, and Disk Cleanup passes that folder by when it clears out files.

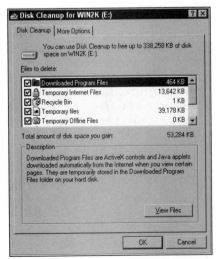

Figure 7-6: Disk Cleanup helps you empty out unneeded files from a number of disparate locations.

Note You can also get to Disk Cleanup from the Drive Properties dialog box. Right-click the desired drive volume, click Properties, and then click the Disk Cleanup button. You bypass the initial Disk Cleanup dialog box and go straight to the results dialog box.

To see exactly what the system found, select one of the items and click the View Files button. The selected folder opens in a separate Windows Explorer window. If you want to clear out the suggested items, click OK and then click Yes at the confirmation dialog box. Within a few seconds, the Disk Cleanup program clears out the marked entries.

Still short on space? Click the More Options tab in the Disk Cleanup dialog box to see two areas: Windows components and Installed programs. Clicking the Clean up button in either of these areas launches the appropriate install/uninstall wizard or facility, as shown in Figure 7-7. To learn more about how to use these facilities, refer to Chapter 3.

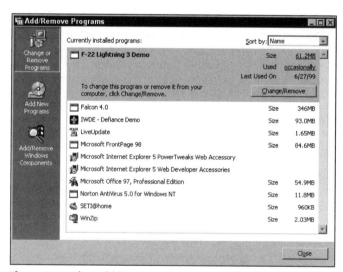

Figure 7-7: The Add/Remove Programs facility has been improved to indicate how frequently installed applications are used, helping you figure out which programs to uninstall.

Disk compression

Maybe you are in a really tight spot. Deleting temp files and removing unused applications just doesn't seem to free up enough space. What next? Well, typically I tell people to see what data files they can offload. Do you have three-year-old scanned images of your family sitting on your hard disk? Try moving those files from your hard disk to a removable medium such as an Zip or Jaz disk, CD-recordable or CD-rewritable discs, or even floppies. Ultimately, though, a new and larger hard disk may well be the answer.

But what if you can't afford a big hard disk or aren't willing to invest in a disk for a machine you might retire in less than a year? In that case, the Windows 2000 disk compression capabilities may help you extend the usefulness of that little drive. Disk compression is hardly new. A company called Stac Software made a killing for a few years by offering on-the-fly compression for PCs running Microsoft Windows. A couple of years later, Microsoft all but killed off Stac by bundling compression right into Window 95.

Disk compression makes your hard disk seem bigger than it actually is by squeezing down files before they are written to the disk. When Windows goes to open a file on a compressed drive, it must expand the file to use it. This trickery happens on the fly and in the background — you never see the compression going on. But you do pay a price for this "free" disk capacity in the form of slower system operation and sluggish disk access. And depending on your system's hardware, the slowdown can be significant, as disk compression consumes considerable CPU resources and memory.

Most critical, Windows 2000 provides disk compression only for drives or partitions formatted using the NTFS file system. (For more on Windows 2000 file system options, see Chapter 23.) If your drives are formatted using the FAT16 or FAT32 file systems, Windows 2000 offers no compression capability. You must convert your FAT partitions or drives to NTFS in order to make use of the Windows 2000 compression capabilities.

Converting to NTFS from FAT

There are a lot of good reasons to use NTFS as your default file system. Advanced security and encryption features, useful event logging, and built-in file- and folder-level compression are among the many advantages of NTFS over FAT16 and FAT32. But if you didn't select the NTFS conversion option during the Windows 2000 upgrade — or your Windows 2000 system arrived with FAT32 partitions — what can you do?

Fortunately, Windows 2000 includes an NTFS conversion utility, accessible from the command line. To run the utility, click Start ➪ Programs ➪ Accessories ➪ Command Prompt. At the command prompt, type **convert c: /fs:ntfs**, where c: is the letter of the specific drive or partition you wish to convert.

If you're trying to convert the drive that contains the Windows 2000 operating system, you are prompted to restart your system before the conversion can take place.

Is NTFS for you? As we've discussed, there are definitely attractive features to this advanced file system, including its large volume support, activity logging, and file- and folder-level encryption and compression. But NTFS isn't a good idea for partitions smaller than 500MB — the high overhead of NTFS makes it a poor fit for small drives. Also, NTFS cannot be used on 3.5-inch floppy disks, although there is no problem moving data between an NTFS volume and standard FAT16 floppy disks.

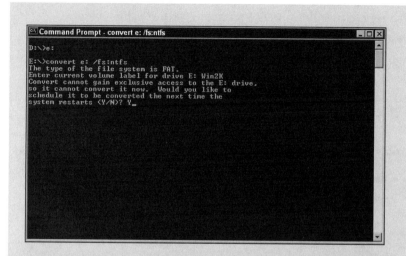

If you are running a multiboot system, converting a partition to NTFS may make it invisible to the other operating systems on your PC. Also, you won't be able to start a conversion unless the drive you convert is locked—that is, no files or applications can be open. If you try to convert the drive containing Windows 2000 itself, the conversion process won't start until you reboot your system.

A few words of warning. In no case should you take a file system conversion lightly. Any problems during the process—say, a sudden power outage—could render your partition unreadable. Also, converting from FAT16 or FAT32 to NTFS is a one-way street. The only way to get back is to purchase a third-party utility such as PowerQuest's PartitionMagic or to reformat the partition and start over from scratch. So back up your data before you start.

Using disk compression under Windows 2000 is surprisingly easy. Here's the quick way to compress an entire drive:

1. Double-click My Computer.

2. Right-click the NTFS-formatted drive you want to compress. Select Properties from the shortcut menu.

3. On the General sheet of the drive Properties dialog box, check the box labeled Compress drive to save disk space.

4. Click OK.

Of course, you may not want to compress an entire drive. After all, compression degrades overall system performance. So what about compressing select folders or files? For example, you might maintain an archives folder where you keep all old documents and records that you rarely open but need to keep handy, just in case. Such a collection of files is a perfect candidate for the big squeeze. Here's how to compress a folder on an NTFS-formatted drive:

1. Use Windows Explorer or browser to navigate to the desired folder.

2. Right-click the folder or file you want to compress and select Properties.

3. If the folder or file is NTFS formatted, the General sheet of the drive Properties dialog box includes an Advanced button. Click it.

4. In the Advanced Attributes dialog box (shown in Figure 7-8), check the box labeled Compress contents to save disk space.

Figure 7-8: It's almost too simple. Just click the Compress contents to save disk space checkbox to enable NTFS-based file- and folder-level compression.

5. Click OK to close the dialog box and then click OK at the Properties box to kick off compression.

Note   Windows 2000 can compress only files and folders that are *not* protected using encryption. If you secure your files via encryption, you cannot use compression on those files. And if you elect to compress files, you cannot secure them.

Unless you've specifically set Windows 2000 to display compressed files in a different color, there's really no obvious way to tell compressed files and folders from uncompressed ones. However, if you right-click one or several compressed files or folders and click Properties, you see an indication on the Properties dialog box. Figure 7-9 shows how Windows 2000 provides both the original size of the file and the compressed size. While JPEG, GIF, and ZIP files won't shrink, many XLS, DOC, TXT, and HTML files shrink by a factor of two or more.

Tip   To quickly tell compressed items from uncompressed ones, click Tools ➪ Folder Options in any Windows Explorer or browser window. Click the View tab and then click the checkbox labeled Display compressed files and folders with alternate color (it's the first entry in the Advanced settings scrolling list box). Click OK, and the Explorer window updates. The color of icon text for compressed files goes from default black to blue.

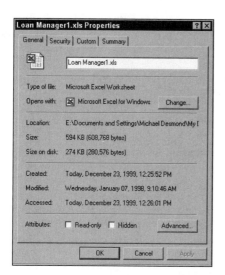

Figure 7-9: The amount of disk space consumed by a large Excel spreadsheet—nearly 600K uncompressed—shrinks by more than half when compressed using Windows 2000 NTFS compression.

Windows 2000 disk compression is an extremely flexible tool for easing hard disk constraints. For example, if you want to preserve top performance while reducing space used by older files, you can easily create a separate archive folder where you keep all your aging documents and files. Set compression for this folder and any files in it. Then, when you feel you don't need regular access to certain files any longer, drag them over to the compressed archives folder you created. Windows 2000 automatically compresses files moved to the folder, often reducing consumed disk space by half. Similarly, when you move a file from a compressed folder to an uncompressed one, Windows 2000 will automatically decompress the moved file.

Of course, files in that folder remain accessible to Windows 2000 and applications. The only concern is that the processor overhead involved in opening and closing compressed files can degrade system performance. But by limiting compression to the oldest files, you can still save space while ensuring that your day-to-day work proceeds smoothly.

Note Don't worry about sharing files with others. When you copy a compressed file to another medium—say, to a network, onto a floppy disk, or even into an e-mail message—Windows automatically uncompresses the file and transfers it in native format. The result: You don't give up compatibility with other users.

Using Microsoft Backup

Whether you want to protect your valuable data or free room on a crowded hard disk, the Windows 2000 Backup facility is a terrific resource. Unlike earlier versions of this built-in program, Backup in Windows 2000 is quite capable. It enables you to schedule backups at regular intervals—say overnight, so you avoid degraded performance during the day—and you can save files to a variety of media types. Backup also features a wizard interface to guide you through the process of backing up and restoring data.

Note   Microsoft Backup is a useful utility, but you may want to spend money on a third-party backup program for several reasons. Perhaps most notable is the fact that Backup will not copy files that are open or in use. That makes backing up files on a schedule something of a hit or miss process, since the system won't copy anything that is being used. You'll also find that backup software tailored for specific drive types may offer useful feature or interface tweaks to help make managing backup routines easier.

To open Backup, click Start ➪ Programs ➪ Accessories ➪ System Tools ➪ Backup. You see the Welcome sheet of the tabbed Backup interface window, which invites you to use the step-by-step Backup Wizard to make data backups. Be aware that you must have appropriate user rights or log on with an administrator account in order to use the Backup application.

Backup types

To work with Backup, it helps to understand the various types of backup routines. There are five backup types that you can use, and each takes a different approach to saving files. Using Normal backups, for example, provides maximum protection by copying all the selected files to the backup medium, but it can take a long time (and multiple disks or cartridges) to copy all the files. Incremental backups, by contrast, speed backups by only copying files that have changed since the last backup. Table 7-2 provides a quick explanation of your backup choices.

Table 7-2	
The Five Backup Types	
Type	**Description**
Normal	Backs up all selected files and then clears the archive bit for each file, which tells Windows 2000 that the file has been backed up. Normal backups give you the capability to restore files quickly because the most current files are stored on a single tape or tape set.
Copy	Copies all selected files but does not clear the archive bit for each file, indicating that the file has not been backed up. Copying is useful if you want to back up files between normal and incremental backups because copying does not invalidate these other backup operations.

Type	Description
Differential	Backs up files created or changed since the last normal (or incremental) backup. It does not clear the archive bit for each file, indicating that the file has not been backed up. Differential backups take longer to complete as the week progresses, but restoring operations are relatively quick because it only requires the last full backup tape and the most recent differential tape.
Incremental	Backs up only files created or changed since the last normal (or incremental) backup. It clears the archive bit for each file, indicating that the file has been backed up. These backups are quicker than differential backups, but restoring operations may take longer. You need the last full backup tape and all the incremental backup tapes since the last full backup.
Daily	Backs up all selected files that have been modified the day the daily backup is performed. This option does not clear the archive bit.

So what type of backup is best for you? Obviously that depends. Conducting normal (or full) backups can consume a lot more time and a lot more media than busy IT professionals can afford. But for home users, such backups may be the most fail-safe way of preserving valuable data.

Personally, I usually back up with the Incremental option because this reduces the number of disks I need to keep on hand and does a quick job of preserving any file changes. I then occasionally (say every two weeks) supplement the incremental backups with a Normal backup that essentially takes an up-to-date snapshot of all my files. Then it's back to Incremental backups for a couple weeks before yet another Normal backup. Rinse, repeat, rinse. You get the idea.

Now I'll step you through the process of backing up and restoring files.

Backing up files

Follow these steps to create a backup of a specific folder or file set:

1. Click Start ➪ Programs ➪ Accessories ➪ System Tools ➪ Backup.

2. In the Welcome sheet of the tabbed Backup interface, click the Backup Wizard button. Click Next. (Alternatively, click the Backup tab to immediately select drives, files, or network data to back up.)

3. In the What to Back Up dialog box, select the appropriate radio button. In this case, select the middle item, Back up selected files, drives, or network data.

4. Select the drives or files you want to back up. Use the left window to navigate to the desired folders. Click the plus (+) sign next to items to expand the tree listing.

5. When you see the folder you want to back up in the right window, move your cursor over the box to the right of the item. The cursor turns into a checkmark. Click the box, and a check appears. The folder is marked for backup. See Figure 7-10.

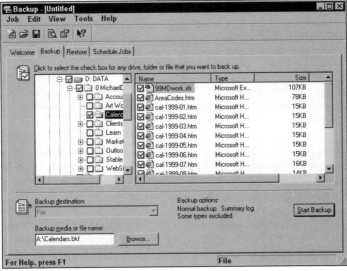

Figure 7-10: Microsoft Backup shows the drives, folders, and files you've selected and makes it easy to tweak your backup roster by unchecking items.

6. Repeat this process for any additional folders or files and then click Next.

7. Tell Backup where to copy backed-up files. You can directly enter the path and filename in the text box or click Browse to navigate to the desired medium. Click Next.

8. The Backup Wizard now displays summary information about your backup job. Click Advanced to select the backup routine type (it's set to Normal by default).

9. In the Type of Backup dialog box, select the type of backup you want to perform from the drop-down list box.

10. If you are on a network and have files that have been moved to remote storage, check the item at the bottom to back these items up. Click Next.

11. Check the Verify data after backup checkbox. The time you spend to verify that a backup has succeeded is well worth it, believe me.

12. You can speed your backup and reduce the number of required cartridges or disks by checking Use hardware compression if available. Keep in mind that compressed backups can be restored only to drives that support this compression. And in many cases, this option is not available. Click Next.

13. In Media Options, decide whether to add the current data to the existing set (top radio button) or to replace the existing set with the current backup (lower radio button). Click Next.

14. The Backup Label dialog displays two text boxes, one for a backup label and one for a media label. Accept the default entries — which imprint the system time on your backup and media — or enter your own data. Click Next.

15. Time to schedule your backup. Select the Now radio button to have the backup run right now or click the Later item to schedule the backup.

16. When you click the Later radio button, you are be prompted to provide your user password. Enter and confirm your password and click OK to proceed.

17. In the Job name text box, enter an appropriately memorable description and then click the Set Schedule button.

18. Select the frequency of backup in the Schedule Task drop-down list box. Figure 7-11 shows the options available in this list, as well as the other scheduling controls.

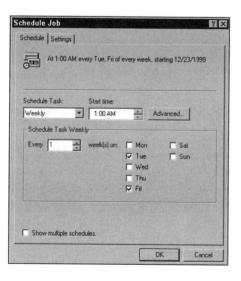

Figure 7-11: Fine-tune the timing of your backups so they don't impair system or network performance. This backup is scheduled to occur every week on Sunday night, typically a slow time on most corporate networks.

19. If you selected Daily, Weekly, or Monthly, enter the desired time of backup in the Start time spinner entry.

Note   You can even set multiple schedules and repeat runs for your backup job. To create multiple schedules, click the Show multiple schedules checkbox. The icon and date stamp at the top of the Schedule Job sheet change into a drop-down list box with the current job selected. Click the New button to create a new job. Then use the frequency and time controls to set the second schedule. Repeat as desired. If you need to drop one of the multiple schedules, select it from the drop-down list box and click the Delete button.

To make the backup task run repeatedly — say, to create multiple instances of the data to protect against sector failures — click the Advanced button. Click the Repeat task checkbox, set the frequency of repetition by entering a number in the Every box, and then select a time scale of minutes or hours. Use the Time or Duration controls to set a deadline for repeat jobs. The bottommost checkbox forces any running job to stop without finishing as soon as the deadline arrives.

20. Click the Settings tab to set rules for when the scheduled job starts based on system conditions. It's a good idea to activate the checkbox labeled Stop the task if it runs for. Enter a reasonable duration in the hours spinner control to keep long and nasty backup jobs from monopolizing a system for hours on end.

21. In the Idle Time area, tell Backup to start the scheduled job only if the system has been idle for a set time. Click the Only start the task checkbox and then enter a value in the minute(s) spinner control. Enter a larger value in the second spinner control. This tells Backup how long to wait for the set period of idle time before abandoning the job. The last checkbox in the Idle Time area stops a backup job if the system gets used while a job is underway.

22. The Power Management area is critical for mobile users because an ill-timed backup can quickly drain batteries. If you are using scheduled backups on a laptop, activate both checkboxes to avoid scheduled backups while the notebook is running on batteries.

23. Click OK to return to the When to Back Up dialog box. Click Next.

24. Click Finish to put your backup settings into effect. The scheduled backup job begins when the system clock reaches the assigned time.

Restoring files to disk

Maybe your hard disk went south unexpectedly, or perhaps you need to move all your files to a new system. In either case, Backup makes it easy to restore the data you've saved. Here's how to restore files.

1. Click Start ➪ Programs ➪ Accessories ➪ System Tools ➪ Backup.

2. Click the Restore tab. You will see a tree view of files and folders you've backed up, as shown in Figure 7-12. Click the box next to the desired backup set — a checkmark appears in the left pane as well as in all the underlying individual files in the right pane.

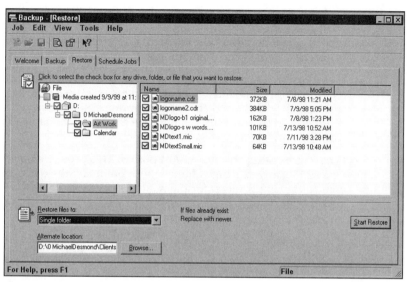

Figure 7-12: Navigate the tree view interface to restore individual files, individual folders, or the entire backup set. You can also restore to the original location or alternative locations, or write all files to a single folder.

3. Once you've selected the files and folders to restore, select the location where you want the files restored. By default, Backup writes back to the original location; however, you can choose to restore to a single folder or an alternative root folder location. In both cases, a file path text box appears beneath the drop-down control.

4. Click Tools ⇨ Options and click the Restore tab to tell Backup how to handle existing files during restore. Choose the top radio button if you don't want to replace files on the PC; choose the middle button to replace files only when the files on the PC are older than those in the backup set; or choose the last button to replace all existing files with the ones in the backup set.

5. Click OK to return to the Restore sheet and then click Start Restore.

6. At the Confirm Restore dialog box, click the Advanced button to bring up the Advanced Restore Options. Here you see four checkbox items:

   a. **Restore security:** Check this option to restore files and folders with the original NTFS security settings. You must restore from and to an NTSF volume for this item to be active.

   b. **Restore Removable Storage database:** Check this option to manage media such as tapes, tape libraries, and removable disc media. This option replaces the existing database stored in the systemroot\system32\NtmsData folder with information in the backup set. If you do not use removable storage to manage media, leave the checkbox unmarked.

    c. Restores junction points: Check this option to restore both the junction points for data on mounted drives as well as the data itself. If this option is deselected, only the junction points pointing to the data will be restored, which means that data itself may or may not be available.

    d. When restoring replicated disk sets : Check this option if the data you are restoring is replicated to other servers, via the file replication service (FRS). Failure to choose this option could cause FRS data not to be replicated to other servers because the restored data appears to be older than the data on the other servers.

    e. Preserve existing volume mount points: This prevents Backup from overwriting any existing volume mount points on the drive, partition, or volume that is the target for the restore operation. If you are restoring to a newly reformatted drive or partition, deselecting this option lets you restore the volume mount points stored in the backup set.

7. Click OK and then click OK at the Confirm Restore dialog box to kick off the restore operation. The Restore Progress dialog box displays information during the transfer, as shown in Figure 7-13.

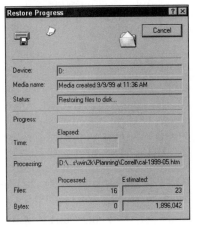

Figure 7-13: The Restore Progress dialog box displays useful information such as the number of files and bytes being transferred. You can compare these against estimated totals to gauge the progress of the restore.

8. When the transfer is complete, click the Report button to view a text file log of the restore operation.

9. Click Close to compete the process. The data is fully restored.

Of Mounted Drives and Junction Points

Mounted drives are useful for network administrators and others who need to have more than the 26 drives supported by Windows 2000. Drives are mounted at an empty NTFS folder and are assigned a path rather than a drive letter. For example, if your system has an NTFS-formatted volume with the drive letter C, and a second hard disk identified by the drive letter D, the second disk can be mounted at an empty folder named C:\DRIVE2. The drive can then be accessed directly through the path C:\DRIVE. Even if you remove the drive letter D, the second disk drive continues to be available through the mounted drive path.

One useful application of drive mounting is to assign a dedicated drive to serve as the Windows 2000 temp file directory. By assigning a second disk drive to the NTFS folder C:\Temp, all temporary files end up on this drive. The result: Greatly reduced disk activity and file fragmentation on your primary drive, yielding improved system performance. Similarly, you can mount a drive to C:\Program Files to provide ample room for applications.

When you mount a drive, Windows 2000 creates a link from the NTFS folder to the drive called a junction point. In essence, a junction point is a pointer to a physical location on another hard disk or storage device. Note that you need to have administrator level rights in order to set up a mounted drive using the Disk Management applet.

Summary

Windows 2000 places more demand on hard disk capacity and performance than any Microsoft operating system before it. Fortunately, Windows 2000 also bolsters the disk management offerings over previous versions of the OS. The result: You can actively monitor and manage your drives to ensure adequate performance and useful operating life. Just as important, a bulked-up backup application means that most users can rely on the built-in tools to perform system backups.

Among the concepts and issues we covered in this chapter:

✦ A rundown of Windows 2000's many storage-related utilities and tools, including Check Disk, the text-based CHKDSK, and Disk Cleanup

✦ A tour of file systems, including the NT File System (NTFS), which offers advanced features such as activity logging and file- and folder-level encryption and compression

✦ An introduction to the improved Microsoft Backup program, as well as a step-by-step guide to performing data backups and restores

✦ A look at mounted drives, which help you extend and manage the storage capabilities of Windows 2000 and preserve optimal performance

In the next chapter, we delve deeper into the diagnostic and tuning facilities of Windows 2000. There you learn how to recover from disaster, protect yourself from inevitable failures, and periodically update Windows 2000 with the latest updates from Microsoft. Whether you are a novice or an expert, the next chapter is among the most important chapters in this book.

✦ ✦ ✦

Fixing and Updating Windows 2000

Every time Microsoft introduces a new operating system, it is touted as the end all and be all of reliable operation, convenient management, and powerful features. Of course, the truth is a lot less appealing. Windows NT 4.0 Workstation — Microsoft's previous flagship business operating system — received numerous patch fixes and five major service pack (SP) updates over its life. While some of these updates actually improved the feature set, the majority of this activity fixed issues such as program bugs, security holes, and Year 2000 compliance issues.

In fact, for a Windows NT 4.0 machine to be considered fully protected against Y2K issues, it needs to be running NT 4.0 Service Pack 5 (SP5). Given all the time, effort, and potential trouble that goes into any operating system update across many networked PCs, many IT managers may be tempted to forego an NT 4.0 update altogether and simply shell out some extra cash for Windows 2000.

However, there are a lot of reasons why upgrading to the new system may not happen. Service Pack updates are typically free for download or available at a nominal price for physical media. Updates also don't ratchet up the hardware requirements of the platform the way moving to Windows 2000 does. And while any new service pack should be fully qualified for operation on the network, the process of qualifying a service pack update is much less rigorous and time consuming than testing out a whole new operating system.

All that said, Windows 2000 offers a way for IT managers and individuals to sidestep the parade of bug fixes and service packs and immediately jump to the most advanced version of Windows for business. But just because you've updated to Windows 2000 doesn't mean updates and troubleshooting are a thing of the past. On the contrary, adjusting to a new operating system can mean you do more tweaking and fixing than ever. And of course, you can expect additional fixes and tweaks as Microsoft hones its new product and adjusts for vulnerabilities and flaws.

This chapter guides you through the new Windows 2000 environment so that you can effectively update, fix, and enhance Windows 2000 as the need arises.

Recovering from System Crashes

System crashes are, quite simply, among the most calamitous and stressful events that can occur in a computing environment. For an end user, nothing is more frightening than seeing his or her system — and all its valuable data — suddenly crash. Fortunately, the NT technology that Windows 2000 is built upon makes such painful failures quite rare compared to Windows 95 or Windows 98.

Anatomy of a system crash

The stability of Windows 2000 is tied directly to how the operating system manages memory for applications. Each application is afforded dedicated memory space in which to operate. This prevents one application from barging in on the memory space of another application or, worse, the operating system — a classic source of fatal system crashes. Because of the hard-line memory protection scheme of Windows NT/2000, even poorly coded programs have a tough time crashing other programs or the operating system itself. Figure 8-1 provides a graphic representation of the Windows 2000 memory model.

Note   Windows 2000 may make it tough for programs to crash other programs or the operating system, but it can do little to protect a poorly written application from itself. If you have a program that crashes frequently during certain operations, it may be the type of program that would crash whether you're running it under Windows 98 or Windows 2000. What Windows 2000 does is prevent self-destructing apps from spreading their problems to other parts of the system.

Unfortunately, this wonderful architecture does not prevent your system from crashing — it only reduces the number of crashes. System crashes occur when the operating system or system hardware causes the computer system to experience a catastrophic failure. In Windows 2000, system crashes almost always result in what is not-so-affectionately known as the *Blue Screen of Death*, or BSOD. The Blue Screen of Death gets its name because it appears as a blue screen background with a large amount of text displayed. This text is essentially a memory dump and looks something like this:

```
Stop: 0x0000000A (parameter1, parameter2, parameter3, parameter4)
IRQL_NOT_LESS_OR_EQUAL*** Address <x> has base at <x> -<filename>
```

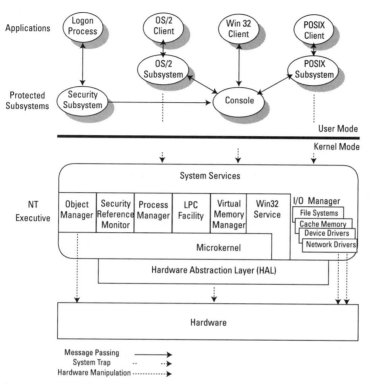

Figure 8-1: Windows 2000 keeps many crashes at bay by preventing applications from inhabiting memory space used by the operating system and applications.

Decipher Screen Dumps

The Blue Screen of Death may at first glance look like a wall of hieroglyphics, but take a moment to look more closely, particularly at the first two lines of the display. It can help you figure out exactly what crashed. Here is an example:

```
STOP 0x0000001E KMODE_EXCEPTION_NOT_HANDLED Address fef65475 has
base at fef62000 - CPQDISP.DLL.
```

Note that the KMODE_EXCEPTION means that the kernel mode hit an error it could not handle. You can also see that the file that crashed the kernel is CPQDISP.DLL, which tells you that the display driver is most likely to blame (CPQDISP.DLL is a display adapter driver file—ComPaQ DISPlay).

Why does BSOD occur? Isn't Windows 2000 supposed to be stable? Yes, but that doesn't mean it is not vulnerable to crashes. Under the Windows 2000 system architecture, the basic functions of the operating system occur in the Executive Services of the kernel mode. While that may be a mouthful to say, essentially it means that the memory space that application (also called *user mode*) code uses is kept separate from the memory space used by the basic functions of the operating system (called *kernel mode*).

✦ **User mode:** Enables applications to work within their respective subsystems while keeping activities separate from low-level system operations. It also prevents direct access to hardware (such as printers and modems) and can render many old DOS applications unusable in Windows 2000.

✦ **Kernel mode:** Enables low-level system components such as the Security Manager, Virtual Memory Manager, I/O services, and graphics operations to occur. Kernel mode also contains the hardware abstraction layer (HAL) that provides a standard interface for applications accessing hardware. It also enables support for multiple platforms, though Windows 2000 today is being supported only on the Intel architecture.

If user mode is violated, Windows 2000 simply terminates the offending thread and reports an error. The rest of the system sails along blissfully, and there is really no risk of a crash or failure. However, if a driver or system process violates the integrity of the kernel mode, you can expect to see a Blue Screen of Death. For example, the Beta 3 version of Windows 2000 running on my laptop caused the system to crash to a blue screen each time I shut down. The error indicated that power management was to blame. Something in the power management interface was clearly violating the Windows 2000 kernel mode, resulting in the BSOD.

Note   Don't confuse system crashes with application faults. Poorly written applications often crash because the application may eat up too much memory or execute illegal instructions. But the failure itself is limited to that application and does not impact the operation of other apps or the operating system itself. In some instances, an application can cause the user interface to "lock up," and in most cases, this does not cause problems with the underlying services. However, the only way to recover the GUI is to reboot the machine.

To help minimize the effect and, more appropriately, to help you recover from a system crash, Windows 2000 has a number of options from which to choose.

Tweaking startup and recovery settings

The first option is to change the startup and recovery settings, which are accessed from the System icon in the Windows 2000 Control Panel. To get there, click Start ➪ Settings ➪ Control Panel and double-click the System icon, or right-click the My Computer icon on the desktop and click Properties from the context menu. Then click the Advanced tab and click the Startup and Recovery button to go to the dialog box pictured in Figure 8-2.

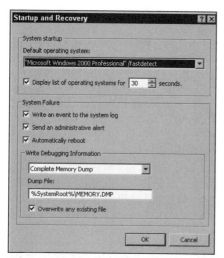

Figure 8-2: Tell Windows how to respond to a system crash — even make your PC reboot automatically — from the Startup and Recovery dialog box.

The Startup and Recovery dialog box includes controls for adjusting the way Windows 2000 behaves during startup and immediately after a system crash. In this case, the Recovery area in the lower half of the dialog box is of particular interest. If you want to glean as much information as you can from a system failure, you should check all of the checkbox controls.

✦ **Write an event to the system log:** If the system encounters a crash (Microsoft refers to these as *STOP errors*), it records the event in the system log of the event viewer. You can find this under the Event Viewer by clicking Start ➪ Programs ➪ Accessories ➪ Administrative Tools and clicking Event Viewer. The information in the Event Viewer may or may not be helpful because often times the log simply indicates that the system unexpectedly stopped. Well, you *knew* that already!

✦ **Send an administrative alert:** Checking this control tells Windows 2000 to send an alert to the Administrator group if the operating system experiences a STOP error. The alert uses the same sending mechanism as the NET SEND command, sending a pop-up message to the desktop of members of the local Administrator group. Note: The Messenger and the Alerter Services must be started for administrative alert to work. Check your services icon in the Control Panel.

✦ **Write debugging information to:** This option tells Windows 2000 to write the contents of system memory at the time of the crash to a file. If you are experiencing STOP errors (that is, the dreaded Blue Screen of Death), make sure this option is checked. For advanced users, the information contained in the memory dump can help you sleuth the cause of the problem. But even ordinarily users may be able to discern some information. Note that the page file (your virtual memory setting) must be as large or larger than your physical RAM. In addition, your system partition must have enough available space to write the contents of physical RAM to disk. (The contents of physical RAM are actually the debugging information.)

✦ **Automatically reboot:** This option is designed to minimize downtime in the event of a STOP error. If you have chosen to write debugging information to disk, Windows 2000 automatically restarts the PC when it is finished. Otherwise, if a STOP error is encountered, Windows 2000 pauses for about five seconds and then reboots.

The memory dump contents are more than gibberish. If you have a service contract with Microsoft, you can send the contents of the memory dump file to Microsoft support for review and analysis. This can help support staff get at the source of the problem quickly.

Note

I check the option Overwrite any existing file item in order to preserve disk space. Each memory dump is approximately the size of the physical memory in your PC — often 128MB or more on many Windows 2000 systems — so multiple memory dumps can rapidly consume hard disk space. The file created contains the image of BSOD as well as the contents of the physical memory. But leave the Write kernel information only option unchecked. This option may slow down the memory writing process, but it ensures you get a complete picture of the system state at the time it went down.

Once you've set up Windows 2000 to keep a close eye on system lockups or STOP errors, as Microsoft refers to them, click OK. Note that you must restart the computer for these changes to take effect.

How to restart Windows 2000 when it won't start

The section title may sound completely contradictory, but the fact is, at times you may have to find a way to get into Windows to fix a problem that prevents Windows from starting. This situation can be fairly serious and rather scary for novices. Part of the problem is that Windows 2000 does not have the safety net of a text-based operating system running beneath it. In Windows 98, for example, you can always boot into DOS and tinker with files and data from the command prompt. The solution with Windows 2000 is a bit less clear.

System Crash Recovery Tips

Beware device drivers: Device drivers can be the root of all evil. Do not be afraid to remove or disable a device that you think could be related to the problem. You can always reinstall it.

Update your drivers: A related issue. You should always get updated drivers for any new hardware *before* you install it. Always check with Microsoft or the hardware vendor for the most up-to-date driver version. This foresight can save you serious headaches by helping you avoid compatibility issues.

Reapply service packs: Always reapply any service packs after you update hardware or install new software. Sometimes drivers or application installations overwrite system files (although Windows 2000 does a good job of protecting against this). Reapplying the latest service pack after an installation can help minimize problems.

Get knowledgeable: Check out Microsoft online knowledge base support at `http://sup-port.microsoft.com/support`. If you have experienced a Blue Screen of Death, have the first two lines of the display available. Someone often has encountered the same error before, and Microsoft has posted a fix for it.

Check memory: If your system continues to crash, you may have a physical memory problem. Try removing RAM one piece at a time to see if the problem still occurs. Note though that today's RAM is fairly high quality, and it is becoming increasingly rare that memory is a problem. It is worth your while to eliminate it as a problem. Also, adding RAM might be a good idea if you notice slowdowns after adding new services.

Reboot automatically: If you leave your system unattended, but running, be sure to click the reboot automatically option in the Startup and Recovery page of the System Properties dialog box. Otherwise, your system waits for user intervention to restart. Be sure to have Windows write debugging information to disk, so that you can capture information about STOP events.

Check the event logs regularly: Check the event logs for errors. Also run a Check Disk on your hard drive to ensure that no file (a driver file perhaps) has been corrupted. Corrupted files can often lead to instability in the system. You should also regularly defragment your hard disk (using Windows' Disk Defragmenter) to ensure optimal performance.

Read the List: Make a point to check the Hardware Compatibility List before adding or updating any hardware on your Windows 2000 system. Device incompatibilities are among the prime culprits of system failure.

Caution   Botched hardware installations are among the leading causes of unrecoverable system crashes under Windows. If you are installing a new hardware device, particularly a new add-in card, be prepared to face a troubleshooting scenario. Always use hardware and drivers approved by Microsoft, which can be found on the Hardware Compatibility List at `www.microsoft.com/hcl`. Refer to Chapter 4 for more information.

So what do you do if you find that Windows 2000 bails out of the startup routine, leaving you staring at a frozen screen or a scary text-based error message? Well, first of all, do not panic. Microsoft has included some useful tools for getting back into Windows 2000 even when the startup routine seems completely scrambled. The most valuable resource is the Windows Safe Mode, a specially tailored profile that enables Windows 2000 to dodge a lot of the resource conflicts that may prevent normal operation.

Windows 2000 includes a variety of safe modes to choose from, each of which is tailored for a specific challenge or task:

✦ Safe Mode

✦ Safe Mode with Networking

✦ Safe Mode with Command Prompt

✦ Enable Boot Logging

✦ Enable VGA Mode

✦ Last Known Good Configuration

✦ Directory Service Restore Mode

✦ Debugging Mode

If your system has crashed and you encounter an error message during startup, pause for a moment. Try powering the system down and starting it up again. Powering down and up can sometimes resolve problems related to a partial Plug-and-Play detection or incompletely flushed memory store.

Tip   If you encounter a show-stopping problem, take an extra moment to power your system all the way down. Physically toggle the power button, wait a moment until you hear the fan spin down, and after five to ten seconds, press the power button again. Doing so helps ensure that system memory isn't being corrupted by a partial power down or other transient effect.

First I tell you how to enter one of the Windows 2000 safe modes. In the next few sections, I explain the different safe mode options.

1. Power down your PC, wait a few seconds, and then power it up again.

2. Watch the screen carefully for any messages that might indicate a BIOS-related or hardware-related problem. If your system locks up before any disk activity occurs, the BIOS or a failed system-critical hard device (such as RAM) may be at fault. If a hardware piece has failed and caused a STOP error, it generally manifests itself with an error message before the bootloader screen appears. After a few seconds, the boot selector screen should appear.

3. Press F8 when the boot selector appears. (Note that this is a major change from NT!) You now see the Advanced Options text menu, which presents a number of choices on how to load Windows 2000 Professional.

With Windows 95 and 98, Microsoft provided one safe mode, which loaded only the pieces essential to running the operating system. Items such as advanced video, networking, and printing were disabled. Windows 2000, however, enables a number of different safe mode options, which can be useful if you want to try to retain networked resources, for example, during your troubleshooting. System administrators often need network access to quickly install new software to an ailing PC, for example.

4. Use the cursor keys to highlight a selection and press Enter. Windows 2000 boots into the safe mode environment you selected.

Safe Mode

Safe Mode loads Windows 2000 using a minimum number of drivers. The operating system uses the default VGA driver and settings to eliminate video problems and does not load network or other drivers that are not essential to system operation. While you lack many features in this mode, you are able to uninstall applications that may be causing the problem. Figure 8-3 shows what the display looks like in Safe Mode.

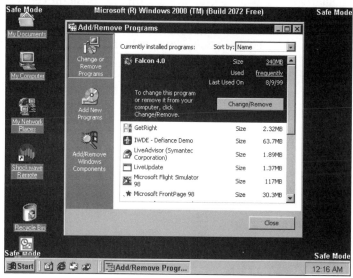

Figure 8-3: It ain't pretty to look at, but the low-resolution display of Safe Mode at least enables you to access Windows facilities such as the Device Manager and the Add/Remove Hardware Wizard.

Safe Mode with Networking

Similar to the basic Safe Mode, this selection loads network drivers during startup. Use this mode if you know your network is not the problem and you need to access resources over the network. Network administrators, for example, can greatly speed recovery if they are able to access resources (such as device driver software) that can be installed over a LAN connection. Without network access, software must be loaded from physical CD-ROM media.

Enable VGA Mode

This mode is made especially for video driver goof-ups. All normal services are started, including network connections and device drivers for audio, scanners, printers, and the like. However, this mode starts the system using the standard VGA graphics driver to specifically isolate graphics-related problems. So, in a sense, it is not a safe mode; rather, it sets up normal system operation with least common denominator graphics. If you installed an incorrect video driver by mistake, or if you think the driver is corrupt, you can recover easily from the problem by running in this mode. Windows 2000 employs the default VGA driver when the operating system starts, enabling the system to work and you to change or reinstall the video driver.

Safe Mode with Command Prompt

This mode is particularly useful when a graphics or other problem prevents the graphical interface from loading. Expert users may also feel most comfortable working from the command line, which is considerably faster in responding than is the graphical interface. As with baseline Safe Mode, only the most basic files and drivers are loaded.

Enable Boot Logging

Often, troubleshooting is all about sleuthing, figuring out exactly what went wrong and where. The Enable Boot Logging option kicks off a normal boot process (that is, all services, drivers, and files are loaded) but keeps tabs on the process by writing all activity to a log file, calledNTBTLOG.TXT. If you need to figure out why your system isn't booting normally, the Enable Boot Logging mode makes it possible to find the broken piece.

Last Known Good Configuration

The Last Known Configuration option restores your system to a state identical to that used the last time the PC successfully booted. Specifically, Windows 2000 restores the Registry key HKEY_LOCAL_MACHINE\SYSTEM\CURRENTCONTROLSET when you invoke the Last Known Good Configuration.

But don't be in too much of hurry to log in. Here is the important part: Windows 2000 assumes that if you are able to log into the system, then the configuration is good, but that might not be the case. Once you log in, Windows 2000 replaces the previous Last Known Good Configuration with the current configuration, and you may compound your problem. The lesson: You should wait before logging into Windows 2000 to see if an error occurs.

Note

Why does waiting matter? When Windows 2000 loads, it initiates the user interface — including the login prompt — before all the device drivers have had a chance to initialize. For this reason, it may take a few minutes after the login dialog box appears for an error to present itself.

Also, after adding new hardware devices to the system or changing existing device drivers, users should wait a few minutes before logging on. If an error message pops up after a couple minutes, the users at this point can still safely power down the system via the power button and reboot with the Last Known Good Configuration option.

Tip

If you have installed new hardware onto your system, reboot the PC and wait for a while before you log in. If Windows 2000 crashes, restart again using the Last Known Good Configuration. Remember that the Last Known Good Configuration is drawn from the last time someone logged in, so be careful.

Directory Service Restore Mode

This option is not valid for Windows 2000 Professional. The mode works only with Windows 2000 Server, Advanced Server, and Data Center Server versions.

Debugging Mode

This option starts Windows 2000 using the Debugging Mode, which sends informative debug code through the serial port for collection by another computer. Software developers frequently use debug code to discover behaviors in applications and work-in-progress code. In the case of a serious system crash, the Debugging Mode can help you zero in on the culprit and address the issue. The average user and even advanced users do not need to use this feature.

These are tools that can help you diagnose and solve a system crash, but they should be used with care. The various safe modes enable you to successfully start your system even in the face of a fatal hardware or software conflict, while diagnostic tools such as boot logging help advanced users and administrators sleuth for trouble. The useful Last Known Good Configuration boot option may be particularly helpful because you can invoke this option during startup to boot from the last version of the Windows Registry that was able to successfully boot the system.

Using the Recovery Console

Inside of Windows 2000 is a new tool that was not in Windows NT: the Recovery Console. The Recovery Console is a command-line system console that looks like DOS but enables you to manipulate the Windows 2000 environment without launching the graphical user environment. The console enables you to stop and start services, fix the master boot record, format drives, and replace system files. You can run the Recovery Console to help recover from system crashes that may have disabled your system. Again, this feature, like the Debugging Mode, may be more than an advanced user ever uses. However, it is good to know that such a tool is accessible if needed.

While the Recovery Console is certainly a tool for more advanced users, even novices may find themselves in a bind where they cannot recover from a crash. In these instances, the Recovery Console makes it possible to regain system control. Otherwise, your only other option may be to reinstall Windows 2000 from the CD-ROM. Of course, noodling with this facility isn't something that should be taken lightly—novices should consider getting help from a system administrator or expert user.

Normally the Recovery Console can be run only from the original four setup disks or from the Windows 2000 Professional CD. However, it can be added as an item in the boot selector. If you are experiencing frequent problems or are testing beta software or hardware that can cause severe problems, it may be a good idea to add the Recovery Console to your boot selector display.

The following directions walk you through installing the Recovery Console as a boot-time option:

1. Place the Windows 2000 Professional CD-ROM in your CD-ROM drive.

2. Click the Start menu and choose Run.

3. In the dialog box, type **<CD-ROM DRIVE LETTER>\I386\WINNT32.exe /cmdcons**.

4. A dialog box (shown in Figure 8-4) appears asking you to confirm the installation for the Recovery Console. Click Yes.

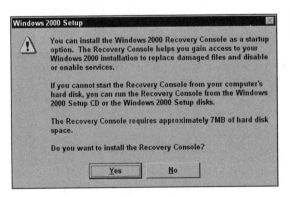

Figure 8-4: If you do nothing else, protect yourself against disaster by creating a Recovery Console for your system.

5. A Window 2000 setup dialog appears and automatically begins copying files. When the routine completes, click OK. You must restart for the Recovery Console to become available.

To boot into Recovery Console, the user must select Microsoft Windows 2000 Recovery Console at the boot menu. The Recovery Console has no fancy graphics. Rather, you find yourself back in the days of DOS, slinging command-line parameters and reading text screens. The good news is that the console enables interaction with system resources when Windows 2000 is too broken to even load its graphical environment. To exit the Recovery Console, type **exit** at the command prompt.

Many commands are available in the Recovery Console (which is started either using the setup disks or adding to the boot selector menu), including several that are identical to commands used under MS-DOS. I've provided a list of some of the most useful commands and their functions. For a complete listing of commands, see the Recovery Console help files or type **help** from within the Recovery Console environment. Remember these are advanced features and should not (note the *should*) be necessary.

✦ **Disable:** Disable *Service name* — Enables you to disable a system service or driver. You can disable a service that may be causing problems — for example, to cease a service that causes the GUI to freeze up. You must know the name of the service to disable it. Use the command Listsvc to find out what services are running. Example: disable Messenger.

✦ **DiskPart:** diskpart */add /delete device name partition name* — Enables you to manage the partitions in your system. If you omit any parameters in the command, Windows 2000 brings up a graphical interface that helps you add or delete partitions by showing available partitions and free space. Think of this as a scaled down Disk Manager. Example: diskpart delete D.

✦ **Fixboot:** Fixboot *Drive letter* — Writes to the specified drive's system partition a new boot sector (the area on the disk that contains information for the OS to access the hard disk, enabling the system to boot up). This works only on X86-based computers. This may be necessary if you accidentally install a second OS and it rewrites the boot sector. Example: Fixboot C:.

✦ **FixMBR:** Fixmbr — Repairs the master boot record of the boot device. The master boot record contains information that enables the BIOS to find the boot sector on the hard disk. Master Boot Records have been known to become corrupt, sometimes due to a viral infection. This command can help you recover the master boot record to restore system operation. Example: Fixmbr.

✦ **ListSvc:** Listsvc — Lists all the services and drivers available on the system. It can be used to identify whether or not certain services are a problem when trying to run Windows 2000. Listsvc is useful to help identify which service to shut down using the disable command. Example: Listsvc.

✦ **SystemRoot:** SystemRoot — Sets the current directory to the system root, usually the Winnt\System32 directory on your hard drive. This command is provided so that in the case of multiple Windows 2000 installations, you can access the correct system directory. Nothing can hold up a repair process like making changes to the wrong file!

Note

What is a service, exactly? It's a program, routine, or process that performs a specific function in the system in order to support other programs. Services generally operate close to hardware level and are unseen by the end user. If you have Administrator-level access to your PC, you can view the various services in the Component Services management console. Click Start ➪ Programs ➪ Administrative Tools ➪ Component Services. The dialog box that appears lists all the available services and shows their status, such as whether or not they are currently running.

Use the Recovery Console carefully. And make sure you have backed up any important data. If you do find yourself in the position of trying to recover from a crash with the Recovery Console, be sure that the command you issue is appropriate to the problem you are having. If you have any questions when trying to recover a system using the Recovery Console, it's a good idea to contact a system administrator or Microsoft technical support before proceeding.

Emergency Repair Disks

The emergency repair disk (ERD) is nothing new to Windows NT, and this useful tool has been carried into Windows 2000. The ERD saves important system files to a diskette in case a catastrophic failure disables the system. The Windows 2000 ERD should be used to help repair a damaged Windows 2000 system that cannot start. It is used in conjunction with the four setup disks created by the installation (or they came with your Windows 200 software). The ERD is so important that it should be updated each time you make a change to the system. If you add any new hardware, install a new application or make any major changes, you should update the emergency repair disk. To create an ERD, use the following steps:

1. Open Microsoft Backup by clicking Start ➪ Programs ➪ Accessories ➪ System Tools ➪ Backup.

2. Click Tools ➪ Create an Emergency Repair Disk, as shown in Figure 8-5, or click the Emergency Repair Disk button on the Welcome page of the Backup dialog box.

3. Insert a blank, formatted diskette into your A:\ drive.

4. There's an option in the Emergency Repair Diskette dialog box to create a Registry backup for the diskette. If you don't have another Registry backup handy, check this checkbox. Click OK.

5. It takes a while to copy the files to the diskette. Once the copy is complete, click OK to finish the operation.

6. Remove the diskette, label it as an emergency repair disk, and note the date of creation on the label, to save you the agony of deciding if the disk is any good. Store the disk someplace safe and hope you never have to use it.

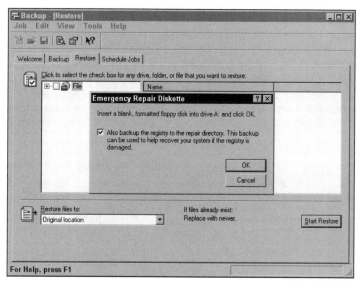

Figure 8-5: Oddly enough, the emergency repair disk creation facility is hidden in the Backup applet.

If possible, make an ERD before and after you make a change to your system. That way you can always try to recover either way. Any changes to the Windows 2000 environment (to the hardware or the system, and so on) should include an update to the ERD. The ERD can really save your skin.

Caution   The ERD contains security information such as user names and encrypted passwords. If this disk falls into the wrong hands, your passwords can be compromised. Keep the ERD in an accessible but secure place!

Follow these steps to use the ERD to recover your system:

1. Insert startup disk #1 (referred to as the *boot disk*) that came with your Windows 2000 program and restart the computer.

2. You are initially asked to continue the installation of Windows 2000. Press Enter to continue.

3. Next you are asked whether to continue with a fresh installation or repair an existing installation. Press R for Repair.

4. You are asked to indicate the type of repair or recovery operation. Press the R key to repair a damaged Windows 2000 installation.

What's in the ERD?

The reason the ERD is so important is that it contains some important Registry and configuration files. The ERD contains the files found in the \Winnt\Repair directory.

It's worth noting that several of the Registry files contain so-called hives, Microsoft terminology for a portion of a Registry subtree. As defined by Microsoft: "A hive is a discrete body of keys, subkeys, and values that is rooted at the top of the registry hierarchy. A hive is backed by a single file and a .log file, which are in the systemroot\System32\Config or the systemroot\Profiles\username folders." Hive files are typically found on disk in the systemroot\System32\Config folder. You can also find the user profile for each user registered on the computer stored in the systemroot\Profiles folder. Hives can be moved from one system to another—they are just files, after all—but must be edited using Registry Editor.

The following files are stored on a complete ERD:

✦ AUTOEXEC.NT: Used to set up environmental variables at boot time, including CD-ROM access, input devices, resident programs, and drivers. Similar in function to the old DOSAUTOEXEC.BAT file, it loads apps or drivers in your DOS session.

✦ CONFIG.NT: Similar to AUTOEXEC.NT, except that it provides environment variables similar to those in the old DOSCONFIG.SYS. Use it to set parameters in your DOS session, such as memory settings.

✦ DEFAULT._: The default user profile. A source for the desktop settings.

✦ NTUSER.DAT: The new user profile. Source for new users to retrieve desktop settings.

✦ SAM._: The security account manager Registry hive. This is the piece of the Registry where all of your security information is stored! Keep this disk in a secure place!

✦ SETUP.LOG: The setup log used when Windows 2000 boots. When the boot logging option is activated, SETUP.LOG is used to record activity as files are loaded.

✦ SOFTWARE._: The software Registry hive. Maintains information about installed software. This file is a major piece of the Registry!

✦ SYSTEM._: This system Registry hive maintains a listing of all the hardware drivers and services that are used in Windows NT.

5. Two options are presented, Fast Repair and Manual Repair. Select the one that suits your situation:

Choose Fast Repair to automatically fix any Registry, boot sector, or system files. No user intervention is required when you choose this option. It is the recommended option for fixing your system because it is comprehensive and, if your ERD is up to date, causes no problems with your current settings.

If you choose the Manual Repair option, you are prompted to repair each individual component, including the Windows 2000 system files and the disk boot sector. The manual option does not enable you to repair the Registry, so if a Registry problem is at the source of your system woes, the Fast Repair option is the way to go.

7. When you hit Enter to continue (using either option), Windows 2000 proceeds to repair the components you chose by copying the necessary files from the ERD and replacing the required ones on the hard disk.

8. After the copying is finished, Windows 2000 prompts you to restart the system. If all went well, the offending piece of your system has been replaced, and the system is functioning correctly.

However, it is possible that the problem you are experiencing is not related to what is contained in the ERD. So the emergency repair process may not always be successful. However, I do recommend at least trying it before throwing in the towel and reinstalling Windows 2000.

Using the Windows Update Web Facility

With Windows 95 and Internet Explorer came the idea of Web updates. Essentially Web Update enables you to incrementally upgrade Windows via the Internet. While the transfer may be a bit slow over a modem, these online upgrades can be a helpful tool. You must have an Internet connection for the Windows Update facility to function!

Imagine a world free of typing FTP server addresses, receiving CD-ROM updates, or downloading patches. While the Windows Web Update may not eliminate these things, it may cut down on them by enabling you to automatically receive Windows 2000 updates from Microsoft. Web Update is intended to act as an online extension of the operating system, helping to cut down on the time and expense of system maintenance.

The Web Update Web site, shown in Figure 8-6, is a convenient, powerful, and simple tool to use. With a single click, you can connect to the Internet, contact Microsoft, and automatically install the latest updates, device drivers, and add-on applications that Microsoft has to offer. It beats the living daylights out of sifting through hundreds of Web pages at the Microsoft site looking for the latest device driver or update.

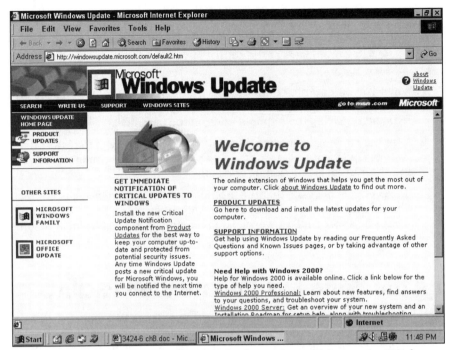

Figure 8-6: Step right up to timely upgrades from Microsoft's interactive Windows Update Web site.

Microsoft in Your Kitchen

With that glowing review in mind, there always seems to be a potentially sinister side to such a service as the Windows Update. Keep in mind that Windows Update performs its magic by enabling Microsoft's servers to scour your system configuration and compare your profile against the latest updates. Is there a potential risk with Microsoft reading your hard disk and sorting through your Registry? Perhaps more of a concern, what if someone figures out a way to tap into the Windows Update facility for malicious purposes? These concerns are legitimate!

Microsoft swears that it is not gathering, much less using, any information through the Web Update site. Is this true? Well, if it were not, it would not be the first time that Microsoft gathered information from users without disclosing the fact. Ultimately, the choice is yours. The Internet is a public domain, and information is frequently pirated and stolen. If you truly wish to be 100 percent safe, don't use the Windows Update facility. There is simply no way to otherwise ensure that Microsoft is not making use of the information found in your system.

The good news is that you aren't stuck if you decide to abstain from the Windows Update Web site. Microsoft offers product updates to licensed users in the form of CD-ROM discs available for a nominal fee.

Visiting the Windows Update Web site

So what is Windows Update really? The feature is a combination of components. The first component is the Web site itself, located at `http://windowsupdate.microsoft.com` and reachable in one of two ways:

✦ Open Internet Explorer and manually type in the URL.

✦ Click the Start button and then click Windows Update found near the top of the Start menu, as shown in Figure 8-7.

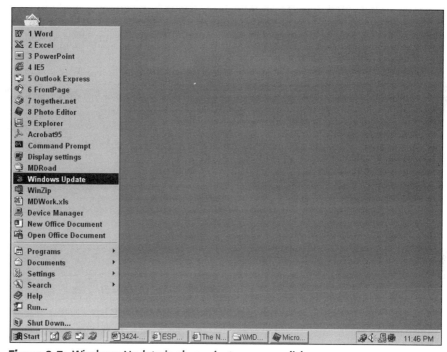

Figure 8-7: Windows Update is always just a mouse click away.

The Web page displays the options available within Windows Update. You probably want to visit the Product Updates link. However, the Support Information page is also worth mentioning. It contains frequently asked questions about Windows Update, known issues, and other options that can prove useful in troubleshooting a problem with Windows Update. Be sure to read the information in this section if you are having specific problems with the Windows Update service.

Types of Windows updates

Clicking the Product Updates link takes you to a list of items that can be updated on your PC as shown in Figure 8-8. Note that your system is being scanned for installed components as this page loads — that's why it can take a little while. The updates (called the *catalog* by Microsoft) are split into the following multiple categories:

✦ **Critical Updates:** These updates fix known issues that affect your computer. Download and install the updates found in this section. I do recommend ensuring that the fix is appropriate for your system prior to updating. For example, it is not necessary to download the latest update for encryption if encrypted data is not important to you. You can investigate the issue further by checking out `http://support.microsoft.com`. You should note that on occasion, software vendors have been known to install fixes that cause more problems than they fix!

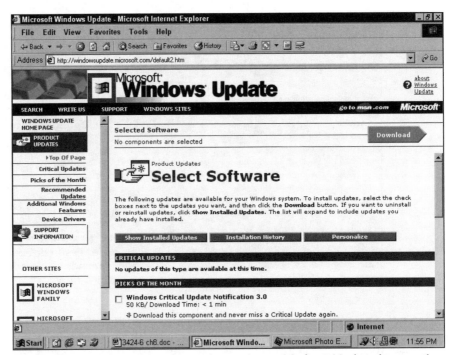

Figure 8-8: If you do nothing else, make a point to visit the Critical Updates section of the Windows Update Web site. It could save you a lot of headaches from known bugs.

✦ **Picks of the Month:** The Picks of the Month section contains software that Microsoft has picked for special attention. Mostly these selections are add-ons to the current operating system that target a certain market of user. Examples are extended fonts and more accessibility options.

✦ **Recommended Updates:** Recommended Updates are just what they seem. Microsoft thinks this update has value, but the update may not apply to everyone. Encryption packs are a good example of a Recommended Update.

✦ **Additional Windows Features:** These additional features are not fixes but rather extras that you can add to your system. FrontPage is a good example of an Additional Windows Feature.

✦ **Device Drivers:** Microsoft maintains a listing of new device drivers. Device drivers, as you have already learned, are pieces of software that enable the operating system to interact with a specific piece of hardware. It is occasionally necessary to update or add a device driver for a new or previously unsupported piece of hardware. If you cannot find a driver here, always remember to check the vendor's Web site.

If you find an update or addition at the Windows Update site that you want, simply click the checkbox and then click the download button in the upper-right portion of the screen. The update downloads and then installs automatically.

Caution   Avoid trying to download and install multiple updates at a time. Users have reported problems when trying to set up multiple components in a single pass. See the Known Issues section of the Windows Update Web page for more information.

Scheduling critical updates

If checking the Web site every month or so is too much of a hassle, you can receive critical updates automatically. One of the recommended Picks of the Month is the Windows Critical Update Notification 3.0. If you haven't installed this one yet, I suggest you do. The Critical Update Notification application automatically checks the Windows Update Web site for new critical updates.

When you install the Critical Update Notification program, the program scans your computer at a prescheduled time. The Critical Notification scan is listed as a task in the Scheduled Tasks applet (invoked by clicking Start ➪ Accessories ➪ System Tools and clicking the Scheduled Tasks icon). Microsoft recommends that you do not modify the task. But for your knowledge, the task scans your system (the executable file is WUCRTUPD.EXE and is found in the \SYSTEM32 directory) for the current updates every five minutes. The scan itself is not intrusive nor hardware intensive, so do not fret about loss of system resources or a memory drain. The impact is minimal. In fact, if you are a laptop user, the scan doesn't even run if you are on battery power. Nor does the scan run if you are not connected to the Web.

If you are connected to the Internet and a new Critical Update is available (remember that the Critical Updates Notification program has scanned your system and knows what updates you have), you receive a download prompt. You can choose to download the update immediately or postpone the download for a later time.

Disabling Windows Update

In some instances, a network administrator may not want the Windows Update facility available to end users. Microsoft has included a way to remove the update feature from Windows 2000. Altering the local policy of the computer through the Microsoft Management Console (MMC) enables you to remove the update feature. For more information on the standard MMC interface used by administration tools, see Chapter 2. Here's how to disable Windows Update:

1. Start the MMC by clicking Start ⇨ Run and typing **MMC** in the text box. Click the OK button in the Run dialog box to launch the console interface.

2. Click Console ⇨ Add/Remove Snap-in choice to bring up the next dialog box. Click the Add button.

3. Scroll down to the Group Policy item in the Available Standalone Snap-ins box and click it, as shown in Figure 8-9. Click the Add button.

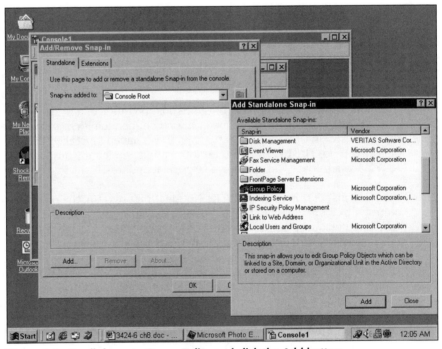

Figure 8-9: Scroll down to Group Policy and click the Add button.

4. Click the Finish button (accept the defaults of any dialogs that appear).

5. Click the Close button and then click the OK button. You return to the Console interface, where the Local Computer Policy item is now listed in the Tree view.

6. Navigate down to Local Computer Policy (on the left side of the split screen) to User Configuration as shown in Figure 8-10. Double-click it.

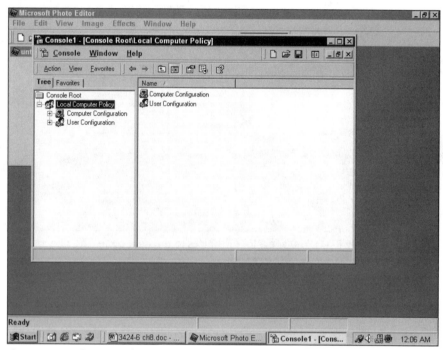

Figure 8-10: The Console now features a new entry under the Local Computer Policy tree header. Select User Configuration.

7. Folders appear in the right pane. Double-click the Administrative Templates entry.

8. Finally, double-click the Start Menu & Taskbar entry. You see the screen shown in Figure 8-11.

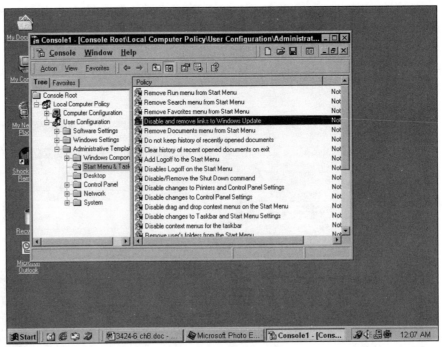

Figure 8-11: You see a lot of choices in the right pane. The one you need should be near the top, as shown here.

9. Double-click the entry marked Disable and remove links to Windows Update. The dialog box shown in Figure 8-12 appears.

10. Click the Disabled option and click OK. Exit the MMC.

Windows Update is a powerful tool, if you can get past the Orwellian Big Brother stigma often associated with such sites. While some perceived risk is involved with this feature, its benefits clearly outweigh the exposure.

Using Device Manager

If you have spent any time troubleshooting Windows 95/98 or Windows NT, you have spent time with Device Manager. This invaluable resource lets users view properties for virtually every hardware device in the system. Fortunately, Windows 2000 incorporates Device Manager, allowing users to use their hard-won device management and troubleshooting skills with the new operating system.

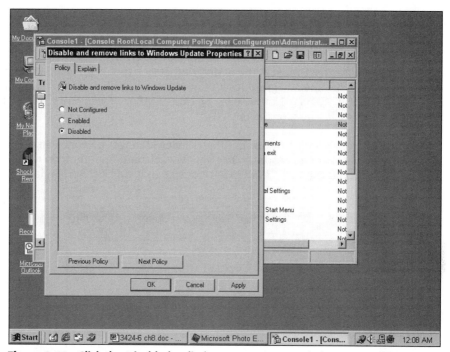

Figure 8-12: Click the Disabled radio button to prevent Windows 2000 from going to the Windows Update Web site.

Microsoft has moved Device Manager within Windows 2000, but it's still there. You can open Device Manager in one of the following ways:

✦ Click Start ➪ Settings ➪ Control Panel, double-click the System icon, click the Hardware tab and click the Device Manager button.

✦ Right-click the My Computer icon on the Windows 2000 desktop, click Properties from the fly-out menu, then click the Hardware tab and click the Device Manager button.

✦ Right-click the My Computer icon, click Manage from the fly-out menu. In the right pane of the Computer Management dialog box, click the Device Manager item. The Device Manager list of devices appears in the left pane.

Tip

Do you expect to use Device Manager often? You can create a desktop shortcut or Start menu icon that instantly launches the facility. Right-click the desktop and click New ➪ Shortcut. In the Create Shortcut dialog box, type **C:\WINNT\system32\devmgmt.msc** in the Type the location of the item text box. (Be sure to substitute the specific drive and directory name of the Windows 2000 directory on your system.) Click the Next button. In the Type a name for this shortcut text box, enter a short name (say, Device Manager) for the icon and click Finish. A new shortcut icon now appears on the desktop called Device Manager. Double-click this icon, and the Windows 2000 Device Manager launches.

The Penny Tour

Launch Device Manager, and you see the window displayed in Figure 8-13. As you can see, Device Manager lists the various device types. Click the plus (+) symbol next to each entry to reveal the underlying device that is installed. In this case, you can see the specific graphics adapter that is installed (the Trident Video Accelerator 9525DVD). Double-clicking this or other device entry brings up the properties dialog box for the device.

More importantly for troubleshooting, Device Manager provides an update if a device is not working properly. The yellow exclamation point icon next to the PCI Device entry in Figure 8-13 indicates a device that isn't properly enabled.

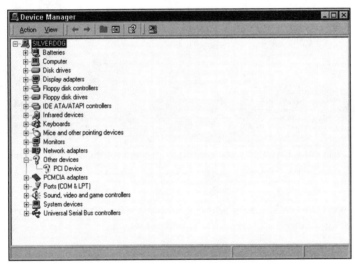

Figure 8-13: Device Manager does more than display the hardware installed on your system; it also updates you if things aren't working properly.

Device Manager's Many Views

One of the powerful aspects of Device Manager is its ability to let you look at several aspects of your system configuration. There are four different Device Manager system views that can be accessed by click the Views menu. They are:

✦ **Devices by type:** The default view, this setting shows devices organized by type, such as network adapters and mice and pointing devices. This is the most intuitive way to seek out properties for a specific device.

✦ **Devices by connection:** Displays devices organized by the type of connection, such as the motherboard or the PCI bus. Useful to compare devices that are driven off a single connection.

✦ **Resources by type:** Shows the status of allocated system resources, such as direct memory access (DMA) channels, interrupt request (IRQ) lines, and memory addresses. This makes it easy to see all devices that might be sharing or competing for a specific system resource, such as IRQs.

✦ **Resources by connection:** Displays the status of allocated system resources, this time by connection type.

To select any of these views, simply click View and the matching command from the drop-down menu. The display in the Device Manager window will update to reflect the new organization, as shown in Figure 8-14. Nothing has changed between Figure 8-13 and Figure 8-14 except for the view.

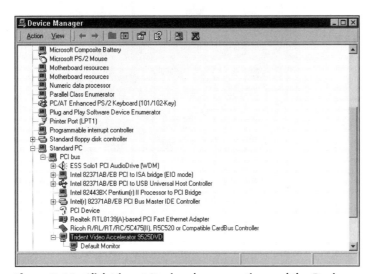

Figure 8-14: Click View ➪ Devices by connection and the Device Manager display changes to show components arranged by their links to the system.

Note   Switching views under Device Manager only changes the way system resource and device information is presented. In all cases, you are able to drill down to the underlying device properties dialog boxes to edit settings and view configuration details.

Accessing Detailed Device Information

One of the most useful aspects of Device Manager is its ability to let you drill down on individual devices and components. Figure 8-15 shows the device properties dialog box that appears when you double-click the listing under the Mice and other pointing devices type. This dialog box presents information in the Device status text box, and offers tabs to let you view and adjust resources settings, review and work with driver software, and even access advanced device capabilities.

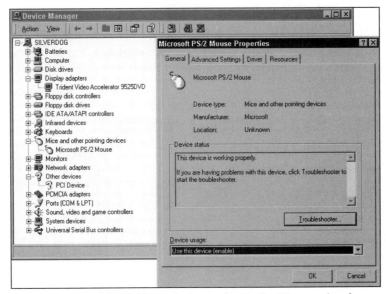

Figure 8-15: Double-clicking a device under Device Manager invokes that device's properties dialog box.

Most devices that users will tend to interact with include three tabs:

✦ General

✦ Drivers

✦ Resources

What appears in the properties dialog box may differ based on the specific operation and nature of the device being reviewed. That said, you will see a number of common facilities.

The General page

As shown in the Figure 20-15, the General page presents the working status of the selected device. You also see the device manufacturer and other information displayed at the top of the dialog box.

One useful feature is the Device usage drop-down control, which lets you turn off the device and free up the resources it consumes. To disable a device, click the Device usage drop-down control and select Do not use this device (disable). Click OK, and the device will no longer be operable. In addition, any IRQs, DMA channels, and system memory dedicated to the device are freed for the system to use.

Why disable a perfectly good device? Well, if you find that your modem isn't working, it may be because your mouse and modem are trying to use the same COM port resources. By disabling the mouse, you can see whether or not the modem begins to behave normally. If it does, a resource conflict is probably at the source.

Note   Not all devices can be disabled. For example, if you have one graphics adapter installed in your system (as most do), disabling that adapter would effectively disable your system. In these cases, you'll find that the Device usage control is grayed out.

The Driver page

As its name suggests, the Driver page gives you access to the driver software used to allow the device and operating system to talk to each other. At the top of the page is displayed useful information like the driver version, date, and manufacturer (as shown in Figure 8-16). Below are three buttons:

Figure 8-16: The Driver page does more than present useful information; it lets you update devices with the latest driver software by clicking the Update Driver button.

✦ **Driver Details:** View the specific paths and filenames of the drivers used to enable your hardware. Useful for confirming if you have the latest drivers or if drivers are causing a compatibility problem.

✦ **Uninstall:** Lets you manually uninstall a device, freeing all system resources and removing the drivers from the system.

✦ **Update Driver:** Launches the Upgrade Device Driver Wizard. Follow the steps presented in the wizard to find updated drivers either on disk or from the Microsoft or manufacturer's Web site. This facility is excellent for keeping your PC up to date.

The Resources page

Finally, the Resources page of the device properties dialog box shows you what system resources the device is using. Figure 8-17 shows this page. At the top of the page is the Resource settings scrolling window, which enumerates the various resources being consumed by the device. In some cases, you may have to scroll through the list to see all the resource listings in this box.

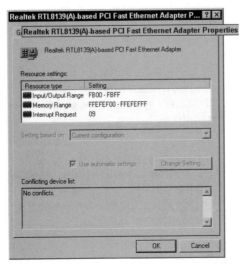

Figure 8-17: Get the lowdown on what system resources a device is using by clicking the Resources page.

At the bottom of the dialog box is the Conflicting device list text box, which displays the name of any device using the same resources as the device you are viewing. This text box makes it easy to hone in on device conflicts that may have caused you to drill down on a particular device.

In between, shown grayed out in Figure 8-17, is the Setting based on drop-down list control, the Use automatic settings checkbox, and the Change Settings button. In most cases, these items will be inactive, because Windows 2000 Plug and Play requires that resources be dynamically allocated by the operating system and the system BIOS.

If these controls are active, you can alter a device's configuration by clicking the desired resource in the Resource settings scrolling list box and clicking the Change Setting button. In the dialog box that appears, you can then enter a new IRQ, DMA, or memory address value to replace the one that was there before.

Caution   Just because you can change a device setting doesn't mean you should. When you input your own setting, you establish a static resource setting for that device, which can run afoul of the dynamic resource environment present in Windows 2000's Plug and Play environment. Establishing static settings can, therefore, create incompatibilities that cause device or system failures.

Printing Device Manager Reports

Device Manager is also a good place to produce a quick inventory of your system. Simply click View ➪ Print to go to the dialog box shown in Figure 8-18.

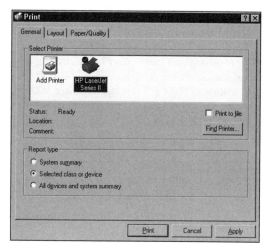

Figure 8-18: Select from any of three report types when printing out configuration data.

The Print dialog box presents three report types. They are:

✦ **System summary:** Prints a summary of devices, including product version, bus type, and resource information such as IRQs and memory addresses.

✦ **Selected class or device:** Prints a report specific to the selected device or hardware type. The report includes device name, device driver location, version and manufacturer information, and resources allocated to the device, such as I/O ports and memory addresses.

✦ **All devices and system summary:** Prints a report for each device or hardware type installed on your computer as well as a summary of your system. Be warned: If you have a lot of devices installed on your system, the resulting print out can be rather large.

Using the Windows Troubleshooter

The Windows 2000 operating system contains an extremely useful help file. Microsoft has gone to great lengths to provide in-depth how-to lessons in the Help system, and I recommend that you make full use of them. They cover just about every aspect of Windows 2000 Professional, including hardware, security, e-mail, and many other important topics. You can access the help file associated with a current dialog box or screen by pressing the F1 key at any time. However, the troubleshooters can give you the most assistance when system problems arise.

You were introduced to the troubleshooters in Chapter 4 when you learned about adding hardware. In this chapter, I go into more detail.

The troubleshooters ask questions pertaining to a particular issue, taking a logical step-by-step approach to problem resolution. For example, clicking the Video Troubleshooter invokes a dialog box asking if your screen is flickering, if there is no video, or if the multiple monitor feature is not working. Clicking one of the items brings up a second dialog box for further clarification. Eventually (you hope) the troubleshooter provides a solution.

As you might guess, however, Microsoft can't anticipate every problem. So many problems and topics are simply not covered by the troubleshooters. Also, troubleshooters often yield options or resolutions that don't fit your situation.

Here is a list of the troubleshooters that might come in handy:

✦ **Display:** Helps flesh out problems with your current graphics settings. Graphics settings are pretty straightforward, and the troubleshooter has a tendency to tell you to download new drivers. This is a common solution in many of the troubleshooters.

✦ **Hardware:** Helps with peripherals such as CD-ROM drives, mice, and network adapters. This troubleshooter takes you down many different paths to help resolve your hardware problems. It may take you to the Device Manager, which can be a helpful tool.

✦ **Internet Connections:** Assists in connecting to an ISP. The troubleshooter covers issues such as login problems, TCP/IP problems, and script error messages.

✦ **Modem:** Troubleshoots common modem problems.

✦ **MS-DOS Programs:** Helps find out why your current DOS programs are having trouble.

✦ **Multimedia and Games:** This troubleshooter is limited to joysticks, DirectX, and game installations. It checks your DirectX version, joystick installation, and game installations.

✦ **Networking:** Troubleshoots TCP/IP and its configuration.

✦ **Print:** Troubleshoots installation of printer drivers and general printer configuration. It is a good resource to help you solve printing problems.

✦ **Remote Access:** Solves common remote access problems when you're dialing into other networks.

✦ **Sound:** Helps resolve common sound driver issues.

✦ **System setup:** Assists with common installation issues.

You can access all the troubleshooters from a single place by clicking Start ⇨ Help and then clicking the Contents tab in the Windows 2000 Help dialog box. Click the Troubleshooting and Maintenance item to see the list of troubleshooters shown in Figure 8-19.

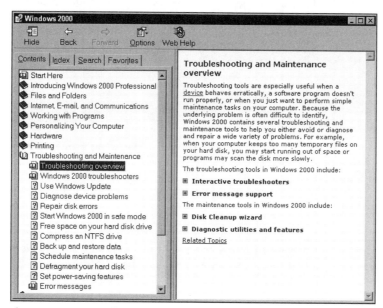

Figure 8-19: An embarrassment of troubleshooters. Hopefully somewhere in there are the answers you need.

The troubleshooters are good tools and can help you resolve problems in many Windows 2000 components. However, because only so much can be anticipated, you may find yourself frustrated by circular answers or resolutions that are not appropriate. Don't blame Microsoft on this one; they can only anticipate so much.

Device Manager

A long-time companion to Windows 9x, the Device Manager is a hardware configuration lifesaver. Previous versions of Windows NT did not include a Device Manager, and you were left to your own devices trying to configure hardware components or trying to resolve hardware conflicts. With the Device Manager, you are seeing the hardware components as they report themselves to Windows 2000. Memory ranges and IRQs are configurable here. You should note that because Windows 2000 supports Plug and Play, many of the hardware device configurations are alterable from the Device Manager. This is a long way from the days of dip switches and DOS-based configuration programs.

The Device Manager is launched from the Microsoft Management Console (MMC). The Device Manager provides a hierarchical view of the installed hardware components. Note the different categories of hardware listed, modems, network adapters, video adapters, and so on. By expanding the category, you can see the installed hardware components. Double-clicking the icon brings up the properties dialog box that contains the configuration information for that hardware piece. Included is a tab for the device driver.

Summary

System recovery is hardly a pleasant topic to cover, because no sane person wants to face a catastrophic system crash. But with Windows 2000, Microsoft has provided a number of recovery options that can help you weather the bad times. More important, Windows 2000 is robust enough that you just may not often have to face a show-stopping crash.

You can tilt the odds in your favor by following a few basic rules. Always be sure of what you are installing and get the latest drivers. And always, *always*, check the Microsoft Hardware Compatibility List before installing new hardware. And in case things do go wrong, keep an emergency repair disk handy and back up your data frequently.

Among the things we did in this chapter:

✦ Took a tour of Windows 2000's many and varied diagnostic and system management tools, including Device Manager, logging facilities, and boot options.

✦ Stepped through disaster recovery techniques, including using the Recovery Console feature, the Emergency Repair Disk, and safe modes.

✦ Reviewed available resources to help you prevent and fix crashes, such as the Microsoft Hardware Compatibility list and the Windows Update feature.

Now that you've learned how to make an inoperable system accessible again, we next cover how to make a working system even more accessible. The next chapter discusses the accessibility features of Window 2000, which enable those with disabilities to effectively work with their PCs.

✦   ✦   ✦

Make Windows 2000 Accessible

Windows 2000 Professional includes several features designed to make the operating system more accessible and easier to use for people with handicaps, disabilities, or other physical limitations. If you have trouble hearing system sounds, Windows can display visual warnings. If you have trouble reading the screen, Windows can enlarge the text, switch to high-contrast colors, and even narrate the contents of menus and dialog boxes for you. If you have trouble using certain key combinations on a keyboard, Windows can modify the way the keyboard reacts to key presses. The Narrator and On-Screen Keyboard utilities are new features of Windows 2000, as is the Utility Manager that enables you to automatically activate those utilities when you start Windows.

Although the Windows 2000 accessibility features are intended to address certain special needs, they are often helpful to ordinary users as well. In much the same way that wheelchair ramps at public buildings are a boon to anyone with a stroller, shopping cart, or delivery hand truck, Windows' accessibility features can come in handy for all sorts of other situations. Visibility enhancements, for example, intended to assist visually impaired users, can also help laptop computer users with screens that are difficult to read under poor lighting conditions.

Using the Accessibility Wizard

Windows 2000 Professional includes a sizable list of accessibility features and options. To assist you in selecting and configuring the appropriate accessibility features, Microsoft created the Accessibility Wizard. Of course, you can enable or disable the various features and adjust the options and settings manually if you want (the other sections in this chapter show you how), but the Accessibility Wizard is a great place to start for a quick checklist of the available options and how they can help you. The Accessibility Wizard asks you a series of questions and then enables and configures various accessibility features based on your responses.

To use the Accessibility Wizard, follow these steps.

1. Launch the Accessibility Wizard by choosing Start ➪ Programs ➪ Accessories ➪ Accessibility ➪ Accessibility Wizard. The welcome page of the Accessibility Wizard dialog box appears.

2. Click Next to advance past the welcome page of introductory text. The Text Size page of the Accessibility Wizard appears as shown in Figure 9-1.

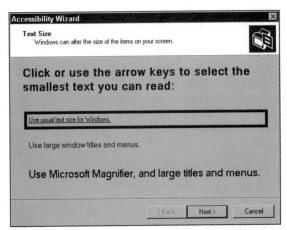

Figure 9-1: Picking a text size in the Accessibility Wizard.

3. Click the sample of the smallest text that you can read comfortably. Your choices include normal text size, a larger font that results from changing font or screen resolution settings, and the very large text you get when you use the Microsoft Magnifier utility. (You learn all about the Magnifier later in this chapter.) When you've made your choice, click Next, and the Display Size page of the Accessibility Wizard appears as shown in Figure 9-2.

4. Confirm (or change) the display settings. Based on your text size selection on the previous page, the Accessibility Wizard suggests changes in your display or suggests using Microsoft Magnifier. You can accept the wizard's suggestion or click the checkboxes to select one (or more) of the other options: changing your Windows font size, changing to a lower display resolution, or using Microsoft Magnifier. Click Next when you've made your selection. The Set Wizard Options page of the Accessibility Wizard appears as shown in Figure 9-3.

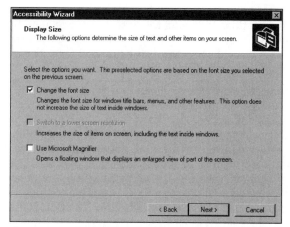

Figure 9-2: Confirming display options in the Accessibility Wizard.

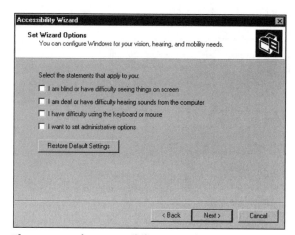

Figure 9-3: The Accessibility Wizard options quiz.

5. The Accessibility Wizard asks a number of questions to determine which accessibility features are likely to benefit you. Click the checkboxes for the statements that apply to you — whether vision, hearing, or keyboard/mouse operations enhancements — and then click Next. The Accessibility Wizard page that appears next depends on the options you select.

Note

Don't be intimidated by Accessory Wizard terms such as *blind* and *deaf*. Just check the first option if you want to use vision enhancements, the second for sound replacements, the third for keyboard alternatives, and the last option if you want to adjust settings for activating and deactivating the accessibility options. You can choose any combination of the options on this page. Check them all if you want to explore all the options the wizard controls.

6. Work through the remaining screens, setting your preferences and making choices. Refer to the sections following these steps for explanations of your many options. When you're finished, the Default Accessibility Settings page enables you to choose whether or not to save the setting for the current user profile only or to apply this setting to all new user accounts.

7. Click the Save Settings button if you want to save your accessibility settings to a file. If you click the Save Settings button, Windows opens a Save As dialog box where you can specify where you want to save the file. Click Save to close the Save As dialog box, save the file, and return to the Accessibility Wizard. You can take the resulting file to another computer (that supports the same display capabilities) and use it to configure that computer with the accessibility options you've selected. If you don't want to create an accessibility settings file (you don't plan to use another computer), simply click Next without clicking the Save Settings button. The Completing the Accessibility Wizard page appears as shown in Figure 9-4.

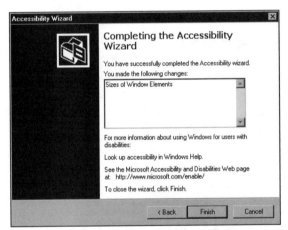

Figure 9-4: The final page of the Accessibility Wizard.

8. Click Finish to close the Accessibility Wizard dialog box and apply the settings you selected. The wizard displays a summary of your changes in the list box. If you see something on the list that you don't want, use the Back button to step back to the page where you can change that setting or use the Cancel button to leave the wizard without making any changes.

Visibility options

If you check the I am blind option, the Accessibility Wizard gives you several ways to adjust the display so visually impaired users can see the screen more easily.

The first option enables you to select a scroll bar and window border size as shown in Figure 9-5. Pick the smallest size that you can easily see.

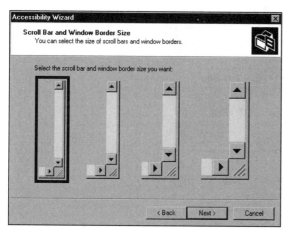

Figure 9-5: The Accessibility Wizard Scroll Bar and Window Border Size page.

Note To adjust the scroll bar, window border, and icon sizes manually, use the settings on the Appearance tab of the Display Properties dialog box. Open the dialog box by right-clicking the desktop background and then choosing Properties from the pop-up menu.

Windows also enables you to set the icon size, shown in Figure 9-6, and the color display, shown in Figure 9-7. Select a high-contrast color scheme from the Color Scheme list box to see a sample of the colors in the Preview box. For more information on the high-contrast options available through the Accessibility Wizard, refer to the section "Accessing Accessibility Features in the Control Panel," later in this chapter.

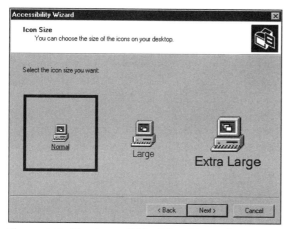

Figure 9-6: The Accessibility Wizard Icon Size page.

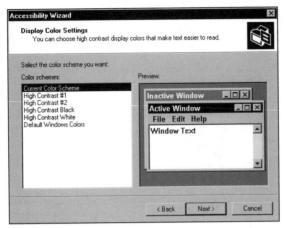

Figure 9-7: The Accessibility Wizard Display Color Settings page.

Note You can select the same color schemes (and others) on the Appearance tab of the Display Properties dialog box. Open the dialog box by right-clicking the desktop background and choosing Properties from the pop-up menu.

Windows also enables you to change the color — white, black, or inverting — and size of the mouse cursor as shown in Figure 9-8. If you choose the Inverting option, the mouse cursor color, which is normally black, changes dynamically, depending on the background color of a page. For example, if the mouse cursor is on a black background, it inverts to white so you can see it easily. If you want to go back to the original cursor size and color, click the Current Cursor button.

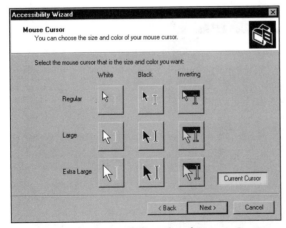

Figure 9-8: The Accessibility Wizard Mouse Cursor page.

Audio options

If you check the I am deaf option, the Accessibility Wizard asks if you want to enable the SoundSentry. The SoundSentry monitors your system and displays an onscreen message when it detects a system sound. You can add more functionality by turning on the ShowSounds option. ShowSounds works with some programs to display captions for verbal messages and sounds generated by those programs. For more details about SoundSentry and ShowSounds, refer to the section "Accessing Accessibility Features in the Control Panel," later in this chapter.

Keyboard and mouse options

If you check the I have difficulty using the keyboard or mouse option, the Accessibility Wizard gives you several choices for changing the way you work with these devices.

✦ StickyKeys enables you to create key combinations that use the Ctrl, Shift, and Alt keys by pressing the keys sequentially instead of simultaneously.

✦ BounceKeys causes Windows to ignore repeated keystrokes.

✦ ToggleKeys alerts you with a sound when you press the Caps Lock, Num Lock, or Scroll Lock keys. It's intended to serve as a warning in case you press any of these keys accidentally.

✦ Extra Keyboard Help displays tooltips and other supplemental instructions for using the keyboard when the instructions are available in programs.

✦ MouseKeys enables you to use the numeric keypad keys on your keyboard to control the mouse pointer.

✦ Mouse Button Settings, shown in Figure 9-9, enables you to set the mouse for right- or left-handed use.

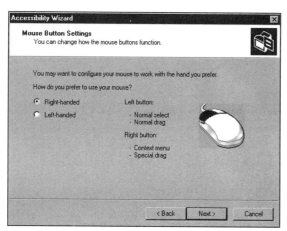

Figure 9-9: The Accessibility Wizard Mouse Button Settings page.

✦ Mouse Pointer Speed enables you to use a slider to increase or decrease the speed of the mouse pointer.

Note

You can also adjust mouse buttons and mouse pointer speed and select cursor sizes using the Mouse Control Panel applet in the Windows Control Panel. Click Start ➪ Settings ➪ Control Panel and double-click the Mouse icon to access these and other mouse settings.

For more information on the keyboard and mouse options available through the Accessibility Wizard, refer to the section "Accessing Accessibility Features in the Control Panel," later in this chapter.

Administrative options

In addition to the visual, audio, and mouse/keyboard options, the Windows Accessibility Wizard enables you to set some overall parameters. If more than one person uses the accessibility-enhanced machine, you might want Windows to turn off the settings automatically when you're finished using the machine. On the Set Automatic Timeouts page, shown in Figure 9-10, you can adjust the timeout period by entering a number in the minutes box. You can also choose to leave the accessibility features on at all times.

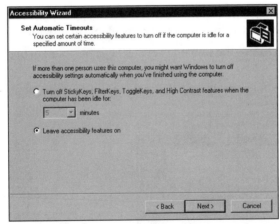

Figure 9-10: The Accessibility Wizard Set Automatic Timeouts page.

Just the beginning

The Accessibility Wizard enables you to activate and configure most of Windows' main accessibility options, including some display properties and mouse settings that aren't strictly accessibility options, even though they have a significant accessibility impact.

However, the Accessibility Wizard doesn't cover all the options. Other accessibility utilities — Narrator, On-Screen Keyboard, and Utility Manager — aren't included in the wizard, and configuration settings are available through the Control Panel that enable you to fine-tune several of the other accessibility options. The remaining sections of this chapter cover these additional options.

Using Magnifier

High-resolution display settings are great for creating room for lots of open windows on your desktop. Unfortunately, the text and icons get smaller as screen resolution gets higher. And that can be a problem if you have trouble reading small text onscreen. To make the onscreen text more legible, first try adjusting the display settings to use a lower screen resolution. (See Chapter 16 for information on adjusting display settings.) If a lower screen resolution doesn't make the onscreen text big enough for good legibility, then the Magnifier utility is the answer.

Magnifier adds a special panel to your desktop that displays an enlarged image of the area around the mouse pointer. The Magnifier utility, shown in Figure 9-11, is like looking at a book through a magnifying glass. A selected portion of the page (desktop) is enlarged significantly, thus making it easier to read. In Figure 9-11, the Magnifier panel is positioned across the top of the screen, which is the default location.

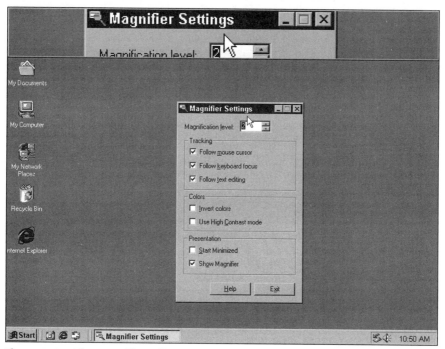

Figure 9-11: The Magnifier utility at work.

To start Magnifier, click Start ⇨ Programs ⇨ Accessories ⇨ Accessibility ⇨ Magnifier. (You can also use the Utility Manager, discussed later in this chapter, to start Magnifier automatically when you start Windows.) Windows adjusts the desktop to make room for the Magnifier panel across the top of the screen by moving desktop icons and open windows down.

When you first start Magnifier, Windows displays a disclaimer noting that the Magnifier utility is limited and you may need a more robust utility (click OK to dispose of the message), then the Magnifier Settings dialog box appears. You can adjust the settings in the dialog box to change the behavior of the Magnifier utility. The following list summarizes the Magnifier configuration options:

✦ **Magnification level:** Determines the degree of enlargement of the image in the Magnifier panel. The default value of 2 is usually adequate, but you can enter any number between 1 and 9.

✦ **Follow mouse cursor:** Causes the image in the Magnifier pane to display the desktop in the vicinity of the mouse pointer.

✦ **Follow keyboard focus:** Causes the image in the Magnifier pane to display the area that has the focus because of keyboard entries. For example, when you press the Tab key to select areas and options in a dialog box, Magnifier displays the selected option.

✦ **Follow text editing:** Causes the image in the Magnifier pane to display the text being entered or edited at the text-editing cursor (the flashing vertical bar cursor).

Note   You can select any combination of Magnifier's tracking options. They may seem contradictory, but in normal usage, you don't use the mouse pointer, make keyboard selections, and edit text simultaneously. Selecting all three tracking options means that the Magnifier shows the active portion of the screen, no matter how you create that activity.

✦ **Invert colors:** Displays the contents of the Magnifier pane in inverted colors — black appears as white and vice versa.

✦ **Use High Contrast mode:** Switches the entire display to the high-contrast mode color scheme and fonts.

✦ **Start Minimized:** Starts Magnifier with the Magnifier Settings dialog box minimized.

✦ **Show Magnifier:** Controls the Magnifier panel. Unchecking this option hides the Magnifier panel. (I can't imagine why you'd want to do that and still leave the Magnifier utility running.)

In addition to choosing the configuration in the Magnifier Settings dialog box, you can change the way Magnifier appears on your desktop by manipulating the Magnifier pane itself.

✦ Click and drag the edge of the Magnifier pane to make it larger or smaller.

✦ Click and drag the Magnifier pane to move it to a new location. If you drag it to another side of the screen, the Magnifier pane attaches itself to that side of the desktop. If you drag it to the center of the screen, the Magnifier pane becomes a conventional, resizable window with a standard title bar.

Close Magnifier by clicking the Exit button in the Magnifier Settings dialog box.

Using Narrator

The accessibility features I have discussed so far were available in previous versions of Windows. Narrator, on the other hand, is a new addition that debuts in Windows 2000. Narrator takes a different approach to assisting users who have trouble reading text onscreen. Instead of enlarging the text or increasing its contrast, Narrator uses a synthesized voice to "read" the contents of menus, dialog boxes, and program windows. If you have trouble seeing onscreen text, you can hear it with Narrator.

To start Narrator, click Start ➪ Programs ➪ Accessories ➪ Accessibility ➪ Narrator. (As with Magnifier, you can also use the Utility Manager to start Narrator automatically when you start Windows.) A message box noting the limitations of the Narrator utility appears and Narrator begins reading its contents. Click OK to close the Microsoft Narrator message box, then click the Narrator button on the task bar to display then Narrator dialog box (see Figure 9-12). Narrator begins to speak, reading the name of the dialog box and announcing the status of the options.

Figure 9-12: The Narrator dialog box.

Caution You must have a Windows 2000-compatible sound card and speakers properly installed and configured in order for Narrator to work. See Chapter 17 if you need more information about setting up your sound card.

Narrator's synthesized voice sounds a little strange at first, with its unusual pronunciation of some words and its slightly unnatural pacing and pauses. Still, Narrator isn't hard to understand once you get accustomed to the way it describes onscreen options. First, Narrator reads the name of the currently active option, followed by its description and status, and then continues with instructions for changing the option.

For example, Narrator's announcement of the first item in its own dialog box is "Announce events on screen. Checkbox checked. To uncheck, press spacebar." When a new dialog box or window appears, Narrator reads all the options and button labels available in that dialog box.

The options in the Narrator dialog box enable you to control Narrator's behavior. The four checkbox options are self-explanatory:

✦ Announce events onscreen

✦ Read typed characters

✦ Move mouse pointer to the active item

✦ Start Narrator minimized

Change the sound of the Narrator voice by clicking the Voice button to open the Voice Settings dialog box shown in Figure 9-13. Select a base voice and language from the Voice list box (if more than one voice is available). Adjust the settings in the Speed, Volume, and Pitch spin boxes by clicking the up and down arrow buttons in each box. With Narrator announcing each change as you make it, you hear the effects of your changes immediately. Click OK to close the Voice Settings dialog box and make your changes permanent.

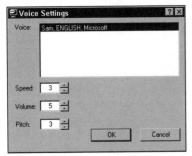

Figure 9-13: The Voice Settings dialog box.

Tip Reducing the speed setting slows the Narrator voice to a pace that's a little easier to understand. Then, when you get used to using Narrator, you can increase the speed to work quicker.

To turn off Narrator, click the Exit button in the Narrator dialog box and then confirm the action by clicking Yes in the Exit Narrator box.

Using On-Screen Keyboard

If you have trouble using the regular keyboard but can use a pointing device, Windows 2000's new On-Screen Keyboard utility is just the thing for you. The On-Screen Keyboard utility does just what its name implies — it provides an onscreen rendition of the standard computer keyboard.

Click Start ➪ Programs ➪ Accessories ➪ Accessibility ➪ On-Screen Keyboard to open the On-Screen Keyboard window shown in Figure 9-14. A message box noting the limitations of the On-Screen Keyboard utility also appears. Click OK to close the message box.

Figure 9-14: The On-Screen Keyboard window.

Clicking a button in the On-Screen Keyboard window has the same effect as pressing the corresponding key on the keyboard. Windows types the character, selects the option, or takes whatever action is associated with the keystroke. To use the modifier keys (Shift, Ctrl, and Alt), simply click the modifier key first, followed by the key you want to modify. For example, to execute the Ctrl+S key combination with the On-Screen Keyboard, simply click Ctrl and then click *s*.

You can use the On-Screen Keyboard to enter text, make selections, and navigate through just about any dialog box, document, or program window. Basically, anything you can do with the regular keyboard, you can do with the On-Screen Keyboard. Its window normally stays on top so it's accessible even when other windows are open and active.

The menu commands available for the On-Screen Keyboard enable you to customize the program in several ways:

   ✦ Click File ➪ Add to Utility Manager to include On-Screen Keyboard in the Utility Manager program, which enables you to automatically start the major accessibility utilities (Magnifier, Narrator, and On-Screen Keyboard) when you start Windows.

   ✦ Select the keyboard layout using the commands on the Keyboard menu. You can select a standard or enhanced keyboard, a regular or block layout, and 101, 102, or 106 keys.

✦ Click Settings ⇨ Always on Top to toggle the Always On Top feature on or off. When Always On Top is active, the On-Screen Keyboard window remains on top of all other windows even when another window has the focus.

✦ Click Settings ⇨ Use Click Sound to toggle sounds on and off. Selecting this option causes the On-Screen Keyboard to make a clicking sound when you click each key button.

✦ Click Settings ⇨ Font to open the Font dialog box where you can select the font the On-Screen Keyboard uses to label its key buttons.

✦ Click Settings ⇨ Typing Mode to open the Typing Mode dialog box shown in Figure 9-15. The options in the Typing Mode dialog box enable you to specify how you want to select buttons from the On-Screen Keyboard window.

• The Click to select option is the default and requires a mouse click to select each keystroke.

• The Hover to select option enables you to select keys by simply pointing to a button with the mouse pointer. The keyboard button changes color when you point to it; then, after a predefined interval, the highlighted button is selected automatically without requiring a click of the mouse button. Set the Minimum time to hover value to determine how long the pointer must hover over a button before the On-Screen Keyboard selects the key. (Try one second.)

• The Switch or key to select option enables you to use a joystick or other device to select keys in the On-Screen Keyboard window. If you select this option, set an appropriate value in the Scan interval box and click the Advanced button to open another dialog box where you can select the device or keyboard key you want to use.

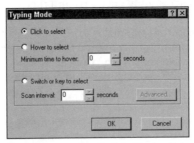

Figure 9-15: The Typing Mode dialog box.

Starting Accessibility Utilities with the Utility Manager

The Utility Manager enables you to automatically start your choice of the three major accessibility utilities — Magnifier, Narrator, and On-Screen Keyboard. You can also use Utility Manager to conveniently monitor the status of those same utilities and start and stop them at will.

Here's how to launch and set options in the Utility Manager:

1. Click Start ⇨ Programs ⇨ Accessories ⇨ Accessibility ⇨ Utility Manager. The Utility Manager dialog box, shown in Figure 9-16, opens.

2. To start a utility that isn't running, select the utility in the list box and click Start. To stop a utility that is running, select the utility and click Stop.

3. Use the checkboxes beneath the Start and Stop buttons to set the selected utility to start automatically with Windows or whenever you start the Utility Manager program.

4. Click OK to close the dialog box.

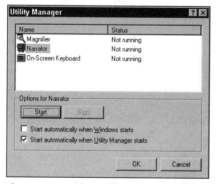

Figure 9-16: The Utility Manager dialog box.

Tip

For a quick alternative to using the normal Start Menu command to open Utility Manager, try using the Windows key shortcut (press Windows+U) to display the Utility Manager dialog box.

Accessing Accessibility Features in the Control Panel

In addition to the major accessibility utilities such as Magnifier, Narrator, and On-Screen Keyboard, Windows 2000 includes an assortment of accessibility options designed to do such things as make keyboards easier to use for someone with limited finger dexterity. If you went through the section "Using Accessibility Wizard," in the first part of this chapter, you've already been introduced to most of them.

However, you don't have to go through the Accessibility Wizard to access Windows' accessibility options. The Accessibility Options icon in the Control Panel enables you to select and configure the individual accessibility options you want to use, including some accessibility options that are not included in the Accessibility Wizard.

Accessibility Options

Click Start ➪ Settings ➪ Control Panel to open the Control Panel window and then double-click the Accessibility Options icon to open the dialog box shown in Figure 9-17. The Accessibility Options dialog box has five tabs:

✦ **Keyboard:** Includes the StickyKeys, FilterKeys, and ToggleKeys options

✦ **Sound:** Includes the SoundSentry and ShowSounds options

✦ **Display:** Includes the high-contrast options

✦ **Mouse:** Includes the MouseKeys option

✦ **General:** Includes the Automatic reset, Notification, SerialKey devices, and Administrative options settings.

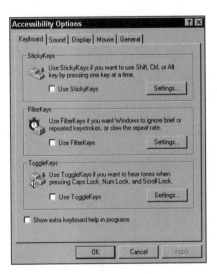

Figure 9-17: The Accessibility Options dialog box.

StickyKeys

The Sticky Keys option enables you to build keystroke combinations such as Ctrl+S and Ctrl+Alt+Delete by pressing the keys sequentially instead of simultaneously. This option is a real boon for users who have trouble pressing multiple keys at the same time because of limited finger dexterity. It's also helpful for anyone who needs to use the keyboard with only one hand. That includes able-bodied people who want to use the keyboard with one hand while doing something else (such as shuffling papers or counting items on an assembly line) with the other hand.

To enable the StickyKeys option, click the Use StickyKeys checkbox on the Keyboard tab of the Accessibility Options dialog box. For fine-tuning, click the Settings button in the StickyKeys area to open the StickyKeys Settings dialog box shown in Figure 9-18. The dialog box includes the following settings, which you can turn on or off by clicking the checkbox next to each option:

✦ **Use shortcut:** Enables a keyboard shortcut (pressing the Shift key five times) for turning StickyKeys on or off.

✦ **Press modifier key twice to lock:** You can lock a modifier key (Ctrl, Alt, or Shift) by pressing it twice. Press the key again to turn off the lock.

✦ **Turn StickyKeys off if two keys are pressed at once:** Disables StickyKeys if a modifier key and a normal key are pressed simultaneously. In other words, if someone presses an ordinary key combination, StickyKeys shuts down, and the keyboard returns to default operation.

✦ **Make sounds when modifier key is pressed:** Provides audible feedback to confirm when a modifier key is pressed.

✦ **Show StickyKeys status on screen:** Adds an icon to the system tray when StickyKeys is on.

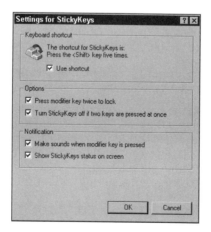

Figure 9-18: The Settings for StickyKeys dialog box.

Adjust the settings in the Settings for StickyKeys dialog box as desired and then click OK to record the settings, close the dialog box, and return to the Accessibility Options dialog box.

FilterKeys

The FilterKeys accessibility option filters out repeated keystrokes that result from pressing and holding a key too long or inadvertently pressing a key multiple times (a potential problem for people with hand tremors).

To enable the FilterKeys option, click the Use FilterKeys checkbox on the Keyboard tab of the Accessibility Options dialog box. Like you can with StickyKeys, you can adjust an assortment of optional settings for FilterKeys by clicking the Settings button beside the Use FilterKeys option and editing the settings in the Settings for FilterKeys dialog box shown in Figure 9-19. The available options are as follows:

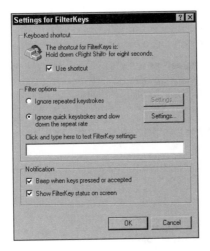

Figure 9-19: The Settings for FilterKeys dialog box.

+ **Use shortcut:** Enables a keyboard shortcut (press and hold the right Shift key for eight seconds) for turning FilterKeys on and off.

+ **Ignore repeated keystrokes:** If a key is pressed and released rapidly, Windows accepts the first keystroke and ignores the rest. (This is called *BounceKeys* in the Accessibility Wizard.) If you select this option, you can click the Settings button beside the option to open an Advanced Settings for FilterKeys dialog box where you can set and test the time period. Drag the slider to adjust the lockout period, and then click OK to record the setting and return to the Settings for FilterKeys dialog box.

✦ **Ignore quick keystrokes and slow down the repeat rate:** Selecting this option actually enables two options called RepeatKeys and SlowKeys. Click the Settings button beside the option to open another version of the Advanced Settings for FilterKeys dialog box as shown in Figure 9-20.

The RepeatKeys settings in the upper portion of the dialog box override the keyboard repeat rate settings in the Keyboard Control Panel when the FilterKeys option is active. For RepeatKeys, you can select No keyboard repeat or Slow down keyboard repeat rates and then use the sliders to adjust the repeat delay and repeat rate times.

In the SlowKeys area, use the slider to adjust the length of time a key must remain depressed before Windows accepts the keystroke.

✦ By carefully adjusting the RepeatKeys and SlowKeys settings, you can effectively filter out extraneous keystrokes that result from inadvertently pressing a key multiple times or pressing the wrong key. The result is a slow and deliberate typing pace with few errors, even if your hand trembles and shakes. After adjusting the options in the Advanced Settings for FilterKeys dialog box, click OK to record the settings and return to the Settings for FilterKeys dialog box.

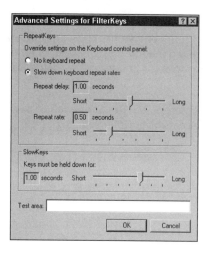

Figure 9-20: This Advanced Settings for FilterKeys dialog box enables you to control keystrokes.

✦ **Beep when keys pressed or accepted:** Causes Windows to sound a beep each time you press a key.

✦ **Show FilterKey status on screen:** Displays an icon in the system tray portion of the taskbar when the FilterKey option is active.

After adjusting the settings in the Settings for FilterKeys dialog box, click OK to record the settings and return to the Accessibility Options dialog box.

ToggleKeys

The ToggleKeys option helps prevent inadvertent use of Caps Lock, Scroll Lock, and Num Lock by sounding a beep when you press any of these keys. Click the Use ToggleKeys checkbox on the Keyboard tab of the Accessibility Options dialog box to activate the option. Click the Settings button next to the option to open the Settings for ToggleKeys dialog box.

The dialog box contains a single option—Use shortcut—which enables a keyboard shortcut (holding down the Num Lock key for five seconds) that turns the ToggleKeys option on and off. After adjusting that lone setting, click OK to close the Settings for ToggleKeys dialog box and return to the Accessibility Options dialog box.

SoundSentry

The SoundSentry option displays visual warnings when your computer makes a sound. With SoundSentry, you are aware of the audible alerts Windows sounds, even if you can't hear them. Obviously, SoundSentry is designed to assist users with hearing difficulties. However, it is also useful if you have system sounds muted to avoid disturbing others, such as when you're using a laptop computer on a late-night airline flight.

To activate SoundSentry, click the Use SoundSentry checkbox on the Sound tab of the Accessibility Options dialog box (shown in Figure 9-21). Next, click the Settings button beside the option to open the Settings for SoundSentry dialog box.

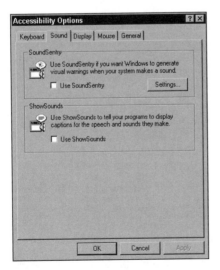

Figure 9-21: The Sound tab of the Accessibility Options dialog box.

Then choose the visual warning device you want to use from the Warning for windowed programs drop-down list box. You can choose between flashing the active caption bar, flashing the active window, or flashing the desktop. After selecting an alert, click OK to close the Settings for SoundSentry dialog box and return to the Accessibility Options dialog box.

ShowSounds

The ShowSounds option instructs programs to display visible captions for the sounds and speech that they generate, assuming that the program has such captions available. To activate the option, click the Use ShowSounds checkbox on the Sound tab of the Accessibility Options dialog box.

High Contrast

The High Contrast option switches the Windows display to a color scheme and font selection designed for high visibility. This is another Windows accessibility option that often finds uses beyond its originally intended purpose. The High Contrast option is designed to enable visually impaired users to quickly configure a system to use high-visibility colors and fonts and return the system to normal just as quickly when another user needs to access the system. However, laptop users who must sometimes use their systems under difficult lighting conditions can also make good use of the High Contrast option to improve screen legibility and then switch back to normal under better lighting. In fact, any computer user can employ the High Contrast option to instantly switch to any alternate color scheme.

To activate the High Contrast option, click the Use High Contrast checkbox on the Display tab of the Accessibility Options dialog box. Click the Settings button to open the Settings for High Contrast dialog box shown in Figure 9-22. The dialog box offers the following options:

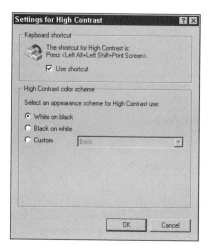

Figure 9-22: The Settings for High Contrast dialog box.

◆ **Use shortcut:** Enables a keyboard shortcut (Left Alt+Left Shift+Print Screen) for turning the High Contrast option on and off.

◆ **High Contrast color scheme:** You can choose from white on black, black on white, or Custom. If you choose the Custom option, you can select a color scheme from the adjacent drop-down list box, which includes all the color schemes available on the Appearance tab of the Display Properties dialog box. So your high-contrast color scheme does not have to be high contrast at all. It can be any color scheme you want to be able to invoke with the High Contrast shortcut key.

After making your selections in the Settings for High Contrast dialog box, click OK to close the dialog box, record your settings, and return to the Accessibility Options dialog box.

MouseKeys

The MouseKeys option offers a keyboard-based alternative to the ubiquitous desktop rodent. MouseKeys is not just for people who have trouble using a mouse for one reason or another; it's for anyone who prefers to keep both hands on the keyboard instead of reaching for a mouse or other pointing device. Activating the MouseKeys option enables you to control the mouse pointer using the keys of the numeric keypad.

The following list describes the effect of pressing the various keys:

1	Moves pointer diagonally down and left
2	Moves pointer down
3	Moves pointer diagonally down and right
4	Moves pointer left
6	Moves pointer right
7	Moves pointer diagonally up and left
8	Moves pointer up
9	Moves pointer diagonally up and right
/	Selects left (main or primary) mouse button
*	Selects both mouse buttons
-	Selects right (secondary) mouse button
5	Clicks selected mouse button
+	Double-clicks selected mouse button
Ins	Clicks and holds selected mouse button for drag operations
Del	Releases selected mouse button to complete drag operations

To activate the MouseKeys option, click the Use MouseKeys checkbox on the Mouse tab of the Accessibility Options dialog box. To fine-tune the settings for the MouseKeys option, click the Settings button to open the Settings for MouseKeys dialog box as shown in Figure 9-23. The following options are available in the Settings for MouseKeys dialog box:

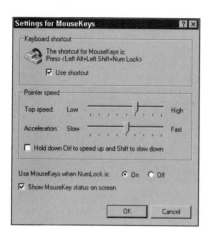

Figure 9-23: The Settings for MouseKeys dialog box.

✦ **Use shortcut:** Enables a keyboard shortcut (Left Alt+Left Shift+Num Lock) to turn the MouseKeys option on and off.

✦ **Top speed:** Drag the slider left or right to decrease or increase the maximum speed of the mouse pointer.

✦ **Acceleration:** Drag the slider left or right to decrease or increase the rate at which the mouse pointer picks up speed when you press and hold a direction key down.

✦ **Hold down Ctrl to speed up and Shift to slow down:** Click the checkbox if you want to use the Ctrl and Shift keys to modify the speed of a mouse pointer.

✦ **Use MouseKeys when NumLock is:** Select On or Off to designate the status of the numeric keypad when using MouseKeys.

Tip

If you have a standard keyboard, you probably want to configure MouseKeys to use the numeric keypad when Num Lock is off. That way, the MouseKeys option replaces the function of the numeric keypad keys when they are serving as arrow keys, Home, End, and so on. Because the standard keyboard includes dedicated keys for those functions, you're not likely to need to duplicate those functions with the numeric keypad. Toggling Num Lock on disables the MouseKeys option and enables you to use the numeric keypad to enter numbers quickly.

✦ **Show MouseKey status on screen:** Displays an icon in the system tray of the taskbar when MouseKeys is active.

After adjusting the options in the Settings for MouseKeys dialog box, click OK to close the dialog box, record your settings, and return to the Accessibility Options dialog box.

Controlling Accessibility Options

The General tab of the Accessibility Options dialog box (shown in Figure 9-24) offers several options for controlling how you activate the accessibility options. The following list describes the available options:

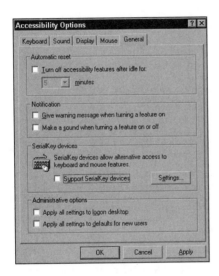

Figure 9-24: The General tab of the Accessibility Options dialog box.

✦ **Automatic reset:** Click the checkbox if you want to disable all accessibility options automatically if the computer remains idle for a specified period of time. If you choose this option, you can specify the time delay before the automatic reset takes effect by making a selection from the minutes drop-down list box.

✦ **Notification:** The two checkboxes in this area enable you to tell Windows whether and how to notify you when you turn accessibility options on or off.

✦ **SerialKey devices:** The Support SerialKey devices option enables you to select and configure alternative input devices such as foot pedals. To activate the alternative input device, click the checkbox and then click the Settings button to open a dialog box where you can select the port to which the device is attached and set the appropriate baud rate for the device.

✦ **Administrative options:** These two options enable you to specify whether you want the current accessibility option settings to apply to the current user's profile and or become the default settings for new users that you add to your system.

After adjusting all the settings in the Accessibility Options dialog box, click OK to close the Accessibility Options dialog box and apply the selected settings to your system.

Summary

Recent versions of Windows have included an assortment of features designed to improve accessibility of the operating system for users with a wide range of limitations and disabilities. Windows 2000 continues the tradition and adds to it by providing some new accessibility features. Narrator is a text-to-speech utility designed to assist visually impaired users by reading aloud the contents of menus, dialog boxes, and other Windows. On-Screen Keyboard provides users who have difficulty using a traditional keyboard with an alternative way to enter text and keyboard commands in Windows.

Topics covered in this chapter include:

✦ Using the Accessibility Wizard to configure Windows' accessibility options

✦ Improving display readability with the Magnifier utility

✦ Using the Narrator utility to read the contents of menus and dialog boxes

✦ Typing with your mouse using the On-Screen Keyboard utility

✦ Controlling accessibility utilities with the Utility Manager

✦ Customizing the Accessibility Options with the Control Panel

In the next chapter I cover adding and maintaining the fonts on your system.

✦   ✦   ✦

Fraternizing with Fonts

Windows 2000 comes with a set of preinstalled fonts that would have been the envy of a graphic designer not too many years ago. But nowadays, having an assortment of fonts available for all of your applications is something computer users take for granted.

Sophisticated font-handling technology is built into Windows 2000. As a result, all of your applications (and Windows itself) can share the same fonts and use them for both onscreen display and printed output on almost any printer. Gone are the days of printer-specific fonts that had to be separately installed in each application and onscreen preview fonts that didn't match printed output. TrueType font technology has been a feature of Windows for years. Now, Windows 2000 introduces OpenType, the successor to TrueType, which supports an enhanced version of TrueType fonts and extends the same font handling capabilities to Type 1 (PostScript) fonts as well.

This chapter shows you how to use these built-in tools to manage your font collection. The Windows technology for handling fonts and delivering them to the screen and to your printer is completely automatic. No user intervention is required.

Understanding Fonts

Back in the days when a simple typewriter was the main tool for preparing documents, you couldn't do much to make text look better. Today's computers provide the power and flexibility to enhance the appearance of your documents with a variety of different fonts and text treatments. You have lots of options for how you want your text to appear onscreen and in your printed documents. Having lots of options also means having lots of choices to make — and learning terminology to describe those choices. Here's a quick rundown of some of the terms you encounter as you work with fonts and type:

✦ **Typeface:** A full set of characters (letters, numbers, punctuation marks, and special characters) that share a distinctive appearance due to design details such as thickness of lines, the presence or absence of serifs and other embellishments, and subtle variations of the standard letter shapes. Typefaces have names such as Arial, Tahoma, and Times New Roman.

✦ **Serif:** A small embellishment at the ends of the lines forming a letter. A typeface that incorporates serifs in the design of the letters is called a *serif font*. Times New Roman is perhaps the best known example of a serif font.

✦ **Sans serif:** Literally, without serifs. A descriptive term for a typeface that does not include serifs. Arial is probably the most common sans serif font. Sans serif fonts are sometimes referred to as *block letters*.

✦ **Font:** Originally, a font was a set of typesetting characters, all of the same typeface and the same size. Now that computers use one master file to produce characters of a given typeface in any size, the terms *font* and *typeface* have become synonymous. Windows uses *font* (perhaps because it's shorter).

✦ **Size:** Type is sized by height. The size is measured from the top of the tallest letters to the bottom of the *descenders* (the tails of characters such as *g* and *y* that hang down below the other letters), not the height of the capital letters as you might expect. Type sizes are traditionally expressed in points.

✦ **Points:** A unit of measure traditionally used by typesetters and graphic designers. There are approximately 72 points to an inch. Therefore, each line of 72-point type occupies approximately one inch of *vertical* space. To put it another way, six lines of 12-point type fit in one vertical inch.

✦ **Caps:** The large letters of the alphabet. Caps is short for *capitals*, also known as *uppercase*.

✦ **Lowercase**. The small letters of the alphabet.

> **Note**
>
> Here's an interesting bit of trivia: The terms *uppercase* and *lowercase* come from the traditional practice of storing old-fashioned metal and wood type characters in drawers called *cases*. Each typeface was stored in a pair of drawers. The capital letters were stored in the top drawer (the *upper case*), and the small letters were stored in the bottom drawer (the *lower case*).

✦ **Style:** Refers to variations on a standard typeface such as the attributes bold, italic, and bold italic.

✦ **Bold:** A style variation in which the lines forming the characters are thicker than those of the standard typeface. Using the **bold style** gives text more emphasis by making it look darker and heavier.

✦ **Italic:** A style variation in which the characters are slanted. Using the *italic style* is another way to give text more emphasis.

Note

True italic typefaces are separate versions of the basic typeface, designed to take advantage of the slanted style to achieve a calligraphic or script-like appearance. Technically, the term *oblique* is used by typographers to describe a simple slanted variation of the base typeface. When you select the italic style of a given font, Windows uses a true italic typeface if one is available; otherwise, Windows automatically generates oblique characters as needed by slanting characters from the basic typeface.

✦ **Monospaced font:** A font in which every letter, number, and punctuation character takes up the same amount of horizontal space, like the fonts on an old-style typewriter or text-only computer terminal. `Courier is an example of a monospaced font`. Monospaced fonts are also called *fixed pitch* fonts.

✦ **Proportional font:** A font in which horizontal space is allocated to each letter in proportion to its shape. For example, a lowercase *i* is much narrower than a cap *W*. Most fonts are proportional fonts.

✦ **PANOSE:** A system for describing characteristics of fonts so that appropriate substitutions can be made when the specified font isn't available. For example, the Arial typeface looks similar to the Helvetica typeface even though there is no similarity in their names. If you create a document on one computer using Helvetica and then transfer the file to another computer that doesn't have Helvetica installed, Windows uses the PANOSE Matching System to select Arial as the best substitute and uses Arial to display and print your document.

Over the years, several different technologies have evolved for rendering fonts, displaying fonts onscreen, and printing text using various fonts. Windows 2000 supports several different kinds of fonts and font files:

✦ **TrueType:** The original *Windows font* format. TrueType fonts contain instructions that define the outline shape of each character in a typeface. There is no need to store separate font files for each type size or separate font files for onscreen display and for printer output. Windows uses the TrueType outlines to generate images of text characters at any size and does so on the fly.

✦ **OpenType:** The successor to TrueType, OpenType fonts are also outline fonts that Windows can use to render text for onscreen display and for output to any Windows 2000-supported printer. OpenType is more than a font file format, it's also a new font-rendering technology that enables Windows 2000 to use TrueType and Type 1 fonts as well as OpenType fonts.

✦ **Type 1:** This scalable outline font format developed by Adobe for use with PostScript printers is often called *PostScript*. In previous versions of Windows, you needed a special utility program (Adobe Type Manager) to use Type 1 fonts in Windows, but now you can install and use Type 1 outline fonts in Windows 2000, just like TrueType fonts.

Tip

Windows 2000 and OpenType enable you to use Type 1 fonts on non-PostScript printers, just as though the Type 1 fonts were TrueType fonts. That's a pretty slick trick.

✦ **Vector fonts:** Fonts that render text characters from a mathematical model. Sometimes called *stroke* fonts, vector fonts are primarily intended for use with CAD programs and plotters. Windows 2000 comes with three vector fonts installed: Modern, Roman, and Script.

Vector fonts are designed to print letters composed of thin lines. Printing those lines with a plotter pen creates readable text. However, printing them on a laser printer or other high-resolution output creates lines that are so thin that they almost disappear.

✦ **Raster fonts:** Characters are composed of patterns of dots optimized for display or printing at a specific size on a particular output device. Windows 2000 supports raster fonts for compatibility with legacy programs that require them. Windows also uses its own raster fonts for onscreen display of text in dialog boxes and such. Raster fonts normally don't appear on the font lists in your programs.

Finding and Viewing Installed Fonts

Windows 2000 stores fonts in a special folder — creatively named Fonts — that is a subfolder in your main Windows folder. The default path name is usually C:\Windows\Fonts or C:\Winnt\Fonts. The Fonts folder contains an entry for each font that is installed and accessible by Windows and your Windows applications.

You might have other font files scattered about in various folders on your system. However, until they are installed in the Fonts folder, they aren't accessible to Windows.

You could open an Explorer window and drill down to the Fonts folder to view its contents. However, it's easier to get to the Fonts folder through the Control Panel. Click Start ➪ Settings ➪ Control Panel. When the Control Panel window appears, double-click the Fonts icon to open the Fonts folder window as shown in Figure 10-1. The figure shows a few TrueType and Type 1 fonts installed in addition to the default assortment of OpenType and Vector fonts.

At first glance, the Fonts folder looks like a fairly typical folder window, generously populated with icons for the various fonts that are installed on your system. One difference that isn't immediately obvious is that the label under each icon is the name of the font rather than the filename. (That's an important distinction because some font files have impossibly cryptic filenames.) The symbols on the icons in the Fonts folder indicate what kind of font each icon represents. Table 10-1 gives a rundown of the icons you're likely to encounter.

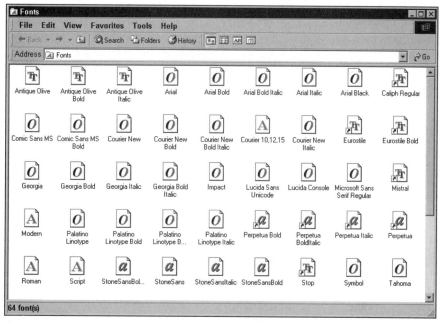

Figure 10-1: The Fonts folder is a standard folder window with a few extra touches.

Table 10-1
Fonts Folder Icons

Icon	Font It Represents
O	OpenType font file
TT	TrueType font file
A	Vector font file and other legacy font formats such as printer-specific fonts
a	Type 1 (PostScript) font files
TT	Shortcut to a TrueType font file stored in another folder
a	Shortcut to a Type 1 font file stored in another folder

Not all the fonts installed on your Windows 2000 system must be stored in the Fonts folder. To access a font, Windows needs an icon in the Fonts folder, but that icon doesn't have to represent the font file itself. Instead, the icon can be a shortcut that points to a font file stored in another location. Notice that a few of the font icons in Figure 10-1 have the distinctive arrow in the lower-left corner marking them as shortcuts.

Sorting the contents of the Fonts folder

The default view of the Fonts folder is the large icon view shown in Figure 10-1, but that's not the only way you can view the contents of the Fonts folder. Buttons on the Font folder's standard toolbar, described in Table 10-2, give you easy access to four different views. You're already familiar with three of them; one of them is unique to the Fonts folder.

Table 10-2
Font Folder Toolbar Buttons

Icon	View	Description
	Large Icons	Each font or shortcut in the folder is represented by a large icon and a name as shown in Figure 10-1. You can also select this view by choosing View ⇨ Large Icons.
	List	Each font or shortcut in the folder is represented by the font name with a small icon next to it. The smaller icons make it possible for many more fonts to be displayed in the Fonts folder window. You can also select this view by choosing View ⇨ List.
	Details	Each font or shortcut in the folder is represented by the font name with a small icon next to it, like the List view but with added columns of information for each font as shown in Figure 10-2. Although the format of the Details view in the Fonts folder is similar to the corresponding view in other folder windows, the information displayed in the columns is different. Notice that there are separate columns for font name and filename, plus columns for file size and modification date. You can also select this view by choosing View ⇨ Details.
	Similarity	This view is unique to the Fonts folder. In the Similarity view, you can select any installed font (select the font from the List fonts by similarity to drop-down list box), and Windows lists the other installed fonts rated by how similar or dissimilar they are to the selected font. Figure 10-3 shows a listing of fonts rated by their similarity to the Trebuchet font. You can also select this view by choosing View ⇨ List Fonts by Similarity.

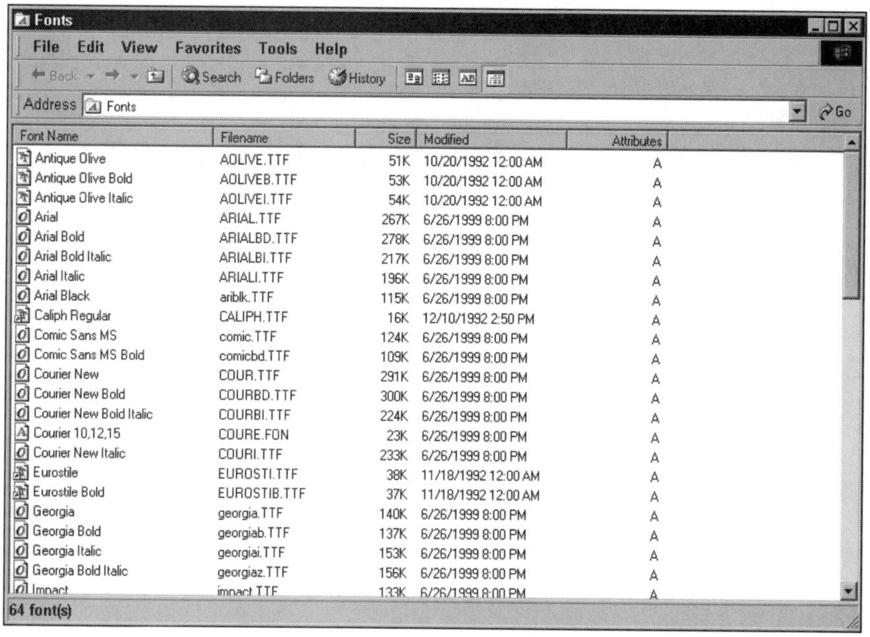

Figure 10-2: The details listed in the Fonts folder are a little different from other folders.

Note Windows bases its similarity rating on the PANOSE font-matching information in each font file. That information is included in all newer TrueType and OpenType font files and in some Type 1 files. However, some of your older font files may not include PANOSE information, and Windows can't rate those fonts.

Note Remember that it is the font name, not the filename, that normally appears in the Fonts folder window. As a result, the Details view is the only place you can see the filenames for your fonts without opening the Properties dialog boxes for the individual fonts.

No matter which view you select, you can simplify the font list somewhat by choosing View ➪ Hide Variations. When you select this option, Windows does not display the bold, italic, and bold italic variations of a basic font. As a result, fonts such as Arial show up in the Fonts folder as a single item instead of four separate items (Arial, Arial Bold, Arial Italic, and Arial Bold Italic). The Hide Variations option is a toggle. A checkmark appears beside the Hide Variations command on the View menu when it is active. To display all the font variations, just choose the command again to switch it off.

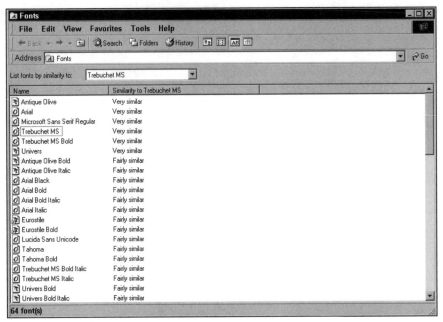

Figure 10-3: The Similarity view helps you locate fonts that look similar.

Note

Not all fonts have separate font files for bold, italic, and bold italic variations. Some fonts consist of just a base font file, and Windows fattens the characters to create a pseudo-bold or slants them to create a pseudo-italic (oblique) variation as needed. Some fonts, such as script typefaces and symbol fonts, simply don't have italic or bold variations.

Viewing font samples

Font designers give fonts names that are distinctive but not very descriptive. As a result, the font name under an icon in the Fonts folder window doesn't tell you much about what the font looks like. Sure, you're probably acquainted with fonts such as Arial, Courier New, and Times New Roman. But do you remember exactly what the Georgia, Tahoma, and Verdana fonts look like? I thought not!

Fortunately, Windows 2000 includes a handy font viewer that you can use to preview the fonts on your system. Simply double-click the icon for a font file to display the selected font in a Windows Font Viewer window such as the one shown in Figure 10-4. The Windows Font Viewer displays the font name, information about the font file, an uppercase and lowercase alphabet, and sample lines of text in several sizes. After viewing the font, click Done to close the Windows Font Viewer window.

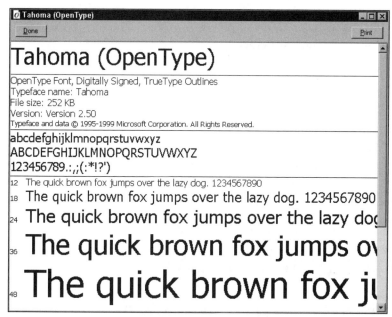

Figure 10-4: With the Windows Font Viewer, you can preview font samples.

Tip

The Windows Font Viewer can display samples of any font file that you can access with Windows Explorer, not just the fonts installed in Windows. You can view fonts in other folders, on other disks, and on network drives. As long as Windows supports the font file, you can view it by double-clicking the font file icon in any folder window. You can use the Windows Font Viewer to preview fonts located on other drives before you install them.

Printing a font sample

An onscreen font preview is handy, but you might also need a printed sample of your fonts for offline reference. The Windows Font Viewer can fill that need.

View a font in the Windows Font Viewer and click the Print button to open the Print dialog box. (Of course, you must have a printer installed in order to print font samples.) Select the printer you want to use and any other options (such as the number of copies you want to print) and then click Print to close the Print dialog box and send the font sample page to the printer. The resulting font sample page looks similar to the one shown in Figure 10-5 and is essentially the same as the onscreen sample shown in the Windows Font Viewer (refer back to Figure 10-4).

Tahoma (OpenType)

OpenType Font, Digitally Signed, TrueType Outlines
Typeface name: Tahoma
File size: 252 KB
Version: Version 2.50
Typeface and data © 1995-1999 Microsoft Corporation. All Rights Reserved.

abcdefghijklmnopqrstuvwxyz
ABCDEFGHIJKLMNOPQRSTUVWXYZ
123456789.:,;(:*!?')

12   The quick brown fox jumps over the lazy dog. 1234567890

18   The quick brown fox jumps over the lazy dog. 1234

24   The quick brown fox jumps over the la

36   The quick brown fox jump

48   The quick brown fo

60   The quick brow

72   The quick brc

Figure 10-5: A printed font sample page.

Installing New Fonts

Windows 2000 comes with a good basic assortment of fonts. In addition, many popular programs install additional fonts along with the program software. And one of the great things about Windows font handling is that once a font is installed, it's available to all your Windows programs that access fonts, not just to the program that installed the font. After installing a few major programs, you may find that you have quite an assortment of fonts installed in Windows.

You don't have to depend on fonts that come with various programs though. You can buy and install individual fonts on your own. Fonts are available from several companies that specialize in fonts, clipart, and other computer graphics products. You can download freeware and shareware fonts from many sources on the Internet. In addition, your corporate computer support or graphics departments may have fonts available that you can use for producing company documents. Whatever the source of the fonts you want to install, the process for installing them is the same. Just follow these steps:

1. Open the Fonts folder window by clicking Start ⇨ Settings ⇨ Control Panel and then double-clicking the Fonts icon in the Control Panel window. Alternatively, you can open an Explorer window and drill down to the Fonts folder inside the Windows folder on your primary disk drive.

2. Choose File ⇨ Install New Font. The Add Fonts dialog box appears.

3. Select the location of the font files you want to install. First select the drive from the Drives drop-down list box and then select the folder in the Folders list box. After you select the folder, Windows scans the specified folder searching for font files and displays the results in the List of fonts list box. Be patient; scanning the folder can take awhile, depending on the speed of your system and the number of files in the target folder. Figure 10-6 shows the Add Fonts dialog box displaying an assortment of TrueType fonts.

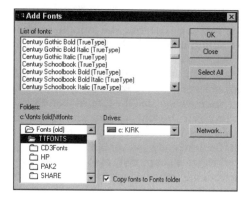

Figure 10-6: Windows displays the list of fonts that are available for installation.

4. Select the font or fonts you want to install. You can select an individual font by clicking its name in the List of fonts list box. You can select multiple fonts by Ctrl+clicking additional fonts. To select all the fonts in the target folder, click the Select All button.

5. Click the Copy Fonts to Fonts folder option to check (or clear) the checkbox. The default setting is to automatically copy the selected font files to your Fonts folder. However, you can install fonts *without* copying the font files to the Fonts folder. If you clear the Copy Fonts to Fonts Folder option, Windows leaves the font files where they are and installs the fonts by adding shortcuts to those font files into the Fonts folder. For example, you may prefer to organize your font files in a series of folders and subfolders on a different drive in your system. In that case, installing fonts with shortcuts saves some disk space by avoiding having duplicate files in the Fonts folder as well.

6. Click OK. Windows closes the Add Fonts dialog box and installs the selected fonts in the Fonts folder.

Tip   As an alternative to using the Add Fonts dialog box, you can drag and drop font files from another folder window into the Fonts folder. Open the Fonts folder and the folder containing the font files you want to install. To install a font, drag its icon from the target folder window and drop it into the Fonts folder window. Windows copies the font file to the Fonts folder and installs the font.

Removing Fonts

Fonts are fun to use, and having a lot of them to choose from seems like a good idea. However, you can have too much of a good thing.

Having too many fonts on your system can create so much clutter that you have trouble finding the font you want to use. Having an excessive number (hundreds) of fonts installed on your system can even have a negative impact on performance.

Fortunately, it's easy to remove fonts. All you need to do is remove the unwanted font file or shortcut from the Fonts folder by deleting the font file or shortcut or moving it to another folder. Either action uninstalls the font.

Caution   Use caution when deleting fonts from the Fonts folder. Remember that in most cases, the font files themselves are stored in the Fonts folder. When you delete a font from the Fonts folder, you not only uninstall the font so that it's not available for use within Windows, you also delete the font file from your system. Unless you have another copy of the font file stored somewhere, you won't be able to change your mind and restore the font. Consequently, you should always copy the font file to another folder on your hard drive, to a floppy disk, or to a Zip disk or other storage medium before deleting it from the Fonts folder. As long as you have a copy of the font file, you can always reinstall it.

Using Special Characters with Character Map

The characters you can access directly from the keyboard account for only a little more than half the characters in a typical font. Others, such as the copyright symbol (©), fractions ($^1\!/_4$, $^1\!/_2$, $^3\!/_4$), boxes and bullets (•), and so on, have no keyboard counterpart — at least, not anything you can enter with a single keystroke. You can enter these characters from the keyboard by pressing and holding the Alt key while you type a four-digit number on the numeric keypad, but that's not always a practical solution. Let's see, is $^1\!/_4$ Alt+0188 or Alt+0189?

The problem is bad enough with typical fonts. It's even worse with the special symbol fonts such as Wingdings. The entire font is composed of symbols and other special characters. Many of them are linked to standard keyboard keys, but how can you remember which symbols are mapped to which keys? Very few people use these special characters and symbol fonts often enough remember the proper keystrokes and sequences without some kind of reminder.

When you need to enter special characters, the Character Map applet comes to the rescue. It's one of the standard assortment of small utility programs installed automatically with Windows 2000. Character Map is an onscreen chart of all the characters available in a given font. You can use the chart as a reference, or you can copy and paste characters from Character Map into your documents.

To use the Character Map applet to add special characters to your document, follow these steps:

1. Open Character Map by clicking Start ➪ Programs ➪ Accessories ➪ System Tools ➪ Character Map. Windows opens the Character Map dialog box shown in Figure 10-7.

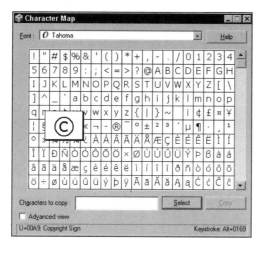

Figure 10-7: Character Map provides easy access to special characters hidden away in your fonts.

2. Select the font you want to use from the Font drop-down list box. Character Map displays the characters available in the selected font.

Note   By default, Character Map opens with the font that is currently in use already selected. So if you are editing text in the Arial font in WordPad, when you open Character Map, the characters available in the Arial font appear.

3. Select the symbol or character you want to add to your document. Clicking a character in the Character Map chart displays an enlarged version of the character. The keystroke or key sequence required to produce that character appears in the lower-left corner of the Character Map window. Double-click a character or click the Select button to add the selected character to the Characters to copy box near the bottom of the Character Map dialog box.

Tip   You can use the key sequence shown in Character Map to enter the selected character into your document. To do so, simply switch back to the document window and type the key sequence to enter the desired character. For example, pressing Alt+0169 inserts the copyright character (©) in most fonts. Touch typists often prefer using the keyboard whenever possible instead of using the mouse to click menu commands.

4. Click the Copy button to copy the selected character from the Characters to copy box to the Windows clipboard.

5. Switch back to your document window, position the cursor where you want to insert the special character, and press Ctrl+V (or choose Edit ➪ Paste or right-click and choose Paste from the pop-up menu that appears) to paste the special character from the clipboard into your document.

You can use Character Map and the Windows clipboard to insert special characters into just about any Windows application. You're most likely to use the technique with your word processing program, but it works equally well with spreadsheets, graphics programs, Web page editors, and anything else that accepts text input from the Windows clipboard.

Summary

Windows 2000 includes built-in font-rendering technology that provides matching fonts for onscreen display and for output to any Windows 2000-supported printer. The capability to do this with TrueType fonts has been a hallmark of Windows for years. Windows 2000 expands the supported font formats to include Type 1 fonts as well.

Windows 2000 comes with a nice assortment of fonts preinstalled. You can add to that assortment with fonts that are automatically installed when you install various software programs and with fonts you add yourself. Installing, viewing, and removing fonts in the Windows Fonts folder is a simple matter of working with icons in a folder window that is remarkably similar to other folder windows where you manage other kinds of files.

This chapter concludes Part II of this book. In the next part, you learn how to connect Windows 2000 to the Internet, and Chapter 11 explains how to set up a modem.

✦   ✦   ✦

Windows 2000 and the Internet

◆　◆　◆　◆

◆　◆　◆　◆

Setting Up Modems

It's 2000, folks, so I'm not going to lead into the first chapter of the Internet section with a sermon on how important the World Wide Web and the Internet have become. I think anyone who reads this book (heck, anyone who watches TV) has gotten the message.

And if you run Windows 2000, you have more ways to get to the Internet than ever before. Whether you're still riding a sluggish analog modem (like me), zipping along on DSL or cable, or pushing bits over a network through the company's T1 or T3 line, Windows 2000 is ready to make the connection. What's more, Windows 2000 Professional enables you to do such things as

- ✦ Share a single Internet connection among several networked machines

- ✦ Link to remote networks using secure, virtual private network (VPN) connections

- ✦ Create multiple, customized dial-up sessions

- ✦ Use two or more modems to create multiple links to an ISP, producing a higher bandwidth connection

- ✦ Provide remote connectivity to the host system via Remote Access Service (RAS)

Notable among these features is the capability to share Internet connections over a network and integrated support for VPN connections. Both are new to Windows 2000 and offer important capabilities in an increasingly connected world.

Setting Up Modems

A PC without a modem or other communications device is like an airplane without wings — a sleek and powerful vehicle with no place to go. Of course, virtually all PCs sold into the home over the past year have come equipped with modems, while corporate PCs enjoy shared connections to the Internet over a local area network (LAN).

Still, Windows 2000 upgraders may face the prospect of a modem installation. Why? For one thing, Windows 2000 (as well as Windows NT) won't work with as vast a selection of hardware as Windows 98. If your existing modem doesn't appear on the Windows 2000 Hardware Compatibility List (HCL), chances are good it won't work when you upgrade. Some systems may also be equipped with 28.8 Kbps or 33.6 Kbps modems. Given the amount of time even casual users spend on the Internet, a step up to a 56 Kbps modem can save time and possibly money (in the form of connect time charges).

Note   If you have fast digital Internet access available in your area, you should definitely look into it. The benefit of a digital Internet connection can't be overstated. Of course, you need to make sure that the hardware and software — which sometimes come from the service provider — support Windows 2000.

So many modems

The steps involved in installing a new modem can differ markedly depending on whether the modem is an external or internal model. In fact, there are so many variations that it can get a bit confusing. Among the common modem types are the following:

✦ Internal ISA card

✦ Internal PCI card

✦ External serial port (shown in Figure 11-1)

✦ External USB port

Cross-Reference   For more on the various bus and port types supported by Windows 2000 PCs, see Chapter 4.

If you are considering a new modem, my recommendation is to go with an external model that hooks into a USB port. Windows 2000 offers complete USB support, which means USB devices are now an attractive option. Modems don't move enough data to warrant an ISA bus connection, much less a fast PCI bus link, and internal add-in slots are often in short supply. The external serial port, meanwhile, is targeted for extinction by Microsoft and Intel — your next PC may not have a serial port at all.

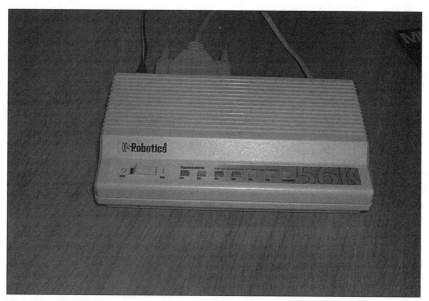

Figure 11-1: Why get an external modem? For one thing, it's easy to share with other laptop and desktop PCs, and the status lights can help you troubleshoot lost connections.

Note   USB is not available on many older PCs—those sold more than two years ago. However, these same older PCs are unlikely to be suitable platforms for serious Windows 2000 use. The result: I expect most Windows 2000 users will have access to USB devices and will want to take advantage of them.

More than fear of early obsolescence drives the USB decision. USB products offer all the benefits of an external modem, including helpful status lights, a power switch for recovering from lockups, and the capability to share the modem among PCs. What's more, USB modems don't have separate power cords because they draw their juice directly from the USB wire. But wait, there's more. Plug-and-Play USB devices automatically configure themselves when hooked into your system, avoiding the clumsy COM port wrestling that often occurs with serial port modems. Had enough? I thought so.

Caution   After all that, I toss out this warning to IT professionals outfitting hundreds of desktops. USB hardware can get a bit twitchy, depending on your platform configurations. You should check with your desktop system vendor to see what specific USB modems are rated to work with your systems.

Installing modems

As with so many other installations, modem setup has been greatly simplified by the Windows 2000 Plug-and-Play capability. The dark days of NT, where you picked around to find a free IRQ or COM port, are just about gone. I'm not saying you should completely trust an operating system to get all the configuration details right, but I've found that Windows 2000 can handle most modem installations just fine.

Of course, there are several types of modems, as noted previously. External modems can connect to serial or USB ports, or can even come in svelte PC Card form factors for notebook PCs. Internet modems typically plug into ISA add-in cards, though most products are transitioning to the PCI bus as fewer and fewer new desktop PCs provide ISA slots.

The good news is that, physical handling aside, the steps for setting up a new modem are very similar among the different modem types. Once you've installed an internal ISA or PCI card modem and started up the machine, the steps for installing drivers and detecting the hardware are the same as those for external serial or USB modems.

Let's step through the installation of a new modem:

1. First, consult your modem documentation to get familiar with the product components and setup procedures.

2. An internal modem should be plugged it into the appropriate ISA or PCI slot, whereas an external modem should be connected to the serial or USB port.

   Note

   Of course, you should shut down the PC before removing the case to install an internal modem or any other internal device. Make sure the ISA or PCI card is securely fitted in the slot and that you screw the backplate to the PC chassis to prevent slippage. Once your modem lines are properly connected, power up the PC. Windows 2000 will automatically detect the new device at startup.

3. Next, connect any power and phone lines to the modem. Remember that internal modems and external USB modems don't have separate power cords since they draw electricity from the bus port or slot.

4. For external modems, turn on the modem power switch.

5. If this is a USB modem or an internal modem, Windows will likely detect the new device automatically. Serial modems, however, may or may not be detected. If not, launch the Add New Hardware Wizard by clicking Start ➪ Settings ➪ Control Panel and double-clicking the Add/Remove Hardware icon.

6. Click Next to kick off the wizard. At the next dialog box, make sure the Add/Troubleshoot a device radio button is selected and click Next.

7. There is plenty of disk work and waiting around as Windows goes looking for the new device. After a few moments, a dialog box should announce that it has found your device. Click Next to install it.

8. Windows asks if you want to search for a driver (lower radio button) or select from a list of products (upper radio button). You know the hardware, so select it from the list. Click Next.

9. You'll probably see your modem model displayed in the window, indicating that Windows 2000 found a default driver. But the CD-ROM or diskettes that came with your modem probably has a more recent driver than those on the Windows 2000 CD-ROM. Insert the media and then click Have Disk to use the drivers that came with the modem itself.

10. Click the Browse button at the next dialog box to go to the drive (probably D:\ or higher letter assignment for CD-ROM based installations) and assign the proper .INF file. Click OK, then click Next to proceed with the install.

11. Once installed, you should be able to use your modem. Close the dialog box.

Manual installation

If Windows fails to find your modem, you likely have a device that is not working or is not supported by Windows 2000. You can try to manually install the device. In some cases, this will allow Windows to detect the device and work normally. In many instances, however, you'll find that Windows either won't work with the device or there is some problem with the port assignment or cable that prevents the modem and your PC from communicating.

To manually install a modem, do the following:

1. Repeat Steps 1 through 5 in the preceding section.

2. Click the radio button labeled No, I want to select the hardware from a list, and then click Next.

3. In Hardware types, click Modems and click the Next button.

4. Select your modem maker in the Manufacturers scrolling list box, and select the modem model in the Modem scrolling list box. Click Next.

5. If you are installing drivers from provided disks, click the Have Disk button and navigate to the .INF file, click OK, and then click Next to kick off the install.

In some cases, a misassigned COM port may be the culprit. To manually set the COM port for the modem, open the Phone and Modems Options item in the Control Panel, click the Modems tab, and then click Properties. Click the Advanced tab and then click Advanced Port Settings. Now enter the port number you want to assign in the Com Port Number control. If you don't see this control, your modem doesn't support a change.

Is this thing working?

I've been using Windows 95, Windows 98, and NT 4.0 for as long as they've been around. And during that time, I've been well trained to seek out my modem settings in the Windows Control Panel. But with Windows 2000, the comforting Modem icon is gone. Where do you turn?

Look in the Control Panel again, closely. You see an icon called Phone and Modem Options. That's the ticket. To kick off a quick test, do the following:

1. Double-click the Phone and Modem Options icon to see a dialog box with three tabs, General, Modems, and Advanced. Click the Modems tab.

2. You now see a dialog box listing your installed modems (in most cases, just one device), and the COM port each modem is attached to. Select the modem item you want to test and click the Properties button.

3. In the dialog box that appears, click the Diagnostics tab. Here you can actively test the modem and see if the PC and modem are talking to each other.

4. Click the Query Modem button. This action sends a series of AT commands to the modem.

Note   AT commands is short for Attention commands. AT commands are used to automatically configure modem behavior before a session. For example, your system can send an AT command string that tells the modem to pick up the line on the first ring or to wait for a dial tone before dialing out. Vendors typically use their own specific AT command sets, so it is important that Windows 2000 has properly identified your modem. Otherwise, these AT commands may not be recognized.

Device Manager listens in as the PC sends data to the modem and determines how the modem responds. A dialog box pops up telling you to wait while the test completes.

If you have good interaction, a bunch of cryptic entries appear in the lower window, as shown in Figure 11-2. The Command column shows the specific AT instruction the system has sent to the modem, while the Response column displays the result from the modem. Some of the commands may come up with entries such as COMMAND NOT SUPPORTED. Don't panic, it probably means your modem doesn't recognize certain, rarely used AT commands.

Usually, if something is wrong, your modem won't respond at all, and an error message tells you as much. If you don't get this error message, scroll through the lower window to view the results. If you see responses such as OK, your modem make and model, and other details, you are in like Flynn, and it's time to set up a dial-up session.

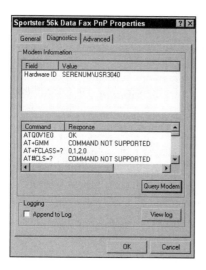

Figure 11-2: If you see a series of AT codes and other text in the Response window, you and your modem are in business.

If the modem failed to respond, you face some troubleshooting. Among the most prevalent causes of a failed diagnostic run are the following:

✦ The modem is not properly configured for available system resources.

✦ An improper driver has been assigned to the hardware.

✦ The modem has not been turned on.

✦ The connecting cable is loose or unattached.

✦ There is a physical fault with the modem or cable. For example, you may have the wrong cable type installed, such as a null modem cable rather than a serial modem cable.

If you find yourself struggling to get the modem to work, it's time for you to pay a visit to the section "Troubleshooting Modems," later in this chapter.

Note   Another way to get to these same, and a few additional, modem controls is through the Device Manager. The problem is, Microsoft has moved this most useful of resources (I place that decision in the "what were they thinking?" department.) To get to the Device Manager, click Start ➪ Settings ➪ Control Panel and double-click the System icon. Then click the Hardware tab and finally (finally!) click the Device Manager button.

Tip   Get to Device Manager fast with this shortcut. Right-click the My Computer icon on the desktop, click Manage from the context menu, and then click the Device Manager item in the left pane of the Computer Management dialog box. There you are!

OK, *there's* the modem icon, shown in Figure 11-3. Click the plus sign (+) to see the specific device and then double-click the device item to get at the Properties dialog box. You should see five or six tabs: General, Modem, Diagnostics, Advanced, Driver, and in some cases, Resources. Three of these, General, Driver, and (optionally) Resources, offer driver-specific information and services that are not available through the Phone and Modem Options icon on the Control Panel.

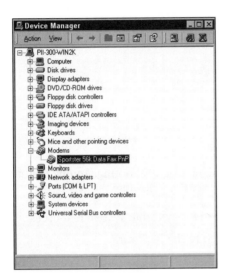

Figure 11-3: The Modems entry in the Device Manager may be a chore to get to, but the payoff comes in the form of additional tools in the device Properties dialog box.

Support for Fast Connections

The last 12 months or so have been incredibly important for online access. Every day, more and more people connect to the Internet using fast and affordable digital connections. Cable modem access, digital subscriber line (DSL) service, and satellite-based access are all growing more popular.

The problem is, the digital picture is still murky. In some places, consumers can choose from two or more different service providers or technologies, while the next town may have access to only slow analog modem service (just ask me, I know).

The first thing you need to do is understand your options. In broad terms, the world falls into two camps: those with digital access and those without. The most prevalent connection types are:

✦ Analog modems

✦ ISDN (Integrated Services Digital Network)

✦ ADSL (Asymmetric Digital Subscriber Line)

✦ Satellite

✦ T1

Figure 11-4 gives you a quick idea of the performance differences among these connection types.

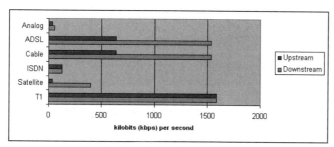

Figure 11-4: Speed thrills: upstream and downstream data rates compared.

Note   What are upstream and downstream data rates? *Upstream* refers to the bandwidth available for data moving from your network device to the network. *Downstream* refers to data coming from the network to your device.

As you can see, going digital can pay a hefty benefit when it comes to Internet access. A typical ADSL modem setup can pump nearly 20 times more data upstream than can the fastest analog modem. The downstream disparity is higher still, at more than 27 times faster. Expect to pay more for digital options — particularly for adapter hardware if it is not provided as part of the service.

For example, say you want to download a 22MB file, about the size of a typical Web browser. On an analog 56-Kbps modem, that download would take 54 minutes under ideal conditions (no line noise, little communications overhead such as that encountered with certain protocols). In reality, such a download would probably take 70 minutes or so. That same file, downloaded via cable modem or DSL, would ideally take less than 2 minutes to transfer, assuming you have 1.5 Mbps downstream data rates. Again, in reality that transfer would take 3 minutes or so, but still more than an order of magnitude less time than the analog modem needs.

More than raw data rates come into play, too. Digital connections almost always enjoy more responsive behavior — known as *shorter latency* — than analog modems. The reason: Converting between digital and analog format takes time, and the presence of line noise and other interference often requires bits to be sent several times. So where an analog modem can take a quarter second (250 milliseconds, or 250ms) or more to get a response over the Internet, DSL or other digital connections can perform the same task in less than a tenth of a second (25ms). Initiating a connection is also faster — in fact, DSL is always connected, eliminating the need to dial up at all. Even with ISDN, which does require a connection sequence, the process is much faster, with none of the noisy and time-consuming screeching that modems engage in.

Tip
If you are an avid online game player, a digital connection is well worth your trouble. Gamers playing over low-latency digital connections enjoy an enormous tactical advantage over those connected via analog modem. Digital connections enable you to see the action sooner—sometimes a quarter or half a second sooner—than your analog adversaries. That can add up to a lot of easy frags in games such as Deathmatch Doom or Quake Arena.

Whether or not your local phone, cable, or Internet access provider has gotten around to bringing digital service to your neighborhood, Microsoft has made fast access a part of Windows 2000. Drivers for popular DSL and cable modem devices are included in the operating system, increasing the chances that you can smoothly set up a digital adapter.

Making sense of the options

A discussion of the many Internet access alternatives on the market could easily consume this entire book, and it's easy to see why. While there is one flavor of analog phone service, the digital options are numerous, overlapping, and changing. No fewer than six or seven viable DSL alternatives are available, as well as a slew of additional approaches for low-cost DSL access. ISDN users must puzzle through single or dual Bearer (or B) channel offerings, while cable users contemplate the benefits of hybrid fibre coax and bidirectional access over analog services that force you to use a modem for upstream communications.

I could go on and on, but suffice it to say that the digital access picture in 1999 remains a muddy mess. Personally, I'm guessing it will be 2002 or 2003 before we have a good, solid direction that will pare down competing access options and begin to create a few marketwide standards in North America. Table 11-1 gives you a snapshot comparison of the various options.

Table 11-1		
The Pros and Cons of Comms		
Access type	**Pros**	**Cons**
Analog	Most affordable, universal standard, virtually all ISPs offer modem hookups, 56-Kbps modems sufficient for basic Web browsing and e-mail.	Low data rates, high latencies, and long connect routines make modems a time-consuming option; while analog modems are rated for 56 Kbps, FCC rules limit actual performance to about 52 Kbps to 53 Kbps.

Access type	Pros	Cons
ISDN	Reliable digital connection; fairly rapid logon; good availability in most greater metropolitan areas.	Slow compared to DSL and cable; service is typically quite expensive and installations are usually hair-raising.
ADSL	Fast, always-on digital connection works over existing phone wires in your home (you can even talk and send data at the same time); service can cost as little as $40 with ISP fee included.	Slow rollout by the telcos means limited accessibility, complaints about service blackouts, and botched installations; usually requires that your PC have a network card installed; always-on connection invites snoops and hackers.
Cable modem	Fast, always-on digital connection usually works over existing cable coaxial wires (you may need an upgrade), availability improving quickly, service costs as little as $40 with ISP fee included.	Shared access by those served by the neighborhood distribution point (known in cable parlance as the *head end*) poses two problems: performance degradation as usage increases, and the possibility that others might intercept your Internet packets; cable providers may use external cable modems that require a network card (though USB devices are becoming available), and tales of botched installations abound; always-on connection invites snoops and hackers.
Satellite	Best and only high-speed option in many rural and even suburban areas; one dish can provide Internet access and satellite TV reception.	Requires a modem connect upstream, so uploads are slow; dish must have line of sight to satellite; distance to satellite introduces latency; service and installation are expensive compared to cable or DSL.
T1/T3	The corporate choice; always-on service is equally fast upstream and downstream; suitable for Web hosting and publishing. T3 is used for the most bandwidth-intensive environments, such as for Internet service providers (ISPs) and large companies.	Very expensive, access limited outside of business districts.

Note   Many fast, digital access alternatives require you to install a dedicated network or other adapter into your PC, adding complexity and the potential for hardware conflicts to your list of worries. Fortunately, support for USB is growing among makers of cable modems, DSL adapters, and satellite access providers. Using a USB connection to link to your comm adapter makes a lot of sense, but you should be sure to check that the provider's equipment offers Windows 2000 compatibility. Check the Windows 2000 Hardware Compatibility List (HCL) at www.microsoft.com/hcl and ask your provider.

Fast access checklist

The fact is, nifty digital Internet access technologies are of no use to you if you can't get at them. Readers who live in enlightened areas of the country such as Silicon Valley, Seattle, and the Route 128 loop around Boston crow about the benefits of DSL and cable modem access. But the fact is, many of these areas don't enjoy much competition when it comes to access technologies. An area is likely to have either cable or DSL but rarely both.

In other words, you can do all the research and digging around you want, but the fast access you ultimately pay for is the one that you can actually get. To that end, it pays for you to first make sense of your local market. Call your local phone and cable providers to get an update on their access plans and keep an eye on local coverage regarding deployments. Better yet, if you do business with a local ISP, call them. They are likely to have an up-to-date picture of the emerging access scene.

ISDN

1. Call your local phone company and inquire about ISDN availability, rates, per-minute tariffs, and the incremental cost for using a second Bearer channel, commonly called a B channel. You need to employ two B channels (each of which provide 64 Kbps of bandwidth) to achieve a 128 Kbps data rate.

2. Check with your ISP about ISDN service availability and rates. If your current ISP doesn't offer ISDN, check with a regional or national provider. Depending on where you are, the likelihood of getting ISDN access is quite good.

3. Before you order anything, have the phone company conduct a loop qualification test. This test determines if you are close enough to a phone switch and if your local phone lines are good enough to support ISDN signals.

4. Be prepared to wait. It can take phone companies quite some time to get a technician out to install an ISDN line and set up the new jacks. Installation can also be quite harrowing. You need to know all the nitty-gritty details of your ISDN adapter and of your telephone company's local ISDN switch before you set up.

Note

So how do you get this information? Your phone company should be able to tell you the specific make and model of the switch serving your ISDN line. At that point, you can positively research an ISDN adapter that will work with the telco's switching hardware—in some cases, an ISDN modem may not be able to work with a switch at all! Call the ISDN modem maker for details on the model you are considering. In the worst case, you may find that you must replace a perfectly good ISDN modem because it is incompatible with the telco switch you connect to.

ADSL

1. Call your local phone company and your long-distance carrier to inquire about DSL service availability and rates. You may also need to dig around to find out if a third-party telco has plans to deploy DSL in your area.

2. If DSL service is to be provided, check with the carrier regarding its ISP package. Typically, DSL access comes as a bundle: You get a DSL modem, physical wire and jack installation, and ISP service as part of the deal. That means you likely have to switch ISPs if you want to move to DSL.

3. Again, be prepared to wait. Telephone companies are backed up in their efforts to deploy DSL services, and waits can be as long as three or four months. Once the installation occurs, be prepared for some added complexity because your carrier may need to install a network card in your PC.

4. Consider keeping your ISP as a backup. Reports of service outages and botched installations abound. You might keep your current ISP account and your analog modem for the first two or three months, just in case prolonged outages occur.

5. Be aware of security issues. DSL is an always-on service, which means that your system is always present on the Internet. If someone decides to poke around your PC, and you haven't properly secured your system against intrusion, you could be facing real trouble.

Cable

1. Call your local cable company to inquire about cable modem service availability and rates. Find out if the carrier is offering all-digital, bidirectional service. If not, you may need an analog modem to send upstream data, which greatly reduces the benefit of cable access. If the service does require a modem, you might reconsider and wait until digital cable or DSL arrives.

2. As with DSL, check with the cable carrier regarding the ISP package that is included with the service. You likely have to switch ISPs if you want to move to cable.

3. Inquire about security. Cable systems work by broadcasting packets to all users connected on the neighborhood head end (much the way Ethernet works). The cable adapter that the carrier provides can filter out packets not bound for other users, but the broadcast model can invite unauthorized

hacking and snooping. The provider should provide hardware that encrypts packets as well as filters that prevent you from seeing packets bound for other destinations. And like DSL, cable is always on, so your system may be more prone to intrusion than on a dial-up connection.

4. And once again, be prepared to wait. Cable companies are also backed up in their efforts to deploy cable modem service, and waits can be as long as three or four months. Once the installation occurs, be prepared for some added complexity because your carrier may need to install a network card in your PC.

5. Consider keeping your ISP as a backup for the first couple months. If you run into problems with your cable Internet access, you can fall back to your dial-up connection quickly.

Satellite

1. DirecPC is the only satellite Internet access game in town, but you can order it from a wide range of stores and distributors. Shop around to find the best deal and perhaps pick up a nifty rebate on the cost of the dish. Expect to pay about $200 for the dish, provided you honor a two-year service contract.

2. Before you buy anything, walk outside, face south, and look at what you see. If your south access is blocked by tall trees or buildings, you may be out of luck. The DirecPC satellite sits in geosynchronous orbit about 22,000 miles over Mexico, and your dish requires line-of-sight access to the bird. The further north you are, the tougher it is because the satellite rides closer to the horizon. The most direct access and the strongest signal strength are in Texas and surrounding areas.

3. Consider getting an installer to mount and point the dish. Finding the satellite can be a difficult task — believe me, I've tried — and the DirecPC installation kit offers only rudimentary tools for getting the task done. Have a qualified DirecPC or DirecTV installer do the task for $100 or $200 (you may be able to get this paid for in the purchase) unless you are a hardy do-it-yourself type.

4. DirecPC offers ISP service to simplify matters, but you should consider your experience with your existing ISP. You can use the service while dialing into a third-party ISP.

T1 and T3

T1 and T3 service is for professionals. Corporate and branch offices, low-traffic ISPs, and other users of bandwidth all fall into the T1 range. Larger companies and ISPs may need the additional bandwidth of a dedicated T3 line. An entire network of users can typically share a single T1 or T3 line, or the line might be used to connect a Web server to the Internet. In any case, T1 or T3 service is not something you are likely to draw into your home office.

T1 and T3 service can be arranged through consultants who specialize in communications deployments for businesses. One thing is for sure: Expect to pay big bucks for a T1 line. Monthly fees range from $800 to $2,000, depending on your location and usage. T3 service is higher still, ranging up to $10,000 per month

 Cross-Reference For more on setting up TCP/IP settings for Internet dial-up sessions, see Chapter 12.

TCP/IP: A Primer

Anyone who has been around personal computers for more than, say, four or five years knows that communications were once a lot harder than it is today. Then, there was no unifying Internet, with its global networking protocol, to serve as a common target for all applications and devices. Users trying to dial into other computers, networks, or bulletin board services had to often glean crucial information before a connection could be attempted.

What protocol does the target system use? Kermit, X-Modem, Y-Modem? Users even had to go so far as to noodle with physical modem settings. Parity and stop bits had to be aligned with those of the target system or network, for example. The result was that you had even more variables at work than you do today.

Today the common thread is the Transmission Control Protocol/Internet Protocol, better known as TCP/IP. TCP/IP is the root of the Internet, and is the protocol that allows disparate systems, networks, and devices to talk to each other on a global scale. Under TCP/IP, all you need to connect to another machine over the Internet is the IP address of the target.

What is an IP address? It is a (typically) unique numerical sequence that looks like this: 132.198.101.60. Enter this sequence in your browser's address bar while connected to the Internet, and you'll end up at the home page for the University of Vermont. Of course, you can also type http://www.uvm.edu to get to the same place — dedicated servers on the Internet take alphabetic addresses and resolve them into the source numerical addresses.

TCP/IP-enabled devices transact data in a common format called *IP packets*, which contain both data and information about the data (this so-called header information helps devices route and work with packets). Because TCP/IP provides a common way for devices to talk, to manage data transactions, and to address each other, it becomes reasonably easy to connect systems.

With Windows 2000, that prospect is easier still, because the operating system comes with TCP/IP network drivers preconfigured. All you need to do to get on the Internet is gather network information provided to you by your ISP or network administrator. These include one or two IP addresses for the target server(s), possibly a dial-up phone number, and a DNS server IP address to resolve your alphabetic URLs into numeric format. Once these are entered into the dial-up networking facility of Windows 2000, you are good to go.

Exploring Windows Modem Facility

Modems can be persnickety beasts, in part because many users tend to noodle with them so much. Consider the many reasons to mess with your existing modem settings:

✦ The transition from proprietary 56-Kbps technologies (remember x2 versus k56Flex?) to the international v.90 standard required modem firmware and driver updates.

✦ The explosion of new area codes means that many users must change their dialing rules to reflect new local area codes.

✦ Increased Internet usage has motivated many a modem upgrade as users seek faster access.

✦ Mobile users must constantly tweak modem settings to reflect their current location and calling card information.

Perform any of these activities, and you may find yourself wandering around the modem management facilities of Windows 2000. These dialog boxes enable you to do everything from changing dialing rules and phone card numbers to setting the modem speaker volume and creating custom initialization scripts.

As discussed earlier, there are two ways to get to the modem facilities:

✦ Click Start ⇨ Settings ⇨ Control Panel ⇨ Phone and Modem Options.

✦ Click Start ⇨ Settings ⇨ Control Panel ⇨ System, then click the Hardware tab, and click the Device Manager button. Click the + sign next to the Modem item and then double-click the specific device.

While it's quicker to go through the Phone and Modem Options icon in the Control Panel, the Device Manager affords a wider range of controls. Specifically, driver and some troubleshooting dialog boxes are in the Device Manager that for some reason are omitted in the Phone and Modem Options area.

General tab

Access the Modem Properties dialog box from the Windows 2000 Device Manager, and by default you end up on the General page, shown in Figure 11-5. This page displays some useful information, including the device model and manufacturer and the COM port or other resource the device uses. Also, the Device status text box displays a message telling you whether or not the selected modem is working properly—useful for starting troubleshooting efforts.

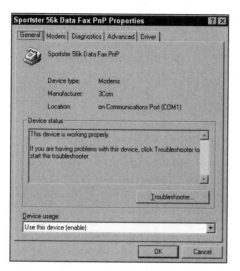

Figure 11-5: The Device Manager Modem Properties dialog box offers access to the Modem Troubleshooter and allows you to disable the modem — features not found in the Control Panel version of the modem facility.

Enabling and disabling modems

The Device usage drop-down list control makes it easy to switch among multiple installed devices, by letting you enable and disable the selected device. For example, you may have two external modems: a slower one that stays connected to your desktop PC all the time and a faster 56-Kbps model that you take with you for your notebook when you travel. Keeping the older modem around makes it possible to dial into your desktop from the road or enables your family to connect while you are gone. Here's how it works.

When you are working at home, you can turn off the slower modem by double-clicking the device in Device Manager and selecting Do not use this device (disable) from the Device usage drop-down list. Click OK, and your system ignores the modem and frees up its resources. Now plug in the faster 56-Kbps modem that goes with you on your travels, open its Properties page from the Device Manager, and select Use this device (enable) from the Device usage drop-down list control.

Next time you have to hit the road, reverse the process. Select the currently active 56-Kbps modem from the Device Manager and disable it from the Device usage control. Remove the hardware and plug in the old 28.8 Kbps modem. Then just enable the old modem from its Properties dialog box.

Using the troubleshooter

The other prominent feature of the General tab is the Troubleshooter button. Click this button, and Windows 2000 launches its HTML-based Help system. Oddly, the Hardware Troubleshooter pane on the right lacks context (the left pane contains the usual tabbed access to Contents, Index, and Search facilities). You need to select the radio button labeled Windows 2000 doesn't detect my modem from the list and then click the Next button.

At this point, you enter the troubleshooter's branching question-and-answer scheme. The first question: Does Windows 2000 recognize your COM port? Helpful prompts tell you how to figure out which COM port your modem uses, and there's even a quick link to the Device Manager (much, much faster than having to dig for this resource through the Start button).

At the bottom, you tell the troubleshooter whether or not your COM port appears to be working, or you can choose to skip the first question. Once you've clicked the appropriate radio button, click Next to proceed. Based on your response, you get a different troubleshooter window. By following the Troubleshooter, you can often avoid spending hours struggling with common or silly issues — such as forgetting to connect the device.

The Troubleshooter may help a lot of novice users, but it is no miracle worker. All too often, you get the terse statement "This troubleshooter is unable to solve your problem." In other words, you're on your own. For more on troubleshooting, see the section "Troubleshooting Modems," later in this chapter.

Modem tab

The sparsely populated Modem tab gives you a few useful tweaks. Among them are the following:

✦ Speaker volume

✦ Maximum port speed

✦ Dial control

Adjusting speaker volume

The Speaker volume slider bar enables you to adjust how loud the dialing, ringing, and modem screeching sounds are when you're connecting. These noises are useful when you're trying to figure out what might be wrong when connections fail. Hearing that distinctive busy signal tone can answer a lot of questions, for example.

But modem connections are also obnoxiously noisy, particularly if you work in an office or open area of the house. In general, I keep my Speaker volume slider set to on because I work in a private space. But if the noise is a concern — if I need to dial up during a conferencing call, for example — I can quickly move the slider to the Off position, click OK, and silently dial up.

Setting port speeds

The Maximum Port Speed drop-down list control is used to limit the speed at which programs can send data to the modem. You won't usually have to adjust this value because it gets set by default to a rate of 115,200 bits per second, about four times greater than your modem's top upload speed. Why the disparity? Most modems offer hardware compression, which means they can send more raw data over the line than the indicated data rates would make you think.

> **Note** If you are having trouble with the modem, you might try scaling down the maximum port speed from 115,200 bits per second to 57,600 bits per second. This may slow your transfers a bit but may also eliminate buffer overruns that corrupt transfers or force programs to resend data.

Detecting dial tones

By default, Windows 2000 makes your modem wait for a dial tone before it begins dialing. This is done to avoid having your modem run off a long string of tones while somebody else is trying to talk on the phone line. It's also useful to avoid misdials that can occur when a dial tone is slow to come up.

There are situations when dial tone detection is not a good thing, however. For example, if you use your phone company's call-waiting feature, you may get nonstandard dial tones when messages are waiting. My service uses a three-pulse stutter before the normal dial tone begins. While that's enough to tell me when messages are waiting, it confuses my modem when it is set to wait for a dial tone before dialing.

If you run across this problem, turn the feature off by deactivating the checkbox labeled Wait for dial tone before dialing. Conversely, if your kids are stomping on your phone conversations with modem dial-ups, activate that checkbox.

Dealing with diagnostics

I've already talked about the useful diagnostics feature in the modem Properties dialog box. Here I look a little bit deeper at the results produced by the modem query. When you click the Query Modem button, Windows sends a series of commands to the modem, and the device responds. By viewing the response, you can tell whether or not the modem is working.

> **Note** Your modem must be idle to run the query. If you are online, first hang up the connection and then perform the diagnostic.

The following commands are sent in the modem query:

✦ ATQ0V1E0: Initialize query.

✦ AT+GMM: Identify the modem model. Don't be surprised if you get a COMMAND NOT SUPPORTED here; not all models recognize this command.

✦ AT+FCLASS=?: Show the classes of fax communications supported by the modem.

✦ AT#CLS=?: Indicate support for the Rockwell voice command set. Again, this command is not always supported.

✦ ATIn: Display model information, port speed, results from a checksum test, and other data.

Typically, if there is a problem with the sent command, you will see a response of COMMAND NOT SUPPORTED appear in the lower window in the Modem Information area. Otherwise, you will see different responses based on the query. For example, AT+FCLASS=? might return a result of Class 1, which means the model complies with Class 1 fax standards and will work with the vast majority of standalone fax machines on the market.

In addition, the Diagnostics page includes a nice logging feature, which keeps a text-based history of modem activity. This resource can be a huge help when you're trying to hunt down mysterious or intermittent problems. You will be able to sift through this text-based file to find suspect error messages that may lie at the root of the problem.

By default, Windows 2000 Professional writes modem activities to a log file. However, it overwrites the previous log file for each session. If you want to keep a running history of modem happenings, activate the Append to Log checkbox. Now, whenever your modem engages in activity, the system adds to the existing log file. If you keep the checkbox clear, Windows 2000 Professional starts a new log file for the current session, overwriting the previous session information.

Note   Why use the append option? If you are suffering from infrequent but recurring modem problems, a running log file can prove a useful record. Such a complete record enables you to compare behaviors over days and weeks, something that is not possible in the default setting. Just be aware the log file will grow and grow over time. You may want to pare it down occasionally by unchecking the Append to Log checkbox. This will cause Windows 2000 to overwrite the existing (and very large) log file with the information produced in the most recent session.

To read the log file, click the View log button. Windows 2000 opens Notepad with the MODEMLOG_MODEMNAME.TXT file. The file shows driver resources used by the modem and AT command interactions between the PC and modem. There is also a sampling of modem data rates and bytes transferred, which is updated every two minutes. The log file resides in your Windows 2000 home directory, so it is easy to find using Windows Explorer as well.

Get advanced

The Advanced tab is surprisingly sparse, but it provides access to key capabilities. The first thing you see is the Extra initialization commands text box. Here, you can enter AT command codes tailored for your specific modem model or usage. Entries here are sent to the modem after all other standard AT commands, which means you can override default commands using this text box. You need to consult your modem documentation for available command customizations and take care that you don't disable the modem by sending incorrect commands. Modem-specific commands can be used to set up one-time modem behaviors — for example, disabling a pickup on ring setting.

There's more to keep you busy behind the Change Default Preferences button. Click it, and you see two tabs: General and Advanced. The General tab enables you to control automatic disconnects and connection preferences, while Advanced handles some of the obscure parity and stop bit settings that were so important in the long-lost BBS days of Kermit and X protocol transfers.

Setting call preferences

The General tab includes the Call preferences area where you can tell your modem whether and when to disconnect active connections or give up on botched dial-ins. These features can help free up your phone line and reduce connect time charges.

The auto-disconnect facility prevents having a modem accidentally on-hook overnight because it disconnects after a specified period of inactivity. Click the Disconnect a call if idle for more than checkbox so that a check appears. The text box to the right goes active. Now enter the number of minutes you want Windows 2000 to wait before it ends a connection.

Remember, this is idle time I'm talking about here. If you are actively browsing, accessing e-mail, or downloading a large file, that time does not count. Disconnection occurs only after the defined period of inactivity.

The second item cancels a dial-up attempt if a connection is not successfully made within the number of seconds indicated. You can use your personal experience with your ISP to judge how long that figure should be. By shortening the default 60-second setting to 30 seconds, you can save a lot of time by giving up on lost-cause dial-ups.

Setting connection preferences

Next comes the Data Connection Preference area where you have four drop-down list controls: Port speed, Data Protocol, Compression, and Flow control. Figure 11-6 shows the available options in this page.

The Port speed control probably looks familiar because you just saw a similar entry on the Modem tab of the modem Properties dialog box. And in fact, if you change the Maximum Port Speed entry on the Modem tab, this setting changes too. As with that other control, this one is useful for dealing with buffer overruns that can occur when programs send data to your modem too quickly.

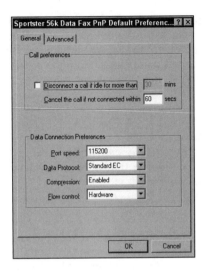

Figure 11-6: Having trouble connecting? You can tailor modem operation to meet specific needs. Just be careful. Most of the world works with the default values displayed here.

The Data Protocol control enables you to select from Standard EC (error correction), Disabled, and Forced EC. You should use Standard EC unless you think the error correction setting is causing timeouts or incompatible connections with the other end. Why? The correcting code prevents confusion that can be caused when bits get jumbled by line noise and interference. While the error-correcting code adds a little overhead to transactions, it can save a lot of hassles.

The Standard EC setting means that your modem and the other modem negotiate the optimal correction method. If you want to limit correction to the v.42 method — the most advanced available — select Forced EC from the list. Finally, selecting Disabled can help you connect more quickly, because protocol negotiation is eliminated, but likely may reduce connection reliability.

Compression comes in two flavors: enabled and disabled. By default, hardware compression is enabled, helping greatly speed the transfer of compressible files such as text, HTML, word processing documents, spreadsheets, and the like. However, modem compression is entirely redundant for previously compressed fare such as GIF and JPEG files, AVI and MPEG movies, or ZIP files. And in fact, compression adds overhead to these compressed file types because it takes time (and sometimes a few extra bits) to apply compression atop these already squeezed file types.

Still, most users should keep the Compression control set on Enabled to ensure optimal transfer rates. Here's the exception: your transfer software is already compressing files or all you send are compressed file types (such as ZIP, GIF, and JPEG files).

Finally, Flow control determines how the flow of data between your PC and the modem is handled. In most cases, flow control is handled in hardware, which is to say, by your modem. If hardware flow control is not supported by your modem (you should check the modem manuals for this information), select Xon/Xoff from the drop-down list box. Because Xon/Xoff may not work with some applications, you may need to use the None option to disable flow control completely.

Changing hardware settings

Click the Advanced tab. Now you see the final stop behind the Change Default Settings button, the Hardware Settings area. Here you find four drop-down list controls: Data bits, Parity, Stop bits, and Modulation. Figure 11-7 shows the Advanced sheet with a typical configuration.

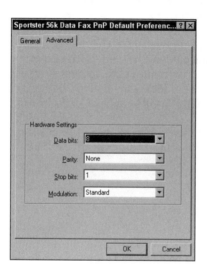

Figure 11-7: Want to talk with the rest of the world? Your best bet is to set Data bits to 8, Parity to None, Stop bits to 1, and Modulation to Standard.

In most cases, your Data bits entry should be set to 8 because this setting is the most common. The value defines how many bits of information are assigned to each character transferred over the wire. In order for transfers to occur, both sides of the connection must share the same data bit setting. In some cases, a BBS might require you to set this value to 7.

The Parity value determines how your modem handles error checking. In most cases, None should be selected here because more sophisticated error-correcting protocols — such as v.42, MNP4, and MNP3 — are now used to verify the integrity of incoming and outgoing data. As is the case with the Data bit setting, both parties must share the same Parity value for connections to work.

The Parity drop-down list contains several selections:

✦ **Even:** Sets parity bit to 0 or 1 so that the resulting number of 1 bits in the packet is always even.

✦ **Odd:** Sets parity bit to 0 or 1 so that the resulting number of 1 bits in the packet is always odd.

✦ **None:** No parity bit used.

✦ **Mark:** Sets the parity bit to 1 at all times.

✦ **Space:** Sets the parity bit to 0 at all times.

Stop bits are used as data mile markers, telling the other side when a complete byte of data has been set. This value is virtually always set to 1; however, some older protocols may require using more than 1 stop bit.

Finally, Modulation determines how your modem translates the digital 1s and 0s of your PC into analog tones that other modems can understand. Both computers must use the same modulation type in order to communicate. In almost all cases, Standard is the setting you want to use. Older modems may use the Bell protocol, while some modems may use the proprietary HST protocol from US Robotics.

Note   Modulation is, in fact, where modems got their name. Modem is simply short for the rather cumbersome phrase *modulate-demodulate*, which describes how modems turn bits into tones and tones into bits.

Doing drivers

The Driver page of the modem Properties dialog box resembles the driver pages of most other devices. The top of the dialog box shows some basic information such as who provided the driver, the date the driver was created and its version, and information about a digital signature, if present. The digital signature indicates whether or not Microsoft has formally tested the software in its labs, which should provide an extra level of assurance regarding reliability.

You can dig a little further by clicking the Driver Details button, which brings up a dialog box listing the modem driver files. You typically see only one or two files in this dialog box.

The Uninstall button is fairly self-explanatory. It removes the driver software — and therefore, the modem — from your system. You might consider removing the driver if you want to install a new one and seem to be having trouble getting the old driver to step aside. You will generally have to reboot after this operation to ensure that the driver is no longer part of your system configuration.

The Update Driver button is a useful facility for any device. That said, modem drivers don't tend to change much. Most modems now use the internationally accepted v.90 protocol for moving data at speeds as high as 56 Kbps. Still, clicking this button brings up the Windows Upgrade Device Driver Wizard that you can use to search for drivers on disk drives or on the Internet.

Creating Dialing Rules

Any veteran notebook user can tell you about the tyranny of dialing rules. As you hopscotch from area code to area code, dialing from phones that require an ever-changing set of prefixes for an outside line, you need to change the modem settings in Windows. Windows 2000 Professional eases things a bit with its revamped Dialing Rules interface. In this section, I step you through the creation and management of different dialing sessions.

You won't find the Dialing Rules interface under the Device Manager's Modem Properties dialog box. You need to go back to the Control Panel to open the Phone and Modem Options icon. Get ready to dive right into the process of rule making.

Setting dialing behaviors

To create a new dialing rule, do the following:

1. Click Start ➪ Settings ➪ Control Panel and double-click the Phone and Modem Options icon.

2. On the Dialing Rules tab of the Properties dialog box, click the New button.

3. Enter a name for this session in the Location name text box. Because this is first session, call it something really creative such as Default.

4. Select the item that applies to you in the Country/region drop-down list box and then enter your local prefix in the Area code box.

5. Set up modem dialing behavior in the Dialing rules area. The two text boxes supply prefixes used to get an outside line — common in offices and hotel rooms. In the top box, enter the prefix for local calls (typically those within your area code, though there are exceptions, as you learn very soon).

6. In the lower text box, enter the prefix used to get an outside line for a long-distance call. Hotels, in particular, use different prefixes.

7. If you have call-waiting on your line, check the box to disable it (the tones this service produce can knock off a connection). Then select the prefix that your local phone company uses to disable call-waiting. If the entry you need is not in the drop-down list, you can enter your own directly by clicking in the box and typing.

8. Finally, select the radio button to have the modem dial using Tone (typical) or Pulse (rare in most connected areas). Of course, Tone is the better choice in all cases.

Okay, that wasn't so hard. You can review the results of your new calling session entry in Figure 11-8.

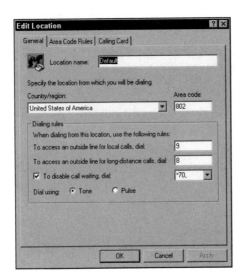

Figure 11-8: The Windows 2000 Dialing Rules resource enables you to set area codes, dial prefixes, and call-waiting.

Click Apply so that you don't accidentally lose all your changes by clicking the Cancel button or the Esc key later in the setup process.

Setting area code rules

Now go to the next tab, Area Code Rules, where you can tell Windows when to treat numbers within the local area code as long distance (commonly known as *local long distance*).

1. Click the Area Code Rules tab and click the New button.

2. In the dialog box that appears, enter the area code in the Area code text box.

3. In this case, assign specific prefixes. Click the second radio button in the Prefixes area. The Add button goes active. Click it.

Note   In the United States, the prefix is the first three digits of a local telephone number. In the number 802-555-4321, 555 is the prefix.

4. In the Add Prefix dialog box, enter the phone number prefix you want to single out and click OK.

5. Now tell Windows what to do. Check the Dial checkbox to have the modem dial a 1 (or other selectable) number before dialing phone numbers starting with the identified prefix.

6. If necessary, click the Include the area code checkbox. This tells Windows to dial the area code — even though the area code is the same as yours — before dialing the number.

7. You can see the results of your work in Figure 11-9. Click OK to make the changes take effect.

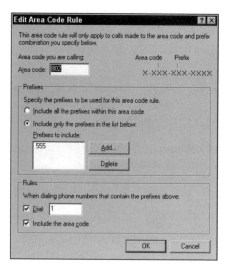

Figure 11-9: My home state of Vermont has only one area code (still!). That means a lot of calls within my area code are actually long distance. Fortunately, with Windows 2000, I can create local long-distance dialing rules based on phone number prefix.

Dealing with calling cards

Perhaps the most important and most frequently used dialing rules feature among notebook users is the Calling Card facility. This tab on the New Location dialog box makes Windows automatically dial long-distance numbers in such a way that the calls are billed to your calling card.

Note

The Calling Card feature is a real lifesaver when you need to call out from a hotel room. As travelers know, virtually all hotels attach brutal surcharges to long-distance calls you place directly to the other party. These charges can run $1 per minute or more. To avoid being robbed — and it is robbery we are talking about — you need to master this feature before you hit the road.

If you primarily use your PC to dial into your ISP, it's likely that the vast majority of your calls are local. But when you need to access your ISP or your desktop PC from a notebook on the road, the calling card feature comes in handy indeed. And if you use Windows 2000's convenient fax applet (more on that in Chapter 5), the capability to charge to a calling card might be useful as well.

Creating calling cards from the default list

There are two types of calling cards in Windows 2000: those that you can select from a list, and those that you must create yourself. Windows 2000 offers nearly 25 preset calling card entries, complete with access numbers for long-distance and international calls, and preset dialing sequences to automate the entire dialing sequence.

Here's how to set up a new calling card that appears in Windows 2000's default list:

1. Click the Calling Card tab.

2. From the Card Types scrolling list box, click the card type and description that match your own. The access number(s) appears in the Access phone number for area.

3. Enter your card's account number in the Account number text box.

4. Enter your PIN in the Personal ID Number text box. The dialog box now looks like the one in Figure 11-10.

5. Click OK or Apply to make the new card active.

When you dial an outside line, your modem uses the credit card information to conduct long-distance calls.

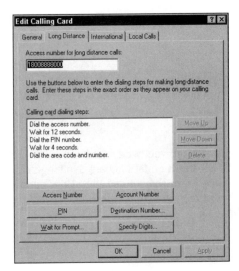

Figure 11-10: In most cases, you can select your calling card from the Card Types scrolling list box.

Creating new calling cards from scratch

But what if your calling card isn't on this long and distinguished list? Fortunately, you can create custom calling card entries that make it possible to mix and match any combination of access numbers, PINs, account numbers, and other variables.

Here's how to create a new calling card entry:

1. Click the Calling Card tab and then click the New button.

2. On the General tab, enter a name for the calling card in the Calling card name text box; then enter your card's account number and PIN in the two boxes below.

3. Some cards may provide different access numbers and other information for international, local, and long-distance calls. Start by clicking the Long Distance tab.

4. In the Long distance calls access number box, enter the access number for normal long-distance calls.

5. In the Calling card dialing steps box, shown in Figure 11-11, use the buttons to construct the automatic actions that go into placing a custom credit card call. Click the buttons under the display window to make the items appear in the Calling card dialing steps box in the order that they need to occur. Use the Wait for Prompt button to have the dial sequence wait for a defined period or for a voice message before moving to the next activity.

6. Use the Move Up and Move Down buttons to the right to juggle the order of actions so that they are set as desired. The Delete button gets rid of a selected action.

7. Click Apply to make the changes take effect.

8. Next click the International tab.

9. You likely have a separate International access number (if you have one at all), so enter it in the International calls access number text box.

10. Repeat step 5, making any changes in the order or content as necessary. Be sure to click the Specify Digits button and enter 011 in the text box so that the dial sequence accesses an international line. This entry (Dial 001) should appear immediately after the initial Dial the access number entry in the Calling card dialing steps list box. When you click the Destination Number button, be sure that the Dial the country code checkbox is checked, as shown in Figure 11-12.

11. Click Apply again.

12. If you need to use a calling card for local calls, click the Local Calls tab now.

13. Once again, enter an access number in the Access number for local calls text box.

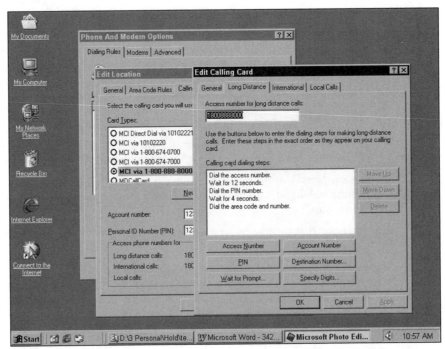

Figure 11-11: You need to make sure the actions in the Calling card dialing steps list box are properly timed and set in the correct sequence. Otherwise, your calls won't go through.

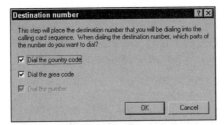

Figure 11-12: Going international? Be sure you set your calling card dialing rule to dial the destination country code.

14. Repeat the steps in step 5. When you click the Destination Number button, be sure that the Dial the country code and Dial the area code checkboxes are left blank.

15. Click OK to return to the base Calling Card page. Scroll down the Card Types list to see your fully customized calling card entry in the scrolling list box, as shown in Figure 11-13.

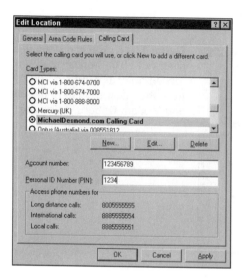

Figure 11-13: There's my custom calling card entry, complete with long-distance, international, and local dialing number entries.

Don't be surprised if you have some trouble getting a calling card connection to work at first. It can take a little tweaking to get the right order, timing, and prompt sequences down. After you've created a new setting, be sure to take a trial run to see if you are able to dial through. Set the speaker modem so that you can hear all the dialing rings, voice prompts, and tones. That way you can tell where any problems occur and tweak your calling card script to match.

TAPI Dancing

You can add a number of drivers and services to your modem settings. These include Telephony Application Programming Interface (TAPI) services that are used by applications to work with telephony and network services. Windows Phone Dialer, for example, uses TAPI to dial numbers, answer incoming calls, and route telephone calls. A sales and contact management application might also use TAPI to automatically dial a number when you click a contact entry.

Support for TCP/IP means that TAPI-aware applications are able to route data over packet-based networks — useful for events such as video conferencing. For businesses, TAPI enables interoperation with everything from fax machines to corporate PBXs (the dedicated boxes that control in-house phone systems).

You can view Windows 2000's installed TAPI services from the Phone and Modem Options facility. To go there, click Start ➪ Settings ➪ Control Panel and double-click Phone and Modem Options. Click the Advanced tab. You see a list in the Providers text box, shown in Figure 11-14, that features several entries. Some examples are described in the following list.

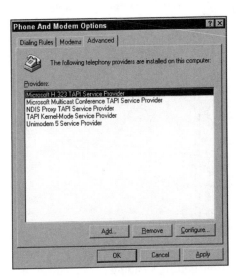

Figure 11-14: You can see a quick snapshot of TAPI drivers and services loaded on your Windows 2000 PC from the Advanced tab of the Phone and Modem Options dialog box.

✦ **Microsoft H.323 TAPI Service Provider:** Enables you to set up firewall and proxy settings for H.323-compliant audio, video, and data conferencing, as shown in Figure 11-15.

The Microsoft H.323 TAPI Service Provider item opens into a dialog box where you can enable proxy and gateway addressing for H.323-compliant conferencing. Check the top checkbox to configure an H.323 gateway, which provides access to shared external ISDN or other switched service lines for conferencing endpoints on the network. Once the box is checked, enter the IP address or server name of the gateway in the text box and click OK.

Activate the lower checkbox to enable calls through a firewall. The H.323 proxy allows users to conduct video, audio, and data conference calls over a network to an outside destination while maintaining network security. Enter the IP address or server name of the proxy server in the text box and click OK to enable this capability.

✦ **Microsoft Multicast Conference TAPI Service Provider:** Enables media broadcast over the network or Internet. When this service is loaded, client PCs on the network can send a video, audio, or data conference to a single server address and have that stream broadcast to all identified addresses on the network.

✦ **NDIS Proxy TAPI Service Provider:** NDIS stands for Network Device Interface Specification and is a Windows driver interface that allows a network card to work with multiple protocols, such as TCP/IP and IPX/SPX. The NDIS Proxy TAPI Service Provider allows client PCs on the network to transfer data, voice, and fax information over multiple protocols.

✦ **TAPI Kernel-Mode Service Provider:** Enables low-level system access for communications processes.

✦ **Unimodem 5 Service Provider:** Unimodem 5 features complete feature parity with Windows 95/98, including full-duplex voice support and enhanced NetMeeting support.

You may see additional providers in this list, depending on the applications and capabilities that have been added to your system. In some cases, you can configure or view information by double-clicking the entry.

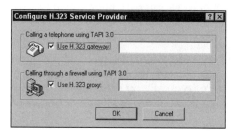

Figure 11-15: H.323 proxies enable you to set up conferencing in a secure environment while gateways make it possible for many networked conferencing stations to share one or more ISDN lines over a LAN.

Troubleshooting Modems

Troubleshooting communications problems can be dirty work. So many variables get involved with connection problems because your modem interacts with the outside world. And it may not be obvious if some form of hardware conflict or a phone line issue is the source of the failure. Is the problem an unplugged wire, a mismatched driver, or perhaps a slow-to-emerge dial tone on your phone? Maybe your ISP is coughing up busy signals.

Here are a few ideas to get you on your way. Of course, you should also consult the Windows 2000 troubleshooter because it steps you through the review process based on your input.

✦ Are all your wires, cords, and cables properly connected?

✦ Is the modem power turned on?

✦ Is your modem installed? Go to Device Manager (Start ➪ Settings ➪ Control Panel) and double-click Modem. Do you see an entry for your modem there? If not, you need to install your modem hardware.

✦ Do you have a recent driver? Check the date in the Driver tab of the Device Manager's Modem Properties dialog box. You may want to update.

✦ Check for COM port conflicts. Double-click the Modem entry in Device Manager, make sure the modem is enabled in the Device usage box, and see what the Device status text box says about its operation. If a specific conflict is noted (say, COM1 is already being used by the mouse), take action to address the issue (by moving the mouse or modem to COM2, for example).

✦ Mystified? Diagnose! If no issue is apparent, click the Diagnostics tab and click the Query Modem button to see if your system and modem interact. If they do, the problem is probably with your dialer, phone line, or ISP.

✦ Check the COM port. Your modem relies on the COM port as the bridge to your system. If it's out, your modem is out. In Device Manager, click the plus sign (+) next to Ports and see if an exclamation point or red X appears in the COM Port entry. If not, your COM port is probably fine. If a character does appear, double-click the item and check the Device status text box to see if Windows identifies a specific conflict or problem. You may also be able to resolve the issue by enabling the COM port in the Device usage drop-down list box.

✦ If there is no COM port entry, you may need to enable the COM port from your system BIOS. You need to consult your system documentation for instructions on entering the BIOS setup application (typically by pressing a key sequence during boot up) and determining what settings are available.

✦ What if the modem is working but tends to lose connections or garble downloads? Try turning down the Maximum Port Speed setting in the Modem tab of the Device Manager Modem properties dialog box. This can eliminate buffer overruns between your PC and modem.

✦ Are you compatible? Make sure your default settings work with those you are dialing into. Click Start ➪ Settings ➪ Control Panel ➪ Phone and Modem Options, click the Modems tab, click Properties, and click Change Default Preferences. Make sure the entries in the Data Connection Preferences area of the General tab and the Hardware Settings area of the Advanced tab, match those of your ISP or other dialing destination.

Summary

For the vast majority of households and even many small businesses and branch offices, modems are the primary way to connect to the Internet. Windows 2000 offers improved modem management and dialing capabilities, as well as welcome diagnostics and interactive help. By learning your way around the Modem Properties dialog box in the Device Manager and the Phone and Modem Options Control Panel facility, you can quickly get online and stay there.

Among the topics we covered here:

✦ A tour of the various digital and analog dial-up and wide-area connectivity options available to Windows 2000 users

✦ A step-by-step guide to setting up and configuring modems under Windows 2000

✦ Weighing modem alternatives, including ISDN, cable modems, DSL, satellite access, and T1 service

✦ Testing modem operation and setting default properties

✦ Creating custom dialing rules and calling card settings

✦ Tips for troubleshooting modem problems

Of course, digital connectivity is a small but growing option in many parts of the United States and the world. Jupiter Communications, a prominent Internet market research firm, estimates that by 2002, about 20 percent of all households will make use of fast, digital connections. Surprisingly, that means that 80 percent of us will be slave to those sluggish, old analog phone lines well into the new millennium. So modem management is not likely to go away anytime soon.

✦   ✦   ✦

Dial-up
Networking

The Internet has proven beyond all doubt that the most compelling thing about computers is their communication capabilities. In fact, desire for Internet access has launched the enormous market for affordable home computers. So-called *free* PCs — systems that users get in exchange for signing a long-term Internet service contract — also owe their existence to the Internet.

The problem is, getting connected to the Internet remains a fairly trying ordeal for most novice- and intermediate-level users. Anyone accustomed to slick graphical user interfaces and helpful step-by-step setup wizards could find themselves hitting a brick wall when it comes to setting up Internet access. Appealing icons and that user-friendly interface give way to cryptic IP addresses, foggy terminology, and laborious entry screens.

Unfortunately, most folks are not ready for the detailed work needed to make Internet connections. This chapter shows you how to master these issues and dial up under Windows 2000.

Setting Up TCP/IP and Network Settings

The Transmission Control Protocol/Internet Protocol (TCP/IP) is the universal language of the Internet. Every server, router, switch, gateway, and client PC on the worldwide network recognizes TCP/IP communications. Heck, even printers, palmtop computers, and some home appliances are becoming fluent in TCP/IP. The result is that tens of millions of computers worldwide are able to share information, trade e-mail, and interoperate. From streaming video broadcasts to low-rent e-mail spam, TCP/IP is the underlying technology that makes it happen.

Windows 2000 can make access to the TCP/IP-driven Internet seem deceptively easy. You click a dial-up icon or simply launch your Web browser, and the system automatically dials into your ISP, creates a connection, and off you go. The reality of the situation is that your system needs to be properly configured to create a smooth dial-up sequence.

ISP basics

Before diving into the step-by-step process of creating a dial-up session, you first need to take a look at the various components that are involved. In addition to a working modem and phone line, here's the laundry list of what you need to make a dial-up Internet connection work:

✦ ISP account and phone number

✦ Login name and password for your ISP

✦ Domain Name Server (DNS) numbers for your ISP

You get the ISP account and phone number from your Internet Service Provider (ISP). When you set up a new account, the ISP provides one or more local phone numbers (known as *points of presence*, or POPs) that you can dial into. You may also be assigned an 800 number for long-distance access. Accounts are typically arranged on a monthly basis, with the fee usually debited directly from a credit card.

In addition, when you set up your account, your ISP provides the information you need to log into your ISP's servers and connect to the Internet. The Domain Name System (DNS) server addresses point your PC to a server (maintained by your ISP) that resolves friendly host names (referred to as *Fully Qualified Domain Names* or FQDNs) into IP addresses. This enables easy text-based references to computers on the Internet that in turn invoke numeric IP addresses (for example, it turns www.amazon.com into 208.216.182.15). For redundancy purposes, you typically get two DNS server IP addresses, one pointing to a primary DNS server and the other pointing to a secondary DNS server. The DNS address itself is an IP address — remember, it's an address to a server on the Internet.

Finally, you probably received an account name and a temporary account password. You need both to log onto your ISP's servers and gain access to the Web. In many cases, you must choose a new password once you've successfully logged on.

Of course, in order to be on the Internet, your PC needs an IP address of its own. Otherwise, there would be no way for servers on the Web to send back the bits that you request. So why haven't I discussed local IP addresses here? Because in almost all cases, your ISP provides this number automatically, using dynamic IP addressing, a common procedure for dial-up ISP accounts.

Note Why not simply use a hard-coded IP address for your PC? The problem is that the world is running out of IP addresses. Even though IP version 4 (the IP version now in use across the Internet) theoretically provides for over four billion individual addresses, addresses are broken into classes to ease routing, reducing the achievable number of addresses. As a result, there are now so many systems, servers, routers, and other devices connected to the public network that there literally aren't enough numbers to serve them all. As a workaround, individual desktop PCs are assigned an IP address only when they log onto the network. When they log off, the IP addresses are recycled and made available for use on other desktop systems. The forthcoming IP version 6 (IPv6) fixes this problem by employing a 128-bit naming scheme. How many potential addresses are we talking about with IPv6? Let me put it this way: For every square inch of Earth's surface, there would be about five available IPv6 addresses. That oughta hold us for now.

This should be enough to get you started . Keep reading for instructions on setting up a dial-up networking (DUN) session under Windows 2000.

Creating a dial-up networking session

If you're used to Windows NT 4.0 or Windows 9x, the news is both good and bad. The good news is that the dial-up networking feature works similarly to the one you are familiar with. The bad news is that Microsoft has made it needlessly difficult to find, and there are enough tweaks to have you fighting old habits for a couple months.

Start the process by finding the dial-up networking feature. Microsoft has tweaked things a bit, combining networking and dial-up settings in a single folder, but this feature remains easy to access. There are two ways to get there:

Click Start ⇨ Programs ⇨ Accessories ⇨ Communications ⇨ Network and Dial-up Connections.

Click Start ⇨ Settings ⇨ Network and Dial-up Connections. The Network and Dial-up Connections window, shown in Figure 12-1, is basically a Windows Explorer window.

1. You're setting up a fresh dial-up connection for your Windows 2000 PC, so double-click the Make New Connection icon.

2. The Network Connection Wizard launches with a welcome dialog box. Click Next.

3. Select the network connection type by clicking the second radio button, labeled Dial-up to the Internet (see Figure 12-2). Click the Next button.

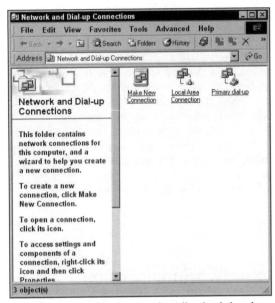

Figure 12-1: Windows 2000 bundles both local area and dial-up networking connections in a single window.

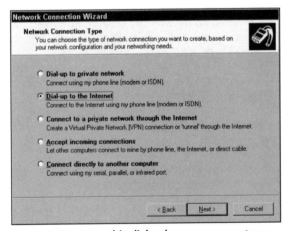

Figure 12-2: From this dialog box, you can set up any number of connections, including the dial-up session you're working on now.

4. Oops. Time for another wizard, this time of the Internet Connection variety, as shown in Figure 12-3. You have three options: Sign up for a new Internet account, transfer an existing account, or set up the connection manually. You're going to be adventurous and click the third radio button to do things by hand. Click Next to proceed.

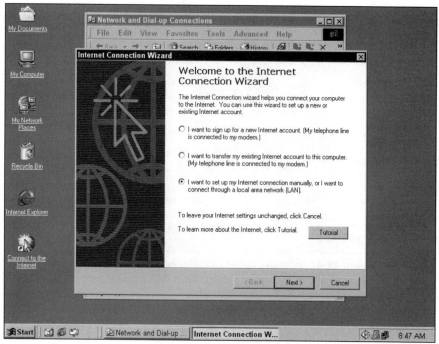

Figure 12-3: You'll need to know a thing or two about how you are connecting to the Internet before you get far into the Connection Wizard.

Note

The Tutorial button shown in Figure 12-3 takes you to a rather slim tutorial that introduces concepts such as the Internet, e-mail, and Internet chat. Unless you've been hiding under a rock for the past five years, you can safely go on without clicking this button.

5. A dialog box asks how you will connect to the Internet, by phone or by network. Assume a modem connection for now. Click the top radio button and click Next.

6. Now you're getting somewhere. Enter the dial-up phone number your ISP provided in the Telephone number text box shown in Figure 12-4. Note that you can enter phone numbers either with or without dividing dashes — the dialer will work with either format. If you've already set up your modem properties, the area code appears. If not, be sure to enter that as well. I suggest you check the Use area code and dialing rules checkbox, as this allows your dial-up sessions to account for long distance calls should you take a notebook on the road, for example.

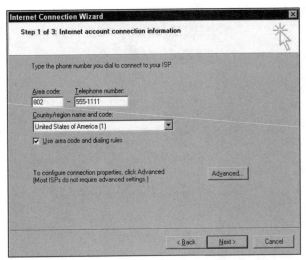

Figure 12-4: Enter the assigned ISP phone number but don't sweat the Advanced button. Most ISPs play by the rules assumed by Windows 2000.

Note

What's behind the Advanced button? A two-tabbed dialog box enables you to select from among connection types (PPP, SLIP, and C-SLIP), of which the Point to Point Protocol (PPP) is by far the most prevalent. PPP is the de facto protocol for Internet connections to ISPs. SLIP, which stands for Serial Line Internet Protocol, is an older technology that was generally used in Unix environments during the early days of dial-up services. Windows 2000 Dial-up client does support SLIP, but I'd advise against using it for general Internet access. You're living in 1992 with that protocol.

The Addresses tab on this dialog box enables you to override dynamic IP addressing as well as automatic Domain Name Server addressing. Of particular interest is the Logon procedure area in the Connection page. More on advanced procedures later.

7. Click Next to see the dialog box where you input your ISP-assigned user name and password. It's pretty straightforward. Enter them in the two text boxes and click Next.

8. Time to give your new connection a name. By default, it's set to read "Connection to *phone number*," where *phone number* is the ISP-assigned number your modem dials. Enter a memorable name, such as "Desktop Dialup" or "EarthLink Dialup," that enables you to differentiate it from other sessions you create later. Click Next.

9. You are now asked to set up an Internet mail account. Make sure the Yes radio button is selected and click Next.

10. Make sure the Create a new Internet mail account radio button is selected and click Next.

Note
It should be no surprise that Windows 2000's dial-up setup routine assumes you'll be using Outlook Express, the e-mail client that comes with the operating system. If you are using Eudora, Pegasus, or other third-party e-mail software, you will need to set up account information directly in those applications.

11. In the Display name text box, enter the name you want to appear on your outgoing e-mails and click Next.

12. Now enter your e-mail address. Your ISP should have assigned you an e-mail address based on your account name. Enter that in the text box. Click Next.

13. Now for some real work. Point Outlook Express at your mail servers by entering the values your ISP gave you here. In the Incoming mail server text box, enter the server name. Next, enter the outgoing server address in the next text box (see Figure 12-5). Click Next.

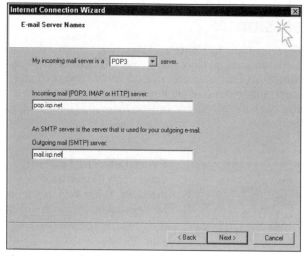

Figure 12-5: The incoming and outgoing e-mail server addresses tell the bundled Outlook Express e-mail client where to look on the Internet for your mail.

14. In the next dialog box, enter your account name in the top text box and your password (typically the same as your Internet logon password) in the bottom text box.

15. Congratulations! You've reached the last dialog box. Click the Finish button to close the dialog box. Note that if you keep the checkbox here checked, your system immediately launches IE5 and tries to jump to the Microsoft Network home page.

If you made a mistake along the way, you will not be able to go back and correct your mistake at this point. You can start over by clicking the Cancel button, but you'll need to reenter all your information. If you click the Cancel button, the Internet Connection Wizard prompts you with a warning dialog box saying that it has not finished setting up your Internet connection and asking if you want to close the Wizard. Click the Yes button to discard all information and start over again. You can also let the wizard finish, open the new connection from the Networking and Dial-up Connections window, and use the Properties pages to correct the mistake.

Once you've completed the wizard, your new connection appears as an icon in the Network and Dial-up Connections window. As you create subsequent connections, additional icons appear to represent them. Double-clicking an icon launches the related connection to connect to the Internet.

Adding advanced options to your new dial-up session

The Advanced button (refer back to Figure 12-4) enables you to access additional options for your dial-up connection. Here you explore this resource in a bit more depth. Assume for purposes of our discussion that you've retraced steps 1 through 6 of the setup procedure, but instead of clicking the Next button after entering your ISP phone number, you click the Advanced button instead. The dialog box pictured in Figure 12-6 appears.

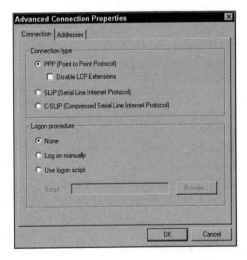

Figure 12-6: The Advanced Connection Properties dialog box is the place to tweak your connections for unusual or specific requirements.

Changing connection types

The Connection tab of the Advanced Connection Properties dialog box (shown in Figure 12-6) enables you to address two issues: the connection type and the logon procedure. By default, connection type is set to Point to Point Protocol (PPP), the dial-up protocol used by virtually all ISPs nowadays.

The Disable LCP Extensions checkbox enables you to turn off requests for Link Control Protocol, which establishes the way data is configured before it is transmitted under PPP. You should keep LCP extensions enabled (control unchecked) in order to ensure that data frames sent over your PPP connection are properly configured.

The SLIP and C-SLIP radio buttons enable you to use variations of the Serial Line Internet Protocol for your dial-up link. SLIP harks back to the early 1990s and is used for remote access to Unix servers. For Internet access today, however, SLIP is a nonstarter and results in much slower performance than PPP (provided, of course, you can even get a SLIP connection with your ISP). The SLIP options are available to ensure compatibility with other platforms and software.

Using scripts

Just below the Connection type area is the Logon procedure area. The radio buttons here enable you to tweak the way the ISP logon step is handled. By default, the top radio button, labeled None, should be selected. This option automatically carries out logon duties and should get you hooked up in most situations.

The Log on manually button forces you to directly input information needed to conduct a logon procedure. These actions are handled automatically when the None radio button is active. The Log on manually option can be useful to troubleshoot logon problems that are not otherwise apparent.

More useful is the last radio button, Use logon script. Click this radio button, and the Script text box at the bottom of the Connection tab goes active. Here you can enter a path and filename of a script file (or use the Browse button to navigate to a script file), a text file that contains commands, expressions, and parameters used to interact with the remote server or ISP.

Why assign scripts to dial-up connections? Actually, in the vast majority of cases, no script is needed at all. ISPs use standard connect procedures that occur seamlessly when using the basic dial-up settings in Windows 2000.

But there are instances where a server or information service may require specific or nonstandard input during the logon process. For example, Microsoft includes with Windows 2000 the script file CIS.SCP to enable PCs to dial into the CompuServe information service using a standard dial-up networking connection. There are likewise several bundled logon scripts with Windows 2000 that enable SLIP connections. Scripts can also be used to automate authentication, such as entering user name and password, during the logon process.

Caution   Scripts are simple text-only files, so they can be relatively easy to create. Just keep in mind that using a script file to automate authentication or other security-related procedures can pose a real threat to your network and servers. Carefully weigh the advantage of scripting authentication steps against the risk posed by unauthenticated server access.

So what exactly goes into a logon script? The text below is the entire contents of the CIS.SCP script file, used to enable Windows 2000 to connect to the CompuServe network through the standard Dial-up Networking facility.

```
;
; This is a script file that demonstrates how
; to establish a PPP connection with Compuserve,
; which requires changing the port settings to
; log in.
;


; Main entry point to script
;
proc main

    ; Set the port settings so we can wait for
    ; non-gibberish text.

    set port databits 7
    set port parity even

    transmit "^M"

    waitfor "Host Name:"
    transmit "CIS^M"

    waitfor "User ID:"
    transmit $USERID, raw
    transmit "/go:pppconnect^M"

    waitfor "Password: "
    transmit $PASSWORD, raw
    transmit "^M"

    waitfor "One moment please..."

    ; Set the port settings back to allow successful
    ; negotiation.

    set port databits 8
    set port parity none

endproc
```

Script files employ a simple syntax that is easy to pick up just by reading scripts. For example, it's easy to see from the preceding script that the semicolon character is used to denote nonactive text—that is, text used for comments, not to be executed by the script.

The set command is used to configure modem settings, and the transmit command is used to send character commands over the line. The waitfor command tells the modem to wait for a specific text-string response before moving to the next operation in the script, enabling script-based interaction with remote sites.

Setting addresses

Click the Addresses tab of the Advanced Connection Properties dialog box to see a couple of options for changing Windows 2000 default ISP address handling, as shown in Figure 12-7. By default, Windows 2000 expects your ISP to provide both an IP address and a DNS address when you log on. This is the way the vast majority of Internet connections work, and it most likely will work for you.

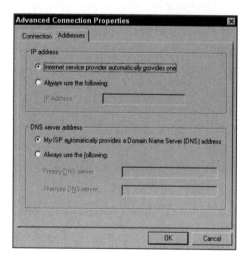

Figure 12-7: By default, Windows 2000 assumes that your ISP will provide a dynamic IP address, which changes each time you log on.

That said, you may be in a situation where your system has a static IP address, which means the address remains the same even when you reconnect to your ISP. In that case, you need to click the radio button labeled Always use the following. The IP Address text box goes active. Enter the permanent IP address that your ISP or network administrator system assigned to you.

Tip   Remember, if you are dialing in from a networked PC, your Internet connection IP address and your network IP address are not the same thing. In fact, they must, by definition, be different, since each host on a TCP/IP network requires a unique IP address. If you duplicate the IP address, you won't be able to create successful network connections.

The DNS server address area enables you to manually define a Domain Name Server for your dial-up sessions. Click the Always use the following radio button to activate the two DNS fields. Enter the primary and alternate IP address assigned you by your ISP or network administrator for the Domain Name Server in the appropriate text boxes. Click OK to make the changes take effect.

Setting up network-based Internet access

Networks have become ubiquitous, from large 10,000-seat corporate networks to home networks consisting of two or three PCs. The upshot is that many PCs don't dial into the Internet at all—they connect through a server on the network. To handle this situation, Windows 2000 uses the same Network Connection Wizard that you use to create modem connections. Here's how:

1. Launch a new session by double-clicking the Make New Connection icon in the Network and Dial-up Connections window.

2. The Network Connection Wizard launches with a welcome dialog box. Click Next.

3. Select the third radio button to connect through the LAN and click Next.

4. At the next dialog box, click the second radio button and click Next.

5. By default the top checkbox is enabled, telling Windows 2000 to automatically detect a proxy server on the network. Click Next.

The rest of the process is identical to setting up a modem-based connection. Of course, not all network-based Internet connections are so simple. Network administrators may need to tailor proxy rules and access, using the Use automatic configuration script to enable the system to read its configuration from a server-based script file. This facility lets administrators set up proxy servers, which can filter requests to control access to Web sites, limit external access to internal resources, and even speed Internet transactions. In order to do so, you need to enter the network address of the script file in the Address text box as shown in Figure 12-8.

The Manual Proxy Server checkbox enables you to assign individual proxy servers for different network protocols, as shown in Figure 12-9. You can also use a single proxy server for all the protocols, by checking the checkbox control at the bottom of the dialog box.

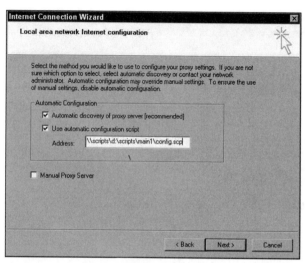

Figure 12-8: Windows 2000 makes it easy for network administrators to modify client Internet access using proxy servers. These servers can enhance security, control Web access, and boost network security.

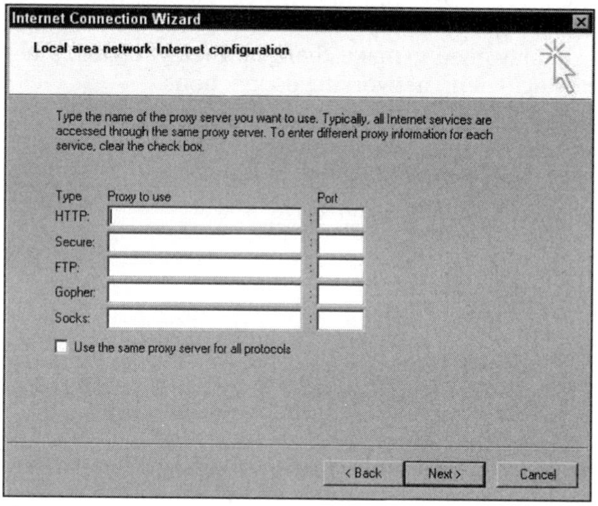

Figure 12-9: Enter the IP addresses or server names of individual proxy servers for HTTP, FTP, and other protocol traffic, including secure traffic.

A Word About Proxies

Most individual Windows 2000 users won't have to worry about setting up proxy servers. The company network administrator will configure your desktop system to connect to any proxy servers set up on the network. Still, it is helpful to know what these servers do.

In essence, proxy servers act as gatekeepers to the network. They sit between individual client systems on a network and the outside world, where they can filter packets, serve up data, secure resources, and streamline transactions. The Figure 12-9 shows proxy servers for different types of network activities, including file transfer protocol (FTP) and secure transactions. Network administrators can focus resources on specific tasks by configuring proxy servers to a specific type of transaction.

So will you need to configure Windows 2000 to communicate through proxy servers? Again, that's a question for a network administrator. But if you are accessing the Internet through a shared connection over a LAN or need to shield external traffic from your internal network for security reasons, a proxy server is likely involved.

Tweaking Your Dial-up Sessions

Once you've got a dial-up connection set up, you may need to update a few more options. You can edit your dial-up networking connection to account for calls from the road, for example, or you may need to make changes when you go to a new ISP. Here's how to edit your existing dial-up networking connections.

Right-click the dial-up network connection icon you want to edit. The properties dialog box for the connection appears, sporting five tabs:

✦ General

✦ Options

✦ Security

✦ Networking

✦ Internet Connection Sharing

The General tab is the starting point and enables you to jump to a number of powerful facilities. Figure 12-10 shows the various entry points.

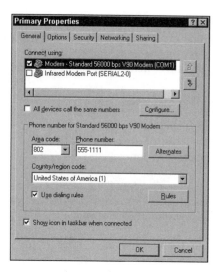

Figure 12-10: Adjust dialing rules, configure your modem, and create alternate dial-up numbers from the General tab.

The General tab

At the top of this page, you should see the name of your currently installed modem, the device that this dial-up networking connection uses to reach the Internet. Click the Configure button to jump to the Modem Configuration dialog box for your modem. This dialog box, shown in Figure 12-11, features controls that enable you to adjust the operation of your communications hardware.

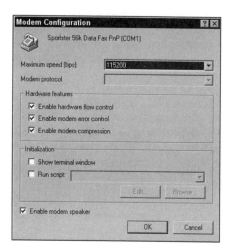

Figure 12-11: Tailor modem hardware properties directly from the dial-up connection.

Configuring the modem

In the Maximum speed area, the default 115200 bps setting should work for everyone, but if you are experiencing connect troubles, try paring this number back to 57600. That may eliminate buffer overruns caused by data coming from your PC too quickly.

In the Hardware features area, you can use the three checkbox controls to toggle some key features on and off. You should keep all these checked unless your ISP or network administrator specifically indicates otherwise. Likewise, if you're having problems making connections, you may want to tweak these settings, but only after you rule out more obvious issues. The controls are

- ✦ **Enable hardware flow control:** Determines how data is handled, either through the modem's hardware or through software. Users should check this item by default, unless some conflict indicates otherwise.

- ✦ **Enable modem error control:** Additional bits are used to help verify that packets are received intact.

- ✦ **Enable modem compression:** Reduces the amount of data moved over the wire by compressing data as it hits the modem.

The Initialization area changes the way your modem behaves at logon. The Show terminal window checkbox simply tells Windows 2000 to display a text-based window that shows all the commands being passed back and forth during logon. The Run Script drop-down list box enables you to select from script files used to automate actions during logon. For example, you can create a script that automatically inputs your user name and password to eliminate the need to type it in at each logon — at the expense of security, of course.

Finally, the Enable modem speaker checkbox turns noisy dial-ups on and off. Defaulted to on, this control means that you can hear your modem screeching over the phone line to make a connection. That's useful for troubleshooting problems and makes for a nice aural prompt as to when you are actually online, but it's also plain loud. Turn it off if you rarely need to sniff out dial-up problems.

Click OK on the Modem Configuration dialog box, and you land back in the General tab of your dial-up connection properties dialog box. The next area you see is the Phone number area, which includes entry controls for area code, phone number, and country/region code. Here you should see your ISP phone number.

Using alternate phone numbers

But what if you are having trouble dialing in? Perhaps you're getting chronic busy signals, or a line is simply not working. Here's how to add alternate phone numbers, which your modem dials if the first number does not work.

1. Click the Alternates button to go to the Alternate Phone Numbers dialog box shown in Figure 12-12. You should see your primary ISP phone number in the Phone numbers list.

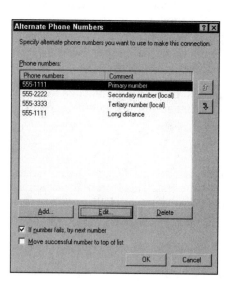

Figure 12-12: Enter additional phone numbers here so Windows can try another line if the primary ISP phone number fails.

2. To add additional numbers, click the Add button.

3. In the Add Alternate Phone Numbers dialog box, click the Use dialing rules checkbox. This action activates the Area code drop-down control at the top of the dialog box.

4. Enter the area code and phone number of your ISP in the appropriate boxes at the top of the dialog box. Also select the appropriate country/region code for your number.

5. For clarity, type a quick note in the Comment text box. It can be helpful if you intend to enter a lot of alternate phone numbers and need to sort through them later. Click OK.

6. Back at the Alternate Phone Numbers dialog box shown in Figure 12-12, you now see your new numbers. Note that your comments are displayed here too, making it much easier to figure out the entries.

7. If you want to tweak any of these numbers, select the number from the list and click the Edit button. You land back in the same dialog box you just came from (though it is now named Edit Alternate Phone Number) so you can change the number, comment, and other properties.

8. Finally, set the order of numbers by selecting the desired number and clicking the Up and Down arrows to the right of the Alternate Phone Numbers window.

Note   Windows 2000 tries numbers in the order they appear in the Alternate Phone Numbers window of this dialog box, so take your time to set up the proper order. If you have a lot of trouble getting a consistent hook-up, consider checking the Move successful number to the top of list checkbox. This automatically assigns the last good number as the primary ISP number. Most likely, over time you'll find a line that works better than the rest. Just remember to keep all your alternate local phone numbers; otherwise, Windows may assign a long-distance number as your default, causing you to run up expensive phone bills.

9. If you want to remove any numbers, select them and click the Delete button. Otherwise, click OK to accept the list and return to the General tab of the dial-up properties dialog box.

Create dialing rules

One of the most powerful aspects of the Windows 2000 dial-up networking feature is its capability to provide rules for dial-up access. This feature is particularly useful for long-distance dialing, such as when you take a notebook PC on the road, for example. Dial-up rules are covered in detail in Chapter 11, but I provide an overview here.

On the General tab, click the Rules button, which brings you to the Dialing Rules page of the Phone and Modem Options dialog box, shown in Figure 12-13. If multiple dialing locations are listed in the Locations window, click the one you want to update and then click Edit. Now you land in the Edit Location dialog box, where there are the following three tabs.

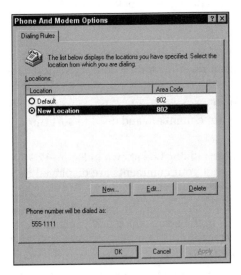

Figure 12-13: The capability to use multiple dialing rules means that frequent travelers don't have to manually input numbers when they dial in from the road.

✦ **General:** Enables you to set special dial prefixes for disabling call waiting and getting an outside line from a hotel or office. This is also the place where you can change the local area code or country location setting. Figure 12-14 shows this useful dialog box.

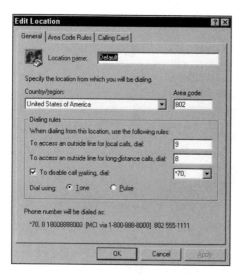

Figure 12-14: Disable call-waiting to eliminate those abrupt line kick-offs, and use the dialing prefix text boxes to get an outside line when calling from hotels or offices.

✦ **Area Code Rules:** Useful for local long-distance dialing, when numbers inside your area code actually require you to dial 1 plus the area code or 1 plus the number. This page enables you to tell Windows 2000 which prefixes (the first three numbers of a seven-digit phone number) to treat as local long-distance calls.

✦ **Calling Card:** Enormously useful for travelers, this page enables you to make long-distance calls using a calling card number and PIN. Select from prebuilt entries or build your own sequences that include access number, phone number, PIN, and other required elements. Figure 12-15 shows an entry for a typical calling card.

You can also create new rules from the Dialing Rules page by clicking the New button. Doing so creates a new listing in the Locations window of the Dialing Rules page. When you set your dial-up connection, you must make sure, however, that you've selected the proper rule set for your connection. Otherwise, your calls may not go through properly.

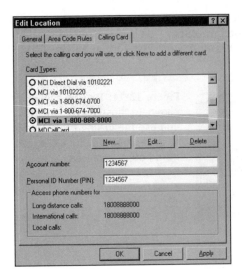

Figure 12-15: Mobile users rely on the Calling Card page because they can configure their dial-up connections to automatically dial long-distance using a calling card.

The Options tab

The Options page of the Connections Properties dialog box is the place where you can tweak logon security and manage connect behaviors. Figure 12-16 shows a typical configuration for a dial-up networking connection.

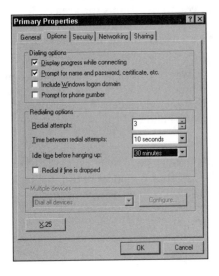

Figure 12-16: By default, Windows tries to dial into a number three times before moving on. You can easily change these settings if you are not so patient.

Dialing options

The Dialing options area at the top of this page consists of four checkbox controls. These checkboxes specifically manage the way Windows 2000 dials into a connection and provide useful tweaks for enhancing the security of dial-up networking connections:

✦ **Display progress while connecting:** Dialing into an ISP can take a few seconds — sometimes, many seconds — so displaying a status dialog box can be helpful. I always keep this setting checked myself.

✦ **Prompt for name and password, certificate, etc.:** Windows 2000 can authenticate dial-up attempts before ever firing up the modem if you check this control. This control is also useful if a physical security device — such as a smart card reader or thumbprint scanner — is used for authentication prior to dialing.

✦ **Include Windows logon domain:** Used in conjunction with the Prompt for name and password control, checking this control requires users to identify the Windows domain they belong to. Under Windows NT and Windows 2000, domains are used to demarcate areas of a network. Users can find out what domain they belong to by contacting their network administrator.

✦ **Prompt for phone number:** This control provides yet another layer of security, by forcing the user to always input the ISP phone number before dialing it. This setting makes it that much tougher for bad guys to crack into your Internet account, since they would need immediate access to the ISP phone number to get into your account.

Redialing options

The top part of this page covers logging on, while the lower half is all about trying again. As any seasoned Internet surfer knows, ISP phone lines sometimes don't work. Modem lines get jammed during busy periods, resulting in annoying busy signals, or sometimes you get kicked off because of line noise or a network error. This section helps you deal with these ugly realities:

✦ **Redial attempts:** Sets the number of times that Windows tries a number that doesn't work before giving up and going to an alternate number or ceasing dial-up operations altogether. Three is the default.

✦ **Time between redial attempts:** The default 30-second pause is intended to give a remote modem or line enough time to become clear, but this setting really applies more to fax machines and other one-to-one point calls than it does to ISPs, which typically maintain a fleet of modems. Move this figure down to 5 or 10 seconds to enable more rapid redialing.

✦ **Idle time before hanging up:** Protects you against eye-popping connect time charges or blatant phone line hogging. If no activity—such as file downloads or Web browsing—occurs during the time period allotted, the modem hangs up.

✦ **Redial if line is dropped:** Check this option to have Windows reconnect after an unplanned interruption. Note that setting this option won't cause your modem to redial if you hang up the connection or if the Idle time control ends the link.

Finally, what's that X.25 button lurking in the corner? X.25 is an old online messaging protocol still used by many corporate networks. Although the entire world has flocked to TCP/IP, you may need X.25 capability to be compatible with some networks and users. Click the button, and you see the X.25 Logon Settings dialog box, shown in Figure 12-17.

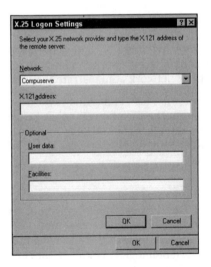

Figure 12-17: Tell Windows 2000 what network to use for X.25 transmissions and your X.121 address, which is the equivalent of a phone number for this aging protocol.

Again, most users won't need to set up X.25 messaging, but if you do, you first need to identify the network that will carry your traffic. Click the Network drop-down list control and select the appropriate network. Then enter your X.25 "phone number" in the X.121 address text box.

The Optional area enables you to input information that may be needed for custom configuration. Check with your network administrator regarding the need for entries in the User data and Facilities text boxes. Click OK to return to the Options page.

The Security tab

If you are a network administrator, you are paid to be afraid. Afraid of careless users who leave their machines open to misuse by others, afraid of crafty hackers who lift corporate data and damage networking systems, and afraid of constantly expanding networks that now provide points of entry from any place on the globe. The Security tab of the Connection Properties dialog box is where users and administrators alike can help beat these fears. Figure 12-18 shows the many options you can use to enhance dial-up security.

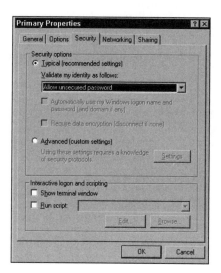

Figure 12-18: Although the Typical setting includes the usual user name and password authentication, you can do a lot better by tweaking this dialog box.

Basic settings

By default, the top radio button is active, which tells Windows to use typical dial-up authentication. The Validate my identity as follows drop-down control enables you to select from three settings, in escalating order of security:

✦ **Allow unsecured password:** With this, the default setting, your password is sent to the remote server over the line in unencrypted format. There is a risk that a focused and determined attacker could read your authentication information in this setting.

✦ **Require secured password:** Protects against password lifting by encrypting your password. This setting activates both checkboxes. The top checkbox uses your Windows logon name and password as part of the logon process (useful for remote networking), and the second checkbox enables you to specifically mandate encrypted remote connections. This second option is useful in high-risk environments.

✦ **Use smart card:** Select this option if your network requires hardware-based authentication to log on. Again, you can require an encrypted server-client link to maintain utmost security.

Advanced settings

If you have some specific security needs, click the Advanced radio button and then click the Settings button. This takes you to the Advanced Security Settings dialog box shown in Figure 12-19.

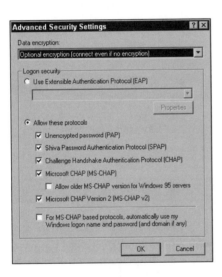

Figure 12-19: Network administrators can ratchet up the security of the logon process by using protocols such as CHAP that encode logon information.

The drop-down control at the top of the dialog box enables you to tailor user logons to require encryption, not require encryption, or make it an option. Using these controls, administrators can ensure compatibility or ratchet up security.

But most of the business gets done in the Logon security area, where a raft of checkbox controls are active if you click the Allow these protocols radio button (which is active by default). Here's what these checkbox controls mean:

✦ **Unencrypted password (PAP):** The default, text-based transfer format used for most dial-up connections and needed to connect Windows 2000 to many non-Microsoft-based servers.

✦ **Shiva Password Authentication Protocol (SPAP):** Another unencrypted logon protocol that is used specifically for Shiva servers.

✦ **Challenge Handshake Authentication Protocol (CHAP):** Uses the secure Message Digest 5 (MD5) protocol to transform logon data into a unique form that cannot be reversed. Enables systems to send authentication information without actually sending the password.

✦ **Microsoft CHAP (MS-CHAP):** Tweaked form of the secure CHAP logon technology that enables Windows workstations to connect to Windows servers running Remote Access Service (RAS). MS-CHAP will not work with Unix and other non-Windows servers.

✦ **Microsoft CHAP Version 2 (MS-CHAP v2):** Integrates secure logons with the password and user name management so that entries don't have to be entered twice. A change to your user name and password is immediately made to your MS-CHAP settings as well. MS-CHAP will not work with Unix and other non-Windows servers.

The last checkbox enables you to specify that the Windows 2000 logon information and domain be used under MS-CHAP for remote access. This is useful for systems that are connecting remotely to your local network.

The Networking tab

As an end user, the Networking tab is a place you may visit often. The Networking tab stores all the information needed to make connections to the remote server and get onto the Internet. You can also install additional protocols here. Figure 12-20 shows a typical setup.

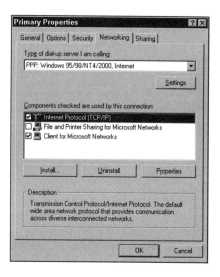

Figure 12-20: You see a number of components listed, but the Internet protocol item is the one that concerns you here.

The drop-down control at the top of the dialog box shows the selected protocol. For Internet access, this control should display "PPP: Windows 95/98/NT 4/2000, Internet", representing the Point to Point protocol used for almost all dial-up Internet connections under Windows 2000.

Click the Settings button underneath this entry to see the PPP Settings dialog box shown in Figure 12-21. Here you see some familiar checkbox controls, such as Enable LCP extensions (identical to the LCP extensions options in the dial-up options Modem area) and Enable software compression.

The last checkbox enables your PC to set up a multilink connection to remote servers, which can yield improved bandwidth for higher audio and video quality over the connection. Of course, you need two or more modems to create these multiple links, as well as multiple ISP accounts for the multiple links.

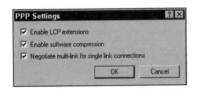

Figure 12-21: The first two checkbox items are identical to features in the dial-up network connection dialog box.

In the middle of the dialog box is a window that displays the various networking protocols currently installed for the dial-up networking connection. You should see Internet Protocol (TCP/IP) listed here. If you don't, and you've selected the PPP option in the drop-down control above, then TCP/IP is not installed on your system. You won't get far with your Internet access if the protocol for Internet communications is not installed. Here's how to add a protocol such as TCP/IP:

1. Click the Install button.

2. In the Select Network Component Type dialog box shown in Figure 12-22, click the Protocol entry and click the Add button.

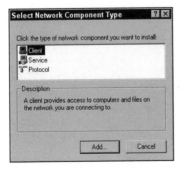

Figure 12-22: Add network savvy to your PC by selecting from among protocols, services, or client components.

3. In the Select Network Protocol dialog box, click the TCP/IP item or other desired protocol and click OK.

4. Windows 2000 installs the new networking protocol. A dialog box displays a status bar as the new components are loaded. In some cases, you may have to insert the Windows 2000 CD-ROM to allow the protocols to be written from disc.

Follow the same procedure to add a new service (such as quality of service capability) or client component. Once TCP/IP is set up, you can use the Properties button on the dialog box to peer under the covers. Click it, and you see the dialog box displayed in Figure 12-23. As you can see, the dial-up connection is set to automatically obtain an IP address from the ISP, using the specific DNS server addresses entered in the boxes below.

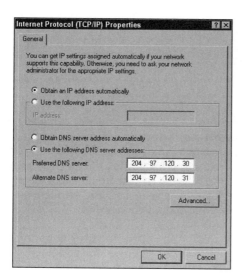

Figure 12-23: If you can't access the Internet, the TCP/IP Properties dialog box is the first place you should visit. Make sure that you are using dynamic or static IP as required by your ISP and that your DNS servers are properly addressed.

Continue your digging by clicking the Advanced button, which brings you to the Advanced TCP/IP Settings dialog box shown in Figure 12-24. The four tabs address different aspects of TCP/IP operation for this dial-up connection.

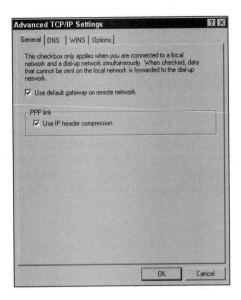

Figure 12-24: Dig deeper to solve problems in the Advanced TCP/IP Settings dialog box.

The General tab

Right off the bat, you hit an important control with the Use default gateway on remote network checkbox. This checkbox controls operation for systems that sit on a network and also dial into the Internet. When you check this control, your system will send any data that is not bound for a destination on the local area network over the dial-up connection to the Internet. If you are having problems connecting to the Internet and this checkbox is not checked, the problem may be that data is not being forwarded over your dial-up connection.

The PPP link area includes one checkbox that controls whether or not your connection uses IP header compression. IP header compression compacts the ancillary data that travels along with the information in packets in order to reduce data transfers. By default, this checkbox is set to on because header compression is commonly supported by ISPs. Again, if you are experiencing problems and this item is unchecked, try checking it and connecting again.

The DNS tab

The DNS tab takes its cue from the General TCP/IP Properties dialog box where the preferred and alternate DNS server addresses are stored. As you know, DNS servers resolve URLs into the numeric-format addresses used by the Internet. You see these addresses in the scrolling list box at the top of the DNS page. The topmost entry is the primary DNS server and is the first one your system will check with when resolving URLs. Subsequent secondary DNS servers can also be set up. You can shuffle the order here by clicking the desired server entry and then clicking the Up and Down buttons to the right of the window. Figure 12-25 shows this dialog box at work.

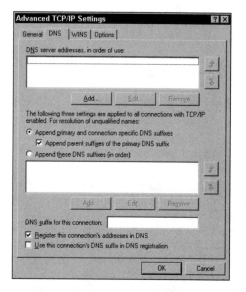

Figure 12-25: Make sure you have set your DNS server addresses in the order specified by your ISP in order to achieve reliable operation.

If you find a DNS address error, you can quickly correct it here. Click the Edit button and type in the proper address in the dialog box shown in Figure 12-26. You can also delete an extraneous, old, or incorrect DNS server address by selecting it and clicking Remove.

Figure 12-26: Enter a new or edited DNS server address to make sure your system is able to translate IP addresses and Web URLs.

The bottom half of the DNS page addresses resolution of unqualified DNS names. For example, say you type the term "intranet" into your browser. When your system sends this "unqualified" URL to the DNS server, it will be unable to provide a URL. (For example, a name such as "intranet" is not itself a qualified domain name, whereas "intranet.com" is.)

To enable Windows to work with partial URLs, click the radio button labeled Append primary and connection specific DNS suffixes. By entering specific suffixes (such as intranet.com), your system will stitch together the partial URL with the suffix and send it on to a DNS server for address resolution.

By contrast, you can click the lower radio button to append specific DNS suffixes in a determined order. Thus, your unqualified intranet DNS search could be set to search through the DNS suffixes you identify. To set suffixes, do the following.

1. Click the lower radio button and then click the Add button.

2. In the dialog box that appears, enter the DNS suffix in the TCP/IP Domain Suffix text box and click OK.

3. Repeat this process for each DNS suffix that you wish to specify.

The new suffixes now appear in the box just below the Append these DNS suffixes (in order) label. The up and down arrows can now be used to set the priority of the suffixes, by moving entries up or down in the order.

The WINS tab

The WINS tab enables you to establish, edit, and remove WINS addresses. What is WINS, you ask? The term is short for Windows Internet Naming Service, a name resolution system that determines what IP address is associated with a specific network computer. Unlike DNS, WINS is limited to Windows systems; you typically won't be using WINS name resolution with ISPs, as many employ Unix servers, and those that use Windows can't assume that Windows-based clients are at the other end. Still, WINS can be very useful for network administrators, because it uses a distributed database to track computer names and associated IP addresses. When a change to a computer name or property occurs, WINS updates the information across the enterprise, helping reduce naming confusion, lost resources, and other trouble that can occur when managing lots of client PCs.

As mentioned previously, if your PC is used to connect to the Internet via an ISP, there probably will be no WINS setting enabled. However, for larger local area networks, your network administrator may elect to use WINS to resolve computer IP addresses. To add WINS, click the Add button in the WINS page of the Advanced TCP/IP Settings dialog box, shown in Figure 12-27, and then enter the IP address of the server in the dialog box that appears. Click Add, and the new WINS server entry appears in the list box.

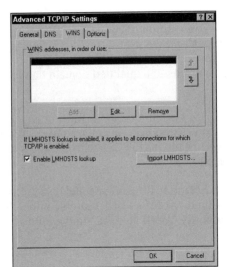

Figure 12-27: Network administrators can use WINS to automatically resolve system names and find resources on Windows-based networks, but ISPs don't need anything assigned here.

Note This chapter deals with dial-up networking, by which users are connecting Windows 2000 PCs to an ISP. For more in-depth coverage of WINS resolution for systems on a local area networks, see Chapters 19 and 20.

Securing communications

You've already learned about securing logons to your ISP. The IP Security dialog box, shown in Figure 12-28, enables you to secure all IP-based communications by using IPSEC. To get here, click the Options tab and then click the Properties button. By default, the Do not use IPSEC radio button is activated because most Internet resources do not employ packet security. You can, however, click the Use this IP security policy radio button and then select Client (Respond Only) from the drop-down control. This action causes IPSEC to be used only when a server provides a secure connection. Otherwise, transactions happen in the clear.

Note What is IPSEC? It stands for *IP Security* and is a set of protocols that enables secure communications over the Internet or other IP network. IPSEC works through public key encryption, in which the sending and receiving devices share a public key. The receiving party obtains a public key and authenticates the sender using digital certificates.

IPSEC is interesting because it forms the basis for emerging *virtual private network* (VPN) implementations. A pair of encryption modes — Transport and Tunnel — can be tailored to the desired task. Transport mode encrypts the data portion or payload of each packet while leaving the header alone; this allows proxy servers and other devices to act on Transport mode–encrypted packets based on their header information. For example, packets that are identified as coming from the company CEO might get high priority on the network. The more secure Tunnel mode encrypts both header and payload. This prevents nefarious parties from seeing any of the source, destination, or other ancillary information about the payload. Unfortunately, it also prevents network services from using this data to make decisions on delivery.

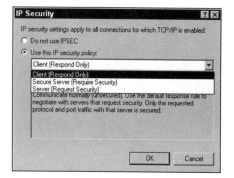

Figure 12-28: Beef up security using the IPSEC data security standard.

Internet connection sharing

Finally, you come to the last tab on the dial-up networking connection properties dialog box, Internet Connection Sharing. Shown in Figure 12-29, this tab offers an intriguing feature for home and small office users who want to share Internet access over a LAN. Click the top checkbox, and your Windows 2000 machine acts as an Internet access server, enabling connected clients to reach the Internet through its one connection.

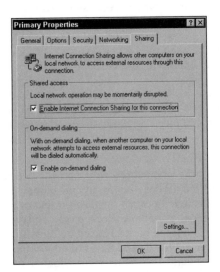

Figure 12-29: Setting up Internet connection sharing is ludicrously easy under Windows 2000. Check the top checkbox, and your Windows 2000 PC will change network settings to enable shared access among systems.

Caution   There is a catch: Internet Connection Sharing requires that your Windows 2000 machine act as a DHCP allocator for your network, assigning IP addresses to other systems on the LAN. In so doing, it not only changes your local system's IP address, it also updates the IP addresses of all the clients on the network. The result: Your existing IP addresses will be overwritten, which could wreak havoc if you rely on known IP addresses to make remote connections or share resources. Also, Internet Connection Sharing is intended for small office and home networks, not corporate LANs. Never *ever* enable this feature on an existing network with other Windows 2000 Server domain controllers, DNS servers, DHCP servers, or systems configured for static IP.

Cross-Reference   For more on IP address management, see Chapters 19 and 20.

The lower checkbox lets you allow other PCs to automatically dial onto the Internet using your Windows 2000 host. It's a good idea to check this box—otherwise remote users will only be able to get shared Internet access when your modem or other access device happens to be connected. Once you've enabled this option, clients on the network can independently dial into the ISP via the Windows 2000 PC's modem to access a Web site, e-mail, or other Internet resource.

You may also want to enable applications or services to access the Internet through the shared connection. You may have shared contact lists or spell check libraries on a remote network, for example, that applications need to access. Click the Settings button to view the Internet Connection Sharing Settings dialog box. In either the Applications or Services tab, click the Add button to access a dialog box, shown in Figure 12-30, that enables you to name the application or service that requires access.

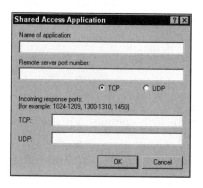

Figure 12-30: Prepare applications and services on your networked PCs for Internet connectivity by enabling them from the Internet Connection Sharing Settings dialog box.

In both cases, you need to contact your network administrator to find out the appropriate TCP and UDP port numbers to use to connect applications to systems. To add a shared access application, do the following:

1. In the top text box, enter an easily recognized name for the application you want to take advantage of shared access.

2. In the Remote server port number text box, enter the port number of the server where the shared application resides. You'll probably need to get this information from a network administrator, since he or she typically designates a port on the host that is available for providing access to the host system.

3. In the TCP and UDP text boxes, enter the port numbers on your home network that the application will connect to. Some applications require only a TCP or a UDP port number, whereas others may require both.

Working with an Active Dial-up Session

So far you have seen how to tweak and update the dial-up networking operation, including the way the connection works when you are dialed in. Here you learn how you can work with active sessions. Start by dialing into your ISP using a connection you've already created.

Click Start ➪ Settings ➪ Network and Dial-up Connections and double-click the appropriate dial-up networking icon from the window that opens.

Tip   I personally find the new dial-up networking location hard to locate and work with, so I moved my dial-up connections to the Start menu where I can quickly access them. Do this by opening the Network and Dial-up Connections window and dragging the appropriate icon over the Start button. Hold it there until the Start menu opens and then move up the menu list to where you want your dial-up shortcut to appear (a black bar indicates where the new icon will go). Release the left mouse button. A dialog box tells you that a shortcut will be created. Click Yes. Now you can quickly launch a dial-up networking connection by clicking Start and then the connection icon. You can also use the same approach to drag and drop a shortcut onto your desktop for quick access.

Checking dial-up status

You can check the status of your current connection in several ways. By default, Windows puts a connection icon in the taskbar tray . You can tell when data is being exchanged when the display screens on the little computers in the icon blink black and blue.

Hold the cursor over this icon to see information about the current connection as shown in Figure 12-31: connection name, connection data rate, and the total bytes sent and received. If you suspect that a transfer has died or the connection has locked up, you can quickly scan for any changes in the amount of data traded by hovering your mouse cursor over the icon. If no change occurs, the link has probably gone south.

Figure 12-31: Hover the mouse cursor over the connection icon to get a quick summary of your active Internet connection.

Using the Status dialog box

Dig a little deeper by checking out the network connection Status dialog box. There are a couple ways to get there:

✦ Double-click the connection icon in the taskbar tray.

✦ Click Start ➪ Settings ➪ Network and Dial-up Connections. Right-click the network connection currently being used and click Properties from the shortcut menu.

You see the dialog box shown in Figure 12-32. The Connection area shows whether or not the connection is currently online, the amount of time the connection has been active, and the download speed.

Note The Speed item displays the top speed going upstream or downstream. So on a 56 Kbps modem or an ADSL link, for example, the top speed represents the download data rate. Upstream data rates are typically slower for these connections.

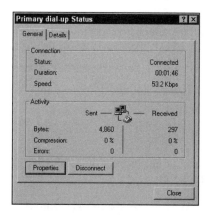

Figure 12-32: Get the lowdown on connection speed, bytes traded, compression rates, and other useful stuff from the connection Status dialog box.

In addition, the Activity area of this dialog box offers a real-time display of connection activity. Download a file from the Internet, and the Sent and Received Bytes fields update to show the new totals transferred. The system icon on the dialog box also flashes trademark blue to indicate data moving through the modem. The Compression field is useful for showing how effectively your modem is reducing data transfers over the wire, while the Errors field indicates problems in the transmission that required a retransmission. A high error rate can be indicative of a severe line noise problem or other issue.

Click the Details tab to see useful information about your connection and TCP/IP settings, as shown in Figure 12-33.

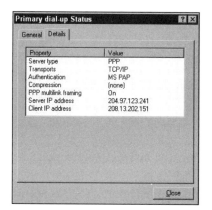

Figure 12-33: Review your connection settings for the current call on the Details tab.

✦ **Server type:** Indicates PPP, SLIP, or other connection type.

✦ **Transports:** Typically TCP/IP because this is the Internet. Local area network connections may show NetBEUI or other protocols here.

✦ **Authentication:** MS PAP (or PAP) is short for Microsoft Password Authentication Protocol and is the standard, clear text authentication protocol. Secure environments might use CHAP, MS-CHAP, or other variants.

✦ **Compression:** Indicates if compression is being used in the current connection.

✦ **PPP multilink framing:** Implements enhanced bandwidth by enabling multiple connections to the server. Defaults to on.

✦ **Server IP address:** This is the IP address of the ISP's Internet server you are connected to.

✦ **Client IP address:** This is the IP address of your connection, typically assigned by the ISP server for this individual connection.

To close the Status dialog box, click the Close button. To disconnect from the Internet, click the Disconnect button.

Note   The Close button only closes the Status dialog box. It in no way disrupts your connection or causes the modem to hang up.

Summary

There is no doubt about it. Since the introduction of Windows 95 in 1995, dial-up networking has become the workhorse component for connecting to online resources. In fact, dial-up networking has become so ubiquitous, that with Windows 2000, Microsoft now models local area network access against this feature. The result is that both local area and dial-up networking connections behave similarly, a move that might cause some short-term confusion but should make life easier down the road.

I've covered an awful lot of concepts here, and even slewed into the wooly world of local area networking. Among the things you've learned:

✦ The various underlying protocols that make Internet access possible, including TCP/IP, IPSEC, and others

✦ The process of creating new dial-up sessions, as well as managing existing ones

✦ Exciting new features in Windows 2000 such as Internet Connection Sharing and shared application access

✦ How to monitor Internet connections and enable features such as security and scripting

In the next chapter, you learn a bit more about putting your hard-earned Internet connection to work, by reviewing the bundled Web browser that comes with Windows 2000 — Internet Explorer 5.0.

✦　　✦　　✦

Using Internet Explorer 5.0

Microsoft Windows 2000 operating system arrives at the conclusion of one of the greatest turnarounds in corporate American history. It was 1995, and Microsoft just wasn't getting it. Marc Andreesen and company had parlayed a graphical Web browser into one of the most successful initial public offerings in history, as Netscape dominated the infant market for Web browsers and enjoyed unprecedented market share, support, and goodwill. Microsoft, meanwhile, stooged around with its clumsy Microsoft Network (MSN) information service, and Bill Gates evangelized such dead-end ideas as the information superhighway and interactive TV.

Fast forward to fall 1999, and the Internet is absolutely everywhere. Web URLs appear in car advertisements and news shows, and ISPs are giving PCs away to people who sign extended Internet access contracts. E-commerce, software distribution, financial services and stock trading, and a host of other activities are being reshaped by the ubiquitous public network. Amazingly, Microsoft is leading the way.

In just four short years, Microsoft went from an Internet also-ran to the dominant player in the browser market. One reason for the astounding comeback is the success of Microsoft's Internet Explorer Web browser software. Now in version 5.0, Internet Explorer accounts for the majority of new browser installations.

Windows 2000 Professional shows how IE5 achieved such success. Like previous versions of Internet Explorer, IE5 is bundled with the operating system and is installed whether you want it or not. Microsoft argues that IE5 is simply part of the operating system, but others contend that such bundling constitutes predatory practices.

Anatomy of a Web Browser

What exactly goes into a Web browser? A Web browser is essentially an application designed to display Web pages and content. Figure 13-1 shows the IE5 interface and a typical Web page. Early browsers displayed HTML and JPEG and GIF image formats, but contemporary browsers go a lot further than that. Today, IE5 handles a variety of media and data types:

Figure 13-1: Just can't wait for SportsCenter? ESPN.com, one of the Web's premier sites, serves up fresh sports news on the Web.

✦ **HTML:** Code embedded into text that describes how Web pages look—the backbone of the World Wide Web.

✦ **JPEG and GIF images:** Compressed graphics file formats used to display in Web pages everything from high-quality photographs to tiny icons. JPEG stands for Joint Photographic Experts Group and is a format best for photo-quality images. GIF stands for Graphics Interchange Format and is a format best suited to small images.

✦ **Streaming video and audio:** Specially formatted and highly compressed digital video and audio that begins playing through the browser even as parts of the media file continue to download.

✦ **Java applications:** Downloadable program code that the browser interprets and runs on the desktop PC. Java is hardware independent. The same program code runs on many platforms, including Windows, Macintosh, Linux, and Unix.

✦ **ActiveX controls:** Modular, downloadable programs that users install into their IE5 browser to add functionality. ActiveX works only with Windows-based systems.

More recently, both the IE5 and Netscape Navigator browsers include support for emerging and important Web technologies. Among the new features are the following:

✦ **Dynamic HTML (DHTML):** Enables consistent designs and dynamic content through use of style sheets and database integration.

✦ **Extensible Markup Language (XML):** Where HTML describes how things look, XML describes what things are. XML makes smart searches and rich machine-to-machine data interchange possible.

✦ **Secure Sockets Layer (SSL) encryption:** Enables e-commerce and other applications by scrambling transmissions to protect them against eavesdroppers.

Finally, both IE5 and Navigator 4.5 offer additional opportunities to display and interact with data, documents, and services on the Internet. Perhaps most well known is the concept of Navigator plug-ins, small programs that users can download and install to add functionality to the base browser. Microsoft's version of plug-ins, called *ActiveX controls*, ups the ante for Web browsers because ActiveX turns the browser into a platform for other applications. In a sense, the browser becomes a micro–operating system.

You can add literally thousands of additional components to your browsers. Among the most prevalent are the following:

✦ **Macromedia Flash:** Enables browsers to display low-bandwidth, visually engaging animation using vector graphics. Figure 13-2 shows an example of a Flash animation.

✦ **Macromedia Shockwave:** Browsers can play back Shockwave presentations consisting of animation, video, and sound.

✦ **Virtual Reality Modeling Language (VRML):** Enables the display of interactive 3D scenes and objects, using the browser as the interface.

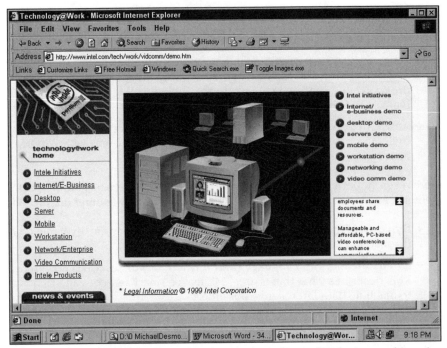

Figure 13-2: Flash animations, such as this one from the Intel Web site, use bit-saving vector graphics to produce images over the Web.

As you can see, Web browsers have come a long way in just four years. And no doubt they will continue to go further still.

HTML renderer

The first and most important thing a Web browser must do is quickly and accurately display HTML code as Web pages. Here's how it works.

IE5 goes through an HTML document looking for tag pairs such as <b></b>, <h1></h1>, <font size=2></font>. These tags, which are embedded within the readable text content of an HTML document, determine the look of the page. For example:

The HTML line <i><b>This is a test. </b></i> looks like this:

This is a test.

Add a few changes — <center><u><i><b>This is a test. </b></i></u></center> — and you get this:

This is a test.

All these tags specifically relate to font formatting (bold, italic, underline) and paragraph formatting (align center), but additional tags enable more complex layouts. Perhaps most useful for designers is the versatile table tag set, which enables Web pages to display multicolumn tables and even nested tables within tables. These layout tags can be combined with useful attribute tags to create effects such as background colors, table border thickness and color, and table height and width. You can even format individual cells in a table.

Tip   Want to see what's going on behind the scenes in a Web page? You can quickly view the HTML code for almost any page by simply clicking View ➪ Source, as shown in Figure 13-3. IE5 opens the Notepad application with the HTML text source code loaded.

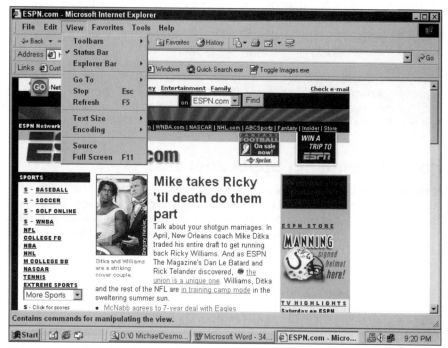

Figure 13-3: View the HTML code behind a Web page by clicking the Source command under the View menu.

Web site source code is just a click away under the View menu of IE5. Of course, no Web page is complete without hyperlinks. In fact, hyperlinking is what made the Web the compelling medium it is today, because it enables users to drill down through content, seek additional information, and explore. Creating links in HTML is relatively simple. Following is an example of simple HTML code that produces a click-through link:

Visit the <a href="http://www.MichaelDesmond.com">MichaelDesmond Communications Web site</a>.

In your browser, you see:

Visit the <u>MichaelDesmond Communications Web site</u>.

When you move or rest the mouse pointer over a link, the mouse pointer changes into a hand. Click the underlined text, and your browser opens the page for the referenced URL. URL stands for Uniform Resource Locator, the familiar www addresses used to access Internet Web sites. You can extend the capabilities of links to open pages in a separate window or to launch the user's default e-mail program with the encoded e-mail address in the To field of the e-mail message.

All this is fine and good, but issues can come up. For example, the speed at which a browser can parse HTML code and text and turn it into a displayed page is an important consideration. Early versions of Internet Explorer were often slower than their Netscape counterparts. Sluggish HTML decoding is particularly a problem in complex pages with large tables and many images.

IE5, by contrast, features an extremely efficient HTML parser that significantly improves performance over the previous 4.0 version of the browser. Intelligent caching and prioritized page output particularly help speed display of large tables. The result is snappier response on both fast and slow Internet connections.

Host for container applications

Netscape made the term *plug-in* a well-known phrase in Internet parlance. In fact, much of Netscape's early success was defined by the extra value end users got by downloading add-in applications and applets to do such things as display vector-based animation, video, and 3D scenes. Before long, a cottage industry of plug-in software vendors had sprung up to help extend and enhance the capabilities of the Navigator browser platform.

The folks at Microsoft are no dummies, and they quickly saw the enormous value and potential market spin opportunity that a plug-in architecture of their own could create. So Microsoft took its existing OLE 2.0 (Object Linking and Embedding version 2.0) technology, rechristened it ActiveX, and touted it as an extension platform for Internet Explorer. Figure 13-4 shows an ActiveX car racing game running within Internet Explorer. It was a clumsy match and fraught with issues, but Microsoft backed up its marketing move with serious developer support and the usual prolonged financial investments. Just as important, ActiveX offered powerful hooks into the Windows environment and its applications—something plug-ins could not fully provide.

ActiveX even got some help from Netscape, which struggled to provide reasonable support and structure for its plug-in developer community. Programming documentation was sparse, vendor support proved hard to come by, and the architecture seemed too loosely defined to support the early, runaway interest in plug ins. The result was that plug-in support began to wane and ActiveX development bloomed.

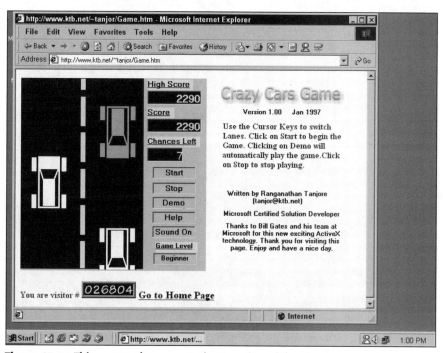

Figure 13-4: This screen shows an ActiveX version of the simple computer game Crazy Cars.

Joltin' Java! Working with Applets

To paraphrase Churchill, Java is an enigma wrapped inside a mystery. Is it a programming language, an operating system, or something in between? Will it drive future PCs, end up embedded in next-generation VCRs, or perhaps power mission-critical business-to-business server applications? Or will it do all these things and more?

These questions are still being answered, but first, you need to get past the dictionary definition. Java is — for now — a programming language that enables developers to create modular, downloadable code that executes on the client system. Importantly, Java is intended to be a "write once, run everywhere" development language, making it a perfect match for the many types of computers and operating systems on the Internet. Interactive 3D clocks, traceroute programs, and editable charts are common examples of Java applets. The figure shows one example running in an IE5 browser.

Continued

(continued)

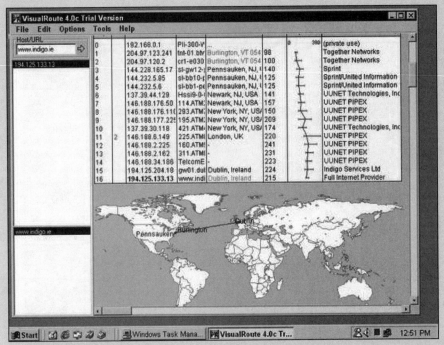

This Java-based graphical trace route application provides a world map view of your Internet transactions.

Unlike ActiveX controls and Navigator plug-ins, which you download and install on your PC, Java applications can run on the fly. That is, you click a Java applet item, the code downloads into your system memory, and the program runs. When the program is completed or is closed, the application is purged from memory; it leaves no indication it was ever on your PC. This approach avoids problematic system updates and also enables a key security feature.

You see, Java is designed to run in a *virtual machine* (VM), a kind of digital sandbox inside system memory that is kept separate and distinct from your operating system and applications. Unlike ActiveX controls, Java applications cannot modify system files and resources because these reside outside the Java VM. This approach eliminates a key danger point because downloadable code can be used for nefarious purposes, whether to wipe out hard disk drives or steal valuable information. Java's architecture is supposed to resolve these concerns, but because of enterprising Java hacks, users should not let down their guard.

Another characteristic of Java is that it is an interpreted language, meaning that code arrives at your machine in raw form, and it is up to your browser or other Java container application to mold that code into a format that runs on your machine. It is this interpreted approach that enables one code set to work on many platforms. But interpreting code on the fly takes time and processing power, which is why Java applications can be so darn slow.

In order to make Java happen, Web browsers need to include a Java compiler, code that converts raw Java code into executable format. The first Java compiler in Internet Explorer (version 3.0) was dreadfully slow compared to rival Netscape Navigator. IE4 improved matters significantly, drawing even with Navigator, while IE5 adds further enhancements that make it faster than Navigator.

Unfortunately, it seems that Java may have a clouded future in Microsoft products, including Internet Explorer. The figure below includes a Web page with a real-time date field in the upper-left corner—a simple piece of embedded Java code powers the date display. A recent court ruling forced Microsoft to adhere to Sun Microsystems' (Java's founder and leading voice) definition of Java development code. The court decision means that Microsoft cannot introduce Windows-centric optimizations to its Java development tools, a key underpinning for Microsoft to make Java hew to the Windows market strategy.

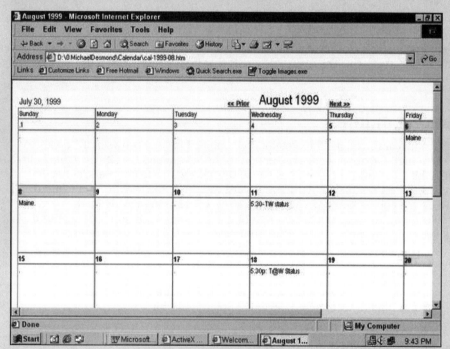

Simple Java code can be incorporated into HTML pages to create displays such as the real-time date on this Web-based calendar.

Suddenly, Microsoft has no vested interest in supporting Java functionality. After all, Microsoft already has ActiveX controls to provide the modular functionality of Java applets and COM+ (component object model +) programming tools to create server-side applications and environments. If Microsoft can't leverage Java to make Windows a more compelling environment, all Java support does is enable a competing development and operating platform.

Continued

(continued)

What's the upshot of all this? While Internet Explorer includes an advanced just-in-time Java compiler, future versions of the browser may not offer this capability. If you try to download and run a Java application, your browser might not recognize the code. It's quite possible that users will have to install a third-party Java compiler and interface to reintroduce Java capability in future versions of Windows PCs. Only time—and a few Microsoft court appeals—will tell.

Living with Internet Explorer

Enough of the background. It's time to dive in and see how to make Internet Explorer work. The good news is that IE5 is far superior to the browsers that came before it because it adds necessary tweaks and enhancements to the already-capable Internet Explorer 4.0 platform. The message here is that it's a lot easier to improve a good product than it is to create a whole new product that is perfect.

Getting online

First things first, you need to get yourself online. Like any browser, IE5 needs to know something about your connection to the Internet so that it can actually find the public network. Microsoft has eased this task with the Internet Connection Wizard, a fairly simple and straightforward setup routine that prompts you to choose the connection type, set network behaviors, and provide further details. Provided you know a minimal amount of information about your network or dial-up connection, you should have little problem getting IE5 to find the Internet.

There are two main connectivity scenarios:

✦ **Dial-up:** Your PC uses an analog modem, DSL adapter, cable modem, or other directly connected device to link to your ISP.

✦ **Network:** Your PC is connected to a network, which itself is connected to the Internet.

Creating a dial-up connection

Here's how to set up Internet Explorer to link to the Internet over your preexisting dial-up networking (DUN) connection.

1. Click Tools ➪ Internet Options.

2. Click the Connections tab. If you've already created dial-up networking connections on your computer (as detailed in Chapters 11 and 12), the Dial-up settings list box will show one or more DUN connections. Click the one you want to set IE5 to work with.

3. To automatically have IE5 dial in when it's launched, click the bottom radio
button (labeled Always dial my default connection) and click Apply or OK.

Note

If you have a notebook PC, you may sometimes connect to the Internet over a
modem and other times over the local area network. In this case, click the radio
button labeled Dial whenever a network connection is not present, as shown in
Figure 13-5. This option tells IE5 to first look for the presence of a local area network (LAN) connection to the Internet. If no such link is available, it then dials in
over the modem using the DUN session identified in the Dial-up settings list box.
You may also want to turn off automatic dialing by clicking the Never dial a connection radio button if you tend to browse documents on your hard disk and don't
always need an Internet connection for IE5.

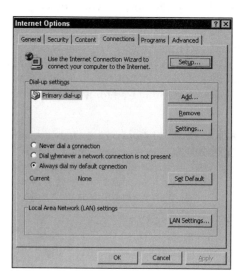

Figure 13-5: The Connections tab
enables you to assign a dial-up session
to Internet Explorer, as well as tailor
connections for network or modem
use — or both.

Creating a network connection

Windows 2000 is a business desktop operating system, so it's quite likely that
Internet connections are implemented over a local area network (LAN) rather
than a slow analog modem or other direct peripheral connection. LAN connections
Internet — typically a fast T1 or even T3 connection that hosts all the Internet
access in a company or branch office.

IE5 is able to take advantage of fast LAN connections. However, to ensure that
only authorized traffic travels to and from the LAN, most networks feature a
proxy server. A proxy server acts as an intermediary between the client PC
and the Internet, intercepting all packets and sending them to the proper
destination. Among other things, proxy servers can deny client access to
specific Internet addresses, filter certain types of inbound traffic, and track
Internet usage by clients on the LAN.

For IE5 to work under such an environment, it needs to be properly configured to send packets to the proxy server, which then directs traffic to the appropriate IP addresses. So when you enter **www.cnn.com**, for example, IE5 sends the request to the proxy server. The proxy looks at the destination, checks it against any policies or rules that might be in place, and then sends the request onto the Internet. The incoming response hits the proxy, where it is examined before it is forwarded to the client on the LAN.

To make IE5 work on a LAN with a proxy server, set the program as follows:

1. Click Tools ⇨ Internet Options and click the Connections tab on the Internet Options dialog box.

2. Click the top radio button, labeled Never dial a connection. Many laptop users may want to select the middle radio button, which dials only when the network connection is not present.

3. Click the LAN Settings button.

4. Most networks allow proxy servers to be automatically detected. Click the Automatically detect settings checkbox at the top of the LAN Settings dialog box. Figure 13-6 shows this dialog box configured for a fully protected network.

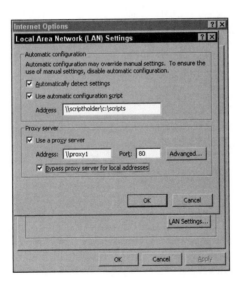

Figure 13-6: Network administrators can create online scripts to control multiple IE5 configurations and set up proxies to protect against intrusion or inappropriate Web browsing.

5. If you store up-to-date IE5 configurations on your network, also check the Use automatic configuration script checkbox and then enter the URL of the script file in the text box.

Note   Why should LAN administrators use configuration scripts? Because they ensure that all IE5 browsers on the network play by the same set of rules. The script can determine the IE5 home page—such as a corporate intranet site—or the current proxy settings and location. When you make changes to the network or policies, a single update to the configuration file addresses all browsers on the network.

   6. Click OK for the changes to take effect.

Using the automatic detection capabilities of IE5 often doesn't cut the mustard. The proxy may not be detectable, or configuration scripts may not be provided on the network, for example. Just as important, your network administrator may need to closely tailor proxy server settings to address traffic based on different protocols or to handle a mix of internal and external traffic.

If you need this level of control in your IE5 browser settings, you need to dig a bit deeper.

   1. In the Internet Options dialog box, click the Connections tab and then click the LAN Settings button.

   2. In the Proxy Server area, click the Use a proxy server checkbox.

   3. Enter the IP address of the proxy server in the Address text box and then enter the port number (frequently 80) in the Port text box as shown in Figure 13-6. Get this information from your administrator.

   4. To speed browsing of resources on the secure LAN, such as the corporate intranet, activate the checkbox labeled Bypass proxy server for local addresses. This setting enables internal addresses to be resolved directly, rather than being routed through a proxy.

If you do specify the proxy server address, you can drill down further by clicking the Advanced button. Click this button to bring up the Proxy Settings dialog box, shown in Figure 13-7. Here you assign a specific proxy server and port address for individual protocol traffic according to the following options:

   ✦ **HTTP (HyperText Transfer Protocol):** The bulk of Internet traffic, including most Web browsing.

   ✦ **Secure:** For secure and encrypted transactions.

   ✦ **FTP (File Transfer Protocol):** Used for file uploads and downloads to and from FTP sites on the Internet.

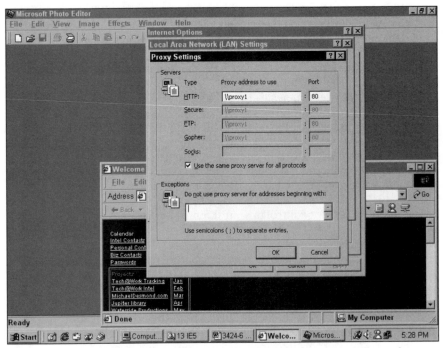

Figure 13-7: Set up individual proxy servers for different protocol traffic on the network. You can also use the text box in the Exceptions area to identify resources that can bypass the proxy server.

> ✦ **Gopher:** Used for access to Gopher servers, which present contents in a hierarchically structured list of files. This is a protocol used before widespread adoption of Web-based search engines.
>
> ✦ **Socks:** Provides a simple firewall for TCP traffic moving through a proxy server by hiding client-side IP addresses and checking inbound and outbound packets.

Again, you need to check with your network administrator to see what settings, if any, you need to set in the Proxy Settings dialog box. Of course, you need a working network connection for this type of connectivity to work. But once it's set up, you will find that network-based connections to the Internet can be fast, reliable, and secure — a huge boon for busy network administrators who must ensure easy, but protected, access to the Internet.

Browsing basics

One of the reasons the Internet has become so pervasive is the relative simplicity of Web browsing. While plenty of complexity is involved in setting up and tweaking an Internet connection and functionality, the actual act of browsing the Web is refreshingly easy. You view text and graphics onscreen and click displayed links (denoted by underlines and color) to move to other Web pages.

About the most difficult challenge to browsing the Web is actually *finding* useful stuff. At last count, more than 100 million Web pages were on the Internet, ranging from the frivolous (personal home pages, Hollywood star tributes) to the professional (secure e-commerce services, industry portals, and corporate Web sites). Fortunately, there are a lot of search engines you can use, and some nice touches newly integrated into IE5 can help you on your way.

Getting around

By default, Internet Explorer opens to (surprise!) the Microsoft Network home page. You are prompted to set up a personal information page, which can be useful. You are prompted to enter your time zone and ZIP code (or outside the United States, your region and city). You then select from a list of general topics, activating specific information services and sources, before updating your MSN site. The result: If you keep MSN as your home page, you will see personalized news, weather, and other information every time you launch Internet Explorer 5.0 We'll come back to setup a little later in this chapter, but for now, let's talk about the basics of getting around the Internet using Internet Explorer 5.0.

There are several ways you can move around the Internet in IE5:

✦ Click a link on a Web page.

✦ Enter the Web address (called a Uniform Resource Locator or URL) in the Address box of the Address bar. Note that if you've visited a site before, IE5 will automatically display that URL in a drop-down list beneath the Address bar, allowing you to click it if you wish.

Tip

Here's a great time-saving tip for manually entering URLs into IE5. Instead of schlepping the mouse pointer all the way to the Address bar to enter the address, just press Ctrl+O or Ctrl+L. Then type the URL into the text box in the Open dialog box, shown in Figure 13-8, and click Enter. IE5 immediately starts downloading the indicated page. Also note that you can generally leave out the `http://` portion of the URL. Just type **www.cnn.com**, for example.

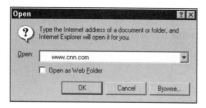

Figure 13-8: Your next Web site is only a few keystrokes away.

✦ Click the Forward or Back buttons on the Standard Buttons toolbar. Note that this only works after you've moved among Web pages.

✦ Right-click the current Web page and select Forward or Back from the shortcut menu. As with the Forward and Back buttons, you must have navigated through Web pages for these commands to be available.

✦ Click the Address drop-down list box and select a previously viewed page listed there.

✦ Click the Favorites menu item and then click any saved page addresses in the list . Or click the Favorites button to display your list of Favorite Web sites in a left pane window. To close this pane, click the X button that appears at the top-right corner of the pane in the Favorites title bar.

✦ Click the History button in the Standard Buttons toolbar. In the left-pane area that appears, navigate to the site you want to visit and then click the specific Web page in the list, as shown in Figure 13-9. Again, to close the left pane, click the X button that appears at the top-right corner of the pane.

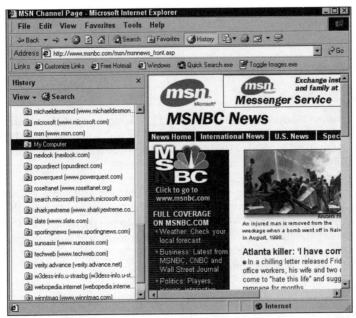

Figure 13-9: Click the History button, and IE5 displays a list of Web sites you've visited in the left pane of the browser. Click a link to jump to any of the displayed sites.

As you can see, there are a *lot* of ways to get from here to there on the Web using IE5. And in fact, IE5 generally offers multiple ways to perform frequent tasks. For example, you can refresh a Web page to reload the HTML document over the Internet) in any one of three ways:

✦ Click the Refresh button.

✦ Click View ➪ Refresh.

✦ Press F5.

Likewise, you can stop a page transfer by clicking the Stop button , clicking the View ➪ Stop menu command, or pressing Esc. Any of these actions achieves the same result — stopping a page transfer in midstream. Just be aware that you may end up starting at a blank IE5 screen if the new page has partially loaded. In this case, you can navigate using the Back button to return to the original page, enter a new URL in the Address bar, or click on a page stored in your Favorites list, among other options.

Browsing a page

Get your bearings by seeing what it takes to browse a Web page. For purposes of this example, visit my company home page at www.MichaelDesmond.com. Here's how to visit and browse:

1. Open Internet Explorer by double-clicking the Internet Explorer icon on the desktop or by clicking Start ➪ Programs ➪ Internet Explorer.

2. Type **www.michaeldesmond.com** in the Address bar and click Go (or alternatively, press Enter).

3. Once the page loads, use the vertical scroll bar on the right side to move down the page. Figure 13-10 shows what the page looks like.

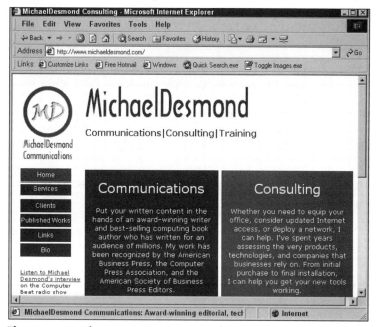

Figure 13-10: The pages you view may change, but the scroll bars, icons, menus, and other elements stay the same.

4. Jump to another page on the site using one of the links. There are two ways to navigate around this site: Either click the colored icons along the left side of the screen or click the text-based links at the bottom of the page. Click the Bio icon.

5. You should see a new Web page displayed in your IE5 window. Again, clicking along the gray bar on the right side of the page scrolls you down the page. Pressing the Page Down and Page Up keys does the same thing.

6. Hop back to the home page. Click the Back button that appears in the Standard Buttons toolbar, just beneath the File menu item. You've returned to where you started.

Tip

Here's another timesaver. Instead of mousing to the Back button, just press Alt-Left arrow key. No surprise, pressing Alt-Right arrow key mimics the action of the Forward button. Another way to move back and forth is to right-click the open Web page and select Forward or Back from the shortcut menu.

Getting there and back again

One of the most challenging aspects of the Web is its vastness. The parade of links invites you to follow one item after another, leaving lots of pages in your wake as you plow down into a certain topic or area. As you saw in the brief navigation example, the Back button (and its counterpart, the Forward button) can come in very handy when you're trying to retrace your steps.

These buttons work because IE5 keeps track of your steps as you move around the Web. But if you've visited dozens of sites, it can take quite a while to click the Back button 20 or more times and wait for IE5 to catch up with you by loading those previously visited pages. Fortunately, you can jump back (or forward, for that matter) in time.

To move back several sites, click the arrow next to the Back button. A list of previously visited sites drops down, as shown in Figure 13-11. Click the bottom-most site to move back as far as possible along your tracks. If this action doesn't get you all the way back, click the arrow next to the Back button again, and another drop-down list of site names appears. To continue digging further back, click the bottom-most entry and click the arrow next to the Back button again.

Figure 13-11: Right-clicking the Back and Forward buttons enables you to jump over several previously viewed sites.

Once you've backtracked, you can quickly jump forward by repeating these steps, only using the Forward button instead. Your browser jumps instantly to the site you select. Once you hit the end of the Back or Forward button lists, the button grays out and becomes inactive.

Alternatively, you can click View ⇨ Go To. A fly-out menu displays a list of sites you've visited during your session. Click any of these to jump directly to the selected sites. You can also click the drop-down arrow on the Address bar to display a drop-down list of Web site URLs you've entered during the current session — click one to go to that site. Other options on this menu include Home Page, which brings you back to the default starting page your browser opens when launched, and the Back and Forward menu items, which behave just like their button counterparts.

Seek, and ye shall find

So you can move around in a straight line through the Internet, but how do you find the sites that interest you? Well, that's where Web search engines and services come in. By going to these sites, you can enter terms of interest into a general search form or drill down through hierarchical indexes of topics to find what you need to know.

For example, say you want to do research on a telescope purchase. At Yahoo, you could enter the word *telescope* directly into the search text box at the top of the Yahoo home page and click the Search button. Or better yet, you could focus the search by entering the terms *telescope* and *astronomy*, thus eliminating references to field telescopes that are used for bird watching and hunting.

The problem with this approach is that you actually have to go to the search engine site — in this case, www.yahoo.com — to get recommendations for other sites. Not only does that take extra time, but it can be something of a hassle to browse to multiple recommended sites because you must constantly go back and forth from Yahoo's search result listing to each different site.

IE5 (like IE4 before it) fixes this inconvenience by incorporating a search service directly into the browser. You are still reaching out over the Internet to a Web-based service, but you can access this service directly from the browser without trudging off to a different Web site. And best of all, you can see and click your result links in a separate column of your IE5 browser, and you view the pages in the main window. The result is much more convenient and less confusing Web searches.

To kick off an IE5 search, just enter the word *go* followed by the search word or words in the Address bar. In this example, a search for information about telescopes, Figure 13-12 shows what the Address bar should look like. Here are the many ways you can make the telescope search happen:

Figure 13-12: Kick off a Web search inside your browser by typing **go telescopes** in the IE5 Address bar.

✦ Click your mouse on the Address bar, enter the words *go telescope*, and click the Go button (or press Enter).

✦ Press Ctrl+O or Ctrl+L and enter the words *go telescope* in the dialog box and click OK or press Enter.

✦ Click the Search button on the toolbar. In the left-pane Search facility, enter the word *telescope* in the text box and press Enter. To close this pane, click the X that appears in the top-right corner of the pane.

Note

These different methods return different results. For example, the Address bar search, by default, searches using the MSN search engine, while the IE5 Search button accesses a variety of search engines. This is different from the IE4 AutoSearch feature, which employed the Yahoo search engine. Needless to say, you get different results from these different searches. Figure 13-13 shows the results of a quick search using the default MSN search engine.

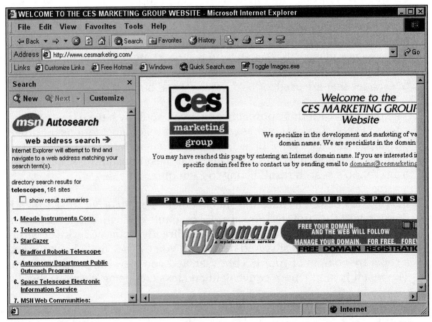

Figure 13-13: This Web page shows the results after entering "go telescopes" in the IE5 Address bar, which invokes the MSN search engine.

You have plenty of relevant hits here, including Meade Instruments Corp., the largest maker of amateur telescopes on the market. But the top-most hit—shown in the Web page display pane—is a domain name reseller of all things. Web searches can be tricky business. Now tailor your IE5 search. First, click the X at the top-right corner of the Search pane (if it's still open), then click the Search button on the toolbar. The left Search pane appears, as shown in Figure 13-14. At the top of the pane are five radio buttons:

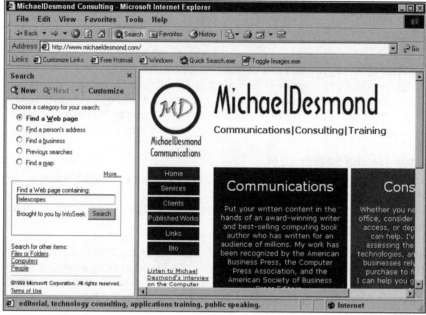

Figure 13-14: Find and seek: The Search pane offers a slew of different search options, making IE5 a one-stop shop for finding information on the Web.

✦ **Find a Web page:** Provides a list of links relating to the term entered in the text box.

✦ **Find a person's address:** Returns the address and phone number based on personal information you enter.

✦ **Find a business:** Returns the address and phone number of businesses. May also return a graphical map with directions to the office.

✦ **Previous searches:** Stores your previous searches, which you can relaunch by clicking the links.

✦ **Find a map:** Brings up a graphical map based on an address or place name.

Click the appropriate radio button to tailor your search. The Web page searches option is selected by default, but you can change it by simply clicking another radio button and then entering data into the text boxes that appear. These text boxes change based on whether you are doing a quick Web site word search or are entering complete addresses for the map and person search modes.

In addition to these default radio buttons, you can click the More link to show three more categories. These appear under the initial five and also include radio buttons to select the type:

✦ **Look up a word:** Turns the Web into your personal dictionary, thesaurus, or encyclopedia.

✦ **Find a picture:** Searches the image database of Corbis (a company owned by Bill Gates, not coincidentally) and returns a list of clickable thumbnail images in the search pane. Note that you have to pay $3 per image to download the high-resolution version without the Corbis watermark.

✦ **Find in newsgroups:** Looks up messages in Internet newsgroups that are indexed by Deja.com, a service that archives the contents of thousands of Internet newsgroups and allows you to search them by keyword, topic of interest, and other parameters. This is a good way to find answers to questions or discussions regarding a wide range of issues.

Customize the Search tool

You've taken a good look at the kinds of search resources available in IE5, and they seem pretty impressive. But you can also customize this resource, going under the hood to see and set exactly which Internet search engines and services are used during searches.

Click the Customize button at the top of the Search pane. The Customize Search Settings dialog box opens as shown in Figure 13-15, displaying a section for each of the radio button items and subitems shown in the expanded Search pane (click the More link to expand this pane). Use the scroll bar on the left to move down the page. As you can see from the checkboxes next to each listed service and engine, IE5 takes a catch-all approach to searching the Web. General Web page searches use no fewer than seven search engines. In addition, there are three search services that search for people and two mapping services.

Figure 13-15: IE5 packs a lot of search engines into jobs you kick off with the Search button, returning much more comprehensive results than those produced by the Address bar's Go searches.

With Internet searches, though, you can have too much of a good thing. To slim down your results, uncheck some of the listed search engines. Slimming down searches helps speed response (and can reduce spurious returns), but you will likely miss some listings you would otherwise see.

You can also change the search engine used when you type **go searchterm** in the IE5 Address bar. The default is the MSN search engine. Click the Autosearch settings button at the bottom of the dialog box. In the dialog box that appears, shown in Figure 13-16, select the search engine you want to use from the drop-down list box.

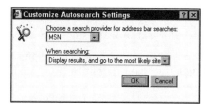

Figure 13-16: Don't like the MSN search engine? Select from any one of nine search engines for your speedy Address bar searches.

Caution   Changing search engines changes the types of returns you get from your Go searches. Yahoo, for instance, is a directory service that returns hits from sites that have registered with its widely used service. AltaVista and others, on the other hand, actually burrow through the Web to find all content relating to your search.

Note that changing the default may change the appearance of the search results. The default MSN Go search loads the most likely Web page into the main IE5 pane, while other hits are listed as links in the Search pane. Switch to Yahoo, however, and the linked hits are displayed in the main page only.

You can also shut off the Go search feature by doing the following:

1. Open the left Search pane in IE5 and click the Customize button at the top of the pane.

2. In the Customize Search Settings dialog box, click the AutoSearch settings button.

3. In the dialog box that appears, click the When searching drop-down list control and click Do not search from the Address bar.

4. Click OK twice to close the dialog boxes and put the changes into effect.

If you want to return to the IE5 defaults, open the Customize Search Settings dialog box as indicated above and then click the Reset button. Click OK to close the dialog box. Note that in order to turn Autosearch back on, you must specifically reinstate the capability by clicking the Autosearch settings button in the Customize Search Settings dialog box. Then select the appropriate item (default is Display results, and go to the most likely site) in the drop-down list control.

Setting your home page

By default, IE5 whisks you off to the Microsoft Network service when IE5 starts and prompts you to set up a personal page. Whether it's a convenience or an annoyance is for you to decide. But you definitely don't have to stick with Microsoft's home page. In fact, my IE5 home page isn't on the Internet at all; it's a local HTML file on my hard disk that is loaded with links and URLs that I use frequently. It's a fast-loading jumping point to other destinations.

You can set your own home page easily. Click Tools ➪ Internet Options. At the top of the General page is the Home page area, which includes the URL of your current home page in the Address text box. There are two ways to set a new home page:

✦ Manually enter the new URL into the Address text box and click OK or Apply.

✦ Use IE5 to load the Web page you want to use as your home page, open the Internet Options dialog box, and then click the Use Current button. Again, click OK or Apply.

If you've changed your home page but decide that you really want MSN as your start point after all, click the Use Default button. Another option is to have no home page at all. Click the Use Blank button, and when you launch Internet Explorer, the browser displays a generic blank page HTML file, which sits on the local hard disk.

Tip   As I mentioned, I use a local HTML file for my home page. It loads faster, doesn't get confused by a disrupted Internet connection, and is readily customizable using any HTML editor. The easiest way to set a local file as your home page is launch the page from the Windows browser or Explorer by double-clicking it. When IE5 opens the file (since it is associated with files with an .HTM or .HTML extension), click Tools ➪ Internet Options and then click the Use Current button to set the local file as the default. The Address box text reads something like `file:///C:/My%Documents/Home.html`, as shown in Figure 13-17.

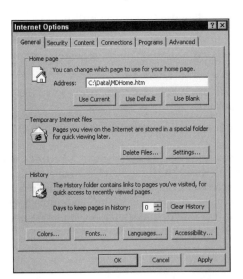

Figure 13-17: Whether you hand-type the URL or click the Use Current button, the URL of your home page appears in the Address text box of the Internet Options dialog box.

Securing Internet Explorer

We live in a connected world. The Internet enables you to download files and applications, access news and information, manage your finances, and correspond with others across the globe — all from the comfort of your home and office. But the immediacy of the public network also poses dangers. Unwanted parties may try to pay a visit to your system through your Internet connection, or companies may want to limit Web access to prevent unproductive use of company bandwidth.

Internet Explorer comes armed with a host of facilities that can do everything from block sites to demand authentication. This section shows you how to limit your exposure to Internet-based risks and dangers. Most of the work occurs on the Security tab of the Internet Options dialog box, shown in Figure 13-18. To get there, click Tools ➪ Internet Options, and then click the Security tab.

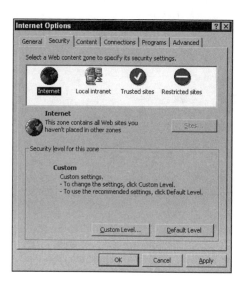

Figure 13-18: The Security tab offers plenty of ways to customize security and filtering for any audience.

Working with zones

Start by creating browsing zones for IE5. This feature enables you or a network administrator to distinguish trusted places on the Internet from untrusted ones. For example, when you visit the Fidelity or Schwab brokerage Web sites, you want to enjoy full access to Java applets and ActiveX controls. You may also need to enable *cookies* — files that Web sites use to identify you and track your activities — to access these secure services.

Of course, the environment can change when you are off casually browsing the Web. If you are digging around for information about, say, aviation, you may not want the Web site owner to be able to tell who you are by placing a cookie on your hard drive. And in many cases, you may want to protect yourself against possible attack or intrusion by locking out programming features such as ActiveX controls.

A tour of IE5's zones

Figure 13-18 shows the various zones that are available. Each has a default configuration, but you can also tweak them as you like. Here are the four zones:

✦ **Internet:** The catch-all zone that covers Web sites that you have not identified in other zones. Security level is Medium.

✦ **Local intranet:** Contains all the Web sites residing on an intranet. The security level is Medium-Low.

✦ **Trusted sites:** The least secure zone, only sites you completely trust should be assigned to this zone. The security level is Low.

✦ **Restricted sites:** The most secure zone, this one is best for sites that you feel could pose a threat to system security or data. The security level is High.

What does the security level do, exactly? The four security levels enable different levels of restrictions on such things as ActiveX downloads, cookie use, and the like. Table 13-1 describes the levels.

Table 13-1 Security Levels		
Security level	**Zone used by**	**Description**
High	Restricted sites	Safest but least functional. Cookies disabled, ActiveX downloads and execution disabled, file downloads disabled, font downloads on prompt only, program launches disabled, download unsigned ActiveX controls disabled.
Medium	Internet	Safe and functional. Cookies enabled, ActiveX downloads on prompt, file and font downloads enabled, launch programs on prompt, download unsigned ActiveX controls disabled.
Medium-Low	Local intranet	Like Medium but without most prompts. Cookies enabled, ActiveX downloads on prompt, file and font downloads enabled, launch programs on prompt, download unsigned ActiveX controls disabled.
Low	Trusted sites	Minimal safeguards and few prompts. Cookies enabled, ActiveX downloads on prompt, file and font downloads enabled, launch programs on prompt, download unsigned ActiveX controls enabled.

By default, all sites you visit are handled as part of the Internet zone. That means when you go on the Internet, you are probably interacting with Web sites using the Medium security level setting. That's not so bad, actually. At Medium level, IE5 prompts you before downloading ActiveX controls, installing desktop items, or launching programs or files; however, cookies are enabled, and ActiveX controls run once they're downloaded.

By default, all your browsing takes place in the Internet zone, at Medium-level security. You can assign sites to specific zones from the Internet Options dialog box. Here's how to do it:

1. Click Tool ⇨ Internet Options and click the Security tab.

2. Click the Trusted sites icon or the Restricted sites icon and click the Sites button.

3. Type the URL of the desired site into the text box at the top of the dialog box that appears, as shown in Figure 13-19.

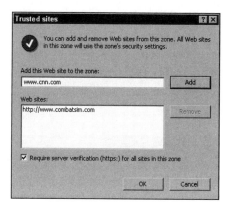

Figure 13-19: Enter as many sites as you want in the Trusted sites list. IE5 takes an extremely lax security posture whenever you visit these sites.

4. Click Add to move the new URL into the Web sites list box.

5. Repeat steps 3 and 4 to add any additional Web sites.

6. If you are adding sites to the Trusted sites list, a checkbox labeled Require server verification is available. Keep this checked if you want to ensure that all connections to trusted Web sites are handled in a secure fashion.

7. Click OK.

Tip

You can easily add sites that you visit to the Restricted sites and Trusted sites zones. Just browse to the site and click the Tools menu item. Then click either Add to Trusted Zone or Add to Restricted Zone. When you go to the Security page of the Internet Options dialog box and open the list for Trusted sites or Restricted sites, the new site appears there.

When you browse to a site that you've placed in your Trusted or Restricted site zones, you see an icon and text on the right side of the IE5 status bar, which appears along the bottom of the window. This icon identifies the current site as either restricted or trusted.

In general, the default security settings should work fine. Prompted access means you know if an ActiveX control or other procedure is requested, but cookie use means you can access virtually any Web site or service (some sites, including Microsoft's download services, require cookies, for example). When you visit unindexed sites, you see a globe icon in the status bar with the word *Internet* next to it.

There are exceptions, however. If you tend to visit hacker sites, for example, you may want to specifically disable programmatic entities like ActiveX controls and Java applets. In this case, you can assign a specific URL to the Restricted Sites zone and rest assured that an invisible ActiveX control isn't going to execute on your system and pass valuable information to the site. In fact, at the time of this writing, disabling ActiveX functionality was a suggested workaround for a known security hole in IE5. By the time you read this, a downloadable patch should address this weakness.

The Cookie Conundrum

There is a lot of talk about cookies, but what are they exactly? Cookies are small text files that Web sites can leave behind on your hard disk as a means of recognizing you when you return. Web site owners use cookies as a valuable source of information, enabling them to track activities and tailor content to each user.

If you think of cookies as a kind of animal tag, you're on the right track. When park officials tag a bear or eagle, they do so with the intention of learning the animal's habits and perhaps taking actions based on patterns they see among tagged animals. Web site cookies essentially act as digital tags, enabling site owners to take actions based on the behaviors they track in your cookie file.

Of course, a lot of people don't *want* to be tracked like an animal in the wild; they prefer to keep their browsing habits to themselves. By disabling cookies (whether by selecting a high security level or by manually disabling the cookie feature specifically), users can prevent a digital tag from being placed on their hard disks.

To disable cookies, click Tools ⇨ Options, click the Security tab, and click the Custom Level button. In the Security Settings dialog box, scroll down to the Cookies section and click the two Disable radio buttons in that section. Click OK, wait for the browser to update its settings, and click OK again to close the Internet Options dialog box. Now any cookies a site tries to place on your hard disk will be turned away.

The one problem is that some sites actually require cookies to work at all. These sites either use cookies as part of the user authentication process or mandate cookie use as a means of extracting valuable user data in exchange for a valuable "free" service, such as Microsoft's Office update facility on its Web site. But very often, cookies are just thrown onto hard drives as another way to measure and track user behavior.

There is a middle ground. You can tell IE5 to prompt you when a cookie is sent to your system. The problem is there can be so many cookie requests that the prompting quickly overwhelms your browsing efforts. That's where IE5's zones come in. You can easily assign a low security setting to those few sites that you are willing to accept cookies from in exchange for a service. The rest of the sites can then be handled by the Internet zone, which you can tweak to not accept any cookies at all. The result is that you get access to services you need while keeping the vast majority of cookies where they belong—in the Web site provider's jar.

Tweaking zones

As you click each of the four zone icons, a slider bar appears along the lower-left side of the Internet Options dialog box. This slider reflects any one of the four default security profiles. By moving this slider, shown in Figure 13-20, you can bolster or reduce the level of security for a given zone. Once you've adjusted the slider, click OK or Apply for the changes to take effect.

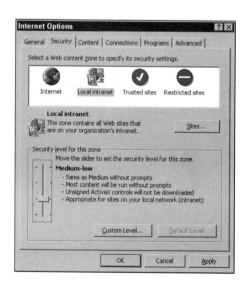

Figure 13-20: With the useful security level slider, you can quickly customize IE5's zones to suit your needs.

Caution Be aware that if you crank up security levels some pages may not work properly. In particular, lack of cookie access causes some pages to reject authentication, downloads, and possibly other functions.

If you decide later that you need to return to IE5 default zone settings, just open the Internet Options dialog box to the Security tab, click the affected zone, and click the Default Level button. The zone you edited snaps back to the settings it had originally.

You can get down and dirty with zone features by clicking the Custom Level button. For example, to tweak your security settings for the Internet zone, first click the Internet icon in the top window and then click the Custom Level button to see a comprehensive rundown of security options in the Security Settings dialog box, shown in Figure 13-21. Most of the items present three choices: Disable, Enable, and Prompt.

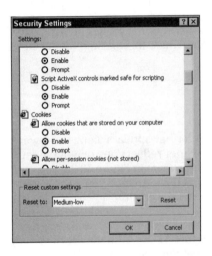

Figure 13-21: Need to get specific? Click the appropriate radio button for each security item to customize the way IE5 treats sites assigned to specific zones.

Use these definitions of the available security elements to help you decide whether to enable or disable the feature or have IE5 prompt you before allowing a transaction or event to occur.

✦ **Download signed ActiveX controls:** Controls transfer of ActiveX applications and controls that have been approved by Microsoft. These ActiveX controls should carry a digital signature, which is a public key assigned by an independent distributing authority. Digital signatures assure users that the ActiveX control comes from a verifiable source.

✦ **Download unsigned ActiveX controls:** Manages transfer of ActiveX applications and controls that have not been digitally signed by Microsoft or other authorized body.

✦ **Initialize and script ActiveX controls not marked as safe:** Dictates the behavior of ActiveX controls that are of unknown origin or intent. Enable overrides the safety setting and allows ActiveX controls to run.

✦ **Run ActiveX controls and plug-ins:** Controls the behavior of all ActiveX controls and Netscape plug-ins, regardless of origin. The Administrator-approved option enables only ActiveX controls or plug-ins that have been identified to the system by a network administrator.

✦ **Script ActiveX controls marked as safe for scripting** ActiveX scripting allows developers to integrate the behavior of several ActiveX controls and Java applications to extend functionality. This setting lets you determine whether an ActiveX control (that has been recognized as safe) can interact with a script.

✦ **Allow cookies that are stored on your computer:** Determines whether your system accepts cookies from Web sites. Used to control persistent cookies that are stored on your hard disk.

✦ **Allow per-session cookies:** Determines whether your system accepts cookies from Web sites. Used for cookies that last just during the current browsing session. Once you close Internet Explorer, the cookie files are deleted.

✦ **File download:** Enables or disables file downloads from Web sites.

✦ **Font downloads:** Controls downloads of fonts from Web sites.

✦ **Java permissions:** Controls the amount of access Java applets have to files, folders, and network connections. For more on Java, see the next section, "Setting Java Permissions."

✦ **Drag and drop or copy and paste files:** Enables or disables the capability to copy files from Web sites onto your system.

✦ **Installation of desktop items:** Controls whether or not applications or components can be installed on the Windows 2000 desktop.

✦ **Launching programs and files in an IFRAME:** Determines if applications and files can be launched when an IFRAME tag references a directory from within HTML.

✦ **Software channel permissions:** Low safety allows e-mail notifications, auto downloads, and auto installations, while medium limits to e-mail notification and auto download. High safety disables all these channel distribution features.

✦ **Submit nonencrypted form data:** Determines if data input into online forms may be sent over the Internet in nonsecure format.

✦ **Userdata persistence:** Enables automated authentication into Web sites by remembering related passwords and user names.

✦ **Active scripting:** Determines whether script code on a page in a zone is run.

✦ **Allow paste operations via script:** Determines whether scripts can be used to access the Windows Clipboard.

✦ **Scripting of Java applets:** Determines whether applets are exposed to scripts within a zone.

✦ **Logon:** Provides four options for logging onto sites requiring authentication. Anonymous logon does not provide user names or passwords, while the Prompt for user name and password enables the user to enter logon information. The two Automatic logon settings attempt to use the current Windows 2000 user name and password to authenticate sites.

Setting Java permissions

The Security Settings dialog box, under the Microsoft VM (for Java virtual machine) section, contains an entry entitled Java permissions. This entry features five options: Custom, Disable Java, High safety, Low safety, and Medium safety. These settings control how much — if any — downloaded access Java applets enjoy to system files, folders, and network resources. If you click the Custom radio button, however, a new button — Java Custom Settings — appears below the Settings list box in the Security Settings dialog box. With this button, you can tailor the behavior of Java applets in your IE5 configuration.

When you click the Java Custom Settings button, you are taken to a dialog box, shown in Figure 13-22, which includes two tabs: View Permissions and Edit Permissions. The View Permissions tab displays settings specified by your network administrator. Permissions are needed to enable Java applets to access requested system resources; otherwise, applets may be denied access and cannot run. Typically, you are prompted when a Java application is denied access to a requested resource, such as when it attempts to write a file to disk.

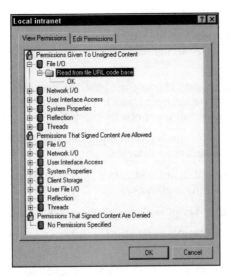

Figure 13-22: Review IE5's Java security settings on the View Permissions tab.

The View Permission page has three sections. Double-click a permission item under any section to view the specific permission status and settings. The three sections are the following:

✦ **Permissions Given to Unsigned Content:** Defines what unsigned Java applications (whose source may be unknown) can do on the system.

✦ **Permissions That Signed Content Are Allowed:** Defines access afforded to Java applications that have been verified by a trusted source.

✦ **Permissions That Signed Content Are Denied:** Defines restrictions to Java applications that have been verified by a trusted source.

Once you've reviewed your settings, you can click the Edit Permissions tab to alter them. Figure 13-23 shows this dialog box. The Edit Permissions page has two topic areas, Unsigned Content and Signed Content. Under each is an overall setting.

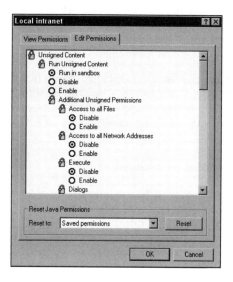

Figure 13-23: If you run Java code served by a local intranet, you probably don't need all the restrictive Java protections. You can change a lot of them here.

✦ **Unsigned Content:** The Run Unsigned Content item is set by default to Run in sandbox. This means that all Java applet access to system information, network addresses, dialog boxes, and execution is disabled.

✦ **Signed Content:** The Run Signed Content item is set by default to Prompt. This means that Java applets can access system information, network resources, and other facilities, provided the end user clicks a dialog box announcing the access request.

In both the Unsigned Content and Signed Content areas, all the specific permissions are set to match the overarching setting. So if the Run Signed Content permission is set to Disable, all the specific unsigned Java content permissions below it are set to Disable as well. If you set the overarching setting to Run in sandbox, however, you can then individually enable permissions, giving access to specific facilities, such as printing, for example.

Finally, you can change Java permissions at a single pass, using the Reset to drop-down list control. This causes all the Java permissions to hew to one of three preset templates (low, medium, and high security) or to a saved, last-known permissions profile.

Managing access

The Internet can be a rather unsavory place. It contains, for example, an explosive amount of Web-based pornography, not to mention hate sites and other extreme content. To help you control access to such sites, Internet Explorer plugs into a Web site rating system managed by the Recreational Software Advisory Council on the Internet (RSACi) that profiles site content. You can use these profiles to restrict user access based on four RSACi criteria: language, nudity, sex, and violence. Each of these criteria is rated on a five-point scale, ranging from 0 (innocuous) to 4 (extreme).

Setting RSACi filters

To view or edit access settings, open the Internet Options dialog box (click Tools ➪ Internet Options) and click the Content tab. Click the Enable button in the Content Advisor area at the top of the dialog box. The Content Advisor dialog box opens to display the four RSACi categories, as well as a slider bar that you can use to set the filter.

To restrict access to offensive material, do the following:

1. Select the first category you want to filter by clicking it.

2. Click the slider handle and drag it to the right, as shown in Figure 13-24. The further to the right you drag, the more content passes through the filter. By default, the slider is set to 0, which accepts literally no offensive content.

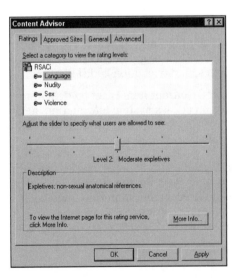

Figure 13-24: The capability to filter content is a boon for parents and others concerned about explicit material on the Internet.

3. Click OK or Apply.

4. If you haven't already, assign yourself a supervisor password in the Create Supervisor Password dialog box. Enter a password, confirm it, and then click OK.

5. A dialog box confirms the change. Click OK.

Now when you try to browse a Web page that doesn't pass the RSACi category filter, you see a Content Advisor dialog box. This dialog box displays the RSACi filter level for the requested site, as well as the source of the rating. A Password text box is provided to enable the supervisor to override the filter setting. By clicking the bottom radio button and entering the password, the supervisor overrides the filter only for the specific browsing session. Clicking the top radio button enables permanent override access to the entire requested site, while the middle radio button opens permanent access to only the specific page that prompted the Content Advisor dialog box.

To adjust settings, do the following:

1. Click Tools ⇨ Internet Options and click the Content tab.

2. Click the Settings button.

3. Enter the supervisor password in the dialog box and click OK.

4. In the Content Advisor dialog box, select the desired RSACi categories and make any desired changes by moving the slider bar.

5. Click Apply or OK.

Note

You can disable content filtering entirely by clicking the Disable button on the Content tab of the Internet Options dialog box. Of course, you have to provide the supervisor password.

Creating lists of approved or disapproved sites

The Content Advisor does more than just restrict access to rated pages. It provides a handy way for you to limit access to Web sites over your corporate LAN. A network administrator might, for example, limit online grazing by specifically denying access to sites such as sports and news sites or job search sites.

To identify a site you want to restrict, click the Approved Sites tab in the Content Advisor dialog box. Then enter the URL of the site in the Allow this Web site text box. Click the Never button. The site appears in the list box with a red icon next to it as shown in Figure 13-25. Users of this Web browser are no longer able to access this site as shown in Figure 13-26.

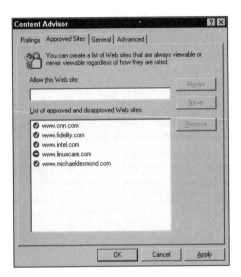

Figure 13-25: Quickly create a list of approved and disapproved sites in the Content Advisor dialog box.

Figure 13-26: When a user tries to visit a site blocked by the Content Advisor rating or Approved Sites list, a dialog box announces that the site is unavailable. If you have a supervisor's password, you can override the protection.

You can also use this dialog box to enable access to sites that might otherwise be blocked by the RSACi service. For example, perhaps you have set the violence filter, but your son still wants to visit sites about his favorite computer game, Quake Arena. Enter **www.quake3arena.com** in the Allow this Web site text box, click Always, and then click OK to exclude this site from the filter.

Note
The Content Advisor feature is nice, but it's really not intended to serve as a network administrator's tool for shaping corporate Internet access. If you are tasked with managing Web access for large numbers of users, you should look into installing software at the proxy server that can detect URLs and compare them against an approved list. That way, you have to change the list only once — at the proxy — and it affects all client systems working through it.

Working access

Click the General tab of the Content Advisor dialog box for some tune-up features for access controls as shown in Figure 13-27. The User options area includes two checkboxes. The top checkbox, when active, enables users to visit sites that fail to return an RSACi rating. Checking this option prevents spurious Web site lockouts but at the risk of allowing offensive material to pass through. The lower item, when checked, enables supervisor-override for sites that do not pass the filter. If you uncheck this box, users no longer get the opportunity to enter a supervisor password to see the site.

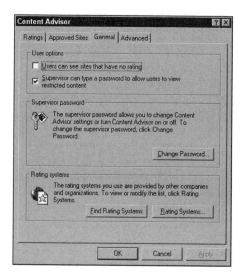

Figure 13-27: Change passwords, tweak site protections, and update site rating sources on the General tab of the Content Advisor dialog box.

The next area is a simple change password facility. Click the Change Password button and then enter your existing password into the dialog box that appears to authenticate yourself. Next, enter the new password in each of the two text boxes and then click OK.

Finally, the Rating systems area enables you to change Web site ratings systems you use for your filters. The RSACi rating system is the default, but you can click the Find Rating Systems button to bring up the Microsoft Internet Explorer rating system page at `http://www.microsoft.com/windows/ie/ratings.asp`. This might be useful if you want to employ a rating system that is tailored to a specific area of interest or content.

You can also add and remove rating systems by clicking the Rating Systems button. This action launches the Rating Systems dialog box, where you see the currently installed rating systems in the list box. You can install a new rating system from a local or network drive by clicking the Add button and navigating to the appropriate .RAT file. To remove a rating system, select it in the window and click Remove.

Using certificates

More and more, Web browsers are becoming conduits for conducting e-business. Every day, millions of dollars worth of orders are transacted over the Web, often using secure, encrypted data links between a corporate Web server and a standard Web browser. To make these transactions happen, however, a level of trust must be established between the buyer and the seller.

A key underpinning to this trust development is the idea of certificates — secure and verified digital documents that establish the identity of the other party (see Figure 13-28). Not just anyone can distribute certificates. Rather, certificates are issued by so-called *certificate authorities* (CAs), companies that specialize in acting as a clearinghouse for identification services. The largest certificate authority is VeriSign.

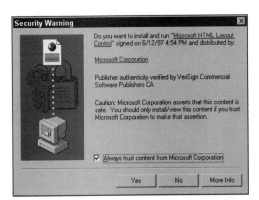

Figure 13-28: Microsoft uses certificates to verify the authenticity of downloadable components such as ActiveX applications. Because nefarious ActiveX components can potentially be harmful to your PC, the use of certificates enables users to download applets with confidence.

Getting a Personal Security Certificate

It's no surprise that large companies such as Microsoft want to adopt digital certificates. After all, these firms have a lot to gain if they can help establish the Internet as a viable medium for commerce. With digital certificates, end users are able to trust that companies on the Internet are who they say they are.

But what about your own identity? How can you verify that you are who you say? Companies such as VeriSign offer digital certificates for individuals. For $9.95 per year, the VeriSign Class 1 digital ID authenticates your e-mail address, provides a listing in VeriSign's public directory, and gives you $1,000 of protection coverage against loss incurred by any issues with the digital ID.

To obtain an ID, you must fill out a form that includes name, address, phone, and e-mail information. You also have to provide credit card information for billing. Once you receive the digital ID, you install it on your system. At that point, you are able to send and receive encrypted, secure e-mail enabled through your Public Key Infrastructure digital ID.

Access information about digital certificates from the Internet Options dialog box. Click the Certificates button to go to the Certificates dialog box.

At the top of the dialog box is the Intended purpose drop-down list box. Select from the list to view certificates that have been installed to match that specific purpose. Client Authentication, for example, applies to certificates issued to verify identity. Secure Email entry applies to certificates that enable encrypted e-mail messages.

The tabbed box underneath the Intended purposes drop-down list box presents certificate entries for Personal, Other People, Intermediate Certification Authorities, and Trusted Root Certification Authorities. Under each tab, you see the certificates or the certificate authorities installed for each entry, as shown in Figure 13-29. The Personal tab enables you to view your own certificate, while with the Other People tab, you can see certificates that others have shared with you as a way to verify their identity.

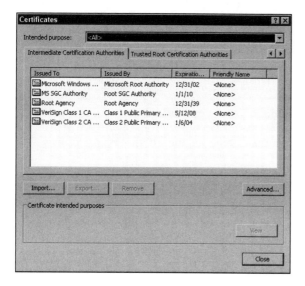

Figure 13-29: The tabbed Certificates dialog box enables you to view your own certificates, as well as those from other users and from certificate authorities.

To import a certificate file, click the Import button to open the Certificate Import Wizard and then click Next at the screen that appears. You need to provide the filename and path for the certificate file, either by entering it in the File name text box or by navigating to it using the Browse button.

Note   Digital certificates can be imported from a number of file formats:

Personal Information Exchange-PKCS #12 (.PFX and .P12 extensions)

Cryptographic Message Syntax Standard-PKCS #7 Certificates (.P7B extension)

Microsoft Serialized Certificate Store (.SST extension)

You may need to export a certificate if you wish to share it with a non-Windows system. To do so, do the following:

1. Select the certificate to export and then click the Export button. The Certificate Export Wizard launches. Click the Next button.

2. To export the certificate with your secure private key information, click the top radio button. You have to protect your private key by providing a password later in the process. If you do not wish to export the key information, click the bottom radio button.

3. Click Next and then select the file formats to save to and the characteristics to enable. Note that the options change based on whether or not your are exporting the private key with your certificate.

4. Click Next. If necessary, enter a password and click Next.

5. Enter a filename in the File name text box. You may want to use the Browse button to navigate to a specific folder. Click Next.

6. A dialog box displays the results of the export. Click Finish to close the process. The file can now be sent to or installed at the destination.

Customizing

Internet Explorer 5.0 improves on its predecessors in a variety of ways. It is more versatile and flexible than earlier versions. From offline browsing to handy customizations, IE5 seems to offer a solution for every problem.

AutoComplete

The AutoComplete feature eases Web site navigation by automatically guessing what you are typing in the Address bar based on what you've typed in the past. For example, if you frequently visit the Fidelity financial services Web site, IE5 beats you to the punch when you start typing the URL. As you enter the URL, a drop-down list appears beneath the Address bar, with URLs that match what you've entered so far. Of course, if you dump the contents of the IE5 History folder, the AutoComplete feature won't know of these previously viewed sites and won't prompt you.

Happily, the browser doesn't fill in the rest of the URL directly in the Address bar, something I find quite distracting. Rather, you can view the drop-down list of selections, as shown in Figure 13-30, and choose at any time to simply click one of the displayed options instead of completing your typing.

Figure 13-30: Start typing a URL, and IE5 presents a handy list of addresses that match what you've typed so far.

In addition to prompting you during URL input, IE5 can also store forms data and your user names and passwords. These features can really help speed access to frequently visited secure sites, but they do pose a security risk. After all, anyone with access to your running PC could access your secure Web sites using the AutoCompleted password and user information.

You manage the AutoComplete feature from the (where else?) Internet Options dialog box. Click Tools ➪ Internet Options and then click the Content tab. Click the AutoComplete button to see the dialog box shown in Figure 13-31. Three checkbox items are in this dialog box:

Figure 13-31: Make your Web browsing easier by having IE5 store passwords and autocomplete URLs. Just be wary of the security issues.

✦ **Web addresses:** Turn IE5's Web address completion facility on or off. Uncheck if you don't want people to see where you've browsed.

✦ **Forms:** If you've entered data in a Web-based form in the past, you can see your input whenever you return to the form page. The forms data is stored in encrypted format on your hard disk and is protected from access by Web sites. Sites only see forms data that you send. This option is off by default.

✦ **User names and passwords on forms:** For sites that require logon, this option stores your user name and password and automatically fills in the logon form. This option is on by default, but you may want to uncheck this box to keep your access secure. Also, uncheck the Prompt me to save passwords checkbox if you don't want to get a dialog box each time you enter a password at a new site.

Use this same dialog box to tighten up your browser security. Click Clear Forms to wipe out any saved forms data. For example, online orders may contain credit card information and other valuable personal data. Clicking Clear Forms removes this data from your system. The Clear Passwords button does just that, removes all stored passwords from your browser. Once you clear your passwords, you need to actively provide passwords to sites that you once breezed into, but at least your access is more secure.

Setting applications

I don't know about you, but I spend a lot of time running my Web browser. What's more, the browser is becoming the launch point for more and more other tasks. From data entry to e-mail, I seem to start more tasks than ever from IE5. IE5 provides an easy way to control the associated applications that can launch to perform certain actions. Located in the (yes, uh huh) Internet Options dialog box, the Programs tab gives you a one-stop shop for setting applications under IE5.

Each task includes a drop-down list box that displays all installed applications pertaining to the specific function. As shown in Figure 13-32, there are application assignments for six functions:

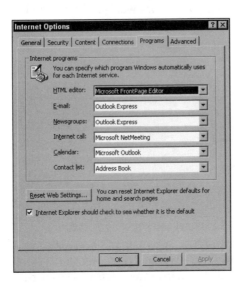

Figure 13-32: Tailor what programs launch when IE5 is used to invoke an e-mail client, kick off HTML editing, and perform other tasks.

✦ **HTML Editor:** Assigns the program to run whenever you click the File ➪ Edit menu command while viewing a Web page in IE5.

✦ **E-mail:** Assigns the e-mail client to run when you click a mailto link on a Web site.

✦ **Newsgroups:** Assigns the news reader application to run when you click a link to an Internet newsgroup.

✦ **Internet call:** Specifies what Internet-based conferencing and calling software to use. Microsoft NetMeeting is the default.

✦ **Calendar:** Sets your calendar program. Microsoft Outlook is the default if you have it installed on your PC.

✦ **Contact list:** Sets your address book program. The Windows Address Book is the default, and Microsoft Outlook shows up here if it is installed.

In addition, the Reset Web Settings button enables you to reestablish Internet Explorer as the default system Web browser. This button works only if you've installed another browser after you disabled IE5 and want to return to the original settings. Clicking the button, for example, kicks Netscape Navigator out as the default browser and puts IE5 in its place. It also resets defaults for your search engines and home page.

Tip You can access your mail and newsreader programs from IE5 by clicking Tools ⇨ Mail and News and then selecting the appropriate item from the fly-out menu.

Finally, the checkbox at bottom turns on the IE5 nag-o-matic feature. If you have another Web browser that you've established as the system default, a dialog box asks you if you want to restore IE5 as the default every time you launch IE5. By default, this checkbox is active (hardly a surprise). Uncheck the box to avoid unwanted dialog boxes when you switch browsers.

Browsing offline

One welcome addition to IE5 is improvements in the way it handles offline browsing. Microsoft has changed the clumsy channel model of IE4, providing a much more straightforward way to synchronize sites on the Internet with the offline versions stored on your hard disk. You now have several ways to handle offline browsing:

✦ Synchronizing content

✦ Downloading content

✦ Browsing from cache

Synchronizing content

The most powerful option is synchronizing content. This feature enables you to identify a Web site or pages in a site and mark them for download to your hard disk. HTML pages, images, ActiveX controls, Java applets, and all other page elements are poured onto your hard drive, where IE5 can then reproduce the complete site browsing experience over a local connection. You can also schedule and automate synchronizations. Who needs this kind of feature? A short list includes the following:

✦ Frequent travelers who want to browse Web content while on airplanes or otherwise away from Internet connections

✦ Users on slow Internet connections, because downloading large files can be performed overnight

✦ Anyone keeping track of updated site content

Setting up automatic synchronization

The following text shows how to set up a site to be available offline.

1. Browse to the site you want to access offline.

2. Click Favorites ➪ Add to Favorites.

3. Check the Make available offline checkbox and click Customize.

4. Click Next.

5. Click the No radio button if you only want to synchronize the open page or click the Yes radio button to have IE5 also cache all linked pages.

6. If you clicked Yes, tell IE5 how far it should follow links for downloaded content (up to three links deep).

7. If you want to synchronize pages manually, keep the top radio button selected. Otherwise, click the lower radio button and click Next to create a schedule.

8. To create a schedule, use the first spinner control to set the interval (in days) for updates and then enter the time of day for the download to occur.

 Tip   In order to avoid gumming up your Internet connection and burdening system performance, it's best to schedule downloads for off-hours, such as overnight. Another benefit is that Internet traffic moves faster because fewer people are online. Of course, you need to keep your PC on to perform these kinds of off-hours downloads.

9. Enter a name for the schedule and then check the checkbox so that your PC can automatically dial in to your ISP when the scheduled download time comes around. Click Next.

10. If the site you're downloading requires a password, click the Yes radio button and enter your user name and password in the text boxes. Click Finish.

11. You return to the Add Favorite dialog box. Click OK to register this favorite page with IE5.

Once you click OK, you see a dialog box noting the download progress. Depending on the amount of data stored at the site or page you are working with, this download can take a while. Once complete, the page is available from your hard disk.

Manually synchronizing Web pages

If you've set up a schedule for your page or pages, your system automatically connects to the Internet and grabs the data, keeping a fresh version on your hard disk. But what if you need to leave for a flight at midday, and your synchronized data is already 12 hours old? You can manually synchronize Web pages. Here's how:

1. Click Tools ➪ Synchronize.

2. In the Items to Synchronize dialog box, make sure the pages you want to synchronize are in the list box and have a checkmark next to them.

3. To minimize download time, uncheck any items you do not want to synchronize in this session.

4. Click the Synchronize button. The dialog box shows the progress and informs you when synchronization is complete.

Saving pages for offline viewing

What if you don't need to synchronize an entire site? Say you need to grab a couple of pertinent Web pages containing some HTML-based reports you want to review on a flight. The best approach is to use IE5's vastly improved Save As capability. In the past, clicking File ⇨ Save As saved only the HTML portion of a Web page to the targeted media. Now, by default, IE5 saves a working replica of the selected Web page.

So if you're viewing a report that's loaded with GIF and JPEG images, HTML text, and even ActiveX controls, you don't have to leave all that behind. Nor do you have to laboriously find, copy, and save images to your disk to keep images with the file. Just click File ⇨ Save As, give the file a name on your local disk drive, and click OK. The HTML file is saved as normal. But IE5 also creates a subdirectory (named to match the HTML file) that contains all the related images and controls.

When you open the file from your hard disk, all the image links are preserved. You can see graphs, photos, and all graphical elements without having to spend time pulling these elements down individually. Now that's much better.

Browsing offline

Browsing offline content is easy. If your system is away from an Internet connection, IE5 prompts you at launch to connect. In the dialog box, click the Browse Offline button. If a URL is available for offline browsing, the page is loaded from the hard disk when you enter its address in the Address bar.

If you attempt to browse to a page that has not been downloaded to disk, the browser brings up a dialog box offering to connect to the Internet. To dial in, click the Connect button. Otherwise, click Stay Offline. Just be aware that IE5 is not able to load the unavailable page and simply continues to display the current page.

To take your offline browsing session back online, click File ⇨ Work Offline. The Work Offline command, which is checked in Figure 13-33, will then be toggled off (so that it is unchecked). IE5 will then establish a connection according to its configuration.

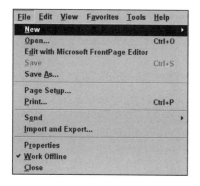

Figure 13-33: You can also go offline by clicking File ⇨ Work Offline. A checkmark appears next to the Work Offline menu command until you tell IE5 to go back online.

Advanced settings

Finally, at the end of the Internet Options dialog box is the Advanced tab. Here is a long scrolling list of IE5 characteristics and settings as shown in Figure 13-34, and each of them has an associated checkbox control. To activate an entry, simply click the item so that the box to the left of the entry title is checked. To turn off an entry, click it so that the box is unchecked. About a million items are listed in this box, so I don't go into them all here. But here is a rundown of topics that are addressed from this control:

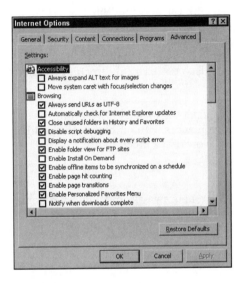

Figure 13-34: The long and distinguished list of options in the Advanced Settings window provides a vivid display of IE5's incredible flexibility.

✦ **Accessibility:** Enables you to enhance readability of text.

✦ **Browsing:** Controls how IE5 behaves.

✦ **Underline links:** Controls appearance of links on Web pages.

✦ **HTTP 1.1 settings:** Manages compatibility with the older HTTP 1.0 protocol on some Web sites by turning off HTTP 1.1 features.

✦ **Microsoft VM:** Controls the behavior of the Java Virtual Machine that is part of IE5.

✦ **Multimedia:** Enables you to adjust how IE5 offers access and services for video, audio, animation, and images.

✦ **Printing:** Enables you to turn on printing of background colors and images.

✦ **Search from the Address Bar:** Controls the formatting of search results when you kick off searches using the Address bar go command.

✦ **Security:** Sets behaviors surrounding digital certificates, temporary files, and secure status warnings.

There's a lot to wade through here, so it's easy to mistakenly set a behavior. Fortunately, the Restore Defaults button at the bottom of the dialog box quickly returns you to IE5's original settings with a single click.

Summary

Unbelievably, there's still ground I haven't covered here. I could go on and on about customizable toolbars, advanced settings, Favorites management, and file handling, but quite honestly, doing so would require a book dedicated solely to Internet Explorer. In fact, entire books *have* been written about this powerful Web browser software.

This chapter has hopefully given you a solid introduction to IE5, particularly to such intriguing features as security, network connectivity and management, and digital certificates.

Among the topics we covered here:

✦ The basics of HTML and Web navigation using Internet Explorer 5.0.

✦ Setting up and configuring Internet access from IE5, including the use of proxy servers to secure networks and speed access.

✦ Customizing IE5, including the interface, security settings, and program associations.

✦ Using IE5 to conveniently search the Web.

This chapter is only the first in my extended coverage of Windows 2000's Internet talents. In Chapter 14, I'll give you the grand tour of Outlook Express 5.0, the impressive e-mail program that comes with Windows 2000. From nifty HTML message formatting to sophisticated rules handling, Outlook Express offers all the features you need to manage your e-mail.

✦   ✦   ✦

Outlook Express Explained

No doubt about it: E-mail makes the Internet go around. From corporate executive offices to home PCs linked up via AOL accounts, e-mail remains the most used online application. In fact, e-mail traffic continues to grow. Not only are more and more users sending more messages, they are also sending more attachments to those messages. The result: Terabytes (that's thousands of gigabytes, folks) of valuable data are being traded via e-mail.

Not surprisingly, Microsoft bundles an e-mail client with Windows 2000 Professional that enables users to contribute to all that growing Internet e-mail traffic. In fact, the Outlook Express e-mail client application is a fine program that, like Internet Explorer, has improved greatly over the years. Today, it offers advanced features and capabilities to make even hardened e-mail veterans such as myself quite happy.

What is Outlook Express? In short, it is a full-featured e-mail client and Internet newsgroup reader. From this application, you get several advanced features:

✦ Multiple e-mail accounts and identities

✦ Advanced rules and folder handling for automatically managing messages

✦ Archiving

✦ Support for text formatting, images, and other HTML messages

Note   You might be wondering what the difference is between Outlook Express (which comes as part of Windows 2000) and Outlook 2000 (which can be purchased separately as part of Microsoft Office 2000 or on its own). Microsoft positions Outlook Express as a lightweight (and free) version of these programs. But don't be fooled. As an e-mail client and newsreader, Outlook Express can stand toe-to-toe with either of these flagship programs. The real difference is in the extended functionality you get with Outlook 98 and 2000. Both programs include advanced group-oriented features such as calendaring, group address books, and personal information manager (PIM) features. If you need to share schedules and contacts among the members of a group, or are looking for a one-stop shop to track, schedule, and manage events and people, Outlook 2000 is your best bet.

You can launch Outlook Express under Windows 2000 in several ways:

✦ Click the Outlook Express micro-icon in the Quick Launch toolbar.

✦ Click Start ➪ Programs ➪ Outlook Express.

✦ Launch Internet Explorer, click Tools ➪ Mail and News, and click the appropriate command to launch the mail or newsreader interface.

One of the most attractive aspects of Outlook Express is its ease of use. Over the years, Microsoft has done a fine job of improving the interface, adding key features and generally making Outlook Express a platform most users can live with. Figure 14-1 gives you a quick peek at the Outlook Express interface.

In fact, I recently shifted from Outlook 98—Microsoft's full-featured mail client, calendar program, and Address Book—to Outlook Express 5.0. The reason is because I prefer to handle contact and schedule information in other applications, and Outlook 98 as a mail client simply doesn't offer much in addition to what Outlook Express offers.

Working with E-mail Accounts

Before you delve into setting up an account and using the powerful features of Outlook Express, you need to understand some e-mail issues and become familiar with the Outlook Express interface.

Mail protocols at a glance

E-mail is by far the most prevalent and important network application. Both individuals and corporations now rely on e-mail for day-to-day communications as much as they do on reliable phone service. For most individuals, e-mail access comes in the form of accounts provided by Internet Service Providers (ISPs), companies such as AOL, Mindspring, and Earthlink that provide the modem dial-in numbers and online servers to enable people to connect their PCs to the public network.

New Message
Forward   Print   Send and Receive All

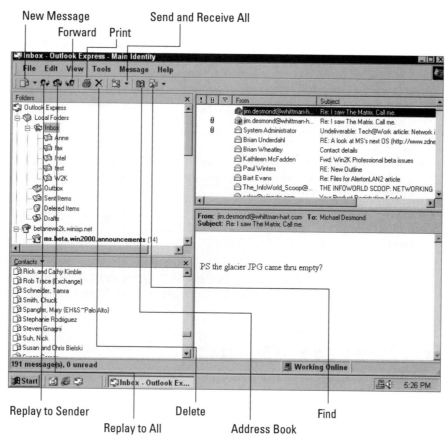

Replay to Sender   Delete   Find
        Replay to All   Address Book

Figure 14-1: A sensible program layout helps make Outlook Express easy to use.

So before Outlook Express can be of use to you, you need to have a working e-mail account. In most cases, e-mail is based on Post Office Protocol 3.0, or POP3. POP3 is a protocol that provides communications between mail clients (such as Outlook Express) and mail servers (such as Microsoft Exchange) over the public network. It also provides an inexpensive option for ISPs, because e-mail typically stays on the ISP servers for only a short time. When you download POP3 e-mail to your hard disk, the data is usually wiped from the ISP server—your inbox and messages all reside on a local hard disk. In addition to easing storage and management overhead for ISPs, POP3 provides fast, local access to your mail data because you don't have to send queries and commands to an e-mail Inbox sitting out on the Internet somewhere.

Note   Outlook Express and other e-mail clients can actually be set to leave messages up on the POP server. This means you could, conceivably, access e-mail messages much the way IMAP and Web-based e-mail systems do—by reading content directly off the server. However, most POP3 accounts are intended to store and forward mail to the client destination, freeing up the server. And while you can tell Outlook Express not to clean messages of the server, your ISP may purge messages that are more than a few days old.

Outlook Express supports three e-mail protocols:

◆ **POP3:** As described, this protocol moves all mail files to the client. That makes for fast, local management, but the files are accessible only from the client PC that downloaded them.

◆ **IMAP:** The Internet Messaging Access Protocol stores messages on the server so that any properly configured PC can be used to access all the e-mail in your Inbox.

◆ **HTTP:** Used for Web-based mail applications, such as Microsoft HotMail that is offered as part of the Outlook Express setup. As with IMAP, your e-mail Inbox resides on a server, where it can be accessed from any properly configured PC.

Creating a new POP3 account

Needless to say, an e-mail program isn't much use if you don't have an e-mail account set up. The account setup steps tell Outlook Express where to look on the Internet for your incoming messages, as well as where to go to transmit outbound messages.

Outlook Express also offers support for multiple accounts and e-mail identities. That means if you have several e-mail accounts, you can work them all from a single e-mail software and from a single session. What's more, you can also create multiple personalities, essentially tailoring identities under a single account so that people who correspond with you see a specific identity. This can be useful, say, if you use your e-mail account for both business and personal use, or if you have several family members using the same Internet account.

The first step is to set up your e-mail account and identity. The first task is to point Outlook Express at the remote e-mail server that handles your mail. This information—the server addresses for your inbound and outbound mail, as well as your user name and password—doesn't come from Windows 2000 or Outlook Express. You need to get this information from your mail provider before you get started.

Assuming you have the server addresses and your authentication information in hand, here's how to set up an Outlook Express e-mail account:

1. From Outlook Express, click Tools ⇨ Accounts to open the Internet Accounts dialog box. The All tab, shown in Figure 14-2, lists all the installed accounts, including Web-based directory servers and your e-mail settings.

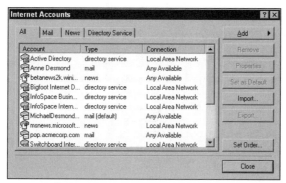

Figure 14-2: Don't mind the selection of preinstalled Web directory services. Click the Add button to input your e-mail settings.

2. Click the Add button and on the fly-out menu that appears, click Mail.

3. The Internet Connection Wizard launches. In the text box, enter the name you want displayed in your outgoing e-mail messages and click Next.

4. If you already have an ISP account (as I assume here), click the top radio button (labeled I already have an e-mail address that I'd like to use). Enter your working e-mail address. The typical format is name@isp.net. Click the Next button.

5. The vast majority of e-mail accounts use POP3 mail servers. If this is the case for you, select POP3 from the drop-down list box.

6. Next, enter the name of the mail server used for incoming traffic. Most POP3 mail servers have names such as pop.isp.net. You can also enter the numeric IP address of the incoming mail server in this box, if you have that information.

7. Finally, enter the simple mail transfer protocol (SMTP) server name, used to transact your outbound mail. Again, a numeric IP address may also be used. A typical POP3 name is mail.isp.net. Figure 14-3 shows what the dialog box should look like. Click Next.

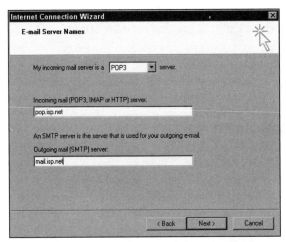

Figure 14-3: They call it a wizard, but you need to know a thing or two about your e-mail account to connect Outlook Express to your e-mail server.

8. Enter your ISP account name and your ISP password in the text boxes in the next dialog box. These entries are used to verify your identity to the ISP's mail servers. To protect your password, Outlook Express will only display a series of asterisks when you type. Type carefully and make sure you have the Caps Lock key off. If you enter your password incorrectly, your e-mail will not work.

9. If your ISP requires Secure Password Authentication, activate the checkbox at the bottom of the dialog box.

10. Click Next to go to the final dialog box. Note that if you made a mistake, you can click the Back button in any of the wizard dialog boxes to return to a specific point to correct information. Clicking Next successive times will return you to the final dialog box, where you click the Finish button to compete the process.

Outlook Express takes you back to the Internet Accounts dialog box. Only this time, you are looking at your newly created mail account. You can test your e-mail by clicking Close to exit this dialog box and then clicking the New Message icon at the far left of the toolbar. In the From field of the message window, you should see the name you entered into the Display Name text box. Enter your newly entered e-mail address in the To field of the message, type the word *test* into the Subject text box, and click Send. Click the Send/Receive icon to transmit the message from your Outbox.

If you get an error message saying the account or server can't be found, you may have entered something incorrectly. Click Tools ➪ Accounts, click the Mail tab, and double-click the newly created account. Click the Servers tab and look closely at your Incoming and Outgoing mail server entries, as well as your Account name and Password text box entries. Do you see any misspelled words or mixed-up assignments? If so, fix them, click OK, and try sending the message again.

Tip

One thing I often do is mix up the inbound and outbound server information. So check to see that your incoming POP3 mail server and your outbound SMTP mail server entries aren't mixed up.

If the message gets out, you're in good shape. That means Outlook Express at least found your SMTP server and was able to offload the message from its Outbox. Wait a few minutes and click the Send/Receive icon again. In most cases, you should see your new message show up in your Inbox. If not, it may be taking its good time getting into the queue. Check the server again in a few minutes by clicking the Send/Receive icon on the toolbar.

Setting up an HTTP account

What if you are using one of the many free e-mail services offered on the market? Yahoo Mail, RocketMail, and HotMail are a just a few of the many options. Most of these use HTTP-based mail servers, which store your messages on a central server. You access your Inbox via a Web browser.

But what if you have, say, your work e-mail in Outlook Express and your personal e-mail through a Web-based service? Rather than go off to multiple places for your e-mail, you can have Outlook Express collect everything in one place. Here's how to make Outlook Express the inbox for your Web-based e-mail:

1. From Outlook Express, click Tools ⇨ Accounts to open the Internet Accounts dialog box.

2. Click the Add button and on the fly-out menu that appears, click Mail.

3. The Internet Connection Wizard launches. In the text box, enter the name you want displayed in your outgoing e-mail messages and click Next.

4. If you already have an e-mail account, click the top radio button and then enter your working e-mail address. The typical format is name@e-mail.com. Click Next.

Note

If you are using Microsoft's preferred Hotmail service, click the lower radio button and click Next. (The drop-down list box offers only Hotmail, no surprise.) Click Next and then Finish. If you did not indicate that you have an existing Hotmail account, you are whisked off to sign up for one online using a wizard interface. For those with an account, you must provide your account user identification (your e-mail name without the @hotmail.com) and your password.

5. Now select HTTP from the top-most drop-down list box, shown in Figure 14-5. If this is a previously setup Hotmail account, select Hotmail in the lower drop-down list box. Otherwise, select Other.

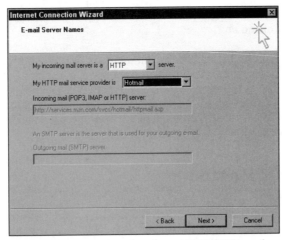

Figure 14-4: You can select from HTTP, IMAP, and POP3 mail service. When you select HTTP, Outlook tries to herd you toward Microsoft's free HotMail e-mail service.

6. In the Incoming mail text box, enter the URL of the server used to handle HTTP-based e-mail. Click Next.

7. Now enter your user name and password. Click Next, then click Finish at the last dialog box to complete the setup process.

Finishing account touches

The wizard guides you through pointing Outlook Express at a specific mail server and getting down your basic information, but it leaves out a few useful steps. Before you can consider your account setup under Outlook Express complete, you need to go through a couple of additional steps:

1. Open the Internet Accounts dialog box by clicking Tools ➪ Accounts. Click the Mail tab.

2. Double-click the account entry you just created to open its Properties box.

3. Give your new account a unique name by entering it in the text box at the top of the General tab, shown in Figure 14-5. This name makes it easier to identify the account in the Internet Accounts dialog box.

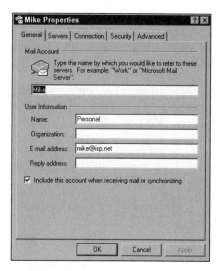

Figure 14-5: See what's missing? Go back to your account setup and add your organization name and your reply-to e-mail address if it's different from your sending address.

4. Both the Name and E-mail address entries in the General page should already be filled out, but you can update them now if necessary.

5. If you use this e-mail account for business, enter the company name in the Organization text box.

6. Redirect replies to your messages to a different address by entering the information in the Reply address text box. This is akin to sending a letter from vacation in Florida, but writing your Michigan home address as the return address on the envelope.

7. The checkbox at the bottom of the page should be activated. If not, Outlook Express doesn't check this account when you click the Send/Receive icon on the toolbar.

8. Click OK or Apply to make your changes take effect.

Working with multiple accounts

One of the most welcome features of Outlook Express is its capability of managing multiple e-mail accounts. This capability means you can use a single e-mail reader to manage e-mail for dozens of different e-mail addresses, whether they all belong to you or they are distributed among many people. Why is multiple e-mail account support helpful? Here are a few reasons:

✦ Makes it possible to use a single e-mail program for PCs used for both work and recreation.

✦ Small business users can create and maintain multiple accounts for their Web sites. So general inquiries go to `info@company.com`, direct e-mail goes to `worker.name@company.com`, and service requests go to `help@company.com`.

✦ Other family members can access their e-mail accounts from a single home PC.

✦ Enables quick access to infrequently used e-mail accounts, such as old CompuServe accounts that are kept around as a backup, in case the primary e-mail account servers should fail, for example.

Setting up multiple accounts in Outlook Express is easy. In fact, all you do is repeat the steps I've described previously for creating a new e-mail account but input the unique information for the second, third, or subsequent account.

Tip Be sure that you assign unique account names to newly created accounts. Otherwise, as you accrue multiple listings in the Accounts dialog box, you may get confused as to which account belongs to whom. By default, the wizard assigns a generic name based on the name of the ISP for the account. You can quickly change that after you've completed the wizard by double-clicking the new item and typing a unique name in the text box at the top of the account's General tab.

Once you've created your multiple accounts, you want to set one of them as the default. The default account is the one Outlook Express automatically assumes is to be used whenever you use shortcut keys or icons to create a new message, for example. Save yourself time and confusion by selecting your most often used account from the Mail tab list and then clicking the Set as Default button.

Of course, multiple accounts means multiple e-mail sources, destinations, and perhaps users. And that can mean confusion. Outlook Express offers rules and folder capabilities to help stem the tide of mail. You learn more about e-mail management later in this chapter.

Once you have set up multiple accounts, the way you send and receive mail changes. The Send/Receive icon features a little down arrow that you use to select from the choices Send and Receive All, Send All, and Receive All. Click this arrow after setting up your multiple accounts, and the fly-out list grows to include an individual item for each account. Figure 14-6 shows you what it looks like. This way, you can choose to download e-mail for only your primary account, while ignoring all others.

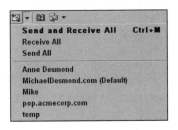

Figure 14-6: Click the small arrow on the Send/Receive icon to whip up a specific transaction — send, receive, send *and* receive — or to send and receive messages for a specific account.

Identities: One system, many users

When Outlook Express is set up with multiple e-mail accounts, it is often used by multiple people. The problem is, while you can read and send e-mail on your account, so can the other folks using Outlook Express. And if you're running a business on a home PC, the last thing you want is your neighbor's kids waltzing through your Inbox looking at contract proposals and payment schedules.

Fortunately, Outlook Express anticipates this dilemma and enables you to create multiple identities. When you create identities, you essentially create separate sandboxes for each user to work in. That way, your son and his friends can't see your business correspondence when they are sending e-mail, and you don't have to wade through their e-mail traffic when you are at work.

Caution   While the Identities feature includes a password option for restricting access to identities, it is hardly secure. Users operating within their own identity, for example, can quickly gain access to your messages and Address Book using the Import feature. Within seconds, they can be looking at all your data. The simple message: If security is a concern, you should not share your PC in an unsecured environment.

Creating a Second Identity

By default, all your work occurs in the Main Identity. To create a second identity — I call it Public — do the following:

1. Click File ⇨ Identities and click Add New Identities from the fly-out menu.

2. In the New Identity dialog box (shown in Figure 14-7), enter your name in the top text box.

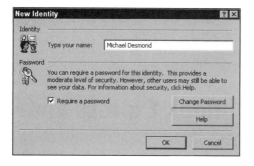

Figure 14-7: Quickly whip up a second, distinct identity for Outlook Express. Just don't let that password feature fool you; your e-mail Inbox could be easily exposed.

3. Click the Require a password checkbox. Now enter the password twice and click OK.

4. Click OK again. If you want to switch to the newly created Public identity, click Yes. Outlook Express opens to the default start screen for the new identity.

To switch between identities, click File ➪ Switch Identities, and then click the identity you want to activate in the Switch Identities dialog box. If the identity requires a password, the Password text box displays so you can enter it. Click OK to make the switch.

Controlling Identity Behaviors

You can also manage how identities behave. For example, you may want Outlook Express to default to the Public identity you just created so that your e-mail doesn't end up onscreen when the e-mail program restarts. Here's how to do this:

1. Click File ➪ Identities ➪ Manage Identities.

2. In the Manage Identities dialog box, make sure the Use this identity when starting a program checkbox is activated.

3. Select the identity you want to start with Outlook Express from the drop-down list box as shown in Figure 14-8. Click Close.

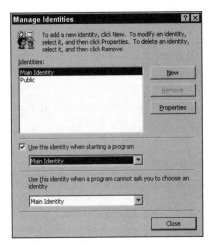

Figure 14-8: Quickly pick which Outlook Express identity bubbles to the top when you launch the program.

The Basics: Using Outlook Express and Making Sense of E-mail

Now that you have set up your accounts and identities, it's time to actually use the program. In this section, you learn how to create and view messages, organize your correspondence, work with attachments, and tailor the Outlook Express interface to your preferences.

Creating an e-mail message

Here's how to create a new message and send it off. First, you must launch Outlook Express, typically by clicking Start ➪ Programs ➪ Outlook Express or by clicking the envelope icon in the Quick Launch toolbar. Once the program launches, do the following:

1. Click File ➪ New and select Mail Message from the fly-out menu. You can also press Ctrl+N or click the New Message icon at the far left of the toolbar. A new message window appears, as shown in Figure 14-9.

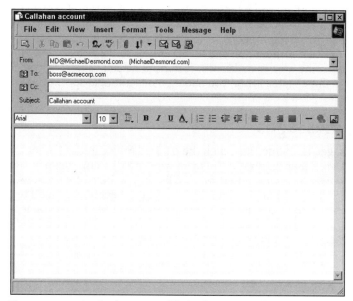

Figure 14-9: Outlook Express fills in the From field on its own, but you need to provide the rest.

2. If you have multiple e-mail accounts, use the drop-down list control in the From field to select the account to send from.

3. Click Tab to move to the To field and type the e-mail address. If this address is already in your Address Book, Outlook Express automatically fills in the address as you type.

4. Repeat this step for anyone you want to include on the Cc (carbon copy) line.

5. Click in the Subject field or tab to it. Enter some descriptive text, keeping in mind that this is what your recipient sees in their Inboxes.

6. Click in the main text area and type your message.

7. Click File ⇨ Send Message. You can also click the Send Message icon on the left side of the toolbar or press Alt+S.

Once you create an e-mail message, it goes to the Outlook Express Outbox, awaiting upload to your mail server. This is a useful feature because it bundles e-mail traffic and uploads it all at once, which is much more efficient than immediately uploading each e-mail over an analog modem. This also means you can have a last crack at a message even after you "send" it. Could the Outbox enable you to make a career-saving edit to a message? Who knows, but there it is.

Note   Before going further, you need to understand the first law of e-mail: Don't anger your recipients. Outlook Express tempts you with all sorts of fancy e-mail templates, graphics, layout options, and other doodads. But unless you are sure that all your fellow e-mailers can, and want, to receive these bells and whistles, you should resist the urge to make such features a default setting. As you go through the rest of this chapter, I warn you about possible trouble spots.

Viewing messages

Viewing messages is simple. Just click the desired folder in the Folder List, and the messages in that folder display in the main window. Click message headers or use your cursor keys to move up and down the list. If you have the preview pane enabled (which it should be, by default), you can see each message's text as you select its header in the pane above it. If you can't see the preview pane, turn it on by clicking View ⇨ Layout, check the Show preview pane checkbox, and click the OK button. Unchecking this box causes the preview pane to disappear.

To open a message, double-click the header. The message opens in a separate window that includes a context-sensitive toolbar for tasks such as replying and forwarding. Move to other messages by clicking the Previous and Next icon buttons or by clicking View ⇨ Previous Message or View ⇨ Next ⇨ Next Message.

To forward or reply to a message, click the message header in Outlook Express and then click the appropriate icon button (Reply, Reply to All, or Forward). The message opens in a new window, with a blank area inserted at the top to enable you to start typing your message. If you are replying, the e-mail addresses are already inserted into the To field. If you are forwarding a message, however, you need to input the address.

Getting organized

If your Inbox is anything like mine, new messages pile up fast, fast, fast. Fortunately, Outlook Express makes it easy to stay organized by enabling you to create folders and move messages. A good place to start is by creating a few folders beneath the Inbox folder that you can use to store messages by topic or source.

1. Click the Inbox item in the Folder List view of Outlook Express.

2. Right-click the Inbox and select New Folder from the shortcut menu, or just click the Inbox and click File ➪ New ➪ Folder from the menu bar.

Tip   You can also create new folders by using a keyboard shortcut. Press Ctrl+Shift+E.

3. In the Create Folder dialog box, shown in Figure 14-10, enter the new folder name in the text box. Make sure that the Inbox folder item is highlighted in the lower window. Click OK.

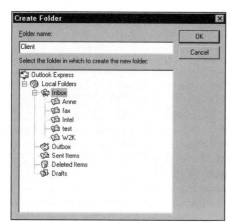

Figure 14-10: Give your new folder a descriptive name.

The newly created folder now appears in the Folder List pane just below the Inbox. The Inbox item gains a small icon that indicates if its subfolders are rolled up or visible.

To move a message from your Inbox into your new folder, first select the Inbox from the Folder List. Then click the header of the message you wish to move in the main window and drag it over to the new folder. Let go of the mouse, and the message disappears from the message header list for the Inbox. You can also right-click a message and click Move to Folder on the shortcut menu. In the Move dialog box, shown in Figure 14-11, click the destination folder and click OK.

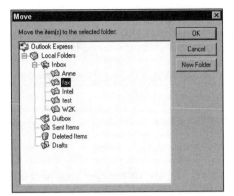

Figure 14-11: The Move dialog box enables you to drill down through a directory tree of folders to decide where to shift messages.

Tip   Moving too soon? If you want to move a message and decide you need a new folder, use the Move to Folder command to open the Move dialog box, shown in Figure 14-12. Then navigate down the tree view by clicking the plus signs (+) to expand folder listings and highlight the existing folder under which you want your new one to exist. Click the New Folder button, enter a name in the text box, and click OK. The new folder appears, highlighted, in the Move box. Click OK to shift the selected message to the newly created folder.

Of course, moving messages one at a time can get downright tedious. To move a range of contiguous messages, click the first message in the group, then scroll down using the scroll bar on the right side of the window to the last message you want to move. Press the Shift key and click the last message header. The range of messages is now highlighted. Let go of the Shift key and click and drag the messages over to the new folder. When you release the mouse button, all of the selected messages land in the new folder.

But what if you want to move all the messages from a certain person? It can get a bit trying having to scroll through the entire Inbox list clicking and dragging individual messages. Fortunately, you can quickly sort the mail list in various ways by clicking a column header in the message header pane. Clicking the From column header once sorts all entries alphabetically by sender, as shown in Figure 14-12, while clicking it a second time sorts entries in reverse alphabetical order. Similarly, you can click the Subject column and the Received column to change sorting rules and orders.

You can do more than shuffle messages around. Select one or more message headers in a folder, and you can perform the following actions:

✦ **Delete messages:** Click Edit ➪ Delete or right-click the messages and click Delete. Also, pressing Del or Ctrl-D does the same thing.

✦ **Move or copy messages to another folder:** Click Edit ➪ Move to Folder or Edit ➪ Copy to Folder. You also can right-click messages and click Move to Folder or Copy to Folder.

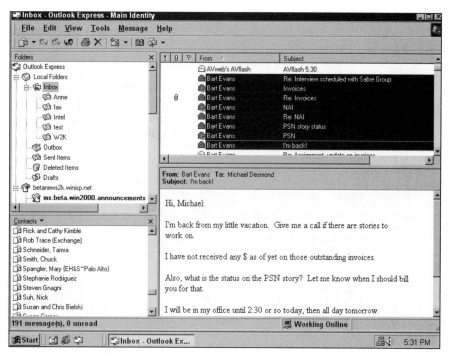

Figure 14-12: On the move: Speed housecleaning chores such as moving messages to new folders by sorting messages and selecting entire ranges.

Working with attachments

Attachments are one of the killer apps of the e-mail world. For one thing, the capability of sending an e-mail with an attached document or file means that deadline busting writers — such as myself — can wait until the absolute last second to send out manuscripts. More to the point, businesses can quickly distribute documents to employees, and families can send digital photos via e-mail to relatives. In a word, attachments are good.

To attach a file to a message, first repeat steps 1 through 6 in the section "Creating an E-mail Message," earlier in this chapter. Once you are looking at your completed message, all you need to do is add the attachment. There are several ways to do so:

✦ Click Insert ↔ File Attachment and use the Insert Attachment dialog box (shown in Figure 14-13) to navigate to the desired file. Make sure you select the file or files you wish to send with the message, and click the Attach button.

✦ Click the Paperclip icon button on the toolbar to open the Insert Attachment dialog box.

✦ From Windows Explorer, click the desired file and drag and drop it over to the message window.

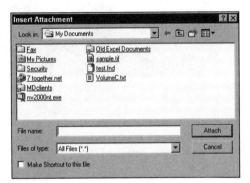

Figure 14-13: In the Insert Attachment dialog box, you can grab files from your hard disk and other drives.

Once you've attached the file, a new field called Attach appears below the Subject field in the message window. The Attach field includes the filename, its size, and the related Windows icon for the application.

Note   Many ISPs limit the size of file attachments in an effort to reduce congestion, and the ISP's mail server rejects any messages that violate their attachment rules (often attachment sizes in excess of 1MB). Also, big file attachments can be a chore for those on analog modems. Use a compression program such as PKZip to squish files down to size. For images, consider using highly compressed formats such as JPEG or GIF.

Tailoring the way Outlook Express looks

You've covered the basics of making, sending, and viewing e-mail messages. Now you can delve a bit into controlling the way Outlook Express behaves. There are plenty of options and controls, many of which can help you tailor the flexible Outlook Express interface to your needs.

When you first launch the program, you see the slow-loading Outlook Express splash page, shown in Figure 14-14. This page contains links that immediately enable you to start creating and reading mail messages, creating and reading Internet newsgroup posts, and working with the Outlook Express Address Book.

The page looks nice, but really you end up working inside the standard folder views anyway. Keep reading for tips on how to make things work your way.

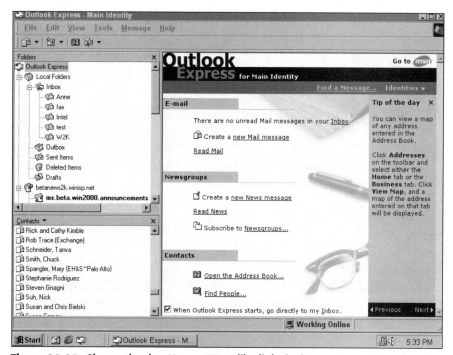

Figure 14-14: Slooow loader: Happy HTML-like links invite you to create and read e-mail, but the veneer soon falls off and you get longer load times to boot. Stick with the Inbox.

Tailoring the interface

The first thing I do is set up Outlook Express so that I can quickly navigate the various mail, newsgroup, and Address Book services. Click the View menu and click Layout. In the Window Layout Properties dialog box is a series of checkbox items. Figure 14-15 shows a view of the Outlook Express interface with all the options on.

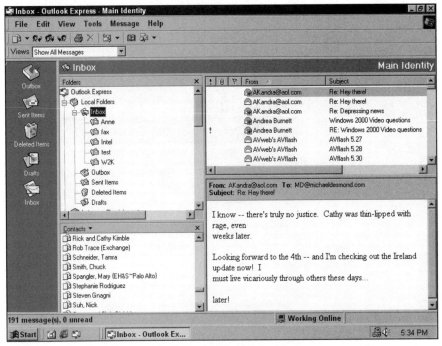

Figure 14-15: The full-on Outlook Express interface gives you many—too many—ways to navigate to various folders and functions.

The following rundown explains how the Window Layout Properties controls affect this interface, and Figure 14-16 shows the dialog box:

✦ **Contacts:** Displays your Address Book listings in the bottom-left corner of the application window. I tend to leave this turned off because addresses I input get auto-filled by Outlook Express.

✦ **Folder Bar:** Displays a static horizontal bar above the messages box that identifies in large type the currently selected folder. I leave this off because I can tell what folder I'm in from the Folder List.

✦ **Folder List:** Displays the list of default and created folders (Inbox, Outbox, Newsgroup folders, and so on) at the upper-left part of the working area. I keep this option turned on so I can see all my folders and resources at a glance.

✦ **Outlook Bar:** Redundant with the Folder List and consumes space. I leave it turned off.

✦ **Status Bar:** Displays useful information along the bottom of the screen about the selected folder, including number of messages, number of messages unread, and online status.

✦ **Toolbar:** Displays the useful icon bar across the top of the application window (just under the menus). I leave this option on.

✦ **Views Bar:** Enables you to filter displayed messages by those that are read or unread. I leave it off, but this option can be useful to help you focus on new or unread messages, particularly if your Inbox tends to fill up with messages.

The other key element of the Window Layout Properties dialog box is the Preview Pane area. By default, when you select a message in Outlook Express, it displays the text in a window at the bottom of the application window. If you uncheck the Show preview pane checkbox, however, this window goes away, providing a lot more room for viewing your message list.

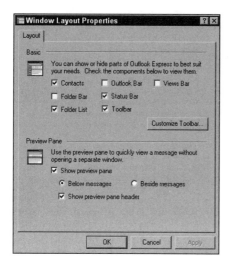

Figure 14-16: Use the convenient checkbox controls and the Apply button in the Window Layout Properties dialog box to quickly preview your interface tweaks.

I always keep the preview pane on, so I can quickly browse message contents without having to double-click message headers and open and close separate windows. But you can noodle with the layout of the preview pane. Outlook Express normally puts the pane beneath your message headers, but you can place it over to the right instead—not an option I prefer, but it's there. Also, I always check the Show preview pane header checkbox because this option enables me to see at a glance who sent the message I'm browsing. Figure 14-17 shows what my preferred interface settings look like.

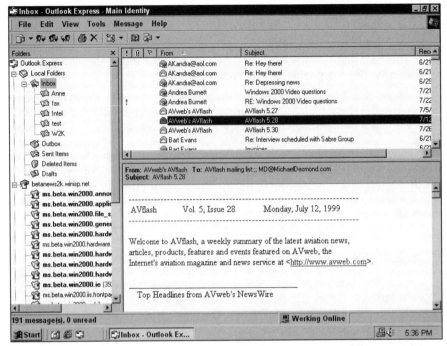

Figure 14-17: This screen is a compromise, offering easy access while preserving screen space for viewing messages.

Setting message layout properties

Outlook Express also enables you to gussy up your e-mail messages by producing output based on HTML. No more 12-point Courier output for me, thanks. Now you can send messages with multiple fonts, formatted and colored text, and in-line links to Web sites and e-mail addresses. The result is e-mail that looks and acts a lot like the Web documents people are accustomed to viewing in their Internet browsers every day.

Caution

HTML-based messages may look good, but be aware that a significant portion of the world doesn't use HTML-aware e-mail clients. For those folks, your fancy layouts and designs are lost at best. At worst, some of your recipients may see gobs of HTML code in their text-only messages, making your e-mail missives quite difficult to read. Remember that first law of e-mail I mentioned at the beginning of the chapter?

To enable rich-mail messages, the first thing you need to do is enable HTML message formats on the Send tab of the Outlook Express Options dialog box, shown in Figure 14-18. Here's how to do it:

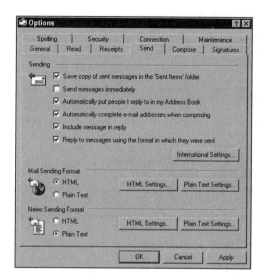

Figure 14-18: Set your default font styles, background designs, and other eye-catching HTML elements on the Send tab.

1. Click Tools ➪ Options and then click the Send tab.

2. In the Mail Sending Format area, click the HTML radio button and then click the HTML Settings button.

3. In the HTML Settings dialog box, shown in Figure 14-19, make sure the Send pictures with messages checkbox is activated.

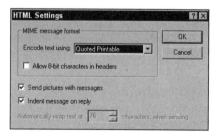

Figure 14-19: Tailor your HTML message layouts from the HTML Settings box. The Indent messages control, for example, helps readers keep track of long message threads.

4. I also usually keep the Indent message on reply checkbox set because this option helps the recipient distinguish old messages in the thread from the latest one.

5. Keep the Encode text using drop-down list box set to Quoted Printable and clear the Allow 8-bit characters in headers checkbox. This provides compatibility with extended character sets.

6. Click OK and then click OK or Apply to have the changes take effect.

Next, set the default behavior for new messages. Attributes such as font size, type, color, and background images can all be set from the Compose tab of the Options dialog box. To set the standard font, simply click the top Font Settings button and then select the appropriate font type, style, size, color, and other formatting settings from the Font dialog box, shown in Figure 14-20. Click OK to return to the Compose tab.

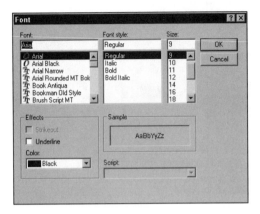

Figure 14-20: Look familiar? The font controls for Outlook Express look a lot like those found in word processors.

Using stationery

The next step is to set the default HTML stationery for your messages. What exactly is stationery, you ask? In Outlook Express, it's a graphical background design for e-mail messages. Figure 14-21 shows an example of an e-mail message created with stationery.

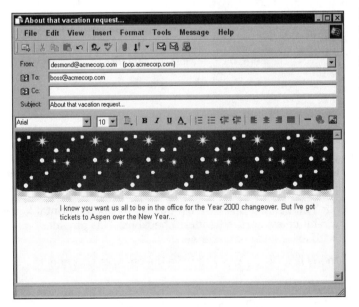

Figure 14-21: Colorful backgrounds, graphical borders, and fancy text are all hallmarks of a stationery-laden e-mail message.

You can fire out e-mails that include graphics that range from subtle and tasteful to absolutely garish. And in fact, Microsoft offers a selection of stationery designs that cover this range. To see what I'm talking about, go back to the Compose page of the Options dialog box (click Tools ➪ Options and click the Compose tab). In the Stationery area click Select. You should see a list of HTML files in the Select Stationery dialog box shown in Figure 14-22. Click one, and you get a preview of the image in the window to the right. Browse through the choices until you see one you'd like to feature in all your outbound e-mail.

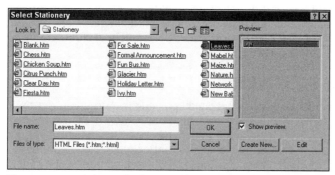

Figure 14-22: Microsoft gives you lots of stationery templates to choose from. The Preview pane enables you to quickly browse the templates, and you can even edit templates to suit your tastes.

Note   Stationery can be cute and even attractive, but the appeal can wear off fast. First, stationery adds bits to every message you send. In addition, many e-mail readers interpret the stationery as an attachment, meaning that the messages going to some of your recipients appear to have documents appended to it. That can lead to some confusion and perhaps frustration on the part of your recipients. These issues are a couple things to keep in mind.

This same dialog box gives you the opportunity to create a new stationery (click the appropriately labeled Create New button) or to make alterations to an existing stationery file (via the Edit button). Clicking Create New kicks off a simple wizard that enables you to choose an image file, select a background color, set font positioning and type, and make other tweaks. Once you save the file to the Stationery directory, you can use it as your stationery. The Edit button, by contrast, opens the selected stationery template in your default HTML editor software (or Notepad, if no HTML editor is installed).

Working With Rules and Filters

I'm sure you've heard the ubiquitous complaint. Though it has been just a few years since many companies discovered e-mail, already *everyone* complains about how full their inboxes are. I know I'm a culprit. I grouse about the barrage of incoming e-mail as much as the next person.

Fortunately, Outlook Express includes tools for managing the flood. The powerful Rules feature enables users to create filters that do things like direct incoming messages to specific folders and delete or move older messages. There are even special rule features that block messages from specified parties — an effective tool against unwanted spam. Let's take a tour of these extremely useful features.

Creating a new e-mail rule

Fortunately, I have a defense against the e-mail onslaught. And if you're running Microsoft Outlook Express, you have it too. Click the Tools ➪ Message Rules ➪ Mail menu command to open the New Mail Rule dialog box shown in Figure 14-23. Use this dialog box to create an e-mail rule that automatically checks incoming messages and moves anything from your boss to a specific folder. Let's step through the process of creating a simple e-mail rule.

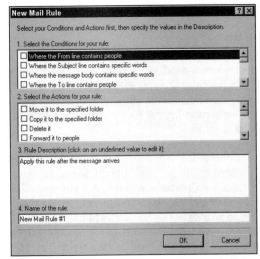

Figure 14-23: The New Mail Rule dialog box lays it all out for you.

1. Click the Tools ➪ Message Rules ➪ Mail menu command to open the New Mail Rule dialog box. In the top window (labeled Select the Conditions for your rule), click the square checkbox to the left of the item labeled Where the From line contains people. A new line appears in the third box down.

2. In the second window (labeled Select the Actions for your rule), click on the square check box to the left of the top selection, labeled Move it to the specified folder Once again. A new line appears in the third window.

3. Now that you've set the stage, it's time to fill it with actors. In the Rule Description window, click the link "contains people" that now appears.

4. The Select People dialog box appears, as shown in Figure 14-24. In the top text box, enter the e-mail address of your boss. You can also click the Address Book button to select one or more e-mail addresses from your Address Book.

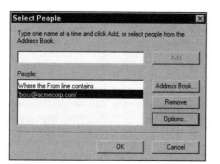

Figure 14-24: Once you enter the full or partial e-mail address you want to filter, click the Add button to place the filter in the People list. You can enter additional filters or click OK to set the new filter.

Tip   Want to filter every message *except* those from your boss? Click the Options button and then click the radio button labeled Message does not contain the people below. (Figure 14-25 shows you what the dialog box looks like.) Click OK to return to the Select People dialog box. After you set this option, any rules you apply affect all messages except those that match what you entered in the Select People dialog box.

Figure 14-25: Set reverse rules by entering a filter value, clicking the Options button, and then clicking the radio button labeled Message does not contain the people below.

5. Click OK to return to the New Mail Rule dialog box. In the Rule Description window, click the link "specified folder".

6. In this example, the Move dialog box appears, prompting you to select a folder to move the matching messages into. Double-click the Local Folders item to see all of the Outlook Express folders. Click the one you want to use and click OK.

7. Click OK to return to the New Mail Rule dialog box. Name your new rule by typing the name into the Name of the rule text box at the bottom of the window.

8. Click OK. The new rule appears in the Message Rules dialog box as shown in Figure 14-26, and a description of the rule appears in the bottom window.

Figure 14-26: Your new rule appears at the bottom of the list. Select the rule, and an editable description appears below. Just click the hyperlinks to change filter values directly from the Message Rules dialog box.

9. Run the rule right away by clicking the Apply Now button. Click OK to run the rule next time you download new messages.

You can repeat this process to handle any number of contingencies. Move, delete, copy, or forward messages based on who sent them, whom they are addressed to, any text that's in the Subject line, and even message size. If you need to create new rules, take your time to scroll through the available conditions and actions to see exactly how you can manage your mail.

Create an out-of-office rule

You can create pretty sophisticated filters by applying multiple conditions and actions to your rules. For example, instead of just adding a Where from condition, you can double-click a second or third condition and add it to the mix. In this case, we'll create a rule that detects messages from the boss and automatically does two things: tells your boss you received the message and forwards the original message to a second e-mail address.

Before we create our new rule, we need to craft a response message for the boss:

1. In Outlook Express, click the New Message icon in the toolbar to open a new message windows.

2. In the Subject line, enter something appropriate like, "I've received your message."

3. In the text line, enter any additional text, perhaps indicating that you check this e-mail account every six hours or daily over the weekend. This will let your boss know that you will see the message soon.

4. Now save the message by clicking File ➪ Save As. In the Save Message As dialog box, give the message a name (say, boss1.eml) and click the Save button. You may want to navigate through the browser window to store the message in a certain folder.

5. Now close the saved message by pressing Esc or by clicking the close window icon at the top-right of the message window.

Okay, we've saved a response message for our boss. Now it's time to actually lay down the rules. Here's what to do:

1. Click Tools ➪ Message Rules ➪ Mail.

2. In the Select the Conditions for the Rule window, click the check box next to the item labeled Where the From line contains people.

3. In the Select the Actions for your Rule window, click the checkbox next to two items, the ones labeled Forward it to People and Reply with message.

4. Now, in the Rule Description window, click the link "contains people".

5. In the Select people dialog box, enter your boss' e-mail address in the text box labeled Type one name at a time. Click the Add button to place the address in the list and click OK.

6. Next, click the link "people" inside the item Forward it to people. In the Select People dialog box, enter the address you want to forward the message to in the Address text box. This might be your home e-mail address to ensure that you get urgent messages at home over the weekend.

7. Time to call up that automated response to your boss. Click the "message" link inside the item Reply with message.

8. In the Open dialog box, find the message you just saved, click it, and click the Open button. The New Mail Rule dialog box now displays that filename and the path of the selected message on your disk.

9. In the Name of the Rule text box at the bottom of the dialog box, enter a unique name for the rule (something you can easily recognize). Click the OK button.

The Boss Response rule now appears in the Mail Rules tab of the Message Rules dialog box. The box next to the new rule should be checked, indicating that the rule is active. The next time your boss sends a message, he or she will immediately get a quick response from your e-mail program. In addition, a copy of your boss' message will be sent to your personal e-mail address, ensuring that you get the message quickly.

So your new rule may look for e-mails from your boss that include the name of an important project in the subject line and are marked urgent. Then, you could set the rule to do more than just shuffle the message to your Boss box. Double-click additional entries in the Action window to forward the message to the AOL e-mail account you use at home in the evenings, for example. You could even send a reply to your boss saying that their e-mail arrived after you left the office, but that the e-mail has been forwarded to your home account as well. Figure 14-27 shows a complex rule.

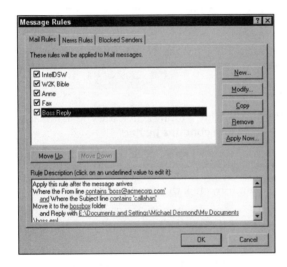

Figure 14-27: This rule not only moves messages from your boss to a specific folder, it also detects a specific word in the Subject line and sends an automatic response.

When you create a new rule, it often doesn't quite behave as you planned. Maybe you mistyped a text string, or messages are going to the wrong folder. You can fix these problems quickly by editing existing rules. Click Tools ➪ Message Rules ➪ Mail and select the rule you want to edit from the Message Rules dialog box. Then click the Modify button. Once again the Edit Mail Rule dialog box opens, where you can click the rule links to change behaviors. Click OK and OK again to make the new changes take effect.

Managing rule orders

Outlook Express rules execute in the order they appear in the Mail Rules dialog box, and this can be an issue. For example, you may have one rule that moves all mail from your boss to a Boss folder, and a second one that deletes all mail with the words "quick cash" in the subject. So what happens if your boss sends you an e-mail about an urgent loan deal you're handling titled "client needs quick cash"? One of two things can occur:

✦ The message is deleted as soon as it arrives, and you never see it.

✦ The message is moved to your Boss folder where you can read it later.

The result depends entirely on the order that you've arranged your rules. If the delete quick cash rule sits above your Boss rule in the Message Rules dialog box, the message is deleted before the second rule can act. The result is that you miss an important message, and the client fumes at lack of funding.

If, however, the Boss rule comes first, the message is shepherded into your Boss folder before the delete rule can take a hack at it. The result is that you may get a couple of unwanted spams forwarded from your boss about get-rich-quick schemes, but at least you won't miss that urgent loan message.

To move rules up or down in the Message Rules dialog box, select the rule you want to affect and click the Move Up or Move Down button. Each click moves the rule one space in the queue. Repeat the process for each rule until you have your rules in the order you want them. Click OK to make the new order take effect.

Caution

Let this example serve as a warning to the limitations of rules. It's easy, when noodling with the rules interface, not to realize how the various rules you create might interact. It's a good idea, therefore, to review all your existing rule conditions and actions each time you make a change, just to make sure you don't accidentally perform unwanted actions. And remember, rules are automatic. You could sail on for weeks or more before you realize that messages from a certain person or with certain words in the subject line are missing.

The Bozo filter

No full-featured e-mail program is complete without a Bozo filter. Bozo filters (yes, named after the clown) are used to squelch the annoying, distracting, and just plain unwanted missives from specific people or groups. Bozo filters can be particularly useful if you need to stop spam from filling your Inbox, for example, or if you just want to do away with the aggravation of reading annoying posts.

To apply the Bozo filter — more politely known as the *Blocked Senders feature* — do the following:

1. Click Tools ➪ Mail Rules ➪ Blocked Senders List. You are now in the Blocked Senders tab of the oh-so-familiar Message Rules dialog box.

2. To add a person or group to this filter, click the Add button.

3. In the Address text box, enter a specific e-mail address if you need to filter out an individual. Or you can enter a domain name (for example, `acmecorp.com`) to filter out all mail from an organization.

4. Next, click the appropriate radio button to knock this person or group out of your e-mail Inbox, your newsgroup reader, or both.

5. Click OK and don't forget to wave bye-bye, now. That's one person or group you won't be hearing from again. Figure 14-28 shows a short Bozo filter list.

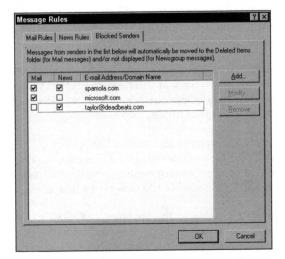

Figure 14-28: The Blocked Senders list enables you to block e-mails, newsgroup postings, or both.

Note   The Blocked Senders List is really just a rule that reads the From line of incoming e-mails and deletes matched entries. Obviously, this is a rule you yourself could create very quickly. One thing this feature does do, though, is enable you to Bozo-filter both e-mail and newsgroups in a single pass. More important, the Bozo filter is designed to handle a large and growing list of persona non grata.

Using the Newsgroup Reader

The explosive growth of the Web has made Internet newsgroups an underappreciated online resource. But anyone who works in the computing business can tell you that these online discussion groups have a lot of good (and some not-so-good) aspects. Newsgroups are essentially online bulletin boards where people from around the world can read and create postings and message threads.

Need to find a driver for an aging modem? Someone on a hardware newsgroup may know the answer. Can't figure out how to make Windows Internet Name Service (WINS) reliably resolve computer names and addresses on your network? You can find a lot of fellow sufferers and maybe a few effective tricks and strategies if you post a message to the proper newsgroup.

Sounds good so far, right? The problem is, about a kajillion newsgroups are out there, with topics ranging from PC-based flight simulators and supercomputing hardware, to politics and sports, all the way out to extremist hate groups and worse. In other words, it's not always a pretty place.

The beauty of newsgroups is that you need to see only the groups you want to see. The result is that you can sign up for newsgroups that help you stay current and active in your professional career, hobbies, or other interests.

Finding and using newsgroups

The first step is getting Outlook Express to find all those thousands of newsgroups. You see, newsgroups don't exist on the Web, though you can find Web-based discussion forums that closely mimic what newsgroups do. Rather, newsgroups exist on servers scattered across the Internet, and their posts and threads are updated continually over the public network.

To see a newsgroup, then, you have to find your newsgroup server. And once you do that, you can use a handy filter to zero in on available groups. But the first step is to find the server. Like e-mail, newsgroup access is defined by your ISP, who keeps a server handy to host updates and manage your connection. So start by finding your newsgroup server.

1. Click Tools ➪ Accounts and click the News tab on the Internet Accounts dialog box.

2. Click the Add button and then News.

3. Enter your name as you'd like it displayed in your newsgroup message headers. Many posters use aliases instead of their real names.

4. Click Next and enter your e-mail address if you want people to be able to respond to your posts.

Tip   Newsgroups are often trolled by spammers — purveyors of bulk e-mail services — who use them to strip out valuable e-mail addresses from posters. If you post to a newsgroup using your real e-mail address, the amount of spam you receive may increase greatly. To flummox the spam merchants, type your e-mail address with an extra element that will cause e-mail sent to the bogus address to be returned. For example, I entered "MD@spamfree.MichaelDesmond.com", as shown in Figure 14-29. The "spamfree." element derails all spammers.

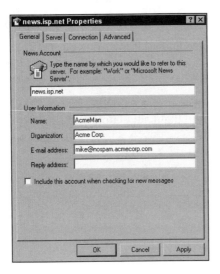

Figure 14-29: Confound would-be spammers by tinkering with your return address. Newsgroup-savvy users know enough to remove the nospam comment, but it's enough to confuse programs gathering e-mail addresses.

5. Click Next. In the text box, enter the name or IP address of your ISP's newsgroup server. Typically, the name conforms to a something like news.isp.net. You need to get this information from your ISP.

6. Click Next and then click the Finish button at the next dialog box to complete the process.

7. From the Internet Accounts window, click the Close button to close the window.

Now that you have access to a newsgroup server, it's time to subscribe to a few newsgroups. Click Tools ➪ Newsgroups (or press Ctrl+W). The Newsgroup Subscriptions dialog box displays all the currently setup newsgroup servers (you can link to multiple servers, just as you can link to multiple e-mail servers). In the main window, you should see a lengthy list of newsgroups.

You can scroll down this list to browse what's available, but the best approach is to enter a term into the text box at the top of the dialog box. For example, if you want information about sailing, try typing that term in the text box. The list in the window is then slimmed down to match your term, as shown in Figure 14-30.

When you find a newsgroup of interest, click its entry and then click the Subscribe button. An icon appears next to the subscribed newsgroup. Outlook Express now keeps the newsgroup in its list. Now click the Go to button at the bottom of the dialog box to download the message headers from the newsgroup server.

Once the newly subscribed newsgroup has been downloaded, you can browse postings by clicking the headers. It takes some time for a newsgroup to load if it contains a lot of messages.

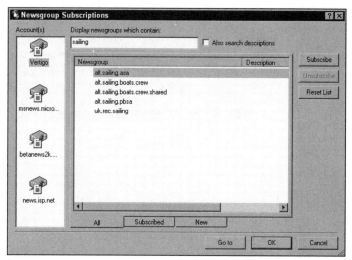

Figure 14-30: Tens of thousands of newsgroups are on my newsgroup server, but only five relate to sailing.

Managing newsgroups

By default, Outlook Express downloads 300 message headers at a time. So it would take that massive flight sim newsgroup nearly 20 separate downloads to be fully represented on the newsgroup reader! The 300-message limit does reduce the amount of time you spend waiting on downloads, however, because you can't read messages while the newsreader is downloading posts. To download another batch of message headers, click Tools ⇨ Get Next 300 Headers.

Tip
To increase (or decrease) the number of postings downloaded at one go, click Tools ⇨ Options and click the Read tab of the Options dialog box. In the News area, change the number in the spinner dialog box to the desired amount. Click OK or Apply, and you're all set.

Downloading message headers from different newsgroup forums can get time consuming. Fortunately, Outlook Express enables you to quickly update groups of newsgroups, or *synchronize newsgroups*, as it is called in the application. To do so, click the newsgroup server entry in the Folders box. (It's the item that sits above all your newsgroup items in the hierarchy.) The right pane refreshes to show the installed newsgroups, as shown in Figure 14-31, and includes information about the number of messages present and unread in the newsgroups.

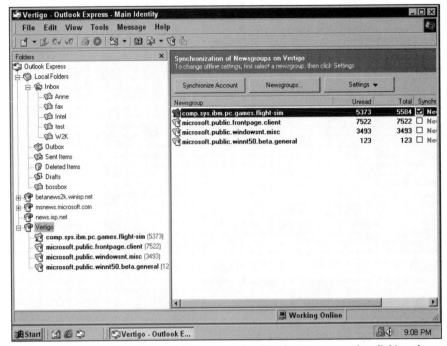

Figure 14-31: You can quickly review your subscribed newsgroups by clicking the newsgroup server in the left pane and then viewing the overview information in the right pane.

To synchronize a newsgroup—that is, to download all the new messages and get entirely caught up—click the newsgroup in the right-pane list and click the Synchronize Account button. The download dialog box shows progress, as depicted in Figure 14-32.

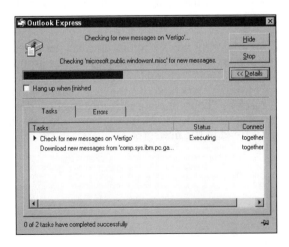

Figure 14-32: Monitor your download progress. Busy newsgroups can take a long time to synchronize over modem connections.

In addition, the Settings button enables you to assign synchronization characteristics to a selected newsgroup. Click a newsgroup entry in the right pane, click the Settings button, and then select from the drop-down menu. By default, messages don't synchronize, but you can tell Outlook Express to synch up headers only (to limit data transfers), new messages only, or all messages.

Finally, to get rid of newsgroups, simply unsubscribe from them. Right-click the newsgroup you want to ditch in the Folders pane and click the Unsubscribe command from the shortcut menu. The newsgroup immediately disappears from the list under the server. Now that wasn't so hard, was it?

Summary

I could go on for a couple of hundred pages with all the features that Microsoft has packed into its Outlook Express e-mail client. Though it's bundled for free in Windows 2000 and also comes with the freely available Internet Explorer 5.0 Web browser, Outlook Express is a professional quality e-mail client. Whether you want a simple e-mail program to pick up messages from your personal mailbox or are running a small business and need access to many accounts, Outlook Express is up to the challenge.

We certainly covered a lot of ground here. Among the high points:

✦ An introduction to the workings of various e-mail protocols, including POP3, IMAP, and Web-based e-mail systems.

✦ Exploration of the Outlook Express interface, including customization features.

✦ Step-by-step review of Outlook Express rules to filter and manage e-mail traffic.

✦ An introduction to using Outlook Express to access Internet newsgroups.

In the next chapter, our exploration of Windows 2000's Internet capabilities continues. Chapter 15 covers the versatile NetMeeting application, which provides audio, video, and data conferencing capabilities. It can even be used as a remote control application for Windows 2000 PCs.

✦   ✦   ✦

Conferencing with NetMeeting

With Windows 2000, Microsoft has taken the kitchen sink approach to operating system design. I mean, absolutely everything you could ever want is in there. Web browser and e-mail? Check. Administrative tools? Check. Image editing and word processing applications? Check. So why should I be surprised that Windows 2000 comes complete with an audio-, data-, and video-conferencing application?

And what an application! Microsoft NetMeeting is the leading Internet conferencing application, and it can be hugely useful depending on your needs. Whether you want to make video calls to the family during long business trips or need a way to give presentations over the wire, the NetMeeting 3.01 software included with Windows 2000 has something for you.

Getting Started with NetMeeting

NetMeeting is a full-featured, multifaceted conferencing application and environment that enables you to conduct conferencing over local area networks (LANs), wide area networks (WANs), and the Internet. Here are some of the things you can do:

✦ Use audio links to talk to others over a network.

✦ Use video to conduct video phone calls.

✦ Share applications and documents.

✦ Collaborate on documents using shared applications.

✦ Transmit and receive files over the NetMeeting call.

✦ Use the shared Whiteboard to sketch out ideas and copy and paste content for viewing.

✦ Use the Chat feature to send text messages back and forth.

In This Chapter

Setting up NetMeeting

Using directories and other resources to find users

Making audio and video calls

Transferring files during calls

Using NetMeeting to remotely control PCs

To launch NetMeeting, you need to dig down into the Communications section of the Start menu. Click Start ➪ Programs ➪ Accessories ➪ Communications and click the NetMeeting entry. Figure 15-1 shows what the menu looks like.

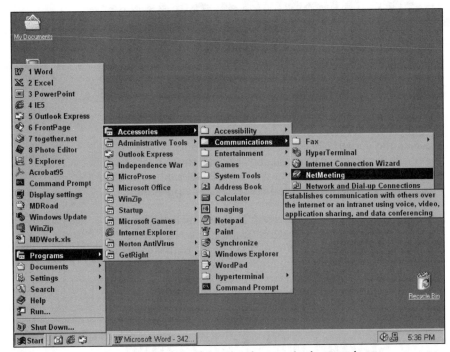

Figure 15-1: NetMeeting isn't exactly front and center in the Start button menu, so you may want to create a more convenient shortcut if you frequently use the application.

Setting up NetMeeting for the first time

The first time you launch NetMeeting, you are prompted to enter a good deal of information. The reason: NetMeeting needs to create online connections and link with online conferencing directories, and the program needs some way to enable others to recognize you online. Here are the steps in the setup process:

1. Click Start ➪ Programs ➪ Accessories ➪ Communications and click the NetMeeting entry.

2. Click Next at the welcome dialog box. In the dialog box shown in Figure 15-2, enter your information into the First name, Last name, E-mail address, Location, and Comments text boxes. Keep in mind that this information may be visible to others in public or private directories. Click Next.

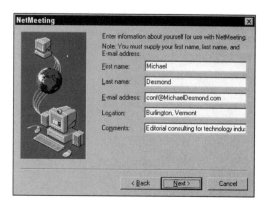

Figure 15-2: The Comments field is included in your directory listing, so it's a good idea to put useful information there.

3. The next dialog box prompts you to choose whether or not to log onto a directory server when NetMeeting starts. Use the drop-down control to select a directory server. The default is Microsoft's directory. Directory servers enable users to find people online.

Note

If you want to keep a low profile, make sure the lower checkbox control is checked. This enables you to log onto a directory server to review entries while keeping your name off the list. See Figure 15-3.

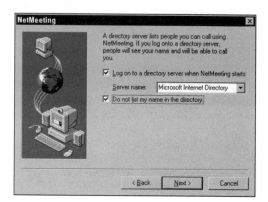

Figure 15-3: Checking the two checkboxes enables you to access the Internet directory while keeping your own name off the list.

4. Click the Next button. At the next dialog box, click the radio button matching your online connection. This setting is important because it tells NetMeeting what kind of bandwidth it can expect to have available for demanding video calls. See Figure 15-4. Click the Next button.

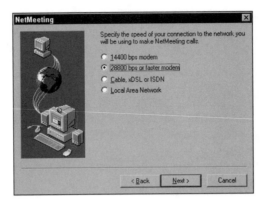

Figure 15-4: Tune NetMeeting to work with your specific online connection — in this case, a 56 Kbps modem.

5. Remember my complaint about NetMeeting being hard to find? On the next setup screen, check the top checkbox to put a NetMeeting icon on your desktop or check the lower checkbox to put an icon in the Quick Launch portion of the taskbar. Click Next.

Tip   Put an end to clutter! Microsoft wants you to create two icons — one on the desktop and one in Quick Launch — for launching NetMeeting. Why do they default both choices to on? For your own sake, turn at least one of these off.

6. The setup program tells you that it is about to test the audio. Make sure that you close any programs that play or record audio because NetMeeting must have exclusive access to audio resources during its test. Once you've closed any open applications that require access to audio resources, click Next.

7. Test the audio by clicking the Test button beneath the slider bar. You should hear a funky sample sound. Click the Stop button (the Test button toggles to Stop) to end the test. If you didn't hear anything, try dragging the slider to the right. If all seems well, click the Next button. Figure 15-5 shows this dialog box at work.

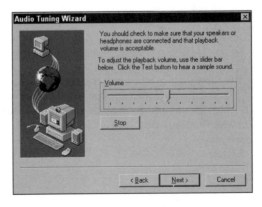

Figure 15-5: The slider bar enables you to tweak the volume to a level that's comfortable for you.

8. Now test your system microphone. The dialog box in Figure 15-6 shows the text you are supposed to read into the microphone. As you read, a line level bar shows signal strength. Try to keep the signal out of the lowest and highest ranges by adjusting the recording volume. Click the slider bar and move it to the left (quieter) or right (louder). Click Next when you are done.

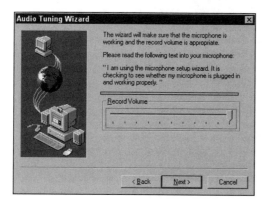

Figure 15-6: Read the provided text into your microphone. If you don't think you're getting proper recording levels, try tweaking the slider bar.

Note If for some reason Windows is unable to record the audio, you see an error dialog box telling you that the microphone may not be plugged in. You are prompted to fix the microphone and click Back to attempt the recording test again.

9. NetMeeting informs you that you have tuned the program settings. Click the Finish button.

Tip Not sure if you've got the audio set properly? Don't worry, you can always go back and tweak it later by selecting Tools ⇨ Audio Tuning Wizard from the NetMeeting menu.

Once you click Finish, NetMeeting automatically launches. It takes a little while for everything to get initialized, so be patient. You should see the default NetMeeting interface window shown in Figure 15-7.

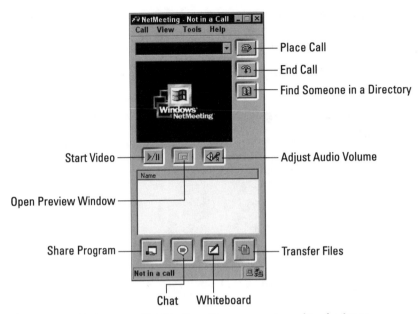

Figure 15-7: Welcome to NetMeeting. Once you get used to the icons scattered about the compact interface, conferencing becomes a snap.

Hardware handicaps

If you've managed to complete the steps in the previous section — and they really are quite simple, to Microsoft's credit — you're ready to place a conference call. But first, let's look at a couple issues that can affect your ability to take advantage of NetMeeting.

NetMeeting enables any two networked computers, whether they are on the Internet, LAN, or WAN, to connect and share data, documents, and resources. What's more, NetMeeting is able to interoperate with other conferencing software and end points that use the industry-standard H.323 conferencing specification. That means that NetMeeting can conduct audio and video conferences over the network. To make this happen, your PC needs to be outfitted with the proper hardware. Here's what you want:

✦ Monitor-top video camera that connects to a USB or serial port

✦ Full-duplex audio adapter with speakers

✦ Microphone

Most home PCs sold over the past two years have come with speakers and sound hardware, but many corporate systems lack this hardware. Without audio hardware, you won't be able to speak with a remote party. You can, however, use the data-sharing features of NetMeeting, such as Whiteboard, application sharing, and Chat.

One step beyond audio is the video-conferencing capability of NetMeeting. Hook up a compatible video camera to your PC, and you can conduct video calls over the network. Not convinced that video calls make sense? Keep in mind that cameras can be used to capture high-resolution still images of documents and products that you hold in front of the camera, enabling remote parties to quickly view objects over the wire.

Video conferencing is neat stuff, but it can gobble up network bandwidth fast. If you intend to use NetMeeting on your corporate network, make sure you inform your network administrator what you're up to. Otherwise, you could kick off a network bandwidth crisis if your coworkers also start making video calls.

If you want to use NetMeeting in the office, you may need to look into a hardware upgrade. While many corporate PCs may lack complete audio hardware, virtually all come without a video camera. The good news is that you can quickly and easily add video cameras to Windows 2000 systems via the USB port. USB's Plug-and-Play capability should make installation a snap. Just plug the unit in, supply the related drivers and applications from the accompanying CD-ROM, and you're off.

Of course, it's not always that simple. Before purchasing a video camera, make sure you check to see that it's listed on Microsoft's Hardware Compatibility List at www.microsoft.com/hcl. While Windows 2000 can play host to USB devices, those devices must come with Windows 2000-specific drivers. Only the HCL can assure you that such drivers are available.

Making the call

Okay, enough talk. NetMeeting is running on your PC, and at the very least, you can kick off a data conference. Here's how to make a call to another PC on the local area network.

You learn the various ways to connect to other systems in the section, "Getting in Touch with Others," later in this chapter. For now, I just want to show you what a connection looks like.

When it comes to Internet-based networking, the most basic unit of identity is the IP address. Your network may feature a cavalcade of system names, domain names, and user names, depending on your local setup. But no matter where you are, you can almost certainly form a link with another PC by using its IP address. Think of it as the "phone number" of the other system.

You can place a call in two different ways. Launch NetMeeting and then do one of the following:

✦ Click Call ➪ New Call. In the Place a Call dialog box, enter the IP address of the PC you wish to connect to and click the Call button. You can also enter the name of the computer on a local area network in the box.

Note   The IP address is the numeric address that identifies a computer or device to other computers on a network or the Internet. You can typically find IP addresses for systems on a network by checking with your network administrator. If you know the name of a system on the network, you can connect using the name.

✦ In the drop-down control at the top of the standard NetMeeting interface, enter the IP address of the PC you wish to connect to. Figure 15-8 shows what a typical IP address entry looks like. Then click the yellow phone icon at the top-right corner of the interface.

Figure 15-8: You need to know the IP address or system name of the remote system if you want to connect without using a directory or other listing.

In either case, the machine you're calling makes a telephone ringing noise, and the dialog box in Figure 15-9 appears on your screen. Once the remote party accepts the call, the dialog box disappears. The NetMeeting window now lists the online parties in the Name box.

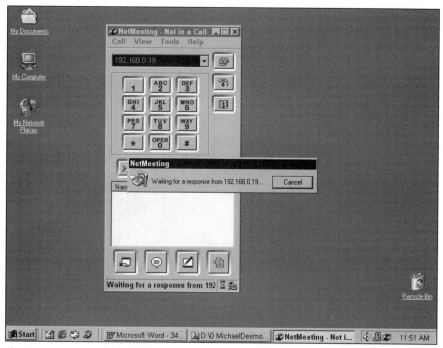

Figure 15-9: NetMeeting informs you that it's trying to reach another party. If you want to stop the call, click the Cancel button.

If you enter an incorrect IP address or system name, a dialog box eventually appears with the message that the other party is not able to accept NetMeeting calls. Double-check the information and try again. On the other hand, if the other party declines to accept your call or was not at their PC to answer, a dialog box appears telling you that the call was not accepted.

Note   NetMeeting does not distinguish between a call that is refused (the other party actually clicks a button to ignore the call) and a call that is not answered. In both instances, the dialog box simply says "The other party did not accept your call."

Receiving a call

The old saying goes that it's better to give than to receive. But when it comes to using NetMeeting, receiving is certainly easier to do. All you need to do is click the Accept button in the small dialog box shown in Figure 15-10. This dialog box pops up as soon as a call comes in.

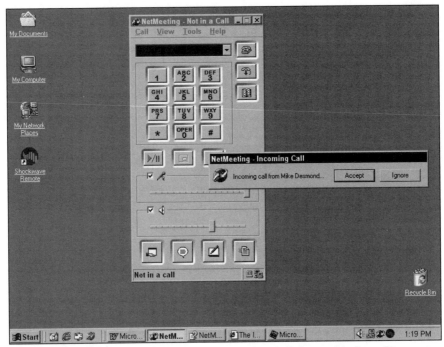

Figure 15-10: Click the Accept button to immediately link up with the calling party or click Ignore to refuse the call.

Of course, you can also decline to answer the call by clicking the Ignore button. It's worth noting that the caller isn't specifically told that you turned down the call.

You may want to automatically accept all calls, even when you are away from your machine, so others can call in to transfer files to your hard disk or prepare presentations for viewing later. To do so, click the Call menu and Automatically Accept Calls. A checkmark appears next to this menu item, indicating that all calls will be accepted.

There is a catch: In order to receive calls, NetMeeting must be running. By default, NetMeeting runs only when you invoke it, which means you could miss a lot of calls. You can set NetMeeting to always launch when Windows 2000 starts. Click Tools ➪ Options and, on the General tab, click the radio button labeled Run NetMeeting in the background when Windows starts. Click OK. NetMeeting is now always ready to accept calls, whether or not you are ready for them.

Getting in Touch with Others

Of course, no conferencing product is worth much if you can't get in touch with others. NetMeeting provides a number of ways to find and link with other parties. Here's a quick list of ways to connect with another NetMeeting user:

✦ Public directory server listing

✦ Computer IP address

✦ Computer name

✦ Telephone number

✦ E-mail address

✦ Address Book listing

NetMeeting also gives you several options that make it easier to place conference calls.

Using Microsoft Internet Directory

The foremost resource available to you is the Microsoft Internet Directory service, which works with the Internet Locator Server (or ILS) to create a universal directory of NetMeeting addresses. This directory provides a searchable listing of logged-on NetMeeting end stations and includes useful information ranging from name and e-mail address to succinct comments about the user. By default, NetMeeting logs you onto the Microsoft Internet Directory, giving you access to directory listings and making you available to others logged onto the directory (provided you make yourself available to the directory).

Note

If you use NetMeeting over a LAN, directory servers do not appear in the list. The same holds true if you transact outside calls through a gatekeeper, conferencing management software that lets network administrators monitor and control conferencing traffic over the network. For more information, contact your network administrator.

Here's how to search for another NetMeeting user using the Microsoft Internet Directory service:

1. Launch NetMeeting.

2. Click Call ⇨ Directory or click the directory icon (the icon with the image of a book—it's the third one on the right side of the interface).

3. The Find Someone window appears. Enter the information you want to search by in any of the following fields: First Name, Last Name, Location, E-mail address, and Comments. Figure 15-11 shows what a typical search looks like.

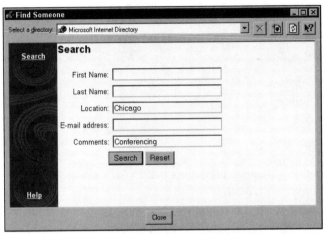

Figure 15-11: I've entered a broad search for anyone located in Chicago who has placed the word "Conferencing" in their online comments. If you are looking for a specific person, be sure to enter their name or e-mail information.

Note

The search fields are self-explanatory, but navigation is made difficult by nonstandard window behavior. For example, the Del button does not remove selected text (you need to use Backspace), and Tab does not move you to the next field.

4. Click the Search button. After a brief period, you see a matching list of NetMeeting users currently connected to the Internet as shown in Figure 15-12. The Attributes field indicates whether the site offers data, audio, and/or video conferencing.

5. Place a call by clicking the Connect With link at the top of any of the addresses. NetMeeting places the call and links if the other party accepts the call.

You don't have to use the default Microsoft Internet Directory server, however. To change the directory service, click Tools ➪ Options and go to the General tab of the Options dialog box. Click the Directory drop-down control and select another listed directory, or enter the directory server name into the control. Click OK to enable the new directory.

Tip

There are many more directories than the default Microsoft service. To gain access to a large list of NetMeeting directories, go to the NetMeeting Zone Web site at http://www.netmeet.net/bestservers.asp.

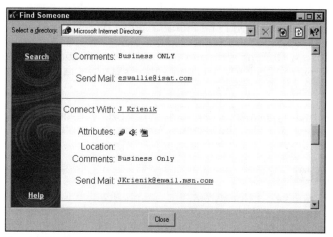

Figure 15-12: A new search turns up a business that supports video, audio, and data conferencing. The red star on the system icon indicates that this user is currently in a call.

Adding other directories

As the preceding tip illustrates, you don't have to be satisfied with Microsoft's directory listing. To gain access to another directory server, simply enter the server address into the Select a directory drop-down control of the Find Someone dialog box. The best way to add a new directory is to click Call ➪ Directory, enter the directory server address into the drop-down control, and press Enter. The Find Someone dialog box updates to look like the one in Figure 15-13 once the directory contents have downloaded.

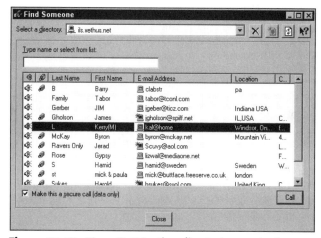

Figure 15-13: Many NetMeeting directories are topic or geography specific, but all feature the familiar columnar layout that provides at least a little insight into listed devices or computers.

Entering a directory name into this dialog box is a one-shot deal. Next time you go back to NetMeeting, the directory won't be there. To add a directory so that you can select it every time you click the Call ⇨ Directory menu command, you need to go elsewhere. Click Tools ⇨ Options and enter the new directory address in the Directory drop-down control. Click OK. The new address is now part of NetMeeting's list of available directories.

To access your new directory, just click Call ⇨ Directory (or click the Call icon) and select the new entry when you click the Select a Directory drop-down control.

Removing directories

To remove a directory you've previously entered, simply delete it from the Find Someone dialog box. But first, you must make sure the directory you want to delete is not set as the default — NetMeeting won't let you delete the default directory. The default directory is the one that appears at the top of the Directory drop-down list. Here's how to remove a directory:

1. Click Tools ⇨ Options and review the Directory drop-down list.

2. If the directory you want to remove is at the top of the list (and is displayed when the list is not expanded), click the drop-down list and select another directory. Click OK.

3. Click Call ⇨ Directory. In the Select a directory drop-down list, select the directory you want to remove from the list.

4. Once the directory is displayed, click the X icon next to the drop-down control. The directory entry is removed.

Creating address books

A real problem with public directory servers is that they tend to attract a lot of undesirable folks looking for explicit video calls. The last thing you want to see when searching for the NetMeeting address of your coworker in Las Vegas is half a dozen offers for racy video calls.

You can avoid the seamy underside of public directories by simply hardcoding addresses that you use frequently into your Windows Address Book. The Outlook Express e-mail client integrated into Windows 2000 includes a separate NetMeeting tab in the Properties dialog box for each Address Book entry.

Note   The Windows Address Book is not part of NetMeeting; rather it's part of Outlook Express. However, the Address Book includes hooks for NetMeeting users, providing a tab for each entry that is specific to NetMeeting use. That means you can quickly make a NetMeeting call while using Outlook Express.

Here's how to add a NetMeeting call address to an Address Book entry in Outlook Express:

1. Open Outlook Express and click the Address Book icon on the toolbar.
2. Navigate to the contact you want to edit and double-click the entry.
3. Click the NetMeeting tab in the contact Properties dialog box.
4. Enter the contact's conferencing server and conferencing address in the two boxes, as shown in Figure 15-14. Click the Add button.

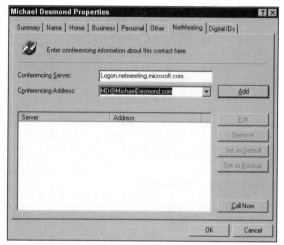

Figure 15-14: These two entries give NetMeeting the information it needs to find a remote conferencing party.

Tip

You can find conferencing server and address information by plucking it from a Microsoft Internet Directory listing. After you find the desired entry in a search, right-click the hyperlinked name next to Connect with: and click Copy Shortcut. This copies the combined ILS server name and user e-mail address to the Windows clipboard. Then right-click the Conferencing Server text box in the desired Address Book entry and click paste. Next you must split up the two parts of the pasted information. Select the e-mail portion of the pasted entry (for example, name@isp.net), right-click, and select cut. Right-click in the Conferencing Address drop-down box and click Paste. Finally, pare down the server information so the Address Book can read it. Delete the "callto:" from the front of the server address and remove the slash (/) character at the end. Congratulations; you just filled in all the server and address information.

5. Test the new address right away by clicking the Call Now button at the bottom of the Address Book entry. NetMeeting places a call to the user.

6. If everything works, click OK to make the change take effect.

As you begin conferencing with more and more coworkers and friends, be sure to enter their NetMeeting information into your Outlook Express Address Book. Before long, you have a single place to keep track of e-mail, phone, and NetMeeting contact information.

Speed calls with SpeedDial

Microsoft has tried to make using NetMeeting a lot like using a phone. It includes a comforting phone-like interface with the familiar numeric keypad, right down to the star (*) and number sign (#) keys. The call and hang-up icons along the right side of the window also reflect the telephone theme. So it's no surprise that Microsoft included a speed-dial feature in NetMeeting.

SpeedDial is a quick and easy way to add contacts you are currently hooked up with to a shortcut list of callers.

To create a speed-dial entry, do the following:

1. In NetMeeting, Click Call ⇨ Create SpeedDial.

2. In the Create SpeedDial dialog box, type into the Address text box the directory server name and e-mail name in the format as follows: directory server name/e-mail name (for example, ils.microsoft.com/someone@ someone.com).

3. If this is an Internet-bound call, keep the Call using drop-down list set to Directory. For LAN-based calls, select Network from this drop-down list.

4. Click the Add to SpeedDial list radio button and click OK. If you want to be able to call this person directly from the desktop, click the Save on the desktop radio button and click OK; an icon will appear on the desktop that automatically launches NetMeeting and calls this address.

When you create your first SpeedDial entry, a new listing called Speed Dial appears in the Find Someone dialog box (accessed via Call ⇨ Directory). To access a SpeedDial entry, click Call ⇨ Directory, select Speed Dial from the Select a directory drop-down control. Your Speed Dial entries appear in the list box below, as shown in Figure 15-15. Click the desired entry and click Call. You can also double-click an entry to place a call.

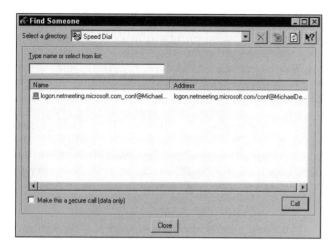

Figure 15-15: The Speed Dial feature gives you instant access to end points directly from NetMeeting.

Using NetMeeting

Okay, so you've found people to conference with. It's time to take advantage of the features NetMeeting offers. Not only can these features enhance your call experience, but they can protect you as well. Security features such as data encryption ensure that only authorized parties can see the data you trade during a conference call.

Using the data-conferencing features

The best place to start is with the set of data-conferencing features in NetMeeting. These features are available to any online NetMeeting user, regardless of whether or not you have set up a microphone or speakers.

- ✦ **Application sharing:** Share access to documents over the wire. Remote callers can collaboratively edit and create documents online.

- ✦ **Data transfer:** Quickly send files from point to point, using a dedicated transfer protocol.

- ✦ **Whiteboard:** Sketch out ideas and share clipboard contents using this common drawing space.

- ✦ **Chat:** Don't have audio capability or an available phone to augment your NetMeeting session? Chat enables you to type messages to your call partner in real time.

All about application sharing

Sharing applications is perhaps the most powerful feature of NetMeeting. With a click of a button, you can provide complete remote access to all sorts of documents and programs. Jointly tweak numbers in a spreadsheet or perform real-time edits on a work-in-progress memo. Application sharing makes it happen.

To prevent the confusion that can occur when two users simultaneously try to move a mouse or type text, NetMeeting toggles active control between parties. When the remote party gains access (by clicking Control ⇨ Request Control in the Application Sharing window), the host's mouse and keyboard are frozen within the shared application window. To grab active control back, the host need simply click a mouse button. The remote user's shared application window stops providing access to the document.

To share an application with a remote caller, do the following:

1. Open NetMeeting and connect to the other party.

2. Open the application and document you want to share.

3. Click the Share Program icon (the left-most icon along the bottom edge of the NetMeeting display) or click Tools ⇨ Sharing.

4. In the Sharing dialog box pictured in Figure 15-16, select the application you want to share in the list box. Click the Share button.

5. To enable sharing, click the Allow Control button. It immediately toggles to Prevent Control, and the two checkbox controls beneath it go active. The remote party only has view-only access until you click this button.

6. To provide instant access to remote parties, click the checkbox labeled Automatically accept requests for control. Now you won't have to click a confirmation dialog box to enable the other party to dive into your shared application.

Tip   You can temporarily eliminate remote control without actually clicking the Prevent Control button. Click the Do not disturb checkbox. Although the remote user sees that the viewed application is controllable (the word Shared appears in the application's title bar), attempting to request control yields a dialog box saying that the host is busy. Once you're ready to offer control to others, uncheck the box. The change in state happens immediately — there's no need to click the Close button. This can be useful if you need to step away from your PC for a moment and don't want to hand over control of your apps to remote parties.

Figure 15-17 shows a PC controlling a Microsoft Word application session based on a remote system. Note how the controlled application is accessed within an application sharing window.

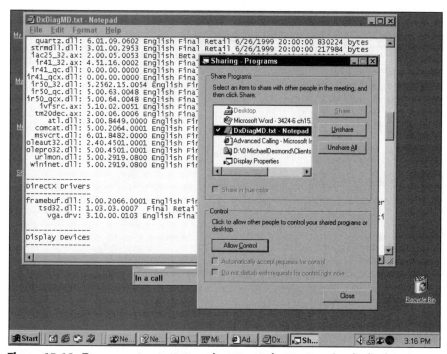

Figure 15-16: Tune remote access to suit your needs. Want to simply display a PowerPoint presentation over the wire? Click the button in the Control area so that it toggles to Allow Control. This gives the remote party view-only access to your apps.

Use NetMeeting as a remote control package

If you think that's something, try this. Click the Unshare All button in the Sharing dialog box. Now click the Desktop item at the top of the list box and click the Share button. The remote computer now enjoys complete access to your entire PC. Why click the Unshare All button to start? Because NetMeeting only provides Desktop access when all other sharing sessions are shut down.

This feature is more important than you might think. By setting up NetMeeting to provide control to the Windows 2000 desktop, you essentially gain features from remote control packages such as Traveling Software LapLink Professional and Symantec PC-Anywhere. With desktop access enabled, a remote system can move and delete files, format hard disks, open and close applications, change system settings, even access the Windows 2000 Registry. This is a great tool if you need to access all your work PC resources from home, for example.

Caution

Obviously, the powerful desktop control feature can put your PC at significant risk. A remote user who is able to take over your desktop can masquerade as you in the network, enjoying all your account privileges and access. Of course, all your local data is accessible as well. Always be very careful about who has desktop control.

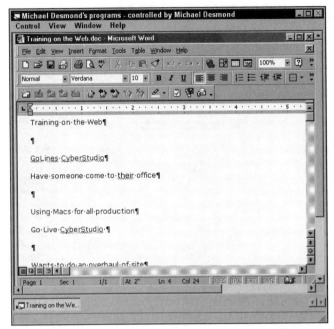

Figure 15-17: Application sharing lets a remote PC take complete control of a single application or even the entire system.

You can configure NetMeeting to act a lot like a remote control package by setting up password-protected access to your PC. If you're on the road, this capability enables you to use NetMeeting to call into your office PC and enjoy full access to all the data and services on the system. Forgot an important file? You can quickly transfer it from the remove hard drive using the Remote Desktop Sharing feature.

Of course, both PCs must have NetMeeting installed. In addition, you need to configure your system to listen for remote control requests from authorized parties when NetMeeting is not running. Here's how to turn your PC into a remotely controllable resource:

1. Click Tools ➪ Remote Desktop Sharing.

2. In the dialog box that appears, check the Enable Remote Desktop Sharing checkbox and click Wizard.

3. Click the Next button and then click the Yes radio button. This enables a password-protected screen saver to lock out other parties who might otherwise walk up to your PC and gain control of it. Click Next.

4. The Screen Saver tab of the Display Properties dialog box appears, as shown in Figure 15-18. Select the screen saver type you want and set the delay. Make sure you check the Password protected checkbox. Click OK.

5. Congratulations — you're ready to achieve remote control over your PC. Click Finish to make the settings take effect and then click OK to close the Remote Desktop Sharing Settings dialog box.

6. In the taskbar tray, right-click the new NetMeeting remote control icon and click Activate Remote Desktop Sharing.

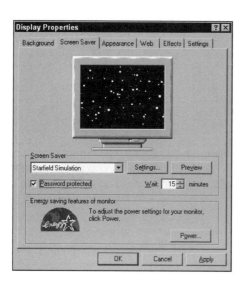

Figure 15-18: Look familiar? It's the standard screen saver tool from the Display Properties dialog boxed.

On the remote system, you must set NetMeeting to perform secure calls. Doing so causes NetMeeting to encrypt all data (but not the video or audio) that is transacted between the systems. Click Tools ⇨ Options and clicking the Security tab. As shown in the dialog box in Figure 15-19, click the checkbox below the Outgoing Calls entry. Click OK. If you fail to perform this action, the host system will refuse your call.

The next time you call in with NetMeeting to this system, a dialog box like the one shown in Figure 15-20 appears. You must enter an administrator user name, a password, and the proper domain information in order to access the desktop. Once you do, you see a Meeting Properties dialog box (Figure 15-21) that outlines exactly what you can and cannot do during your session. The remote desktop appears in the application window.

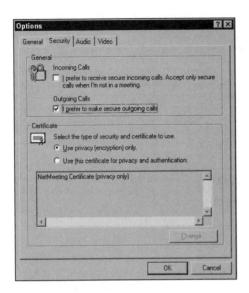

Figure 15-19: You must secure your outgoing transmissions for remote desktop sharing to be available from your PC.

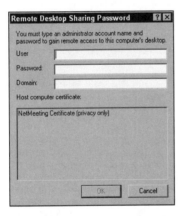

Figure 15-20: Enter an administrator-level user name and password, as well as the appropriate domain information, to access the remote system.

Figure 15-21: The Meeting Properties dialog box shows that I'm unable to make or receive NetMeeting calls when connected to the remotely controlled desktop. This helps preserve a secure environment.

Note When the remote PC is controlling the host, local access at the host is lost. So even if a coworker walked up and physically tried to use the mouse or keyboard, neither would work. However, the screen displays any activity that goes on.

To end a remote control session, click the hang-up icon on the NetMeeting interface. Control now returns to the host PC.

Tip When you return from a trip, it's a good idea to turn off the remote desktop-sharing feature, if only to prevent an unauthorized party from trying to take over your PC. Right-click the NetMeeting system tray icon and click Turn off Remote Desktop Sharing.

Using Chat

Chat lets you send typed messages in real-time to the other connected party—a useful resource if you don't have a working audio connection or a free phone line. To use Chat, initiate a call and then click the second icon from the left along the bottom of the NetMeeting window (or click Tools ➪ Chat). A simple dialog box opens. Enter text into the Message text box and click the icon to send the text to the other system. Your entry appears in the top text box.

Remote entries also appear in the top text box. As shown in Figure 15-22, name headers identify who sent what in the Chat window. If you don't want to send a chat item out to everyone during a multiparty call, click the Send To drop-down control and select the individual user name from the list. Then type your text and click the icon to send the private message.

Figure 15-22: The Chat dialog box gives you a running thread of who said what.

You can ease readability and the difficulty of tracking sessions by using the Options dialog box shown in Figure 15-23. Click View ➪ Options. From here you can add date and time stamps to messages (in addition to the usual user name), alter the layout of text messages, and change font types and colors to help you keep track of different types of messages.

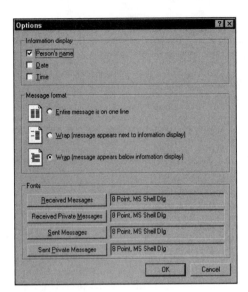

Figure 15-23: Tweak the Chat display to help you keep track of different messages and users.

Working with the Whiteboard

The Whiteboard feature of NetMeeting is essentially a modified Windows Paint application designed to enable multiple users to work on the same canvas. To launch the Whiteboard, click the Whiteboard icon at the bottom of the NetMeeting window (third from left) or click Tools ➪ Whiteboard.

Figure 15-24 shows the Whiteboard application at work. As you can see, it looks almost identical to the Windows Paint applet, except that you have a few additional icons for shared clipboard elements, multiple pages, and the like.

The clipboard features of the Whiteboard are particularly helpful for pulling onscreen data into the Whiteboard for viewing and sketching over. Copy and paste sections of your desktop or copy entire open windows with the useful Select Window and Select Area icons. The Remote Pointer icon (the little hand icon on the vertical toolbar) enables you to draw the other caller's attention to items onscreen. You can even save your onscreen work and access it later.

Transferring files

The File Transfer function in NetMeeting enables you to quickly move a file between systems engaged in a conference call. To send a file, simply click the Add Files icon (the left-most icon just under the File menu command), select the file from a standard navigation window, and click Add. As shown in Figure 15-25, the file appears in the list box of the File Transfer dialog box.

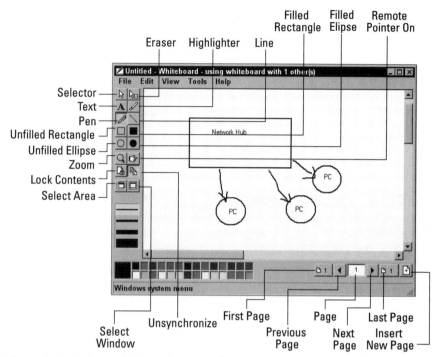

Filled Rectangle   Filled Elipse   Remote Pointer On

Eraser   Highlighter   Line

Selector
Text
Pen
Unfilled Rectangle
Unfilled Ellipse
Zoom
Lock Contents
Select Area

Network Hub

PC

PC   PC

Windows system menu

Select Window   Unsynchronize   First Page   Page   Last Page

Previous Page   Next Page   Insert New Page

Figure 15-24: The Whiteboard is extremely easy to use and is a good place to sketch out ideas or cut and paste graphics for joint review.

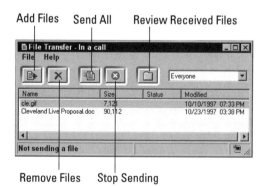

Add Files   Send All   Review Received Files

Remove Files   Stop Sending

Figure 15-25: You can send multiple files to other parties from the File Transfer dialog box.

To send a file, click the send icon (third from left) on the File Transfer dialog box. The display updates to show the status of the transmitted files, by adding the word *Sent* to the Status column of each file. Delete files from this dialog box listing by clicking the file and clicking the Remove Files icon (the second icon from the left).

To receive a file from another party, you don't have to do anything. Once the other party kicks off a transfer, you see the dialog box shown in Figure 15-26, which indicates file transfer progress, the filename, and the origination point. Once the file downloads, you can immediately launch it by clicking the Open button. If you want to open the file later, click the Close button. To delete the file right away, click the Delete button.

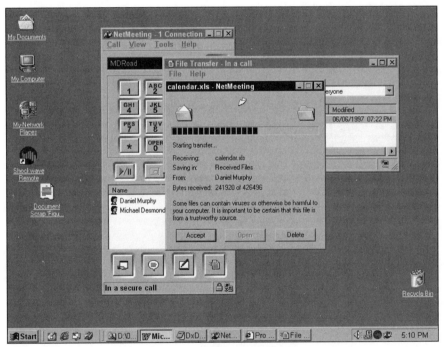

Figure 15-26: You can track progress of file transfers and see where they are coming from.

To open files that you've received previously, click the View Received Files icon in the toolbar (the right-most icon that looks like a yellow folder). This opens a folder in the NetMeeting program folder called Received Files, which is the default target for files sent to you by others.

Tip   You can change the destination folder. Click File ➪ Change Folder and then use the tree hierarchy dialog box shown in Figure 15-27 to select a new target folder. Click OK, and NetMeeting now shuffles all received files to the new spot.

Figure 15-27: Use the Change Folder feature to place downloaded files where you want them, not where NetMeeting thinks they should be.

Setting audio

NetMeeting enables audio conferencing over a LAN or Internet connection. Audio conferencing is actually a valuable feature for two key reasons:

✦ It consumes a tiny fraction of the bandwidth required by video.

✦ Virtually all home PCs and many business PCs are outfitted with speakers, though you'll likely have to purchase a separate microphone.

To adjust your audio settings, click Tools ➪ Options and click the Audio tab. You see the dialog box shown in Figure 15-28.

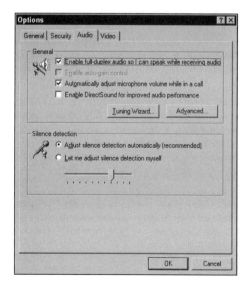

Figure 15-28: Adjust audio settings to improve conference performance.

You should definitely check the checkbox controls in the General area of the Audio page. You may find some of these checkboxes grayed out, however, if your audio hardware doesn't provide the required features to enable these capabilities. Among the neat features:

✦ The full-duplex checkbox enables parties to engage in telephone-like conversation, rather than having to wait for the other to stop talking before being able to speak.

✦ The automatic microphone adjustment control enables your system to adjust for changes, such as when you move closer or further away from the microphone.

✦ If your hardware is compatible with Microsoft DirectSound and has the proper drivers installed, be sure to enable DirectSound capability because its accelerated features can reduce latency in the audio signal. That means fewer drop outs, stutters, and other distracting interruptions.

Finally, the Silence detection area enables you to noodle with NetMeeting's capability to adjust to ambient noise. To reduce bandwidth demand, NetMeeting tries not to encode what it considers to be background noise. That filtering eliminates large amounts of network traffic and can be a real timesaver on slow analog phone connections.

By default, NetMeeting does this filtering automatically. However, if you notice that other parties are experiencing drop outs when you speak, it might be because the automatic detection is failing to detect your voice when you speak softly. To take control of this setting, click the lower radio button and then drag the slider control. You can experiment with the control to find a setting that yields best results.

The General tab of the Options dialog box also contains two buttons: the Advanced button and the Tuning Wizard button. Click the Advanced button to select a specific audio codec to apply to NetMeeting conferences. Audio codecs provide compression and decompression of audio data — critical for preserving quality and bandwidth. However, both parties in a call must employ the same codec in order to interoperate. The Advanced Compression Settings dialog box, accessed by the Advanced button, lets you tell NetMeeting which codec to use. For example, you can specify a better compression algorithm (for higher audio quality) that you know is installed on the other party's computer, where NetMeeting might go with a less capable, but more widely available, compression scheme.

Click the Tuning Wizard button to kick off the wizard that NetMeeting invokes the first time it is launched. This is quite useful if you change your microphone or move to a new office where noise levels are higher or lower — any situation where the initial audio level settings might need tweaking.

Setting video

Click the Video tab on the Options dialog box to see the page shown in Figure 15-29. NetMeeting has a number of useful features that can improve the quality of the video you send and receive:

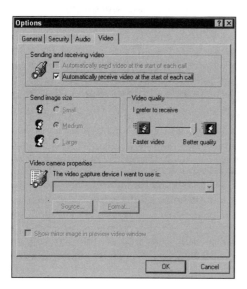

Figure 15-29: The Video page lets you enable video calls, set image size, and even trade off image quality for higher frame rates.

The Sending and receiving video area controls whether or not NetMeeting immediately attempts to create a video link. When checked, the top checkbox indicates that NetMeeting immediately sends video when launched. The lower checkbox, when checked, enables NetMeeting to receive video right away. Typically, I leave both of these unchecked. During calls, I manually tell NetMeeting to begin receiving and sending video by clicking the Start Video button that appears just beneath the keypad area of the NetMeeting interface window.

The Send image size area controls the size of the video image you send over the wire. You can reduce the bandwidth your call consumes by clicking the Small radio button to reduce the number of pixels used to create the video image. By default, NetMeeting uses the Medium image size, which sends a video window that is 320 by 240 pixels in size. Clicking the Large radio button boosts the video window size to 640 by 480, resulting in a much more detailed video image. The small image is 160 by 120 pixels.

Tip

If more than one person is participating at each end of the call, you should consider using the Large image size option. The additional pixels help ensure that individual faces are detailed enough to be recognizable.

The Video quality area helps you get the most from your incoming video. To get higher visual detail, move the slider bar to the right, but frame rates fall as a result. For higher frame rates and smoother playback, move the slider to the left. The compromise is less detailed images.

Finally, the Video camera properties area enables you to select which video input device to use to capture your side of the conference. Click the drop-down list and click the device you want to use. Of course, this assumes you have multiple video devices to choose from.

The Source button enables you to adjust the behavior of the selected input device. The video preview window must be open for the Source button to be active. To open the preview window, click the Picture-in-Picture button that appears just beneath the keypad in the NetMeeting interface window. You will now see your local video feed appear in a window on screen.

Once you've opened the preview window, click Tools ➪ Options, click the Video tab, and click the Source button. The dialog box that appears actually comes from your specific video device software. You should follow the documentation and help material for your camera or input device in order to configure settings for the device.

If your device lacks a configuration interface you may still be able to tweak settings using the Format button. This button provides access to generic video settings.

Click to set video-capture card properties. You must be previewing a video image in the Video window to make this button available. The dialog box that appears when you click this button comes from the capture device's software. If the Source dialog box facility is not complete, the Format button can be used to adjust the device's setting.

Security

Several security options are available in NetMeeting, all of which are available from the Security tab of the Options dialog box. Figure 15-30 shows this page of the dialog box.

Note   The security features of NetMeeting only affect data transfers. Video and audio are not encrypted.

The security features of NetMeeting are simple, yet powerful. The General area of the Security page includes two checkboxes, which determine whether or not NetMeeting employs encryption during online calls. Check the Incoming Calls checkbox to prevent unsecured calls from being accepted by your system. Why? Well, it can prevent a coworker from accidentally trading proprietary information in the open during a NetMeeting conference.

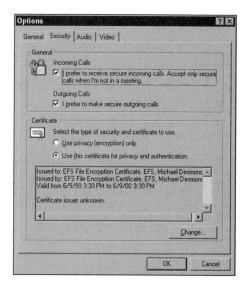

Figure 15-30: Prevent unauthorized parties from accessing data traded during your conferences by setting security for incoming and outgoing calls.

To secure all the calls that you make against snooping, check the Outgoing Calls checkbox. Again, NetMeeting will encrypt all the data transacted between systems in the secure call (though it won't encrypt video and audio) to prevent interception by third parties.

Both these settings use digital certificates to enable encryption under the so-called public key encryption (PKE) scheme. The settings for the underlying certificates are found in the Certificate area of the Security page. Users have two options:

✦ Use privacy (encryption) only
✦ Use this certificate for privacy and authentication

By default, NetMeeting only encrypts data. Using this mode is very simple. To enable privacy all you need to do is check the checkboxes in the General area. NetMeeting automatically supplies the digital certificate to create secure links between parties.

For more on digital certificates and their use, see Chapter 13.

However, if you need to go a step further and verify that other parties are who they say they are, you need to click the Use this certificate radio button. The scrolling text box beneath the radio button updates to show the currently installed certificate used to validate your identity to other parties.

In some cases, you may have been issued multiple certificates by issuing parties. If that's the case, you may need to change the currently installed certificate for one that will be recognized by parties you interact with. To change the certificate, click the Change button. In the Select Certificate dialog box, select the certificate to use from the list and click OK. The new certificate will now appear in the scrolling text box.

Summary

NetMeeting is one of the most powerful examples of Windows 2000's kitchen sink approach to operating system functionality. NetMeeting provides all the benefits of data, audio, and video conferencing directly within Windows 2000. By taking the time to master this application, you can use it to do everything from making video calls to making online presentations. Transfer files, share applications, even remotely control PCs over the wire.

In this chapter, we covered NetMeeting's many features, including:

✦ An overview of the conferencing capabilities of NetMeeting

✦ A guide to finding other conferencing parties using online directories, Address Book entries, and direct address inputs

✦ Creating remote control sessions between NetMeeting-equipped systems

✦ Setting security features under NetMeeting

✦ Configuring audio, video, and other settings

With NetMeeting, we conclude our tour of Windows 2000's Internet capabilities. In Chapter 16, we cover the display capabilities of Windows 2000, including some intriguing advanced features such as dual-monitor support.

✦   ✦   ✦

Graphics and Multimedia

Setting Up the Display

In This Chapter

Setting resolutions and other graphics modes

Updating display drivers

Making use of multiple displays

Installing and set up graphics adapters and monitors

Selecting graphics drivers suited to your mission

Seeing is believing. And Windows 2000 Professional certainly gives you a lot to look at. From advanced 3D graphics and video capabilities to powerful multimonitor display support, Windows 2000 expands your visual horizons. The display enhancements are a lot more than just pretty colors and eye candy. In fact, the improved display handling can provide a big productivity boost for everyone from busy executives to time-pressed application developers.

Of course, the display subsystem can also be among the most troublesome in the PC. In the past, users have had to keep up with rapid graphics board driver updates as vendors sought to squash bugs and resolve incompatibilities. In this chapter, you learn why the dreaded *driver du jour* may well become a thing of the past. That doesn't mean that graphics struggles are completely abated. You need to stay alert to common problems.

Windows 2000 also incorporates powerful 3D graphics and video-handling capabilities. For more on these multimedia and gaming technologies, see Chapter 18.

Setting Display Modes

The most common graphics-oriented update is changing resolutions, color depths, and other settings. Windows 2000 makes graphics-mode changes easy. The tool for changing the display characteristics is the Display Properties dialog box that you access by double-clicking the Display icon in the Control Panel. Alternatively, you can right-click any open space on the Windows desktop and click Properties to open this dialog box.

A number of things in the Windows 2000 interface represent changes from Windows NT, including the Display Properties dialog box. Let's take a look at this bulked up facility. Figure 16-1 shows the dialog box with its six (count 'em!) tabbed pages. For noodling with display modes, the only tab of interest is the one labeled Settings. Click it.

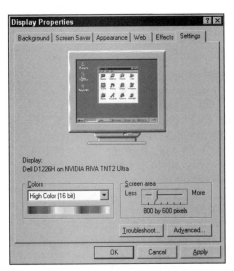

Figure 16-1: The Settings tab of the Display Properties dialog box contains all your display management tools, including controls for resolution, color depth, and troubleshooting.

Figure 16-1 shows the various elements included in the Display Settings dialog box. Most prominent is the monitor graphic, which provides a graphical representation of how the selected resolution setting will look. By watching the graphic while sliding the Screen area slider bar, you can get a good sense of just how much more information you can view by scaling up resolutions.

The graphic is just for show, but a variety of working controls warrant introducing.

Setting color depth

The Colors drop-down list box enables you to determine how many colors your graphics card displays on the monitor. The more colors you can display, the more realistic the graphics appear onscreen. This is particularly true for images, digital photos, games, and other graphics that incorporate a broad range of colors.

The color choices displayed in the Colors drop-down list box may vary depending on the graphics card and driver installed in your system. Table 16-1 lists the most common color settings and some recommendations.

Table 16-1 Color Depths Defined		
Selection	*Number of Colors*	*What You Get*
16 Colors	16	Lowest setting, often used in Safe Mode for troubleshooting graphics problems. Many current programs do not run in 16 (4-bit) color mode.
256 Colors	256	Poor display of images and photos, many games and some productivity applications won't run; Windows dialog boxes and base graphics look fine.
High Color (16-bit)	65,356	Best compromise setting. Images generally look good, and memory load is manageable.
True Color (24-bit)	16.7 million	Displays all the colors the eye can perceive but requires more memory, particularly at high resolution. Required for photo editing.
True Color (32-bit)	4.3 billion	Sometimes offered in lieu of 24-bit color. No real image quality benefit over 24-bit color, and memory demand is even higher.

It's worth noting that all current (and even most aging) CRT monitors can display the full 16.7 million colors of 24-bit color mode. While older graphics boards may lack the memory to push true color at resolutions higher than 800 by 600 pixels, you won't have to worry about your display.

That said, most older CRTs lack sufficient screen area to comfortably display the Windows 2000 interface and applications. I typically recommend a 17-inch CRT for those who multitask programs.

So how do you change colors? It's as easy as clicking the Colors drop-down list box and selecting the mode you want to display.

1. Select the desired color depth from the drop-down list box.

2. Click Apply or OK to make the new color setting take effect.

3. A dialog box asks you to confirm the change. Click OK to proceed or Cancel to abort the change. The screen goes blank for a moment. You should then see the desktop with the new color setting and a dialog box asking if you want to keep the change.

4. Click Yes to keep it or No to go back to the original color setting. If you don't click either button, the desktop returns to the original color setting after 15 seconds.

Note Why the 15-second delayed return? Well, if your graphics card can't handle the new setting, it may fail to display any graphics at all. And it can be downright difficult to get around Windows in the dark. This feature ensures that users can get their original settings back even if their screen goes black or gets scrambled when set to the new color depth.

Changing resolution

The next stop is the Screen area slider control. This intuitive little control enables you to adjust the fineness of the display on your monitor. Sliding it to the right stuffs more, smaller pixels into the display space, and moving the slider to the left reduces the pixel count while boosting pixel size.

Basically, changing the resolution comes down to how much information you want to fit into the finite display space. The higher the resolution, the more application windows, document text, and spreadsheet cells you can fit into a given screen. But you can have too much information. Try using a 15-inch monitor with graphics set to 1280 by 1024 resolution. You'll find yourself squinting at teeny tiny little icons and flirting with a major headache. A much more comfortable setting for smaller monitors is 800 by 600. Figure 16-2 shows how the view changes when you adjust resolution. Table 16-2 gives you an idea of what resolutions are best for specific sizes of monitors.

Note You may have noticed that 15-inch LCD displays are often designed to natively handle 1024 by 768 resolution. The reason for the higher typical pixel count is that LCD display sizes reflect the true viewable diagonal measurement of the screen. CRT monitors, by contrast, are measured by the total diagonal tube measurement, a portion of which is obscured by the plastic monitor frame (called a *bezel*). In addition, because CRTs have a hard time precisely displaying pixels at the far edge of the screen, a portion of the visible glass also may go unused. The result: A 17-inch CRT and a 15.1-inch LCD offer similar viewable areas. Despite this fact, LCD screen take up considerably less desk space.

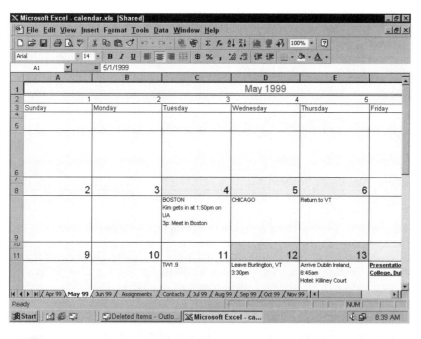

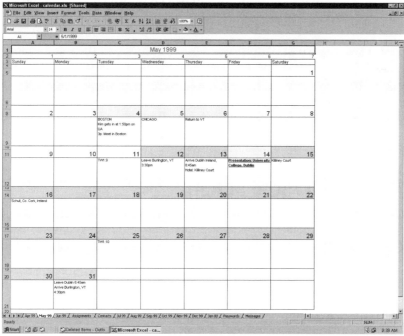

Figure 16-2: What a difference a few pixels can make. Notice how much more of the Excel-based monthly calendar you can see when the screen resolution is set to 1280 by 1024 pixels compared with 800 by 600 pixels.

Table 16-2
Common Resolution Settings and the Best CRT Tube Sizes

Resolution in pixels	CRT tube size
640 by 480	14 inch
800 by 600	15 inch
1024 by 768	17 inch
1280 by 1024	19 inch
1600 by 1200	21 inch +

Changing resolution is a similar process to changing color depth. It may also be something you do occasionally. A higher resolution setting can be quite useful for detailed graphics work, for example, while a lower resolution is optimal for reading text. Windows 2000 can switch resolutions without forcing a reboot, so you can readily tailor your display to the task at hand. Here's how:

1. Click the Screen area slider bar control and drag it to the desired setting.

2. The text beneath the slider updates to reflect the selected resolution as you move the control. Once you've selected the desired resolution, click OK or Apply.

3. Once again you see the confirmation box. Click OK and then wait a moment for the screen to blank and come back up in the new setting.

4. If all looks good, click Yes to keep the settings. If the display looks distorted or doesn't suit your needs, click No to return to the previous setting.

Again, if you fail to click Yes or No within 15 seconds, Windows assumes something is wrong and restores the previous resolution.

Behind the Advanced button

But wait, there's more. Clicking the Advanced button brings up a slew of graphics controls. And depending on what graphics card and driver set you have installed, what you see in the ensuing dialog box can vary widely. Some board vendors, such as ATI, Matrox, and Diamond, typically load you up with custom utilities that do everything from adjusting refresh rates and color output to enabling changes in the graphics chip clock speed.

Typically, you can expect to see the following tabs:

✦ **General:** Set font size and tailor the way Windows 2000 responds when resolutions and color depths are changed.

✦ **Adapter:** View and change graphics card drivers and resource settings; access the troubleshooter.

✦ **Monitor:** Check monitor drivers, access the troubleshooter, and set refresh rates.

✦ **Troubleshooting:** Dial down graphics acceleration to resolve conflicts.

✦ **Color Management:** Select a color profile to tweak monitor output.

The following sections go through each of these tabs in detail.

Setting font size

The first thing you see after clicking Advanced is the General tab. In the top area, called Display, click the Font Size drop-down list box to change the way characters look in places such as the Windows 2000 toolbar, various dialog boxes, and program title bars.

I typically stick with the Small Fonts setting to conserve screen area for real work, but the Large Fonts setting can help enhance legibility, particularly at high resolutions. At this setting, the fonts are 25 percent larger than the default Small Fonts setting.

You can even tailor font sizes by selecting Other from the list, which takes you to the Custom Font Size dialog box shown in Figure 16-3. You can adjust font size from as little as 20 percent of normal (truly unreadable) up to 500 percent larger than normal (truly gargantuan).

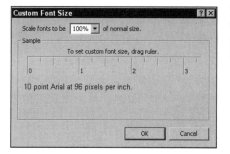

Figure 16-3: Drag the nifty font ruler to scale font sizes up or down, click a preset magnification, or simply enter a magnification value.

Cross-Reference For more on font sizing and other accessibility features, go to Chapter 5.

In all cases, you get a dialog box telling you that you must restart Windows to make the font changes take effect. That turns what seems to be a minor little tweak into a fairly serious change because rebooting a Windows 2000 box can mean disrupting network operation or other work.

Reacting to change

The Compatibility area includes three radio buttons that control how Windows reacts when you change resolutions and color depths. The choices are, in order from top to bottom:

✦ **Restart the computer:** Tells Windows 2000 to restart after a change in display settings.

✦ **Apply the new display:** Tells Windows to change settings without restarting. This is the default setting.

✦ **Ask me before applying:** Tells Windows 2000 to confirm display setting changes before they go into effect. The system restarts after the change.

I keep my system set to the second option. This setting enables me to make quick changes to resolution and color depth—something I do fairly frequently—without the disruption of rebooting the system. The third option adds another confirmation step before making changes, but I honestly think plenty of confirmation is built into the process already.

In some cases, you want to select the top option, however. On-the-fly color depth and resolution switching is convenient, to be sure, but the operation can confuse some systems and graphics cards. If you discover problems occurring during or after a graphics-mode switch, try repeating the operation with a reboot in between. You may find that your system isn't up to changing settings on the fly. Newer PCs and graphics hardware typically have no trouble with this feature, so an upgrade will probably clear things up down the road.

Exploring graphics drivers

The Adapter tab holds the configuration controls for your graphics board and drivers. Here you can confirm board information, perform driver updates, and kick off the Windows 2000 Display Troubleshooter.

I frequently use the Adapter tab when I'm perplexed by graphics upgrade problems. For example, Windows 2000 may insist a certain card is installed when I know it's not. By going to this tab, shown in Figure 16-4, I can get a lot of valuable information right on the main screen:

✦ **Chip Type:** Typically displays the model number or variant of the graphics accelerator chip—the CPU of your graphics card.

✦ **DAC Type:** This is the digital-to-analog converter that determines how flicker-free your CRT image can be, among other things.

✦ **Memory Size:** Measured in megabytes. The more the better, of course.

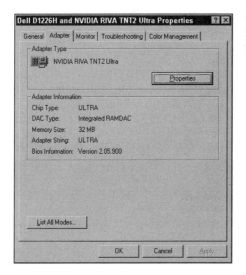

Figure 16-4: The graphics board information displayed here can help you puzzle through setup conflicts.

   ✦ **Adapter String:** Displays any text that your card vendor has elected to include in the onboard BIOS.

   ✦ **Bios Information:** Displays vendor and version information, which is useful for tracking down BIOS-related instabilities.

As you can tell from Figure 16-5, not all these fields contain useful (or sometimes, even any) information. To dig a little deeper and actually make some changes, click the Properties button. The three-tabbed graphics adapter properties dialog box appears.

Note   There are actually two ways to get to this properties dialog box—through the Display Properties interface (as we are doing now) and through the Device Manager. To access these controls from Device Manager, do the following: Right-click the My Computer icon on the desktop, click Manage, and in the Computer Management window that appears, click the Device Manager item in the left pane. In the right pane, click the plus (+) symbol next to Display adapters, then double-click the specific display device that appears beneath it. The same dialog box now appears that was invoked when you clicked the Properties button in the text above.

The General tab

Clicking the Properties button lands you on the General tab of another dialog box where you can see the status of your board. If you find yourself stuck in ugly VGA resolution, you may be able to glean some information from the text in the Device status scrolling text box.

If you are having trouble, the Troubleshooter button can help you puzzle through some common scenarios. For more on troubleshooting graphics issues, see the section "Using the Troubleshooting tab" later in this chapter.

Finally, the Device usage drop-down list box enables you to disable the graphics card. It's generally not a good idea to disable the one device that actually enables you to see the operating system interface, but this control can have its uses. For example, I routinely use two graphics cards to drive a pair of monitors (a natural fit for my schizophrenic lifestyle). But sometimes I want Windows 2000 to forget about the second card, such as when I need to take screen shots of the display for such projects as, well, this book. If both monitors are active, capturing a screen shot yields an extra wide graphic that represents the combined area of the two displays. By disabling one card, I'm able to take single screen captures, without resorting to turning off the PC and pulling out the second graphics card.

Viewing and changing driver information

The next tab is the Driver tab. This useful sheet includes the following text at the top of the box:

- ✦ **Driver Provider:** Company name
- ✦ **Driver Date:** Always vital to know when trying to find the latest and greatest fix or feature
- ✦ **Driver Version:** Another key to comparing your drivers against the state of the market
- ✦ **Digital Signer:** Indicates if the graphics driver has been signed by Microsoft or an approved vendor

Note Of these items, the most interesting is the Digital Signer. Microsoft is using digital signatures as a way to ensure that IT managers and others can identify drivers that have been approved. Drivers that have a signature have passed muster in Microsoft's assurance labs. The drawback is that getting Microsoft certification takes some time, so signed drivers are generally not the newest on the market. For those looking for cutting-edge features — or simply trying to get past a difficult conflict — nonsigned drivers may be the only solution.

Can't get enough? Then click the Driver Details button to bring up a list of the graphics board driver files (and their locations on the hard disk) loaded into Windows 2000. File version information is also here. Again, this can help you ascertain if you installed the proper driver version.

Click OK to back out of the Driver Details dialog box. You could click the Uninstall button, but doing so would probably be foolish. Unless you run a multimonitor system like I do, uninstalling your graphics board could render you effectively blind. But if you absolutely, positively want to uninstall your drivers, this is the place to do it.

Finally, the useful Update Driver button launches the Upgrade Device Driver Wizard. Click Next at the Welcome screen and then follow the wizard's lead as it prompts you to search for suitable drivers (on the Web, your hard disk, or a CD-ROM or floppy). You can also pick through the list of known drivers included on the Windows 2000 CD-ROM.

Because graphics drivers change so frequently, you may use the Driver Update facility quite a bit. If you are anxious about reliability, it's a good idea to stick with Microsoft-approved drivers. But if you crave the newest features and best performance, you can generally get a jump on the action by using the latest drivers that may not be approved yet.

A look at system resources

Last stop is the Resources tab, where you can see all the down-and-dirty system resources information about the board. IRQ assignments, if any, and system memory address ranges are typically displayed here in the Resource settings scrolling list box. Other device types often provide options for changing these settings, but you won't enjoy any such privileges with the graphics board. You can't change anything on this tab, you can only view the information, as shown in Figure 16-5.

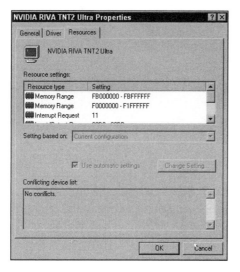

Figure 16-5: Look but don't touch. Notice how the Change Setting button and other controls are grayed out?

Perhaps most helpful is the Conflicting device list at the bottom of this tab. If your graphics card and other device are trying to grab the same IRQ or memory space, you may be able to get a heads-up here.

Setting monitor refresh rates

The Monitor tab is another useful stop because it enables you to update driver software and alter the behavior of your display device. The most important aspect of the dialog box is the Refresh Frequency drop-down list in the Monitor Settings area. Click this control, and you can pick from a list of supported refresh rates, as shown in Figure 16-6.

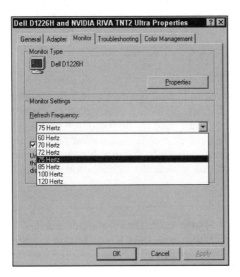

Figure 16-6: Windows 2000 makes it easy to change the refresh rate on your display and prevent a lot of headaches in the process.

Why is refresh frequency (more often called *refresh rate*) so important? The refresh rate setting determines how many times each second your graphics card and monitor team up to repaint the image on your screen. A typical monitor refreshes the image 70 or more times each second.

The reason for all this frantic screen activity is that the pixels on your CRT monitor don't stay lit by themselves. They must be constantly bombarded by a beam of electrons (fired from the back of the CRT) that are tailored to produce the desired brightness. If that beam hits each pixel on the screen less than about 70 times per second, the rise and fade of pixel brightness across the monitor face becomes perceptible in the form of extremely annoying image flicker.

Don't believe me? Try this. Click the Refresh Frequency control and select the lowest value, typically 60 Hertz on most adapters, from the list. Click Apply. If you're prompted to confirm the change, click OK and then watch what happens when the screen comes on. See that intense flicker? To see how bad it can really get, try displaying a screen with a bright white background, say a word processing document. Ouch!

Caution Unless you enjoy courting danger, I suggest you check the box labeled Hide modes that this monitor cannot display. With this box checked, the Refresh Frequency drop-down list control only displays refresh rate settings that the currently installed monitor is designed to handle. Don't get me wrong: I'm a big fan of full disclosure. But enabling this dialog box to present refresh rates beyond what your display can support is asking for a blown CRT. Accidentally click an unsupported 120 Hertz setting, for example, and your graphics board could send a superfast signal that very quickly burns out your monitor's electronics. That's an expensive click of the mouse!

Now set the refresh rate to a more comfortable level — say 75 Hertz or even 85 Hertz, if your monitor can handle it. The image immediately settles down and becomes a lot easier on the eyes. Whenever possible, you should set refresh rate as high as you can manage, particularly if you tend to spend a lot of time reading or otherwise looking at the screen.

Click the Properties button on the Monitor sheet to see a driver information dialog box similar to the one you just reviewed for graphics boards. Here you see the monitor make and model and a Device status scrolling text box that reports any known problems. The Troubleshooter button whisks you off to the help-based Windows 2000 Troubleshooter facility, while with the Device usage drop-down list control, you can disable the monitor.

Note Drivers for a monitor? CRT monitors are analog devices that consume no system resources (such as IRQs) and therefore don't need to be managed by the operating system, so it may seem odd to have a driver loaded. But the monitor driver serves an important role. It tells Windows 2000 and your graphics card what resolution and refresh rates the display can handle. It also makes your life as a user easier, since the driver enables Windows 2000 to report back available refresh rates at each color and resolution setting.

Click the Driver tab to find any available driver information, but expect to find little, if anything, displayed here. If you need to upgrade the existing driver or perhaps replace a generic driver with one specific to your monitor, click the Update Driver button to launch the Upgrade Device Driver Wizard.

Using the Troubleshooting tab

The next stop in the graphics properties dialog box is the Troubleshooting tab, shown in Figure 16-7, where a single slider bar control awaits. This slider enables you to ratchet the hardware acceleration features of your graphics card up or down. By default, the slider is set to full, and you should leave it right there unless you have a situation that makes a change necessary.

Note   What is graphics acceleration? Essentially, your graphics board takes common Windows display tasks and offloads them from the central processor. Filling in colors, moving dialog boxes and other objects, even drawing advanced 3D shapes all occur on your graphics board. Your processor, meanwhile, can concentrate on other tasks. The result: Faster system performance and better-looking graphics. The problem is, conflicts can occasionally occur between the operating system and graphics hardware—particularly when that graphics hardware is more than three or four years old.

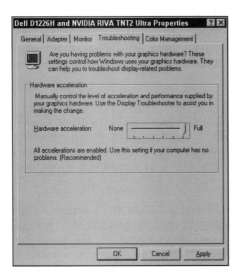

Figure 16-7: Desperate? You may be able to crawl out from under some show-stopping conflicts by tuning down graphics acceleration, but you pay a price in performance.

So when should you fool with the Hardware acceleration slider? Any time you have a graphics-related problem, you might consider it. But first I'd explore more mundane issues, such as driver files, hardware conflicts, or just plain botched configurations. Of course, it doesn't take much to push a slider to the left, so give it a try if your display is flaking out.

Note   If turning down graphics acceleration is your only recourse, you should probably look into replacing your graphics hardware. The existing card is likely too old or too incompatible to be reliable for everyday use. Just be sure to check the Windows 2000 Hardware Compatibility List (HCL) before buying any replacements. The HCL is on the Windows 2000 CD-ROM (in the support folder) and at www.microsoft.com/hcl.

Working with color profiles

The Color Management tab enables you to load and select color profiles for your monitor. This feature won't quicken the pulse of Excel spreadsheet users, but it's of real use to graphics professionals and others who need to match the colors on their screens with the colors produced by a printer or service bureau. A color management system makes it possible for displays and printers to agree upon the output produced by each.

Here's how it works. Windows 2000 comes with a bunch of files that contain detailed information on the behavior of different monitor types. If your monitor is included, you can load color profile files (*.ICM) that are stored in the System32\ Spool\Drivers\Color folder. Once loaded, the color profile provides data needed to translate characteristics such as color, hue, saturation, and brightness for a color management system.

To install a color profile, click the Add button and select the appropriate .ICM file from the resulting dialog box. Then click the Add button in the Add Profile Association dialog box to load the profile. If you like, before you load a profile, you can view information by right-clicking one of the .ICM files in the dialog box and clicking Properties from the context menu. In the Properties dialog box, click the Profile Information tab (shown in Figure 16-8) to see what device the profile is intended for and who created the profile.

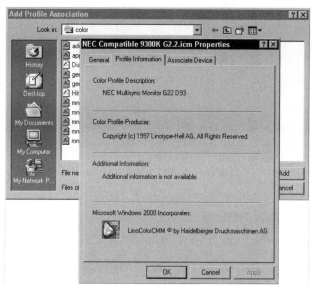

Figure 16-8: Get past the confusing filenames to see exactly which display device a profile file is tailored for.

Windows 2000 comes with a selection of pre-existing .ICM files; however, your monitor maker may provide a profile for your specific display. In this case, in the

Add Profile Association dialog box, navigate to the supplied floppy disk or CD-ROM containing the .ICM file for your display.

You can install multiple profiles, as shown in the scrolling list text box in Figure 16-9. To switch the active profile, select the desired file and click Set As Default. The ability to switch among multiple profiles can be useful if you have multiple display devices (using Windows' multi-monitor support, for example). To nuke a profile, select it and click Remove.

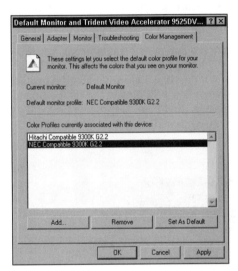

Figure 16-9: The Color Profiles list box in the Color Management page makes it possible to select from one or more associated color profiles.

Note   Color management is an incredibly complex issue that seems to consist of one part art, one part alchemy, and about six parts rocket science. Personally I'm amazed the stuff works at all. Microsoft must consider color profiles a chancy thing because they restrict access to this feature to those with Administrator rights.

What you see is what you get

This tour of the Display Properties dialog box and its various spinoffs shows you some of the basic and advanced graphics-handling talents of Windows 2000. But depending on your specific system, you may get a lot more than what is discussed here. Graphics board vendors such as Matrox Graphics, Diamond Multimedia, Hercules, and ATI Technologies typically bundle utilities and tools that extend the capabilities of Windows 2000.

What are you likely to see? In many cases, these vendors build onto the Display Properties dialog box, adding tabs that offer extended features. Existing tabs may get an overhaul as well, so you may see additional controls and information on many of the screens I've discussed here. And don't be surprised if a graphics-specific micro-icon lands in your taskbar tray after you install a board driver. The icon can give you one-click access to display properties — a welcome shortcut for habitual tweakers.

Using Multiple Displays

Multimonitor support was one of the lauded features of Windows 98, even though it was rarely used. The reason is that most Windows 98 users are consumers or line-of-business productivity users, not the type of hardcore computer users likely to shell out several hundred dollars for a second monitor and graphics board. And while Windows NT appealed to that high-end crowd, it lacked the advanced display support. Now Windows 2000 finally brings this valuable feature to the people who need it most, such as programmers, Web developers, graphics junkies, and financial pros.

The multimonitor feature bears a little explaining. As you know, PCs use a graphics adapter to send images to the monitor. With multimonitor support, a PC is able to house two or more graphics adapters, and each of them can push images to a monitor. With Windows 98 you can install two graphics cards to work with two displays. Windows 2000 ups the ante considerably, hosting up to 10 graphics adapters and 10 displays.

What makes multimonitor support really cool is that you can stitch together multiple graphics adapters and monitors to create a single, very large Windows desktop.

In fact, the benefit of multiple monitors is similar to the benefit of owning a large 19- or 21-inch CRT display. The extra screen real estate enables you to see background applications such as e-mail, an FTP download session, or a Web browser while still having space to actively work on a Word document on the main screen. The extra screen space also means less scrolling around in spreadsheets, documents, and Web pages.

Why not just use a single graphics card with a really large monitor? It's a good question. I still recommend that users go for at least a 17-inch CRT if they intend to run Windows 2000 for any sort of important work (19 inches is even better, believe me), but the benefits of multiple displays are pretty compelling:

  ✦ **See detail with context:** A designer can display an overall page view on one screen, while zooming in for detailed work on a graphic on the second screen.

  ✦ **Monitor multiple applications:** Scan your e-mail inbox without switching out of Word, or keep active tabs on a big rendering job while you're crafting memos.

✦ **See more, more, more:** Span a monster Excel spreadsheet across two or more screens—no more torturous scrolling.

✦ **Manage, tweak, and improve:** Perform and monitor important housekeeping operations—such as disk defragmentation, virus checking, and data backup—in the background without switching out of your main applications.

✦ **Play games better:** Some games enable you to set up multiple views in separate monitors. Keep an overhead strategic view at your side even as you wade into the action.

✦ **Wring use out of old components:** If you bought a new system or upgraded your current one, you may have an extra graphics card and monitor lying around unused.

✦ **Extend application interfaces:** For complex digital content creation apps like PhotoShop and CAD programs, the second monitor can be used to house all the various icons, toolbars, and other interface elements. Detailed graphics can then be displayed on the other high-resolution display.

One of my confederates uses Photoshop 4—he puts the image on the main 19-inch display at 1280 by 1024 resolution and all of the button bars on the second monitor.

Is multimonitor for me?

Before you get too excited, first take a look at what's needed to make multiple monitors work on a PC. The multimonitor feature requires that card vendors tweak their drivers to ensure operation. Also, many older cards lack the necessary hooks to work with two or more graphics cards in your PC.

The first thing to do is to check the Windows 2000 Hardware Compatibility List (HCL). The HCL text file is in the Support folder of your Windows 2000 CD-ROM, or you can browse the up-to-the-minute listing at Microsoft's Web site at www.microsoft.com/hcl.

Note   Be sure to look specifically for compatibility with the multimonitor feature of Windows 2000. A graphics board can appear on the general Windows 2000 HCL but not qualify for multimonitor support.

You also need to assess your system configuration to make sure you have a place for your second graphics card. Multimonitor operation works only with a combination of PCI and AGP bus-based cards; those aged ISA-based adapters do not work. And because motherboards provide only a single AGP slot, you must make sure that your PCI bus is up to spec for multimonitor operation. Specifically, the PCI implementation on the motherboard must conform to PCI version 2.1, and the slot used to house the graphics card must provide full bus-mastering capability. Most PCs sold in the past three years provide PCI 2.1 compliance—check your system documentation to confirm this.

Caution   Windows 98 upgraders be warned. Just because you have multiple displays working with Windows 98, don't assume the hardware can pass muster for Windows 2000 Professional. Windows 2000 uses a very different implementation from that incorporated in Windows 98. According to Microsoft, the Windows 2000 approach is better and more reliable. The problem is that it may not be compatible.

Getting started

As it turns out, installing a second graphics card into a Windows 2000 system is virtually identical to installing a single card. I'm not going to rehash all the steps involved in installing a new card here — read all about it in the next section of this chapter — but I do cover the unique aspects of setup. Specifically, once your new card is up and running, you have some decisions to make to fully enable and tailor the multimonitor display.

Tip   Make sure you place PCI graphics cards as close as possible to the system chipset and CPU. If your only free PCI slot is at the far end, don't hesitate to move less demanding devices such as network or audio cards to that outside slot. Fast graphics cards are not tolerant of the subtle timing mismatches that can occur when they are placed an extra six inches or so from the clock source. If you notice strange onscreen behavior — ranging from pixel debris (stuck pixels) to blank screens — make sure you have all your graphics cards placed as close to center as possible.

When you start your system with a second graphics card, the text screen with BIOS information appears on only one screen. Don't panic; the second screen should come around once the Windows GUI loads. Once you get into Windows, you can start tweaking your preferences such as which screen holds the Windows logon dialog box.

Of course, to see all this, you need a second display installed as well. Fortunately, hooking up that second monitor is as easy as plugging in a power cord and a 15-pin VGA connector. If everything is working properly, you should be staring at two screens (or more!) that display the Windows 2000 background. One of the screens (the primary display, in Windows parlance) hosts the taskbar, desktop icons, and the Windows logon dialog box. When you launch applications, by default they open on this screen. The other screen — the secondary display — has an uncluttered desktop.

Here's where things get neat. Try this. Open a folder or application window (not maximized, just open). Click the title bar and drag it to each edge of the screen until you see the window slide across onto your other display. That's right, Windows stitches the two monitors together and treats them as a seamless whole. You can drag objects back and forth between the monitors and even leave windows straddling across displays, as shown in Figure 16-10. This is indeed very cool stuff.

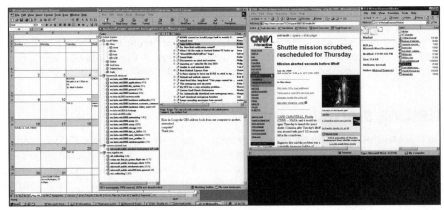

Figure 16-10: Back in the straddle again: Heavy-duty multitaskers love the capability to stretch work across two screens.

Setting up a multimonitor system

Once you're done ogling the multimonitor feature, you may notice some annoying quirks and interesting challenges. For example, you may find that sliding an object off the right side of your primary display causes it to pop up onto the secondary display that sits to the left of the primary — hardly intuitive. What's more, program windows can get lost in no-man's land, forcing you always to leave them in maximized mode to see them at all. Smart management and a bit of extra care can prevent these problems.

Virtually all your management of multiple displays occurs in the Settings tab of the Display Properties box. To get there, right-click an open area on the Windows desktop, select Properties, and then click the Settings tab. Right away you should notice a significant change to the Settings tab as shown in Figure 16-11.

In the following sections, I show you how to manage your many monitors.

Who's the alpha dog?

The first thing you should do is decide which monitor/graphics board combination you want to be the primary display for Windows 2000. The primary display is the one that hosts the Windows logon dialog box, displays newly launched windows and applications, and contains Windows desktop elements such as the taskbar and icons.

> **Note**
>
> You may notice at boot up that the text-based BIOS information displays on your secondary monitor. That's perfectly normal. The BIOS makes its own decision about which monitor to use independent of Windows 2000. For example, the BIOS will typically assign PCI-based graphics cards a higher priority than AGP-based devices and display BIOS-related boot information on that monitor. Once Windows 2000 loads, however, the primary monitor lights up, and the logon dialog box appears there.

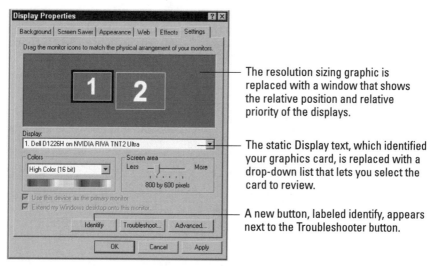

The resolution sizing graphic is replaced with a window that shows the relative position and relative priority of the displays.

The static Display text, which identified your graphics card, is replaced with a drop-down list that lets you select the card to review.

A new button, labeled identify, appears next to the Troubleshooter button.

Figure 16-11: Windows 2000 makes multimonitor management a simple point-and-click affair.

If you are happy with the primary display that Windows 2000 assigned, you don't have to do anything. But if you want to change the display, here's how to do it:

1. Select the monitor/graphics board combination you want to promote from the Display drop-down list box. (The number *2* or a higher number appears in front of the device information listing.) Or you can click the numbered box corresponding to the desired monitor/graphics board combination.

2. Beneath the Colors area, click the blank checkbox labeled Use this device as the primary monitor. The text and checkbox immediately gray out.

3. Click Apply or OK to make the selected card/monitor pair the primary display set.

No restart or confirmation is required to make this switch. Indeed, nothing changes except that the place where new windows spawn changes. To switch back to your original primary display, just repeat this process for that monitor.

Get in place

A more problematic issue is lining up monitors the way you want. After all, it can be disconcerting to have your mouse cursor disappear off the right edge of the right-hand screen only to appear on the left edge of the left-hand screen.

Fortunately, Windows 2000 makes it easy to change the virtual position of the displays. Just click your mouse on the desired display box in the window on the

Settings tab, drag the box where you want it, and let go. The two (or more) display boxes snap into position. You can align displays vertically (top to bottom), horizontally (left to right), and even diagonally (shown in Figure 16-12). To make the new layout take effect, click Apply or OK. The displays may blank for a moment and then come back.

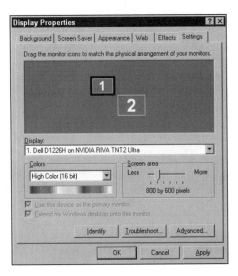

Figure 16-12: Diagonal displays may seem odd, but add two more graphics cards, and you could set up your monitors in four-square fashion.

You may notice that one of your boxes is smaller than the other. This reflects the relative pixel resolution of the different displays, with a larger box indicating a higher resolution. This representation is helpful because it enables you to see how the displays line up to form a virtual desktop.

For example, back in Figure 16-11, the display boxes shown on the Settings tab are lined up evenly across the top. If you move your mouse cursor left to right along the upper edge of the left monitor, it slides right through and along the upper edge of the right monitor. But notice how Figure 16-11 shows the lower edge of the left monitor dropping below the right one. If you sweep your cursor along the bottom edge of the left monitor, going left to right, it hits the edge and goes no further. Why doesn't it move along into the right display? Because as far as Windows 2000 is concerned, the right display ends about 200 pixels above the lower edge of the left screen. It's all a bit confusing at first, but you quickly get accustomed to it.

Tip

It's easy to lose track of which screen is which, particularly if you have three or more displays working. Click the Identify button in the Display Properties dialog box to call up large onscreen numbers that show display priority. Figure 16-13 shows what you see.

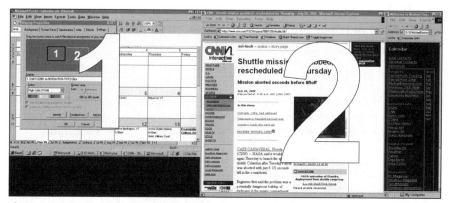

Figure 16-13: Need to figure out which screen is which? The Identify button brings up a none-too-subtle display to answer your question.

Setting Up Graphics Hardware and Software

Graphics cards are among the most frequently upgraded components in the PC. At the same time, they are also a common source of show-stopping conflicts and problems. After all, when your graphics card isn't working, neither are you. That makes installing a new graphics card a fairly serious proposition, and one that veteran upgraders know to approach with care.

At the same time, the benefit of a graphics card upgrade has rarely been greater. New cards and graphics chips offer quantum leaps in 3D graphics performance and functionality over products introduced just 12 months before. At the same time, falling memory prices mean that many new boards are shipping with 16MB and 32MB of fast synchronous DRAM. Here's something to think about: I have more memory in my primary graphics card than I did in the hard drive of my first IBM PC. Wow.

Note   Because it's a corporate-minded operating system, Windows 2000 won't enable just anyone to walk up and perform hardware upgrades. In order to successfully load new drivers, you must be logged on with Administrator rights.

Installing the new card

Before you install a new card, you have to remove the old one. Of course, it's a good idea to conduct at least a full data backup prior to a hardware upgrade. Once you've done that, make sure you have everything you need, typically consisting of the following:

✦ New graphics card

✦ CD-ROM or floppy diskettes with card drivers, utilities, and bundled software

✦ Card documentation

✦ Philips head screwdriver

Remove the PC case and use the screwdriver to free the card from the PC's backplate. Grasp the front and back of the top edge of the card and pull upward evenly. Use a little rocking motion forward and back if the pins are tight.

Set the old card aside and place the new one in the proper slot (typically the same one that housed the old card). Press evenly at the front and back of the top edge of the card until you seat it firmly in place. Make sure the card is sitting level in the slot and the backplate is flush with the back of the PC chassis. Now plug the 15-pin VGA monitor connector into the VGA out port on the back of the card—make sure it's in there firmly. Put off screwing the card in and replacing the case until you know the new hardware works.

Now light it up. Turn on the PC and keep a sharp eye on the monitor for unusual screen activity. If you see the usual text-based BIOS information and other boot information on the screen, congratulations; you've passed the first hurdle. The BIOS has recognized the new card, and your PC is successfully pushing bits through it to your monitor. These are good things.

When the logon screen comes up, make sure you log on using an account with Administrator rights. During startup, Windows 2000 should detect your new graphics card and automatically install the drivers needed to operate the device. Note that you may have to insert your Windows 2000 or graphics board driver CD-ROM into the CD-ROM drive to load the files. You can direct Windows to look for drivers in a specific area, including a floppy diskette or CD-ROM. Once the graphics hardware is configured, you need to restart to make the changes take effect.

Of course, you need to secure the new card. Make sure you screw in the backplate of the card to ensure a tight fit in the slot. Also close the case in order to ensure proper airflow around the graphics board, system processor and other components that may be prone to overheating. Be sure the system is shutdown when performing these actions.

Safe Mode for troubled upgrades

While Windows 2000 Plug and Play should automatically detect a card switch when it boots up, be prepared for headaches caused by a botched detection. If your system displays a blank screen or fails when it tries to boot, work around the problem by entering the Windows 2000 Safe Mode.

Safe Mode is useful because it uses a no-frills configuration that can sidestep problems that cause boot failures. Notably, this mode uses a default VGA driver, which lacks any form of acceleration or high-resolution support, but should work with the vast majority of cards on the market. So even if Plug and Play munged the new hardware detection, you can use Safe Mode to get back to the Windows interface to install drivers and restart. Here's how to enter Safe Mode, just in case.

1. Start your PC.

2. When you see the message "Please select the operating system to start," press F8.

3. A list of options appears in the text-based display. Select the Safe Mode option (typically basic Safe Mode as opposed to Safe Mode with Networking or Safe Mode with Command Prompt) and press Enter.

4. If you have multiple operating systems, select the desired OS and press Enter.

Right off the bat, you notice that the boot sequence now displays text detailing the activity during this phase. When the Windows graphical interface appears, it is in a low-resolution mode. Of course, the good news is that you can see Windows at all. Now you can go about installing the new driver from the included disk or CD-ROM. Right-click the desktop, click Properties, and click the Settings tab in the Display Properties dialog box. Click the Advanced button, the Adapter tab, and the Properties button. Finally, click the Driver tab and click the Update Driver button to launch the Upgrade Device Driver Wizard.

 Tip Safe Mode is good for a lot more than fixing graphics upgrades. Anytime you have a show-stopping conflict or problem (for example, after a program or device installation), Windows 2000 Safe Mode provides a way to regroup and address the problem.

Driver update strategies

Any power user can tell you that graphics board drivers make or break performance. From PowerPoint slide shows to Deathmatch Quake, the responsiveness of your PC is often defined by the quality and age of the graphics board drivers. For this reason, you should always stay on the lookout for the latest non-beta driver software. While such awareness is helpful for all your PC devices, it is especially critical for graphics boards. After all, a new driver can do more than boost frame rates; some updates fix troubling bugs and add support for intriguing features.

So graphics drivers are important, but should you jump onto hardcore gaming Web sites to find the latest beta driver for your graphics card with a fast Nvidia TNT2 Ultra chip? Well, that depends on your priorities. Are you desperate for an extra five or so frames per second in Quake Arena so your display doesn't bog down during big battles? If so, download away. But if you use your PC to get work done, you are much better off being conservative.

Remember, graphics drivers play a role in virtually every operation on your PC. And broken graphics drivers can turn a perfectly good system into an inoperable box. Here are a few considerations to keep in mind.

Strategies for professionals

You use your Windows 2000 PC for spreadsheets and presentations. Performance is important, but when push comes to shove, it's downtime that causes consternation. In this case, you want drivers that are solid and stable and have a complete set of features.

Fortunately, Windows 2000 is able to help ensure PC operation by identifying drivers that have passed muster at Microsoft's quality assurance labs. These drivers include a digital signature that serves as a seal of assurance (but not approval) for the driver. Network administrators and business users should generally limit their driver upgrades to those that feature a digital signature.

How do you know a driver has been tested and signed by Microsoft? The best way is to download drivers from approved sources, including the Microsoft Hardware Compatibility List (HCL) or the board vendor's Web site. Microsoft's HCL provides links only to approved device drivers, making it a good place to hunt down your device and find a safe driver. The problem is, it can take a while to search through the HCL because it includes every Windows 2000 device that has proven to be compatible.

A quicker way might be to download from the board vendor's Web site. While board makers may feature both signed and unsigned Windows 2000 drivers, reputable companies clearly indicate which is which. You may see a brand new driver posted on the vendor site with a note saying that it is unsigned, while the six-month-old, signed driver is posted right next to it.

Windows provides ways to catch unsigned drivers. During the driver upgrade, Windows 2000 looks for a driver signature. If it fails to find one, a dialog box warns you that the driver is unsigned and asks if you want to halt the upgrade.

Once a device driver is installed, you can look for a digital signature on the graphics board Properties dialog box, as shown in Figure 16-14. It takes a little digging to find the dialog box, so here are directions:

1. Right-click the desktop and click Properties.

2. Click the Settings tab and click the Advanced button.

3. Click the Adapter tab and click the Properties button.

4. In the dialog box that appears, click the Driver tab. You see a text entry called Digital Signer. If the words *Not digitally signed* appear here, you want to look for a signed driver.

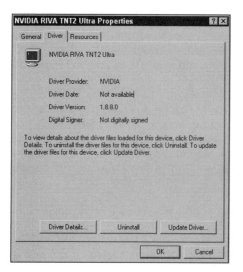

Figure 16-14: Uh-oh, looks like Microsoft hasn't given my current graphics board driver the official going over. Not to worry, I haven't experienced a graphics-related crash since installing the new driver version.

Strategies for the performance-obsessed user

Signed drivers may warm the cold hearts of network administrators, but enthusiasts scoff at the notion. Getting a Microsoft-tested driver can take months, during which time you may be running your PC on slow, incomplete, or just plain buggy graphics board drivers. In fact, if your current drivers are suffering from bugs or other failings, the wait for a signed driver can do more harm than good.

The fact is, millions of people lead perfectly normal lives using drivers that are untested and unsigned by Microsoft. That's because any driver a board vendor releases has likely undergone extensive quality assurance testing in the vendor's lab before release. Certainly, no board vendor wants to invite the tidal wave of angry support calls that a botched driver release can create!

So if you want the latest features, fixes, and performance, by all means grab the newest drivers you can — signed or not. You won't find any of these fresh drivers on Microsoft's Web sites, though. You need to go straight to the source — your board vendor.

What's more, you can cut the corner even further by bypassing the board vendor's drivers and instead using drivers made by the manufacturer of the graphics chip on the board. Graphics chip companies such as S3, Nvidia, and 3dfx sell their chips to other companies, which then build boards and drivers for users to buy. Typically, the drivers written by the board vendor are based on code supplied by the chip maker (after all, the chip maker knows the capabilities of the hardware better than anyone). The upshot is that advanced performance features are likely to appear first in the reference drivers supplied by the chip maker.

Caution Before you get too driver-happy, be aware that a generic driver from your board's chip vendor likely lacks features. In some cases, using generic drivers can disable useful features such as video capture, custom board setting software, and the capability to display images on a TV. Make sure you research the full impact of any new driver before you install it.

What's more, graphics chip vendors often release beta versions of their newest drivers to elicit useful feedback in the general market. Beta drivers can be particularly useful if you are running a brand new operating system that has yet to attract a large number of drivers. If you find yourself anxious to get at the latest driver software, it helps to understand how a typical drive update pattern unfolds. Here's the short story:

✦ Graphics chip maker releases beta version of reference driver for its chip.

✦ Graphics chip maker releases shipping version of reference driver for its chip.

✦ Board vendor add tweaks to the reference driver and releases the new driver for its board.

✦ Microsoft tests the vendor-released driver and issues a digital signature if it passes.

All this is fine and good, but it can take six months for that hot, new reference driver to crawl through the food chain and appear as a signed product. That's a long time to wait when you consider that PCs sometimes get replaced in as little as two years or less, depending on the performance demands of the user.

 Tip Sometimes, the best place to find out about new drivers isn't on the vendor Web sites, but on Web sites and Internet newsgroups related to your specific graphics hardware or related application. Owners of boards based on Nvidia chips can learn about the latest releases—including rumors and innuendo—at sites such as www.rivazone.com. You can also find informal test results at any number of useful hardware sites, including www.tomshardware.com, www.anandtech.com, and www.shakyextreme.com.

Summary

No question about it, there's a lot to see in Windows 2000. Perhaps the most exciting new feature is multimonitor capability, which lets you open up a lot of new viewable area by running a second graphics card and monitor side-by-side with the existing combination. Plug-and-Play technology and support for on-the-fly color and resolution switching both make working with graphics easier than under Windows NT. So what is important to remember about graphics under Windows 2000? Here's the short list:

✦ Setting resolution, color depth, and refresh rates from the Display Properties dialog box

✦ Using the Update Driver facility to upgrade your graphics driver software

✦ How to install and set up graphics adapters and monitors

✦ How to install and manage multiple displays

✦ Troubleshooting graphics problems and using Safe Mode

✦ Understanding the graphics driver pecking order and tailoring your driver choices to your needs

Ultimately, the graphics subsystem is among the most critical in virtually every aspect of PC operation. Performance, stability, and user interaction are all defined by your graphics hardware and driver software. By understanding how the graphics subsystem works under Windows 2000, you can extend and enhance the useful life of your PC.

In the next chapter, our exploration of multimedia capabilities under Windows 2000 continues. In Chapter 27, we examine audio and video features, including recording and playback of these multimedia file types.

✦　　✦　　✦

Working with Audio and Video

Personal computers, even those used in a business
setting, have undergone a multimedia transformation
in the last few years. Continuing this trend, Windows 2000
Professional comes with a complete assortment of audio and
video tools built right into the operating system. You don't
have to purchase a single thing to have access to the majority
of audio and video formats in use today on the Internet, in
applications, or for fun. It's like having a high-powered stereo
right on your desktop!

In this chapter, you learn the basic hardware and software
requirements that enable you to enjoy audio and video,
and you learn about some of the most popular multimedia
formats. You also learn how to access your audio and video
settings in Windows 2000 Professional and how to use the
multimedia applications shipped with Windows 2000.

Your Minimum Daily Multimedia Requirements

In order to see images, hear sounds and music, or watch
videos, you must install some basic hardware and software
components in your computer and set them up correctly.
These are the minimum components:

> ♦ A graphics card to process information and display it
> on a monitor

> ♦ A monitor to display output processed by the
> graphics card

> ♦ A sound card to translate binary computer data into
> analog audio output

✦ Device drivers to enable your hardware to communicate with Windows 2000

✦ Speakers or headphones to deliver sounds you can hear

✦ Codecs to compress and decompress audio and video files (Oops, I gave that one away. I was going to make you wait until later to tell you what *codec* stands for.)

✦ Software to manage and play audio and video files

Hardware requirements

Figure 17-1 shows the hardware on my computer as displayed in the Device Manager. Notice that I am viewing the devices by type, and I have selectively expanded the tree to show my multimedia devices. You can access your Device Manager by clicking Start ⇨ Settings ⇨ Control Panel, and then choosing System, selecting the Hardware tab, and choosing Device Manager. Notice also what hardware the Device Manager doesn't show: my speakers or microphone.

Note   Another way to get at your hardware is to right-click My Computer on your desktop, select Properties, choose the Hardware tab, then select Device Manager.

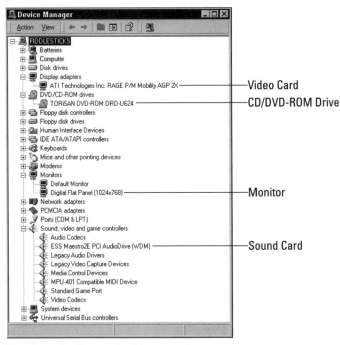

Figure 17-1: The Device Manager shows my multimedia hardware.

Because you learned about setting up your graphics card and installing the correct drivers in Chapter 16, I won't cover the subject again. Suffice it to say that if your graphics card and monitor are not working correctly, you will have trouble seeing videos.

Cross-Reference   If you need help installing or configuring your graphics card (also known as a *display adapter*) or monitor, refer to Chapter 4 or Chapter 16.

Your sound card, sometimes referred to as an *audio card*, receives binary audio data and converts it to an analog form, amplifies it, and sends it to the speakers.

Note   Many of today's computers have the functionality of a high-end sound card built into the motherboard, eliminating the need to take up an expansion slot for an add-on audio card.

Sound cards can also synthesize sound, mix sound from various sources, simulate musical instruments, and convert analog sound from a microphone or other input source into digital form to manipulate and save as a binary data file.

Speakers or headphones are the final link in the chain from sounds being played to your ear hearing them. As I mentioned earlier, they are not listed in the Device Manager. These devices are connected to the sound card but require no drivers or software to run them. The sound card handles these connections by itself without the help of the system. If the sound card is set up correctly, the devices connected to it should work properly.

Speakers take the analog signal from your sound card and translate it into the physical realm of moving air with a frequency and amplitude you can actually hear. Speakers come in all sizes and shapes, from the common little cubes you can put on your desktop to larger and more sophisticated systems with subwoofers and powered amplifiers. Headphones are obviously a benefit in a crowded office situation or at home if you don't want your spouse or family to be bothered by the noise.

Optional hardware not required to play audio or video files, but certainly helpful if you want to expand your capabilities, includes the following:

✦ Microphone

✦ Video input device

✦ CD-ROM drive

✦ DVD drive

You need a microphone and a video camera or input device if you want to record sounds and video or use the audio and video capabilities of Microsoft NetMeeting, which is discussed more fully in Chapter 15. These devices enable you to create multimedia files, and not just play them back.

You need a CD-ROM or DVD drive if you want to play CD audio or DVD movies, but neither is required to play audio and video files. Their job is to provide access to more and different types of multimedia files. Software is also distributed on CDs, and to a lesser extent DVD disks.

DVD stands for Digital Video Disc (sometimes called Digital Versatile Disc) and is cosmetically similar to a CD but can be double-sided and stores much more information. DVD drives and disks look a lot like their CD counterparts, and since DVD drives can read and play CDs, you don't need to worry about installing a CD drive if you already have a DVD drive. The two types of DVD are DVD-Video and DVD-ROM. DVD-Video stores movies and audio while DVD-ROMs contain data. The difference is similar to a data CD and audio CD. DVD storage can range from over 1GB to 17!

Multimedia software

All the hardware in the world won't do you any good if you haven't installed the appropriate software. For multimedia, essential software falls into two categories: codecs and applications.

Note   I've left out device drivers in this section, which are obviously necessary and provide the interface from your hardware components to Windows 2000. If you need help installing or configuring your hardware, read Chapter 4.

All about codecs

The problem with audio and video in the digitized world is size. When you consider how much space it takes to digitize sound and video, you quickly realize that you could easily fill your entire hard drive with audio and video files.

The size of a sound file is dependent on three things:

✦ The sampling rate or frequency, normally expressed in Hertz, or cycles per second

✦ The number of bits per sample

✦ The number of channels

The concept of sampling is critical to understanding digital audio. Back in the old days when record albums and cassette tapes were the formats of choice for the audio enthusiast, no one had to bother with sampling because recordings were analog. When you make an analog recording, you are literally taping a continuous stream of sound.

Digitized recording is very different! Instead of recording everything, you *sample* the audio every few thousandths of a second (that's where frequency comes into play) and record only the characteristics of that sample. Everything in between these samples is gone forever. The good news is that there is a practical limit to the number of samples per second required for a digital recording to sound like the real thing. This is much like going to the movies. When you see a movie, you are seeing snapshots taken about 30 times per second played back at the same rate. Everything in between these frames is lost, but when it's played back at 30 times a second, you see a continuous stream of pictures.

The number of bits per sample is also an important factor in the size of an audio file and has a direct correlation to the quality of the presentation. A recording that uses an 8-bit sample can record 256 discrete values, or steps, in sound levels. When you compare that to the virtually unlimited sample-rate of analog recording, being able to discern only 256 levels of sound doesn't sound like much. For most purposes, however, it is acceptable. For higher fidelity, 16-bit samples are used. A good comparison is with the number of colors you can display on your monitor. If you set your graphics card to a color depth of 256 colors (which is 8-bit color), you can get by most of the time. Really good color comes into play when you ramp that up to 65,000 colors (16-bit), 16 million colors (24-bit), or 4 billion colors (32-bit). The reason is that your monitor can display many more colors if you use more bits to process the color. It's the same thing with sound sampling. More is better, but more means larger files.

Finally, the number of channels is important; it's what differentiates mono (one-channel) from stereo (two-channel) sound. Monophonic sound may come out both speakers, but it is still only one channel, like AM radio. Stereophonic sound contains two channels that, when used effectively, capture depth of sound by having slightly different content coming through both channels. The major drawback to stereo is that the second channel doubles the size of a file.

Note   You can have more than two sound channels, but I have discussed only mono and stereo to provide the general idea of what goes into sound file size and quality. More channels can be added to produce surround sound and add special effects.

Multimedia Math

CD audio is a high-quality sound you can use as a benchmark to see how large sound files can be. CDs can contain approximately 650MB of information. To put this number into perspective, you were able to install the *entire* Windows 2000 Professional operating system from one CD. In fact, the prerelease CD I used contains 380MB, far less than the 650MB it could contain.

The 650MB of data translates into approximately 74 minutes of CD-quality audio. Assuming 3 minutes and 30 seconds as the average length of a song, 21 songs can fit on a CD. If you do the math, each second of CD audio takes just over 150 bytes of disk space.

665,600 bytes (650MB × 1024 bytes) divided by 4,400 seconds (74 minutes × 60 seconds/minute) = 151.27 bytes per second

See what I mean about the length of quality audio?

For video files, the major factors determining file size are sound, resolution, and color depth.

Although sound adds quite a bit to the size of a video file, videos can be incredibly boring without it. The quality of the sound determines how much extra size the sound adds to the video file.

Resolution refers to the size of the video being displayed, in pixels. The more pixels, the larger the file. Large videos also require more processing to push enough frames in a second to achieve the perception of full-motion video.

Color depth affects video sizes the same way that the number of bits per sample affects audio files. The more colors required to display each frame of the video, the larger the file. Increasing the number of colors also increases the workload on the computer to process the information.

The solution to large audio and video file sizes is the compressor/decompressor processing (codec) algorithms. You know how to compress or archive files on your hard drive to reduce the file sizes. Similarly, audio and video files are compressed, and the technology used to compress and uncompress them so you can hear and see them is the audio or video codec. Codecs rely on hardware (your CPU, sound card, and graphics card), software processing, or a combination of the two to compress and decompress the raw data so the files are smaller and require less bandwidth to transmit over the Internet or other networks.

It helps to know which codecs you have because if you don't have the right one for a particular file type, you won't be able to hear or view it.

Note   Most audio and video applications, such as the Windows Media Player, RealPlayer G2, and QuickTime, install the codecs that enable you to see and hear their respective files. If you haven't installed an application or if you have an outdated codec, you have to find a player or the correct codec and install it.

The following steps show you how to find the audio and video codecs installed on your system and do some minor configuring.

Finding audio codec information

Normally you don't need to worry about the codecs installed on your system. If you can play the types of multimedia files you are interested in (such as .WAV audio files or .AVI movies), then you have the correct codecs. If you are having problems playing multimedia or are recording multimedia (and want to use a specific codec), then knowing what codecs you have becomes more important.

1. Click Start ⇨ Settings ⇨ Control Panel.

2. Select Sounds and Multimedia.

3. Choose the Hardware tab as shown in Figure 17-2.

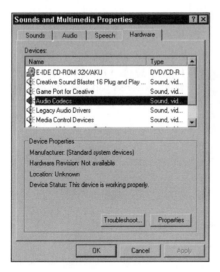

Figure 17-2: The Hardware tab contains information about your hardware and codecs.

4. Select Audio Codecs. The Audio Codecs Properties dialog box displays on the General tab.

5. Select the Properties tab to see the list of codecs installed on your system. See Figure 17-3.

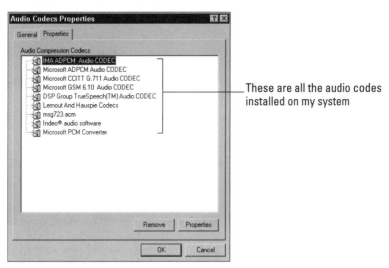

Figure 17-3: The Properties tab lists each codec and enables you to select them individually for more information.

6. Select a codec and click the Properties button to see more information about the codec as shown in Figure 17-4.

Figure 17-4: I have burrowed down to the point where I can see the properties of an individual codec.

The Properties dialog box shown in Figure 17-4 enables you to change a codec's priority or disable it entirely. Changing the priority enables you to decide what order Windows 2000 uses codecs if more than one is capable of compressing and decompressing the file type. The Settings button allows you to change the settings associated with the codec, which for audio normally involves adjusting the maximum real-time conversion rates for compression and decompression. In general, you should not have to change this setting unless you are troubleshooting.

Finding video codec information

Finding information about video codecs is similar to the steps you just followed for audio codecs.

1. Open the Control Panel and select Sounds and Multimedia.

2. Choose the Hardware tab and select Video Codecs.

3. Select Properties to display your video codecs as shown in Figure 17-5.

4. Select a codec and click the Properties button to see the information on a particular codec as shown in Figure 17-6.

Figure 17-6 shows that the information supplied about video codecs is sparse compared to what you find on the audio side. You can, however, see if the codec is working properly, find copyright information about the codec, and in a few cases modify the settings. For the most part, the settings button (if enabled) simply displays copyright information about the codec. Unlike audio codecs, you can't change the priority of video codecs, nor can you turn them off without removing them from your system.

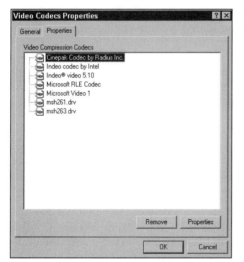

Figure 17-5: These are the video codecs installed on my system.

Figure 17-6: Video codecs require less customization than audio codecs.

Now that you know the hardware you need to play sound and video and have learned about codecs, it's time to delve into the types of multimedia files you may come across, how you can enjoy them in Windows 2000 Professional, and how to optimize your multimedia experience.

Playing popular multimedia formats

Just as other data files — such as documents created in Microsoft Word or spreadsheets created in Microsoft Excel — are formatted differently and distinguished by a unique three-letter extension, audio and video files are not all the same. When media files are created, the data is manipulated, compressed, and stored in different ways.

Your first, and easiest, choice is to use the Windows Media Player to play audio and video files. The Media Player supports several native Windows file formats, versions of RealAudio and RealVideo streaming media, MPEG files, MIDI files, and earlier QuickTime media. The following material summarizes the types of files you can play in Windows Media Player.

✦ **Windows Media Formats:** .AVI, .ASF, .ASX, .RMI, .WAV. These formats are recognized as being native to Windows, and the two most popular are .AVI video files and .WAV sound files.

✦ **RealNetworks' RealAudio and RealVideo (version 4 or below):** .RA, .RAM, .RM, .RMM. RealNetworks has created RealAudio and RealVideo files that are streaming audio or video clips. These are found on the Internet and are optimized for play as the files are being downloaded. That means you don't have to download the entire clip in order to start it.

✦ **MPEG:** .MPG, .MPEG, .M1V, .MP2, .MPA, .MPE. Motion Pictures Experts Group (MPEG) is a platform-independent audio and video format. There are many extensions for the various types of MPEG files, but .MPG or .MPEG are the most prevalent.

✦ **Musical Instrument Digital Interface (MIDI):** .MID, .RMI. MIDI stands for Musical Instrument Device Interface, and these files are platform-independent audio that simulate musical instruments.

✦ **Apple QuickTime (version 3 or lower):** .QT, .AIF, .AIFC, .AIFF, .MOV. Quick-Time is a multimedia format created by Apple and is now in version 4. The Windows Media player can play anything created using QuickTime version 3 or earlier.

✦ **UNIX formats:** .au .snd.

If you need to play QuickTime 4 files, you will have to visit the Apple Web site (www.apple.com) and download the Windows-compatible QuickTime 4 Player. Likewise, if you need to play the latest media from RealNetworks, you should go to www.real.com and download the Windows RealPlayerG2.

Note Web browsers such as Microsoft Internet Explorer 5, which is bundled with Windows 2000, are also capable of presenting multimedia. They are able to do this by using plug-ins, either as part of the system, installed with the browser, or downloaded and installed separately. Internet Explorer uses the Windows Media Player to play most audio and video files within the browser and does not require you to install anything extra or launch other programs. For more information on using Internet Explorer 5, refer to Chapter 13.

MP3 is the new online craze. It's a new audio format that is both highly compressed and high quality. These files average about a minute of music per megabyte of size. MP3 files end in .MP3 and can be played by the Windows Media Player or other players available online such as LiquidAudio.

Note If you double-click a multimedia file and it doesn't open, that means Windows 2000 Professional doesn't recognize the file type. To hear or see the file, return to where you found it (a Web page, for example), find out what software you need, and then download and install it if you really want to hear or see the file. This situation shouldn't happen often. Windows 2000 recognizes and plays many multimedia types without any trouble at all.

Configuring Sound and Optimizing Performance

There isn't much you need to do to configure your system for optimal sound performance if you have reasonably capable hardware. However, if you like to endlessly tweak your system, you can modify some settings.

Optimizing Windows 2000 Professional for your speakers

Windows 2000 has the capability to produce sound optimized for the type of speakers that you have installed in your system. You should identify the correct type of speakers that you have in order for Windows 2000 to be able to perform this task. The key benefits are getting the highest quality audio that your setup can achieve and taking advantage of a more advanced sound setup such as quadrophonic speakers or surround sound.

1. Click Start ➪ Settings ➪ Control Panel.

2. Select Sounds and Multimedia to display the Sounds and Multimedia dialog box.

3. Select the Audio tab. The dialog box shown in Figure 17-7 appears.

4. In the Sound Playback portion of the dialog box, click the Advanced button.

5. Select the Speakers tab.

6. In the Speaker Setup pull-down list, choose the type of speakers you have, as shown in Figure 17-8. If you're not sure what type of speakers you have, select a few from the list and look carefully at the central graphic. It will change to illustrate the selected speaker setup. Notice in the figure that I am selecting Desktop Stereo Speakers, and the illustration shows two speakers on a desktop beside a monitor. If I were to choose Stereo Headphones, the image would change to a drawing of headphones.

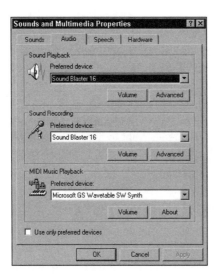

Figure 17-7: Use the Audio tab to configure your audio playback and recording preferences.

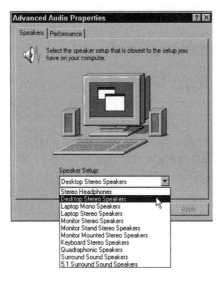

Figure 17-8: Windows gives you quite a few speaker setups to choose from.

7. Click OK to accept changes and close the dialog box, Cancel to close the dialog box and ignore your changes, or Apply to save your changes but keep the dialog box open.

Changing audio playback hardware acceleration

Audio playback hardware acceleration sets the amount of hardware acceleration Windows 2000 expects your sound card to perform while playing audio. If you are experiencing audio difficulties, you may wish to lower the acceleration level and see if that is causing the trouble. Conversely, you may wish to experiment with higher settings to improve audio playback performance.

1. Open the Control Panel and Select Sounds and Multimedia.

2. Select the Audio tab, and in the Sound Playback portion of the dialog box, click the Advanced button.

3. Select the Performance tab.

4. Select the level of hardware acceleration you like. Figure 17-9 shows the four available levels of hardware acceleration. Settings range from None to Full. You should select Full if you wish to enable all hardware acceleration features, Standard to enable only DirectSound features, Basic to enable only required features, or None if you have problems at all other levels. A general rule of thumb is to try to get the most hardware acceleration you can in order to take advantage of any hardware acceleration your sound card is capable of without experiencing audio problems. This ensures you are maximizing your audio playback performance.

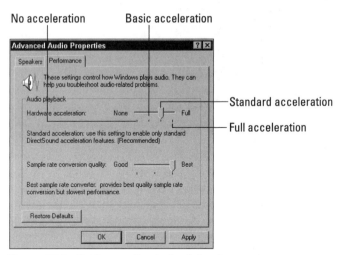

Figure 17-9: Setting audio playback hardware acceleration levels.

Caution Not all sound cards are equally capable of hardware acceleration. Read your documentation to see if you should be aggressive when making these changes.

5. Click OK to accept changes and close the dialog box.

Changing the sample rate conversion quality

Sample rate conversion quality is a tradeoff between a higher audio sample rate and system performance. The more you sample audio, the more your system has to work to convert and play it. If you have a system that is extremely fast or you need the highest quality audio playback possible, you should choose the best sample conversion rate.

1. Open the Control Panel and Select Sounds and Multimedia.

2. Select the Audio tab and, in the Sound Playback portion of the dialog box, click the Advanced button.

3. Select the Performance tab.

4. Select the sample rate you like. Figure 17-10 shows the three available levels of sample rate conversion quality. Settings range from Good to Best.

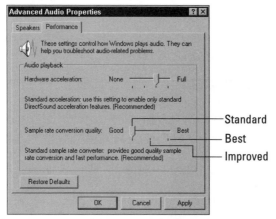

Figure 17-10: The Standard sample rate converter is recommended because it provides faster performance.

5. Click OK to accept changes.

Note

You can change the hardware acceleration for recording operations by clicking the Advanced button in the Sound Recording portion of the Audio tab in the Sounds and Multimedia Properties dialog box. The hardware acceleration and sample rate conversion settings are the same as those for audio playback except they are applied to recording.

Although the preceding material is important, the real fun begins when you start using sound and video to liven up your computing experience. Therefore, the rest of this chapter is devoted to setting sounds to Windows 2000 events and the three multimedia applications that come installed with Windows 2000: using the CD Player which plays audio CDs, playing other audio and video files with the Windows Media Player, and recording and saving your own sounds with Sound Recorder.

Setting Sounds

Windows 2000 plays sounds for certain system events such as Windows startup and error alerts. You can completely customize the audio feedback in Windows. Here are your options:

✦ Adding and removing sounds from specific events

✦ Saving your customized sound setup as a sound scheme

✦ Loading and using other sound schemes

✦ Turning event sounds completely off

Note   Microsoft defines an *event* as "a significant occurrence in the system or an application that requires users to be notified or an entry to be added to a log." This seems a bit drastic because some of the events are as simple as minimizing or maximizing a window.

Assigning a sound to an event

Assigning a sound to an event is an easy way for you to customize the way Windows 2000 alerts you to a system or application event such as receiving new e-mail or when Windows 2000 starts. You can go wild and crazy and purchase audio samples of your favorite television show or movie or download them from the Internet. You can even record your own sounds using Sound Recorder and assign them to events.

1. Click Start ➪ Settings ➪ Control Panel.

2. Select Sounds and Multimedia. This action opens the Sounds and Multimedia Properties dialog box on the Sounds tab. Events are listed in the Sound Events portion of the dialog box. The events with speaker icons already have sounds assigned.

3. Select the event you want to have a sound. The name of the sound currently assigned (if it has one) is displayed in the Name field below the Sound Events window as shown in Figure 17-11.

4. Use the Name pull-down list box to select a sound, as shown in Figure 17-12. Listen to the sound by clicking the play arrow immediately to the right of the Name pull-down list box.

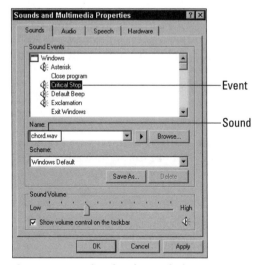

Figure 17-11: The chord sound plays at every critical stop.

Figure 17-12: These sounds (all wave files) are located in the Media directory in the Windows 2000 program directory.

5. If you can't find any sounds you like on this list, click the Browse button to search for sounds that may be in a different location on your hard drive.

6. Click OK to accept any changes and close the dialog box.

Removing a sound from an event

If you get tired of hearing a sound every time an event occurs, you can remove it without affecting other event sounds. During the writing of this chapter, I recorded a few sound bites and assigned them to common Windows 2000 events such as minimizing and maximizing windows. Over time, I became tired of hearing myself say "Minimizing" and "Maximizing" so I removed them.

1. Open the Control Panel and select Sounds and Multimedia.

2. At the Sounds tab, select the event that has a sound you want to remove.

3. On the Name pull-down list box, select None.

4. Click OK to accept your changes.

Creating and saving a sound scheme

As you assign new sounds to events and remove others, you are creating a customized sound scheme. A *sound scheme* refers to the collective set of event-sound combinations that you have either created or modified. Sound schemes can be named and saved, allowing you to have multiple schemes that you can switch to at any time without losing the settings that belong to a specific scheme (providing you have saved it, of course). You may not need more than one, but as they say, variety is the spice of life.

1. Open the Control Panel and select Sounds and Multimedia.

2. At the Sounds tab, assign or remove sounds from as many events as you want.

3. Click the Save As button to save your scheme. When the Save Scheme As text box appears, type a name for your new sound collection as shown in Figure 17-13.

Note Figure 17-13 shows that Windows gives you no option for saving your sound scheme in a location. This is because Windows 2000 stores all of these values in its Registry and not in a separate file.

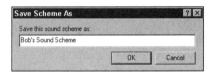

Figure 17-13: Save a sound scheme so you can switch to others and not lose this setup.

Loading a sound scheme

Loading a sound scheme involves switching to an existing sound scheme that either came with Windows 2000 (No Sounds, Windows Default, or Utopia Sound Scheme) or one that you have created to replace the scheme currently in effect. If you have made any changes to your current sound scheme and want to keep them, you should save that sound scheme before selecting a new one.

1. Open the Control Panel and select Sounds and Multimedia.

2. At the Sounds tab, select a sound scheme from the Scheme pull-down list box as shown in Figure 17-14.

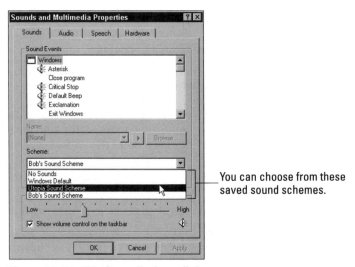

You can choose from these saved sound schemes.

Figure 17-14: Windows displays all the available sound schemes.

3. Click OK to accept your changes.

Note

You can record your own sound bites using the Sound Recorder or download them from the Internet as long as they are in wave format. I bought a cheap microphone and, much to my wife's chagrin, recorded burps and other disgusting sounds to play every time we minimize or maximize a window. Needless to say, that didn't last long!

Using CD Player

Not only can you use your CD drive to install software and reference information contained on data CDs, you can also use it to play audio CDs.

Try it out. Grab your favorite audio CD and put it in the drive. Windows 2000 recognizes it as an audio CD, launches CD Player automatically, and begins playing the CD. Easy! If this is the first time you've played a particular CD, Windows 2000 asks if you want it to download information about the CD from the Internet. See Figure 17-15. Notice that you can set the CD player to either download information about the CD currently loaded into the player or set the CD player to always download information from the Internet whenever it detects a new CD in your player. If you have a network connection with Internet access, Windows 2000 will retrieve the information with nary a hassle. If you have a dial-up connection to the Internet, Windows 2000 will launch your dial-up connection, connect automatically, and download the information.

Figure 17-15: Do you want to connect and download track info?

Note   To disable the autoplay feature, press Shift after you've inserted the CD into the drive and have begun to close the door.

Internet options galore

An exciting feature of the CD Player is the capability to go directly to the Internet, download track information, and search for more information on an album, song, or artist. Figure 17-16 shows the Internet menu, which is accessed by selecting the expandable Internet menu on the CD player (shown in Figure 17-17).

Figure 17-16: Your connection to the world of music is in your CD Player.

Every time you insert a new CD (also called a new album) into the CD player, you have the option of immediately downloading information about the CD and all the songs on the CD. If you choose to cancel the Download option, you can use the Internet menu to perform this activity at a time of your own choosing by selecting Internet Í Download track names. If you don't have a CD in your drive, you can still access the Internet menu to visit Internet music sites (Tunes.com or Music Boulevard), but the options to download album information or find information about an album are disabled.

If you have a CD in your drive, you can search the Net for information about the artist, the album, search the Rolling Stone Web site for information about the artist, and view Billboard's reviews of the album and artist. Select Internet ⇨ Search the net and expand the menu to choose a specific option.

The Internet music sites menu opens up to a submenu and provides two shortcuts that will launch your Web browser and connect to either Tunes.com or Music Boulevard. You will be taken to the main page of their Web sites where you can fully enjoy their services.

The last three items on the Internet menu are shortcuts to search for information on Rollingstone.com and Tunes.com. The Album search option searches Tunes.com for the album you currently have in your player.

Note   Not all CDs have information available on the Internet, and information about CDs that have been re-released with extra tracks could be incorrect. Your mileage may vary.

Playing with all the buttons

If you want to do more than sit and listen to the CD, refer to Figure 17-17 and the following discussion to learn about all the buttons and displays on the CD player and what they do.

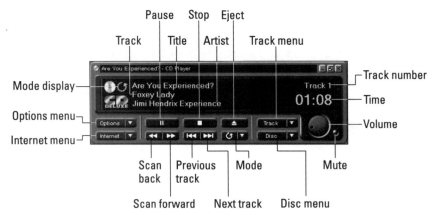

Figure 17-17: Jimi's in the house, and I've downloaded all the album and track information.

The CD Player displays several bits of information about audio CDs loaded into your CD drive. The CD (also called *album*) title is topmost in the CD Player display, with the track (or song) title beneath it and the artist at the bottom. Just to the left of the CD title is a display that tells you what mode of play you are currently using. On the right-hand side of the main display the track number and time is displayed. The time can be displayed in any of four formats: the time elapsed on the track, the remaining time on the track, the elapsed time of the CD, and the time remaining on the CD. Click the time display to toggle between the different time formats.

Note   Several of the displays and menus show specific information about the CD that you have in the player. Therefore, to display the correct values, you must have either downloaded information from the Internet or entered it manually. If you have done neither, the player displays the CD title, artist, and track name as "New Title", "New Artist", and "Track *n*" (where *n* is the track number), respectively.

In addition to the information displays, controls are provided to allow you to operate the CD player. There are controls that you can use to play the CD just as you would a real CD player as well as special menus that allow you to configure the CD player and access Internet options.

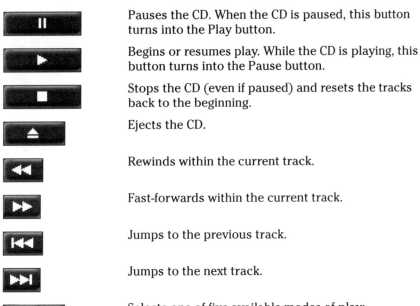

Pauses the CD. When the CD is paused, this button turns into the Play button.

Begins or resumes play. While the CD is playing, this button turns into the Pause button.

Stops the CD (even if paused) and resets the tracks back to the beginning.

Ejects the CD.

Rewinds within the current track.

Fast-forwards within the current track.

Jumps to the previous track.

Jumps to the next track.

Selects one of five available modes of play:

Standard mode	Plays each track in order or plays your custom playlist.
Random mode	Plays tracks in a randomly selected order.
Repeat Track mode	Repeats the current track.

Repeat All mode	Puts the CD in a continuous play loop, starting at the beginning once the CD is finished.
Preview mode	Plays small clips from each track, enabling you to browse the contents of an audio CD without having to continuously click Next Track.

Track ▼	Lists all the tracks on the CD or customized playlist and the time of each song.
Disc ▼	Changes CDs if you have a multiple-disc CD player.
(volume knob)	Raises or lowers the volume. Click the button and move your mouse to raise or lower the sound.
(mute button)	Mutes the sound. The CD keeps playing, but the sound is turned off.
Options ▼	Accesses the CD Player options, covered in detail in the next section.
Internet ▼	Accesses the Internet, covered in the previous section.

Configuring the CD Player

The CD Player has a host of configuration options that are accessible by clicking the Options button on the front panel of the player. The main options menu, shown in Figure 17-18, includes three configuration options: Preferences, Playlist, and Tiny View.

Figure 17-18: Use the Options menu as a starting point to configure the CD Player.

Each item on the menu redirects you to dialog boxes where you can set up the CD Player the way you want it.

Setting your preferences

Choose Preferences to bring up a dialog box that enables you to change player and album options, or see and edit your playlists. Figure 17-19 shows the Player Options tab.

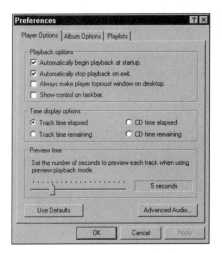

Figure 17-19: The Preferences dialog box is CD tweak heaven.

Here you can choose to start or stop playback automatically, set the CD Player to always be the top window on your desktop, change the time display options, or put a CD control in the taskbar.

Note Adding a CD Player remote control to the taskbar is pretty neat but deserves a bit of explanation. Left-click the icon to pause or resume play of the CD. Right-click to bring up the entire CD Player menu.

You can also set the Preview time by moving the slider from left to right to decrease or increase the time that each track plays in Preview mode before going on to the next track.

Click the Advanced Audio button to display the dialog box shown in Figure 17-20. If you have more than one CD drive, you can set the mixer and volume control for one.

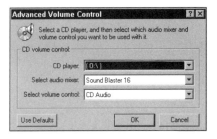

Figure 17-20: Not what I was expecting but still a functional way to assign an audio mixer and volume control to your CD-ROM drive.

The Album Options tab on the Preferences dialog box, shown in Figure 17-21, enables you to set options for downloading information about your CDs.

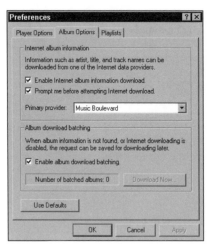

Figure 17-21: "Album options" should probably be renamed "Internet options."

You can enable or disable Internet downloading, choose an information provider, or set the CD player to perform batch downloads.

The Playlists tab of the Preferences dialog box, shown in Figure 17-22, enables you to view CD information stored in the CD Player database to create and edit playlists. For those of you who are interested, the database is stored in a Microsoft Jet Database called DeluxeCD.mdb.

Note   The easy way to access playlists is to choose Playlist from the Options menu of the CD Player.

Figure 17-22: My own music database!

The CD currently in the player is shown at the top of the list, followed by the rest of your database. Expand or contract the track information for each album in your database by clicking the plus (+) or minus (–) sign next to the CD. You can sort your database according to album title (the default) or artist. To sort by artist, click the checkbox under the display window.

Creating a playlist

Playlists define the order that songs are played from an audio CD. By default, the CD Player plays the songs in the original order that they appear on the CD. An advantage to using the CD Player is being able to modify this order and save it so that every time you play a CD the songs play in your customized order. You can also change the name of the CD and the artist from the Playlist Editor.

1. Open the Playlist tab of the Preferences dialog box. You can jump directly here by selecting Options ➪ Playlist from the main CD Player interface or by selecting Options ➪ Preferences and then choosing the Playlist tab.

2. Select a CD.

3. Click the Edit Playlist button to bring up the CD Playlist Editor shown in Figure 17-23. The tracks are initially listed in the order that they appear on the CD.

Figure 17-23: The CD Playlist Editor with the default playlist loaded.

Note You don't need the CD Playlist Editor to change the track names. In the Preferences dialog box on the Playlists tab, select a track and then press F2 to edit the name. I had to edit some track names because the information on the Internet for one of my CDs was incorrect. If you need to edit the artist or CD name, you have to use the CD Playlist Editor.

Tip

4. To rearrange the order in which tracks are played, first select the track you want to move and release the mouse button. Select the track again and drag it to the desired position. Figure 17-24 shows a drag and drop in action.

You can select multiple adjacent tracks by holding the mouse button down as you select them or selecting the top one, holding down Shift, and then selecting the bottom one. If you want to select nonadjacent tracks, select the first one and then hold down Ctrl as you select the others. Remove tracks by clicking the Remove button.

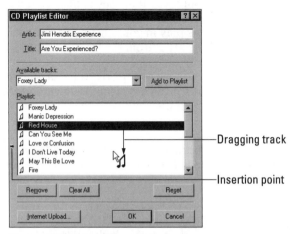

Figure 17-24: Perform minor changes by dragging and dropping tracks.

5. If you want to start from scratch, click the Clear All button to blank the Playlist display. Select tracks one by one from the Available tracks drop-down list and click the Add to Playlist button. As you add tracks, they show up in the Playlist window.

6. When you are finished, click OK to save your changes, Reset to revert back to the original playlist, or Cancel.

Choosing Tiny View

One final configuration you might want to use is Tiny View. As shown in Figure 17-25, this option changes the CD Player interface so that it takes up very little screen space. To change back to normal view, select the Maximize button.

Figure 17-25: Mini-me's CD player, otherwise known as Tiny View.

Using Windows Media Player

The Windows Media Player, as mentioned earlier, can play many different types of audio and video files.

The easiest way to start the Windows Media Player is to double-click a media file. If the player recognizes and can run the file, you're in business. If it can't and the file is a valid audio or video file, the player asks if it can download the appropriate codecs.

To start the Media Player without loading a multimedia file, click Start ➪ Programs ➪ Accessories ➪ Entertainment ➪ Windows Media Player.

The Windows Media Player interface is clean and intuitive as shown in Figure 17-26.

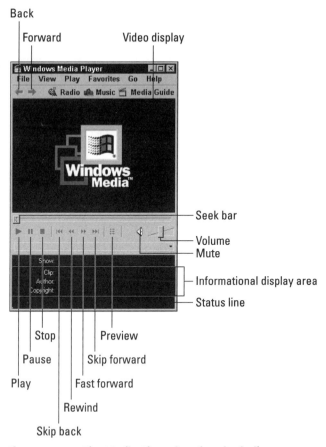

Figure 17-26: The Media Player interface is similar to a VCR or stereo.

To change the size of the player interface, select View menu and choose Standard, Compact, or Minimal. The Compact view eliminates the audio or video information shown at the bottom of the application, and the Minimal view reduces the size of the player to just the video screen and the buttons that operate the player.

To configure and customize the Windows Media Player, select the View menu and choose Options. The five tabs on the Options dialog box enable you to configure the player to suit your needs.

The Playback tab, shown in Figure 17-27, controls the volume, balance, playback features, and video zoom.

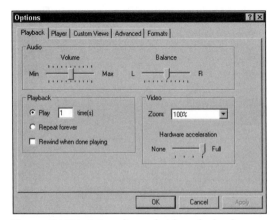

Figure 17-27: Set audio and video playback preferences on the Playback tab.

The Player tab, shown in Figure 17-28, controls whether the Media Player opens a new player for every file or opens new files in the same player. You can also set display options for the player to include player size, making it always the top window, remembering your last zoom setting, and showing the controls when the player is in full screen mode.

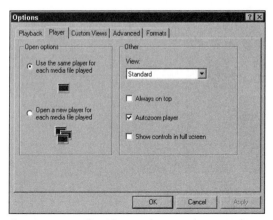

Figure 17-28: The Player tab controls general Media Player behavior.

If you aren't satisfied with the three views that come with the player, you can customize them in the Custom Views tab. Figure 17-29 shows the possible options for the Compact and Minimal views.

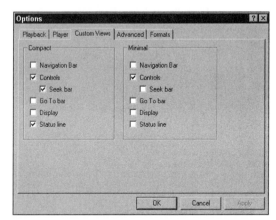

Figure 17-29: Create your own views by selecting the items to appear.

The Advanced tab, shown in Figure 17-30, enables you to change streaming media options.

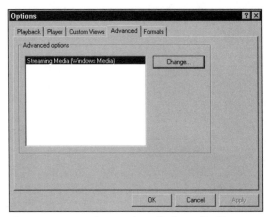

Figure 17-30: Select an installed media filter (highlighted) and then choose Change to access advanced options.

There isn't much to this tab until you click the Change button, which brings up the Streaming Media dialog box that enables you to set advanced playback settings for streaming media, as shown in Figure 17-31.

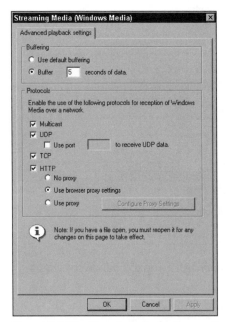

Figure 17-31: Changing streaming media buffering and protocol options.

The Formats tab, shown in Figure 17-32, enables you to assign media types to the Media Player. By default, the Media Player will automatically launch and play files of the type checked in the Formats tab when you double-click the media file. If you install other media players such as Apple's QuickTime Player, these associations will be changed and you may not be able to play them in Windows Media Player by double-clicking the media file. You can use the Formats tab to change the file association back to the Windows Media Player if you wish.

Using Sound Recorder

To record sound from a microphone or your CD player, use the Sound Recorder. To launch the Sound Recorder, click Start ➪ Programs ➪ Accessories ➪ Entertainment ➪ Sound Recorder. To start recording through a microphone, click the Record button and begin speaking (or singing!) into the microphone. The Sound Recorder displays the sound on its central display, as shown in Figure 17-33.

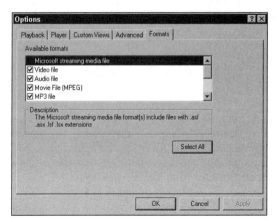

Figure 17-32: Uncheck the formats you don't want the Windows Media Player to play.

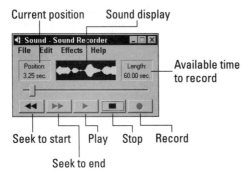

Current position   Sound display

Available time
to record

Seek to start   Play   Stop   Record

Seek to end

Figure 17-33: See Bob talk into
the Sound Recorder.

When you are finished, click the Stop button. If you decide to record more, click
the Record button again, and Sound Recorder begins recording at the spot where
it stopped earlier. When you are really finished, make sure to select File ➪ Save or
File ➪ Save As to save your file for future use. The default directory is My Documents, but you can choose to save the file anywhere you please.

The process for recording from CDs is the same except an audio CD has to be in
your drive and playing. With some careful timing, you can record clips from
any song you like.

Sound Recorder also comes with editing capabilities and a few special effects. You
can copy and paste portions of a recording into another one, mix them, and delete
portions of the recording by using the commands found in the Edit menu. You can
also create special effects such as increasing or decreasing the volume and speed,
adding echoes, or reversing the recording through the Effects menu.

Using Volume Control

To gain complete control of the sound volume, use Volume Control. To launch
Volume Control, click Start ➪ Programs ➪ Accessories ➪ Entertainment ➪ Volume
Control. The interface is shown in Figure 17-34. Notice that you can control each
output device separately.

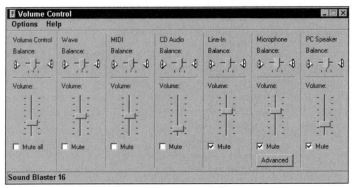

Figure 17-34: Volume Control enables you to increase or decrease volume, as well as change the balance.

You can also control your overall system volume by selecting the speaker icon in the system tray (located in the taskbar). Left-clicking the speaker enables you to move a volume slider up or down to raise or lower your volume. You can also mute your sound from this dialog box. Right-clicking the speaker opens a menu where you can choose to open the full-blown Volume Control.

Summary

In this chapter you've learned how to take advantage of the audio and video capabilities of Windows 2000 Professional.

✦ The general requirements for playing audio and video files include a sound card, speakers, display adapter, monitor, device drivers, codecs, and software applications.

✦ Codecs compress and decompress audio and video files so they take up much less space and bandwidth.

✦ The entry point for configuring audio and video is the Sounds and Multimedia Control Panel.

✦ You can use sound schemes to assign sounds to specific Windows and application events.

✦ CD Player is an amazing, free software application that plays CDs and can even download CD information from the Internet.

✦ Use the Windows Media Player to play most media files.

✦ You can record sound clips with the Sound Recorder.

Audio and video certainly add much to the pleasure of using a computer, but there is a lot more coming! DirectX is a Microsoft technology that enables you to experience high-quality 2D and 3D graphics, video, immersive music, and theater sound. Chapter 18 will lead you on a DirectX tour through DirectDraw, Direct3D Graphics, DirectSound, DirectSound3D, DirectInput, DirectPlay, and DirectMusic.

✦　　✦　　✦

DirectX and Gaming

A lot of folks may be surprised to see a chapter in the *Windows 2000 Professional Bible* with the word *gaming* in it. After all, Windows 2000's progenitor — the straightlaced Windows NT 4.0 operating system — is about as much fun as an accountants' convention. Microsoft may have stapled the attractive Windows 95 interface onto NT 4.0, but from the kernel on up, it has always been a business-first product, tailored to the grim mission of powering faceless server applications and keeping systems running 24 hours a day.

Not that there's anything wrong with that. After all, Windows 95 and 98 have done an admirable job of carrying forward the consumer torch. Plug and Play helped ease bitter memories of intractable hardware conflicts while a spic-and-span interface became more Mac than, well, the Macintosh. And consider this: Just four years after Windows 95 was launched, the scourge of DOS-based games has been eradicated from the market. I mean, that's the biggest news since the eradication of polio.

Okay, so I exaggerate a little. But the fact is, Windows 9x and NT 4.0 have done a respectable job of engaging their specific markets. Microsoft has long had a plan, a road map, a vision even, that someday the two divergent Windows paths would converge. Posited as far back in 1995, the idea was for Windows NT and Windows 9x to merge sometime in 1998 or 1999 under the code name of "Cairo." Needless to say, such grand things have not come to pass under the timetable Microsoft intended, but the vision itself remains.

Windows 2000: The Microsoft merger

With Windows 2000, you are in fact looking at the first serious expression of that merged vision. Oh, NT 4.0 may have tickled a bit of consumer interest with its appealing interface, snappy

Start button, and oh-so-desirable stability, but those were cosmetic steps. Windows 2000 is the first operating system that offers a truly compelling blend of features plucked from each stream. You want Plug and Play *and* granite stability? It's there in Windows 2000. What about ironclad security *and* an easy-on-the-eyes interface? Yup, got that too.

Windows NT 4.0 fumbled at some of these missions, but Windows 2000 sticks them both. More to the point, Windows 2000 finally crosses the chasm of game play. Eye-popping 3D graphics, silky smooth animation, and widespread compatibility with gaming hardware make Windows 2000 a potentially explosive gaming platform.

The upshot of all this is that for the first time, there is no clear-cut reason to buy Windows 9x for one environment and Windows NT for another. In the vast majority of cases, Windows 2000 can address both missions.

The glue that binds these worlds together is a set of technologies called *DirectX*. Launched by Microsoft back in 1995 with Windows 95, DirectX technologies are operating system components, hardware drivers, and related resources that enable advanced multimedia and gaming applications to run on Windows 9x-based PCs. From 2D graphics acceleration to full-motion video and real-time 3D, DirectX has enabled new levels of hardware-accelerated performance in the Windows environment. The DirectX suite of technologies extends as well to user input (DirectInput), networking (DirectConnect), and music (DirectMusic).

These DirectX components have long existed under Windows 95 and 98. Starting with NT 4.0, however, Microsoft began to migrate them to its premier business operating system. The effort started with DirectDraw — the DirectX component in charge of 2D graphics acceleration — enabling enhanced performance for NT 4.0 systems.

Windows 2000 comes outfitted with DirectX 7.0, the newest version of this technology. DirectX 7.0 is the most capable, feature-rich, and performance-friendly version of DirectX yet. That is, until DirectX 8.0 arrives.

Note   Windows 2000 marks a big change for the NT side of the Windows family. While NT 4.0 incorporated some DirectX components, it typically lagged a version or two behind Windows 9x, and some features weren't available at all. With Windows 2000 and DirectX 7.0, Microsoft has established multimedia parity between its consumer and business operating systems.

The DirectX lineup

Multimedia capabilities under Windows are often bundled under the DirectX rubric. DirectX is not a single technology or component of the operating system; rather, it is a suite of components and drivers that addresses a broad range of functions. The DirectX components include the following:

✦ **DirectDraw:** 2D graphics and video acceleration

✦ **Direct3D:** 3D graphics acceleration

✦ **DirectInput:** Input devices, including joysticks and gamepads

✦ **DirectPlay:** Network connections for multiplayer gaming

✦ **DirectSound:** Audio playback

✦ **DirectSound3D:** Positional audio effects

✦ **DirectMusic:** Dynamic music scores

In all cases, DirectX components enable advanced functions and capabilities while maintaining the Windows platform's high level of compatibility. In the past, game software and application vendors wrote directly to the underlying hardware, an intractable situation because so many different devices have to be addressed. DirectX enables software vendors to develop in the familiar Windows environment, where software features are abstracted from the hardware that runs it.

For example, a 3D game that wants to draw bitmap textures on top of a 3D object doesn't tell the graphics card what to do. Rather, it tells Direct3D what it wants. Direct3D then passes along commands to the graphics card, which itself is tailored to interact with Direct3D. The result is that a wide range of Direct3D-compatible software can work with a wide variety of Direct3D-compatible graphics hardware.

DirectDraw and Direct3D graphics

The most visible and well-known DirectX components are DirectDraw and Direct3D. These two DirectX subsets are responsible for making Windows 2000 fast, colorful, and good to look at. They also enable Windows 2000 to play host to many of the most sophisticated 3D games.

Graphics under Windows 2000 are handled via three separate subsystems:

✦ Graphic Device Interface (GDI)

✦ DirectDraw

✦ Direct3D

The Graphics Device Interface (GDI for short) is the base-level graphics engine of Windows and has been around as far back as Windows 3.x. The GDI graphics interface offers the advantages of being well known and highly compatible, but it lacks the efficient structure and acceleration support to enable high-quality graphics. Today, GDI remains an integral part of basic 2D graphics display, but most of the innovation is occurring in DirectX and Direct3D. Figure 18-1 shows a typical screen that stresses the DirectDraw components.

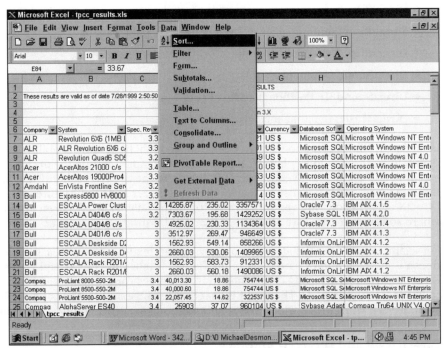

Figure 18-1: GDI enables accelerated performance by doing such things as stashing in memory the portion of the screen obscured by this drop-down menu. When the menu disappears, the hidden part of the screen can be refreshed without pausing to go to system memory.

Note   Actually, GDI underwent a big change with the arrival of Windows NT 4.0 when Microsoft moved GDI from the Win32 subsystem to the Windows NT Executive. This action put graphics operation into Ring 0, the most direct access available to system components, enabling enhanced performance and lower memory overhead. Having GDI run in kernel mode under Windows NT and now Windows 2000 does present an element of risk because graphics subsystems now share address space with memory, I/O, and other OS-critical components. The potential for a poorly designed driver to crash the OS — a definite no-no for Windows 2000 — is one reason why Microsoft now certifies drivers.

GDI is not actually part of the DirectX suite, but DirectDraw and Direct3D are. These two components provide advanced graphics-handling features that turn that staid, 2D windowing interface into a stage for full-motion video, colorful animation, and real-time 3D graphics.

If you don't play a lot of games or frequently render 3D graphics, DirectDraw is the area that may get the most work in your Windows 2000 setup. DirectDraw enables applications to access a drawing surface close to graphics hardware, while still providing a compatibility layer between hardware and applications. Block transfers (called *bit blits*), page flipping, and access to graphics memory are all enabled by DirectX to speed responsiveness of 2D graphics and animation.

But the big news with DirectX 7.0 and Windows 2000 is the Direct3D component of the suite. Direct3D is the graphical interface used by game and application programmers to put rich, real-time 3D graphics onscreen. I'm talking intense, edge-of-your-seat stuff. Check out Figure 18-2. Believe it or not, that's Falcon 4.0, arguably the most visually and technically advanced flight simulator available for the PC. And it's running on Windows 2000, courtesy of Direct3D.

Figure 18-2: Fox three! Texture mapping, alpha blending, atmospheric effects, and other accelerated 3D graphics capabilities are now supported under Windows 2000.

In order for Direct3D to work reasonably well, however, you need a graphics card that's up to the task. Microsoft has been furiously upgrading its Direct3D application programming interface (API) over the past three years, advancing it from a slow, clumsy, and difficult platform to one of the most effective 3D programming interfaces on the market. The result is that more games and more graphics cards now come tailored for Direct3D graphics than for any other technology.

Note   Direct3D does enable older cards and systems to display 3D graphics by using the host processor to handle tasks that might otherwise be processed by a graphics card. Direct3D uses an emulation layer to detect the presence of hardware-accelerated feature support and to send operations to the appropriate hardware. If you have a hot new graphics card, you can get stunning results and fast frame rates, as the Direct3D module relies on your dedicated accelerator to do the job. But if your graphics card is older, the lack of hardware support means Direct3D sends its tasks to the CPU. Not only do things go much more slowly, Direct3D strips out visual fidelity in order to reduce the burden on the system. The result is very poor game play.

The upshot is that if you want gut-wrenching 3D, you're going to have to purchase a graphics board with advanced 3D graphics features to get it. Anything more than a year old is typically missing key features that enhance visual realism and enable high frame rates for smooth action. What's more, 3D graphics acceleration is advancing more quickly than any other component of the PC, including the processor. A year from now, your brand new graphics card probably will sit far behind the curve.

Don't believe me? Check out Microsoft's plans for DirectX 8.0. While tweaks are planned to some of the other subsystems, it's 3D graphics that get the lion's share of the attention. DirectX 8.0 will incorporate advanced 3D technologies that were acquired as part of a technology agreement with workstation vendor Silicon Graphics. These technologies include those used by high-end mechanical CAD and other applications.

In addition, the next Direct3D will support hardware-accelerated lighting and geometry operations, tasks that today are handled by the CPU. Direct3D will enable properly equipped graphics cards to take over many of these operations to further enhance realism and performance. Also expected is support for scene graphs, which enables complex and flexible 3D scenes by describing them as objects instead of as thousands of individual triangles. The upshot will be even better cool graphics running at silky smooth frame rates.

DirectSound and DirectSound3D

The other portion of the DirectX effort currently getting a good deal of work is audio. DirectSound, DirectSound3D, and now DirectMusic have all been improved. DirectSound is the basic audio interface for Windows 2000. Like Direct3D, an emulation layer detects audio hardware capabilities and assigns tasks accordingly.

A low-end audio card, for example, might rely on the CPU to produce the instrument sounds of a MIDI score. A higher-end card, by contrast, relieves CPU overhead by doing this processing directly on the board, often in a 2MB or larger store of memory on the card itself. DirectSound is able to detect the presence of accelerated hardware and make sure these features are used.

More recently, DirectSound3D has become important to game play, as more and more software makers seek to create an immersive experience. DirectSound3D enables a pair of speakers to produce the illusion of sound all around the user. Complex algorithms tweak the audio output to simulate the sound of helicopters moving overhead in conjunction with what you're viewing onscreen. It can also be used to greatly enhance the sense of immersion, by creating music that seems to envelop the listener. The result is added realism without the prohibitive expense of a surround-sound audio system.

The most recent addition to the audio spectrum is DirectMusic, an interface that enables programmatic control of a music score. The possibilities for game makers are stunning. Rather than play a canned set of soundtracks that might be cued based on when the player enters a room or level, programmatic audio changes according to the dynamics of game play. Get jumped by evil beasties, and the music score suddenly picks up to a frenetic pace that matches your situation. Once you've blasted through the bad guys, the music again settles down to a spooky score.

DirectMusic provides a lot of flexibility for programmers because they can vary the scores . For example, you won't have to listen to the same fast action music playing in a monotonous loop. Rather, the music changes subtly throughout the course of the game, to maintain freshness. Unlike some of the other DirectX technologies, DirectMusic does not expect or rely upon hardware acceleration. Rather, it serves as a power application enabler for software developers.

DirectInput

DirectInput is the component in charge of game controllers. Joysticks, game pads, steering wheels and flight yokes, and even foot pedals and head-mounted displays can all be addressed using DirectInput. Importantly, DirectInput provides a common interface for both application support and driver development. For users, that means exotic hardware such as head-mounted displays are much more likely to be supported by games if DirectInput is used by the hardware. Why? Because adding support for a new hardware type through the DirectInput scheme is a lot easier than writing in support from scratch.

DirectPlay

DirectPlay is the game-centric communication component of DirectX. It provides a common API that software developers can use to quickly link games over a network or modem connection. The facility includes native support for TCP/IP networks such as the Internet and many Ethernet LANs, as well as for Microsoft's fast NetBEUI protocol for small local area networks. Direct modem connections are also supported by the DirectPlay facility.

DirectPlay doesn't get a whole lot of attention, but it could be the most important DirectX component because it makes possible a lot of Internet-based game play. In the past, game vendors were forced to create their own communications modules, often with mixed results. DirectPlay helps level the playing field, reducing the hassle and expertise required to create online games, both for software developers and end users.

Using the DirectX Diagnostic Tool

Because DirectX is an API and a suite of operating system components, there really isn't a way for users to directly work with the DirectX technology in Windows 2000. Instead, you see it at work in the graphics, audio, and other subsystems of applications that access DirectX capabilities.

That said, many multimedia programs — and particularly games — require the latest version of DirectX to be installed on your system in order to run. So how do you go about sleuthing your DirectX configuration? I'm glad you asked.

Windows 2000 includes a utility that enables you to detect and test the installed version of DirectX. This can be helpful if multimedia software seems to be having trouble accessing hardware features or isn't running at all. To check your DirectX configuration, click Start ➪ Run and enter **dxdiag.exe** in the Run dialog box to launch the DirectX Diagnostic Tool, shown in Figure 18-3.

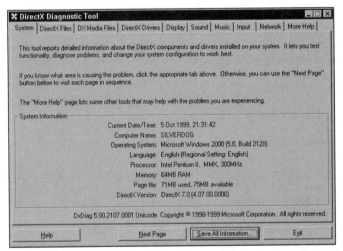

Figure 18-3: Need to know about your DirectX configuration? It's all here for the asking in the heavily tabbed DirectX Diagnostic Tool dialog box.

Alternatively, you can launch the DirectX Diagnostic Tool directly from its location in the System32 folder of your Windows 2000 directory. Find the fileDXDIAG.EXE, double-click it, and the dialog box pictured in Figure 18-3 comes up on your display.

What does this facility enable you to do? Among other things, you can

✦ View information about your system's DirectX setup, including device drivers, component versions, and feature support

✦ Test DirectX features

✦ Disable certain hardware acceleration features (useful for working through compatibility issues)

Once you step through the available features for each of these items, I think you'll find that the DirectX Diagnostic Tool is a thoroughly useful facility for trouble-shooting multimedia performance.

Viewing DirectX information

One thing is for certain, there is a lot to see on the multitabbed DirectX Diagnostic Tool dialog box. Many of these tabs provide access to lists of system files, driver information, and other useful file- and system-level data. By browsing through these pages, you can find out what files provide DirectX functionality, for example.

The System tab

The first thing you see when you launch the DirectX Diagnostic Tool is the System tab, the default opening page for the dialog box. Shown earlier in Figure 18-3, the System tab dishes out lots of general-purpose information such as the system name, operating system version, processor model and speed, and amount of memory. Nothing really shocking here, except that it's all provided in a single, information-filled display — a good start for any troubleshooting effort.

Most useful on this tab is the last field in the System Information window, the DirectX Version. This field shows the version number of DirectX installed in the operating system. If you are having a problem with a game that requires DirectX 8.0, for example, and this screen tells you that DirectX 7.0 is installed, well, there's your answer.

The DirectX Files tab

The DirectX Files tab is the place to review your installed DirectX component files. These are the collected DLL, executable, and system files that make up DirectX under Windows 2000. Figure 18-4 shows what you see on this tab.

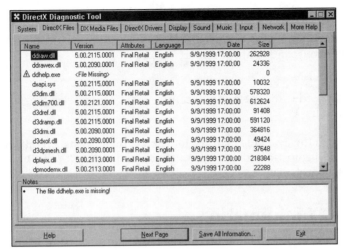

Figure 18-4: Look at the Notes text box at the bottom of the tab to see if any of the installed components are causing problems with DirectX.

The upper list box gives you a detailed directory listing of DirectX component files. Here you can view the name, version number, creation date, and size of DirectX component files, making it easy to compare against published information so you can find corrupted files, for example.

If a problem exists with any of the files, it's reported in the Notes text box at the bottom of the dialog box. For example, if you're running a beta version of DirectX software, this utility detects it and flags the beta- or debug-level files. You want to replace these files with retail versions of the components to possibly resolve compatibility or performance problems.

The DX Media Files tab

One of the key missions of DirectX is to serve as a ubiquitous playback infrastructure for the broad universe of audio, video, and animation media file types that are floating around out there. Figure 18-5 shows how the DX Media Files tab looks. The information here is presented the same way as on the DirectX Files tab, right down to the Notes window that flags any problem files in the set.

Tip If you seem to be having trouble running a particular type of media file that you know Windows 2000 should be able to handle—say, MPEG-2 video—the DX Media Files tab is a good place to start troubleshooting. The underlying media file that supports MPEG-2 may have been corrupted, information the utility can give you on this tab. You may be able to reestablish functionality by simply replacing the errant file. Of course, a complete DirectX reinstall could be in order.

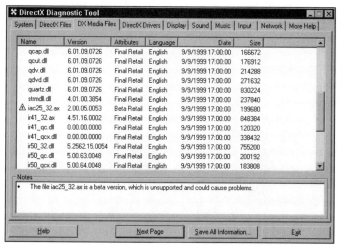

Figure 18-5: Media Player isn't handling all the video types it's supposed to? You may find the answer on the DX Media Files tab.

The DirectX Drivers tab

Next up in your informational tour is the DirectX Drivers tab. Here you can quickly scan all the DirectX-compatible device drivers installed on your system. This is a lot easier than trudging to the individual properties dialog boxes for the graphics card, audio adapter, game controller, and other hardware.

No surprise: the Notes window flags problem driver files. Just as important, the dialog box also flags uncertified drivers, which are drivers that have not passed muster in Microsoft's quality assurance labs. While this doesn't mean that the driver won't work properly — many uncertified ones do — it means that Microsoft hasn't had a chance to confirm its operation under Windows 2000.

Note

If you work in a mission-critical environment, make a point to seek out certified drivers. You invite fewer headaches that way. Individual users, however, can often enjoy greater features and better performance by downloading the latest drivers for their graphics cards, sound cards, and gaming devices.

The Display and Sound tabs

The Display and Sound tabs enable you to interact with your DirectX configuration, and a lot of valuable information also is displayed on these two tabs, as you can see in Figures 18-6 and 18-7. In both tabs, the Notes window displays information about problems the diagnostic program detects. Note that this figure shows two Display tabs because this Windows 2000 features a multimonitor configuration.

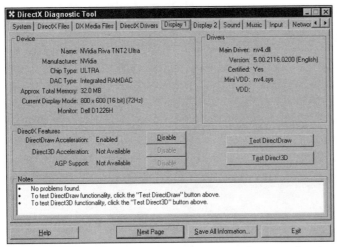

Figure 18-6: The Display page lets you test and set acceleration features. In this case, there are two Display tabs — one for each graphics board installed in this system.

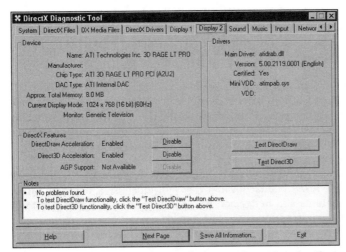

Figure 18-7: Review your audio adapter configuration details, driver version, and other useful information here.

Particularly useful for troubleshooting DirectX-related problems is the information displayed in the DirectX features area of each tab. Here you can quickly find out whether or not your hardware and device drivers incorporate support for advanced features such as accelerated 3D graphics and fast, AGP-based texture mapping. This last feature indicates whether your AGP graphics card, which plugs into the Accelerated Graphics Port slot on the PC motherboard, is able to tap into system memory to store large amounts of data for displaying textures.

Also of interest, these tabs are the first that enable you to tinker with DirectX. You learn about the oh-so-useful testing and configuration-editing features of these tabs in the section "Testing and Configuring DirectX," later in this chapter.

The Music tab

Windows 2000 uses a number of installed devices to produce musical sounds over your sound card or audio adapter. A MIDI synthesizer, for instance, produces the musical notes and scores you hear when you play a .MID file. You can check the status of your installed synthesizers on the Music tab in the Music Ports area, as shown in Figure 18-8.

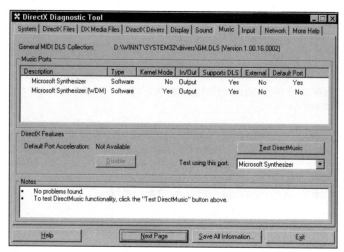

Figure 18-8: Do complex MIDI scores slow down your PC? Check the Music tab to see if perhaps a software-based synthesizer is stealing CPU cycles.

The Input tab

Next up is the Input tab that you use to track the status of game controllers such as joysticks, game pads, and steering columns. DirectInput provides fast and accurate tracking for a broad range of input devices, such as the Microsoft SideWinder Force Feedback joystick, Logitech Wingman Formula Force steering wheel, and other devices. This dialog box, shown in Figure 18-9, has two areas of interest: Input Devices and Installed Drivers.

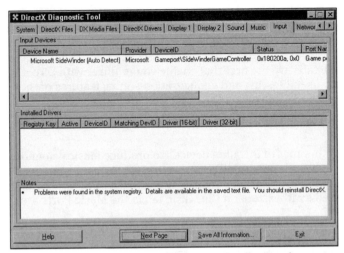

Figure 18-9: Joystick not working? This tab tells you about any problems, such as the one identified in the Notes area.

The Input Devices area identifies individual input devices by type and name, while the Installed Drivers section displays Registry Key information and matches each driver to its related input device.

Tip   In order to work properly, many input devices must be set at the front of the DirectInput queue. That means they have a DriverID of 1. If you are experiencing trouble with a game controller, check its DeviceID value in the Installed Devices area. You may want to change its number (possibly swapping IDs with another, less temperamental device, if multiple controllers are involved).

The Network tab

Any gamer tells you that nothing is quite as much fun as online gaming. Today, most new games incorporate multiplayer capabilities, making it possible for as many as dozens of players to compete or cooperate in a virtual gaming environment. The DirectPlay component of DirectX enables game and other software makers to quickly plug their software into a standard multiplayer gaming facility.

When you click the Network tab, you see the page shown in Figure 18-10. The various types of available supported connections for DirectPlay are displayed in the top list box. If you have any DirectPlay-savvy applications, they are shown in the second list box. (The word *lobbyable* in the title of the second list box means that users are able to gather in a virtual lobby to organize game play before entering the actual gaming environment.)

Again, the Notes box flags any problem files or system states to help troubleshoot failures.

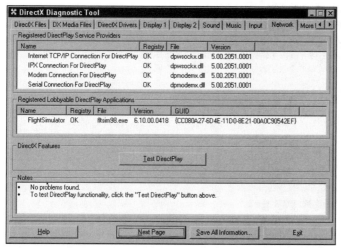

Figure 18-10: Can't get your games to work online? Check to make sure your network, modem, and other interfaces are in working order.

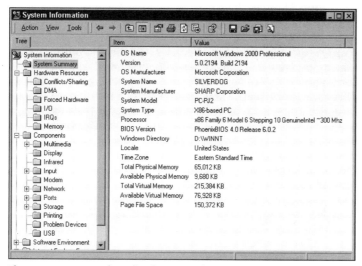

Figure 18-11: Need to dig deeper to hunt down problems and conflicts? You can launch the useful Microsoft System Information tool directly from the More help tab of the DirectX Diagnostic Tool.

The More help tag

Finally, the More help tab can guide you through your troubleshooting. This dialog box may display a list of recommended actions to resolve existing problems, for example. In addition, the MSInfo button gives you quick access to the useful

Microsoft System Information Tool. With this system diagnostic application, which uses the standard Microsoft Management Console (MMC) interface used by Device Manager and other facilities, you can look deep into your system configuration. Figure 18-11 shows the System Information dialog box.

Testing and configuring DirectX

One of the neatest features of the DirectX Diagnostic Tool is its capability to enable you to test system operation. Not sure if your 3D graphics card is able to handle the latest Direct3D-capable games? You're just a Test button away from finding out. Here I go over the testing facilities for DirectX and what they do.

What you see is what you get

Your first stop is the DirectDraw and Direct3D display features. Click the Display tab. In the DirectX Features area are the following items, each with a button labeled Disable next to it:

✦ DirectDraw Acceleration: Accelerated 2D graphics and video

✦ Direct3D Acceleration: Accelerated 3D graphics

✦ AGP Support: Enables the graphics card to access main system memory to store 3D information.

If your graphics card supports any of these features, the Disable button to the right of each is activated. If you are experiencing software crashes during certain graphics operations, you can try to get around them by clicking the Disable button. Doing so forces DirectX to perform the affected operations in software, ignoring any existing hardware in the system. If a hardware compatibility is truly at issue, DirectX software emulation can enable you to run the problem software, albeit at slow frame rates and often much lower visual quality.

Note　When it comes to troubleshooting, disabling DirectX features usually isn't a good long-term solution. Doing so forces Windows 2000 to perform a lot of performance-intensive tasks that would otherwise be handled by the graphics board, stealing CPU cycles and dragging down performance. DirectX also dumbs down operation for nonhardware environments, which means you get lousy looking 3D graphics. What disabling features does for you is give you working access to DirectX applications and perhaps return system operation during tasks that were previously crashing applications.

Testing graphics

Now it's time for a little eye candy. The Test DirectDraw and Test Direct3D buttons on the Display tab invoke a series of graphical operations that stress your display subsystem. Click the Test DirectDraw button, for example, and you get a confirmation dialog box, shown in Figure 18-12, that warns you that the test is about to begin. It can take some time, so don't run this test if you're in a rush.

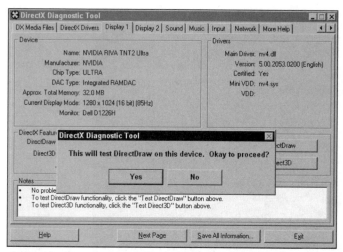

Figure 18-12: Are you sure? Just make sure you have a minute or two to go through the prompted test routine. Windows 2000 needs you to confirm that everything is being displayed properly.

Click the Yes button. You get another prompt, this time asking you to click OK to kick off the first test. You are also told that the first test assesses windowed graphics performance. The following tests occur:

- ✦ A garish display of alternating black and white boxes
- ✦ A bouncing block
- ✦ A full-screen bouncing block

After each test, Windows asks you if what you saw matched the description in the dialog box. If not, click No. An error message shows up in the Notes text box, and you have some troubleshooting to do. If the display and the descriptions match, you can proceed to the next test.

The Direct3D test is similar to DirectDraw except that different images are displayed. This test displays a spinning, multicolored cube onscreen, first in a window and then full-screen. Figure 18-13 shows what this test looks like.

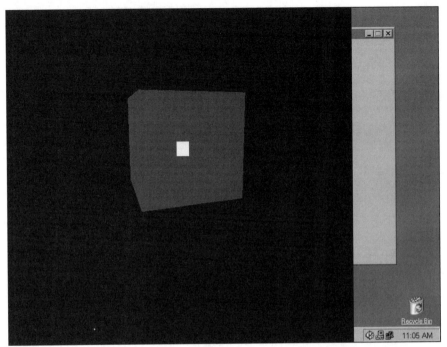

Figure 18-13: It ain't pretty, but it's enough to determine if Direct3D is working on your system.

Can you hear me?

The Sound tab enables you to do two things: set the level of audio hardware acceleration and test DirectSound playback.

To tweak acceleration, click and drag the slider bar control left or right. Dragging it all the way to the right makes maximum use of acceleration for playing back sounds and creating audio effects. Moving the slider to the left places more tasks on the system processor.

Why turn down acceleration? Depending on your hardware, easing off acceleration features can help reduce application crashes and provide access to certain effects that hardware may refuse to play. The penalty comes in the form of slower performance — audio tasks chew up CPU cycles — and lower audio fidelity.

To test performance, click the Test DirectSound button. An initial dialog box informs you that the test is about to begin. Click OK. You should then see a dialog box indicating that DirectSound is playing an 8-bit, 11kHz sound. If you hear the sound, click Yes in the dialog box that appears after it plays. Repeat this process for each step of the test.

If you don't hear a sound, click the No button in the dialog box. The test halts, and an error line appears in the Notes area of the Sound tab, indicating what failed.

Next in line is the Music tab. Here you can click the Test DirectMusic button to see if the synthesizer on the selected port is working. You see the usual dialog box announcement, and you should hear music playing. If you don't, click No at the dialog box, and an error line appears in the Notes area. If you hear music, click Yes. The test ends. Repeat the test for each synthesizer listed in the Test using this port drop-down control.

As with DirectDraw and other display features, you can turn off Music support. Click the Disable button to turn off DirectSound hardware acceleration. If no acceleration is available, the Disable button is grayed out.

Testing for play

Finally, the Network tab enables you to test the availability of online gaming features under Windows 2000. Here's how to test DirectPlay:

1. If you are connected to a network via LAN or modem, click the Test DirectPlay button. The DirectPlay dialog box appears.

2. Click the connection you want to test in the Service Provider list box and then click the Create New Session radio button. Figure 18-14 shows this setup. Click OK.

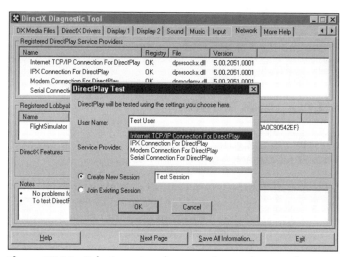

Figure 18-14: Select a network connection and get testing.

3. In the DxDiag DirectPlay Chat dialog box, shown in Figure 18-14, type some text into the text box at the bottom and click the Send button.

4. The text you just entered should appear in the scrolling list box. You can enter additional text and click Send to see it appear, as shown in Figure 18-15.

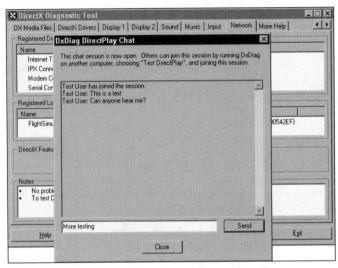

Figure 18-15: You should be able to chat online if you can see any input in this dialog box.

5. Click Close to end the test and return to the DirectX Diagnostic Tools dialog box.

Saving DirectX information

All these tools and features are great. But what if you've encountered a problem that you can't resolve? In that case, a call to technical support may be in order. The DirectX Diagnostic Tool can help you here as well.

The Save All Information button, which is always visible at the bottom of the dialog box, writes your current DirectX system configuration to a text file. It is then a simple matter for you to send that file to your corporate help desk or a vendor's technical support representative for review. Technical support can quickly scan the report for trouble states, as well as get a better sense of your system's multimedia configuration. Figure 18-16 shows a typical report displayed in Notepad.

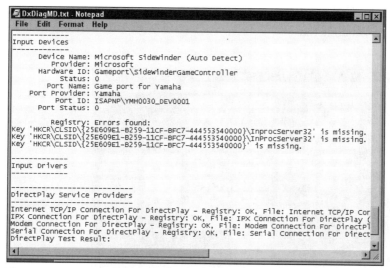

Figure 18-16: See the problem? Looks like DirectX Diagnostics has detected a couple of erroneous Registry entries for my joystick.

To create a text file with your DirectX information, click the Save All Information button and then use the dialog box that appears to name the text file and direct it to a specific drive or folder. That's it.

Fun with Windows 2000

Okay, enough sleuthing and troubleshooting. It's time to check out some of the games that come as part of this operating system. Granted, Windows 2000 is hardly your basic consumer operating system, but that doesn't matter. I know many a business user who has become absolutely addicted to FreeCell, the solitaire-like card game that's part of Windows 98 and the Windows 95 Plus pack. Bad news for productivity minded managers: FreeCell is included with Windows 2000 as well.

Four games are installed with Windows 2000:

✦ **Solitaire:** The timeless classic card game that has robbed corporations of countless hours of productive work.

✦ **FreeCell:** The Solitaire successor, FreeCell offers more ways to win and more ways to get addicted.

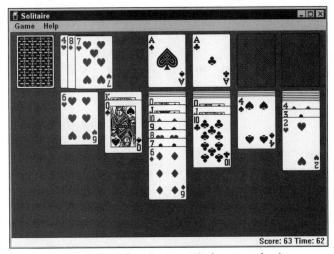

Figure 18-17: Solitaire has been a Windows staple since Windows 3.1. And it's been a monumental productivity waster for just as long.

✦ **Minesweeper:** A long time favorite among Windows users. This simple find-and-seek game is great for kids.

✦ **Pinball:** It looks and plays like a real pinball game. There are even keys for nudging the "machine" left and right. See Figure 18-18.

Figure 18-18: Microsoft's 3D Pinball looks appealing but isn't nearly as addicting as FreeCell or that old favorite Solitaire.

To access any of these games, click Start ➪ Programs ➪ Accessories ➪ Games and then select the appropriate name from the fly-out menu as shown in Figure 18-19.

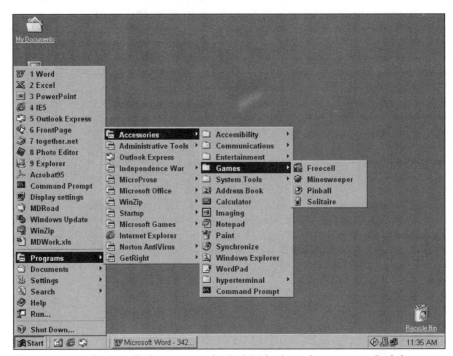

Figure 18-19: The bundled games are buried fairly deep, but you can find them quickly enough, I'm sure.

Summary

Windows 2000 is the direct descendant of Windows NT, so it is a business operating system, designed to run all day every day without failing. But for the first time, Microsoft has managed to inject some cutting-edge fun into this area of its product line, and the results are impressive. Games ranging from Quake Arena to Falcon 4.0 can run under Windows 2000. The secret ingredient is DirectX 7.0

In this chapter, we delved into the workings of the DirectX multimedia and gaming application programming interface suite. Among the topics we covered:

✦ A discussion of how gaming and DirectX multimedia fit with Windows 2000

✦ A tour of the DirectX technologies and what they do

✦ Using the DirectX Diagnostic Tool to review and configure your DirectX settings

✦ A quick review of the games included with Windows 2000

This chapter concludes our discussion of Windows 2000's extensive multimedia talents. In Part V, we'll explore the powerful networking features of Windows 2000. The first chapter of the part, Chapter 19, provides a solid foundation in the basic concepts of networking.

✦   ✦   ✦

Networking with Windows 2000

Networking 101

Networking is all about communication. You can easily grasp the broad concepts of communication because you communicate with other people all the time and intuitively understand the general requirements of communicating thoughts, ideas, and information whether or not you consciously think about the process. If you want to speak to the person in the next cubicle, you can yell over the cube walls. If you want to speak to someone across the country, you can pick up the telephone. Most of the time communication is natural, but when you begin to analyze the process closely, its simplicity diminishes, and its complexity grows. It's the same with networks.

In this chapter, I show you enough about networking to make you dangerous without burdening you with complexities and details you don't need at this stage of your networking career. Mountains of information currently in print and on the Internet explain the concepts and practicalities of networking. Why is there so much coverage? Because networking is a powerful tool for expanding the capabilities of your computer. In addition, the current state of technology makes it relatively easy for anyone to reap the benefits of networking, whether you are a home enthusiast, employed in a small business, or a member of a large international corporation.

As you read this chapter, keep in mind that Windows 2000 Professional has its roots in Windows NT and was designed with networking firmly in mind. Its true power can be achieved only by connecting it to other computers and devices to share information and services.

Networking Basics

A network is two or more computers connected to each other by various pieces of hardware using software protocols and applications to communicate. Because the computers are able to communicate, they can share information. When you connect devices such as printers and servers to your network, you can begin to share other resources and services that might not generally be available to a single computer.

Note   Computer networks came into existence in an era when large computers called *mainframes* ruled the earth and dominated their underlings, called *terminals*. Networks at that time were highly proprietary—optimized for a single operating system—and virtually all computing power was contained in the mainframe. Since then a computer revolution has occurred, leading to a more open computing model based on public standards and extremely powerful personal computers appearing on everyone's desktop. In recent years there has been a movement back toward centralizing the computing power and using network computers with limited capabilities on desktops because those powerful PCs are darned expensive.

Figure 19-1 shows a conceptual network with computers and a variety of available resources. Remember that the point of networking is communicating. Computers in this network are able to share information and other resources. As you add more computers and other devices, your capability to share information and resources among a larger audience is greatly expanded. And if you then connect your network to other networks, the benefits can be staggering.

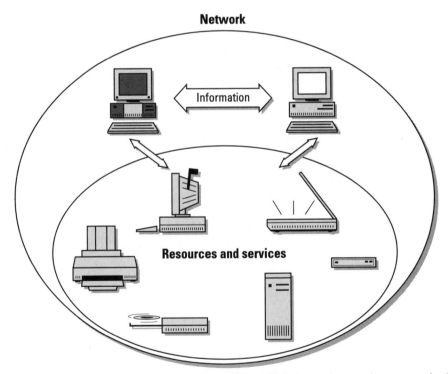

Figure 19-1: This conceptual network is ablaze with information- and resource-sharing possibilities.

Pieces of the network puzzle

All networks share common features that enable them to establish a communications link between the different devices connected to the network:

✦ Transmission media to carry data

✦ Access to the media for devices on the network

✦ Software protocols to regulate communication

✦ Communications software

Because speaking on the telephone is something we all have in common, I use that analogy in Figure 19-2 to show the pieces of the network puzzle, working from the inside out.

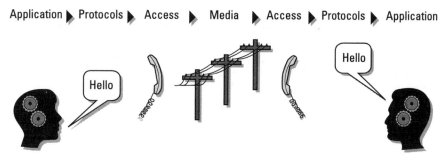

Figure 19-2: These are the general requirements that make networking possible.

The telephone lines in the middle of Figure 19-2 connect telephone networks and enable you to speak to people over the telephone whether they are in the same city or somewhere else in the world. These lines can be cables, radio transmissions, satellite links, or anything else that carries the conversation from one telephone to the other. Along the same lines (no pun intended), all computer networks require a medium for actually sending the data, whether it is a tangible medium such as copper wires and fiber-optic cables or an intangible medium such as radio waves or light. Therefore, the transmission medium is the physical link between the devices of the network. What good is a telephone without telephone lines? Not much! Transmission media currently used in networks include the following:

✦ Coaxial cables

✦ Unshielded Twisted Pair (UTP) cables similar to telephone lines

✦ Fiber-optic cabling

✦ Radio

✦ Infrared

Working out from the media is the telephone, the actual device that connects you to the telephone lines and enables you to have a conversation with another person. In other words, the telephone provides access to the transmission medium and performs the mechanical task of transmitting and receiving your spoken words. Similarly, you need a device that is specifically designed to interface with the type of media that exists in your network and also actually send and receive data. These devices are as follows:

✦ Network adapter cards (also called *network interface cards*) used to connect computers local area networks (LANs)

✦ Channel Service Unit/Data Service Unit (CSU/DSU) devices used to convert digital computer signals to and from digital phone line signals used in wide area networks (WANs)

Moving outward on Figure 19-2 again, one person is on each end of the connection. One person is speaking into the telephone, and the other person is listening. The person speaking must use a language understood by the other party to make the communication meaningful. What's the point of calling someone who doesn't understand you? It's the same for computer networks. Once you have everything hooked up, your computer and other devices need to be able to understand each other as they communicate. This is the realm of software protocols, which are an agreed-upon method for exchanging information. Protocols form a language that enables your computer to encode information and transmit it in a form the recipient can decode and understand. Common software protocols in networking include the following:

✦ Transmission Control Protocol/Internet Protocol (TCP/IP)

✦ NetBEUI

✦ Internet Packet Exchange/Sequenced Packet Exchange (IPX/SPX)

✦ AppleTalk

✦ Point to Point Tunneling Protocol (PPTP)

✦ Dynamic Host Configuration Protocol (DCHP)

Finally, there must be something causing the communication to take place. The human brain illustrates this point in the figure and is what causes you to pick up the phone in the first place. With networking it is the same way, only the brains are different communications software applications that are the reason you are using the network. A few software applications that use networks are:

✦ Operating systems

✦ Web browsers

✦ E-mail clients

Cool things you can do with a network

Whether you're in business, education, or government and use Windows 2000 Professional as an individual or are part of a corporation, there are many benefits from using a network.

A standalone computer is a powerful tool. You can install software applications that enable you to create documents, play games, create artwork, plan a budget, write books, analyze scientific data, and perform many other tasks. As you connect external peripherals such as printers and scanners, you increase your capabilities beyond what your computer has inside its case. At some point, however, you reach a practical limit of what you can attach to your computer. Networking is a way to move beyond your computer and share resources.

Using a network can also change the way you work or at least expand your horizons. Typically people work alone at computers, separated by fuzzy cubicle partitions or office walls. You may work at home, physically removed from others you work with. Networks enable people to collaborate and share information without having to sit side by side.

Here's a rundown of the benefits of using a network, how information is shared, and what kinds of services are available:

File sharing	Having the capability to share files (documents, projects, and the like) can be an enormous benefit because people can work collaboratively on projects. You don't have to shuttle floppy disks around the office or rotate through a single workstation to use the same files.

Caution As with anything, this story has two sides. While sharing files may sound great, you may wish to protect some more than others. Confidential personal information, financial records, and personnel files are probably not the types of information you want floating all over your network. Be sure to read the information on network security found in this and other chapters.

Print sharing	Sharing printers can make printing much more economical for larger groups of people. Instead of buying one printer per computer, you can buy a few good network printers and set them up in a central area with print jobs handled by a dedicated print server or spooled through a workstation.

Application sharing	Another network service is application sharing, or running applications installed on a server on remote workstations. Application sharing not only reduces the number of software packages you have to buy (many programs come with network licenses), but also reduces the amount of time and effort required to maintain and upgrade software. Instead of running around to every machine on the network to perform upgrades, all you have to do is upgrade the application on the server.

Note   Microsoft has a product called Terminal Server that enables Windows 2000 Server to act as an application server. When Terminal Server is installed, all client application execution occurs on the server.

Device sharing	Similar to print sharing is the capability to share other devices such as CD-ROM towers and scanners. A CD-ROM tower is a good solution for providing access to archived data that is infrequently needed. In addition, reference material such as encyclopedias are available in CD format and can be easily shared throughout your network.
Communications services	In today's world, e-mail is an essential service. Whether you have an e-mail server or individual accounts through an Internet Service Provider, setting up and configuring e-mail is a must. E-mail is how the modern world communicates!
Internet access	Instead of buying a modem for each workstation and taking up possibly limited telephone lines, networks can provide access to the Internet for an entire staff. Many people have two phone lines in their house so they can surf the Internet and still use the telephone. When you have tens, hundreds, or even more people in an office who need to use the Internet and communicate by e-mail, networks solve the problem of telephone access.
Network gaming	This one's outside the business aspects of networking, but network gaming is incredibly fun and challenging. I've been playing Quake 3 Area (Test) on the Internet lately, and the challenge of beating human opponents is

more exciting than the prospect of beating the artificial intelligence of the computer opponent found in most games. If you can play during your lunch hour or during off-hours, network gaming can bring a group of people closer together (even if they are demolishing each other like crazy in the game) because they're sharing a common activity that is fun.

The OSI Reference Model

The International Organization for Standardization (OSI) has constructed a model for understanding networking that organizes the networking process into seven interconnected layers that describe how information moves from one computer (or device) across a network to another computer. Each layer has specifically defined, relatively self-contained, networking functions and responsibilities aimed at providing a service to the layer immediately above. The following table identifies the layers and the order they fall within the model:

Layer Description	Number
Physical	1
Data Link	2
Network	3
Transport	4
Session	5
Presentation	6
Application	7

Because each layer communicates both up and down the layer scheme, they all have transmitting and receiving roles in both directions.

The physical layer is responsible for transmitting and receiving data that has been encoded into binary data. It accepts information from the data link layer and transmits it over the transmission media (sometimes referred to as *Layer 0*). It does not process or understand what it is sending. This layer also receives network data and passes it to the data link layer.

Continued

(continued)

The data link layer is responsible for packaging information into binary data packets to be transmitted by the physical layer and for managing, through the use of networking protocols defined by the physical connections in the network, access to the media. When the physical layer receives data packets and passes them to the data link layer, the data link layer verifies the information is intact and acknowledges that fact to the originator.

The network layer establishes the end-to-end route the information travels on the network from the originating computer to the final destination. While the physical and data link layers are concerned only with immediately adjacent network nodes, the network layer sees the entire route the data travels whether to a server in an adjacent room or one across LAN boundaries.

The transport layer maintains the integrity of the data being transmitted and received and controls the flow and sequence of data packets.

The session layer uses network protocols to negotiate and manage requests for network services from applications and the responses to those requests between computer applications.

The presentation layer manages data encoding.

The application layer provides an interface between the end user system and the network services.

Local and wide area networking

One of the most common misunderstandings of the networking novice is the basic differences between a local area network (LAN) and a wide area network (WAN). It boils down to distance and function. A LAN is a network in which the devices are all fairly close to one another and the goal is to connect all the devices. A WAN is a network that spans distances ranging from hundreds of feet to thousands of miles with the purpose of linking together other networks. Both types are networks, but one is a network of devices and the other is a network of networks. Very often you see one or more LANs connected to form a WAN, which is then connected to the Internet, the largest WAN in existence. Figure 19-3 illustrates this point by showing several LANs connected to form a WAN, which is then connected to other WANs.

Network transmission speeds and bandwidth

Network transmission speeds and bandwidth are the subject of endless debates among networking professionals. Everyone tries to squeeze the most speed and efficiency out of their systems because few things are more frustrating than a slow network. As with everything in the computing world, what's fast today is unacceptably slow tomorrow.

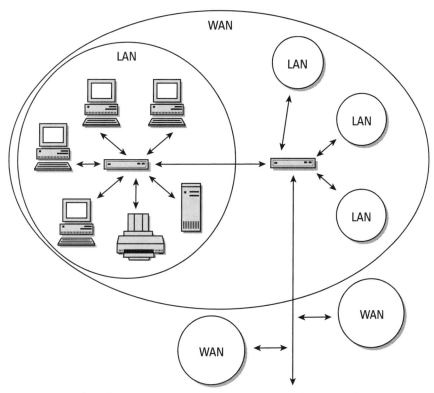

Figure 19-3: The relationship between local area networks and wide area networks.

Transmission speeds are measured in bits per second (bps). When you get more bits than you know what to do with, the notation becomes Kbps, meaning kilo, or thousands of bits per second. The next jump is Mbps, which means mega, or millions of bits per second. Finally is Gbps, or giga, meaning billions of bits per second.

The term *bandwidth* is often misused; it is the potential maximum amount of data that can be carried over a given transmission medium.

Throughput is a more accurate measure of network speed than raw transmission speed measurements because it measures how much data (rather than the flow of bits) is actually being transmitted. Even though a network is rated at 10Mbps, it may not actually transfer 10Mbps of data in all cases and at all times. This is due to the overhead of network protocols, error correction, handshaking, transmission acknowledgment, and other communications that go on behind the scenes to support the data transmission. You can measure your throughput by using the Performance Monitor included in Windows 2000 Professional. Your mileage may vary because throughput is dependant upon factors such as the protocol you are using (such as TCP/IP), the number of clients on your network, the network layer you are monitoring, and your network architecture.

LANs

LANs are probably the most common type of network. They are characterized by the fact that all of the devices within the network are in geographical proximity. In other words, they are local. Most of the time, the computers, printers, hubs, and other devices are actually in the same building.

Note   I use the term *type* to differentiate networks that have different resource access methodologies and hierarchies, *topology* to differentiate the physical or logical arrangement of the connections, and *architecture* to indicate the media access (as opposed to resource access) method.

Types of LANs

There are two major types of LANs: the peer-to-peer LAN and the client/server LAN. LANs can also be a combination of the two. The two types are defined by the way devices attached to the network access resources. In a peer-to-peer network, all devices have equal access. In a client/server network, access to resources being requested by clients, or workstation computers, is controlled by network servers.

The peer-to-peer network

In the peer-to-peer network, shown in Figure 19-4, all computers are equal in status, which is why they are called *peers*. Access to resources on the network is not regulated or controlled because there is no server in a peer-to-peer network. In fact, rather than having a dedicated server, each computer attached to the network can act as a server or client depending upon the situation.

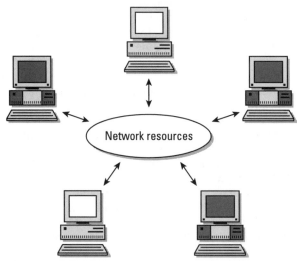

Figure 19-4: Peer-to-peer LANs feature unregulated access to resources.

The advantages of peer-to-peer networking are numerous:

Simple	The peer-to-peer network works great for small networks of only a few computers because it is simple to plan and implement.
Inexpensive	Hardware costs are lower than for other forms of networks, primarily because no server or other expensive networking hardware is required to set up and run a peer-to-peer network.
Easy to install	Because the peer-to-peer network is simple and has relatively few hardware requirements, you only need a limited knowledge of networking software and hardware to set one up. Because peer-to-peer networks are generally small, you don't have to wire your whole building to install one. In addition, support for peer-to-peer networking comes right out of the box with Microsoft Windows 95, 98, NT, and Windows 2000 Professional.
Easy to maintain	Building on the benefits listed previously, supporting a peer-to-peer network doesn't require the services of a paid, full-time network or system administrator.
Fault tolerant	Because peer-to-peer networks don't rely on one critical component that would take the entire network down if it failed, they are considered more fault tolerant than other network types.

Peer-to-peer networks do have limitations, however:

No central services	Because peer-to-peer networks don't have servers, they lose out on the centralized services servers provide such as centralized file storage and networked applications.
Uneven security	Because it has "multiple administrators," the peer-to-peer network is only as secure as its weakest link.
Limited size	Peer-to-peer networks should be kept small and may not meet your requirements.
Lack of standards	Because there is no central networking authority, network operating procedures tend to be made by each individual without necessarily consulting others. This can lead to confusion.
Limited scalability	Adding more computers to a peer-to-peer network eventually brings network access speed to a grinding halt as computers compete for limited bandwidth.

The client/server network

The client/server network has one or more dedicated computers that act as servers. Notice in Figure 19-5 that the server separates resources and services from the workstations. This provides for more regulated use of the network's resources.

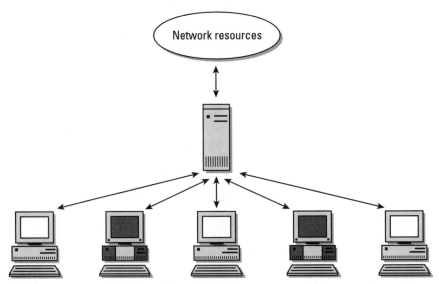

Figure 19-5: In a client/server-based LAN, the server regulates access to resources.

There are several advantages to setting up a client/server type of network:

Easily expanded	Adding more networked devices is relatively easy.
Wide range of services	Having one or more servers provides centralized services such as file storage, print services, access to other devices, and network applications.
Better security	Security can be much better due to centralized management.
Central management	Administration is centralized, and the network administrator performs tasks such as data backups and routine maintenance/upgrades.
Faster	Network access is generally much faster than peer-to-peer networks because each client can communicate directly with the server or other network devices.

Alas, nothing is perfect. Client/server networks also have limitations:

More expensive	Hardware in the form of servers and network operating system software are generally more expensive than the hardware requirements for a peer-to-peer network, and workstations are bought in greater quantity because client/server networks tend to be larger than peer-to-peer.
More difficult installation	Installing and configuring the network operating system on the server can be difficult and time consuming. If more than one server is involved, your commitment increases.
More expertise required	The average person can set up and use Windows 2000 Professional and other workstation operating systems and applications in a peer-to-peer network without too much difficulty. Adding servers and network administration tasks, security, and troubleshooting takes a professional.

Combining peer-to peer and client/server networks

Figure 19-6 shows a network that features a combination of peer-to-peer and client/server networking. Combination networks share elements of the peer-to-peer and client/server network types. In this configuration, workstations grouped together to form a workgroup on a client/server network provide resources among themselves. In reality, many networks use a combination of peer-to-peer and client/server networking. They centralize the resources that need to be used by everyone but segregate specialized resources such as scanners that need to be used by a separate group of people into a peer-to-peer workgroup. In such cases there is no need for the server to manage the resource because of the limited demand for and visibility of the resource.

Major LAN topologies

Now that you know what a LAN is and what types there are, it is time to move to the subject of LAN topology. A *topology* is the physical (and sometimes logical) arrangement of the network connections. Three prime LAN topologies are in use today: bus, ring, and star.

Caution   You can't just pick a LAN topology out of thin air. The architecture (covered later) you choose can restrict or define the topology you must use. The reason topology is covered before architecture is that an understanding of network topologies can help you understand the architectures.

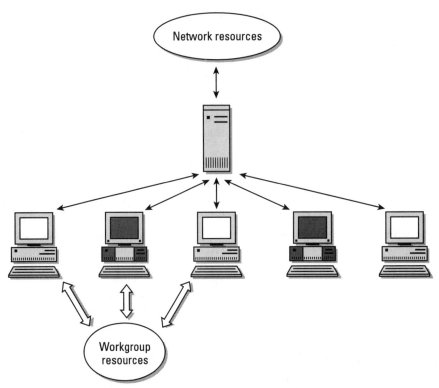

Figure 19-6: This LAN is a combination of client/server and peer-to-peer networking.

The bus topology, shown in Figure 19-7, also known as the *daisy-chain* or linear topology, is created by linking all elements of the network with a single cable called a *backbone*. Each device simply listens to the bus and accepts transmissions directed at it, such as a request for a shared file or printer. One problem with this type of LAN is that a single transmitting device can tie up the entire network and prevent any other device from transmitting. For example, a computer downloading or copying an extremely large file takes over the network during the process of copying the file to the exclusion of all other network requests. Another problem is that if there is a break in the chain due to a cable fault, the entire network goes down, and you are left trying to figure out which link is at fault. A bus topology is more suited to a limited peer-to-peer network, but client/server networks can function using this topology as well. As I will explain shortly, however, bus topologies are becoming less widely deployed in favor of star topologies with both types of networks.

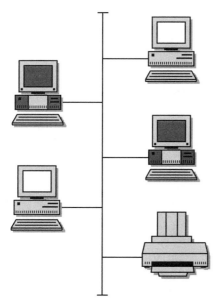

Figure 19-7: A peer-to-peer network using a bus topology.

The ring topology, shown in Figure 19-8, features devices connected in the form of a ring, or circle. Each device has two connections, one to each of its neighbors. One problem is that as more devices are connected, delays in communication increase because there is simply more network to traverse. In other words, because network data may have to go through more cabling and computers attached to the network that may be in between the data source and destination, it takes longer to get there. For example, in a ring network with five computers, the longest distance data has to travel is through four computers and the respective cabling. If I increased the size to 20 computers, the longest distance is dramatically increased. There are few pure ring networks today.

A more popular implementation of the ring topology is the logical ring, or star-wired ring topology. Instead of each computer or device being physically connected to its neighbors, all devices are connected to a centralized device called a *hub*. The ring is maintained by using a circular access method. In other words, access to the network is passed from computer to computer in a circular method, despite the fact that they all share a central connection.

The star topology, shown in Figure 19-9, is the most popular network topology (for both peer-to-peer and client/server networks) because each networked device has a dedicated line to the hub, which serves as the wiring focal point for the network. In other words, the circuit from the device to the hub is used solely by that device and no other, guaranteeing independent access to the media for each device. The star topology is more fault tolerant than the other topologies because if a section fails, it affects only the device that uses that section to connect to the hub.

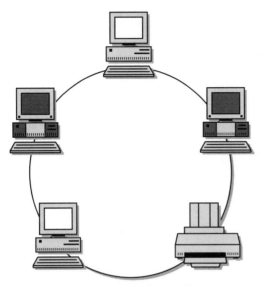

Figure 19-8: The ring topology with a peer-to-peer network.

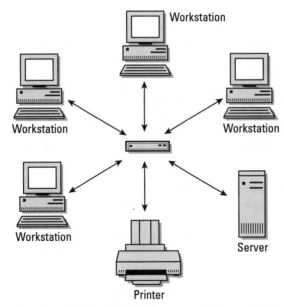

Figure 19-9: This client/server network has a star topology.

Ethernet and Token Ring: popular LAN architectures

Architecture is a term used to define how network devices gain access to the network and the technologies used to provide and regulate this access. The two common LAN architectures in use today are Ethernet and Token Ring.

Note   Ethernet LANs can transmit information up to 100 Mbps (1000 Mbps is in development) while Token Ring LANs are limited to a top speed of 16 Mbps.

Ethernet LANs

Ethernet, developed in the 1970s, is the most popular LAN architecture. Because of its longevity and reliance on open, nonproprietary standards, you can select from a number of stable, compatible, and cost-efficient Ethernet hardware components.

Ethernet networks are primarily wired as a star topology, defined in the previous section. This configuration enables all signals to be concentrated in the hub, and each device has independent access to the network media. There are several types of Ethernet networks, each defined in terms of the network adapters, cables used and attainable transmission speeds.

+ **Thin Ethernet:** Uses 10Base-2 coaxial cabling capable of 10Mbps transmission speeds and requires a network adapter compatible with 10Base-2 cable.

+ **Thick Ethernet:** Uses 10Base-5 coaxial cabling, which is thicker that 10Base-2, is capable of 10Mbps, and requires a network adapter compatible with 10Base-5 cable.

+ **10Base-T Ethernet:** Uses Unshielded Twister Pair (UTP) cabling, which is similar in appearance to a telephone cable; it is also capable of 10Mbps and requires a network adapter compatible with UTP cable.

+ **Fast Ethernet:** Uses UTP and is capable of 100Mbps. Fast Ethernet requires network adapters, hubs, and other network components be capable of transmitting at these speeds and compatible with UTP cable.

Caution   You need to ensure that all peer-to-peer or client/server network hardware (network cards, hubs, and so on) is Ethernet compatible and accepts the cable type you choose (which itself is dependant on the type of Ethernet you select).

Ethernet relies on a technology called Carrier Sense, Multiple Access with Collision Detection (CMSA/CD) to arbitrate access to the media for devices on the network. Each device listens to the network and, if it wants to transmit, waits until no other device is transmitting. If two or more devices transmit at the same time, a collision occurs, and each device waits a randomly chosen amount of time before trying again. Thus, access is not guaranteed to any device because it must wait until there is no network traffic to speak of. In practice, however, this limitation is not much of a problem in relatively small networks.

As the network grows in size and the amount of transmitting increases, collisions become more of a problem. This is why the Ethernet standard imposes a restriction on the number of attached devices in a given network segment as well as the length of the media between devices.

Note   A network *segment* is the part of the network "below" a switch (a device used to connect LANs and form a larger LAN), router (a device used for WAN connectivity), or bridge (a device similar to a switch but able to connect fewer LANs). These devices form a *collision domain* because they all compete for available bandwidth or attention.

Token Ring LANs

Token Ring networks are also a popular LAN architecture and are generally found in IBM-oriented peer-to-peer or client/server networks. The basic topology of the Token Ring is the ring, although logical rings are now the dominant type. (Logical rings, also known as *star-wired rings*, are wired using a star topology.)

In the Token Ring LAN architecture, network access is controlled by the use of a single electronic token that permits a device to "talk" on the network. The token is passed around the network ring from device to device, and when received by a device, one of two events can occur. If the device does not need to transmit, it simply passes the token along to the next device in the ring. If the device needs to transmit, it adds whatever data it has to the token along with destination information and then passes it down the line. When the information gets to the destination, the data is removed, and the token is sent back to the originating device to be recirculated from that point. This process occurs regardless of whether the network is wired with a pure ring or star-wired ring topology.

To help you understand this process, imagine sitting in a ring of 10 people. Each person represents a computer on the Token Ring network. Instead of using a token, you have a pad of paper that you pass from one person to the next, always going in the same order and in the same direction. When the paper is passed to you, it's your turn. You can either write a message or pass the paper to the next person. Nice and orderly isn't it? No one shouts over the voice of anyone else, and everyone gets their turn. The only problem here occurs when someone has to write an extremely long message, or the reply is lengthy. Now add 90 people to your circle. Do you see how it will take longer for you to get the pad of paper and have your turn? These are the two major problems Token Ring networks face.

The prime advantage of the Token Ring architecture is that each device is guaranteed access to the network because the token is passed around in an orderly fashion to every device in the ring.

LAN hardware

LAN hardware requirements are minimal if you are setting up a small peer-to-peer LAN or extensive if you are creating a large client/server LAN that needs access to a WAN or the Internet.

The basic hardware includes the following:

✦ Computer workstations

✦ Network adapter cards for each workstation

✦ At least one hub

Note   Peer-to-peer networks that need access to the Internet may do so by sharing a modem or installing a modem and dedicated phone line to each computer.

✦ Media (cables) that plug into network adapters and connect your computers

You should be familiar with what a computer workstation is so I won't go into this area very much. Suffice it to say that your Windows 2000 Professional computer functions as a workstation, a role that is also referred to as a *client*. Workstations and clients are connected to and request network services from other computers or servers. Workstations should be powerful enough to meet your overall computing needs but do not need raw power to fulfill the role of a network workstation. Servers, on the other hand, generally require additional processing power and memory to manage network services and other server-specific tasks so they should be as powerful as you can realistically afford. Giving you specific advice on how to choose a workstation is difficult to generalize because it depends primarily on what specific tasks you expect to undertake with your computer. Having said that, if your computer can comfortably run Windows 2000 Professional, you should have no trouble with it when it comes to being able to handle networking chores.

Network adapter cards, also known as *network interface cards* or simply *network cards*, are required for connecting workstations to the network. If you are buying new computers for a network, have the network cards preinstalled if possible. That way, you won't have to open the computers and physically install the cards yourself.

Note   When you're buying network cards, it is always a good idea to stick with recognizable name brands and purchase the same cards for all your computers. Having the same card (or at least a card from the same manufacturer) makes figuring out what network card drivers to install much easier in the long run.

Printers also need network cards if you're going to connect them to the network. If you are buying a new printer, look for one labeled "network ready" that has a network card installed. If you already have a printer, check with the manufacturer to see if you can install a network card in that model. You might have to buy a small print port device or upgrade.

Hubs tie your network together. They receive network traffic from a computer they are connected to, regenerate it (to boost its power), and send it to its destination, whether to another computer connected to the hub or through other devices that connect the LAN to a WAN. Hubs come in all sizes, shapes, and prices, but you should pay close attention to how many devices you can connect to one (usually referred to as the *number of ports*) before you purchase it. Small hubs (suitable for peer-to-peer or small client/server networks) can have as few as four ports, and larger, more expensive hubs (for larger client/server networks) can contain upwards of 24 ports.

If you need to connect a large number of devices, consider buying stackable hubs. These are separate hubs that can be connected to form a stack, which can double the number of ports available. The key to stackable hubs is that they form a single logical unit. The fact that there are multiple hubs is invisible to the network.

Another type of hub is the switched hub, which connects two or more LANs to form a single logical LAN with several segments. Switched hubs enable you to have a much larger LAN than would otherwise be possible because the segments divide the network into multiple collision domains, thereby reducing the overall number of collisions and enabling each device to have easier access to the network.

Cables are literally the lifeline of your LAN. There are many types, and the type you choose should be based on the architecture of your LAN and what speeds you need to achieve. Table 19-1 identifies the common LAN cable types.

				Maximum
	Common	Transmission	Cable	Segment
Nomenclature	Name	Speed	Type	Length
10Base-5	Thick Ethernet	10Mbps	Coaxial	500 meters
10Base-2	Thin Ethernet	10Mbps	Coaxial	200 meters
10Base-T	Unshielded Twisted Pair (UTP)	10Mbps	UTP	100 meters
100Base-T4	Fast Ethernet	100Mbps	UTP	100 meters
100BaseFX	Fast Ethernet	100Mbps	Fiber Optic	2 km
100BaseTX	Fast Ethernet	100Mbps	UTP	100 meters

Table 19-1
Common LAN Cable Types

Note I don't discuss wireless LANs or wireless transmission media, but the technology is available. Wireless comes in several flavors: radio, infrared, microwave, and even laser.

So far you have seen all the hardware required to set up a basic peer-to-peer network. The piece of the puzzle that is missing if you want to set up a client/server network is the server.

A server is a computer attached to the network that provides services or access to resources for other computers attached to the same network. Servers also manage user accounts, manage network activity, perform network administration, and manage security for the network.

Depending on the size of your network and the number of requests sent to a server, you may need multiple servers to handle different tasks. Single-server networks are easier to maintain because all server services are contained on one platform. If that server fails, however, and computers have a tendency to fail, your network is dead.

Because of the importance servers play in networking (when they are involved, of course), you should carefully analyze your network architecture (in the general sense), networking goals, and anticipated server workload before you purchase. If your requirements are not intensive and you will not rely on the server to perform mission-critical tasks or store large amounts of sensitive data, then you might be able to get by with a moderately powerful and reasonably priced server. If you want more than this, however, you should bite the bullet and purchase the best, most powerful server you can afford with a corresponding maintenance contract (assuming you have no IT department). This ensures that you have a machine that can handle the workload you intend to put through it, hardware that will not become obsolete overnight, and expert guidance and troubleshooting from the manufacturer.

Finally, if you need to expand the number of computers or devices attached to your LAN or connect two or more LANs to form a WAN, you need additional hardware in the form of repeaters, bridges, routers, or gateways.

Repeaters are a relatively inexpensive way to connect two segments of a LAN that are getting too far apart from each other. As the distance increases, the signal gets weaker, or attenuates. A repeater, as the name states, repeats a transmission, boosting it back to levels necessary to complete its journey. Because repeaters do not perform any other action other than repeating the signal, you can't use them to cross from one type of network to another, such as from an Ethernet to a Token Ring network. For all intents and purposes, the hardware components on either end of the repeater do not know it is there. Its only purpose is to repeat the signal, thus boosting it so that it may travel further.

Bridges are similar to repeaters in that a signal comes in one side, is repeated, and then passes out the other side. What happens in between, however, is different. A bridge can be used to connect LANs of different architectures.

Routers connect networks. The networks can be of different types and use different protocols. Routers talk to other routers. Routers are more fully discussed in the next section "WANs."

Gateways enable communications between completely different environments and are normally specific to the tasks they perform. You can connect a Microsoft-based LAN to an IBM mainframe, for example, with a BackOffice product called SNA Gateway. That particular gateway performs no other task.

WANs

Just as the LAN is designed to link computers, the WAN is designed to link computer networks. Wide area networks come in many different flavors, but the main point of departure from the LAN is distance. WANs span distances far greater than the common LAN, and as a result, different technologies come into play. You can think of a WAN as a network that ties two or more LANs together to form a larger entity. Figure 19-10 illustrates the concept. The largest WAN is the Internet, which ties thousands of computer networks together.

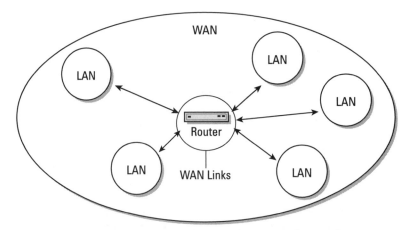

Figure 19-10: A wide area network tying other networks together.

WANs require communications technologies designed to operate over long distances. In general, these are three types of WANs:

✦ Circuit-switched WANs

✦ Dedicated circuit WANs

✦ Packet-switched WANs

Circuit-switched WANs

In circuit-switched networks, which use analog or digital telephone lines, the circuit is established and maintained for the duration of the communications session only. If you are using a dial-up telephone connection, the session lasts as long as you remain connected to the circuit. During the session, the data traverses a path that does not change over the time period you are using the circuit. In circuit-switched WANs, the data being transmitted does not include addressing information (which specifies where to travel along the transmission media to get to its destination) because the path that it travels is a dedicated link as long as the communications session is active. It therefore relies on the underlying circuit-switched technology to provide a transmission path and does not concern itself with those details. In circuit-switched networks, it is up to the receiver to reassemble the data packets in the correct order and perform error control. As soon as the session is terminated, the circuit goes back into a pool of available resources.

A good example of circuit switching is your common telephone circuit. Prior to the moment when you pick up the phone, dial, and establish a connection, the circuit you just occupied was either not in use or just released from use. The circuit you are currently using was not yours to begin with and will be released from your control after you hang up. Likewise, when you initiate a communications session by using your ISDN adapter and connecting to another computer with an ISDN adapter through a circuit-switched network, you are using a circuit that is established only when you make the connection and then terminated when you hang up.

Common circuit-switched connections are available through dial-up telephone lines, Switched-56 (a digital line capable of 56Kbps speeds), and Integrated Services Digital Network (ISDN).

To use dial-up telephone lines, you need modems for each sending and receiving node of your network, and you are limited to a maximum transfer rate of approximately 56Kbps. When you dial and connect, your circuit is established and remains in effect until you end your communications session. Switched-56 requires a special Channel Service Unit/Data Service Unit (CSU/DSU) that dials up and establishes the communications session. A CSU/DSU converts the signals used in computers and LANs to a digital signal compatible with digital phone lines. Using ISDN requires ISDN adapters and CSU/DSUs at each node of your network and is capable of transferring data at a rate of 64Kpbs.

Dedicated-circuit WANs

Unlike circuit-switched networks, where the circuits come and go as they are used (even though the path is static once the session is established), the dedicated-circuit (also called *point-to-point link*) WAN uses circuits that are assigned for its use and available to no one else. This means that you have a permanent physical connection between two points. The advantage here is that the line is available at all times, and you do not have to establish a connection every time you use it.

Common dedicated circuits are the dedicated analog, such as a normal telephone line only capable of carrying much more data at a faster rate due to its quality, a T-1 line, which is a conditioned digital telephone line, and a T-3 line, which is a much larger and faster T-1 line. T-1 lines, although expensive, are widely used in WANs today and are capable of 1.544Mbps transmission speeds. Fractional T-1s, which involve leasing one or more of the 24 individual channels of a full T-1 line, are also available. T-3 lines use fiber-optic cables rather than copper wiring, can transmit up to 45Mbps, and are expensive.

Packet-switched WANs

WANs that rely on packet switching do not use switched or dedicated circuits that establish a single or permanent point-to-point connection. Instead, packet-switched networks transmit data in packets that travel along various routes of a mesh-like web of connections to their final destination. The web is made up of switches that determine which route the packet should take to its destination at that moment in time. When the packets arrive at their destination, they are reassembled in their correct order for further processing.

Figure 19-11 shows a packet-switched network. Notice that there is more than one potential path from the source to the destination. The path is never fixed. Packet switching can be performed using the X.25 protocol, which can use analog telephone lines, or frame relay, which uses T-1 or T-3 lines.

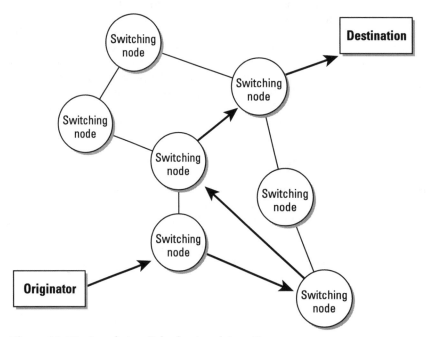

Figure 19-11: A packet-switched network in action.

Of Protocols and Packets

As I mentioned earlier, software protocols are necessary for meaningful communications to take place across a network. Protocols are nothing more than rules that define how communication takes place and are necessary for both LANs and WANs. Some protocols are routable, which means that information about the path from the source to the destination is included with data. This information is used by routers to determine the actual route the data takes through any intervening network nodes. If there is only one possible path from the source to the destination, as is the case in LANs and some WANs, routable protocols are not necessary.

NetBEUI

NetBEUI, which is short for NetBIOS Extended User Interface, was originally developed by IBM as a protocol to be used by local workgroups within a LAN. Microsoft has further refined and developed it to the point where it is the standard Microsoft LAN protocol.

Because it was created for use within one segment of a LAN (and because routers were not so common at the time), NetBEUI is a nonroutable protocol and cannot be used to transport data from one LAN to another or out to a WAN. Because it is built into the Microsoft operating system and not used by other computer platforms, its use is limited to networks (or devices within a network) that use a Microsoft operating system.

For small- to medium-sized networks featuring computers running Microsoft Windows, NetBEUI is a great choice for transporting data within the confines of a LAN.

IPX/SPX

Internet Packet Exchange/Sequenced Package Exchange (IPX/SPX) is a proprietary Novell protocol suite that is routable and thus suitable for use in LANs, WANs, or the Internet.

IPX/SPX, which began life as a LAN protocol, now faces limited support due to its proprietary nature and the overall success of other LAN protocols and TCP/IP. UNIX and Macintosh computers do not use this protocol to communicate with other computers within LANs, instead relying on TCP/IP and AppleTalk (and lately TCP/IP in the Apple community), respectively, and TCP/IP for WAN connectivity.

TCP/IP

Transmission Control Protocol/Internet Protocol (TCP/IP) is the protocol for communicating on the Internet. It is arguably the most important network protocol because you can use it on LANs, WANs, and of course on the Internet. It is really a suite, or collection, of protocols designed to facilitate high-speed communications between large networks (often called *internetworks*) consisting of many wide area networks.

The core protocols of the TCP/IP suite are IP, Address Resolution Protocol (ARP), Internet Control Message Protocol (ICMP), Internet Group Management Protocol (IGMP), TCP, and the User Datagram Protocol (UDP).

In addition to these, application protocols such as HyperText Transfer Protocol (HTTP), File Transfer Protocol (FTP), Simple Mail Transfer Protocol (SMTP), Telnet, the Domain Name System (DNS), Routing Information Protocol (RIP), and Simple Network Management Protocol (SNMP) are used to perform various functions.

Here are the main features of TCP/IP:

✦ It is a routable protocol, which means it can span WANs.

✦ You can run multiple communications sessions using TCP/IP from a single computer. This means you can be using a Web browser, running a Telnet session, and be downloading files with FTP simultaneously – even if every session is communicating to a different network address.

✦ It has built-in support from all the major platforms in use today.

✦ Multiple applications, such as Web browsers, Telnet, and FTP clients run off of the TCP/IP protocol.

✦ Everything that uses TCP/IP must have an IP address.

Each device using TCP/IP must have an IP address. This address is 32 bits in length and is organized into four 8-bit fields, called *octets*. To make it easier to use and remember IP addresses, each octet is converted from binary to decimal.

Figure 19-12 shows an IP address in both binary and decimal notations. You can see from the figure that if you had to remember the binary value for a typical IP address, your life would be much more difficult!

Of Bytes and Men

Why have I chosen to include a sidebar on the decimal and binary numbering systems? Well, first of all, I find it extremely interesting! You may not care about that, so I'll give you another reason: IP addresses (discussed right after this sidebar) are composed of four 8-bit values. To begin to understand the power and limitations of the current method of identifying IP addresses, you should have some knowledge of how binary numbering works. If you choose to learn more about IP numbers, subnet masking, and more advanced IP address topics, this knowledge can serve you well.

Human beings learn to count by using our fingers (and possibly toes). They form a very, pardon the pun, "handy" calculator conveniently carried with you wherever you go. Homo sapiens have developed a numbering system based, therefore, on the number 10. It is called a base-10 or decimal numbering system. Each digit has 10 possible values. For example, a 1-digit number can be any of these possible values:

```
0 1 2 3 4 5 6 7 8 or 9
```

If you add more digits (moving to the left of the original number), the second is called "tens", the third "hundreds", the forth "thousands" and so on. Notice that each digit is an order of 10 greater than the previous digit.

For our purposes, I want you to think now in terms of states. Each digit in the decimal numbering system can have ten states. Each state represents the capability to store data. Having multiple digits increases the total number of states available to store information. A three-digit number in the base-10 numbering system can be any of 1,000 values, or states, from 000 to 999.

Computers do not have fingers or toes, so they cannot learn to count as you have. In fact, the computers that have been designed and built recognize only two values, 1 and 0. Underneath the case, the computer is actually comparing two different voltage levels (some computers recognize changes in voltages), usually 0 and +5 volts. If the voltage is 0v the computer recognizes this as a 0, and if the voltage is +5v, the computer recognizes a 1. I suppose it would be possible to create processors, memory, data storage, and communications devices that can discriminate between ten different voltage levels, but thus far this has been impractical.

This leads me to the fact that our computers use a binary – having two states – numbering system. The smallest unit of storage in the binary system is called a bit, which can contain one of two states, 0 or 1. This is obviously less than the decimal system. Each bit you add expands the total storage capacity by an order of 2.

Ascending one level in binary terminology, you come to the nibble. This is a 4-bit string, able to store 16 discrete values.

A byte (sometimes called an *octet*) is comprised of 8 bits. Because each bit can be either a 1 or 0, the total combination of different values for 8 bits is 2 to the eighth power, or 256.

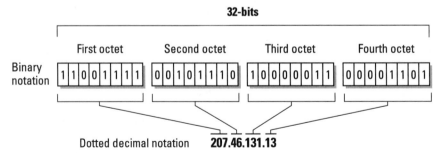

Figure 19-12: The layout of an IP address.

IP addresses are organized into classes in order to identify networks of differing sizes, with each IP address containing a network and a host ID whose lengths are determined by the class of the address. Figure 19-13 presents a graphical view of how IP addresses are classed and the breakout of the network and host IDs.

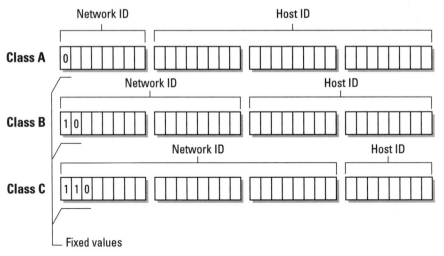

Figure 19-13: IP address classes complete with network and host identification.

If you do the math, you find that there can be 126 Class A networks each with 16,777,214 IP addresses, 16,384 Class B networks with 65,534 IP addresses each, and 2,097,152 Class C networks with 254 IP addresses per network. Table 19-2 shows a few sample IP addresses of the three classes in binary and decimal notation.

Class	Decimal IP	Binary IP

Table 19-2
IP Address Examples in Binary and Decimal

Class	Decimal IP	Binary IP
A	100.42.36.200	01100100 00101010 00100100 11001000
B	150.60.95.1	10010110 00111100 01011111 00000001
C	209.9.32.155	11010001 00001001 00100000 10011011

On a more practical note, your organization probably has a portion of a Class C address or possibly one or more Class C addresses because Class A and B addresses are reserved for large organizations. This means that you are limited to 254 IP addresses per Class C address. Knowing how they work and what IP addresses you can use ensures your network can function using TCP/IP.

AppleTalk

The AppleTalk protocol (actually another suite of protocols) was developed by Apple and is used exclusively on their line of Macintosh computers and Macintosh clones. You can think of it as the NetBEUI of Macs. The best feature of AppleTalk is that it is simple to set up and use.

When Windows and Macintosh computers need to communicate on a network, or if your Macs are connected to the Internet, you need to use TCP/IP.

PPTP

Point To Point Tunneling Protocol, or PPTP, is used to establish a Virtual Private Network (VPN) between nodes across public-switched networks such as the Internet. Using PPTP, you can connect to your Internet Service Provider using TCP/IP and then run a LAN protocol such as NetBEUI through PPTP. PPTP wraps, or tunnels, the LAN protocol within itself.

PPTP is the essential technology behind Virtual Private Networks, which enable you to connect to the Internet via TCP/IP, then connect to a remote LAN, and use the LAN protocols.

DHCP

Dynamic Host Configuration Protocol (DCHP) is a protocol designed to make your life simpler if you have a large TCP/IP-based LAN and is especially effective if you have a limited number of IP addresses. DCHP enables you to centrally manage a group of IP addresses and dynamically assign them to machines as they require connection sessions using TCP/IP.

This is a great idea for two reasons. Assigning unique IP addresses to every device on your network can be a real pain if you have more than a few devices because you must touch each device to configure its TCP/IP setting. It also gives you the flexibility and power of managing all IP addresses centrally, reclaiming unused IP addresses to be used when another device needs it.

If you are using a TCP/IP-based network, all the devices on the network need to have an IP address specifically assigned to them. There can be no duplicates. Going to each machine and physically configuring the TCP/IP properties in a large network is a huge time drain. Not only do you have to assign an IP address to each computer and record it for your records to avoid duplication, you also have to assign IP addresses and every other device on the network, including network hardware such as hubs and routers.

To get DCHP to work on your network, you need a DHCP server, clients set up to use DNS, a pool of IP addresses, and your gateway and subnet mask information.

Setting up the server is beyond the scope of this book, but you should know that all versions of Windows NT and Windows 2000 are ready to use DHCP right out of the box. You need the server because this device manages the IP addresses, and when a workstation boots up, it assigns an IP address to them.

Choosing the right protocol

Choosing the right protocol is an important task because all your networked devices must have compatible protocols installed and configured correctly in order to communicate with each other. The good news is that you can use multiple protocols at the same time and enable the computer to figure out which one to use in a given situation.

For simple LANs with computers using the Windows operating system, NetBEUI works just fine as long as you are not connected to the Internet.

Once you cross into WANs and the Internet, you have to install TCP/IP. You don't have to uninstall NetBEUI for TCP/IP to work; just install TCP/IP over the top of NetBEUI, and everything will work fine.

For heterogeneous networks consisting of a combination of Microsoft, Apple, or UNIX machines, you can use NetBEUI and AppleTalk if the Mac and Windows computers won't be needing to speak to each other. In this scenario, the Macintosh computers can detect and communicate with other Macs, and computers running Windows can do the same with other Windows computers. TCP/IP, however, is the bottom line of compatibility. If your different computers need to communicate with each other, you should rely on TCP/IP.

LANs for Dummies: Setting Up a Small Network

No, this isn't a *Dummies* book, but I just couldn't resist the temptation to use that title for this section! Now that you've read about the different network types and protocols, you might want to create one of your own. In this section, I show you how to design and create a common, inexpensive network with the following characteristics:

✦ Four computer workstations running Windows 2000 Professional

✦ Peer-to-peer type

✦ Star topology with a hub

✦ Ethernet 10Base-T architecture

✦ One modem connected to one computer and shared with the others for Internet access

Nuts and bolts: what you need to get started

For this example, I've chosen a star-wired Ethernet LAN with a hub because it's easy to initially set up and expand in the future. You can easily add computers, other resources, and servers to this type of configuration later if you choose.

Here's a recipe of ingredients you need to build this small network. I've made a few assumptions, so please salt to taste.

Computers	Four IBM-compatible computers to be used as workstations running Windows 2000 Professional (after all, that's what this book is about). This will form a small workgroup that can share documents, a printer, and Internet access.
Printer	One printer with a 10Base-T Ethernet card.
Network cards	Four 10Base-T (UTP) Ethernet cards with a PCI or ISA bus depending on your computer. (Choose PCI over ISA if you have a PCI slot because they communicate with the computer faster). Make sure to get cards that accept UTP cable. These are identified as having an RJ-45 connection.
Hub	One five-port (or larger) 10Base-T Ethernet hub. Make sure to get the variety that is for UTP cable, which is identified by having RJ-45 ports.

Cat 5 UTP cable	Five 25-foot lengths of Category 5 UTP cable for peer-to-hub connectivity. Although you can get by with lower quality cable (Cat 5 is the best), I recommend using Cat 5 to ensure reliable transmissions and upward expandability if you should desire. You can buy cable in mass quantity, but you have to wire the RJ-45 connectors yourself. I recommend getting assembled cables.
Modem	One 56K (56,000 bit per second) modem. I prefer modems of the external variety because you can turn them off to reset them without having to turn your computer off. 56K is the minimum modem speed you should buy, and you should check with your ISP and purchase a compatible modem. If you need faster access, you should consider installing an ISDN modem or leasing a dedicated phone line.

Note   If you don't want to shop for these items separately, package deals are available that include a hub, network cards, cables. There are too many to mention here, but you can find them online at the various computer hardware retailers and outlets. You can also buy computers and printers with network cards installed.

Getting your feet wet (or elbows dirty)

Once you've purchased the necessary equipment, you're ready to actually install your network.

Note   Refer to Chapter 4 and Chapter 20 for more detailed explanations on installing your network cards and configuring your computers to access the network.

1. Physically place the computers and printer in the location of your choice.

2. Install the network cards in your computers and printer and connect your external modem to one computer. If you purchased computers or a printer with network cards, you won't have to install them. You should, however, look at the back of the computer and find the network card. It should have an open port that looks like a telephone jack (but is a bit larger). Connect your modem to a phone outlet with a telephone line.

3. Place the hub in a central location.

4. Connect the network cables to all the computers and printer and then into the ports on the hub. Because you're using UTP, doing so should be easy. Simply insert one end of the cable connector (it looks like a telephone plug) into your network card and then plug the other end (it looks exactly the same, and there is no difference between the two ends) into the hub. Following this, turn the hub on.

5. Turn on the computer that has the modem attached (don't forget the modem, too) and log into the computer. Windows 2000 should detect your network card and modem, automatically install the correct hardware drivers, and automatically set up a local connection for you. Refer to Chapter 4 and Chapter 11 if you need further assistance in installing new hardware. Select Start ➪ Settings ➪ Network and Dial-up Connections ➪ Make New Connection to create a new dial-up connection. Chapter 12 has more information on dial-up networking if you need it.

6. Once you have configured your dial-up connection, test it by selecting the connection and double-clicking it to connect to your ISP, then close the connection after you've successfully connected. Now it's time to set up shared modem access. Right-click the connection (in the Network and Dial-up Connections window) and choose Properties, then select the Shared Access tab. Select Enable shared access for this connection to turn sharing on. Chapter 20 has more information on setting up a shared modem..

7. Now you can turn on all the computers and log into them to ensure they are connected to the network. The easiest way to do this is to select My Network Places from the Desktop, then open Computers Near Me. You should see all four computers in the window.

8. If all your computers are connected to the network, it's time to set up the network printer. You should read thoroughly the documentation that came with your printer to complete this task. Once the printer is set up, you can add a network printer through the Start ➪ Settings ➪ Printers window by choosing Add Printer, then adding a new network printer.

9. When all these tasks are accomplished, you can continue to configure each computer by setting up shared drives, files, and folders, as discussed in Chapter 25.

Securing your network

Security is a prime concern for network administrators. Knowledge is power, and robust security measures all strive to control knowledge of your business practices, products, confidential records, and personal information. You can do several things to improve the security of your network, all of which can be defeated by a determined, well-placed individual bent on cracking into your system. Having said that, you shouldn't throw your hands up in the air and not try! If you make yourself a hard target, then perhaps the hacker will move on to an easier network.

The first, and often overlooked, line of defense is the physical security of your network and attached devices. Can anyone walk into your building and gain access to your computers, servers, hubs, or routers? Hopefully not! From the front door to the location of each computer, printer, and server, you should have barriers in place to thwart illegitimate access, such as locked doors. If you are fortunate enough to have actual offices, all employees should lock their doors when they go home to prevent a person from sauntering in and having a private session with their computer. If the office is set up with cubicles or open workstations, then if possible the entire room should be secured when everyone goes home. Many businesses have electronically encoded security cards that employees must swipe through a reader to enter their building or floor.

If you are running a client/server network, where is your server? Is it sitting out in the middle of the room for everyone to see? If so, you should seriously consider moving the server to a secure room or closet. This is probably your most sensitive piece of equipment and should be highly secure from unauthorized access.

Speaking of access, controlling access to computers and other network components is also a vital part of taking security measures. I am referring not to physical access to a particular machine but to logon access. Consider limiting the time period when people can log onto your network.

Passwords form another important link in the security chain. Although passwords are sometimes a pain to administer, forcing people to accept hard-to-guess passwords is vital. I can't tell you how many times I have been able to guess someone's password! Windows 2000 Professional can be configured to force requirements such as minimum and maximum password length and password expiration time by using Group Policy, which is discussed briefly in Chapter 27.

It is also important to keep abreast of software patches and upgrades for your servers and workstations. When software makers uncover security holes, after a period of development, they patch them. If you aren't running the latest version of your server or workstation software, you could have security holes in your system that you could fix for free.

Finally, know your enemy. If security is a important issue with you, consider investing some time and money learning all you can about your system and how people could hack into it at all points in your network. Devise a plan of attack for dealing with possible break-ins and try to break in yourself. You might find it's easier that you think!

Planning ahead

The design of the small peer-to-peer network I showed you how to build is sound, but you can improve upon several areas if you want to plan for more capabilities in the future. Unfortunately, most of these suggestions cost more money if you decide to implement them at the outset, but they may save you time and money later.

First, you could consider setting aside an area, ideally a large closet of some sort, to be the wiring nexus of your network. You can install a rack (used to mount hubs, routers, and other network hardware) and larger hubs here in the future. Hand-in-hand with this is hard-wiring the cables that run from your computers, printers, and other devices to the hub. A contractor should do this work unless you have done it before. In addition, you should consider installing more hard-wired connections (those that are physically integrated into your building structure) than you currently need so you can easily expand your network in the future.

Another idea is to buy a hub that has more ports than you currently need. If you need four, buy an eight-port hub. If you really want to go hog-wild, you can buy 16-port stackable hubs or even 16-port stackable switched hubs, but these hubs are fairly expensive.

Doctor Mike's Network: A Case Study

Dr. Michael Modesitt, the educational technology coordinator for a school district in Indiana, has been building (as computer networks are rarely finished!) a computer network over the last few years that illustrates many of the networking concepts I have shown you in this chapter. It is a perfect illustration of creating several LANs and tying them into a WAN that has a direct line to the Internet.

General characteristics

Dr. Modesitt works for a school district that has approximately 4,000 students and hundreds of teaching, administrative, and support staff. Virtually all of the administrators, teachers, and support staff have computers on their desktops wired into a building's LAN, and almost every school has computer labs with 15 to 25 computers.

✦ The school district consists of 14 major buildings, most of which are located in a single city, but four elementary schools are out in the county and range from 5 to 20 miles from the center of the city. Figure 19-14 shows the basic geographical layout of the different buildings within the city and county.

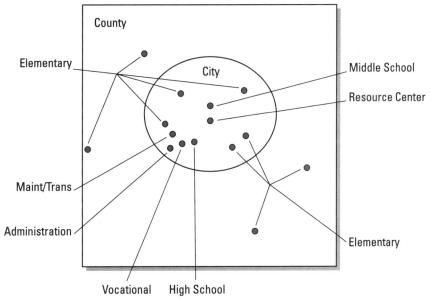

Figure 19-14: The physical layout of the featured network.

The central node

The physical point of Internet connectivity for the entire school district is the Resource Center. As you can see in Figure 19-15, a leased T-1 line passes through a CSU/DSU and into a Cisco 4000 Series router.

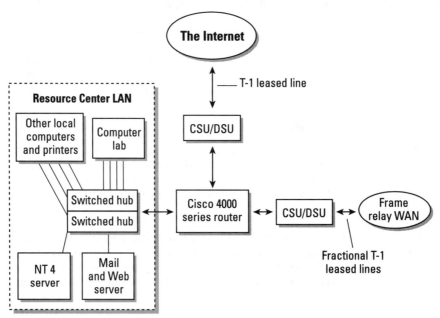

Figure 19-15: Layout of the central node.

All incoming and outgoing Internet traffic goes through this connection, and the router is the master router (or hop router) for the district, storing all routing tables used in the district. Another CSU/DSU is connected to the router that goes out to the frame relay WAN.

The router also has an Ethernet port that is used for the Resource Center LAN. Several important servers that manage district resources are attached to this LAN. The Mail and Web server provides local Web services as well as e-mail accounts. A proxy server, not physically located in the district, is used to control access to potentially offensive material.

Forming the WAN

Each building is connected to the Resource Center by leased lines to form a WAN with a star topology. Most of these are 128K fractional T-1 connections (they have leased a portion of the bandwidth of a full T-1 line, resulting in a much lower cost but also much less bandwidth) with one exception. The Administration building, High School, Vocational School, and Maintenance buildings are close enough together to form a LAN that has a 384K leased line to the Resource Center as its WAN connection.

Figure 19-16 shows the general layout of the WAN with each building having a CSU/DSU and router. All WAN transmissions use the TCP/IP protocol suite.

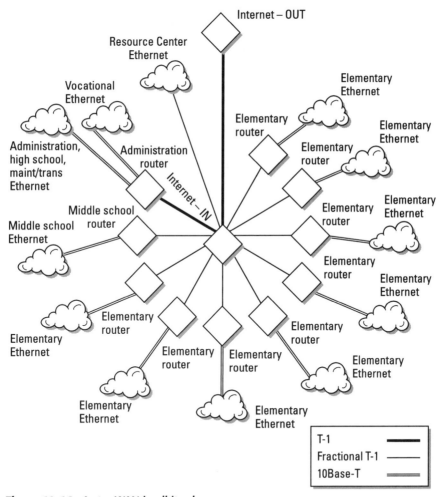

Figure 19-16: A star WAN in all its glory.

General LAN characteristics

Within each building is a 10Base-T Ethernet client/server LAN with a star configuration. Figure 19-17 shows the general layout of a typical LAN within the district.

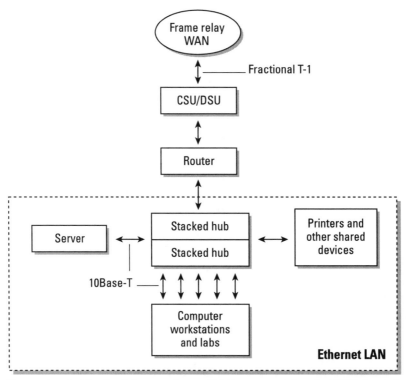

Figure 19-17: The basic layout of a real LAN, connected to the WAN through a frame relay cloud and connected to the Internet through a single point.

Because the elementary buildings all use Macintosh computers, a Macintosh G3 server is at each of these locations, with Windows NT 4 servers present at the Resource Center, High School, and Middle School.

The primary function of the server at each site at this time is to provide application, security, and printer services.

Summary

Wow, what a chapter. I covered a lot of ground and mentioned a lot of buzzwords that are prevalent in the networking world, and I hope you have come away with a better idea of what networking is and even how to build a small network yourself. If I were to test you, the foot stompers would be:

✦ A network consists of two or more computers linked electronically to communicate. Through this communication, you share information, resources, and services.

✦ A local area network links together computers and devices and is normally contained within a building.

✦ A wide area network links together networks over large distances.

✦ Peer-to-peer networks have an egalitarian method of accessing network resources.

✦ Servers control access to resources in a client/server network.

✦ Different wiring topologies are used in networking: the bus, ring, and star.

✦ Ethernet is the most popular LAN architecture.

✦ LANs consist primarily of computers and other devices such as printers, hubs, and cables.

✦ WANs consist of routers, communication media, and CSU/DSUs.

✦ TCP/IP is the communications standard for the Internet but is also used widely in many WANs.

The next chapter shows you how to set up Windows 2000 Professional in a networked environment, how to install the right protocols and services, and how to share files, folders, and drives with other computers in your network.

✦   ✦   ✦

Networking Windows 2000

Networking is supposed to make your life easier, or at least expand your possibilities. The trouble with that idea is that previous versions of Windows (NT and 9x) weren't as user friendly as they could have been when it came to setting up your computer to access a local area or dial-up network. Windows 2000 Professional is supposed to change all that, and believe it or not, it does go a long way toward making the task of networking your computer easier. When you install the operating system or turn on the computer for the first time, it is easy to get up and running on your network. After that it's up to you to make the most of it!

The previous chapter showed you the fundamentals of networking: what networks are and how they are configured. This chapter focuses on step-by-step procedures for using the networking capabilities of Windows 2000 Professional. You learn how to set up your computer on a local area network, configure your protocols, use My Network places, share files and printers among computers, and manage users and groups.

Using Network and Dial-up Connections

The central access point for your Windows 2000 Professional networking settings is Network and Dial-up Connections. You can get there in a number of ways, including two ways to access it from the Start Menu:

1. Click ➪ Settings ➪ Control Panel.

2. Choose Network and Dial-up Connections.

Alternatively,

1. Click Start ⇨ Settings ⇨ Network and Dial-up Connections.

2. Choose Make a New Connection or select an existing one. You can also right-click the Network and Dial-up Connections menu as shown in Figure 20-1 and choose to open or explore the Control Panel.

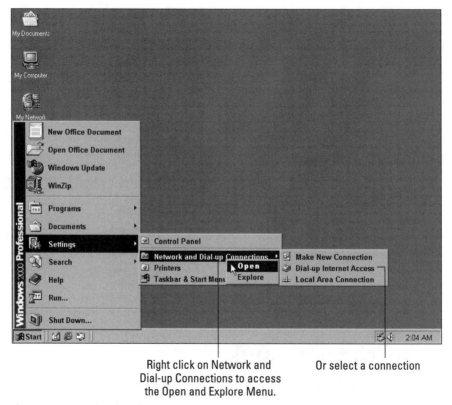

Right click on Network and
Dial-up Connections to access
the Open and Explore Menu.

Or select a connection

Figure 20-1: Right-click the Network and Dial-up Connections menu to see more options.

You can also reach Network and Dial-up Connections from within Windows Explorer:

1. Expand the My Computer tree (if it is not already expanded) by clicking the plus sign.

2. Expand the Control Panel folder.

3. Select Network and Dial-up Connections.

Alternatively, if you're in My Computer or an ordinary folder, you can select Network and Dial-up Connections in the left pane of the window. Figure 20-2 shows an open folder with the See also menu options listed. If you select anything in the window, the menu options are replaced by other context-sensitive information. If you want the menu options back, just click an empty area in the window to deselect the item.

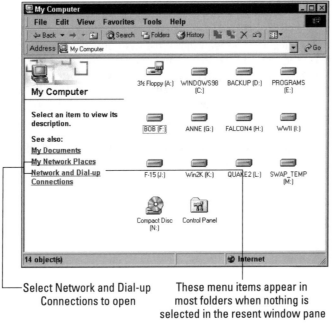

Select Network and Dial-up Connections to open

These menu items appear in most folders when nothing is selected in the resent window pane

Figure 20-2: Network and Dial-up Connections is just a click away from most folders.

Note   Not all folders display these menu items. Folders that are system related tend to display unique information relating to that folder. In addition, if you have disabled Web content in folders, you won't see the menus.

From Network and Dial-up Connections, you can do the following:

✦ Use the Network Connection Wizard to create a new connection.

✦ Open a network connection.

✦ Access the properties of a connection.

✦ Change you computer's identity on the network.

✦ Add additional network components.

✦ Delete a network connection.

The following detailed steps show you how to perform each of these tasks.

Creating a new network connection

If you had a network card in your system (and were connected to a LAN) when Windows 2000 Professional was installed, you should already have a working local area connection (the Windows 2000 term for your local area network), although it may not be completely configured. Therefore, you shouldn't have to create or even start a local area connection. If you do need to create another network connection, the following steps illustrate how to set up any of five available types of connections.

Note   By "not completely configured," I mean that Windows 2000 installs a base set of network protocols and services (TCP/IP, File and Print Sharing for Microsoft Networks, and Client for Microsoft Networks) but does not perform such tasks as setting an IP address or DNS Server address automatically. Therefore, if your LAN uses TCP/IP as a network protocol (internally or for you to establish a connection to the Internet), you have to configure these settings manually.

1. Select Make New Connection. This action launches the Network Connection Wizard shown in Figure 20-3. Click Next.

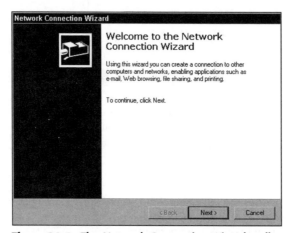

Figure 20-3: The Network Connection Wizard walks you through the connection process.

Note   Click Cancel at any time to abort the process without making changes to your networking setup.

2. On the next screen, you choose a Network Connection Type. Figure 20-4 shows your choices:

Choose Dial-up to private network if you are using a modem or ISDN to connect to a private network. This is different than an Internet connection, which connects to the Internet directly through an Internet Service Provider

(ISP). A private dial-up connection may lead to Internet access ultimately, but these are network resources otherwise unavailable through ordinary ISPs.

Select Dial-up to the Internet if you are setting up a standard dial-up Internet connection through your modem or ISDN line.

Select Connect to a private network through the Internet if you want to create a virtual private network by connecting to an ISP and "tunneling."

Select Accept incoming connections to turn your computer into a host for dial-up access.

Choose Connect directly to another computer if you need to connect two computers through your parallel port using a special DirectParallel cable, serial port, or infrared.

Note

Windows 2000 abides by the Infrared Data Association (IrDA) standards and protocols for infrared data transmission and features the Wireless Link file transfer program, infrared printing capability (IrLPT), and infrared image transfer capability (IrTRAN-P). The IrDA Winsock API supports third-party software and hardware products such as digital pagers. Windows should automatically detect and install infrared drivers if it detects IrDA hardware in your computer.

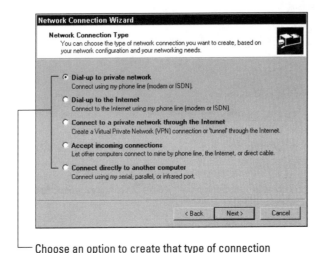

Choose an option to create that type of connection

Figure 20-4: It's time to make a decision about the type of network connection you want.

What happens next depends on the type of connection you choose. If you want to create an Internet connection, refer to Chapter 12 for complete instructions. Similarly, if you want to create a virtual private network, fast forward to Chapter 21. I cover the other three types of connections in the following sections.

Dial up to private network

The Internet is a public network that most people connect to with modems and telephone lines from home and through their network at work. A dial up private network is a network that is not publicly available but may use the same technologies as the Internet. Many corporations and schools have dial-up access to their networks. Setting up this connection is very similar to setting up an Internet connection.

1. Start the Network Connection Wizard.

2. Choose Dial-up to private network and select Next.

3. Enter a telephone number, as shown in Figure 20-5. Continue by selecting Next.

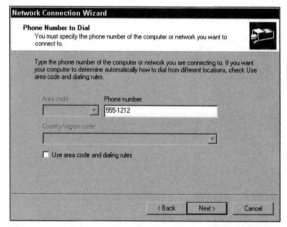

Figure 20-5: Enter the telephone number of the private network for your modem to dial.

4. Identify whether you wish to make this connection available for all users or just yourself and select Next.

5. Name your connection and select Finish.

The Connect Dial-up Connection dialog box launches, as shown in Figure 20-6, and enables you to enter your user name, password, and logon domain for the dial-up private network. Select Properties before you dial and enter any networking information such as your TCP/IP data. Consult the network administrator of the network you are dialing into to confirm that you have the correct values for these items.

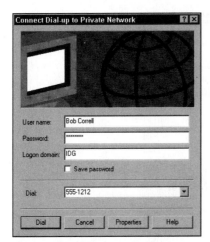

Figure 20-6: Enter your name, password, and domain and then connect to the private network.

Accept incoming connection

Accepting incoming connections enables other people to connect to your computer through a modem, the Internet, or a direct connection. If you already have a local area connection, everyone on your LAN already has access to your computer so you don't need to create this type of connection.

1. The Network Connection Wizard asks you to choose a connection device, as shown in Figure 20-7. This most likely is a modem. If you want to set the modem's properties, click Properties before continuing. When you are ready to go on, click Next.

2. On the next screen, you decide whether or not to enable virtual private connections. This is the reverse of setting up a dial-up connection to a virtual private network. Instead of dialing out, you are choosing to accept incoming calls to create the VPN. Choose your poison and click Next.

3. The next dialog box enables you to select the names of users who can access this connection. These are users that are defined locally for use on this machine. Click the checkbox next to the user's name as shown in Figure 20-8. You can also add local users by clicking the Add button. To change user passwords, click the Properties button. When you're finished, click Next.

Figure 20-7: My modem is the only device capable of receiving an incoming connection so I choose it.

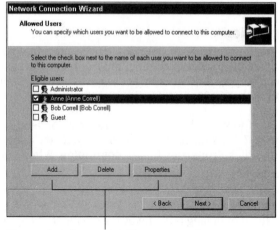

Choose these items to modify your users list

Figure 20-8: Select the users that you want to have access to this connection.

4. The next step is to choose the networking components, or protocols. It's best to accept the default values Windows 2000 supplies. Figure 20-9 shows this dialog box, and you can even install components, if necessary, from this location. When you're finished, click Next.

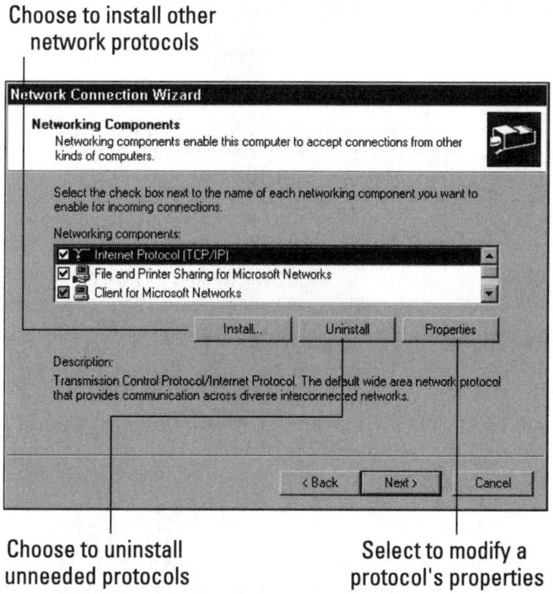

Choose to install other
network protocols

Choose to uninstall
unneeded protocols

Select to modify a
protocol's properties

Figure 20-9: Choose the networking components
your connection supports. The defaults, shown here,
are fine for me.

5. On the last wizard screen, name your connection and click Finish.

Your new incoming connection appears in Networking and Dial-up, and your
computer is now set up to accept incoming connections.

Connect directly to another computer

In some cases it is impractical to set up an entire network due to cost or equipment
limitations, but you still want to connect two computers to share files or printers.
Creating this type of connection enables you to physically connect two computers
to enjoy the benefits of resource sharing as well as identify the host and guest
computers. Direct connections require special hardware to set up. This involves
using one of several types of cables or devices: a serial cable, a DirectParallel cable,
a modem, an ISDN device.

1. The Network Connection Wizard asks whether your computer is to be the
host (has the resources needed by another computer) or guest (needs the
resources of the other computer). Choose Host or Guest, depending on the
role of your computer and click Next. Figure 20-10 shows this dialog box.

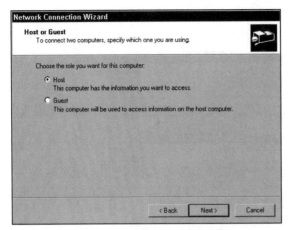

Figure 20-10: Choose Host if you have the resources or Guest if the other computer does.

2. Select a device for the connection as shown in Figure 20-11. You should select the port (LPT or COM) that you are using to connect the computers. Choose Properties to configure the port if necessary. When you're finished, click Next.

Select to view more devices

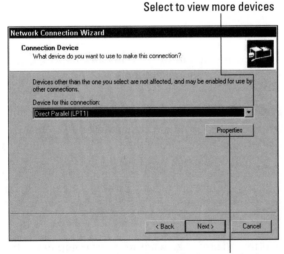

Modify a device's properties here

Figure 20-11: Choose the physical connection type between the two computers.

3. If you selected Guest in step 1 you won't see this dialog box, but if you chose Host, you can select from locally created users to grant them access to this computer via this connection. You can also choose to create this connection for your user profile only or for all people who use this computer.

4. Name your connection and click Finish.

If you've made it this far and the new connection has appeared in Networking and Dial-up Connections, you're done!

Disconnecting from a LAN

Besides creating new connections and connecting to existing connections, another option available in Network and Dial-up Connections is disconnecting from any connections that are currently active.

Note

Hardware profiles, discussed in Chapter 4, are another means to configure selective LAN connectivity. For example, you may have a profile for use at work that uses a network card to connect you to your LAN but have a different profile for use at home.

To disconnect from the LAN, follow these steps:

1. Click Start ➪ Settings ➪ Network and Dial-up Connections.

2. Right-click Local Area Connection.

3. Click Disconnect.

Connecting to a LAN

If you disconnect from your local area network, Windows 2000 Professional remembers and does not attempt to connect the next time you log in. This setup is ideal for mobile users who may not always be connected. To reconnect, follow these steps:

1. Click Start ➪ Settings ➪ Network and Dial-up Connections ➪ Local Area Connection.

2. You're done! There is no second step. Selecting Local Area Connection prompts Windows 2000 Professional to reestablish your network connection.

Setting up shared modem access

You can access other functions through Network and Dial-up Connections, such as the capability to set up shared modem access. Some offices and many homes have only one dial-up connection but multiple computers that need Internet access. Windows 2000 Professional has made setting up modem sharing a breeze.

Caution
You should not use this feature if your computer is on a local network that has Windows 2000 Server Domain Controllers or DHCP servers, or with systems already configured with static IP addresses. The computer with the shared modem becomes the DHCP server for the computers that share its modem and dynamically allocate IP addresses to those machines as they start up. In addition, its own IP address configuration is changed. This procedure is ideally suited for home or small office networks that do not have Windows 2000 Server (or other servers) and that instead rely on the computer that hosts the shared connection to manage the network configuration and Internet connection.

1. Click Start ➪ Settings ➪ Control Panel.

2. Choose Network and Dial-up Connections.

3. Right-click your dial-up connection and choose Properties, as shown in Figure 20-12.

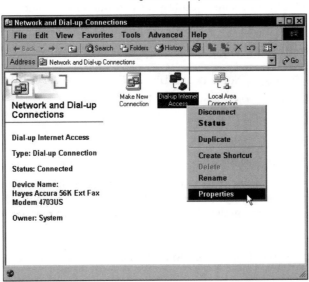

Figure 20-12: Right-click to access your connection's properties.

4. Click the Shared Access tab.

5. Select Enable shared access for this connection to turn on sharing, as shown in Figure 20-13.

6. You have the option of turning on autodialing. Select Enable on-demand dialing if you would like the other computers to be able to fire up your modem when they need access to the Internet.

Enables on demand dialing

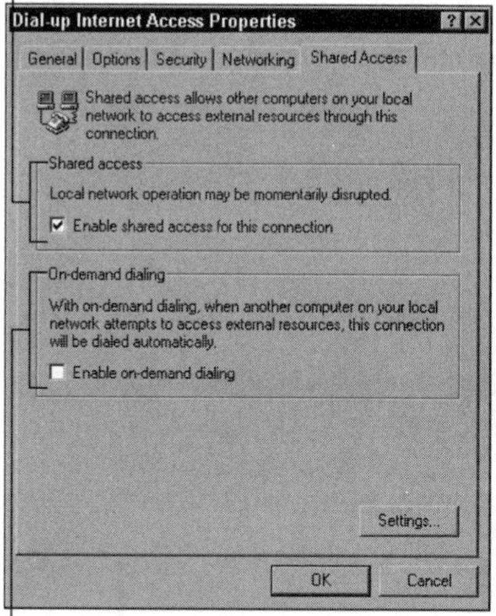

Enables shared access

Figure 20-13: Sharing modems is one click away.

Note

In cases where you need to configure an application for shared access through your connection, select Settings. For most Internet-aware applications such as Web browsers and e-mail clients, this won't be necessary. Games and other applications that can be used over a network may require additional information to work properly through shared access.

Joining a workgroup or domain

A workgroup is a group of computers (and the people who operate them) joined together on a local network in order to work on common projects and share information and resources. This is the lowest level of organization possible on a local network. To join a workgroup, your computer (and all other computers in the workgroup) must be set up with the proper workgroup name. The workgroup name cannot be the same as a computer name, and the default workgroup name is WORKGROUP.

If your computer is part of a domain, which is usually larger than a workgroup and distinguished by the fact that each computer in a domain shares a common directory database, joining a workgroup nullifies your domain membership. Smaller networks, especially those run from home or in a small office, generally use workgroups and not domains as a means of organization.

Caution   If your computer has already been set up by a system administrator, you should not change your network identification.

1. Open Network and Dial-up Connections.

2. Scroll down in the left pane to show the contents at the bottom of the window as shown in Figure 20-14.

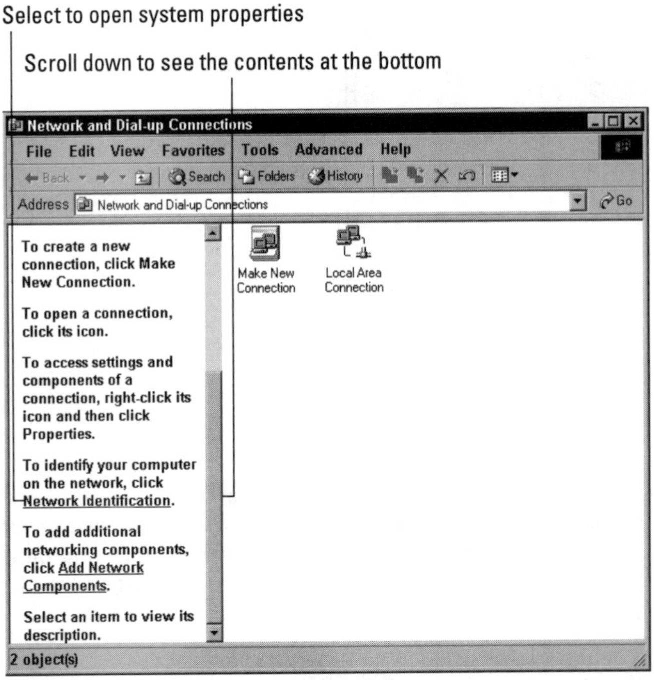

Select to open system properties

Scroll down to see the contents at the bottom

```
Network and Dial-up Connections                          _ □ ×
File   Edit   View   Favorites   Tools   Advanced   Help
← Back  →  🗀  | ◎Search  🗀Folders  ⏱History  ⬚ ⬚ ✕ ⟲  ▦▾
Address 🗐 Network and Dial-up Connections                ▼  ⬭Go

To create a new          🖳          🖳
connection, click Make   Make New   Local Area
New Connection.          Connection Connection

To open a connection,
click its icon.

To access settings and
components of a
connection, right-click its
icon and then click
Properties.

To identify your computer
on the network, click
Network Identification.

To add additional
networking components,
click Add Network
Components.

Select an item to view its
description.

2 object(s)
```

Figure 20-14: Scroll down until you see the Network Identification link.

3. Select Network Identification to open the System Properties dialog box, shown in Figure 20-15. The dialog box opens and automatically displays the Network Identification tab.

4. Click the Network ID button to open the Network Identification Wizard shown in Figure 20-16. Click Next.

5. Select the option that best fits how you use your computer — on a business network or at home — as shown in Figure 20-17, and then click Next.

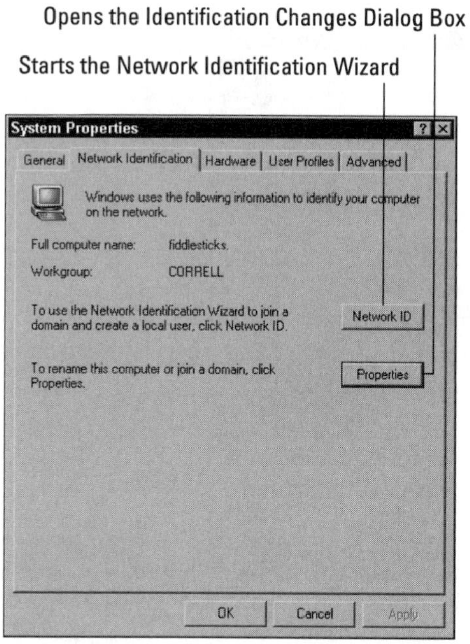

Opens the Identification Changes Dialog Box

Starts the Network Identification Wizard

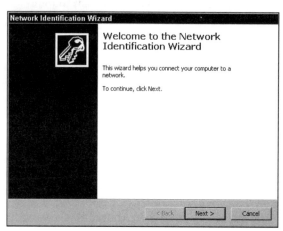

Figure 20-15: System Properties enables you to change your network identification.

Figure 20-16: The Network Identification Wizard steps you through changing your network identification.

6. The wizard then prompts you to identify whether or not your network uses a domain. A domain is an administrative unit by which computers in a network are organized and managed. Because you cannot belong to a workgroup and a domain at the same time, choose the "no domain" option if you wish to join a workgroup. You should choose the "domain" option if you are joining a domain.

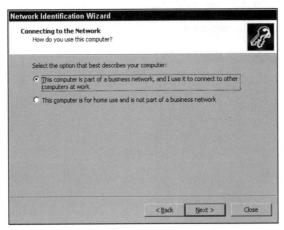

Figure 20-17: Select how you use you computer.

Note Domain names and workgroup names can look similar but in general are identified with smaller organizational structures. A few hypothetical workgroup names are ACCOUNTING or SALES while a domain name can be CASA_LOMA_1.

7. On the next screen, if you are joining a workgroup, change your workgroup name and click Next. If you are joining a domain, you need to enter your user name, password, and the name of the domain you wish to join.

8. Click Finish on the final dialog box. You must restart your computer for these changes to take effect.

Changing your computer name

While workgroup and domain names define what network organization your computer belongs to, your computer's name enables your computer to be identified on the network. When Windows 2000 is installed, your computer is assigned a name that can be lengthy and not intuitive. To make it easier for people to recognize your computer, you can change the name to either identify the primary user or the role the computer plays in your organization. For example, I might want to change my computer's name to something like BOBWIN2KPRO if I wanted people to recognize that this is my computer and I am running Windows 2000 Professional, or I could change it to BOBWEBSVR if I wanted people to understand that I am running a Web server.

1. Open Network and Dial-up Connections.

2. Select Network Identification.

3. Click the Properties button in the System Properties dialog box to open the Identification Changes dialog box, shown in Figure 20-18. This dialog box enables you to change your computer name.

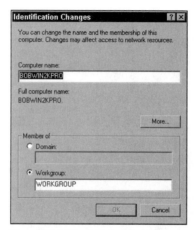

Figure 20-18: Input new values
for computer name, domain, or
workgroup.

4. Enter a new name for your computer and click OK, and you are returned to
the System Properties dialog box, which you can close.

Getting Around My Network Places

If you're familiar with the Network Neighborhood in previous versions of Windows,
you can expect to catch on to My Network Places quickly. And even if you're not
familiar with Network Neighborhood, you are still going to find this process easy.

My Network Places is a folder that has options for viewing computers in your
workgroup or any computer on your network. You can even put shortcuts to
your favorite network items in My Network Places! This feature is so important
that Windows 2000 places an icon for the folder on your desktop, as shown in
Figure 20-19.

You can open My Network Places through a variety of methods:

✦ You can select it from your desktop.

✦ A link to My Network Places is available in nonsystem folders.

✦ My Network Places is in Windows Explorer.

My Network Places appears on your desktop

Figure 20-19: My Network Places is an important system folder for accessing shared network resources.

Figure 20-20 shows the open folder. Notice that the left pane contains instructions and links to other folders, while the right pane contains icons relating to network places or tasks that are labeled Add Network Place, Computers Near Me, and Entire Network.

Adding a network place

If you find yourself accessing a computer on your network or an FTP/Web site, you can create a shortcut to it by adding it as a network place.

Note   Web sites and other folders must be set to share their resources in order for you to create a network place.

1. Open My Network Places.

2. Double-click Add Network Place. This action starts the Add Network Place Wizard that walks you through the entire process.

Select to open the Add Network Place Wizard

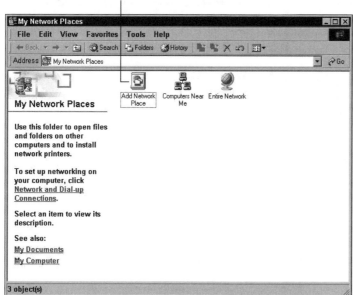

Figure 20-20: The My Network Places folder.

3. Type the address of the location you wish to add, as shown in Figure 20-21. The figure shows the address of an FTP site, but if the location you are connecting to is on your network, you need to type the server name followed by the share point. For example, to connect to place called Library on a server named Win2Kserver, you type **Win2KServer\Library**. When you're finished, click Next.

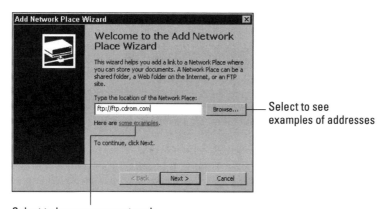

Select to browse your network

Figure 20-21: You can add Web sites, FTP sites, or other resources to your network.

4. If you add an FTP site, the wizard asks if you want to log on anonymously. If you do, make sure the checkbox is selected as shown in Figure 20-22. To provide a user name, unselect the anonymous login and type your user name. When you're finished, click Next.

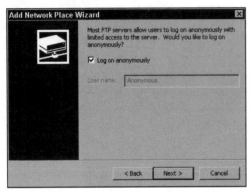

Figure 20-22: Choosing to log in anonymously.

5. Name the connection, as shown in Figure 20-23, and click Finish.

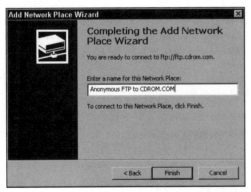

Figure 20-23: Type a name you can recognize.

Your new network place is now located in My Network Places, as shown in Figure 20-24.

Figure 20-25 shows what happens when you double-click the new connection: it opens in the same window as My Network Places. Windows 2000 Professional doesn't have to launch another application!

New shortcut in My Network Places

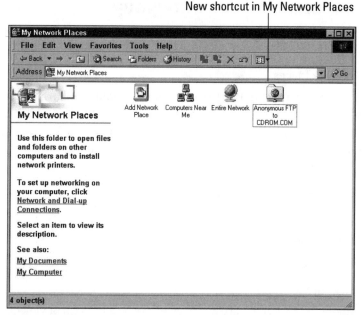

Figure 20-24: To connect to your new network place, double-click it.

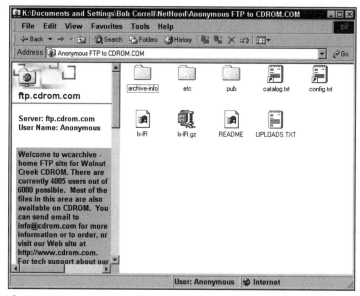

Figure 20-25: Connected to cdrom.com through My Network Places.

Viewing computers in your workgroup

If the other computers in your workgroup have shared resources, you can view them (folders, printers, or other devices) through this easy process:

1. Open My Network Places.

2. Double-click Computers Near Me. The computers in your workgroup are displayed.

3. Double-click a computer to open it. You can see all of that computer's shared folders or printers. To view the contents of a shared folder, open it as you would any other folder in Windows 2000.

Viewing the entire network

The previous series of steps applies to your workgroup only. This procedure shows you how to view your entire network.

1. Open My Network Places.

2. Double-click Entire Network.

3. The next window, shown in Figure 20-26, gives you the options of viewing the entire network or searching for computers or files.

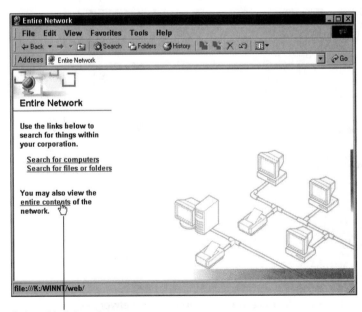

Select this link to view contents

Figure 20-26: Select entire contents to continue.

4. Selecting entire contents opens another folder that enables you to choose the network you want to connect to.

5. Through this link, you can select other workgroups and explore further, ultimately reaching other computers that have shared resources.

Searching Your Network

Being able to find what you are looking for quickly is important even on small networks. Windows 2000 Professional includes a robust search tool that enables you to search for computers, files, and folders on your network

Searching for computers

If you are on a large network with several workgroups, you may forget where a computer you need access to is located. Instead of navigating through the Entire Network tree of My Network Places, you can save yourself some time by searching for the computer by name.

1. Open My Network Places.

2. Click the Search button on the toolbar.

3. In the Computer Name field of the Search pane, type the name of the computer you are looking for and click the Search Now button as shown in Figure 20-27.

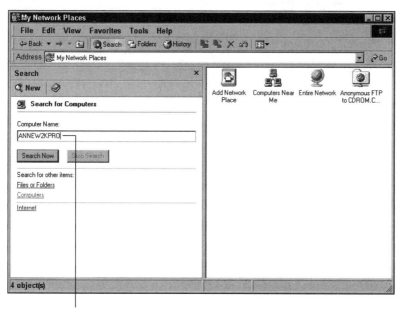

Enter the name of the computer you are searching for

Figure 20-27: Searching for a computer requires the computer's network name.

4. If your search locates the computer, it is displayed in the right pane of the window. To open it, double-click the computer icon.

Searching for files or folders on a network

If you need to find a file or folder on your network but can't remember exactly where it is, you can quickly and easily find it by searching for files or folders on your network.

1. Click Start ➪ Search ➪ For Files or Folders.

Note

If you have a Windows Explorer window open, you can click the Search button.

2. In the Search pane, enter the name of the file of folder you are looking for or enter text that is contained within the file in the appropriate search field.

3. Use the drop-down list control in the Look in field to specify the network drive you want to search.

4. Click the Search Now button.

5. The results are displayed in the right window. Figure 20-28 shows a completed search.

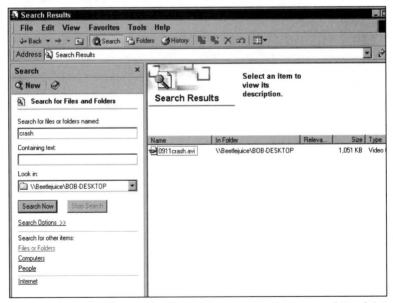

Figure 20-28: The file I am looking for is on a computer named Beetlejuice in the BOB-DESKTOP drive.

Sharing Drives, Folders, Files, and Printers

Being able to share resources is central to networking, and Windows 2000 Professional makes this easy.

Sharing drives

When you share a drive, you are enabling other users to have access to its contents over the network.

1. Open My Computer.

2. Right-click the drive you want to share and click Sharing on the pop-up menu. The drive properties dialog box opens, and the Sharing tab is shown, as illustrated in Figure 20-29.

3. In the Properties dialog box, select Share this folder.

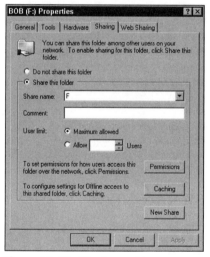

Figure 20-29: Sharing a drive.

Note   Don't be confused by the term *folder* used in the Sharing dialog box. You can choose a drive or a folder to share, and they are both called *folders*.

4. Type a comment if desired. The comment is displayed in My Network Places when View ➪ Details is chosen.

5. Set a user limit if desired.

6. Click the Caching button to set the caching settings. These enable you to set up offline access for the contents of the shared drive.

7. Click OK to finish the process. Figure 20-30 shows what a shared folder looks like. The little hand underneath a drive indicates that drive it shared.

A hand holds a shared drive

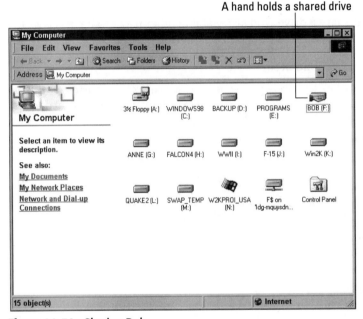

Figure 20-30: Sharing Bob.

Setting permissions on shared drives

For security purposes, you should probably apply permissions to each shared drive or folder to keep unwanted visitors from accessing your files. Permissions are different from passwords in that passwords provide access to the shared drive while permissions define the tasks a person can perform, such as deleting or creating files.

1. Open My Computer.

2. Right-click the drive you want to set permissions for.

3. Select Sharing from the pop-up menu. This opens the Properties dialog box for the shared drive and automatically selects the Sharing tab.

4. Choose Permissions from the Sharing tab, which brings up the dialog box shown in Figure 20-31. By default, Windows 2000 Professional initially sets shared permissions for Everyone, but you can change this setting in the next step.

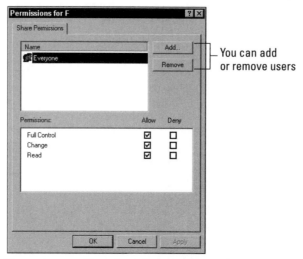

Figure 20-31: Choosing who gets permission to see my shared drive.

5. Click the Add button to add local users or groups, or click the Remove button to remove users or groups. Remember, these are users and groups that are defined on your computer.

6. Select a user or group to change permissions.

7. Click the appropriate checkboxes to Allow or Deny Full Control, Change, or Read.

Sharing printers

Printers are sometimes scarce commodities, and networks enable you to share them. Setting up printer sharing is easy!

1. Click Start ⇨ Settings ⇨ Printers.

2. Right-click the printer you want to share and select Sharing from the pop-up menu.

3. On the Properties dialog box that appears, choose Shared as and name the printer as shown in Figure 20-32.

4. Click OK. Figure 20-33 shows the shared printer in the Printers window.

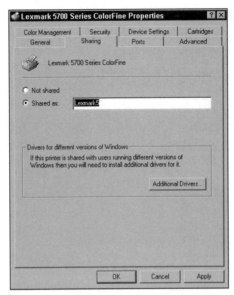

Figure 20-32: Enable sharing and name
the printer. The printer name is the way
people recognize it on the network.

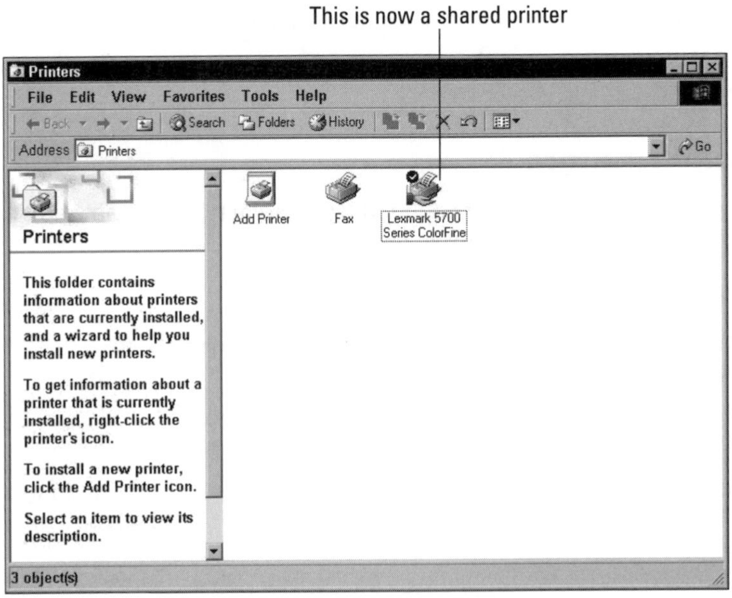

This is now a shared printer

Figure 20-33: Shared printers also have little hands underneath them.

Mapping a network drive

The opposite of sharing a drive on your computer is mapping another computer's drive. Mapping a drive displays a network drive in your My Computer folder or in the folder pane of Windows Explorer. Once you map the drive, you are able to open its contents and work with it just as if it were part of your computer.

This feature is best suited to situations where you share a folder on a network computer and routinely need access to the folder in order to work. You could find and open the folder by searching through Computers Near Me in My Network Places, but mapping a drive makes the folder accessible through My Computer or Windows Explorer.

Note

The owner of the drive you wish to map must share it and enable you to have access to it.

1. Open My Computer, Windows Explorer, or another folder.

2. Select Tools ➪ Map Network Drive.

3. In the Map Network Drive dialog box that appears, assign an available drive letter from the pull-down menu to the resource you are mapping.

4. Just below the drive letter, type the server name and share name in this form: \\server\share. So, for example, if you are connecting to a server named BobServer and a share folder called MyShareFolder, you would type **\\BobServer\MyShareFolder**.

5. Continuing in the same dialog box, select Reconnect at login if you want Windows 2000 Professional to connect to this share at your next session.

6. If you have a different user name or password on the share you are attempting to connect to, select Connect using a different name.

7. Select Finish to conclude the process. Windows 2000 launches a new Explorer window displaying the contents of the mapped drive, and the drive appears in My Computer with the drive letter you assigned in step 3.

Disconnecting a network drive

When you are finished working with the mapped network drive and no longer need access to it, you can remove it from your system. Choosing to do so is largely a matter of personal taste.

1. Open My Computer or Windows Explorer.

2. Find the drive you wish to disconnect.

3. Right-click the drive and choose Disconnect.

Managing Users on a Small Network

Managing users and groups is a vital task even for a small network. By creating groups and adding users, you define the circle of people who can access the computers and the network. In addition, you are able to divide people into groups of people who may have more or less access (or permission to do things) than others.

Setting up login security

I advise everyone to force a login when their computer starts. This keeps a hostile coworker from starting your computer and accessing your files or the network. To set up boot security, follow these steps:

1. Click Start ➪ Settings ➪ Control Panel.

2. Select Users and Passwords, which brings up the dialog box shown in Figure 20-34.

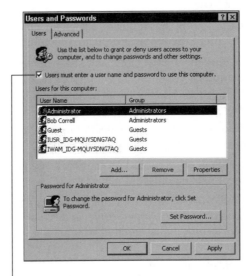

— Select to increase security

Figure 20-34: Users and passwords dialog box.

3. Enable user names and passwords by clicking the checkbox for the option that forces people to enter a user name and password to use the computer.

4. Select the Advanced tab.

5. In the Secure Boot Settings portion of the dialog box, enable secure boot by clicking the checkbox as shown in Figure 20-35. This forces users to press Ctrl+Alt+Del to log into your computer. This guarantees that the logon screen that appears is actually from Windows 2000 and not a utility meant to capture your user name and password in order to steal them.

— Select to increase security

Figure 20-35: Secure boot keeps unwanted visitors from playing with your computer.

6. Select OK to close the dialog box.

Adding users

Each person using the computer has a unique user name and password, and they are assigned to predefined or self-created groups. A group is a collection of people with similar access requirements and computer privileges. Windows 2000 has standard, predefined groups, but you can also create your own. Table 20-1 lists the predefined groups.

To add users, follow these steps:

1. Click Start ➪ Settings ➪ Control Panel.

2. Choose Users and Passwords to display the Users and Passwords dialog box.

3. Click the Add button to add a new user.

4. On the Add New User screen, type the person's user name, full name, and a description, as shown in Figure 20-36. Click Next.

Table 20-1
Predefined Groups

Group Name	Description
Standard User	A member of the Power Users group.
Power Users	Can modify the computer and install programs, but cannot read other user's files.
Restricted User	A member of the Users group.
Users	Can operate the computer and save files, but cannot install programs or make system changes.
Administrators	Full access to the computer and domain.
Backup Operators	Access only to the backup programs.
Guests	Can operate and save, but cannot install programs or make significant changes to the system.
Replicator	Supports file replication in a domain. This group is meant to be used by the system and supports directory replication functions . You should not assign anyone to it other than a domain user to log into the Replicator services of the domain controller.
Users	Can operate the computer and save files, but cannot install programs or make system changes.

This is the name the user will use when logging in

Figure 20-36: Enter the name and description of the new user.

5. On the next screen, type a password and then confirm it by typing it again as shown in Figure 20-37.

Notice the passwords are masked!

Figure 20-37: Enter a password. Make sure to remember it!

6. Select a group for the new user in the next dialog box as shown in Figure 20-38. Click the Finish button.

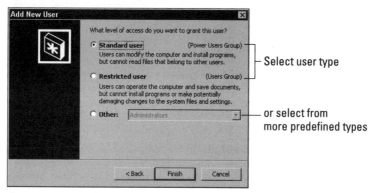

Figure 20-38: Selecting a group for a new user.

The new user now appears in the user list in the Users and Passwords dialog box as shown in Figure 20-39.

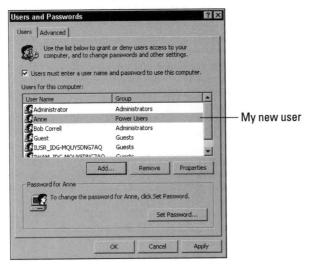

Figure 20-39: My new user appears in the Users and Passwords dialog box with their assigned group.

Summary

I hope you can see there is a lot to this networking thing. Windows 2000 Professional has made it easy to set up your computer to operate on a local network and easy for you to access and use resources on the network. Here are the major points you should remember:

✦ Use Network and Dial-up Connections to create new network connections and change the properties of existing ones.

✦ Use My Network Places to access shared network folders and other computers in your workgroup and to view the entire network.

✦ You can map network drives so they appear in My Computer.

✦ You can also share your drives, folders, and printers.

✦ You can add users and should give them passwords for security purposes.

In the next chapter you learn about Virtual Private Networking (VPN), how to set up VPN access, configure user settings, and secure VPN sessions.

✦   ✦   ✦

Virtual Private Networks

Having remote access to your corporate network is extremely useful. It enables you to work from home or while traveling. In many cases, a server within the corporate network provides this remote access. A modem on your computer then connects to a modem on the remote access server to provide access to the network. If the location you are connecting from is long distance to the remote access server, though, this connection can become expensive.

A Virtual Private Network (VPN) enables you to dial in to any local ISP (which most likely is not long distance) anywhere around the world and establish a connection to the corporate network. In Windows 2000, a VPN connection is set up much like a regular Internet connection, using the Network Connection Wizard.

What Is a Virtual Private Network?

A Virtual Private Network (VPN) uses the Internet or any other public network as a secure transport for a remote access session. It uses a tunneling protocol to send data across the Internet in a secure fashion. Tunneling, by definition, is using one network to transport data for another network. A tunneling protocol encrypts your data and encapsulates it into a packet that can be placed on the public network for transport. In this case, data for your remote network is tunneled through the Internet.

Windows 2000 Professional has the capability to use two different tunneling protocols: Point to Point Tunneling Protocol (PPTP) or Layer Two Tunneling Protocol (L2TP). PPTP encapsulates Point to Point Protocol (PPP) frames (PPP frames are what are sent over the modem when you connect to an ISP) in IP datagrams (IP datagrams are the data sent over TCP/IP networks) to be transported over a TCP/IP network. PPTP provides the services of User Authentication, Data Compression, Data Encryption, and Key Management. These services are discussed in detail later in this chapter. PPTP can function only over a TCP/IP transport network but can carry TCP/IP, IPX/SPX, or NetBEUI traffic.

L2TP functions much the same as PPTP, except it can use TCP/IP, Asycronous Transfer Mode (ATM), X.25, or Frame Relay networks for its transport. It is not restricted to TCP/IP. L2TP also uses different methods to maintain the tunnel and send the encapsulated data at a protocol level. L2TP also supports multiple tunnels with different priorities. For example, video conferencing can run over a tunnel with a high priority to ensure low delay, and an application such as FTP can run over a low-priority tunnel because delay is unimportant. PPTP provides only one tunnel.

VPNs have several advantages over traditional dial-up connections. No long-distance fees are accrued because you can use any local ISP for the dial-up connection. Data sent over the VPN is also encrypted so that it cannot be intercepted. Less equipment is required at the server site because all connections are made through ISPs and the Internet. No modems or extra telephone lines are required. Windows 2000 VPNs support almost all Windows 2000 protocols, such as TCP/IP, IPX/SPX, and NetBEUI so most applications should run as if they were on a local network or over a dial-up connection.

Setting Up VPN Access

Configuring VPNs in Windows 2000 is much easier than in earlier versions of Windows. The Network Connection Wizard automates most tasks involved with configuring a VPN client including adding associated protocols and services. To configure the workstation to access a VPN, follow these steps:

1. Right-click My Network Places on the desktop and then click Properties from the pop-up menu.

2. Double-click the Make New Connection icon.

3. On the first screen of the Network Connection Wizard, click Next to continue.

4. Select Connect to a private network through the Internet and then click Next.

5. If you have a dial-up Internet connection installed on your computer, the next screen is the Public Network dialog box, shown in Figure 21-1. Choose whether or not the VPN connection should dial your ISP automatically. Having the VPN connection dial your ISP automatically is the easiest method, but you can also choose to start the ISP connection manually. If you choose to start the connection manually, before you open your VPN, you must connect to

your ISP as if you were just connecting to the Internet; otherwise, you cannot open the VPN connection. Click Next to continue.

Tip

If you have a permanent Internet connection, such as ADSL, ISDN, or cable modem, set up on your computer, step 5 is not necessary. The dialog box appears only if you have a regular dial-up networking connection installed.

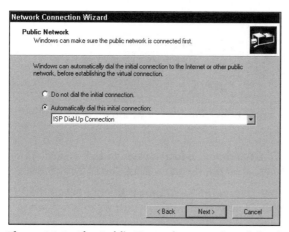

Figure 21-1: The Public Network connection dialog box.

6. The next dialog box asks for the destination address of the VPN server that you are connecting to. If you don't know it, obtain this information from your network administrator. Click Next to continue.

7. Choose whether to make the connection available to all users or only yourself and then click Next. If you choose to make the connection available to all users, anyone who logs on to this system can use this connection. You must have administrative rights on the local machine to make the connection available to all users.

8. The next window is Internet connection sharing seen in figure 21-2.5. From this window, you can make the VPN connection available to other computers on your network. The advantages and caveats of sharing a VPN connection are discussed below under the Sharing tab of the VPN options, but essentially when a connection is shared, other workstations on the network can access the connection. If the Enable on-demand dialing box is checked, the other computers will initiate the connection to the ISP when they are using the VPN, if the ISP connection has not already been made. If you choose to enable sharing, you will be prompted with a window notifying you that the IP address of the computer will be changed to 192.168.0.1. This is discussed further below.

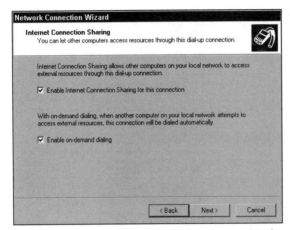

Figure 21-2: The internet connection sharing window

8. Give the connection a name on the next screen of the wizard. You can also choose to add a shortcut to the desktop. Click Next to continue.

9. Enter your user name, password, and domain to connect to the VPN and click Connect. The domain name is the remote Windows logon domain.

Tip   You must be connected to the Internet, either through a dial-up or permanent Internet connection, before you connect to your VPN.

You should now be connected to your VPN and have access to the network resources on the remote network.

VPN Configuration Options

Following the preceding steps should be sufficient to connect to most VPN servers. Some servers, however, may have special configuration options that need to be set. Some configuration options make connecting to the VPN more convenient. To access the VPN configuration options, right-click My Network Places on the desktop and choose Properties from the pop-up menu. This opens the Network and Dial-up Connections window, which contains all defined network connections on this computer. Right-click the VPN connection you want to configure and choose Properties from the pop-up menu.

The Virtual Private Connection Properties dialog box has five tabs that cover various settings related to the VPN connection. The settings provided by default are usually enough to connect to a VPN, but in special cases, properties need to be changed to successfully connect. The administrator of your VPN can inform you of special security and network settings, and other settings can enable the connection to be shared and to change the name of the VPN server if necessary. I go through the options available on each of these tabs in the following sections.

The General tab

The General tab enables you to change the name of the VPN server and the dial-up connection you use to connect. The server name is set in the "Host name or IP address of destination" section. You can also change whether or not the VPN connection dials your ISP and to which dial-up connection it connects in the "First connect" section. The last option on this tab is the Show icon in taskbar when connected checkbox, which displays an icon in the task tray on the right side of the taskbar when the VPN is connected.

The Options tab

The Options tab enables you to change the number of redial attempts and several other display options related to establishing the connection. In the Dialing options section, you can choose whether or not to display the progress while the VPN is connecting, to prompt for the user name and password when the VPN connects, and/or to prompt for a Windows logon domain, which is dependent on the type of remote server. If the remote server is a Windows-based server, you must specify the remote domain you wish to connect to. The Redialing options section enables you to specify the number of redial attempts when the connection fails, the time between attempts, and the idle time before hanging up. The idle time before hanging up is useful if the dial-up connection is paid for on a time basis. If the idle time is set, the connection hangs up when it is not in use. The Redial if line is dropped checkbox forces the VPN to automatically reconnect if the connection is lost.

The Networking tab

The Networking tab enables you to change the type of VPN server from PPTP to L2TP. The default setting is for Windows 2000 to automatically detect the type of server. An example of the Networking tab is shown in Figure 21-3. If your VPN connection is unable to detect the server type, you have to specify it in the drop-down box on this tab. This tab also enables you to change the network services and protocols used over this connection. This can increase throughput over the VPN if certain resources are not needed. If no NetWare servers are on the VPN, for example, disabling the Nwlink IPX/SPX protocol and the Gateway services for NetWare can speed up the connection. By default, all networking components installed on your system are enabled for the VPN. The administrator of the VPN can tell you if any of the protocols on your local network are not used on the VPN and can be disabled.

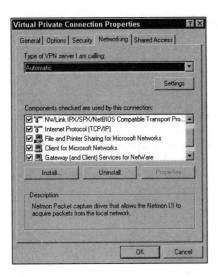

Figure 21-3: The Networking tab of the Virtual Private Connection Properties dialog box.

The Shared Access tab

The Shared Access tab enables other computers on the local network to access resources across the VPN through your computer. Select the shared access checkbox to enable the sharing of the connection. If you want other computers to initiate automatic connection to the VPN, select the Enable on-demand dialing checkbox. This enables your system to act as a "gateway" or "proxy" server for other systems on your network. You should enable shared access if other computers on your network do not have a means (a modem or other Internet connection) to access the VPN. They then have access to the VPN via your system. The caveat to using the shared access feature is that when it's enabled, your system is set to use the IP address of 192.168.0.1. The other computers on your network must be set to use IP addresses in this range or set to get their IP addresses automatically. This feature is meant for small workgroups and not large groups of computers. The Shared Access tab is shown in Figure 21-4.

You must configure the applications and services and their respective TCP or UDP ports for shared VPN connections. Applications are programs on the local network that connect over the VPN connection. Services, by comparison, provide access to other computers on the local network from systems over the VPN. For example, a Web server on the local network needs a service configured to be accessible from across the VPN. For users to be able to use a Web browser across the VPN from the local network, an application must be configured. Some services come configured by default. The procedure for adding applications and services is provided later in this section.

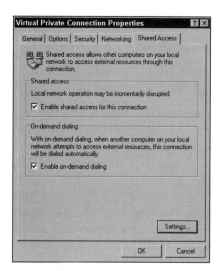

Figure 21-4: The Shared Access tab of the Virtual Private Connection Properties dialog box.

You must provide the TCP or UDP ports for the services or applications you wish to add. The TCP or UDP ports are basically channels that the application uses to send and receive data. The application sends data on the outgoing port and listens for data on the incoming port. The ports used by certain applications or services are sometimes found in the documentation for those applications. Listings of common port numbers are also on the Internet. If you cannot find the port numbers, ask your system administrator. You must have administrative rights on the local machine to configure shared access. This Shared Access Application window is shown in Figure 21-5. The Shared Access Service window is shown in Figure 21-6.

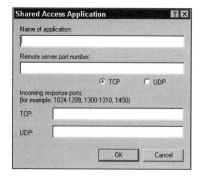

Figure 21-5: The Shared Access Application window showing an example of adding Web browser access.

To add a Web browser application:

1. Click the Settings button on the Shared access tab.

2. Click the Add button from the Applications tab.

3. Give the application a descriptive name ("Web Browser," in our case).

4. Configure the remote server port number, which is 80 for a Web browser. For a Web browser, it's also a TCP port, so the TCP radio button must be selected.

5. Configure the incoming response ports for the application.

6. Click OK.

Figure 21-6: The Shared Access Service window showing an example of adding a Web Server service.

To add a Web server service:

1. Click the Settings button on the Shared Access tab.

2. Click the Add button from the Services tab.

3. Give the service a descriptive name (we use "Web Server").

4. Define the Service Port Number (80 for a Web server, and it is a TCP port).

5. Define the name or address of the computer running the Web server. Here I assume there is a computer on the local network called WEBSERVER that is running the Web server service.

6. Click OK.

You now see the Web Server service in the list. Remote computers now have access to this service.

The Security tab

Windows 2000 VPNs can also use several different authentication protocols. An authentication protocol is what a server in a connection looks for to verify the identity of the calling party (the client). An authentication protocol provides a means of transporting the user name and password over the connection in order for the server to provide access to the client.

Two security risks are involved with VPNs. The first involves authentication. With certain authentication protocols, the user name and password are sent across the connection unencrypted in plain text form. When you are connecting to a VPN over the Internet, this means that your user name and password are traveling over a public network in plain text and are exposed to being intercepted. Windows 2000 uses authentication protocols that use encryption to avoid this problem. Before the authentication information is sent, it is encrypted using a method that the server also understands. This makes intercepting the password futile, as it is very difficult to unencrypt the information. The authentication protocol configuration is set in the Logon Security part of the Advanced Security Settings window. Windows 2000 implementations of PPTP and L2TP use private (or symmetric) encryption keys for most authentication protocols. Private keys are exchanged when the VPN is connected and updated periodically during the connection. With a private key algorithm, the two connecting systems must share the private key that is used to both encrypt and decrypt the data flowing over the connection.

At the bottom of the Logon Security section of the Advanced Security Settings window is a checkbox labeled "For MS-CHAP based protocols, automatically use my windows logon name and password (and domain if any)." This selection enables authentication protocols based on MS-CHAP (or MS-CHAP v2) to use your logon name and password (that you are currently logged in with) to authenticate you on the VPN. This way you are not prompted for the user name and password again when you connect to the VPN. This makes the connection more convenient because you do not need to reenter your logon information. However, it decreases security because if you walk away from your computer when it is logged on, anyone can connect to the VPN without a user name and password. This option should not be checked if you are concerned about the security of the VPN connection. If the VPN connection uses a user name, password, or domain different from your own, this checkbox cannot be selected.

The other security risk involved with VPNs is data encryption. When data travels over a VPN, it must be encrypted, or it is also open to interception on the Internet. Four options are available for data encryption. These are set in the Data Encryption drop-down box in the Advanced Security Settings window.

The No Encryption Allowed option does not use encryption in any case, and if the server requires encryption, the client disconnects. This setting is not recommended because it ensures that your data is sent over the Internet in plain text form, which can be intercepted. The Optional Encryption option connects to the server either with or without encryption. This setting is also not recommended because it is possible to connect with no encryption and send data over the Internet in plain text.

The next two options are the recommended options. Require Encryption and Maximum Strength Encryption both disconnect if the server does not support encryption. This ensures that your data is encrypted when it is transported and is not vulnerable to interception. Maximum Strength Encryption uses a stronger encryption protocol and does not connect to all servers. The Require Encryption option is recommended unless the data you are sending over the VPN is highly secret. Advanced security can be accessed by selecting the Security tab, then clicking the Advanced (custom settings) radio button. Click the Settings button to see the Advanced Security Settings dialog box as shown in Figure 21-7.

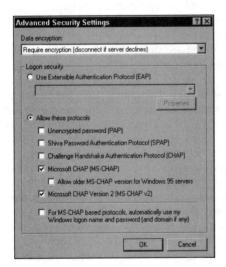

Figure 21-7: The Advanced Security Settings dialog box.

Windows 2000 Professional supports the following types of authentication:

✦ **PAP (Password Authentication Protocol)**: Uses an unencrypted password sent over the Internet. This is the least safe method of authentication because your password is transmitted in plain text and can be intercepted. Use PAP only if the server supports nothing else.

✦ **SPAP (Shiva Password Authentication Protocol)**: A special version of PAP for Shiva clients. Shiva is a brand of VPN server software. SPAP is used only if the VPN server you are connecting to is Shiva based or requires the SPAP protocol. Your VPN administrator can inform you if this is the case. This is also an unsafe protocol because passwords can be intercepted. Use SPAP only if the server supports nothing else.

✦ **CHAP (Challenge Handshake Authentication Protocol)**: Uses encryption to send your password over the Internet. This is the standard method that most servers use for authentication.

✦ **MS-CHAP (Microsoft Challenge Handshake Authentication Protocol):** Is an enhanced version of CHAP that runs on all Microsoft Windows NT servers.

✦ **MS-CHAP v2 (Microsoft Challenge Handshake Authentication Protocol Version 2)**: The next generation of MS-CHAP used on Microsoft Windows 2000 servers uses stronger password encryption for safer authentication.

✦ **EAP (Extensible Authentication Protocol):** An authentication protocol that can use devices such as smartcard readers to verify your identification. Two versions of EAP are available, Transaction Level Security (TLS), which uses external devices such as smartcard readers or certificates, and Message Digest 5 (MD5), which uses a strong password encryption scheme.

EAP provides a secure method of authentication. To use EAP, you must select Use Extensible Authentication Protocol in the Logon Security section of the Advanced Security Settings window. EAP provides three methods of authentication, which are set from the drop-down box under the Use Extensible Authentication Protocol selection. The two selections in this drop-down box are MD5-Challenge and Smartcard or other certificate (TLS) (encryption enabled). MD5 is similar to MS-CHAP in the method it uses to authenticate passwords. MS-CHAP uses an encryption algorithm called MD4, which is less secure than MD5. MD5 uses a larger key to encrypt the data, which makes it more difficult to unencrypt the user name and password without the key.

EAP also enables the use of a smartcard, which is similar to a credit card but has an embedded microchip containing a certificate and is read by a smartcard reader, which must be connected to your system. This way, only the person with the smartcard can access the connection. EAP enables the use of other certificates for authentication. When using the EAP-TLS authentication protocol, public key (or asymmetric) encryption is used. With public key encryption, two keys are used, related by an encryption algorithm for each system, one private and known only to the connecting system, and one public key shared with the remote system. In this method, the private key and public key are used to encrypt and decrypt the data, respectively. This is a stronger method of encryption than private key, because most public keys are signed by a certificate verifying the identity of the public key sender. Certificates are issued by a Certificate Authority, a trusted third party. Certificates are stored in the Windows 2000 Certificate Manager.

To configure the options for the smartcard or other certificates, click the Properties button just below the drop-down box while Use Extensible Authentication Protocol is selected and Smartcard or other certificate (TLS) (encryption enabled) is selected from the drop-down box. The Smartcard or Other Certificate (TLS) Properties window is shown in Figure 21-8. You can select either Use my smartcard or Use a certificate on this computer. If you choose to use a certificate on your computer, it must be installed in the Windows 2000 Certificate Manager.

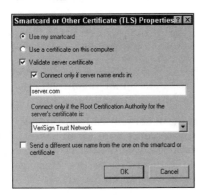

Figure 21-8: The Smartcard or Other Certificate (TLS) Properties window.

From this window you can also choose whether or not to validate the server's certificate. This enables you to verify that the server is who it claims to be. It is possible for someone to set up a server that looks like the server you want to connect to and use it to intercept your data. This option ensures that the server has a certificate that verifies its identity. The Connect only if server name ends in: checkbox enables you to specify the suffix of the server name (that is, server.com) to ensure that the server you are connecting to is the correct one. The Connect only if the Root Certification Authority for the server's certificate is: drop-down box enables you to specify the authority who granted the certificate to the server, if known. This is another method of verifying the server's identity. You can also select Send a different name from the one on the smartcard or certificate if your user name and the name on the certificate are different. In this case you are prompted for your user name when you start the VPN connection.

Summary

Windows 2000 Professional provides a secure method of connecting to remote networks via the Internet using Virtual Private Networks. In this chapter you learned

> ✦ What is a VPN?
>
> ✦ What is tunneling?

✦ What tunneling protocols are available?

✦ How do you set up a VPN connection?

✦ What configuration options are available for VPNs?

✦ How does VPN security work?

In the next chapter, you learn how to use Windows 2000 Professional as a Web server.

✦   ✦   ✦

Using Windows 2000 Professional as a Web Server

U nless you've been living under a rock for the last four years or so, you should already know about the Internet and its star performer, the World Wide Web (WWW). But I'd like to belabor the point anyway! The Internet is the world's largest network, comprised of networks upon networks upon networks. In other words, it's a worldwide network of networks. The World Wide Web, a component of the Internet, is a means of delivering information, entertainment, services, and other electronic transactions over the Internet. Both are open for business 24 hours a day, seven days a week.

Behind the scenes of the WWW sits a multitude of servers that store Web pages and supporting files grouped into entities called *Web sites*. Of course these servers don't just sit there; they manage requests for their resident Web pages and send them on their merry way to the agent that asked for them. This same process that works so well on the Internet can also be used in Local Area Networks (LANs) that use Internet technologies such as the TCP/IP protocol suite. This type of LAN is called an *intranet*.

Perhaps this is a long way of making a point, but here it is. Windows 2000 Professional comes complete with a bona fide Web server that enables you to store, serve, and manage your very own Web site for use on your intranet. You have to create the Web sites, of course, but once you do, you can share information and services over a "Web" between computers connected to your intranet.

Note   Here's an important distinction you should remember as you read this chapter: it's about serving Web pages over intranets, not the Internet. To set up a Web site on the Internet, you should consider upgrading to Windows 2000 Server.

The product that makes this happen is Microsoft Internet Information Services (IIS) version 5.0, which comes bundled with Windows 2000 Professional. In this chapter, you learn how to install and set up IIS, start serving your Web site, manage it with the Personal Web Manager and IIS snap-in, and learn a little bit about FrontPage 2000 Server Extensions.

The Fast Track to Internet Information Services

First let me say that this chapter can serve only as a starting point in your career with IIS. I cannot hope to cover every feature, component, or option at the level of detail that is required for you to get the full benefit of using IIS to publish and manage intranet Web sites. Nevertheless, you will be able to actually use IIS once you finish this chapter. As I said in the introduction, Internet Information Services 5.0 is a Windows 2000 Professional Web service that enables you to publish Web sites for viewing on your intranet.

Note   IIS can also host File Transfer Protocol (FTP) sites. Many of the underlying principles are the same, but this chapter covers only Web sites in detail.

IIS turns your Windows 2000 Professional computer into an intranet Web server. You need the following to install and use IIS:

Local area connection	In other words, computer workstations wired to form a network.
Network adapter card	Your computer has to be a part of the network!
TCP/IP	Your local network must use the Windows TCP/IP protocol suite and connectivity utilities to form an intranet.

If your Windows 2000 Professional computer is already hooked up to your local TCP/IP network, then you're ready to roll. If not, you need to install your network adapter, physically connect it to the LAN, then reboot and set up your local area connection using TCP/IP.

In addition to the basic requirements, Microsoft recommends the following:

✦ Install Domain Name Service (DNS) on your intranet.

Note

DNS maps domain names to IP addresses so you can enter the domain name (such as www.bobcorrell.com) of a computer instead of having to use its IP address. Small networks can do without DNS, but you have to enter the IP address of the Web server unless you configure the HOSTS file in the \%SYSTEMROOT%\System32\ Drivers\Etc directory.

✦ Format drives to be used with IIS with the NTFS file system as opposed to FAT or FAT32.

✦ Use Microsoft FrontPage 2000 as your Web authoring tool.

✦ Use Microsoft Visual InterDev to create interactive Web applications.

Note

The last two may seem like shameless Microsoft plugs for FrontPage and Visual InterDev, but they are more integrated with IIS and Windows 2000 Professional than other third-party Web development products. You needn't run out and purchase them to use IIS however, so the decision is completely up to you. If you are already using other Web authoring tools and don't want to change, that's fine! I have written the chapter in such a way as to not assume you have either of them.

If you've got everything ready, go ahead and install IIS. It's actually very easy!

Installing IIS

Unless you're upgrading from Windows NT 4 and already have a previous version of IIS on your system, IIS 5.0 will not be installed. Grab your installation CD (or a local copy of the Windows 2000 setup files) and put it in your CD drive to get started.

1. Click Start ➪ Settings ➪ Control Panel.

2. Choose Add/Remove Programs.

3. Select Add/Remove Windows Components, and wait until Windows 2000 processes what components you already have installed.

4. Click Next at the first screen of the Windows Component Wizard.

5. On the next wizard screen, select Internet Information Services, as shown in Figure 22-1.

Select IIS

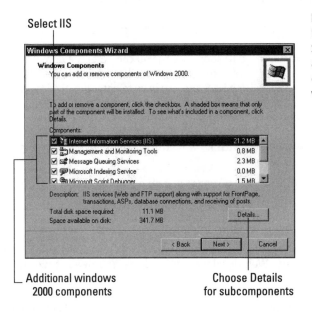

Figure 22-1: Install Internet Information Services from the add/remove Windows components page of the wizard.

Additional windows
2000 components

Choose Details
for subcomponents

6. If you want to choose the IIS components to install, select IIS and click Details. On the resulting dialog box (Figure 22-2), check the components you want to install. If you're happy with installing the complete package, click Next.

Note

Accepting the default IIS setup works just fine, and you don't have to perform any more work to use it. Later in this chapter, I cover some items you can configure.

Choose desired subcomponents

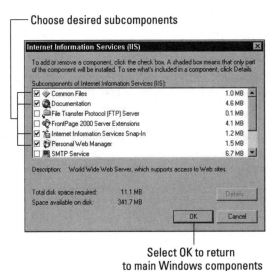

Figure 22-2: Choosing subcomponents of IIS to install.

Select OK to return
to main Windows components

The default installation includes all of the IIS components, but you may wish not to install all of them. In order to help you make the decision of which ones you can safely leave out (or must include), the material below lists the component name, whether it is required, recommended, or optional to install, and a short description of the component.

Common Files (required) includes files required by the IIS program and files required by necessary IIS components.

Documentation (recommended) installs the IIS documentation, which includes information on Web publishing, site content, server administration, and Active Server Pages information.

File Transfer Protocol (FTP) Server (optional) enables you to create and manage an FTP server for file uploading and downloading.

FrontPage 2000 Server Extensions (optional) are server add-ons that enable IIS to use unique FrontPage 2000 and Visual Interdev functions. These extensions are not required to set up and run a Web server that is not optimized for these applications. FrontPage 2000 Server Extensions are covered later in the chapter.

Internet Information Services Snap-In (recommended) installs the IIS administration interface, which "snaps-in" to a Microsoft Management Console (MMC). Although it is only a recommended installation, I would highly urge you to install it. Further information on using the IIS Snap-in is covered later in this chapter.

Personal Web Manager (optional) installs the Personal Web Manager, an easy-to-use tool to administer your Web server. If you are new to IIS, I recommend installing this option and using it first, then upgrading to the Internet Information Services Snap-in as you become familiar with IIS administration.

SMTP Service (optional) is required if you would like to use your Windows 2000 Professional computer as an e-mail server. (SMTP stands for Simple Mail Transfer Protocol.)

Visual InterDev RAD Remote Deployment Support (optional) installs support files needed for developers to install and register server components through Web pages with a remote Visual Studio client. (RAD stands for Rapid Application Development.) Although useful, Microsoft warns of the security implications for your Web site because any Visual Studio 6 developer with author permissions can install and register components.

World Wide Web Server (required) installs the Web server, which is what makes your Web site available on the Internet or in your corporate intranet.

7. When you are finished choosing the subcomponents you want to install, click OK and then click Next to start the installation process.

8. When installation is complete, click Finish.

Once you install IIS, you're ready to begin publishing Web pages immediately. You don't even have to restart your computer!

Making sure it works

After you install IIS, perform this quick check to make sure it is installed correctly and is working.

1. Open My Computer.

2. Select the drive where Windows 2000 Professional is installed.

3. Look for the existence of a \inetpub directory, as shown in Figure 22-3.

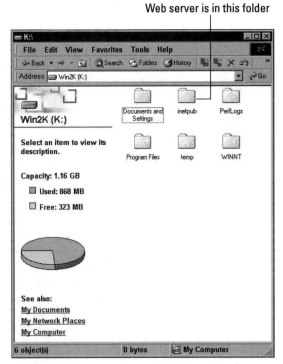

Figure 22-3: Your Web server is located in the inetpub folder.

4. Open the inetpub directory and then the wwwroot directory, as shown in Figure 22-4. You won't see many files here because you haven't published anything yet. Don't worry; you get to that soon. This test is just to confirm that the directories are created and the default content is included.

Root folder of published Web site

Default IIS files

Figure 22-4: The wwwroot folder is the root directory of your Web site.

5. Close your Windows Explorer window and launch Internet Explorer.

6. Enter **http://** followed by your IP address in the Address bar.

Note

If you have DNS installed on your network with your site name registered, you can type in the address of your new Web site, such as `www.bob.com`. You can also connect using your own computer name. In my case that would be `http://bobwin2kpro`.

Figure 22-5 shows that IIS is indeed working, although you have yet to publish any content. Notice that this welcome page appeared without your having to type in an address to this exact Web page. Until you publish content, your site visitors see a construction page, not this IIS page. This is due to the fact that you are using the computer that is running the Web service and are the administrator.

My IP address

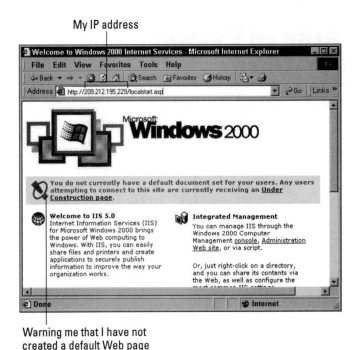

Warning me that I have not
created a default Web page

Figure 22-5: Confirming IIS is working.

Because you don't have any content, IIS launches the IIS help page in Internet Explorer in a separate browser window.

Note   It's a good idea to bookmark the help page so you can easily get back to it.

Publishing Web pages

Now that you've confirmed that IIS is installed and operating, it's time to publish a Web page. Publishing Web pages into the default IIS directory structure couldn't be easier.

1. Create a Web page or Web site. I've created a simple Web page that lists a few fictitious projects I'm working on and links to pages with more information that I could create and put in the same directory as this one with the appropriate file names as listed in the code below.

Note   If you have yet to learn HTML, I encourage you to pick up a book on HTML and start learning or visit the World-Wide Web Consortium (the body responsible for the development of HTML) web site at www.w3c.org. For the time being, I've included a small amount of code to illustrate the point and show you the HTML behind Figure 22-6.

```
<HTML>
<HEAD>
<TITLE>Bob's Workgroup Web Page</TITLE>
<HEAD>

<BODY>

<H1>Projects</H1>

<H2>In-Progress</H2>
<p><A href="feas.html">Feasability Study</A>
<p><A href="mark.html">Market Research</A>
<p><A href="cost.html">Cost-Benefit Analysis</A>

<H2>Planned</H2>
<p><A href="vac.html">Vacation</A>

<H3>Contact:</H3>
<ADDRESS>Bob Correll<BR>
555-1212<BR>
<A href="mailto:correll@noplace.com">E-mail me</A><BR>
</ADDRESS>
```

2. Name the home page DEFAULT.HTM. This naming convention is important if you have not changed the default setup. IIS looks for DEFAULT.HTM as the home page of your Web site.

Note   If you're used to making Web pages with an .HTML extension, be careful here. Make sure to use the extension .HTM and not .HTML, or you will not see your fine handiwork. You can change this association (I get to that later), but for now stick with .HTM for your default page.

3. Copy the file to the \Inetpub\Wwwroot folder of your system hard drive. If you have created a more substantial Web site instead of the page I have used, copy all the files and any subdirectories.

4. Launch your Web browser and enter your address to confirm that the page displays. My example is shown in Figure 22-6.

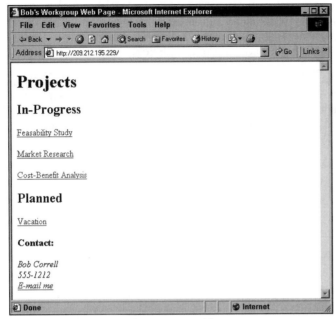

Figure 22-6: My first Web page served by IIS.

Managing Your Web Site with Personal Web Manager

Behind the scenes, IIS runs your Web service with no intervention required. In fact, it is impossible to use IIS to manage itself. If you want to perform any Web site administration such as stopping the Web server or monitoring site statistics, you will have to rely on a tool external to IIS. Windows 2000 Professional comes with an easy-to-use utility called Personal Web Manager (PWM), which can be used to manage your Web site and configure or change the nature of your intranet services.

If you didn't install PWM with IIS, go back to the section "Installing IIS" and follow the steps, making sure you click the Details button and then select Personal Web Manager.

Once PWM is installed you can perform basic tasks such as launching it, starting or stopping Web services, and monitor your Web activity.

Launching PWM

You have to run PWM to use it. Because PWM is a tool used to administer your Web site, you can find it under Administrative Tools in the Control Panel.

1. Click Start ➪ Settings ➪ Control Panel.

2. Choose Administrative Tools.

3. Select Personal Web Manager, as shown in Figure 22-7.

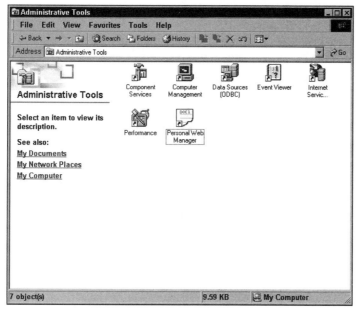

Figure 22-7: The Personal Web Manager is an administrative tool.

4. When PWM launches, tips are shown by default, as shown in Figure 22-8. To start using PWM, close the tip window. You can easily turn off this feature by unchecking the Show tips at startup checkbox.

Note

If you find yourself running PWM a lot, you might consider creating a shortcut and putting it in your startup folder. That way, every time you log into your machine, PWM launches automatically.

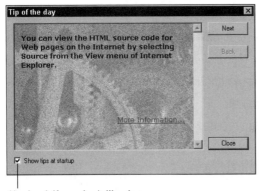

Uncheck if you don't like tips

Figure 22-8: Tip of the day courtesy of Personal Web Manager.

Figure 22-9 shows the main PWM interface. Notice that Web publishing is automatically turned on (as shown in the Main window), and there are three icons on the left side of the interface.

Web page address   Select to stop service

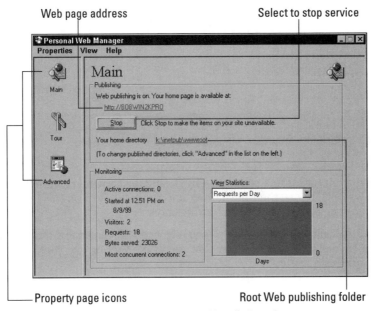

Property page icons   Root Web publishing folder

Figure 22-9: PWM has an easy-to-use, friendly interface.

The Main icon displays the Web publishing and monitoring information that you see in Figure 22-9. You can see the status of your Web server, jump to your Web site by selecting the address, stop the Web service, open the home directory, and monitor site statistics.

The Tour icon launches a tour of the PWM that provides general product information and Web service concepts. I recommend viewing this slide show if you are new to IIS and PWM.

The Advanced icon displays PWM advanced options in the main program window. These options enable you to edit, add, or remove directories within your Web site and other options explained later in this section.

Starting and stopping service

IIS automatically starts your Web service (in other words, your Web site will be available to external users) when you boot up, so starting service is not so much of a problem. If Web publishing is on, your site is "live" and people can display your Web pages in their Web browsers. At times, however, you need to stop service if you want to take your Web site offline and make major changes to the Web pages contained within your Web site or to change your server configuration or settings.

Launch the Personal Web Manager. Click Stop or Start, depending on whether you are stopping or starting service. If your service has already started (you can tell because the Main window will display the message "Web publishing is on"), your only choice will be to stop it. Conversely, if you have previously stopped service (and you see the message "Web publishing is off"), you can only choose to start it again.

Figure 22-10 shows what PWM looks like with services turned off.

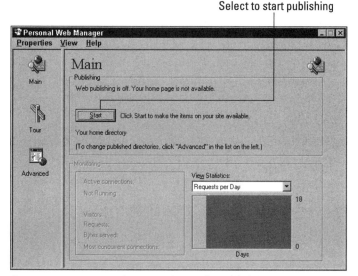

Figure 22-10: PWM after stopping Web publishing.

Showing and using the PWM tray icon

Another useful feature of PWM is the capability to put a PWM icon in your system tray. This way, you can close PWM but still be able to see the status of your service and open PWM with a quick click.

1. Launch PWM.

2. Select Properties ➪ Show tray icon.

When you close PWM, an icon appears in your system tray, as shown in Figure 22-11. You can perform routine tasks such as starting and stopping service by right-clicking the icon and selecting the appropriate menu item. To reopen PWM, right-click the PWM icon and select Properties or double-click the icon in the system tray.

PWM icon

Figure 22-11: The PWM system tray icon.

Monitoring Web site activity

PWM makes it easy to monitor your Web site activity. With PWM open and services running, look at the Monitoring portion of the Main window, shown in Figure 22-12.

Select to change type of statistics graphed

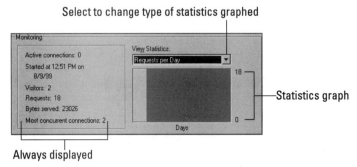

Statistics graph

Always displayed

Figure 22-12: Monitoring Web activity is a breeze with PWM.

The items automatically displayed are the number of active connections, the service start time, and the numbers of visitors, requests, bytes served, and most concurrent connections.

PWM also displays a graph of the connections in the lower-right portion of the window. You can use the drop-down list box above the graph area to choose from four different displays:

✦ Requests per day

✦ Requests per hour

✦ Visitors per day

✦ Visitors per hour

Advanced tasks

The basic tasks you can perform with PWM are, well, basic. They are limited in nature and don't involve changing the configuration of IIS or your Web site. At some point, you may realize you need to do some more tinkering, so this section is for you! Figure 22-13 shows the Advanced Options of PWM.

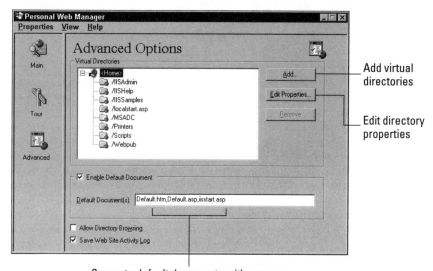

Separate default documents with commas

Figure 22-13: Make advanced configuration changes in the Advanced Options window.

Changing your home directory

By default, the home directory of your Web site is \inetpub\wwwroot, but you can change the home directory. You might want to make this change if you already have set up a Web site in a different directory, for example. IIS enables you to specify only one home directory that contains the files seen by the visitors to your Web site.

1. Launch PWM.

2. Select Advanced.

3. Select <HOME> (which is the root directory) and click the Edit Properties button to display the screen shown in Figure 22-14.

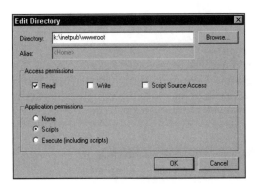

Figure 22-14: Changing my home, or root, Web publishing directory.

4. Enter the path of your new home directory in the Directory field.

5. Select OK to close the Edit Directory dialog box and return to the PWM. Your new home directory takes effect immediately.

Changing default documents

A default document is loaded into a visitor's browser when he or she visits your site or a directory within your site but does not include a Web page name in the Web site address. For example, if I chose to visit www.bob.com, I would be presented with the default.htm document, but if I entered www.bob.com/sales/q3.htm, I would be taken directly to that page. It is a good idea to make sure this feature is enabled so that visitors don't get access errors. If they enter www.bob.com and the default document association does not exist and directory browsing is not enabled, they will get an error indicating they do not have permission to view the files.

1. Launch PWM.

2. Select Advanced.

3. Enter new document names, separated by a comma, as shown in Figure 22-15. The precedence for loading these documents (if more than one is present in the same directory) is the order they are listed in the Default Document field.

Figure 22-15: Changing the default documents that are loaded into a visitor's Web browser.

Note To turn off the default documents feature (not recommended), uncheck Enable Default Document.

Adding virtual directories

While IIS enables only one home directory, you can have as many virtual directories as you like. This convenient feature enables you to include directories in your Web site that are not physically located under your home directory.

1. Launch PWM.
2. Select Advanced.
3. Click the Add button, which brings up the Add Directory dialog box.
4. Enter the path of the directory and an alias name as shown in Figure 22-16. The alias describes how the directory will be displayed in PWM and is the name you should use to refer to the directory in any HTML files. In this example, I have included a Sales directory whose path is K:\Bob\Web\Sales, but because I have chosen Sales as it's alias, the Web address for this virtual directory will be http:\\www.someurl.com\sales.

Directory on my hardrive

Name of directory in Web site

Figure 22-16: Entering the path and alias name of the virtual directory.

5. Enter Access and Application permissions. Access permissions grant or restrict access to files within your Web site from visitor's Web browsers. Read access is the highest level of security, whereas write access allows users to write to that directory. Enabling Script Source Access enables users to view any scripts that may be on the Web site. Applications permissions determine what users can do with program files that may be on your Web site. If you choose to, you can deny them permission to run any application or script on your Web site from their Web browser or grant them permission to run scripts only, or any application.

6. Click OK.

The virtual directory appears under the root Web publishing directory as shown in Figure 22-17.

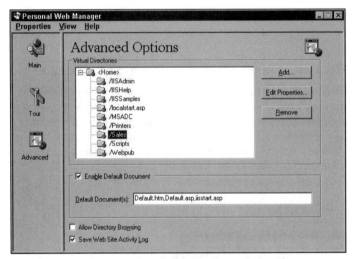

Figure 22-17: The new virtual directory is ready for files.

Changing directory permissions

The default directory permissions are security conscious. They enable visitors to read Web pages at your site and execute scripts but nothing more. You may need to loosen the access permissions or change the application permissions. Most often this is the case when you have created a Web site for use within your company or local workgroup and want people to be able to execute applications on your machine.

1. Launch PWM.

2. Select Advanced.

3. Select a directory. Each directory has it's own set of permissions that must be modified separately.

4. Click the Edit Properties button to bring up the Edit Directory dialog box.

5. Change the access and application permissions to suit your taste. These permissions are the same as those displayed in the Add Directory dialog box.

Enabling directory browsing

Directory browsing enables visitors to navigate the directory structure of your Web site and is disabled by default. You should enable it only if people need to navigate the structure of your Web site much like they would using Windows Explorer to view the contents of a folder on your hard drive. A side effect of enabling directory browsing is that you needn't create any Web pages at all. You can plunk files in your Web site directory structure and people can navigate to them, view them, or download them at will.

1. Launch PWM.

2. Select Advanced.

3. Click the Allow Directory Browsing checkbox at the bottom of the page.

Visitors to your site will be able to see the directory structure of the directories for which you have enabled directory browsing as shown in Figure 22-18.

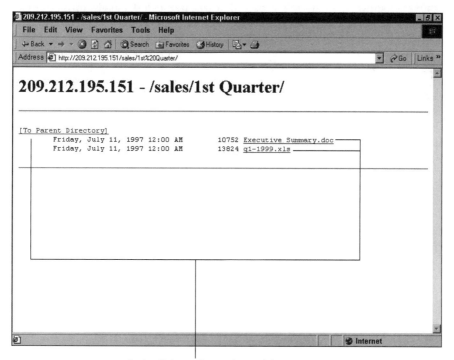

Active links to directories and documents

Figure 22-18: Directory browsing opens up your site, so use it wisely.

Disabling site logging

The site logging function keeps a detailed log of IIS activity as it serves up your Web pages. Site logging is enabled by default, so your option is to turn it off.

1. Launch PWM.

2. Select Advanced.

3. Clear the Save Web Site Activity Log checkbox.

Viewing site logs

Logs of Web site activity are a way to keep track of who contacts your site, when they visited, what pages they viewed, and what errors were returned.

Logs are automatically saved in the \System32\LogFiles\W3SVC1 folder of your Windows 2000 Professional directory. Each file is named using the year, month, and day, so a file created on the August 9 is named ex990809.log. To open, double-click the log file. Figure 22-19 shows a log opened with Notepad.

The logs have five columns of information. The first two columns tell you when and who visited your Web site. The time column displays the time of the visit and the c-ip column displays the IP address of the computer requesting a Web page. The cs-method column indicates the method used to request the Web page, and the cs-uri-step shows the path to the page that was requested. Finally, the sc-status column shows the status returned of the Web page (or other item) request.

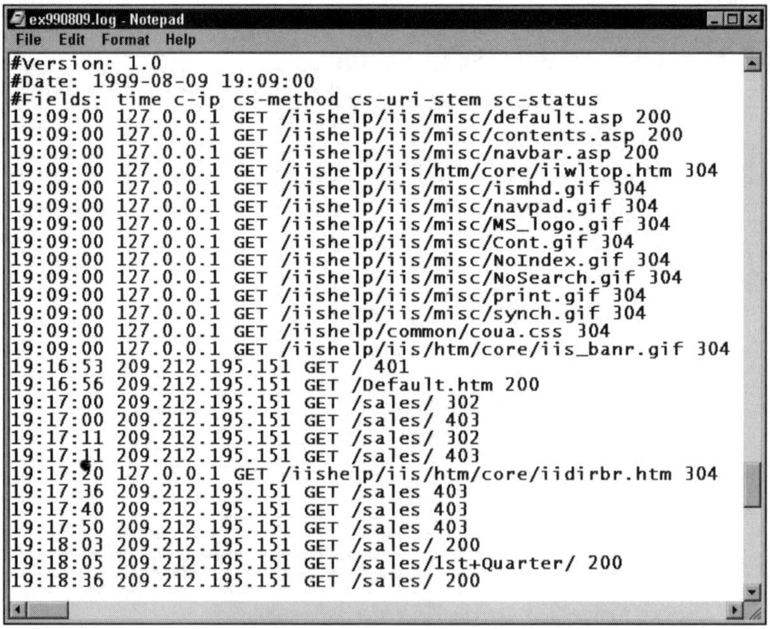

Figure 22-19: My Web log for today.

A good rule of thumb is to keep these logs for a month and then archive them for long-term storage. If you're not that concerned with tracking Web site activity, you needn't worry about keeping them longer than a few weeks.

Managing Your Web Site with Internet Services Manager

The Personal Web Manager is a great tool to use for Web site administration, but it was created with limited capabilities precisely in order to make it easy to use. To unlock the power of administering your Web site you should consider using the Internet Services Manager.

The Internet Services Manager is a snap-in tool (the actual snap-in is called Internet Information Services) to a Microsoft Management Console. Administering Web sites through this tool provides fine control over every aspect of your Web site.

Here's how to launch the Internet Services Manager:

1. Click Start ➪ Settings ➪ Control Panel.

2. Choose Administrative Tools.

3. Select Internet Services Manager to bring up the screen shown in Figure 22-20.

Note   You can also select Start ➪ Settings ➪ Control Panel, choose Administrative tools, and run Computer Management to access the Internet Information Services snap-in. It is located in the Server Applications and Services tree under Internet Information Services. If you would like to create a standalone console for the snap-in, select Start ➪ Run, enter mmc /a, and add the Internet Information Services snap-in to your new MMC console.

By default, the content that populates the IIS tree of Internet Services Manager originates from the local machine. You can change this behavior by right-clicking an item below the default Web site, selecting Properties, and choosing a content location option. The three possible options are local machine, shared folder on another computer, and a redirection to a URL.

You can see from Figure 22-20 that the Internet Services Manager is a far cry from the Personal Web Manager. From this interface, you can perform all the Web site management tasks available through PWM except real-time monitoring of Web site activity. You will have to use other monitoring tools such as System Monitor, Event Viewer, Task Manager, or Network Monitor to view real-time system or site performance.

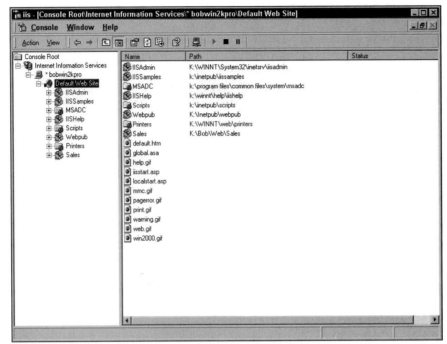

Figure 22-20: The Internet Services Manager, an advanced IIS management tool.

Accessing your Web's properties

If you want to set master properties for all Web sites created on your computer, you can do so by right-clicking the local computer in the console tree and selecting Properties. This action brings up the dialog box shown in Figure 22-21.

The Internet Information Services tab contains a multitude of settings.

Master Properties

Choosing Edit brings up the mother of all configuration dialog boxes. Each tab is explained in this section.

Web Site   Shown in Figure 22-22. Change your site identification, limit the number of connections, and enable logging.

Select to edit Master Properties

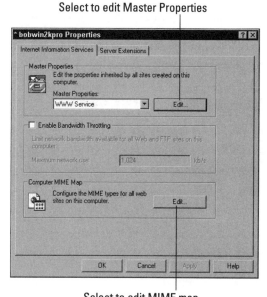

Select to edit MIME map

Figure 22-21: Your Web site's master properties.

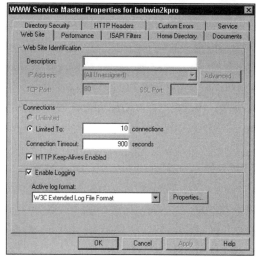

Figure 22-22: The Web site tab includes identification, connection, and logging options.

Performance   Shown in Figure 22-23. Drag the slider to approximate the number of Web site hits you expect per day to tune Web site performance, configure how much bandwidth the site can use, and set a limit for the amount of CPU time that can be devoted to Web services.

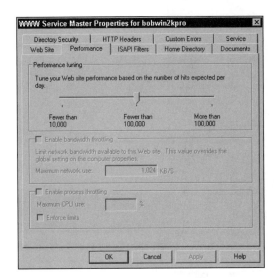

Figure 22-23: The Performance tab.

ISAPI Filters   Shown in Figure 22-24. Add, remove, edit, and change the priority of ISAPI filters. ISAPI filters are programs that respond to events while a Web server request is being processed.

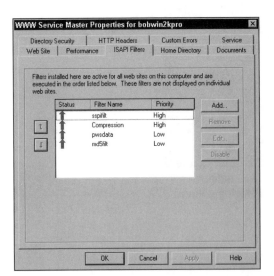

Figure 22-24: The ISAPI Filters tab enables you to add and remove ISAPI filters and change their priority.

Home Directory   Shown in Figure 22-25. Set the properties of the home directory and applications of your Web site.

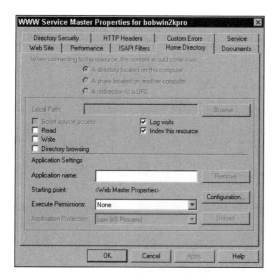

Figure 22-25: The Home Directory tab enables you to manage your Web publishing directory.

Documents   Shown in Figure 22-26. Enable default documents, set their load priority, identify a source location, and enable footer documents. A footer document is an HTML document that will be displayed at the bottom of every Web page a site visitor sees.

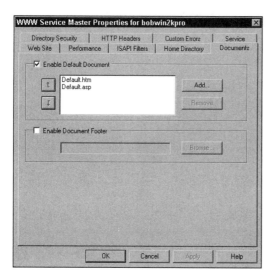

Figure 22-26: The Documents tab allows you to manage default documents and document footers.

Directory Security	Shown in Figure 22-27. Enable access and authentication control, IP address and domain restrictions, and configure secure communications.

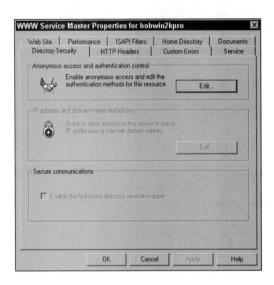

Figure 22-27: The Directory Security tab sets a Web site's security features.

HTTP Headers	Shown in Figure 22-28. Configure how IIS reads HTML headers that identify expiration date, content ratings, MIME settings, and add or edit custom headers.

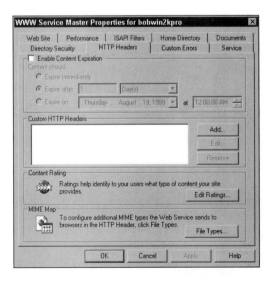

Figure 22-28: The HTTP Headers tab sets the HTML header values returned to a Web browser.

Custom Errors   Shown in Figure 22-29. Identify files to load on HTTP errors. One of the cool things you can do is create your own custom error pages that a user will see and include them here.

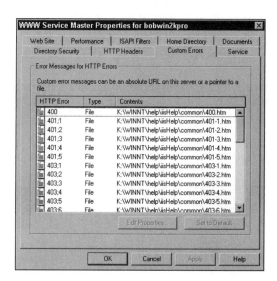

Figure 22-29: The Custom Errors tab enables you to create custom Web pages to display errors to users in their Web browsers.

Service   Shown in Figure 22-30. Configure IIS 3.0 administration and HTTP compression.

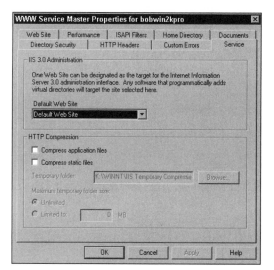

Figure 22-30: The Service tab enables HTTP compression and sets IIS 3 administration options.

Enable bandwidth throttling

Bandwidth throttling   Refer back to Figure 22-21. This limits the total bandwidth that can be used by this computer to serve Web and FTP connections. This is very useful if you want to reserve network bandwidth for other uses and don't want Web or FTP services to take all possible bandwidth.

Computer MIME map

MIME map   Refer back to Figure 22-21. Configures MIME types. Selecting Edit enables you to add, edit, and remove types as shown in Figure 22-31.

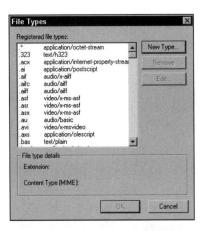

Figure 22-31: The MIME map enables you to assign MIME types.

Stopping, starting, and restarting IIS

One great thing about this version of IIS is that you don't have to reboot your system to stop and restart services. With the Internet Services Manager, you have the option of stopping, starting, and restarting (stopping services immediately followed by starting them again) Web publishing in addition to rebooting the computer hosting the Web server.

1. Launch the Internet Services Manager.

2. Right-click the computer the Web site is hosted on to display the pop-up menu shown in Figure 22-32.

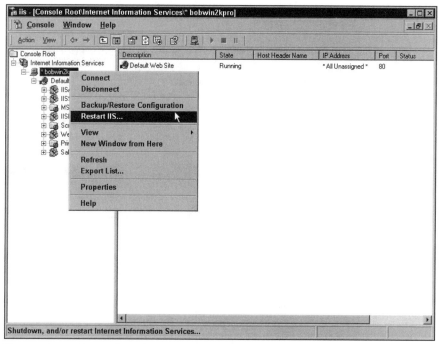

Figure 22-32: Restarting IIS.

3. Choose Restart IIS.

4. Select a restart option, as shown in Figure 22-33. Your options are to Stop Internet Services (if running), Start Internet Services (if stopped), Reboot the Computer, and Restart Internet Services.

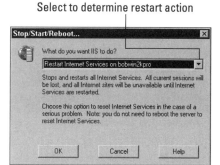

Figure 22-33: Select an option from the pull-down list.

Creating new virtual directories

For the same reasons mentioned earlier in conjunction with Personal Web Manager, you might need to create additional virtual directories for your Web site.

1. Launch the Internet Services Manager.

2. Right-click the Default Web Site.

3. Choose New ➪ Virtual Directory as shown in Figure 22-34.

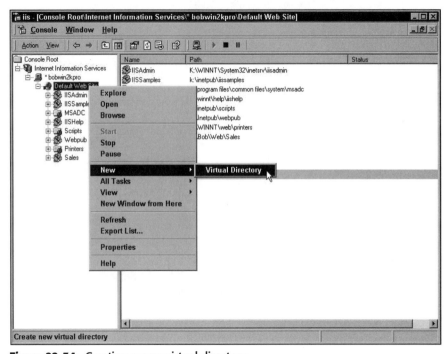

Figure 22-34: Creating a new virtual directory.

4. This action starts the Virtual Directory Creation Wizard. Click Next at the first screen.

5. Enter an alias name as shown in Figure 22-35 and click Next. The alias describes how the directory will be displayed in Internet Services Manager and is the name you should use to refer to the directory in any HTML files.

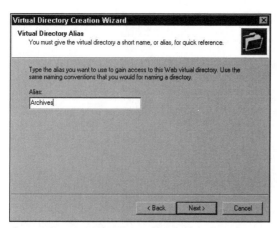

Figure 22-35: Name your alias in the Virtual Directory Creation Wizard.

6. Enter the path to the directory as shown in Figure 22-36.

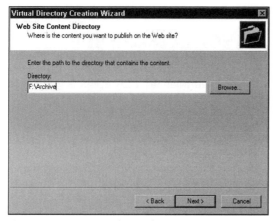

Figure 22-36: Enter the path to your virtual directory.

7. Configure directory permissions as shown in Figure 22-37.

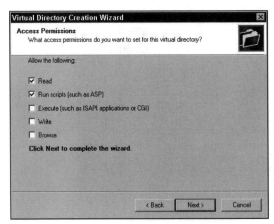

Figure 22-37: Set the directory permissions.

   8. Click Next and then click Finish to complete the operation.

Your virtual directory is created within IIS and is now ready for use!

FrontPage 2000 Server Extensions

Microsoft FrontPage is Microsoft's premier Web site authoring and management tool. It's powerful and easy to use. FrontPage not only enables you to create Web sites that can be used on any server, but it also can use special server add-ons, called *FrontPage Server Extensions*, to increase its functionality in ways such as collaborative Web site creation, the use of hit counters, forms handling, and remote site editing. These extensions must be installed on the server, however, for FrontPage to be able to use them.

Caution   The FrontPage 2000 Server Extensions are compatible only with FrontPage 2000. Do not install them unless you plan to use FrontPage 2000!

Installing FrontPage Server Extensions

If you didn't install the extensions when you installed IIS, grab your Windows 2000 Professional CD and follow these steps.

   1. Click Start ➪ Settings ➪ Control Panel.

2. Choose Add/Remove Windows Components to launch the Windows Component Wizard. Click Next at the first wizard screen.

3. On the next screen, select Internet Information Services and click the Details button.

4. Select FrontPage 2000 Server Extensions as shown in Figure 22-38.

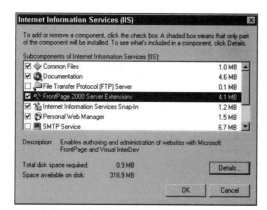

Figure 22-38: Installing FrontPage 2000 Server Extensions.

5. Click OK and then click Next to start the installation.

Administering FrontPage extensions

FrontPage 2000 Server Extensions are administered through a console called Server Extensions Administrator.

1. Select Start ⇨ Settings ⇨ Control Panel.

2. Choose Administrative Tools.

3. Select Server Extensions Administrator.

Figure 22-39 shows the Server Extensions Administrator with the tree expanded.

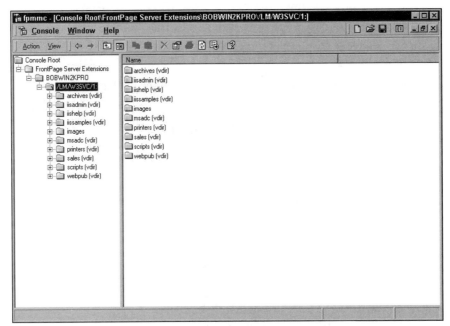

Figure 22-39: Use the Server Extensions Administrator to administer FrontPage 2000 Server Extensions.

Summary

I hope you've gotten a little taste of what's possible by using Internet Information Service 5.0 and Windows 2000 Professional in this chapter. You can install IIS and get a Web site up and running very quickly.

✦ IIS enables you to manage and serve Web pages over your intranet using your Windows 2000 Professional computer as a Web server.

✦ Installing and initially configuring IIS is a breeze through the Add/Remove Windows Components Wizard.

✦ Use the Personal Web Manager to manage your Web site with ease.

✦ If you want total control over your Web site, use the Internet Services Manager snap-in.

✦ FrontPage 2000 Server Extensions are necessary if you are going to host Web sites created by FrontPage 2000 and want to enable special features.

This chapter concludes Part VI. You've seen what networking is all about, discovered how to network Windows 2000 Professional, how to set up Virtual

Private Networking, and turn your Windows 2000 Professional computer into a Web server with IIS. The next part will focus on digging deeper into Windows 2000 Professional, with the next chapter discussing all the choices involved in installing the operating system as well as showing you how to upgrade another version of Windows to Windows 2000, install Windows 2000 Professional from scratch, and run multiple operating systems in a multi-boot configuration.

✦   ✦   ✦

Digging Deeper

◆   ◆   ◆   ◆

◆   ◆   ◆   ◆

Installing Windows 2000 Professional

Installing an operating system is always a daunting task. Operating systems interact with computers at the most basic level, and a mistake or a problem during an upgrade or fresh installation can spell disaster. You must make many choices — correctly — and pay attention to details, or face learning painful lessons the hard way.

Microsoft does what it can to simplify the installation of Windows 2000, but the fact is any user looking to install Windows 2000 faces a confusing array of alternatives. Should you upgrade or install fresh? Can you (and should you) upgrade from any version of Windows, including Windows 3.1, Windows 95, and Windows 98? And what if you have NT already, whether NT 4.0 or the older NT 3.5x? The questions don't stop there because Windows 2000 even enables you to put multiple operating systems on a single PC.

No question, there are a lot of tough choices when it comes to installing Windows 2000. In this chapter, I address the choices you face and point out the potential dangers lurking ahead.

Decisions, Decisions: Install Fresh, Upgrade, or Multiboot?

Windows 2000 is the most comprehensive Microsoft operating system yet, and that extends to the product's support for a wide range of installation options. The wealth of options is a good thing, but it also means you need to plan carefully before you begin the upgrade process. Otherwise, you could end up with an operating system configuration that fails to meet your needs, and you may have no way of getting things back.

The first stage in any operating system upgrade is to conduct a little reconnaissance. You need to know both your system and Windows 2000's system requirements before you make a move. That can take a little digging. Here are a few issues that you must tackle before deciding how you want your Windows 2000 installation to look:

✦ Minimum hardware requirements

✦ Hardware compatibility

✦ Vendor-specific drivers

✦ Data backup

✦ Your needs

Caution Make sure you have a fully licensed copy of Windows 2000. For example, some less-than-scrupulous system makers bundle so-called *gray market* software, including the operating system, with their hardware. If your Windows 2000 software is not officially licensed, you may find yourself out of luck with Microsoft's tech support or, worse, in trouble with the law. The software on pirated or gray market discs may also be out of date (an older version) or even infected with a virus. Network administrators should also make sure to keep tabs on the software packaging, license documentation, and CD key numbers to ensure access to support services and avoid trouble in case of an audit. Remember, all it takes is an anonymous phone call to a software piracy hotline to put your business under the microscope.

Minimum hardware requirements

Before you can install Windows 2000, you need to ensure that your hardware meets Microsoft's minimum requirements for installation. For obvious system items such as RAM and hard disk space, the setup program checks to make certain you meet the minimum requirements. But the setup program can't check everything, so be sure that your system meets or, better, beats the minimum requirements. Here is a quick list of the minimum hardware requirements (as published by Microsoft) for Windows 2000 Professional:

✦ 166MHz Pentium processor or better (Note that AMD and Cyrix are both supported. See the HCL for your particular processor.)

✦ 32MB of RAM

✦ 650MB of free hard disk space on at least a 2GB drive

✦ VGA-quality monitor

✦ Keyboard and mouse

These are the minimum requirements to *install* Windows 2000. The minimum configuration runs the operating system, albeit slowly, but does not handle much else. Applications such as Office 2000 can be downright unusable. A recommended configuration is more like the following:

✦ 266MHz Pentium MMX or better

✦ 64MB to 96MB system RAM or greater

✦ 4GB hard disk with at least 1.5GB of free space

✦ S-VGA (800 by 600) or better monitor

✦ Keyboard and mouse

Windows 2000 is not for the faint of heart, despite Microsoft's minimum configuration. The operating system is memory intensive — much more so than Windows 98, for example — and the operating system and full suite of installed drivers can consume 500MB or more of hard disk space. Older systems run Windows 2000 so slowly that you'll find them all but impossible to use.

Note
Don't believe me? I installed an early beta version on a 90MHz Pentium system with 32MB of RAM and a 3.2GB hard disk drive. While Windows 2000 ran, installing and running any applications on top of it was simply out of the question. I've had much better success on a 200MHz Pentium MMX — hardly a cutting-edge system. The simple message: The better the hardware, the better Windows 2000 runs.

Even if you have a decent midrange PC, say with a Pentium II or Celeron processor running at 300MHz, you may not be out of the woods yet. Many of these PCs shipped with 64MB of RAM. While this is adequate for running Windows 2000 and one or perhaps two other applications, anyone who runs demanding applications or multitasks will experience major slowdowns. The reason is that Windows 2000 itself consumes so much system memory that it forces a lot of program code and data off to disk as virtual memory, resulting in significant performance losses. If youhave a system with a decent processor that experiences severe performance problems, a RAM upgrade to 128MB might be a sensible course of action. The good news is that you can wait until *after* the upgrade to assess the environment and add RAM only when necessary.

Hardware compatibility

The next hurdle you have to clear on your way to starting a Windows 2000 upgrade is compatibility. Anyone who has worked with Windows NT is familiar with the issues and challenges that hardware compatibility can bring. Fortunately, Microsoft has long provided a list of approved hardware devices that have been tested for compatibility with its Windows NT operating system. And thankfully, that same resource is available to users of Windows 2000 as well. Known as the Hardware Compatibility List, or simply HCL, this resource provides an up-to-date index of all the devices and hardware known to work with Windows NT and Windows 2000.

Caution

Important! Windows 2000 may function correctly with a piece of hardware that is not on the list. Your hardware's exclusion is an indication it has not been tested by Microsoft, not an indication that the hardware does not work under Windows 2000. If you want to find out if hardware that is not on the HCL will work, it may be worth installing Windows 2000, but don't be surprised if things go awry. If you call Microsoft for help, the first words might likely be, "That hardware is not compatible with Windows 2000." Remember to always check with your hardware vendor for needed drivers.

The first resource is to run the Windows 2000 Professional Compatibility Tool. The compatibility tool is a utility that checks your hardware and verifies its operation within Windows 2000. The compatibility tool is on the Windows 2000 Professional CD-ROM in the SUPPORT\NTCT folder.

In addition, the Microsoft Hardware Compatibility List is in the \SUPPORT folder on the Windows 2000 Professional CD-ROM. The file is called HCL.TXT. Open this file using Word or another robust word processing program, and you can perform a quick search for the name of the device you want to check. The HCL is too large for Notepad to handle, so use WordPad or a full-featured word processor.

An even better idea is to go online and check the constantly updated HCL information on Microsoft's Web site. You can find it at `http://www.microsoft.com/hcl`. Figure 23-1 shows the HCL search feature at work.

Tip

In fact, I don't use the disc-based HCL.TXT file at all. Remember, your Windows 2000 CD-ROM could be months old by the time it arrives at your doorstep. By using the online HCL resource, you're assured of looking at the latest compatibility data from Microsoft's labs.

Vendor-specific drivers

Many hardware vendors create their own drivers and certify them with Windows 2000. To prove the point, the driver files include a digital signature from Microsoft. This signature is an assurance that the device driver passed muster in Microsoft's labs and is compatible with Windows 2000.

Note

If you use your PC for business or other critical tasks, I recommend you stick with Microsoft-signed drivers. These drivers improve your chances for reliable operation and help keep you in the clear with tech support if problems arise.

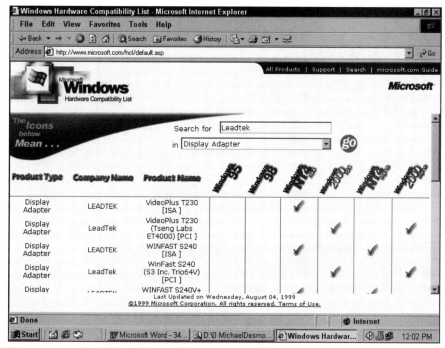

Figure 23-1: The slick online Hardware Compatibility List is *the* place to get the most up-to-date device compatibility information for all Microsoft operating systems, including Windows 2000.

To see if a driver has been signed under Windows 2000, go to the Device Manager and open the properties dialog box. Remember, you need to have Windows 2000 installed before you can perform this operation:

1. Right-click the My Computer icon and click Manage or click Start ➪ Programs ➪ Administrative Tools and click Computer Management.

2. In the Computer Management console window, click the Device Manager item in the left pane. A list of device types appears in the right pane, as shown in Figure 23-2.

3. In the right pane, double-click the device type you want to check. If it is installed, the device appears beneath the item you double-clicked.

4. Double-click the specific device entry. The device Properties dialog box opens.

5. Click the Driver tab of the Properties dialog box.

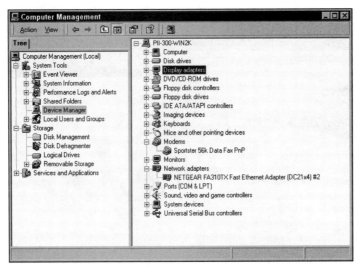

Figure 23-2: The Device Manager enables you to quickly access all your system hardware to check driver status.

You should see a Digital Signer entry on the Driver tab of the dialog box, as shown in Figure 23-3. Next to it you should see an entry such as Microsoft Windows NT Publisher or Not digitally signed. If Microsoft is not mentioned there somewhere, you likely have an unsigned driver. You may want to consider replacing it if reliable system operation is paramount.

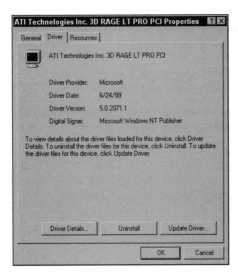

Figure 23-3: Not all devices behave alike, but most include a Driver tab that enables you to check the signature status of the installed driver.

Note Keep in mind that I'm being a bit paranoid here. Unsigned drivers may not have been tested by Microsoft, but typically the device maker has conducted more-than-adequate QA on the code. In fact, unsigned drivers are often simply the latest version of drivers that Microsoft has not yet had the time to test and sign off. A few weeks or months down the road, that very same driver may come with the reassuring Microsoft seal.

Data backup

Okay, now I'm not being paranoid; I'm just being plain smart. If you do nothing else before a Windows 2000 upgrade or installation, you must — MUST — back up any data that you cannot afford to lose. You must do the backup before you begin your installation. Otherwise, the slightest burp in the process could leave you in big-time trouble. I'm going to make a point here by listing just a few things that can cause an installation to go painfully sour:

✦ Incompatible hardware or software

✦ Brief power outage, brownout, or power spike

✦ Aging hardware

✦ Overheating chips and drives

✦ Too little memory or disk space

✦ File system errors

✦ Memory leaks

✦ Stray cosmic rays

✦ Acts of God and just plain bad luck

I think you get the picture. And because this is an operating system upgrade, the potential for disastrous data loss is definitely there. If your installation bombs, there's a good chance you may never see any of the data on your hard disk again.

So before you upgrade, make a complete backup of your data to fresh media. Take the time to verify that the backup and media are in good shape and that data can be read from your backup media. Now, if the worst happens, all you've lost is some time.

In addition, it's a good idea to make use of available recovery facilities before you upgrade. Windows 95/98, for example, can create system recovery diskettes that provide the files you need to gain text-based access to a disabled Windows 95/98 machine. This includes CD-ROM drives, enabling you to quickly reinstall Windows 95/98 in the case of a complete meltdown. Likewise, Windows NT offers emergency repair diskettes that offer similar functionality.

Before you start an upgrade, use the built-in facilities in the existing operating system to create recovery resources. Then, if something goes wrong during or after the installation (particularly for dual-boot systems), you stand a chance of getting your system back to its initial configuration. Combined with a data backup, these actions will protect your hard work.

Weighing your needs

The old adage says that choice is good. Of course, that was before everyone learned a lesson in consumer confusion from the Ma Bell breakup. Have you tried to make sense of your phone bill lately or figure out a cell phone service plan? Sheesh. Installing Windows 2000 can be a bit like puzzling through your telephone billing statement, particularly when you're trying to make sense of whether or not to install fresh. On the other hand, Microsoft has tried to simplify things by actually *taking out* some choices. I look into that as well.

A look at your choices

Windows 2000 really presents a terrific amount of flexibility in terms of system configuration. From the very first step, you can choose from three alternative installation approaches: fresh install, OS upgrade, or dual-boot. Table 23-1 lays it out for you.

Table 23-1 **Installation Choices for Windows 2000**		
Approach	*Available for*	*Description*
Upgrade	Win 95, Win 98, NT 3.51 workstation, NT 4.0 workstation (latest service pack, currently SP6)	Keeps existing data and preferences.
Fresh install	Hard drive is blank, or you are willing to have it reformatted!	Here is the chance to get a fresh start!
Dual-boot	Windows 3.x, Win 95, Win 98, NT 3.51 workstation, NT 4.0 workstation (latest service pack)	Should have a second partition to store Windows 2000.

In some cases, your situation may limit you to one approach, but in most instances, you have a choice to make. The next sections address each of these options so you can decide which path is right for your situation.

The upgrade approach

An upgrade is likely the most popular option for those putting Windows 2000 on existing systems. Why? Because you are able to keep at least some of your current environment settings, shortcuts, and other tweaks. You should also be able to seamlessly keep your client network configuration, meaning you won't have to go digging around for proper system names, domain memberships, permissions, passwords, IP addresses, and the like.

Microsoft has worked hard to make the upgrade to Windows 2000 as painless as possible. And if you are coming from Windows NT 4.0, you'll like what you see. The migration from NT (mind you, NT with the latest service pack) can offer some smooth sailing. Coming from Windows 95 and Windows 98 is a bit more complex, but again, integrated migration tools should be able to pluck information from your Registry to at least keep system settings in place.

Note   If your current operating system is Windows 3.x or NT 3.5x, you might consider a fresh install.

Don't expect too much from an upgrade, though. While your system settings and data remain intact, your programs need to be reinstalled to work properly. Otherwise, the Windows 2000 Registry will have no awareness of applications installed under the other operating system. Without a reinstall, some programs may work (if you launch them manually), but many will not. To achieve a reliable environment, you should get these applications freshly set up on your system.

Tip   You can set up your applications under both Windows 95/98 and Windows 2000 and not lose gobs of disk space. How? After setting up Windows 2000 beside the original operating system, install your applications to the same folders they were originally installed to. For example, if Windows 98 and its applications are on the C:\ drive, and Windows 2000 is on the D:\ drive, reinstall those applications to the appropriate existing folders on the C:\ drive. Doing so will avoid creating duplicate sets of program files on your disk, while still providing Windows 2000 the Registry information it needs to make file associations and other critical functions.

Fresh install

Fresh install is the approach I recommend for most people. Why? Because you really don't have to put that much more time into a fresh install over an upgrade, and you achieve a much cleaner operating environment. Starting fresh means you can eliminate the carcasses of long-deleted applications that still gum up your Registry, while completely wiping clear your hard disk to reduce performance-sapping fragmentation. In other words, you can make your old system young again.

Note   Of course, if you're installing Windows 2000 to a system running OS/2 or to another operating system that Microsoft didn't provide an upgrade path for, you must install fresh.

What's more, a fresh installation by its nature removes some of the complexity from the installation process (that is, from a code perspective). Windows 2000 doesn't need to comb an existing Registry and make guesses about what belongs where. Rather, it starts from a blank slate.

Generally, a fresh install leads to the best system performance and compatibility. But you do face the challenge of backing up and restoring all your data. Perhaps more critically, you must go through and input all your original program and environment settings. That process can take some time and can prove particularly trying because useful things such as Web site passwords and the like are lost. A smart backup approach can help ease the sting a bit.

Dual-boot

Dual-booting is actually amazingly easy with Windows 2000, and I'd recommend it to more folks if the actual task of living with a dual-boot system weren't so complex. In essence, when you dual-boot install Windows 2000, your PC has two person-alities (only one of which it can use at a time): its Windows 2000 brain and its Windows 9x, NT, or Win3.x brain. The two operating systems have virtually nothing to do with each other. That means you must manage two sets of network configura-tions, browser settings, program settings, and the like. It can become a chore, particularly when you update something in the environment and forget to apply changes to both sides of your dual-boot fence.

The payoff, though, is huge for lots of users. Game players, for example, still need Windows 98 to play all the latest games and titles (despite the incorporation of DirectX 7.0 in Windows 2000). By dual-booting, they can work under Windows 2000 and play under Windows 98. Similarly, home office workers can use Windows 2000 for work and leave Windows 98 or other operating systems to the family after hours. This helps isolate home use from critical business resources, so that an accidental folder deletion becomes much less likely.

 Tip

You want total security in one system? Dual-boot Windows 2000 and format the Windows 2000 disk partition using the New Technology File System (NTFS), the advanced file system available with Windows 2000 and Windows NT. NTFS offers features such as file-level compression and encryption and file activity logging — very useful for critical environments where security and reliable operation are val-ued. Now your kids won't even be able to see your Windows 2000 files and resources from Windows 98. That portion of the disk is invisible to the other oper-ating system, eliminating the fear of deleted files or uninvited snooping. You learn more about the intricacies of file systems later in this chapter.

Dual-booting requires a lot of disk space. Not only must you have room for two complete operating systems, you need to install two sets of applications as well. If you intend to install Microsoft Office or another suite on both sides, for example, you want at least 2GB to 4GB per partition.

Upgrading to Windows 2000

Many Windows 2000 users decide to upgrade their current systems. The Windows 2000 setup enables upgrades from Windows 95, Windows 98, or Windows NT 4.0. If you are running Windows 3.x or Windows NT 3.51, you will need to either install Windows 2000 fresh (by reformatting the hard disk) or first upgrade the existing operating system to one that is supported by Windows 2000 upgrade facility.

Remember that the upgrade replaces your existing Windows files. Because Microsoft states that it will no longer support 16-bit applications with Windows 2000, you should review all the applications that you use prior to upgrading.

Note   When I say Microsoft won't support 16-bit applications, it doesn't mean they won't run under Windows 2000. In fact, old apps may run just fine. It's just that Microsoft's technical support probably won't be of much help if you need to hunt down a problem with older software. They're cutting the cord to 16-bit applications, which means you may be on your own.

The benefits of upgrading are fairly obvious, and Microsoft has gone to great lengths to ensure that all of their current operating systems can be upgraded to Windows 2000. This is definitely an option for those who don't like to tinker with installations!

Fiddling with file systems

One thing is for sure: Moving to Windows 2000 could make you an expert in disk file systems. A file system is the structure and rule set used to read, write, and maintain data on your disk drive. Without it, all the bits on your drive would be impossible to find. Windows 2000 offers support for three hard disk file systems:

✦ **FAT:** A close derivative of the original File Allocation Table file system of DOS and later Windows 3.x.

✦ **FAT32:** A 32-bit version of FAT, it supports bigger drives, smaller file clusters, and some neat performance optimization capabilities. Windows 98 and late Windows 95 (OSR2.1) systems offer FAT32.

✦ **NTFS:** Like FAT32, the NT File System is 32 bit and supports big drives and small clusters. But NTFS offers terrific security, compression, and logging features.

Note   Actually, there's a fourth file system involved, the CD-ROM File System, or CDFS. CDFS is the standard file system used for read-only CD-ROM drives, and is common among Windows 95/98, NT, and 2000.

When you upgrade or install Windows 2000, you have to decide what file system to use. While you can certainly keep your existing file system, you could be passing by some huge advantages by not considering a change. Table 23-2 gives you an at-a-glance rundown of the pros and cons of each file system.

| Table 23-2 | | |
| Choosing a File System | | |
File system	**Advantages**	**Disadvantages**
NTFS	File-level security and compression lets you encrypt and slim down files; support for large disks does not cause performance degradation	If you dual-boot, you may not be able to access NTFS partitions from other operating systems.
FAT32	Enhanced version of FAT; supports disks from 512MB to 32GB	Does not have the file-level security; no file-level compression; not as efficient as NTFS.
FAT	Compatible with most operating systems; good for dual-boot with DOS or Windows 3.x	Performance degrades with larger sizes; supports only 2GB or smaller partitions.

Here's the short take: Use NTFS if Windows 2000 is going to be the only operating system you are going to use. It's faster and has the file-level features the other file systems lack. If you are going to dual-boot, use FAT32. It is supported by Windows 95 and later versions. Note that if you dual-boot to Windows 3.1 or DOS, use FAT because Windows 3.x and DOS do not recognize FAT32.

Tip   As I mentioned earlier, in some dual-boot situations, it makes great sense to use NTFS for your Windows 2000 partition and FAT or FAT32 for the other partition. This setup provides the best security for your Windows 2000 files and resources because the OS on the FAT-based partition is unable to even see the area where Windows 2000 resides. If you have family members using your PC for games or Internet access, this kind of dual-boot setup offers great defense against accidental deletions.

Running setup

There are two ways to install Windows 2000 Professional:

✦ Install to a PC with no operating system or an unsupported operating system

✦ Install from a current, supported operating system

In addition, there is the option to dual-boot Windows 2000 alongside another operating system. I'll also cover many of the unique issues and challenges that present themselves in a dual-boot configuration in the sections that follow.

If you were wondering what those four floppy diskettes in the package were for, now you know. If you are installing to an unsupported OS or blank system, you need these diskettes to boot up and start the install process. The CD-ROM-based installation assumes the presence of Windows 3.x, 9x, or NT; it won't work with an OS/2- or Linux-based system, for example.

Tip   Be certain to end any tasks such as antivirus software or other background applications before you run the setup routine. Antivirus routines, in particular, can confuse or abort installations.

Installing to a blank PC or unsupported operating system

If your computer is blank or your operating system is not supported, you must install Windows 2000 from scratch. To do so, you need the Windows 2000 startup disks. These should be provided in the package, but if you don't have them handy, you can quickly create them by running theMAKEBOT.EXE file in the \BOOTDISK directory of your Windows 2000 CD-ROM. If you intend to wipe out an existing operating system to install Windows 2000 fresh, make sure you create these diskettes before you nuke the existing operating system. Otherwise, you'll need to go to another system to create the diskettes. Of course, you will need to have four blank, high-density 3.5-inch floppy diskettes on hand.

Okay, enough jabbering; it's time to get down to the business of installing Windows 2000 step by step.

1. Power down your PC and insert the disk labeled startup disk #1. Power on the computer. The setup routine begins automatically (startup disk #1 is sometimes referred to as the *boot disk*). You see the character-based setup screen, which can by identified by its Microsoft Blue background. The setup program begins loading driver files one at a time.

Note   If your system has a SCSI RAID controller (very few workstations do because they are normally reserved for servers), keep an eye on the bottom of the display during this process. You will see a prompt to press F6. The prompt goes by quickly, so be ready to press F6 to set up your RAID-based system.

2. You swap in each of the four diskettes in turn, while the display shows which files the setup program is loading. During this period, Windows 2000 loads a wide range of drivers for many device types, testing them to see if it gets a response. This hit-and-miss approach enables Windows 2000 to determine the base-level hardware in your computer.

3. After the fourth disk has been accessed, the setup program reports that it is starting Windows 2000 setup. You are prompted to do one of the following: install Windows 2000, repair an existing version of Windows 2000, or exit setup completely by pressing F3.

Note

Quitting setup by pressing the F3 key at this stage causes no harm to your system. Just be aware: This is your last chance to turn back.

4. Next you are prompted to place the Windows 2000 CD-ROM in the drive. Remember, setup has loaded the CD-ROM drivers from the floppy disks, which makes it possible to run the CD-ROM drive. Place the CD-ROM in the drive and press Enter.

5. Time to sign the dotted line. The setup routine requests that you agree to the End User License Agreement. You can choose to accept or not to accept the agreement, but declining means the installation stops. Press Page down to reach the end of the agreement and then press the F8 key to accept it.

6. You are now asked which partition will house Windows 2000. Depending upon your system configuration, it may be necessary to create a new partition or delete an existing partition and create a new one.

Note

When I installed Windows 2000 over a Linux operating system, I had to delete and recreate the Linux partition. Be sure to read the instructions carefully in this section, because a missed keystroke could end up nuking the wrong partition or otherwise mangling your carefully thought-out plans. For example, at one point, setup asks you to confirm the deletion of a partition by pressing L rather than Enter. Just be careful.

7. If you choose to create a new partition, setup now prompts you to format the partition. There are two choices: NTFS or FAT. If your partition is larger than 2GB (2048MB), setup automatically prompts you to format with FAT32.

Note

There are some limitations with FAT32 and Windows 3.1/95. Refer to Table 23-2 for help.

8. Setup now begins formatting the partition. If your disk is 3GB or larger and you have chosen FAT32, go get a cup of coffee. It might be a while.

9. After the format is complete, setup automatically copies files from the CD-ROM to your hard disk. Might be time for another cup of coffee.

10. Once the copying is complete, the screen indicates that a reboot is imminent. Setup counts down for 15 seconds before rebooting. Be sure to pull that setup disk #4 out of the drive before it restarts!

11. After rebooting, Windows 2000 displays the text-based boot selector menu. It should appear as a black screen with white lettering. Windows 2000 Professional should be listed there as the only option. Either you can let the

timer expire and Windows 2000 setup continues, or you can press Enter and receive the same result.

12. You are now entering the graphical phase of the installation. At this point, all flavors of installation act the same. To continue, skip ahead to the section "Common installation routines."

Dual-boot cautions

Dual-boot is a great option. Currently my personal machine boots between Windows 98 and Windows 2000 with no problems. But dual-booting can be dangerous for those who aren't sure what they are doing. Still, if you are in a situation that requires more than one operating system, this is a feature that you cannot live without. Windows 2000 supports dual-booting with the following operating systems:

✦ Windows NT 3.51

✦ Windows NT 4.0 (requires Service Pack 4 or higher)

✦ Windows 95

✦ Windows 98

✦ Windows 3.1

✦ Windows for Workgroups 3.11

✦ MS-DOS

As I said, dual-booting is enormously useful but a bit tricky. So to try to get ahead of the game, keep reading for a few helpful hints for that PC with two brains.

Braving boot sectors

If you intend to dual-boot Windows 2000 with either Windows 95 or MS-DOS, it's best to install the non-Windows 2000 operating systems first. The problem is that Windows 2000 changes your drive's partition boot sector upon installation. If MS-DOS is installed after Windows 2000, the partition boot sector is overwritten, and you won't be able to boot Windows 2000 any longer.

Tip   Is this advice a little too late for you? If so, there is hope. An emergency repair disk can enable you to recover the boot sector settings so that both operating systems once again work.

If MS-DOS or Windows 95/98 is already installed, however, Windows 2000 copies the partition boot sector to a file BOOTSECT.DOS. Next, Windows 2000 creates its own version of the partition boot sector, which it uses to load the Windows 2000 boot loader, or NTLDR. The Windows boot loader is the character-based screen that displays the option of which operating system to load. If you choose the DOS/Windows 95 option, the boot loader loads the original BOOTSECT.DOS, and the non-Windows 2000 operating system loads.

Why all this finagling? This setup actually enables the operating systems to share resources, yet remain unaware of each other. Note that Windows 98 is Windows NT/2000 aware, so you don't have to sweat the order of installation when dual-booting Windows 98 and Windows 2000.

Beware NTFS issues

When making file system choices, you should almost always use the FAT or FAT32 file system on the C: partition of your PC's disk drive. While Windows 2000 supports NTFS, any operating system other than Windows NT 4.0 does not. To avoid confusion and possible loss of data, initially format all your partitions using FAT or FAT32. You can then use the helpful CONVERT.EXE text-based utility to move partitions to NTFS later.

There are other issues with NTFS and Windows 2000 on dual-boot systems. If you dual-boot Windows 2000 and NT 4.0 and both are installed to NTFS partitions, NT 4.0 won't be able to see changes made by Windows 2000. The reason is because when Windows 2000 alters or creates file on its NTFS partition, the file is no longer accessible to any other operating system.

 Caution   Do not install Windows 2000 on a compressed drive. For obvious reasons, installing on a compressed drive is guaranteed to cause problems! And as a side note, Windows 2000 does not support the DriveSpace compression featured in Windows 9x.

A few final cautions

If you install Windows 95 or Windows 98 after Windows 2000, it is possible that these operating systems could have changed hardware settings such as IRQs or memory addresses. Review and record all your hardware resource settings before you add a second operating system. That way you can compare settings between the two should a problem arise.

Finally, a network note: If you dual-boot Windows NT 4.0 Workstation in an NT domain, the NT installation must have a different computer name than the Windows 2000 installation. Even if you try to assign the same name to both personalities of a dual-boot machine, the security IDs associated with the creation of the two accounts will be unique. In other words, you won't be able to quickly replicate permissions by adopting the same name — you need to individually set permissions for each personality.

In any case, it's good practice to assign different names to each side of a dual-boot system, if only to make it clear on the network which operating system is connected.

Creating a dual-boot system

With these tips and cautions fresh in your mind, here's how to create a dual-booting Windows 2000 machine.

1. Boot your PC to the current operating system. If you do not have an OS installed, Microsoft suggests you install the non-Windows 2000 operating system first.

2. Insert your Windows 2000 installation CD-ROM into the drive. If you are upgrading over a network, access the appropriate share resource on the LAN.

3. Run the SETUP.EXE file in the \I386 directory. You should see a dialog box similar to the one in Figure 23-4.

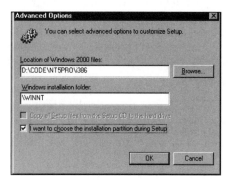

Figure 23-4: The Advanced Options dialog box enables you to point your system at the setup files over a network, useful for office upgrades.

4. Click the radio button labeled Install a new copy of Windows 2000 (Clean Install) and click Next. Figure 23-6 shows this dialog box.

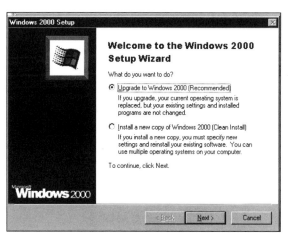

Figure 23-5: By default, Windows 2000 tries to upgrade your existing operating system. You need to click the lower radio button to keep your old OS.

5. You now see another dialog box that demands you accept the End User License Agreement. Read the agreement carefully and click I accept. Or if you do not agree, click the I don't accept this agreement and the installation aborts.

6. The next box has three configuration checkboxes on it. Language (the default is English – United States), Accessibility options (Magnifier and Narrator), and Advanced options. If you have a need for the accessibility or language options, click the appropriate box. However, you should click the Advanced options checkbox.

7. The Advanced options button contains three important items: the location of the Windows 2000 source files, the directory where Windows 2000 should be installed, and the option to have setup copy the CD to the hard drive and choose which partition to install on. Click the checkbox marked I want to choose the partition during setup. Click OK and then click Next.

Caution   This is a very important step. You must check the Advanced Options checkbox in Step 6 and then specify a partition in Step 7. Otherwise, Windows 2000 will most likely treat your installation as an upgrade, effectively wiping out your existing Windows 95/98 or NT setup!

8. Now Windows 2000 asks if you would like to upgrade the partition to NTFS. Answer No to this question. For more information, see the dual-booting tips.

9. Clicking Next invokes a quick file copy and then a dialog box informing you that the system will reboot.

10. When the computer reboots, one of two things happens:

    If your preexisting operating system was Windows NT or Windows 2000, the boot selector appears with a new entry for the setup of Windows 2000. If your existing operating system was Windows 98, a blue screen appears and the setup process begins right away.

10. Setup begins copying files in earnest. When it is finished, it displays a screen rebooting the machine. Setup now enters the graphical portion of the installation. Skip ahead to the section "Common installation routines" for the remainder of the steps.

Upgrading another Windows operating system

Many users will no doubt upgrade to Windows 2000 from Windows 98 or Windows NT 4.0 Workstation. Upgrading an existing operating system is actually quite simple. The setup program detects and installs the correct drivers for all the system hardware. If Windows 2000 cannot support some of this hardware, it reports it.

Note Windows 2000 offers plenty of upgrade paths, but you need to be careful. For example, Windows 2000 Professional will not upgrade an existing Windows NT 4.0 Server system. It will only work with Windows NT 4.0 Workstation.

Follow these steps to upgrade an existing operating system to Windows 2000:

1. Boot your system to your current operating system. If you do not have an operating system installed, Microsoft suggests you install the non-Windows 2000 operating system first.

2. Access your Windows 2000 installation media. This can be the CD-ROM, the code copied to your hard drive, or a network share.

3. Run the SETUP.EXE file in the root directory of the CD-ROM.

4. Click the box marked Upgrade to Windows 2000 (Recommended) and click Next.

5. Here comes the perfunctory End User License Agreement acceptance (be sure to read it!). If you agree, click the appropriate choice and click Next.

6. You are next prompted to upgrade your drive to NTFS. If you do not plan to use any other operating system with this PC, I recommend selecting Yes; otherwise, choose No.

7. Setup begins copying files. When finished, it begins a countdown sequence to reboot the computer.

8. You now enter the character-based mode of setup. After copying files, setup begins examining your hard disk for errors and available space.

9. When finished, Windows 2000 setup copies the installation files to your hard drive.

10. After another reboot, the graphical part of the installation begins. A nice splash screen of Windows 2000 appears and asks you to wait.

That's pretty much it. You are not prompted for any more information. Windows 2000 reboots twice more before running through a few more copying, registering, and component installation routines. But because this is an upgrade, Windows 2000 already has all of the information it needs. You may be prompted for an administrator password if you are upgrading from Windows 98.

Common installation routines

As you no doubt noticed, many Windows 2000 installations share a common set of steps. In order to avoid boring you to death, I've bundled these together right here. These steps pick up where you left off with your installation.

Getting started

1. When starting, setup automatically detects as many devices as possible. This process may take some time, so be prepared to wait. Also, don't panic if the display flickers a bit; that's just Windows 2000 testing the display adapter and monitor.

2. The setup program prompts you to continue with the installation. Click Next.

3. Time to set the, well, time. Setup asks if you would like to customize your Regional settings. The locale settings by default are set to English — United States. Click the customize button if you need to change them. The keyboard setting by default is set to US Keyboard Layout. Click the adjacent customize button if you need to change it.

Names and dates

1. The next dialog box requests your Name and Organization. Because this is the name that appears on every splash screen for almost all of the Microsoft applications installed on your PC, I suggest you think about what you enter in the boxes. Click Next to continue.

2. Setup continues by asking for a computer name and administrator password.

Note

In order to ease administration and network access, be sure to choose a system name that is both descriptive and unique. The administrator password should be something you can remember but is not easy to guess. Anyone who gets the password has instant access to all your files.

3. If you have a modem and Windows 2000 detected it, you are prompted to supply your telephone area code and outside line access prefix, if necessary. Click Next.

4. The date and time settings now appear. This is the system time for Windows 2000. Enter the correct information and your current time zone. On this screen you can also enable the daylight savings time feature.

Network cards

If you have a network card, Windows 2000 setup now begins preparing the networking components. Be aware that if you are upgrading another operating system to Windows 2000, and have working network connections in place, you won't have to worry about these steps. Windows 2000 will automatically assume the existing network settings.

1. Windows 2000 asks if you want to install typical network settings or if you would like to customize them. If you are on a network, you generally must get the relevant network information from your administrator. Items such as default protocol, network client, and any other services need to be addressed.

If you are upgrading to Windows 2000, you do not need to make any network changes; just click Next.

2. Choosing Typical installs the Client for Microsoft Networks and TCP/IP. Typical is recommended for most users.

3. If you need to change the network settings, click the Customize button.

4. The Network components screen appears showing the following: NIC card, MAC address, network client (MS Networks and File and Print sharing), and TCP/IP. Use the Install, Uninstall, and Properties buttons to make changes where needed.

For a discussion of networking concepts, see Chapter 12. For more information about networking Windows 2000-based PCs, see Chapter 13.

5. The last part of the Networking components section prompts you to join a workgroup or domain. A *workgroup* is just a group of computers sharing the same workgroup name on a network. No central authority provides security. Workgroups are most common in small networks. A *domain* is a Windows NT- or Windows 2000-based network that is created to provide centralized security and administration. To join a domain, you need to have an account created by a network administrator. You must also have the appropriate user name and password to access network resources. If you are unsure of what to do, ask your network administrator.

6. Click the Next button to cause the network to start. If you can see your network card, you might see the green link light blinking. That's a good sign because it means data is being traded over the wire.

Final steps

Now another bar graph appears indicating that the setup routine is installing components and performing final tasks. Microsoft offers some status updates by displaying dialog boxes such as the following:

✦ Installing Start Menu Items

✦ Registering Components

✦ Saving Settings

✦ Removing Temporary Files

Now you can finish the job. Windows 2000 setup declares that you have successfully completed the installation. This is a bit of a fib, actually, because there is a bit more waiting around to do. Setup loads and applies personal settings. When finished, the ever-present Getting Started splash screen appears. Okay, this time the installation is really done. Honest.

Advanced Windows 2000 Installations

The vast majority of users will go through the installation scenarios I've described, using the graphical interface and default setup characteristics. But more advanced users, particularly network administrators, might need to assert additional control over the installation process. Windows 2000 provides options for doing this:

✦ Command-line syntax arguments for theWINNT32.EXE executable

✦ Unattended setup

Windows NT command-line syntax

The Windows 2000 setup program is actually a file called WINNT32.EXE found in the I386 directory of your Windows 2000 CD-ROM. You can customize the installation parameters by supplying one of the many switches. Here is a listing of all the options open to the WINNT32.EXE. This information comes directly from the WINNT32.HLP help file.

✦ **/s:sourcepath:** Specifies the source location of the Windows 2000 files. To simultaneously copy files from multiple servers, specify multiple /s sources. If you use multiple /s switches, the first specified server must be available or setup fails.

✦ **/tempdrive:drive_letter:** Directs setup to place temporary files on the specified partition and to install Windows 2000 on that partition.

✦ **/unattend:** Upgrades your previous version of Windows2000 in unattended setup mode. All user settings are taken from the previous installation, so no user intervention is required during setup.

Using the /unattend switch to automate setup affirms that you have read and accepted the End User License Agreement (EULA) for Windows 2000. Before using this switch to install Windows 2000 on behalf of an organization other than your own, you must confirm that the end user (whether an individual or a single entity) has received, read, and accepted the terms of the Windows 2000 EULA. OEMs may not specify this key on machines being sold to end users.

✦ **/unattend[num]:[answer_file]:** Performs a fresh installation in unattended setup mode. The answer file provides setup with your custom specifications.

Answer_file is the specific name of the file being used to provide automated inputs during the setup process. Num is the number of seconds between the time that setup finishes copying the files and when it restarts your computer. You can use num on any computer running Windows NT or Windows 2000.

✦ **/copydir:folder_name:** Creates an additional folder within the folder in which the Windows 2000 files are installed. For example, if the source folder contains a folder called Private_drivers that has modifications just for your site, you can type **/copydir:Private_drivers** to have setup copy that folder to your installed Windows 2000 folder. So then the new folder location is C:\Winnt\ Private_drivers. You can use /copydir to create as many additional folders as you want.

✦ **/copysource:folder_name:** Creates a temporary additional folder within the folder in which the Windows 2000 files are installed. For example, if the source folder contains a folder called Private_drivers that has modifications just for your site, you can type **/copysource:Private_drivers** to have setup copy that folder to your installed Windows 2000 folder and use its files during setup. So then the temporary folder location is C:\Winnt\Private_drivers. Unlike the folders /copydir creates, /copysource folders are deleted after setup completes.

✦ **/cmd:command_line:** Instructs setup to carry out a specific command before the final phase of setup. This would occur after your computer has restarted twice and after setup has collected the necessary configuration information, but before setup is complete.

✦ **/debug[level]:[filename]:** Creates a debug log at the level specified, for example, /debug4:C:\Win2000.log. The default log file is C:\%Windir%\ Winnt32.log, with the debug level set to 2. The log levels are as follows: 0-severe errors, 1-errors, 2-warnings, 3-information, and 4-detailed information for debugging. Each level includes the levels below it.

✦ **/udf:id[,UDB_file]:** Indicates an identifier (id) that setup uses to specify how a Uniqueness Database (UDB) file modifies an answer file (see the /unattend entry). The UDB overrides values in the answer file, and the identifier determines which values in the UDB file are used. For example, /udf:RAS_user,Our_ company.udb overrides settings specified for the identifier RAS_user in the Our_company.udb file. If no UDB_file is specified, setup prompts the user to insert a disk that contains the $Unique$.udb file.

✦ **/syspart:drive_letter:** Specifies that you can copy setup startup files to a hard disk, mark the disk as active, and then install the disk into another computer. When you start that computer, it automatically starts with the next phase of the setup. You must always use the /tempdrive parameter with the /syspart parameter.

The /syspart switch for WINNT32.EXE runs only from a computer that already has Windows NT 3.51, Windows NT4.0, or Windows 2000 installed on it. It cannot be run from Windows 9x.

✦ **/checkupgradeonly:** Checks your computer for upgrade compatibility with Windows 2000. For Windows 95 or Windows 98 upgrades, setup creates a report named UPGRADE.TXT in the Windows installation folder. For Windows NT 3.51 or 4.0 upgrades, it saves the report to theWINNT32.LOG in the installation folder.

✦ **/cmdcons:** Adds to the operating system selection screen a Recovery Console option for repairing a failed installation. It is only used after setup.

✦ **/m:folder_name:** Specifies that setup copies replacement files from an alternate location. Instructs setup to look in the alternate location first and if files are present, use them instead of the files from the default location.

✦ **/makelocalsource:** Instructs setup to copy all installation source files to your local hard disk. Use /makelocalsource when installing from a CD to provide installation files when the CD is not available later in the installation.

✦ **/noreboot:** Instructs setup to not restart the computer after the file copy phase of winnt32 is completed so that you can execute another command.

Unattended setup mode

This section is geared more toward the network administrator. The unattended setup enables you to install Windows 2000 without any user intervention. All that is required is a text file known as an *answer file*. The answer file (created by you) provides the answers to all of the questions that the Windows 2000 setup asks.

The unattended setup mode is designed to help deploy multiple Windows 2000 Professional workstations because it can speed up the process and enable multiple installs to happen simultaneously. There are two versions of the unattended setup mode: upgrade and fresh install.

An unattended upgrade essentially answers Yes to all of the End User License Agreement questions. A sample file can be found on your Windows 2000 CD-ROM in the I386 folder. The file is UNATTEND.TXT. The actual text is below.

```
; Microsoft Windows 2000 Professional, Server, Advanced Server and Datacenter
; (c) 1994 - 1999 Microsoft Corporation. All rights reserved.
;
; Sample Unattended Setup Answer File
;
; This file contains information about how to automate the installation
; or upgrade of Windows 2000 Professional and Windows 2000 Server so the
; Setup program runs without requiring user input.
;

[Unattended]
Unattendmode = FullUnattended
OemPreinstall = NO
TargetPath = WINNT
Filesystem = LeaveAlone

[UserData]
FullName = "Your User Name"
OrgName = "Your Organization Name"
```

```
ComputerName = "COMPUTER_NAME"

[GuiUnattended]
; Sets the Timezone to the Pacific Northwest
; Sets the Admin Password to NULL
; Turn AutoLogon ON and login once
TimeZone = "004"
AdminPassword = *
AutoLogon = Yes
AutoLogonCount = 1

;For Server installs
[LicenseFilePrintData]
AutoMode = "PerServer"
AutoUsers = "5"

[GuiRunOnce]
; List the programs that you want to launch when the machine is logged into for
; the first time

[Display]
BitsPerPel = 8
XResolution = 800
YResolution = 600
VRefresh = 70

[Networking]
; When set to YES, setup will install default networking components. The
; components to be set are TCP/IP, File and Print Sharing, and the Client for
; Microsoft Networks.
InstallDefaultComponents = YES

[Identification]
JoinWorkgroup = Workgroup
```

Summary

Windows 2000 is based on NT technology, and the installation proves just that. The setup program is nearly the same as it is with Windows NT 4.0 but with some improvements. Plug-and-Play support and more upgrade options are just the beginning. There are just a few basic rules to remember when installing Windows 2000:

✦ Know what kind of install you want: fresh (including dual boot), upgrade, or start from scratch.

✦ Choose your file system according to your needs. FAT, NTFS, or FAT32.

✦ BACK UP YOUR DATA PRIOR TO INSTALLING!

✦ Bring a cup of coffee; the install can take a little while.

For the most part, the installation is stable. In the multiple times I have had to install Windows 2000, I encountered only one problem and that corrected itself after a reboot!

In the next chapter, we delve into the various power management features of Windows 2000. In fact, Windows 2000 finally gives the growing ranks of notebook computers the capability to run Microsoft's corporate-level operating system.

✦   ✦   ✦

Power Management

Ask any IT manager, business executive, or traveling sales professional why they use Windows 98 instead of Windows NT on mobile PCs, and you get one answer loud and clear: NT can't do power management. Although notebook vendors have recently released custom power management facilities for their various product lines, no standard power management is built into Windows NT 4.0. The result is that a notebook running Windows NT has an effective battery life that is shorter by half or more than the battery life of Windows 98 systems.

Some IT departments have taken up custom power management solutions to get their notebooks transitioned to NT, but the challenges are many. Custom power management is usually tailored for a specific notebook family. Companies supporting more than one mobile platform have to support more than one power management solution, if solutions are available at all. For notebook lines lacking NT power management facilities, the only real answer was to replace the systems with a product line that enjoyed such support. In either case, migrating laptops to NT often yielded higher operating expenses.

Finally, Windows 2000 Professional makes it possible for both IT departments and individuals to take an industrial-strength operating system on the road. Compatible notebooks running Windows 2000 are able to shut down on specified intervals, blank their screens, idle their hard disks, and go into hibernation. The result is acceptable battery life when running the NT code base.

Power Management Basics

What is power management exactly? Essentially, power management is a set of features and capabilities that enables the operating system or other application to interact with system hardware to reduce power consumption based on predefined rules. Power-savvy notebooks based on Windows 9x, for example, can be set to blank their screens and idle their hard disk drives using standard OS-based features. And different sets of rules can be applied to systems based on their profiles (desktop versus notebook) or environment (plugged-in versus on-battery).

Today, power management is typically based on activity tracking. Windows 2000 or other power-savvy software keeps tabs on system activity, noting when there is a pause in typing or mouse input, for example. When a defined period of time has passed — say, 10 minutes — the software can blank the screen and shut down power to that component. A few minutes after that, the software can be told to idle the hard disk and even put the machine into Sleep mode. Click a keyboard key or wiggle the mouse, and the system reactivates the display and resumes normal operation.

Most power management falls into five common areas:

✦ **Blank the display:** Saves copious amounts of power, particularly on note-books with large 14- and 15-inch *active-matrix* displays, which produce considerable brightness and contrast. Power is cut off to the display. Flat-panel screens recover to brightness quickly, but desktop-based *cathode ray tube* (CRT) monitors can take awhile to warm up if the components are allowed to cool.

✦ **Idle the hard disk:** Physically spinning the hard disk — as well as floppy and CD-ROM drive mechanisms — draws a lot of power. Disks can therefore be spun down to save power. The drawback is that it takes time to spin up a disk in order to read or write data, impairing system performance.

✦ **Slow down the CPU:** No matter how fast you type or read, no one needs 300MHz of processing power to review or enter text into a document. Power management can slow your 300MHz processor down to 100MHz, reducing power consumption. Again, overall performance suffers, particularly in such demanding tasks as presentations and multitasking applications.

✦ **System standby:** This approach basically tells the system to take a nap. The display goes dark, the hard disk and other drives spin down, and even the CPU settles into a quiescent state. Enough power is supplied to keep the contents of system memory fresh, but otherwise the system is inoperable. Recovery from Standby mode is relatively quick because your active work is still in RAM.

✦ **Hibernation:** The next step after Standby is Hibernation. This mode shuts down everything, including the processor and system RAM, to achieve maximum power savings. In fact, a single battery can last for weeks in Standby mode. Before going into hibernation, a snapshot of the system state is sent to the hard disk, so that it can be recovered later. The hard disk storage yields long recovery times — on the order of 30 seconds or more — because the saved profile must be read from a spun-down disk.

Note

Hibernation mode can actually increase power consumption if used improperly. That's because a lot of disk activity occurs when your system state is saved or restored. If you plan to be away from your PC for a short period — say, 5 or 10 minutes — you are better off just putting the notebook into Standby mode.

The Technology Behind Power Management

If power management were easy, it would have been implemented under Windows NT 4.0 a long time ago. The challenge is making the operating system work with all the different hardware that's out there. Both hardware and software need to agree on a common set of rules when it comes to interacting on power issues.

Power management has evolved in baby steps over the years. The Advanced Configuration and Power Interface (ACPI) specification, released in 1996, was the first industry-wide effort to set rules for power management. ACPI enabled widespread adoption by hardware vendors for operations such as intelligent shutdown and recovery.

More recently, the Advanced Power Management (APM) specification has brought full interoperability and an effective feature set to both hardware and software. APM-compliant systems are able to enter and recover from full system hibernation, for example, and provide intelligent interaction between hardware and software.

What do you need to ensure that your notebooks can provide power management under Windows 2000? You need two things:

✦ An APM-compliant BIOS

✦ APM-compliant hardware

Of course, any notebook you plan to use with Windows 2000 should first pass muster on the hardware compatibility list (HCL). Go to www.microsoft.com/hcl to find out if your notebook make and model are present on the HCL. If not, you may still be able to migrate to Windows 2000 on that platform, but the difficulty involved may increase markedly. And the likelihood of power management support goes down as well. You should check with your notebook vendor if you have any questions prior to the upgrade.

Power Management: Not Just for Notebooks

I spend a lot of time talking about notebooks in this chapter, but power management is also an important feature for desktop PCs. Corporate IT departments can realize cost savings by deploying APM-compliant desktop systems. How? For one thing, desktop PCs that power down consume a lot less electricity than those that are on all the time. That may not seem like much when you're talking about a single system, but multiply the savings out over 1,000, 10,000, or more PCs, and big money can be saved. Companies also find that they can reduce costs related to cooling because those big 17-inch CRT monitors aren't pumping warm air into office buildings.

IT departments can also ease their management workload by using APM features to make it easier to access PCs during off-hours. Systems that are physically turned off pose a challenge because administrators must often go to each system and manually turn it on. Systems that are asleep, however, can be accessed normally over the network, enabling software upgrades, system inventory, and other activities during nonworking hours.

Finally, power management can even add an element of security to the workplace. By default, Windows 2000 requires you to reauthenticate when you wake up a sleeping system. That means that if you walk away from your desk, within a set period of time your PC is no longer be accessible to strangers — unless they have your user name and password, that is. The result is that power management narrows the window of vulnerability at the desktop.

In some cases, you may be able to achieve power management compatibility on a platform with power management issues. For example, systems with older BIOS code written prior to 1998 probably lack API compliance, but in many cases, you can obtain a BIOS upgrade from the system vendor to provide full APM functionality on your notebook and desktop systems.

Note   A BIOS upgrade can do more than make your PCs power-savvy. It can help you dodge thorny Year 2000 issues as well. While Windows 2000 is Year 2000 compliant and represents a good solution for eliminating Y2K issues on client PCs, the underlying BIOS code can introduce problems. When checking with your vendor regarding APM-aware BIOS updates, make a point to inquire about Year 2000 compliance as well.

Assessing Power Options

That's enough theory and background. It's time to sink your teeth into power management issues and see whether Windows 2000 can actually solve the notebook power crunch. I start with a quick tour of the power management facilities of Windows 2000.

When it comes to managing the flow of juice in your system, it all begins and ends with the Power Options Properties dialog box. This is where you do everything from create power profiles to monitor battery life. To get to this useful dialog box, go through the Windows 2000 Control Panel. Click Start ➪ Settings ➪ Control Panel ➪ Power Options.

The way this dialog box behaves differs depending on whether or not you have an APM-aware system. The reason is because APM provides more fine-tuned control of power management settings. Figures 24-1 and 24-2 show the default property dialog box for non-APM and APM-enabled systems. Because the APM-aware interface is a superset of the base power management interface, I assume for this discussion that your PCs are APM aware.

Tip If you launch the Power Options Properties box and see only four tabs, don't give up too quickly. To ensure operation, Windows 2000 assumes that your PC lacks APM compliance and therefore does not enable this capability. To enable APM, you need to click the APM tab and look at the Enable Advanced Power Management Support checkbox. If it's not checked, check it now. Then click OK to close the dialog box. Be sure to refresh the settings in the Control Panel by pressing F5 while in the Control Panel window. Then open the Power Options facility again.

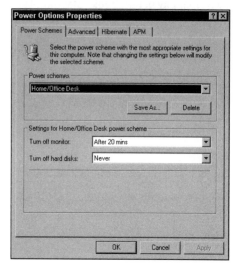

Figure 24-1: The base set of power management features lets you turn off monitors and disks, but not put your PC into power-saving standby mode.

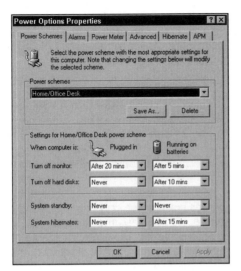

Figure 24-2: Notice the additional tabs on the dialog box when APM has been enabled? The Power Schemes page also adds entries for system standby and hibernation modes.

Note   There's another reason to focus on APM-aware systems. Virtually all notebooks and most desktops sold over the past 18 to 24 months include APM capability. The fact is any notebook older than that is going to have a hard time running Windows 2000 effectively. The result is that the vast majority of notebooks that run Windows 2000 can provide APM features.

When you launch the Power Options icon in the Control Panel on an APM-enabled system, a dialog box with six tabs appears:

    ✦ **Power Schemes:** Set your power-saving parameters here. This is where most of the real work gets done.

    ✦ **Alarms:** Windows 2000 can tell you when battery power is getting low.

    ✦ **Power Meter:** Keep an eye on power levels.

    ✦ **Advanced:** Secure your powered-down PC. This is the biggest benefit.

    ✦ **Hibernate:** Turn your notebook into a power camel by enabling it to go into Hibernate mode.

    ✦ **APM:** Turn APM capability on or off.

Power management is surprisingly easy to manage under Windows 2000, thanks to the clear and concise tools in the Power Options Properties dialog box. I step you through each tab of this resource in the following sections so you can learn how to manage power.

All about power schemes

When it comes to power management under Windows 2000, it all starts and ends at the Power Schemes tab of the Power Options Properties dialog box. The default tab when you launch into Power Options, the Power Schemes tab enables you to choose from prerolled power schemes, create new schemes, and tailor existing ones. Figure 24-3 shows the prebuilt power settings you can choose on an APM-enabled system.

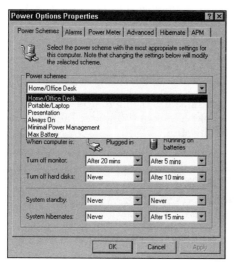

Figure 24-3: Choice is a good thing, no doubt, but the six preset power schemes provided with Windows 2000 seem to lack differentiation.

Note   The Power Options dialog box seems to have a dozen faces. For example, the Power Schemes tab can include up to eight drop-down list elements if your PC includes a battery, features APM, and is set to make use of the hibernation feature. By contrast, many desktops without such power-saving tweaks enabled could present as few as two drop-down controls. Refer to Figure 24-1 to see a basic Power Options dialog box on a system lacking aggressive power management facilities.

Reviewing power schemes

The top-most drop-down list box, labeled Power schemes, enables you to choose from a series of power profiles that were either provided with Windows 2000 or have been created by the user or administrator. By default, Windows 2000 includes six preset power schemes:

✦ **Home/Office Desk:** The default setting turns off the most power-hungry component — the CRT display — after 20 minutes but otherwise leaves desktop subsystems active.

✦ **Portable/Laptop:** Attempts to preserve battery life when a notebook is unplugged by powering down all available settings after just 5 minutes of inactivity.

✦ **Presentation:** Helps prevent the dreaded presentation power-down. All power-saving features are disabled when the notebook is plugged in, and even battery settings are liberal.

✦ **Always On:** The monitor powers down after 20 minutes but the hard disk is always active to ensure quick response.

✦ **Minimal Power Management:** Like the default setting, your key desktop subsystems (aside from display) are always on.

✦ **Max Battery:** Aggressive battery settings shut down your monitor after just one minute and your hard disk after three. Not recommended if you want to read documents on an airplane because the monitor keeps cutting out.

Now that you've got a sense for what each setting is trying to do — not to mention the considerable overlap among them — take a look at the specs. Table 24-1 compares the preset power schemes side by side.

Table 24-1
Power Schemes at a Glance

Scheme	Monitor (plugged/unplugged)	Hard disk (plugged/unplugged)	System standby
Home/Office Desk	20/5 mins	never/10 mins	never/never
Portable/Laptop	15/5 mins	30/5 mins	20/5 mins
Presentation	never/never	never/5 mins	never/15 mins
Always On	20 mins/15 mins	never/30 mins	never/never
Minimal Power Management	15/5 mins	never/15 mins	never/5 mins
Max Battery	15/1mins	never/3 mins	20/2 mins

Creating power schemes

Now that you've reviewed the existing power schemes, you can make your own. Here's how:

1. Open the Power Options dialog box by clicking Start ➪ Settings ➪ Control Panel and double-clicking the Power Options icon.

2. With the default Home/Office Desk scheme selected in the Power schemes drop-down control, click Save As.

3. In the Save Scheme dialog box shown in Figure 24-4, type a new name for your power scheme over the existing one. Click OK.

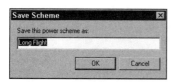

Figure 24-4: Give your new scheme a name before you get too far down the road.

Note

Why save first? One, it's a precaution to ensure you don't accidentally overwrite the original settings. Two, saving at the front makes it easier to save as you go. That way, if you need to drop your work quickly, you can come back later, open the newly saved power scheme, and start where you left off.

4. Back at the Power Options Properties dialog box, start with the settings under Plugged in. I assume you want maximum responsiveness when running off AC power. Start off by setting the Turn off monitor drop-down list control to Never.

5. Powering up the hard disk is a lengthy process, so set the Turn off hard disks drop-down control to Never as well.

6. I'm a bit of a security nut, so I'm going to set my plugged-in PC to drop into Standby mode after 15 minutes. Click the System standby drop-down list box and select After 15 mins from the list. Figure 24-5 shows the long and distinguished selection.

Note

If your system has been set to support Hibernate mode, a pair of drop-down controls appears beneath the System standby controls. As with the System standby setting, you can set a time interval for hibernation that controls when the PC saves your active profile to disk and shuts down. When you start up the PC again, Windows 2000 boots directly to the screen you were on. As a rule of thumb, set System hibernates to an interval longer than System standby.

7. Next, address consumption on the road. To maximize battery life, set the Turn off monitor control to After 3 mins. (I'm sorry, but 1 minute is just too aggressive for me.)

8. Set the Turn off hard disks control to 3 minutes at well.

9. Finally, set System standby to After 5 mins.

10. Click the Save As button again and click OK at the Save Scheme dialog box.

11. Now select the power scheme you want active for this system and click OK or Apply for the new scheme to take effect.

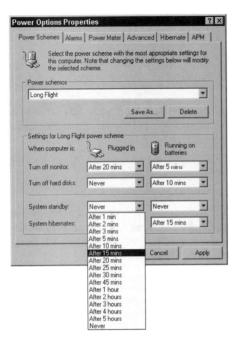

Figure 24-5: An embarrassment of choices confronts you when you want to set shutdown intervals. Personally, I think a simple spinner control—which enables you to type in values—would work better here.

Congratulations! You just rolled your own power scheme. Now when you click the Power schemes drop-down control, you see your new scheme title in the list along with the others. Figure 24-6 shows the final result.

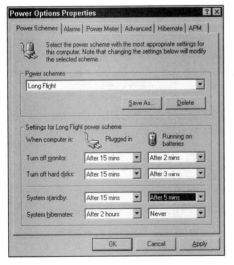

Figure 24-6: Take a moment to review your final results. You want to make sure that you didn't mix up the settings for AC and battery-based operation, for example.

Granted, the list of power schemes is rather long. And by creating a power scheme, you just added to it. To pare down available power options, click the Power schemes drop-down list box, click the scheme you want to remove, and click the Delete button. Windows 2000 prompts you to confirm the deletion. Click Yes, and the system removes the power scheme and returns you to the default Home/Office Desk scheme.

Note

If you're an IT manager, you might consider paring down the Power schemes list to just one or two formally approved schemes for your workplace. Doing so can help ensure that unattended desktop systems remain accessible only for a limited time, for example, and can also help reduce support calls from those who accidentally set power schemes and mistake power savings behavior for a system problem.

Sound the alarm!

Okay, so the section title is a little dramatic. All you're doing here is defining how Windows 2000 tells you when battery power is running low. Don't underestimate the importance of this little feature. Many a presentation and long file download have been rudely interrupted by a system that turned itself off due to a low battery. The Alarm tab of the Power Options Properties dialog box ensures that you don't get caught by surprise.

Figure 24-7 shows the two battery alarm slider controls, the top one for providing an early heads up and the lower one for handling low battery levels. By default, both of these are set to kick up a dialog box warning that you click to confirm that you know the battery status.

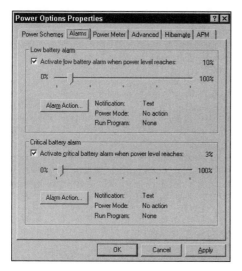

Figure 24-7: By default, Windows 2000 assumes power is low when the battery has reached 10 percent charge and that shutdown is imminent at 3 percent. You can change these settings, however.

Of course, sometimes a text message isn't enough. Perhaps you have an unattended download underway or an unsaved document open. In these cases, you can escalate the warning—from text to an audio alarm—as well as have the system act on its low battery status.

Adjusting alarm settings

Here you learn how to tailor your settings. Personally, I like the defaults that Windows 2000 uses for the low battery level state. However, I think the critical battery alarm settings could be a bit more aggressive. The following steps explain how to make a few changes to the critical alarm properties.

Note   The Low battery alarm and Critical battery alarm facilities are identical in every respect. Use the steps I outline here to set the Low battery alarm settings too.

1. By default, the Activate alarm checkbox is checked. This tells Windows 2000 to pass along a warning. Keep it checked.

2. Now click and drag the slider bar to tweak your definition of low battery power. I live near the edge so I'm going to slide it to the left just a touch to 2 percent.

3. Now it's time to set some behaviors. Click the Alarm Action button to open the Critical Battery Alarm Actions. Figure 24-8 shows you this dialog box.

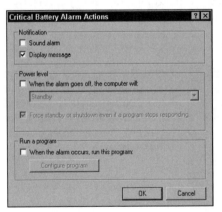

Figure 24-8: Now that you've told the system when to sound the alarm, tell it what to do as well.

4. In the Notification area, the Sound alarm control should be unchecked, and the Display message control should be checked. If things are critical, I want to hear about it. Click the Sound alarm checkbox now. This produces both a text and audible warning.

5. In the Power level area, click the top checkbox control. The drop-down control list below it goes active. By default it is set to put your PC into Standby mode, but click Hibernate instead.

Note

The Standby selection automatically puts your system into Sleep mode. But I've set my critical alarm so close to the edge that I prefer to close things up entirely. That's why the Hibernation command is so useful. This setting physically shuts down my PC but saves the active state so that next time I start up, all my work is restored. I see all the open dialog boxes, applications, documents, and windows just as they were when the battery went critical. If your PC isn't set to provide Hibernate mode, the Power Off command still enables you to safely shut down. In either case, the threat that a sudden shutdown could result in lost data or a scrambled disk is reduced. Figure 24-9 shows the available selections.

Figure 24-9: Hibernate is a terrific option for the auto-shutdown feature. It turns your PC off to ensure no data is lost but sets things up to open as they were on your next start up.

6. Make sure the Force standby checkbox is checked. This keeps your system from just running out of juice if a hung program prevents a normal shutdown/standby sequence.

7. Leave the checkbox in the Run a program area unchecked. I talk more about this in a moment.

8. Click OK to return to the Alarm page and click OK or Apply to make the new settings take effect.

Launching programs at an alarm

One of the more intriguing features of Alarm Settings is the capability to launch an application at an alarm. For example, a low battery warning might cause your PC to perform a quick backup of specific files over a network or to a floppy, Zip, or other drive. Likewise, you could launch a batch program that uploads files to a server.

To take a quick tour of this facility, Click Start ➪ Settings ➪ Control Panel. Double-click the Power Options icon and click the Alarms tab. In the alarm type you wish to work with, click the Alarm Action button. Finally, click the Configure program button in the dialog box that appears. Whew! You should be looking at the dialog box in Figure 24-10.

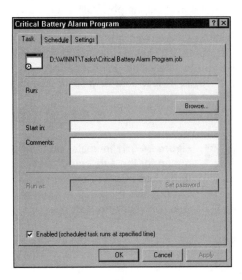

Figure 24-10: Look familiar? This dialog box is identical to the New Task dialog box used by the Windows Scheduler applet to automate tasks.

Here's a quick rundown of the available facilities in the Critical Battery Alarm Program dialog box. Note that this is the same dialog box used by the Windows Scheduler to automate tasks.

✦ To select an application to run, enter the path and filename of the executable in the Run text box. Otherwise, use the Browse button to navigate to the desired file using the standard Browse dialog box interface.

✦ Use the Start in text box to tell programs where to look for associated files that may be needed for the application.

✦ The Comments dialog box simply gives you a place to make descriptive notes. These notes can be helpful for someone who comes across your automated task later and needs to know what it does.

✦ The Run as text box is particularly important because it enables Administrators to run programs from accounts with administrative privileges. This enables activities that otherwise would not be enabled for systems logged on with basic user privileges.

Note   If you are not logged on with an account with administrative privileges, the Run as text box and the related Set password button are grayed out and inaccessible.

Power meter tab

Next in line is the Power Meter tab. Click this tab and you see a page that displays the current battery charge status. By default, a horizontal status bar shows the amount of power remaining, with a percentage value displayed just underneath. Figure 24-11 shows what this status display looks like.

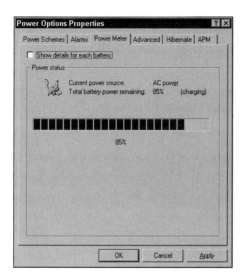

Figure 24-11: Keep watch on available battery life from the Power Meter tab.

If you have a notebook with two batteries installed — as I do as I write this during a cross-country flight — you can click the checkbox at the top labeled Show details for each battery. Doing this causes the status bar to disappear, replaced by a pair of battery icons, each representing one of the two batteries in your system.

Advanced tab

Ironically, the Advanced tab is not so advanced. All you find here is a pair of checkbox controls. The top checkbox enables you to display a power status icon on the taskbar, while the bottom control causes Windows 2000 to prompt you for a password when you power up the system from standby mode. Figure 24-12 shows this simple dialog box in my preferred setting.

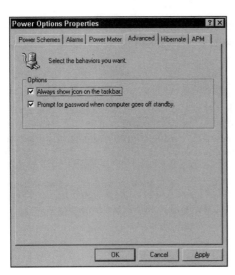

Figure 24-12: I keep both checkboxes activated. The password option, in particular, is important if you want to restrict access to your machine when you walk away from it.

When you check the Always show icon checkbox, an icon representing a power plug (for AC power) or a battery (for, well, battery power) appears in the taskbar tray. The icon informs you immediately whether or not your PC is plugged in. More important, double-clicking the icon launches the Power Options Properties dialog box, enabling you to quickly switch among power schemes, for example.

Hibernate tab

By default, the Windows 2000 Hibernate feature is not activated. The reason is because putting your PC into Hibernation requires tens of megabytes of disk space to store your active state. The Hibernate tab enables you to assess your disk space situation before you enable this feature. Just check the numbers in the Disk space for hibernation area.

If you feel you have enough space available to support this feature, go ahead and click the Enable hibernate support. Figure 24-13 shows you the dialog box, including the estimated disk space requirements. Now when you shut down Windows, a Hibernate option appears. Click this, and the PC takes a while to save the active state to disk. Next time you hit the power button, the system wakes right up where you left off.

Back to the APM tab

You've come full circle back to the APM feature. Clicking the APM tab displays a dialog box that includes a control labeled Enab Advanced Power Management support. Check this box, and APM is enabled, provided, of course, that your system can handle it.

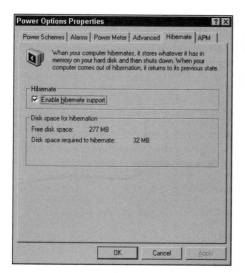

Figure 24-13: Hibernation mode consumes tens of megabytes of disk space to store your active system state. Fortunately, the Hibernate page discloses the likely hit on disk space.

Note   If you have APM enabled and decide to turn it off, you have to perform a system reboot for the change to take effect. Configuration reboots in Windows 2000 are relatively rare (compared to Windows NT, let me tell you!), but when they do happen, they can be disruptive. Fortunately, turning on the APM feature requires no such restart.

Accessing Power Features from Display Properties

At first glance it may not make sense, but your quickest way to setting power-saving properties may be right-clicking the Desktop, clicking Properties from the shortcut menu, and clicking the Screen Saver tab. Now, what do screen savers and power management have to do with each other?

Actually, more than you would think. After all, both screen savers and power management wait for a period of inactivity before doing their thing. And you can use both to effectively lock down unattended systems by requiring a user password before allowing access to the system. In this case, however, access to power-saving features is offered as kind of an extension to the screen saver settings.

Consider this: During the day you might not want to kick in power savings, maybe because users complain about long recovery times. But that doesn't mean you want free access to unattended systems during the day. The solution is to set password-locked screen saver graphics to kick in after a short period of inactivity and back that up with power settings that put systems into Standby mode after, say, two hours.

From the Screen Saver page of the Display Properties dialog box, first set up your screen saver settings. Once you do that, click the Power button, shown in Figure 24-14. You are transported to (surprise!) the Power Options Properties dialog box. Here you can access all the power-saving features of Windows 2000 I've already discussed. When you are done, click OK or Apply to make your changes take effect.

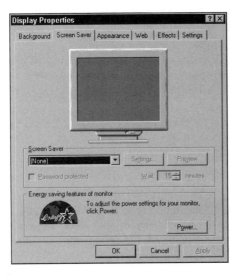

Figure 24-14: Tap into the energy-saving features of your monitor by clicking the Power button next to the Energy Star logo.

Note   You might be wondering what the Energy Star graphic in the Screen Settings page is all about. Energy Star is a program that gave vendors the incentive to market hardware and software that reduced power consumption. Monitors, printers, and PCs all commonly carry the Energy Star seal.

Power-Saving Tips

Windows 2000's power management features can help increase battery life, but they won't solve all your woes. Fortunately, you can take a number of steps to prolong the life of your beleaguered battery. Here are a few:

✦ Whenever possible, use lithium ion batteries. They offer the best charge-to-volume ratio and lack the dreaded *memory effect,* which causes NiCad batteries to lose effective charge unless they are always drained all the way down before being recharged.

✦ Get multiple batteries. Many full-size notebooks can accept a second battery, provided you're willing to do without a CD-ROM drive for the duration of a plane flight. You can double your operating life this way.

✦ Turn off multimedia. If you need to conserve power, the last thing you want to do is send power to speakers or have your CPU working overtime on video clips you really don't need to see.

✦ Look for custom power settings. Your notebook may support battery-friendly tweaks such as modes that lower the CPU clock speed.

✦ Turn down the display. Use your notebook's brightness and contrast controls to ease down your display settings and conserve a little energy.

✦ Unplug PC card devices. It takes juice to keep a network or modem PC card active, generally a waste if you're on an airplane. Remove the PC card for the trip and plug it in when you get to your hotel room.

Summary

Power management is among the most welcome new features for those familiar with Windows NT. Until now, companies and end users often opted for Windows 95/98 on notebook computers, because Windows NT was unable to preserve battery life. Now, with Windows 2000, the most advanced and secure Microsoft client operating system is able to take to the road.

Among the key concepts covered in this chapter:

✦ The benefits of power management for both notebook and desktop computers.

✦ Overview of how to use the Power Management facility in the Windows 2000 Control Panel, including setting up custom power profiles, enabling advanced power management, and other facilities.

✦ The differences among Standby and Hibernation modes and when they are best used.

In the next chapter, we will delve into the world of the Windows 2000 Registry, the central repository for system, device, and application properties. The Registry Hacks chapter will provide useful tips, tricks, and tactics for making system changes by editing the Registry.

✦   ✦   ✦

Hack Happy: Plumbing the Registry

T he Registry is a system database that stores your
computer's configuration. Windows 2000 Professional
relies on the Registry from bootup to shutdown in order to
operate. It is probably the most important collection of files
you have on your computer because without it (or with a
damaged or corrupt Registry), your computer won't be much
more than a doorstop! You ordinarily don't need to worry
about the Registry, how it works, how it is organized, or
especially how to edit it, but a basic law of computing is that if
people can find something, they want to fiddle with it. I know
this for a fact because I can't resist the temptation either!

Caution   I can't stress this point strongly enough: Although there are
a few safeguards to protect you, damaging your Registry
can render your system inoperable! What's more, damaging it is *easier* than you think. Follow the instructions in this
chapter with care!

If you are a fiddler, power user, or system administrator
interested in the inner workings of Windows 2000
Professional, this chapter gives you enough information so
that you can safely work with the Registry and hopefully not
ruin your computer. I introduce you to the Registry and how it
works, show you how to use the tools Windows 2000
Professional provides to edit the Registry, provide information
on how to protect and back up your Registry, and even pass
on a few Registry hacks!

Note   To balance the preceding caution, virtually everyone agrees
that if you really want a high degree of control over
Windows 2000 Professional (previously NT 4), having a
sound knowledge of the Registry and being able to edit it is
critical. In other words, *Be Ye Not Too Afraid*.

Introducing the Registry: How It Works

As I said in the introduction to this chapter, the Registry is a database that
Windows 2000 Professional uses to store important information. In fact, the
Registry contains not just important information but *critically* important
information. From the time Windows 2000 starts to the time you shut it down,
Windows 2000 Professional reads information from the Registry and updates it as
changes are made to the system. The information you can find in the Registry
includes the following:

- ✦ Hardware settings
- ✦ User profiles
- ✦ Desktop settings
- ✦ File associations
- ✦ Folder settings
- ✦ Installed software
- ✦ Computer identification
- ✦ Network settings

To illustrate this point, open your Control Panel as shown in Figure 25-1 by clicking
Start ⇨ Settings ⇨ Control Panel. Just look at all those icons representing options
and settings galore.

Essentially, everything you can modify or configure through the Control Panel (and
other places) is converted into Registry settings that Windows 2000 Professional
uses behind the scenes. Most of the time you want to change your configuration
through the Control Panel or by changing the settings of an application. In fact,
Microsoft would prefer that you change your system settings through the applets
available in the Control Panel; for normal, everyday tasks, this is the safest and
most convenient method. There are times, however, when you have to go to the
Registry itself.

Keys to understanding the Registry

The Registry is a database organized in a hierarchical manner, resembling a tree
with branches and leaves. At the uppermost level, the Registry has five predefined
keys, also referred to as *root keys*. Keys, whether they are root keys or subkeys,
organize the database into manageable divisions. Root keys contain only subkeys,
while subkeys can contain actual data, other subkeys, or both.

Figure 25-1: The Windows 2000 Professional Control Panel, your interface to the Registry.

There are five root keys:

✦ HKEY_CLASSES_ROOT

✦ HKEY_CURRENT_USER

✦ HKEY_LOCAL_MACHINE

✦ HKEY_USERS

✦ HKEY_CURRENT_CONFIG

Figure 25-2 shows the root keys displayed in a Registry editor covered later in the chapter. Notice that in this program, each key looks like a folder in Windows Explorer, complete with indicators that tell you a branch can be expanded.

Note   Each predefined key consists of the prefix *HKEY* (the *H* is a programming convention that refers to a handle, in this case, to a key) followed by an underscore and then the proper name of the key. Instead of running all the words together, Microsoft has separated them with underscores. The predefined key names never change, and they are always displayed in uppercase.

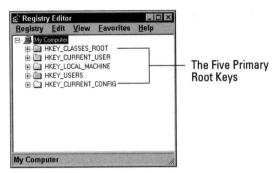

Figure 25-2: Your keys to Windows 2000 Professional.

Each of the root keys serves a purpose and contains several subkeys (which I sometimes refer to simply as *keys*) within its structure. To complicate matters (or simplify them, depending on your perspective), two of the root keys, HKEY_LOCAL_MACHINE and HKEY_USERS, are actual keys while the others are aliases only and refer to branches within the two *real* root keys. For this reason, I cover HKEY_LOCAL_MACHINE and HKEY_USERS first, because if you understand them you can quickly catch on to the others.

HKEY_LOCAL_MACHINE contains keys for the local machine that are applied to any user that logs in. As the name implies, the information contained in this root key is specific to this computer. To illustrate, in Figure 25-3 I have expanded this key to show its immediate subkeys.

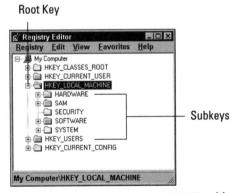

Figure 25-3: HKEY_LOCAL_MACHINE subkeys.

Note The syntax for expressing keys and subkeys is the name of the root key followed by a backslash and then the subkey. Each additional subkey is separated by a backslash, like this:

HKEY_LOCAL_MACHINE\Hardware\Devicemap\Serialcomm

Each of these subkeys in turn serves a specific purpose in the Registry.

The HKEY_LOCAL_MACHINE\HARDWARE key contains information about the hardware installed in your machine. Figure 25-4 shows the keys immediately underneath HARDWARE.

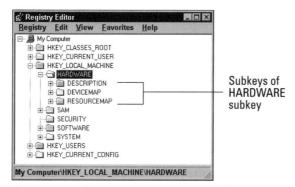

Figure 25-4: The HKEY_LOCAL_MACHINE\HARDWARE key.

The HKEY_LOCAL_MACHINE\SAM (Security Account Manager) key contains security information for users and groups. The contents are hidden from normal viewing in the Registry editors, and this key is edited with the user management tools. This provides an additional level of security from users who might be tempted to edit their (or someone else's) security settings.

The HKEY_LOCAL_MACHINE\SECURITY key contains local security policy. This information is also hidden and cannot be accessed through the Registry editors.

Note If you need to make changes to users, groups, or security settings, open Users and Passwords from the Control Panel or Local Security Policy in Administrative Tools.

The HKEY_LOCAL_MACHINE\SOFTWARE key is a repository for information needed or used by applications installed on the local machine. For a software application to be certified as being "Designed for Windows," it must make use of the Registry. Figure 25-5 shows the SOFTWARE key and its subkeys. Notice that most of the keys are the names of software companies.

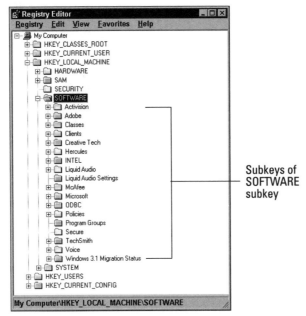

Subkeys of
SOFTWARE
subkey

Figure 25-5: The HKEY_LOCAL_MACHINE\SOFTWARE key.

The HKEY_LOCAL_MACHINE\SYSTEM key, shown in Figure 25-6, contains control
sets and other system information that enable Windows 2000 Professional to
communicate with hardware and provide services.

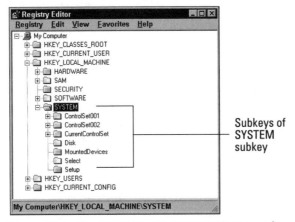

Subkeys of
SYSTEM
subkey

Figure 25-6: The HKEY_LOCAL_MACHINE\SYSTEM key.

Note Thus far all you have seen in the figures have been the keys. I am intentionally hiding any values (the actual settings) in this portion of the chapter in order to focus closely on the organization of the Registry. Don't worry, I get to values shortly!

HKEY_USERS is the root key of all user profiles stored on the computer. For each person who logs onto the computer, Windows 2000 Professional creates a subkey under HKEY_USERS that contains all of their individual configuration data. Except for .DEFAULT, the subkeys under HKEY_USERS are generated dynamically, meaning that you will only see the keys associated with the current user and won't see the user information for anyone else who has logged into the machine. Figure 25-7 shows the HKEY_USERS root key expanded to show its immediate subkeys.

Root Key

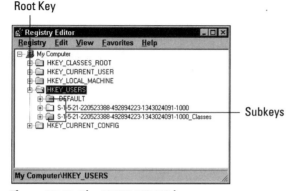

Figure 25-7: The HKEY_USERS key.

The figure shows an HKEY_USERS\.DEFAULT key and two other keys with incomprehensibly long numbers in the name. The HKEY_USERS\.DEFAULT key contains information that controls how Windows 2000 Professional acts when no one is logged in and also is used the first time a user logs onto the machine. Figure 25-8 shows the expanded key.

Windows created the other two keys after I logged onto the computer the first time, and they are loaded every time I use the computer.

Now that you are familiar with the HKEY_LOCAL_MACHINE and HKEY_USERS root keys, the remaining root keys are easy to understand. Remember, the following keys are but subsets, or aliases, to those two "real" root keys.

HKEY_CLASSES_ROOT is a subset of HKEY_LOCAL_MACHINE\SOFTWARE and contains, among other things, file associations and registration information for COM objects. Figure 25-9 shows a portion of this key. Notice that the key contains far too many items to display all at once!

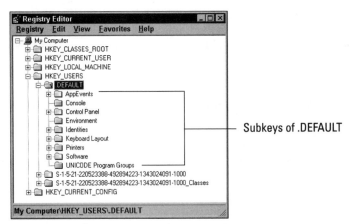

Figure 25-8: The HKEY_USERS\.DEFAULT key.

Subkeys of .DEFAULT

Root Key

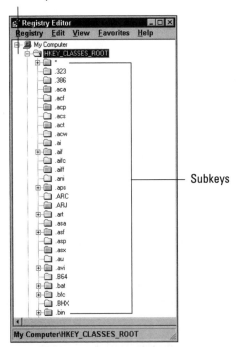

Subkeys

Figure 25-9: A few of the many file associations contained in HKEY_CLASSES_ROOT.

HKEY_CURRENT_USER contains the user profile of the person currently logged into the computer. This profile is extracted from HKEY_USERS. Figure 25-10 shows the HKEY_CURRENT_USER key. If you were to compare this figure with my key under HKEY_USERS (the one with the really long number that doesn't end in _Classes), you would see that they are the same.

Root Key

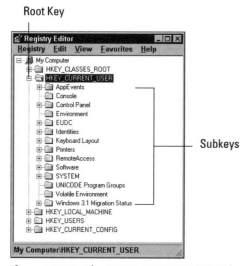

Subkeys

Figure 25-10: The HKEY_CURRENT_USER key.

HKEY_CURRENT_CONFIG, shown in Figure 25-11, contains the hardware profile information built each time the computer boots, and it is also an alias for HKEY_LOCAL_MACHINE\SYSTEM\CurrentControlSet\Hardware Profiles\Current. Although this key also contains a SOFTWARE subkey, with information such as the current font set for your screen resolution, HKEY_CURRENT_CONFIG remains associated with your hardware profile.

Root key   Subkeys

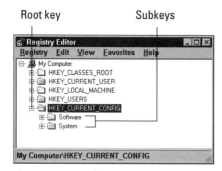

Figure 25-11: The HKEY_CURRENT_CONFIG key.

Understanding Registry entries: Values and data types

Understanding the keys is important, but you're not done yet. All the keys contain values. Values are a three-part construct that define the settings of a given key. In other words, the values define the keys by the data they hold. Refer to Figure 25-12 as you read the descriptions of the three parts of a value:

✦ **Name:** The only way to identify a value is by its name. Otherwise, the Registry would be incomprehensible! Value names are generally created by Microsoft and other software or hardware vendors so that you can tell what the data contained in the value is supposed to do.

✦ **Data type:** One of the first things you learn in programming (if you are a programmer, that is) is that not all data is of the same type. You therefore need a way to differentiate, say, a string of characters from a numerical value. The computer manipulates different value types in fundamentally different ways. Even separating characters from numbers is not enough, however, because not all numbers need to be the same length and occupy the same number of bits. Therefore the Registry contains different data types.

✦ **Data:** While the first two parts of a value are descriptive in nature, the final part is the actual data used by Windows 2000 Professional for the key in question. Depending on the data type, the data can take the form of character strings, binary numbers, and other types explained below.

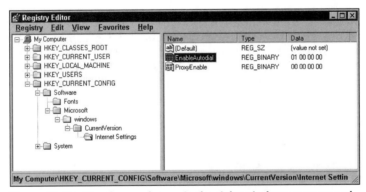

Figure 25-12: The three columns in the right windows correspond to the three parts of a value: it's name, type, and data.

Here are the most common data types in Windows 2000:

- ✦ REG_BINARY
- ✦ REG_DWORD
- ✦ REG_EXPAND_SZ
- ✦ REG_MULTI_SZ
- ✦ REG_SZ

The REG_ prefix indicates a Registry value type. The name following the prefix generally describes the type.

REG_BINARY values contain binary numbers. There is no size limitation. Figure 25-12 shows a REG_BINARY value in the Registry. Although the value name is pretty self-explanatory, it's not always easy to guess what data is acceptable or figure out what a particular binary number actually does.

REG_DWORD values contain 32-bit values expressed in hexadecimal format. Figure 25-13 shows a REG_DWORD value in the Registry in the HKEY_LOCAL_MACHINE\ SYSTEM\Setup key. It indicates my SetupType is 0. Again, although the value name has meaning, the data itself cannot be easily "decoded". In other words, you must have access to other information to adequately explain what the data (in this case, 0), means.

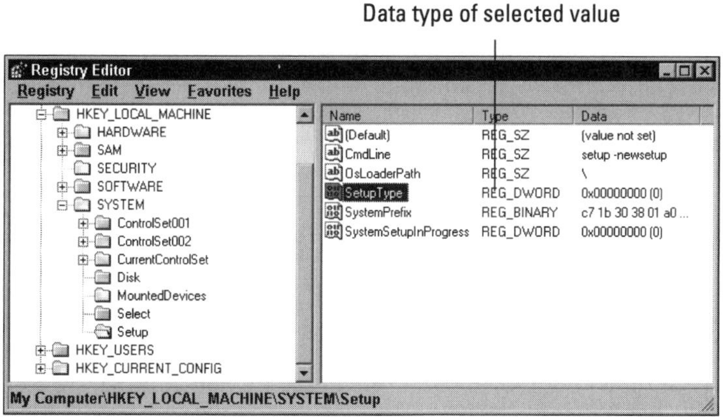

Data type of selected value

Figure 25-13: A REG_DWORD value in the HKEY_LOCAL_MACHINE\ SYSTEM\Setup key.

REG_EXPAND_SZ values contain expandable strings. The most common use of this data type is to enable the replacement of an unexpanded environment variable such as %USERPROFILE% with the actual data. Figure 25-14 shows the value REG_EXPAND_SZ in the HKEY_CURRENT_USER\Environment key. Notice that the value for the environment variable TEMP is %USERPROFILE%\Local Settings\Temp. %USERPROFILE% is expanded to reflect the disk location where user profiles are stored. Expandable string variables eliminate the need to hard-code environment path information in the Registry.

Data type of selected value

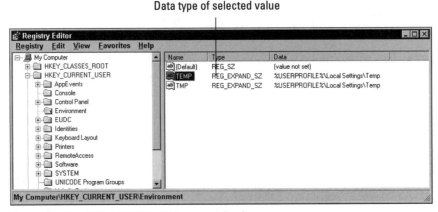

Figure 25-14: REG_EXPAND_SZ is a useful value type.

REG_MULTI_SZ values can contain multiple strings, which are separated by a 0. Multiple strings can also contain expandable values, such as %TEMP%, in addition to strings, in effect combining the REG_EXPAND_SZ and REG_SZ value types into one. The REG_MULTI_SZ value shown in Figure 25-15 indicates that files stored in the temp directory are not backed up or restored. You can't tell this from the value itself, as the value simply assigns the multistring %TEMP%* /s to Temporary Files. You can tell, however, by looking at the key in the status window in the figure.

REG_SZ values contain characters that are handled as a string, not as numbers, even if the string contains numbers. What Windows 2000 Professional (or other software) does with each string depends on the specific key, but REG-SZ values are typically reserved for data not meant to be processed numerically. Figure 25-16 shows a REG_SZ value that contains my video adapter chip name: nVidia RIVA TNT.

Data type of selected value

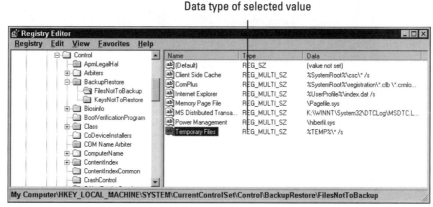

Figure 25-15: A REG_MULTI_SZ value.

Data type of selected value

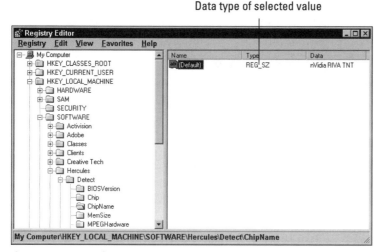

Figure 25-16: Perhaps the most readable value type, REG_SZ.

The Registry gives me the hives

Just when you think you have a handle on the Windows 2000 Professional Registry, I'm going to throw you a curve ball: hives. The truth about the Registry is that it isn't one file, or even two. The Registry is comprised of several files called *hives*. A hive is a file that appears on your hard disk and contains a section of the Registry whose purpose is to store and protect Registry information. When you or Windows 2000 Professional make changes to the Registry, the changes actually take place in the hive files. Because hives are files, you can move them (not recommended!) or back them manually (that is, save copies of them to another location), but you can only edit them through a Registry Editor.

Data Types You Never Hear About

If you do a little spelunking in the Registry, you might run across more value types than I've listed. I don't recommend you fool with any of these values, but I list them to satisfy your curiosity and perhaps save you some time and frustration trying to find out what they mean yourself.

✦ REG_DWORD_LITTLE_ENDIAN: Similar to REG_DWORD in that it is a four-byte numerical value. The difference is that REG_DWORD_LITTLE_ENDIAN signifies the least significant byte is at the lowest address.

✦ REG_DWORD_BIG_ENDIAN: Similar to REG_DWORD_LITTLE_ENDIAN, but this time the least significant byte is at the highest address.

✦ REG_LINK: A string naming a symbolic link.

✦ REG_NONE: This indicates data with no particular type.

✦ REG_RESOURCE_LIST: A device driver's list of hardware resources, used by the driver or one of the physical devices it controls.

✦ REG_RESOURCE_REQUIREMENTS_LIST: A device driver's list of *possible* hardware resources it or one of the physical devices it controls can use.

✦ REG_FULL_RESOURCE_DESCRIPTOR: A list of hardware resources that a physical device is using.

Note To perpetuate the insanity, here's where the word *hives* comes from. *Hives*, according to Microsoft, "were named after their resemblance to the structure of beehives." Okay, right. How many other analogies can you use? Hives, trees, branches, keys, and so on. It would be nice to stick to one overall theme, such as the anatomy of the duck-billed platypus, and leave it alone.

You might assume that each root key has a hive. Wrong! Remember, there are only two real root keys: HKEY_LOCAL_MACHINE and HKEY_USERS. All other keys, even root keys, are derived from these two. Therefore, the hives (four local machine and three user) are made up of the subkeys (with one exception) of these two root keys. The following are the hives on my system as listed in the Registry:

✦ HKEY_LOCAL_MACHINE \Security

✦ HKEY_LOCAL_MACHINE \Software

✦ HKEY_LOCAL_MACHINE \System

✦ HKEY_LOCAL_MACHINE \SAM

✦ HKEY_USERS\.DEFAULT

✦ HKEY_USERS\S-1-5-21-220523388-492894223-1343024091-1000

✦ HKEY_USERS\S-1-5-21-220523388-492894223-1343024091-1000_Classes

Note   The information in the previous list can be found in the HKEY_LOCAL_MACHINE\ SYSTEM\ControlSet001\Control\hivelist key.

The reason I have listed the hives in this manner initially is to reinforce the notion that they are directly tied to the two "real" root keys in the Registry: HKEY_LOCAL_MACHINE and HKEY_USERS. The hives aren't named after the root key, such as HKEY_LOCAL_MACHINE\Security, but you should know which hives represents which root keys.

Notice that the last two keys are my unique identity on this machine. They contain all my user data and file associations.

Now I'm going to explain the individual hives and break them out by their root key associations: local-machine and user related.

The local machine hives look amazingly similar to the keys under HKEY_LOCAL_MACHINE. They are:

✦ Security

✦ Software

✦ System

✦ SAM

Notice that there isn't a hardware hive corresponding to the HARDWARE subkey of HKEY_LOCAL_MACHINE. This is because Windows 2000 Professional builds a hardware list each time you boot your computer. Having a static listing isn't necessary in this case.

Each local machine hive contains information relating to the key it is associated with. The security hive contains the local machine security information, the software hive contains system-wide software configuration data, the system hive contains Windows 2000 Professional configuration data, and the SAM hive contains users and group account security information.

The user hives are:

✦ DEFAULT

✦ ntuser.dat

✦ UsrClass.dat

There is a default user hive because Windows 2000 Professional relies on it to configure the computer the first time any user logs into the machine. Having a static representation of this data makes sense. The ntuser.dat and UsrClass. dat hives correspond to the other two HKEY_USERS subkeys that are the currently logged in user's account. This information is stored in those two files in the user's profile directory.

Now that you know the layout of the hives, it's time to see their supporting files and where they are all stored on your hard drive. Each hive has multiple files associated with it that perform unique functions. You can discriminate what the support files are based on their extension. Table 25-1 identifies the file extensions used by hives.

Table 25-1 **Hive File Types**	
Extension	**Purpose**
None	Most actual hive files have no extension although their support files do.
.DAT	Designates a user hive file
.ALT	Backup copy of the hive
.LOG	Contains changes made to the hive for use in updating and recovery
.SAV	Backup copy of the hive

Not every hive has all of these supporting files, however. Table 25-2 identifies the support files that are used by their respective hives.

Table 25-2 **Hive Support Files**			
Hive	**.ALT**	**.LOG**	**.SAV**
Security	no	yes	yes
Software	no	yes	yes
System	yes	yes	yes
SAM	no	yes	yes
DEFAULT	no	yes	yes
Ntuser.dat	no	yes	no
UsrClass.dat	no	yes	no

You're probably itching to see where they are located and might even want to open them to see what's inside. All the hives except for the unique user account hives are located in the %systemroot%\system32\config directory. The user account hives are located in the Documents and Settings\%username%\ directory.

But before you go find one and try to open one up in something like Notepad to explore it's contents, remember that you can't directly edit hive files. You have to use the Registry Editor.

I'll conclude this section on hives with this thought: As a practical matter, you won't have to deal with hives unless you want to perform a file-level Registry backup or restore using the Windows 2000 Backup utility or other program. If you want to edit the Registry, you must use a Registry Editor.

Protecting and Editing the Registry

The discussion thus far has focused on familiarizing you with what the Registry is and how it is organized. Now it's time to get your elbows dirty and delve into the actual Registry itself.

There are two applications you can use to edit the Registry from a Window-based environment:

✦ The Windows 9x based Registry Editor (REGEDIT.EXE, which I call *Regedit*)

✦ The Windows NT based Registry Editor (REGEDT32.EXE, which I call *Regedt32*)

There is another tool, called REG.EXE, which is part of the Windows 2000 Resource Kit and not installed by default. This is a "Console tool," one that is run from the Windows 2000 Command Prompt. Using REG.EXE, you can perform most of the functions available with the other two applications, such as adding, changing, deleting, searching, backing up, and restoring the Registry.

Note
Oddly enough, they are both called *Registry Editor*, but they are differentiated by their filenames. On a whim, I found the actual executables and right-clicked them to check their properties. The description of REGEDT32.EXE reads "Registry Editor Utility," while the description of REGEDIT.EXE reads "Registry Editor."

Each one has its pros and cons, and you might find yourself using both in different circumstances. In general, Regedit is easier to navigate and search for keys and values, but Regedt32 allows you to edit more value data types. In addition, if you use Regedt32 you can manage Registry security by assigning editing permission to users and groups as well as audit Registry editing. Both tools are covered in this section.

Read this before proceeding!

Once more I need to caution you about editing the Registry. If you do something wrong, you can render your system inoperable. Therefore you should take every precaution and create an Emergency Repair Disk (ERD) and back up your system before you perform any Registry editing.

Windows NT 4 had a little utility called RDISK.EXE that you could use to create an Emergency Repair Disk. To create an ERD using Windows 2000 Professional, launch the Backup utility and choose Create an Emergency Repair Disk from the Tools menu. Although the Registry is too large to fit onto the ERD, you can still use the disk to boot your system in case of extreme emergencies and troubleshoot. To perform a complete backup of the Registry and your system files, you must perform a full system backup that includes the System State. The System State includes the Registry's hive files as well as other important system files.

Note   For a full explanation of backing up data and creating ERDs, refer to Chapter 7.

To backup the Registry itself, launch Regedit and export the entire Registry or launch Regedt32 and save each root key.

Using Regedit

Regedit is a snappy little application that looks and feels a lot like Windows Explorer. You won't find it on your Start menu, and you won't find shortcuts to it anywhere else. To run it from the Start menu, click Start ➪ Run, type **regedit** in the Run dialog box, and click OK. Figure 25-17 shows the Run dialog box.

Type application name

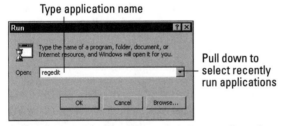

Pull down to
select recently
run applications

Figure 25-17: Type **regedit** and click OK to launch
the application.

If this is the first time you've run it, Regedit opens showing the root keys with nothing expanded. Once you begin to explore, Regedit saves your last location before you quit the program, and when you reopen, it takes you directly to that key.

Learning the interface

Figure 25-18 shows the Regedit interface with subkeys expanded and values listed in the right window pane.

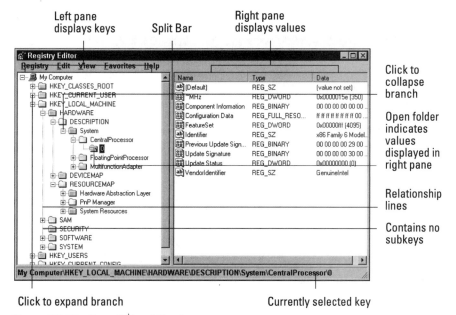

Left pane
displays keys

Split Bar

Right pane
displays values

Click to
collapse
branch

Open folder
indicates
values
displayed in
right pane

Relationship
lines

Contains no
subkeys

Click to expand branch

Currently selected key

Figure 25-18: Regedit in all its glory.

The left window pane displays all the root keys and subkeys displayed as folders. A plus sign beside a folder indicates the tree can be expanded when you click the plus sign. A minus sign beside the folder tells you that the tree is expanded and you can contract it by clicking the minus sign. If no sign is beside the folder, then no other folders are within it. The dashed lines make you aware of where you are and the relationship between the expanded folders. To choose a key, simply select its folder, and the folder opens.

The right pane contains the values assigned to the key you have chosen in the left pane. You can see from Figure 25-18 that I have selected the HKEY_LOCAL_MACHINE\HARDWARE\DESCRIPTION\System\CentralProcessor\0 key, and it has ten values of various types listed. Each value is listed by name with the data type and actual data displayed. To select a value, click the value name. To edit the value (more on this later), double-click the value name.

The status line at the bottom of the window displays the full path of the key you have selected.

You can move the bar that splits the window by moving your cursor over it. When your cursor changes shape (see Figure 25-19), you can click and drag the bar to the location of your choice. This is helpful if you need more space in the left window to see the keys or more space in the right window to see the values.

Select bar   Drag to new location

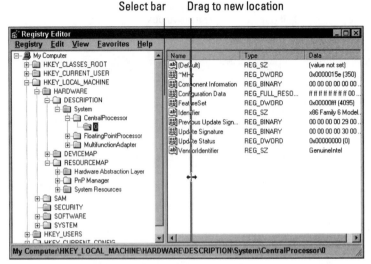

Figure 25-19: Moving the bar.

You can also resize the columns in the right pane by selecting the column divider in the header area and dragging it to suit your taste. This capability comes in handy when you are trying to see the name or data and the value is too long to fit in the allotted space.

If the data is too large to fit, you see ellipses at the point the name, value type, or data is truncated. Figure 25-20 illustrates a situation where each column has shortened entries.

Searching for information

Searching for information couldn't be easier with Regedit. Select Edit ➪ Find, and the dialog box in Figure 25-21 pops up. Regedit allows you to search for values and data in addition to keys, but Regedt32 only allows you to search for keys. This is why most people use Regedit when they need to find a value or data in the Registry.

Type your search term and click Find Next. You can narrow your search by choosing from the options in the dialog box: Keys, Values, Data, and Match whole string only.

When the search is completed, Regedit will expand all the necessary keys to show you the key, value, or data that it has found.

To continue searching for the same value, press F3.

Ellipses indicate
more information

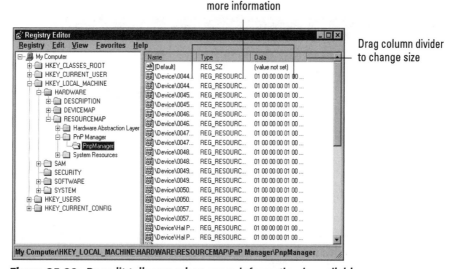

Drag column divider
to change size

Figure 25-20: Regedit tells you when more information is available.

Check options to narrow searches

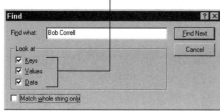

Figure 25-21: Searching for "Bob Correll".

Creating and deleting keys

To create a key, you first need to navigate to the spot in the Registry where you
want the key to reside.

Note   You cannot create, rename, or delete root keys.

For this example, I'm going to create a new key in HKEY_CURRENT_USER\Software.
All you need to do is make sure the key is selected, right-click, and choose New ➪
Key. Figure 25-22 shows this in action.

Selected Key   Right-click to see menu

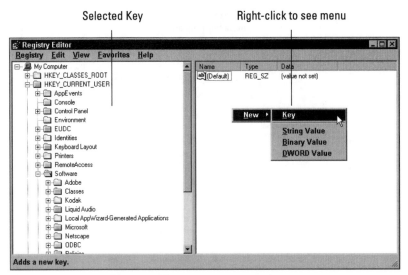

Figure 25-22: Creating a new key.

Figure 25-23 shows the result. There is a new key begging me to rename it. Notice that the key folder is open, and no values for the key are displayed.

New key yet to be named

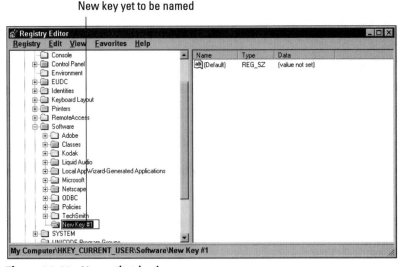

Figure 25-23: Name that key!

To delete a key, right-click its name and choose Delete from the pop-up menu. Windows then asks you to confirm the deletion. If you need to rename a key, right-click the key and choose Rename.

Caution   Notice that Regedit has no undo feature. Once a key is gone, it's gone forever (for our purposes). Deleting a key that contains subkeys and values is just as easy as deleting an empty key. Be careful!

Creating and modifying values

Creating a new value is a two-step process. First you must create the value, and then you need to assign data to it. To create the value, first make sure you're in correct key (the key folder will appear open), then right-click and choose New. Pick the type of value you want. Figure 25-24 shows the creation of a new string value.

Although you can view all the different value types in the Registry with Regedit, one of Regedit's most significant limitations is that you can only create the three types of values shown in Figure 25-24: string (REG_SZ), binary (REG_BINARY), and DWORD (REG_DWORD). If you need to create or edit any other value data types, you must use Regedt32.

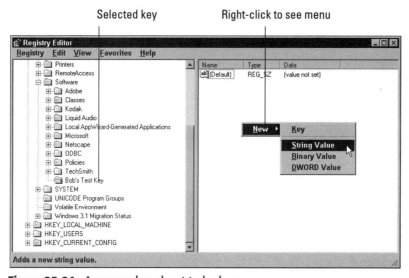

Figure 25-24: A new value about to be born.

Name the value when it appears in the right window pane, then assign data to the value. Double-click the new value name and type the data in the Edit String dialog box as shown in Figure 25-25. The dialog boxes for different data types are all slightly different, but the process is the same.

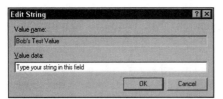

Figure 25-25: Assigning data to a value.

When you're done, click OK, and the Registry updates. Figure 25-26 shows the new value and the data I've just created.

Double-click name to edit valve

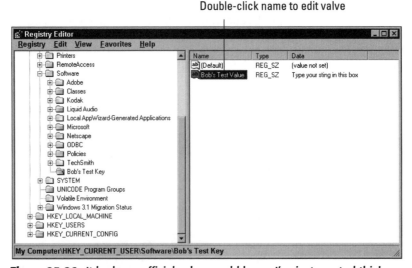

Figure 25-26: It looks so official, who would know I've just created this!

To modify a value, simply double-click the value name and edit the data. The mechanics are simple, but be careful with the data you edit! By entering data that is invalid, you can corrupt your Registry and render your system (or an application) inoperable. In addition, be very wary of editing binary or other numerical values unless you know exactly what the values and the data means.

Importing and exporting

To import Registry information from an external Registry file, select Registry ➪ Import Registry File. The file must be an actual Registry file, not a hive or text file.

Caution Importing strange Registry files can be extremely dangerous. Only import Registry information if you know exactly who created it, why, and what it will do to your system!

To export your Registry, select Registry ➪ Export Registry File. Regedit prompts you to export the entire Registry or the currently selected key, as shown in Figure 25-27.

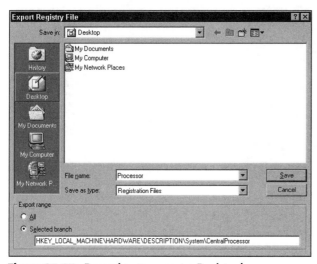

Figure 25-27: Preparing to export a Registry key.

For this example, I have selected the HKEY_LOCAL_MACHINE\HARDWARE\ DESCRIPTION\System\CentralProcessor\0key to export. The figure shows the selected key (branch) at the bottom of the window. I'm going to save this key to the desktop to open and view it. Figure 25-28 shows the exported file on the desktop ready for inspection. You can tell it's a Registry file by the .REG extension and the Registry icon.

Registry Icon   .reg extension

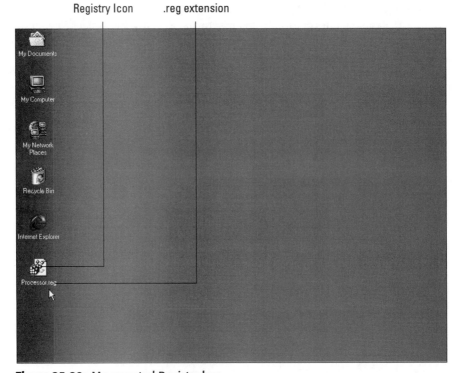

Figure 25-28: My exported Registry key.

Caution   Do not double-click this Registry file. Double-clicking immediately imports it to your Registry! Also, selecting Open with ➪ Registry Editor from the pop-up menu (that you get when you right-click) imports the contents of the Registry file to your Registry. Do not perform these actions unless you mean to.

To open the Registry file and look through it without importing it to your Registry, one method is to right-click the icon and select Open with ➪ Notepad as shown in Figure 25-29.

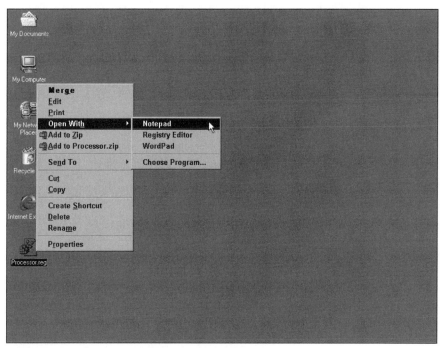

Figure 25-29: Opening a Registry file with Notepad.

Now take a look at the next two figures and compare them. Figure 25-30 shows the HKEY_LOCAL_MACHINE\HARDWARE\DESCRIPTION\System\CentralProcessor\0 key in Regedit, and Figure 25-31 shows the same key in Notepad.

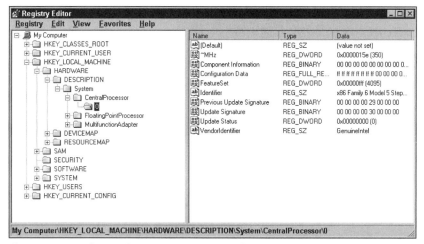

Figure 25-30: The Registry contents in Regedit.

Key   Values

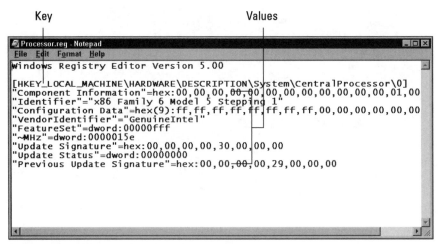

Figure 25-31: The saved Registry key in Notepad.

Notice that the file in Notepad has an identifier at the top: "Windows Registry Editor Version 5.00." This is a change from previous versions of Windows NT where "REGEDIT4" appeared at the top. There is always a blank line following the version information. You can also see that keys are enclosed in braces, and the value names associated with each key are each on a separate line with their data following. The value names are enclosed in quotation marks.

Printing

To print the Registry or selected keys, select Registry ➪ Print menu. A print dialog box gives you the opportunity to print the entire Registry (make sure you have enough paper) or the key you have selected.

Connecting to a remote Registry

Another feature of Regedit is the capability to connect to the Registry on another machine on your network. To do so (assuming you are an administrator with the appropriate privileges), select Registry ➪ Connect Network Registry menu and either enter the computer name or browse for the computer on your network. This enables you to view or edit a remote Registry.

To disconnect, select Registry ➪ Disconnect Network Registry.

Using Regedt32

Regedt32 performs many of the same functions as Regedit, plus a few extras, but uses a different interface. To run it from the Start menu, click Start ➪ Run, type **regedt32** and click OK. Regedt32 launches and opens each root key in a separate window, as shown in Figure 25-32.

Each root key is in a separate window

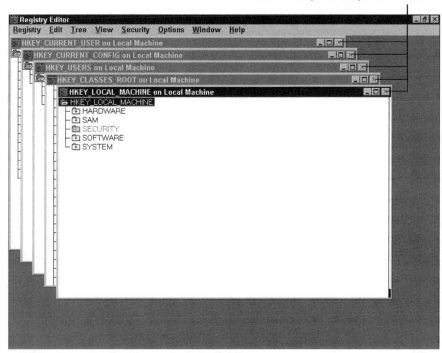

Figure 25-32: The many faces of Regedt32.

Managing the interface

Each window contains a root key, and you can minimize, maximize, cascade, or otherwise arrange the windows to suit your taste. Figure 25-33 shows all windows minimized except for HKEY_LOCAL_MACHINE to better illustrate the navigation and display features.

First of all, the left pane shows the Registry keys as folders, just as in Regedit. Instead of single-clicking a folder with a plus or minus sign to expand the branch, in Regedt32 you have to double-click.

Note   Right-clicking in Regedt32 doesn't do anything, so don't even bother.

The left pane contains the values and data, but they aren't neatly organized into columns as in Regedit. No status bar is at the bottom of the window.

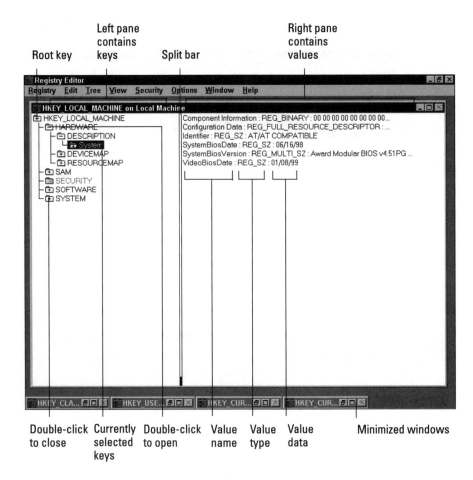

Figure 25-33: Finding out how to use the interface.

Searching for information

You are limited to finding only keys, not data, with Regedt32, which means you have to have a good idea what you're looking for in the first place. You also have to have the root key window open and selected to search in that key. To perform a search, select View ➪ Find Key, type the key name (or fragment) you are looking for in the dialog box, and then click Find Next.

Creating and deleting keys

To create a key, first select the root key window and subkey you want to place your key in. Then select Edit ➪ Add Key. The dialog box asks for the key name and class. Many keys you create do not have a class, but Windows OLE objects must have a unique class identifier.

To delete a key, select it and choose Edit ➪ Delete.

Creating and modifying values

To create values, select the key you want to add a value to and then select Edit ➪ Add Value. Name the value and choose its type. Click OK, and Regedt32 immediately prompts you to enter the data. When you complete that process, the new value is displayed in the right pane.

To modify a value, double-click the value name. A dialog box opens to enable you to make changes.

Assigning Registry permissions, Auditing Registry Changes, and Ownership

As mentioned earlier, Regedt32 has the capability to secure the Registry by assigning permissions, auditing changes made to the Registry, and taking ownership of keys. This is something that Regedit cannot do. In addition, you can set specific permission levels for each key in the Registry.

To assign permissions to a specific Registry key, first choose a root key in the left window pane of Regedt32 and select the key you wish to assign permissions to, then select Security ➪ Permissions from the menu bar. Figure 25-34 shows the dialog box for the HKEY_LOCAL_MACHINE root key.

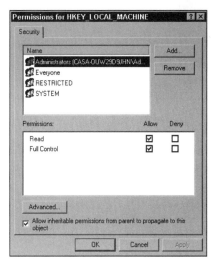

Figure 25-34: Assigning permissions with Regedt32.

Select a group or user (no users are shown in this figure, but you can add them) and change the type of access. The two types of access are Read and Full Control, and you can choose to Allow or Deny.

Read enables a user to open the Registry and see what's inside but not to modify the key or keys that are identified as read-only. Full Control enables users to make whatever changes they like to the Registry, as well as take ownership of it (be in charge of the administration of the key and set security policies for it).

Selecting Advanced from this dialog box opens the Access Control Settings dialog box for the specified key, as shown in Figure 25-35. The three tabs allow you to assign permissions, audit changes to the key, or take ownership of the key.

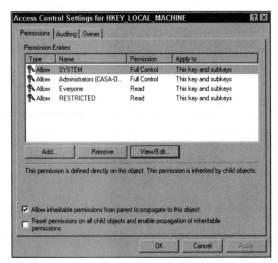

Figure 25-35: Access Control Settings allows you to modify permissions, auditing, and ownership of a key.

Double-clicking a name in the Permissions tab opens another dialog box, shown in Figure 25-36, that allows you to apply more specific permissions to users and groups for the selected key, the selected key and any subkeys, or only the subkeys of the selected key.

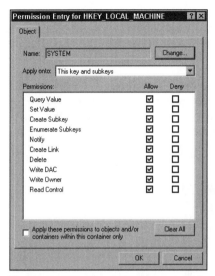

Figure 25-36: Check the boxes beside he options to change individual permissions for this group.

The possible options are:

✦ **Query Value**: Read value entries in a key

✦ **Set Value:** Set value entries in a key

✦ **Create Subkey:** Create subkeys in a selected Registry key

✦ **Enumerate Subkeys:** Identify the subkeys of a Registry key

✦ **Notify:** Enables audit notification when the Registry key is changed

✦ **Create Link:** Creates a symbolic link in a particular key

✦ **Delete:** Enables deletion of a selected key

✦ **Write DAC**: Gains access to a key for the purpose of writing a discretionary Access Control List (ACL) to the key

✦ **Write Owner:** Enables the user to take ownership of the key

✦ **Read Control:** Enables the user to see the security information on the key

The Auditing key allows you to add users and groups you wish to audit. If you have a user or group of users you want to monitor, or if you simply want to track changes made to the Registry, auditing allows you to track successful and failed Registry modification attempts.

The Owner tab, shown in Figure 25-37, shows the current owner of the key and allows you to change its ownership. Taking ownership means that you are defined as the administrator for that key. The owner can set the security for the key, give away ownership of subkeys, and generally be in charge of the key. The owner does not necessarily have to have an administrator account.

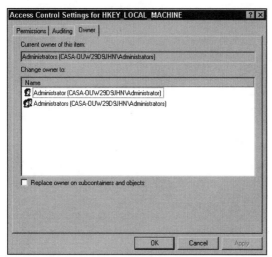

Figure 25-37: Select a new owner and choose Apply to modify a key's owner.

Printing

Printing is similar to printing in Regedit. Simply select Registry ⇨ Print Subtree, and the subtree is immediately sent to the printer. No further options are available from this menu. If you need to configure the printer, select Registry ⇨ Printer Setup first.

Connecting to a remote computer

To open a remote Registry, select Registry ⇨ Select Computer. A dialog box appears to enable you to choose the remote computer. You can open only the two real keys (as mentioned earlier in the chapter), HKEY_USERS and HKEY_LOCAL_MACHINE.

Backing up and restoring Registry data

There are several techniques for backing up the Registry. The easiest method is to open Regedit and select Registry ➪ Export Registry File. Figure 25-38 shows the export dialog box. Notice that I've chosen to export the entire Registry, and I have named the file REGISTRY_BACKUP.

Figure 25-38: Exporting the entire Registry for safekeeping.

If you need to import this into your Registry later, simply select Registry ➪ Import Registry File. This can be an easy way to restore your registry, but it's not that simple. Importing will overwrite keys with the same names but will not remove keys that have no counterpart in the imported file. Therefore, if you have bad data in your Registry and no value in the file that you wish to import that will overwrite the value in question, you're still stuck.

Another method is to identify all your hive files and back them up manually or save them to another location for future use. If you need to find your hive files, open your favorite Registry editor and find the HKEY_LOCAL_MACHINE\SYSTEM\ControlSet001\Control\hivelist key, which identifies your hive files. Figure 25-39 shows my hive list in Regedit. Notice that although there is a value for hardware, there is no hive file associated with it. That's because there isn't one. Also, the user hives are listed in the Registry Editor under the lengthy user identification number. This isn't the actual hive name, but shows you where you can find ntuser.dat and UsrClass.dat for this particular user.

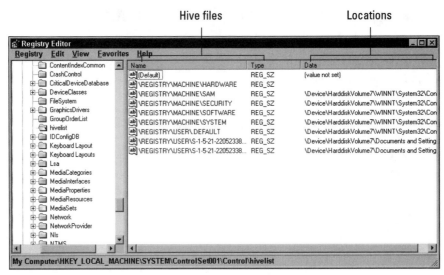

Figure 25-39: Find your hive files and manually back them up.

There is no easy way to restore your Registry. If you have a corrupt Registry, reboot your computer and, when you see the message "Select an operating system," press F8. Select Last Known Good Configuration, press Enter, and then follow the instructions.

The other solution is to boot with an ERD and manually overwrite the old bad hives or perform a complete system restore if the Backup utility is working correctly.

Eight and a Half Registry Hacks

To complete this chapter, I've gathered a collection of Registry hacks from the Internet that aren't too dangerous but enable you to modify the way your system works. Because each one involves editing the Registry directly rather than changing your system settings through the Control Panel, you must use either Regedit or Regedt32 to make the changes. I find Regedit to be the most comfortable for normal Registry editing. Some Registry changes require you to reboot or log out and come back in. When this is the case, I tell you.

Caution These hacks aren't particularly dangerous, but then again, accidents happen. Please proceed at your own risk and make sure you have backed up your Registry in case something goes wrong.

Hack 1: Enabling command-line completion

If you have worked on a Unix machine, you're undoubtedly familiar with a handy command-line feature: auto completion. When you type a directory name or filename from the command prompt, you type only a few letters, press Tab, and your entry is completed. All you need to do next is press Enter. For multiple files or directories with similar beginnings (such as system and system32), the Tab key takes you to the point of differentiation ("system") where you need to type another letter or two (such as "3" if you want to continue on to system32) to tell the processor where to branch.

Here's how to enable command-line completion on your Windows 2000 machine:

1. Open your Registry editor.

2. Navigate to HKEY_CURRENT_USER\Software\Microsoft\Command Processor.

3. Choose the value named CompletionChar.

4. Modify its value to 9.

5. Close your Registry editor.

Note If you want to make this change for all new users, go to HKEY_USERS\.DEFAULT\ Software\Microsoft\Command Processor and make the same change.

Hack 2: Putting Control Panel applets on the Start menu

At times I need to access a Control Panel applet but don't want to go through the hassle of opening the Control Panel and selecting an applet. Having each applet show up on the Start menu is a real timesaver! Here's how to do it:

1. Right-click the taskbar and choose Properties.

2. Select the Start menu Options tab.

3. Under Start Menu Settings, select Expand Control Panel.

4. Click OK or Apply. Figure 25-40 shows the new and improved Start menu with cascading Control Panel applets.

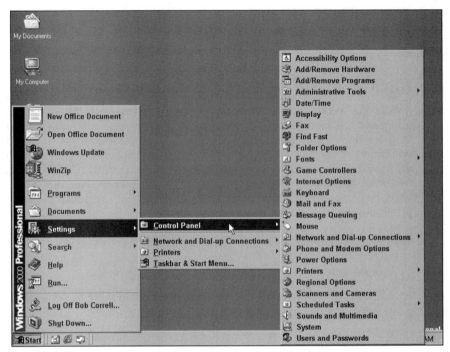

Figure 25-40: Cascading Control Panel applets isn't a hack anymore.

Note

Okay, I cheated on this one (this is the half hack). It has nothing to do with editing the Registry, but I included it to illustrate a point. Many times it is easier to change a setting by finding the Windows-approved method than messing with the Registry. In addition, Microsoft actually does listen to the comments they receive about improving a product. What was once a Registry hack (as this one was) is often integrated into the operating system at its next release.

Hack 3: Changing the Windows 2000 Professional logon screen

When Windows 2000 Professional starts you are initially presented with a logon screen with a dialog box asking for your name and password. The background is the Windows 2000 Professional default desktop background color. If you want to customize this background with a company logo or other wallpaper, follow these steps:

1. Open your Registry editor.

2. Find HKEY_LOCAL_MACHINE\.DEFAULT\Control Panel\Desktop.

3. Select the value named Wallpaper.

4. Edit the string to include the path and filename of your bitmap.

5. Close your Registry editor.

6. Log off Windows 2000 Professional to see the new wallpaper in action.

This wallpaper will be displayed each time the logon screen is present, but when a user logs in their preferences will be implemented and their own desktop will be displayed.

Hack 4: Creating and modifying Windows 2000 Professional tips

Every time you start Windows 2000 Professional, you are presented with tips (assuming you haven't turned this feature off). Changing these tips to suit your organization or yourself is a good way to personalize this feature.

1. Open your Registry editor.

2. Find HKEY_LOCAL_MACHINE\Software\Microsoft\Windows\CurrentVersion\ Explorer\Tips.

3. Edit the data in an existing numbered tip or create more. Figure 25-41 shows the tips in Regedit.

4. Close your Registry editor.

Hack 5: Speeding up the Start menu

When you select the Start Menu and let your mouse hover over a cascading submenu, there is a noticable delay before it pops open and shows you the contents of the submenu. If you would like to decrease the delay time so the menus pop open more quickly, follow these steps:

1. Open your Registry editor.

2. Navigate to the HKEY_CURRENT_USER\Control Panel\Desktop key.

3. Change MenuShowDelay to a smaller number. Figure 25-42 shows the key and MenuShowDelay with the default value.

Tip numbers   Tip text strings

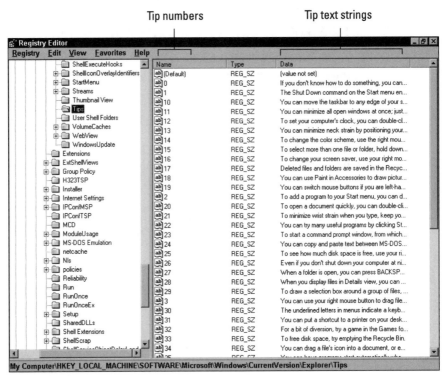

Figure 25-41: Tip-mania just ready to be hacked!

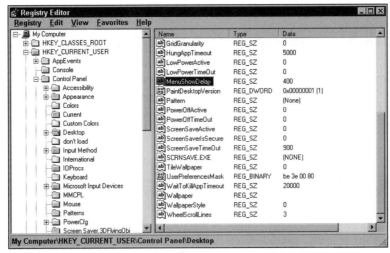

Figure 25-42: Getting ready to turbocharge the Start menu.

Note The default value is 400, or 400 milliseconds. If you want a slower menu delay, set this value larger than 400. You can go up to 1,000, which is a full second.

4. Close your Registry editor.

5. Restart your computer.

Hack 6: Opening a command prompt from an Explorer directory

Sometimes I want to shell out to a command prompt in the directory I'm viewing in Windows Explorer. Most often this happens when I need to run a program from the command line and need to input command line switches to control the program. The following hack shows you how to share the excitement:

1. Open your Registry editor.

2. Find the HKEY_CLASSES_ROOT\Directory\shell key.

3. Create a new subkey called opennew under the shell key.

4. Make the default value Command Prompt in this directory, as shown in Figure 25-43.

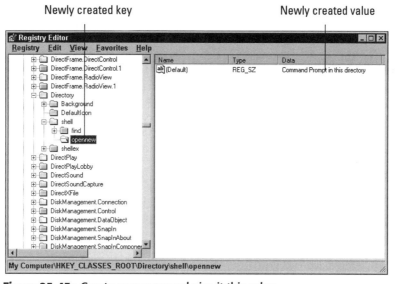

Figure 25-43: Create opennew and give it this value.

5. Create a new subkey within the opennew key called command.

6. Make the default value cmd.exe /k cd %1 as shown in Figure 25-44.

7. Close your Registry editor.

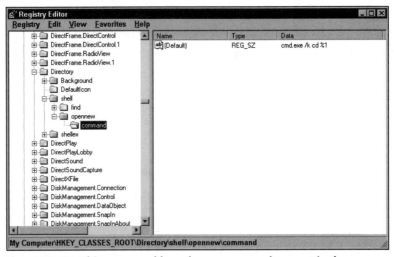

Figure 25-44: This command launches a command prompt in the current directory.

Hack 7: Opening a command prompt from a drive

There are other times when I'm working in My Computer and need to use the command prompt and want it to be open and set to the drive I am interested in. Instead of selecting Start ➪ Programs ➪ Accessories ➪ Command Prompt and then having to switch to the drive you need, you can use this hack to open a command prompt from a drive in Windows Explorer:

1. Open your Registry editor.

2. Find the HKEY_CLASSES_ROOT\Drive\shell key.

3. Create a new subkey called opennew under the shell key.

4. Make the default value Command Prompt in this drive.

5. Create a new subkey within the opennew key called command.

6. Make the default value cmd.exe /k.

7. Close your Registry editor.

You can now select a drive from My Computer or within Windows Explorer and open a command prompt from the new menu as shown in Figure 25-45.

Custom menu item

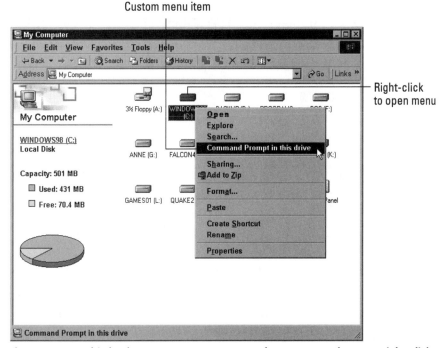

Right-click
to open menu

Figure 25-45: This hack creates a custom menu that appears when you right-click a drive in My Computer.

Hack 8: Changing the computer's registered owner

You get a new computer at work, and someone else is shown as the registered user, making it look like Jane Doe still works there and is doing all your work. Here is an easy hack to make the former user an un-person.

1. Open your Registry editor.
2. Find HKEY_LOCAL_MACHINE\SOFTWARE\Microsoft\Windows NT\CurrentVersion.
3. Change the value of RegisteredOwner to your name.
4. Close your Registry editor.

Hack 9: Refreshing the screen automatically

Sometimes Windows Explorer takes a while to update it's display when you move, add, or delete files, especially if you have multiple windows open. If you get tired of waiting, you can force it to automatically refresh.

1. Open your Registry editor.

2. Find HKEY_LOCAL_MACHINE\SYSTEM\CurrentControlSet\Control\Update.

3. Edit the UpdateMode value to 0.

4. Close your Registry editor.

5. Restart.

Summary

You've learned a lot in this chapter. If you want a deeper understanding of Windows 2000 Professional and the capability to really take control, the Registry is the place you want to be. Here are the main points I covered in this chapter:

✦ The Registry is a database containing all aspects of Windows 2000 Professional configuration data.

✦ There are five root keys in the Registry, each performing a different task.

✦ Each root key contains subkeys that can contain more subkeys and data.

✦ Registry data is comprised of values with a name, type, and data.

✦ Hives are the actual files that make up the Registry and are stored on your hard drive.

✦ Regedit and Regedt32 are the two Registry editors available in Windows 2000 Professional.

✦ You can directly edit the Registry with a Registry editor and nothing else.

✦ To back up your Registry, you need to perform a complete system backup.

✦ You can tweak Windows 2000 Professional performance or options to suit your needs.

Up next is Chapter 26, where you will learn how to use the Windows Script Host to run scripts written in JScript or VBScript from the command prompt or with the click of your mouse.

✦   ✦   ✦

Windows Script Host

With the release of Windows 98, Microsoft introduced the Windows Script Host on a broad scale. Until that time, users of the Windows 9x and NT operating systems did not have any other way to perform automated tasks or do chores other than by writing a batch file, using a compiled application, or installing and using Perl (Practical Extraction and Reporting Language) for Windows NT. Batch files, although useful, are limited in their utility, applications can be expensive to buy or develop in-house, and Perl has yet to catch fire in the Windows realm outside of Web server duty. Something else was needed, a way to execute scripts previously used in standalone applications or contained in a Web page and interpreted by a Web browser. That something is the Windows Script Host, which provides a similar functionality to AppleScript for Macintosh and shell scripts used in the Unix world.

In this chapter, you find out what the Windows Script Host is, discover how it works, try your hand at using it to execute scripts, and even learn a little about VBScript and JScript.

Introducing Windows Script Host

The Windows Script Host (hereafter referred to as *WSH*) is officially defined as "a language-independent scripting host for ActiveX scripting engines on 32-bit Windows platforms." Huh? Tell you what, I'll break all this apart, define everything separately, and then put it back together again later. Hopefully that will make things a bit more comprehendible.

Note

Although Microsoft sometimes refers to the WSH as the Windows *Scripting Host*, the official name of the product appears to be *Windows Script Host*. Most of the documentation directly associated with WSH uses the term *Script*, not *Scripting*.

Understanding the terminology

First I tackle the terms that make up WSH: *Windows, script,* and host.

Windows, which I am limiting to Windows 2000 Professional, is a computer operating system built around a 32-bit Application Programming Interface (API). A 32-bit application uses 32-bit memory addressing and takes advantage of the 32-bit registers on your CPU to provide faster performance than the 16-bit applications of the past. An API is a group of data types, definitions, and functions that programmers rely on to create programs that interface with the operating system. (I suppose it would be simpler to just say Windows is the thing that runs when you boot your computer, but I got carried away.)

Scripts are files that contain command language or high-level programming commands and routines. Script engines interpret the scripts (convert them from something you can read to a form your processor can execute) as they are run rather than compiled into machine-readable code before run time. Scripting has its pros and cons. The syntax and rules of scripting languages tend to be much easier to use than those of formal programming languages and the development process shorter and less involved. The latter benefit is partly due to the fact that scripts have more modest goals than applications created with a programming language. Scripts are far more limited than general-purpose programming languages such as C++ or Java, although they may call upon existing components created by those languages. All in all, scripts serve a useful purpose and are used by a wide audience. The two scripting languages covered in this chapter are Microsoft Visual Basic Scripting Edition (VBScript) and Microsoft JScript.

A host (in this context) is a program that executes another program to interpret a script. The other program, the one doing the script interpreting, is called a script engine. Your Web browser is a good example of a script host because it sends scripts contained within the <SCRIPT> . . . </SCRIPT> tags in a Web page to a script engine for execution. There are actually two hosts involved with WSH, which I get to later.

All right, now I'm going to put all this together into a reasonably understandable definition you can use for WSH:

The Windows Script Host sends uncompiled text files (called scripts) containing high-level programming commands and routines to a script engine for interpretation within the 32-bit Windows operating system environment.

Note   WSH version 1.0 was released with Microsoft Windows 98 and has been available for Windows NT ever since. WSH version 2.0 is currently in beta, and the final version will be shipped with Windows 2000. This chapter is written about the 2.0 version. Other components that may be necessary for the WSH are Visual Basic Script Edition (VBScript) Version 5.0, JScript Version 5.0, Windows Script Components, and Windows Script Runtime Version 5.0.

I want to cover a few other terms in the Microsoft definition previously quoted: *language-independent* and *ActiveX scripting engines*.

To cut to the chase here, in the Microsoft technology arena, *language-independent* describes a quality of ActiveX Scripting. You see, ActiveX Scripting is a standard that defines the relationship between script hosts and engines. It tells programmers how to create these hosts and engines and lays out the ground rules by which they interrelate. When Microsoft defined the ActiveX Scripting standard, they intentionally did so without locking the type of script to be used in the standard. The language of the script is irrelevant if the script host and script engine know how to communicate. The programming problem then turns into one of creating a script engine that conforms to the ActiveX Scripting standard. As of now, only two scripting languages have an ActiveX scripting engine: VBScript and JScript, both Microsoft technologies.

 Note You can easily find the two scripting engines in the System32 subdirectory of your Windows 2000 directory. The VBScript engine is VBSCRIPT.DLL and the JScript engine is JSCRIPT.DLL.

In practical terms, that means you can choose either VBScript or JScript to write scripts that can be interpreted by the ActiveX scripting engines that ship *with Windows 2000. Microsoft is, however, promoting the use of Perl, TCL, REXX, Python, and other scripts if third-party companies or individuals create ActiveX scripting engines for those languages. If the engines are built, the script hosts can run.

Now you have come to a fuller understanding of what the WSH is and is supposed to do. To rephrase the definition a bit, the Windows Script Host acts as language-independent intermediary between scripts and ActiveX scripting engines on the 32-bit Windows operating system. Remember, the WSH isn't the script, and it does not run the script.

Introducing your hosts: WSCRIPT.EXE and CSCRIPT.EXE

Now it's time to bring the two WSH applications out of the closet. I explain how to use both of these programs later, but to understand some of the benefits of WSH, you need some information about the hosts. Windows 2000 Professional has two Windows Script Hosts for you to use:

 WSCRIPT.EXE

 CSCRIPT.EXE

My ActiveX File

To understand what an ActiveX scripting engine is, you first need to know a little about ActiveX. ActiveX is part of Microsoft's overall Active technology, a technology that enables interaction among software components that may be written in different programming languages. Reusable components that use the Component Object Model (COM) are at the heart of Active technology. The Component Object Model is a software architecture defined by Microsoft that ensures software components are written in such a way as to be able to interact with one another in a networked environment, regardless of the language with which they were created. Active technologies include the following:

✦ Active document containment

✦ ActiveX Controls

✦ Active Scripting

✦ Automation

Active document containment enables Active documents (such as a letter saved in Microsoft Word format) to be opened in an Active Document container (such as a Web browser) including original interface features (toolbars, buttons, and so on) from the native document creator. In other words, when I save this chapter in Word format and open it up in Microsoft Internet Explorer, not only is the document itself opened, but the toolbars and buttons used in Word are enabled in Internet Explorer.

ActiveX Controls are controls that are used in Active document containers that add user interface features or other functionality. The System Monitor features an ActiveX Control that can be run in a Microsoft Management Console or opened up in Internet Explorer. The interface and routines that track system activity are an ActiveX Control.

Active Scripting, discussed earlier, defines the relationship between script host and engines as one of language-independence.

Automation (formerly known as Object Linking and Embedding automation) allows objects to be "exposed" other programs and therefore manipulated.

WSCRIPT.EXE enables you to run scripts from the Windows graphical user interface (GUI), using Windows Explorer. Think of the W as standing for *Windows*.

If WSCRIPT.EXE can execute scripts from Windows, the obvious counterpart to it is CSCRIPT.EXE, the command-line script host. Think of the *C* as *command prompt*. CSCRIPT.EXE executes scripts from a command-line interface, enabling more control over host and script properties through the use of command-line switches. In particular, CScript is most useful when little or no user interaction with the script is required.

Benefits of WSH

If you analyzed the definitions of all the terms associated with WSH along with me as well as the two specific hosts, you might already be thinking of the benefits of using the WSH. I list a few here and discuss each afterward.

✦ Scripting integrated with Windows

✦ Two methods of execution

✦ Using multiple files

✦ Script extensions mapped to the Registry

✦ ActiveX interfaces to scripts

✦ Doesn't hog the system

The first benefit is fairly obvious, the raison d'être of the WSH. For the first time, scripting is integrated with Windows. Instead of having to rely on batch files to perform routine or automated tasks, instead of having to rely on Microsoft or third-party developers to know every task you have and provide the needed product or feature, you can create scripts yourself or find them on the Internet. What's more, because scripting is integrated with the operating system, you don't have to run them through your Web browser with its tighter security model.

Additionally, Microsoft has provided two methods for executing scripts, either from Windows or the command prompt. This is nice because it gives you the flexibility of choosing which method suits your or the script's needs.

Another benefit of using the WSH is the capability to call multiple script files that may use different scripting engines from a single Windows Script file. You can put your knowledge of Extensible Markup Language (XML) to good use because Windows Script files contain XML. Windows Script files are covered later in this chapter, but you can think of them as project files that tie together scripts and other functions.

You also don't have to worry about using a specific method or tag in script files to identify them as scripts to the system. With HTML scripting, all scripts have to be enclosed in the <SCRIPT> . . . </SCRIPT> element so the browser can send the contents of the script to the appropriate engine. With the WSH, ActiveX scripting engines are registered in your system Registry, and scripts are identified with a filename extension. The extension determines the appropriate scripting engine for the host to call. Currently, scripts written in VBScript are identified by a .VBS extension, and scripts written in JScript have a .JS extension. Table 26-1 identifies all the types of files handled by the WSH.

Table 26-1
Windows Script Host Extensions

Extension	File Type	Purpose
.JS	JScript	Script file
.VB	VBScript	Script file
.WS	Windows Script	Script project file
.WSH	Windows Script Host	XML control file to specify script properties

The power behind the WSH is the Windows Script Host Object Model. The Object Model provides a direct interface with the ActiveX scripting engines to control script execution and troubleshooting, and to gain access to other helper functions. This feature can significantly expand the power and flexibility of the scripts you write.

Finally, Microsoft is making an effort to point out the low memory requirements of the WSH. Instead of launching and using a Web browser to execute scripts and taking the hit of their larger memory footprints, you can use these small hosts to perform quick but powerful tasks.

What can I do with it?

The answer to this question is up to you. You can do nothing with the WSH and get by pretty well, dabble with it to see if it bears further investigation, or go whole-hog and try to run the universe with it. Well, not quite run the universe, but you can use scripts to get information and automate many tasks. The full range of possibilities depends on the WSH Object Model, the features of the scripting language used, your intelligence, and your creativity.

Note

Sneak a peek at Table 26-3 later in this chapter and browse through the WSH objects, properties, and methods. These illustrate the wide range of specific functions the WSH can perform.

In general, you can use the WSH to run scripts that do the following:

✦ Display onscreen messages or information

✦ Search for information about your computer

✦ Perform network functions

✦ Map network drives

- ✦ Connect to printers
- ✦ List and modify environment variables
- ✦ Edit the Registry
- ✦ Add users and groups
- ✦ Find groups
- ✦ Access your file system
- ✦ Create logon scripts

And much more!

Using WSH to Run Scripts

As I mentioned earlier, the WSH provides two methods for running scripts: through Windows and from the command prompt. You learn the ins and outs of both methods in this section.

Using a Windows interface to run scripts

Running scripts from Windows Explorer is simplicity itself. But, and there always is a but, there are limitations. The primary limitation is the inability to pass arguments or switches to the scripts. This is the same limitation faced by all command prompt applications that Windows 2000 runs. For example, if I were to double-click MEM.EXE in Windows Explorer, the program would run but I wouldn't have a chance to enter any switches, such as /C to classify the data. Although you may run scripts from the Windows interface using WSCRIPT.EXE, you cannot include any arguments that will be passed on to the script itself. For some scripts this isn't a problem (that is, those that do not require command line arguments), but for others, such as a script to create a user account that requires a name and a password in order to run, you must use CSCRIPT.EXE.

There are three methods for running scripts from Windows Explorer:

- ✦ Double-clicking the script file
- ✦ Running the script from the Run command on the Start menu
- ✦ Using WSCRIPT.EXE to run your scripts

Running scripts the easy way

The double-click method is the most intuitive, and you really don't need to know anything.

1. Locate the script you want to run. It can be anywhere on your computer, and you can select it through My Computer, Windows Explorer, the Start menu, the Find menu, or your desktop. Figure 26-1 shows a small script I wrote in VBScript that tells me how much free space I have on one of my volumes. Notice the .VBS extension.

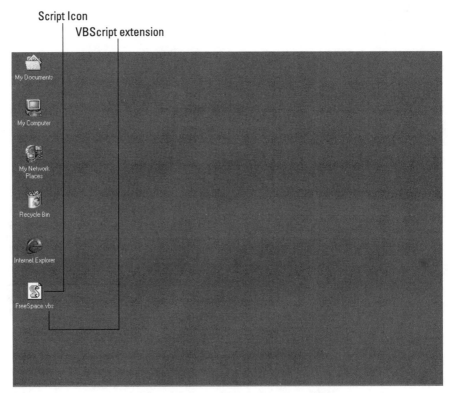

Figure 26-1: Locating the script to run. This one is on my desktop.

2. Double-click the file to run it. Figure 26-2 shows the output of the script.

Figure 26-2: I have just under 70 megabytes of free space – not much left!

Using the Run command

To use the Run command to run scripts, you must know the name of the script and its location if it is not in a location specified in your path environment variable. A path is the complete location of a file, such as C:\DATA\, and the path environment variable stores paths that allow you to execute programs from the command prompt without typing in their exact location. To see what you path environment variable is, open a Command Prompt and enter PATH. To add a location to your path, enter PATH=*location* and it will be added for your current session. If you need to permanently add a path to this variable, right-click My Computer, select the Advanced tab, choose Environment Variables, and under System Variables choose Path and then select Edit. Enter the desired path, select OK, and close all of the dialog boxes.

1. Click Start ➪ Run.

2. Enter the filename, including the extension, that you want to run. Figure 26-3 shows the Run dialog box with my entry.

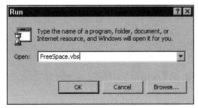

Figure 26-3: Using WScript to run a script from the Run menu.

Note I cheated a bit here and placed the script in the root of my Windows 2000 Professional volume so it would be in the path. Depending on the script's location, you might have to include the full path to the script file for it to run.

3. Press Enter or click OK to run the script.

Forcing WSCRIPT.EXE to run a script

If you want to ensure WSCRIPT.EXE runs a script, you can do so by entering WSCRIPT.EXE before the script you want to execute.

1. Click Start ➪ Run.

2. Enter WScript and the script name as shown in Figure 26-4.

Figure 26-4: Forcing the script to run using WScript.

3. Press Enter or click OK to run the script.

Running scripts from the command line

You can run scripts from the command line in order to get around the limitations of using WScript to execute your scripts. Command-line execution relies on CSCRIPT.EXE to act as the script host.

Running CScript from the command prompt

Running scripts from the command prompt requires that you first open the command prompt. Once you have this window open, you are free to run scripts from the command line.

1. Click Start ➪ Programs ➪ Accessories ➪ Command Prompt. Figure 26-5 shows the command prompt.

2. Type **cscript** followed by the script name as shown in Figure 26-6 (including any necessary script parameters not shown) . You can also enter parameters for CSCRIPT that modify it's execution, which are listed in Table 26-2.

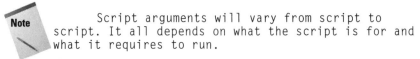

Note   Script arguments will vary from script to script. It all depends on what the script is for and what it requires to run.

3. Press Enter, and the script runs. Figure 26-7 shows the script output. Notice that the output is displayed in the command prompt and not in a window.

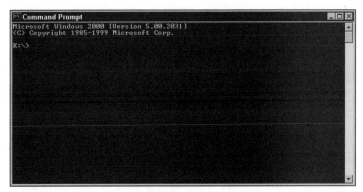

Figure 26-5: The command prompt is ready for input.

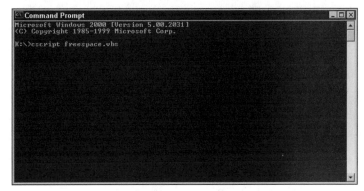

Figure 26-6: Using CScript to run my script.

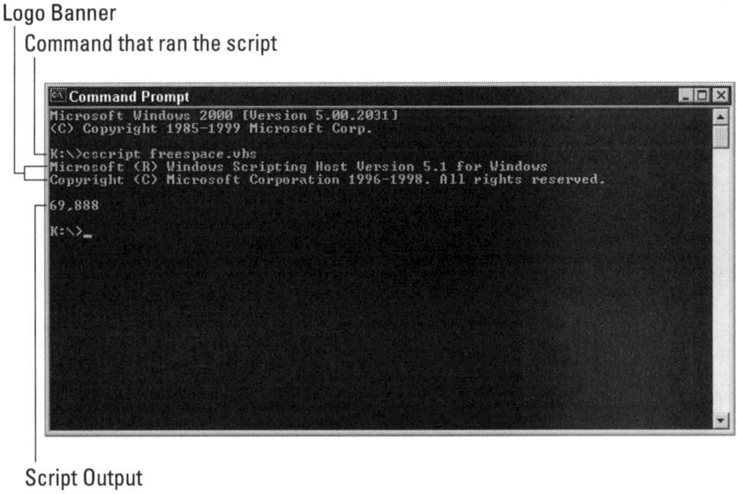

Logo Banner
Command that ran the script

Figure 26-7: This script returns the same value, but this time it is displayed in the command prompt.

Script Output

Table 26-2 contains all the parameters, also called host options, available for use with CScript.

<table>
<tr><td colspan="2" align="center">Table 26-2
CSCRIPT.EXE Host Options</td></tr>
<tr><td>*Switch*</td><td>*Function*</td></tr>
<tr><td>//I</td><td>Interactive mode. Enables display of user prompts and script errors. This is the default mode.</td></tr>
<tr><td>//B</td><td>Batch mode. Suppresses command-line display of user prompts and script errors. Batch mode and Interactive mode are opposite and mutually exclusive.</td></tr>
<tr><td>//T:nn</td><td>Time-out. nn sets the maximum number of seconds the script can run. The default is no limit.</td></tr>
<tr><td>//logo</td><td>Logo. Displays a banner and is the default option. The banner displays copyright and version information.</td></tr>
<tr><td>//nologo</td><td>No logo. Prevents display of an execution banner at run time. //nologo and //logo are opposite and mutually exclusive.</td></tr>
<tr><td>//H:CScript
//H:WScript</td><td>Host selection. Registers CSCRIPT.EXE or WSCRIPT.EXE as the default application for running scripts. If neither is specified, WSCRIPT.EXE is assumed as the default.</td></tr>
<tr><td>//S</td><td>Save. Saves the current command-line options for this user.</td></tr>
<tr><td>//?</td><td>Help. Displays these CScript host options.</td></tr>
<tr><td>//E:engine</td><td>Engine. Executes the script with the specified scripting engine.</td></tr>
<tr><td>//D</td><td>Debug. Turns on the debugger.</td></tr>
<tr><td>//X</td><td>Launches the program in the debugger.</td></tr>
<tr><td>//Job:<JobID></td><td>Runs the specified JobID from the .WS file.</td></tr>
</table>

Setting WScript Host Options

If you are using WScript to execute a script, you can set two options that apply to individual scripts. These allow you to supress the copyright and version information as well as control the script's termination. These are equivalent to the //T:nn and //logo or //nologo options for CSCRIPT.EXE.

1. Right-click a script as shown in Figure 26-8.

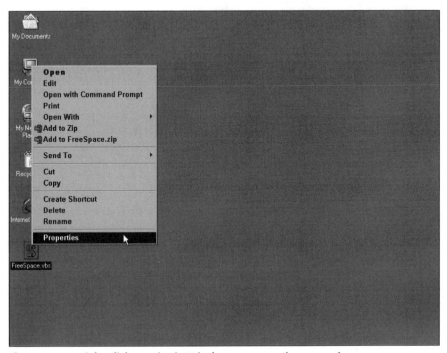

Figure 26-8: Right-click a script in Windows to get at its properties.

2. Choose Properties.

3. Select the Script tab.

4. Choose the properties you wish to modify. Figure 26-9 shows the Script tab and the available properties.

5. Click OK.

This action creates a .WSH file with the host options. Each time the script is run, it checks for the existence of a .WSH file and reads the options. The script is executed accordingly.

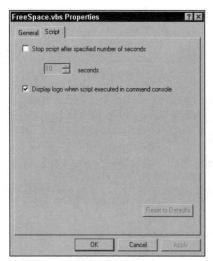

Figure 26-9: You can set the timeout and logo options for scripts run by WScript.

Creating Scripts for WSH

If you've never scripted before, this section serves as a broad overview of the two scripting languages currently compatible with the WSH: VBScript and JScript. It is not possible to demonstrate the fullness of either scripting language or teach you how to script in this book, so I encourage you to seek out additional resources in the form of books or Web sites.

Unlike formal programming languages, scripting is reasonably easy to learn and try out on your own without devoting an extensive amount of time or spending a lot of money. Programming languages, although based on public specifications, are sold as software packages that cost a good deal of money. The software companies have to create a compiler to convert or compile the written code the programmer creates into an executable program or dynamic link library. Software companies also develop extensive reusable libraries of code for use in programming. This takes time and money on their part, and although you can get by without the libraries, you must have a compiler. Scripting has a much "lower bar" for you to cross if you want to try your hand at it. In fact, if you have Windows 2000 Professional, you have everything you need to start scripting right now!

In addition, you don't require (although you may benefit from one) a special integrated development environment (IDE) in order to begin scripting. Integrated development environments are programs that facilitate programming in formal programming languages and usually include extensive examples, help, compiler, and debugger. Everything you need to develop your programs is contained in one integrated environment, saving you development time and money. For scripting, all you really need is a text editor. This is because scripts are written as text files and are not compiled before they can be run. The host takes the text content of the script and sends it to the script engine for interpretation. Of course, you might want to have one or more references available to help you remember the details of the scripting language you are using, but this isn't required.

Defining scripting terminology

This small section cannot hope to teach you every detail of VBScript or JScript, but I would like to highlight a few important terms used in scripting. The three main conceptual components of scripting I discuss are objects, methods, and properties.

If you understand what these are and the relationships between them, you can then read more detailed information concerning a specific scripting language and quickly get a feel for what it is capable of. Then all you need to learn is the syntax (how to write the commands in the correct format) and conventions (how the language references variables, creates functions, the language's data types, and so on) unique to the language.

Objects are a result of the object-oriented programming philosophy of creating a construct that not only holds data but also contains the means to manipulate it. In programming circles, these are called *classes*, but scripting has termed them *objects*. Objects, therefore, are a collection of methods and properties. For example, VBScript has a Folder object that provides access to the properties of folders such as their location, modification date, and size. Contained within the Folder object are methods to manipulate folders, such as moving them, and properties that return information about a folder.

Methods are functions that are members of an object and are used to manipulate the object's data or perform an action. Not all objects contain methods. Using the Folder object example in VBScript, the associated methods enable you to copy, delete, and move folders as well as create text files within them.

Properties are values or a set of values that return information. The VBScript Folder object contains properties that describe the folder in great detail. Among the many properties of the Folder object are modification date, a list of files within the folder, the properties of the parent folder, and the folder's path.

Visual Basic Scripting Edition (VBScript)

Visual Basic Scripting Edition, more commonly known as *VBScript*, is Microsoft's premier scripting language. It is derived from the popular programming language, Visual Basic, and is also related to Visual Basic for Applications. VBScript is the same language whether you use it to write scripts for Web pages using Microsoft Internet Explorer, server-side scripts for use with Internet Information Server, or scripts for use with the Windows Script Host. The only things that change are the objects, methods, and properties unique to each host.

JScript

JScript, sometimes confused with Netscape's JavaScript, is Microsoft's implementation of the ECMA 262 language specification (an international standard for a common scripting language). Microsoft admits that VBScript is more or less a Windows scripting language but has recognized the need to provide a language that conforms to the ECMA standard and is therefore more universal. It has its roots firmly in the Web page and therefore is more limited than VBScript when dealing with your local computer. If you are familiar with Java or JavaScript and know nothing about VBScript, then JScript is a good scripting language to become familiar with.

The WSH object model

An object model provides an interface to a collection of objects, properties, and methods. As such, the WSH object model enables you to directly manipulate the execution of the script as well as certain system objects. An understanding of the WSH object model is crucial to opening up Windows to scripting. Table 26-3 identifies the objects, methods, and properties of the WSH object model.

Table 26-3 WSH Objects, Properties, and Methods	
Object	**Properties**
WScript	Application
	Arguments
	FullName
	Name
	Path
	ScriptFullName
	ScriptName
	Version

Object	Properties
Object	Properties
	Methods
	CreateObject
	DisconnectObject
	Echo
	GetObject
	Quit
	Sleep
Object	Properties
WshArguments	Item
	Count
	Length
	Methods
	None
Object	Properties
WshEnvironment	Item
	Count
	Length
	Methods
	Remove
Object	Properties
WshNetwork	ComputerName
	UserDomain
	UserName
	Methods
	AddPrinterConnection
	EnumNetworkDrives
	EnumPrinterConnection
	MapNetworkDrive
	RemoveNetworkDrive
	RemovePrinterConnection

Continued

	Table 26-3 (*continued*)
Object	*Properties*
	SetDefaultPrinter
Object	Properties
WshShell	Environment
	SpecialFolders
	Methods
	CreateShortcut
	ExpandEnvironmentStrings
	LogEvent
	Popup
	RegDelete
	RegRead
	RegWrite
	Run
Object	Properties
WshShortcut	Arguments
	Description
	FullName
	Hotkey
	IconLocation
	TargetPath
	WindowStyle
	WorkingDirectory
	Methods
	Save
Object	Properties
WshSpecialFolders	Item
	Count
	Length
	Methods
	None
Object	Properties

Object	Properties
WshUrlShortcut	FullName
	TargetPath
	Methods
	Save

A short example

In this section I explain a short sample script I wrote in VBScript. This script, called FREESPACE.VBS, displays the free space I have on one of my drives.

My first task is to create the variables that are going to hold objects and information. I use the Dim command to create variables I reference in the main body of the script:

```
Dim fso, d, myFree
```

I need access to the FileSystemObject in order to access drive properties. I get access by creating a new FileSystemObject:

```
Set fso = CreateObject("Scripting.FileSystemObject")
```

Now that I have created a FileSystemObject, I can catch a unique drive's properties:

```
Set d = fso.GetDrive("C")
```

The next step is to read the actual amount of free space on the drive. Because the value returned is bytes, I want to divide by 1,024 to get megabytes and use the FormatNumber function to format the display:

```
myFree = FormatNumber(d.FreeSpace/1024, 0)
```

Finally, I need to display the returned value. I do so by using the Echo method of the Wscript object.

Listing 26-1 shows the completed script.

Listing 26-1: **FreeSpace.vbs**

```
Dim fso, d, myFree
Set fso = CreateObject("Scripting.FileSystemObject")
Set d = fso.GetDrive("C")
myFree = FormatNumber(d.FreeSpace/1024, 0)
```

```
Wscript.Echo myFree
```

Although this is a simple example, you can see that VBScript obtains information about the system, and the WSH object model provides the means to display it. Listing 26-2 shows the same script written in JScript.

Listing 26-2: **FreeSpace.js**

```
var fso = new ActiveXObject("Scripting.FileSystemObject");
var d = fso.GetDrive("C");
var myFree = d.FreeSpace/1024;
WScript.Echo(myFree);
```

The principles are the same, but the differences in the two languages are obvious even with this short example.

Creating and Using Windows Script Files

In addition to running single scripts with the Windows Script Host, you can also create and use Windows Script files as a form of project file, which are used to manage multiple files and resources in formal programming IDEs. Windows Script files are text files with a .WS extension written in Extensible Markup Language (XML). They enable you to run multiple scripts and access external resources.

Everything in a Windows Script file must be encapsulated in an element. The different elements identify each object in the file and enable you to include additional data. Table 26-4 lists the elements you can use.

Table 26-4
Elements

Element	Description
<?job ?>	Sets error handling and debugging options.
<?XML ?>	The file is treated as strict XML.
<job>	Identifies jobs.
<object>	Creates global objects.
<package>	Encloses multiple job elements.
<reference>	References an external type library.
<script>	Identifies script statements within the Windows Script file.

Summary

This chapter was a broad overview of the Windows Script Host and showed you how it works, how to use it, and a little about how to script for the WSH.

✦ The Windows Script Host acts as language-independent intermediary between scripts and the ActiveX scripting engine on the 32-bit Windows operating system.

✦ You can currently run scripts written in VBScript or JScript.

✦ You can modify the run-time properties of individual scripts.

✦ There are two methods to run a script: from Windows and the command prompt.

✦ The WSH Object Model defines objects with properties and methods that enable you to control script execution and gain access to the system and network.

✦ Windows Scripts are project files written in XML.

So much for the WSH! Chapter 27 is up next and it covers the primary administrative tools you will use with Windows 2000 Professional. Learn how to use the Performance Monitor to monitor your computer's performance, view and manage events, use the Microsoft Management Console, manage users and groups with advanced tools, and install the Windows 2000 Resource Kit.

✦   ✦   ✦

Administrative Tools in Windows 2000 Professional

If you are a power user, system administrator, or tweak-maniac like me, just getting your system running and being generally productive isn't enough. An imperative floating around in your brain exercises itself whenever you boot your system. It prompts you to explore under the hood, figure out the inner workings of your computer, optimize everything possible, and troubleshoot even when there is no trouble. This chapter is for you!

Microsoft Windows 2000 Professional comes with a complete assortment of highly customizable tools that you can spend hours playing with. They enable you to monitor the performance of your computer; alert you when it drops below a certain level; catch hardware, application, and system events that notify you of errors or warnings; manage your computer, users, and groups; and distribute and manage component applications.

I've divided this chapter into two parts. The first part covers the Performance Monitor, Event Viewer, and advanced user management, while the second part covers other administrative tools and the Windows 2000 Resource Kit.

The Performance Monitor is a tool you can use to monitor a wide range of system activities such as disk access, free memory, and CPU utilization. You can view the results in real time or write monitoring data to a log file for later analysis. You can analyze system events, identify bottlenecks, and tweak the system based on your interpretation of the data you collect. What's more, you can even have the Performance Monitor alert you if performance drops below a certain threshold.

Launching the Performance Monitor

To start the Performance Monitor follow these steps:

1. Click Start ➪ Settings ➪ Control Panel.

2. Choose Administrative Tools, which will open the Administrative Tools window of the Control Panel.

3. Select the Performance icon to launch the Performance Monitor.

Choosing Performance launches the Performance Monitor as shown in Figure 27-1. Notice that if this is the first time you've used it, nothing is happening. You have to configure the Performance Monitor to monitor the activities you choose.

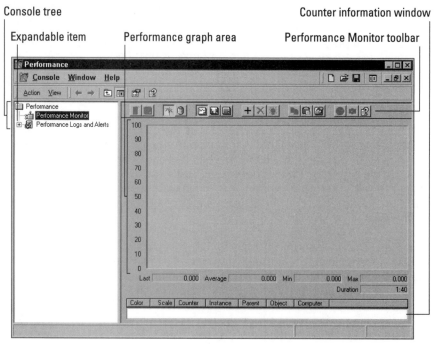

Figure 27-1: Performance Monitor awaits your commands.

Charting and viewing performance data

You can chart the performance of your machine or others on your network in near real time using the graphing function of the Performance Monitor. This capability is ideal for taking a quick, short-term look into a computer as it is performing certain tasks to see the effects on its performance.

Adding counters

First you need to add counters. A counter is nothing more than the specific data associated with a characteristic of a performance object, which is a collection of performance data related to a component of your system. There are several ways to add counters, but because I prefer right-clicking, I cover that one in detail.

1. Right-click in the portion of the window containing the graph, as shown in Figure 27-2. A context-sensitive menu appears.

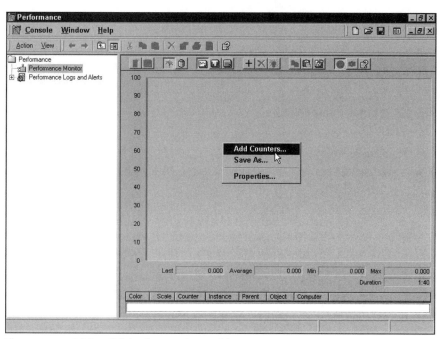

Figure 27-2: Right-click in the graph to add counters.

2. Choose Add Counters. This action brings up the Add Counters dialog box as shown in Figure 27-3. The dialog box is divided into three areas: computer selection, performance object selection, and performance counter selection.

You can also select a remote computer

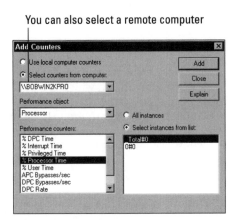

Figure 27-3: Adding counters by selecting a computer, a performance object, and a performance counter.

3. To add counters from the local computer, make sure Use local computer counters is selected. If you want to monitor other computers on your network, choose Select counters from computer and enter the name of the target computer.

4. Select a performance object from the pull-down list. Figure 27-3 shows Processor selected.

5. Select a performance counter associated with the performance object. Figure 27-3 shows % Processor Time selected.

You might be wondering which instance of a counter to add. Some performance objects, such as memory, have only one instance so it doesn't matter if you choose All Instances or choose one of the values from the list. They are all the same. If you have multiple instances of an object, such as CPUs or disks, you have the option of choosing which instance of the object to monitor. Figure 27-4 shows the Physical Disk counter selected to illustrate this point. Notice that you can select all instances of the Physical Disk counter, the total of the instances, or one specific instance or drive. I should note that two of my three hard drives are partitioned into multiple volumes, and thus the Performance Monitor shows the drive letters assigned to the disks.

Select the total or an individual instance

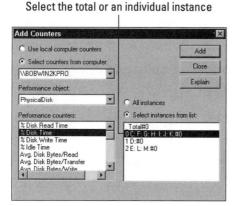

Figure 27-4: Choosing to add one instance from the three available physical disks.

Note

Counter paths are defined as follows:

```
Computer_name\Object_name(Instance_name#Index_Number)\Co
unter_name
```

Or in the case of my physical disk:

```
\\BOBWIN2KPRO\PhysicalDisk(0 C: F: G: H: I: J:
K:#0)\%DiskTime
```

6. Click Add. At this point, the Add Counters dialog box remains open for you to add more counters. When you are finished, click Close.

When you close the Add Counters dialog box, the counter or counters are added to the graph and are dynamically updated at a set interval. Figure 27-5 shows my memory counter charting along as I opened and closed a few programs to see the effect it had on my free memory.

This bar marks the beginning of the monitoring

Numerical readouts are displayed
for the selected counter

Select to stop updating

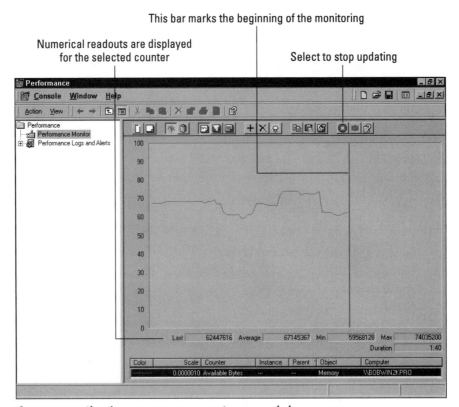

Figure 27-5: Charting memory usage as I open and close programs.

You can add several counters to see the effects of a task or tasks on multiple performance objects. In Figure 27-6, I added Processor Time, Disk Time, and Thread Count to see what happened when I opened and closed a few programs. It might be hard for you to differentiate the counters in grayscale in the figure, but Available Bytes is the line running across the middle, Processor Time jumps around a bit but stays below 70 percent, Disk Time has the high peak in the middle, and Thread Count stays at the top the entire time.

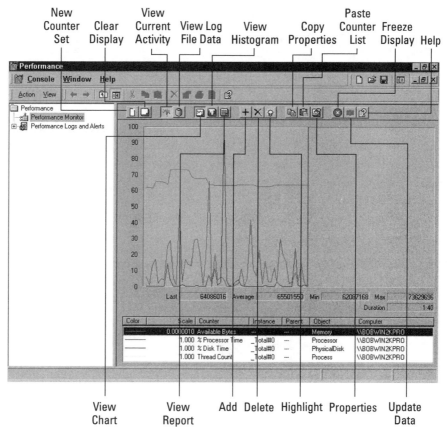

Figure 27-6: Charting multiple performance counters at once.

Deleting counters

If you try out a few counters and decide that one or more isn't measuring what you want, it is easy to delete them.

1. Select the counter in the lower window. In Figure 27-7 I have selected Thread Count because in the previous chart the value didn't change and so I don't think it's useful.

2. Click the Delete button on the toolbar.

This counter is selected

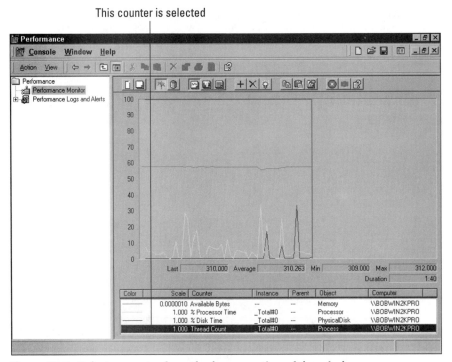

Figure 27-7: Select a counter from the lower portion of the window.

An alternate method of deleting counters is to right-click the graph and choose Properties from the pop-up menu. On the System Monitor Properties dialog box, select the Data tab, shown in Figure 27-8, select the counter you want to delete, click the Delete button, and then click OK to close the dialog box.

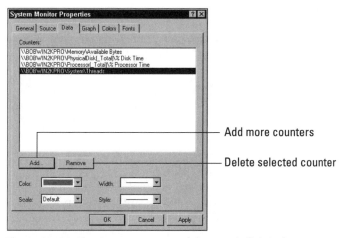

Figure 27-8: Choose a counter to delete and click Delete.

Changing display types

I find the graphical display to be useful, but it can get confusing at times, or maybe you just want a change of pace. You can change the display from a chart to a histogram or a report and back again.

✦ To view performance as a chart, click the Chart Display button on the toolbar.

✦ To view a histogram, click the Histogram Display button (sixth button from the left, currently depressed in Figure 27-9) on the toolbar. Figure 27-9 shows a histogram of my three remaining counters.

Histogram dislays all counters   Data is for selected counter

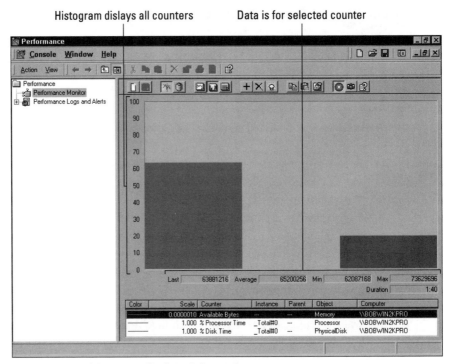

Figure 27-9: A histogram display of the performance counters.

✦ To view as a report, click the Report Display button (seventh button from the left, currently depressed in Figure 27-10) on the toolbar. Figure 27-10 shows a report.

Changing graph properties

If you don't like the display in the Performance Monitor, you can easily change it through the System Monitor Properties dialog box. Open the dialog box by clicking the Properties button on the toolbar or by right-clicking in the chart area and choosing Properties.

The System Monitor Properties dialog box contains five tabs. You've already seen the Data tab. In addition, the dialog box has tabs marked General, Source, Graph, Colors, and Fonts.

The General tab, shown in Figure 27-11, contains the general properties of the Performance Monitor.

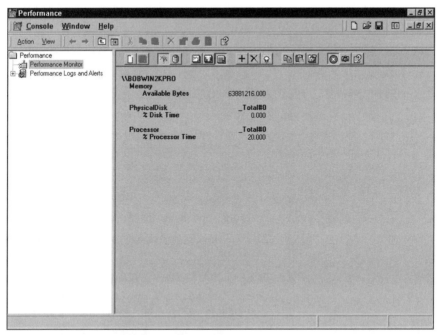

Figure 27-10: A report of the performance counters.

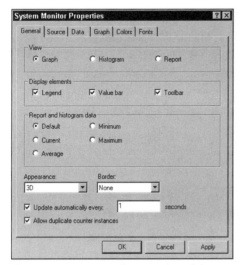

Figure 27-11: General properties of the Performance Monitor.

You can see from the figure that several configuration choices are available. Table 27-1 lists the options and their effects.

Table 27-1 General Properties Options	
Property	**Effect**
View	Switches between Graph, Histogram, and Report displays.
Display elements	Toggles the Legend, Value bar, and Toolbar on or off.
Report and histogram data	Assigns a value type to be presented in the Report display. You can choose between default, current, average, maximum, and minimum values.
Appearance	Changes the display from flat to a 3D look with recessed readouts.
Border	Adds a border to the Report display.
Update	Lets you set the update time in number of seconds or turn automatic updating off and rely on manual updates.
Allow duplicate counter instances	Enables you to monitor duplicate counters.

Use the Source tab, shown in Figure 27-12, to define a data source. Notice that you can choose between current activity and log files. This is different from choosing a computer to monitor. If you want to load data from a log file, choose Log File, find the file, and then select a time range.

The Data tab (previously shown in Figure 27-8) enables you to identify a computer or computers on your network to monitor as well as add or delete counters.

You can also modify the graph properties of each counter in the Data tab. Select the color, line type, and scale that suits your needs.

Figure 27-13 shows the Graph tab, which enables you to title your graph, assign a Y-axis label, turn a grid on or off, and set the graph scale. Figure 27-14 shows the results of entering the values shown in Figure 27-13.

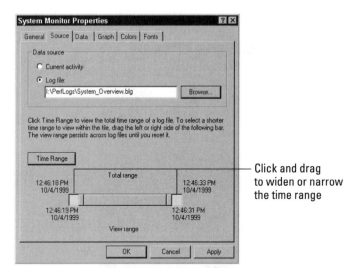

Click and drag
to widen or narrow
the time range

Figure 27-12: Assign a data source to the Performance Monitor on the Source tab.

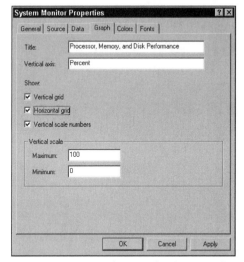

Figure 27-13: Use the Graph tab to set the properties of your graph.

Y-axis label   Title   Grid

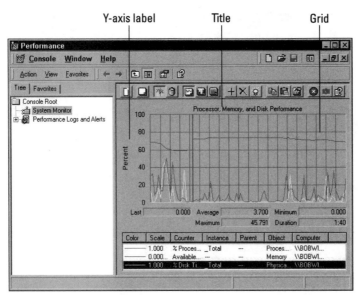

Figure 27-14: I have added a title, a Y-axis label, and a grid to the chart.

Use the Colors tab, shown in Figure 27-15, to change the colors of specific items in the graph and interface.

Drop down list displays more properties

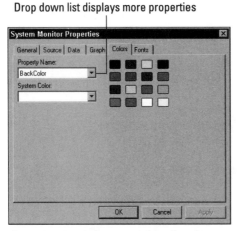

Figure 27-15: Select a graph or interface component and change the color.

The Fonts tab, shown in Figure 27-16, enables you to change the fonts displayed. Font changes affect only the right window pane of the Performance Monitor.

Figure 27-16: The Fonts tab: Am I in Word or in the Performance Monitor?

Viewing the Performance Monitor as a Web page

Because the Performance Monitor relies on an ActiveX control, Microsoft has made it easy for you to save your current configuration, whether a graph, a histogram, or a report as a Web page. This is not just a static image, but a live control that is updated based on the settings you originally chose. To save your graph as a Web page, simply right-click in your graph, and choose Save As. In the Save As dialog box, choose a save location and name your file. The file is automatically saved with an .HTM extension. Double-click the HTML file to open it in your Web browser. Figure 27-17 shows what it looks like. All the controls in the toolbar are active, and the interface works the same as in the Performance Monitor. This example shows a graph, but you can also save histograms and reports.

Note   If you want to create custom Web pages with an embedded Performance Monitor, simply add the counters you wish to monitor in the Performance Monitor, select Save as HTML, then open the HTML file in a text or HTML editor. Once you have the HTML file open, you can add your own HTML code to create a custom Web page. Be careful not to modify the HTML associated with the Performance Monitor ActiveX control. This code is automatically generated by the Performance Monitor and ensures the control displays and monitors correctly.

This is an Active X Control   Functional Performance
                                   Monitor toolbar   Live graph

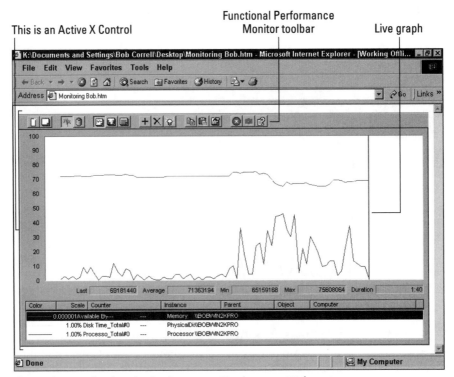

Figure 27-17: Viewing the Performance Monitor as a Web page.

Using performance logs and alerts

So far you've used only a portion of what is available in the Performance Monitor, namely near real-time monitoring of system performance. The Performance Monitor also has the capability to create log files and generate alerts. Log files enable you to automatically collect data on your machine or one connected to your network for analysis at a later time either in the Performance Monitor or in a spreadsheet program such as Excel. You can automatically set alerts to trigger when a counter falls below or rises above a certain threshold and notify you or begin a log file of the current processes.

The Performance Logs and Alerts feature is located in the left pane of the Performance Monitor interface as shown in Figure 27-18. Each item in the left pane functions like a Windows Explorer tree. To make a selection, click the item name. To expand or contract the tree, click the plus or minus sign beside the name.

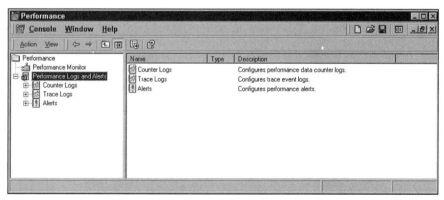

Figure 27-18: Performance Monitor showing the Performance Logs and Alerts.

Creating a counter log

If you want to log certain counters, you need to create a counter log:

1. In the left pane of the Performance window, select Performance Logs and Alerts.

2. Select Counter Logs.

3. Right-click in the right window and select New ⇨ Create New Log Settings from the pop-up menu. The Create New Log Settings dialog box appears.

4. Name your log file in the dialog box and click OK.

5. The dialog box shown in Figure 27-19 appears. Add new counters to the dialog box in the same way you added counters to the Performance Monitor.

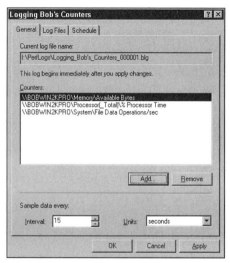

Figure 27-19: Adding counters to log.

6. When you are finished, click OK, and the log file you've created immediately begins logging the data from the performance counters you selected. Your log appears in the display as shown in Figure 27-20.

Note

The log icon is green, indicating that it is active. Red icons indicate logs that are not currently active. Aside from scheduling a start and stop time, you can right-click the log and choose All Tasks ➪ Start or All Tasks ➪ Stop to start or stop the log. This applies to trace logs and alerts as well.

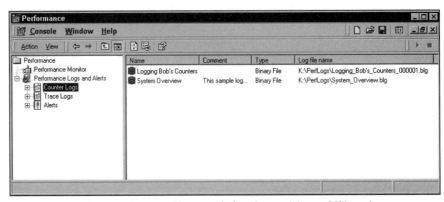

Figure 27-20: The icon is green if currently logging activity, red if inactive.

To modify the properties of the log you just created, simply double-click it (or right-click the log and choose Properties). The General tab enables you to add or remove counters and change the sampling rate. The Files tab, shown in Figure 27-21, enables you to change the log file parameters.

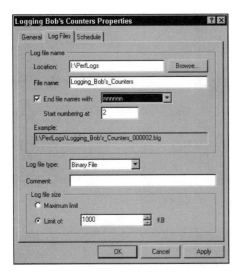

Figure 27-21: Change log file parameters on the Log Files tab.

You can change the log file's location and name, change it's naming convention, change the log file from binary to comma- or tab-separated values, add comments to the log that appear in the Performance Logs and Alerts interface, and set a maximum log file size.

The Schedule tab, shown in Figure 27-22, enables you to set logging to begin and stop at certain times or be controlled manually.

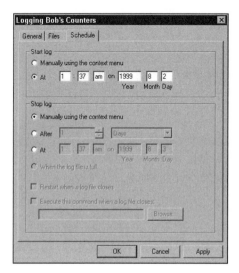

Figure 27-22: Schedule your logging times to coincide with the time period you want to collect data.

Creating a trace log

Trace logs are different from counter logs in that they wait to begin logging until a specific event or activity occurs and then record a continuous log of system activity. For example, you can create a trace log to begin logging when a page fault occurs. You can go back and review the log to help troubleshoot the system.

1. In the left pane of the Performance window, select Performance Logs and Alerts.

2. Select Trace Logs.

3. Right-click in the right pane and select New ⇨ Create New Log Settings from the pop-up menu.

4. In the Create New Log Settings dialog box, name your trace log and click OK.

5. You must now select either a general trace provider (also known as a nonsystem provider) or enable the system trace provider, as shown in Figure

27-23. The system trace provider option uses the Windows kernel trace provider to monitor processes, threads, and other activity.

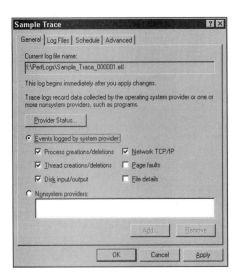

Figure 27-23: Choose system provider to enable your system to log these events.

6. When you're done, click OK, and the trace log appears in the Trace Logs window as shown in Figure 27-24.

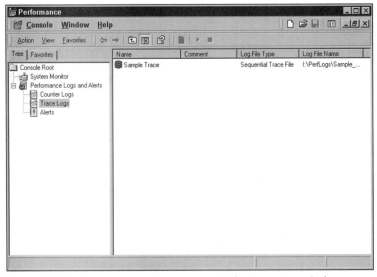

Figure 27-24: The new trace log appears in the Trace Log window.

Trace logs, like counter logs, have options for customizing the logging and log file through the trace log properties. To access the properties, double-click the trace log icon (or right-click the log and choose Properties). You've already seen the General tab of the resulting dialog box, and it also includes a Log Files tab and a Schedule tab that work just like those for counter logs. The fourth tab, Advanced, shown in Figure 27-25, is unique to a trace log.

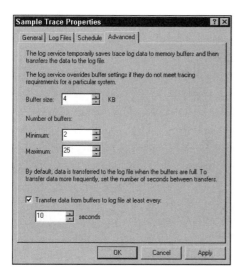

Figure 27-25: Advanced Trace log settings enables you to configure memory buffers.

Buffer size is the amount of memory used to hold the trace data. Minimum buffers sets the minimum number of buffers you want to allocate to the trace log, and Maximum buffers sets the maximum number of buffers. If you want the provider to periodically flush the buffers, select Transfer data from buffers to log file and specify a time interval.

Creating an alert

Alerts notify you when a performance counter rises above or below a certain threshold. Here's how to create an alert:

1. In the left pane of the Performance window, select Performance Logs and Alerts.

2. Select Alerts.

3. Right-click in the right pane and select New ➪ Create New Alert Settings from the pop-up menu.

4. In the New Alert Settings dialog box, name your alert and click OK. The dialog box shown in Figure 27-26 immediately appears.

5. Add counters by selecting Add. This will display the familiar Add Counters dialog box. Once you have added the counters, specify an over or under threshold value as shown in Figure 27-26. Notice that I have chosen two

performance counters, Processor Time and Available Bytes (free memory) and have assigned a value of 1,024 bytes to the memory counter. When my free memory falls below this value, the alert is triggered.

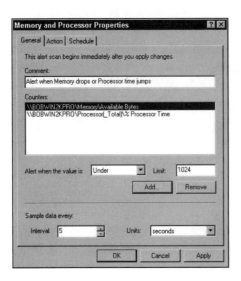

Figure 27-26: Add counters and specify a threshold.

6. Select the Action tab, shown in Figure 27-27, and choose an action to take place if the alert is triggered. I have chosen to log an entry in the application event log, but you can choose to send a network message, execute a command file, or begin logging.

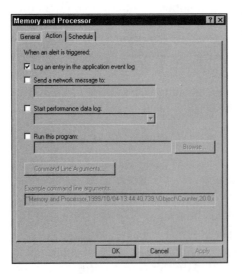

Figure 27-27: Choose an action to occur when the alert is triggered.

7. Click OK to save the Alert. The alert appears in the Alert window as shown in Figure 27-28.

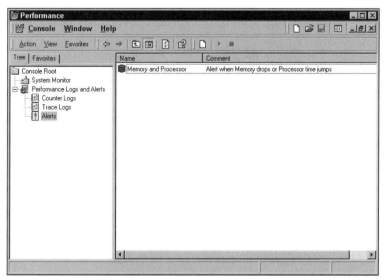

Figure 27-28: The new alert.

On the Schedule tab, you can also schedule times when the alerts are active and inactive.

Figure 27-29 shows the warning that appeared in the Event Viewer (covered later in this chapter) after I triggered the alert.

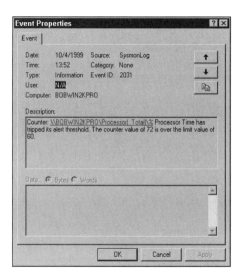

Figure 27-29: The alert triggered and logged an event warning.

Deleting logs or alerts

If you have made a mistake or the log or alert you have created has served its purpose and you want to delete it instead of turning it off, follow these steps:

1. Select Counter Logs, Trace Logs, or Alerts, depending on the log you want to delete.

2. Right-click the log to be deleted.

3. Choose Delete.

Using Event Viewer

The Event Viewer monitors a wide range of software, hardware, and system events as well as security events. You can use the Event Viewer to troubleshoot problems as they arise or prevent problems from getting larger.

Launching the Event Viewer

Here's how to start the Event Viewer:

1. Click Start ➪ Settings ➪ Control Panel.

2. Choose Administrative Tools, which will open the Administrative Tools window of the Control Panel.

3. Select the Event Viewer icon to launch the Event Viewer.

Figure 27-30 shows the Event Viewer.

Figure 27-30: The Event Viewer.

Notice that there are three types of event logs:

✦ **Application log**: Contains events logged by applications such as your Web browser or word processing program. It is up to the application developer to register events for logging.

✦ **Security log:** Contains security events ranging from login attempts to file operations and policy changes. You can specify which events are logged through the Group Policy editor.

✦ **System log:** Contains events generated by the Windows 2000 Professional system components. Because these events are designed into the system, you have no control over them.

Within each event log, five types of events can occur:

Information	This event describes the successful operation of a driver, application, or service.
Warning	Not significant enough to be an error, but not benign like information. Warnings may indicate a problem. Figure 27-31 shows a warning.

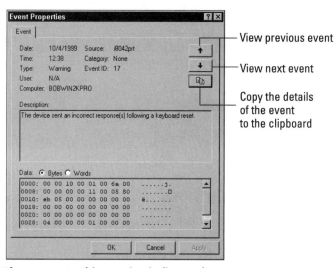

Figure 27-31: This warning indicates the keyboard sent an incorrect response.

Error   Indicates a significant problem. Figure 27-32 shows an error.

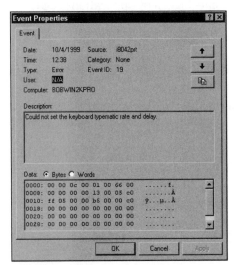

Figure 27-32: A good example of a hardware error with my keyboard.

Success Audit   An audited security access attempt succeeds. Figure 27-33 shows a successful audit.

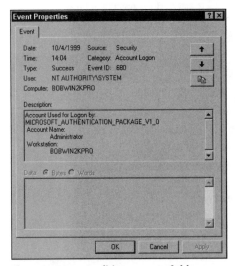

Figure 27-33: Auditing successful logon attempts.

Failure Audit An audited security access attempt fails. Figure 27-34 shows a failed audit.

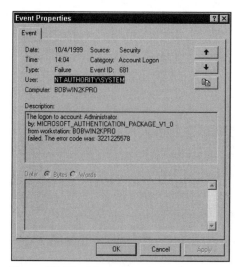

Figure 27-34: Attempting to log in as an unknown user generates a failure audit.

Viewing and managing events

Viewing and managing events is the heart of the Event Viewer. You can ward off trouble before it starts by periodically checking for errors and warnings as well as keep tabs on security.

Browsing logs and viewing events

Scanning through the Event logs is a quick way to see what has happened in your system.

1. Select the log you are interested in (Application, Security, or System). I have selected the System log in Figure 27-35, and it contains a variety of information events, warnings, and errors.

2. Use the scroll bar to move up or down the event listing.

3. Double-click an event to see a detailed description, as shown previously in Figures 27-31 through 27-34.

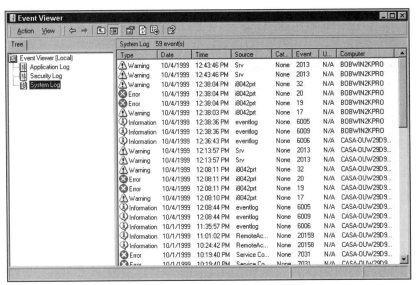

Figure 27-35: Select a log to browse its events.

Searching for events

The Event Viewer has a powerful search tool that enables you to search for broad categories of events or really narrow your search.

1. Select a log.

2. Choose View ➪ Find from the menu bar. Figure 27-36 shows the Find dialog box. Notice that I am searching in my local security log.

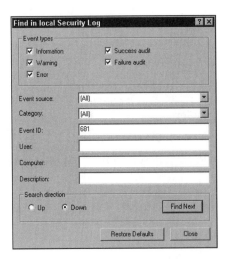

Figure 27-36: Searching for security events by Event ID.

3. Choose a type of event to search for. All of the event types are checked by default.

4. Choose a source and category. All sources and categories are selected by default. Pulling down the Source menu allows you to choose an event source, which is dependent on the log (Application, Security, or System) you are searching in. The Category pull-down menu is also dependant on the log you are searching in.

5. Type an event ID, computer name, user, or description to search for. In this case I'm looking for security events with an ID of 681, which is a failed account logon.

6. Determine the direction to search the log file for the event. The two directions are up or down, with down being the default.

7. Click the Find Next button. Figure 27-37 shows an event that matched my search criteria highlighted in the event listing. I have moved the Find dialog box out of the way, but it is still open and ready to continue searching.

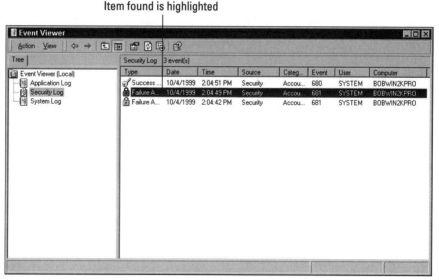

Figure 27-37: My search was successful.

8. If you wish, you can open the event and view it in detail by double-clicking the event. To continue searching, click Find Next until you are finished and then click the Close button to close the dialog box.

Clearing a log

If you have too many events and you want to clean them out, you can clear your logs.

1. Select a log.

2. Right-click the log name and choose Clear All Events. You are prompted to save the log before the events are cleared.

Saving a log

Saving logs is a good idea for archiving interesting or troubling events for future analysis. There are three formats you can choose from when saving logs: Event log format, comma-separated value format, and tab-delimited text format.

1. Choose a log.

2. Right-click the log name and choose Save Log File As.

3. In the Save As dialog box, enter a filename and select the format type for saving your file. Choose from three file formats:

   • **Event log format (.EVT):** Preserves any binary data and enables you to open the saved log in the Event Viewer.

   • **Comma-separated value format (.CSV):** Enables you to import the information (although no binary data is retained) into a spreadsheet. The data is formatted be separating values with commas.

   • **Tab-delimited text format (.TXT):** Similar to the comma-separated value format, but in this case the values are separated by tabs.

4. Click Save.

Exporting log column data

If you don't want to export the actual contents of the events but would like to save the columns shown in the main Event Viewer window, you can choose the option to export log column data. Here's how:

1. Select a log.

2. Right-click and choose Export List from the pop-up menu.

3. In the Save As dialog box, enter a name and choose a file type from the four options:

   • Tab-delimited text (.TXT)

   • Comma-delimited text (.CXV)

   • Tab-delimited Unicode text (.TXT)

   • Comma delimited Unicode text (.csv)

Note   The ASCII and Unicode files have the same extension although they are different character encoding formats. ASCII (American Standard Code for Information Interchange) uses an 8-bit scheme to encode 256 unique characters, while Unicode, developed by the Unicode Consortium, uses a 16-bit character encoding scheme to encode a possible 65,536 unique characters.

4. Click Save.

Customizing event logs

You can modify the Event Viewer interface to suit your needs by changing the sort order of data, hiding columns, filtering events, and selecting other options.

Changing the sort order

Sort order refers to the arrangement of data in the Viewer and can be either ascending or descending. To set or change the sort order, decide which column you want to sort by and follow these steps:

1. Select a log.

2. Select the column you want to sort by clicking it's heading.

Note You can resize the columns by dragging their dividing lines or double-clicking the line between columns to autofit the contents.

3. Click the column heading again to change from ascending to descending. Figure 27-38 shows the System log sorted by the Type column in ascending order. In this sort, Errors are listed first because they're most important, followed by Warnings and Information events.

Triangle indicates sorted field and
whether it is ascending or descending

Type	Date	Time	Source	Category	Event	User	Computer
Error	10/1/1999	10:19:40 PM	Servic...	None	7031	N/A	CASA-OUW29DSJHN
Error	10/1/1999	10:19:40 PM	Servic...	None	7031	N/A	CASA-OUW29DSJHN
Error	10/4/1999	12:38:04 PM	i8042prt	None	19	N/A	BOBWIN2KPRO
Error	9/30/1999	11:59:48 AM	i8042prt	None	19	N/A	CASA-OUW29DSJHN
Error	9/30/1999	11:59:48 AM	i8042prt	None	20	N/A	CASA-OUW29DSJHN
Error	10/4/1999	12:08:11 PM	i8042prt	None	19	N/A	CASA-OUW29DSJHN
Error	10/4/1999	4:14:27 PM	i8042prt	None	20	N/A	BOBWIN2KPRO
Error	10/1/1999	10:19:40 PM	Servic...	None	7031	N/A	CASA-OUW29DSJHN
Error	10/4/1999	4:14:26 PM	i8042prt	None	19	N/A	BOBWIN2KPRO
Error	10/4/1999	12:38:04 PM	i8042prt	None	20	N/A	BOBWIN2KPRO
Error	9/30/1999	12:16:02 PM	i8042prt	None	19	N/A	CASA-OUW29DSJHN
Error	9/30/1999	12:16:02 PM	i8042prt	None	20	N/A	CASA-OUW29DSJHN
Error	9/30/1999	5:54:52 PM	i8042prt	None	20	N/A	CASA-OUW29DSJHN
Error	9/30/1999	5:54:52 PM	i8042prt	None	19	N/A	CASA-OUW29DSJHN
Error	10/1/1999	10:02:21 PM	i8042prt	None	19	N/A	CASA-OUW29DSJHN
Error	10/1/1999	10:02:22 PM	i8042prt	None	20	N/A	CASA-OUW29DSJHN
Error	10/4/1999	12:08:11 PM	i8042prt	None	20	N/A	CASA-OUW29DSJHN
Error	10/1/1999	10:19:40 PM	Servic...	None	7031	N/A	CASA-OUW29DSJHN
Error	10/1/1999	10:19:40 PM	Servic...	None	7031	N/A	CASA-OUW29DSJHN
Error	10/1/1999	10:19:40 PM	Servic...	None	7031	N/A	CASA-OUW29DSJHN
Warning	9/30/1999	11:59:48 AM	i8042prt	None	32	N/A	CASA-OUW29DSJHN
Warning	9/30/1999	6:00:42 PM	Srv	None	2013	N/A	CASA-OUW29DSJHN

Figure 27-38: My System log sorted by event type. Hmm, lots of errors here.

Showing, hiding, and moving columns

If you want to go hog-wild, you can completely customize columns and their order in one fell swoop.

Note You cannot choose to hide the type of event or move it from the first column.

1. Select a log.

2. Select View ➪ Choose Columns from the menu bar to display the Modify Columns dialog box as shown in Figure 27-39.

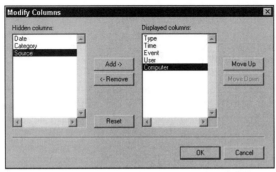

Figure 27-39: If you don't need to see a column or if you want to reorder them, select View ➪ Choose Columns and salt to taste.

3. Add or remove the columns you want to display. In this instance, I have chosen to hide the Source, Category, and Date columns by selecting them and clicking Remove.

4. To change the column order, select a column and click either the Move Up or Move Down buttons.

5. Click OK to accept the changes, Reset to revert to the values present when you opened the dialog box, or Cancel to cancel your operation. Figure 27-40 shows the final result.

Note Hiding and reordering columns affects all three logs. You cannot set column properties for individual logs.

Filtering events

Filter events when you want to fine-tune your viewing to weed out unneeded data or define a time frame of events you wish to inspect more closely.

Note You can set up filters for each log that do not affect the others.

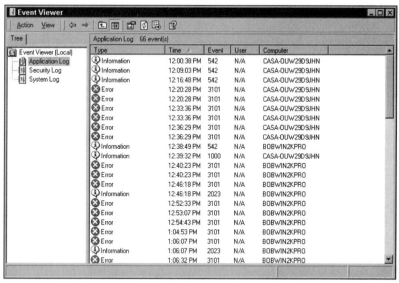

Figure 27-40: The new column structure.

1. Select a log. For this example I have chosen the Application log.

2. Select View ➪ Filter from the menu bar to display the Application Log Properties dialog box shown in Figure 27-41.

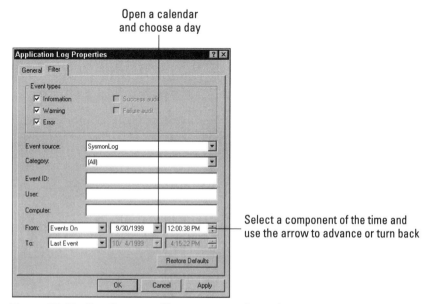

Figure 27-41: Use the event filter to narrow down the events you see.

3. Select a time frame. The controls enable you to select a range of dates and associated times.

4. Select the event types you want to exclude by clicking in the checkbox to remove the check.

5. Select a source, category, user, computer, and event ID to display. If you enter values for these options, you filter out all other values. Figure 27-41 shows a request for all the events registered by the System Monitor Log.

6. Click OK.

Clearing a filter

Here's how to clear the filter for a log:

1. Select a log that has the filter applied.

2. Select View ⇨ Filter from the menu bar.

3. Select Clear.

Setting log options

In addition to filtering events, you can change the display name for a log, fix a maximum size for the file, and set wrapping options on the Application Log Properties dialog box.

1. Select a log.

2. Right-click and select Properties from the pop-up menu to display the Properties dialog box shown in Figure 27-42.

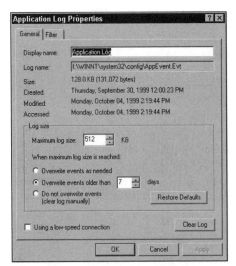

Figure 27-42: Right-click a log to access its properties.

3. Change the display name if desired.

4. Set a maximum log file size.

5. Set event log wrapping options. Overwrite events as needed overwrites the oldest events in order as the file reaches its maximum size. You can also choose to overwrite events older than a given number of days, or set the log not to overwrite any events. In that case, you have to clear it manually to make room for new events if it reaches its maximum allowed size.

6. Identify a low-speed connection. Check this option if the log file is located on a remote computer and you are connecting at a relatively low speed, such as a 56K modem versus a 10Mbs LAN connection.

Microsoft Management Console

The Microsoft Management Console (MMC) is a host that enables you to open existing administration snap-ins and modify the interface or create a console of your own. The tools that exist in the console and the ones you add are called *snap-ins*. These components provide all the functionality for administration.

You've already seen the MMC in action if you've used any of the administrative tools such as the Performance Monitor, Event Viewer, or Computer Management consoles. Each one of these tools uses a specific snap-in to provide its unique functionality.

To launch the MMC from the Start menu, click Start ➪ Run and enter **mmc /a** at the prompt. Figure 27-43 shows the Microsoft Management Console with no snap-ins added.

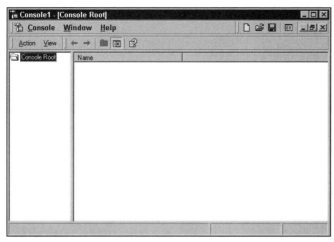

Figure 27-43: A Microsoft Management Console with a clean slate.

You can add or delete snap-ins through the Console ➪ Add/Remove Snap-in menu. Available snap-ins include the following:

✦ ActiveX Controls

Note   The Performance Monitor is an ActiveX Control called the System Monitor Control. ActiveX Controls can be embedded in Web pages.

✦ Certificates

✦ Component Services

✦ Computer Management

✦ Device Manager

✦ Disk Defragmenter

✦ Disk Management

✦ Event Viewer

✦ Fax Service Management

✦ Folder

✦ FrontPage Server Extensions

✦ Group Policy

✦ Indexing Service

✦ Internet Information Services

✦ IP Security Policy Management

✦ Link to Web Address

✦ Local Users and Groups

✦ Performance Logs and Alerts

✦ Removable Storage Management

✦ Security Configuration and Analysis

✦ Security Templates

✦ Services

✦ Shared Folders

✦ System Information

Many of these snap-ins are created by Microsoft although a few are developed by third parties. You can expect more to be available as Windows 2000 matures and companies take advantage of the MMC to build a better mousetrap.

One of the important features of the MMC is the capability to restrict users from modifying a console and creating others.

Here's a list of the available console modes:

✦ **Author mode**: Complete access to all MMC features and the capability to add and remove snap-ins, create new windows, and navigate the entire console tree.

✦ **User mode with full access:** No access to adding or removing snap-ins or saving consoles, but otherwise full access to the console tree and windowing functions.

✦ **Multiple window user:** Similar to User mode with full access but lacks the capability to create new windows or access restricted console tree snap-ins. Multiple child windows are available, but the user cannot close them.

✦ **Single window user:** The same as User mode with full access but without the capability to create multiple windows.

To access the Options dialog box and set the console mode, select Console ⇨ Options from the menu bar and select the Console tab. Figure 27-44 shows the tab with the console mode set to Author mode (the /a command-line switch opens the console in authoring mode).

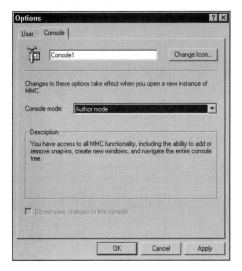

Figure 27-44: Console options showing author mode.

Using the Security Log

To use the Security log, you must turn on auditing through the either the Group Policy or the Local Security Policy administrative tools, both of which are covered in more detail later. Group Policy settings allow you to manage various components of a user's desktop environment, such as what programs appear on the Start Menu, and security settings such as the maximum password age before it expires. The Local Security Policy tool allows you to view and modify local security policies, which are a part of Group Policy.

Opening the Local Security Policy

1. Click Start ⇨ Settings ⇨ Control Panel.

2. Select Administrative Tools, which opens the Administrative Tools window of the Control Panel.

3. Select the Local Security Policy icon to launch the Local Security Policy MMC, as shown in Figure 27-45.

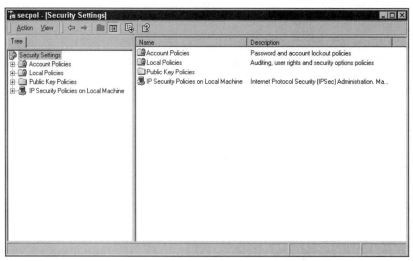

Figure 27-45: The Local Security Policy administrative tool allows you to view and modify local security settings.

Enabling auditing

1. With Local Security Policy open, expand the Local Policies tree in the left window pane and select Audit Policy, as shown in Figure 27-46.

2. Select the attribute you want to audit and double-click it. The Audit Logon Events dialog box displays.

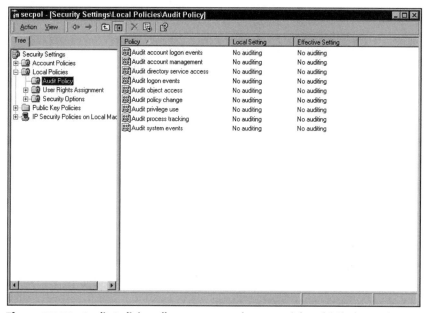

Figure 27-46: Audit Policies allow you to track successful and failed security events.

3. In the Audit Logon Events dialog box, click the checkboxes to include successful and/or failed attempts. Figure 27-47 shows auditing enabled for all logon attempts, whether successful or not.

   The effective policy setting reflects the policy as it currently exists and is applied to the local computer. Once you have made changes to the policy and closed Local Security Policy, the effective policy setting will be updated.

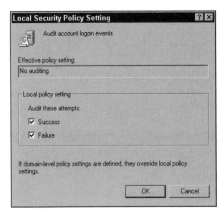

Figure 27-47: Choose the types of events you want to audit.

4. Click OK to set the local policy.

5. When you are finished changing policies, close Local Security Policy for your changes to take effect. If you reopen Local Security Policy, you will see that the Local Policy and Effective Policy settings match.

Advanced Local User Management

The standard tool for managing users and groups provided by Windows 2000 Professional is called Users and Passwords and is located in the Control Panel. Using this tool, you can add and remove users as well as assign them to groups. Another more advanced user management tool called Local Users and Groups is also available. For those of you who need more power in creating or editing users and groups, follow me!

Launching Local Users and Groups

The Local Users and Groups tool is provided as an MMC interface. To open it, you can use the Users and Passwords tool in the Control Panel or create a new MMC and add the Local Users and Groups snap-in. The first method is explained here:

1. Click Start ➪ Settings ➪ Control Panel.

2. Choose Users and Passwords to bring up the Users and Passwords dialog box.

3. Select the Advanced tab and click the Advanced button in the Advanced User Management section to launch the Local Users and Groups Management Console shown in Figure 27-48.

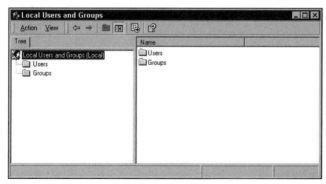

Figure 27-48: The Local Users and Groups console is simple, yet powerful.

Note
To create this MMC yourself, select Start ➪ Run and enter mmc /a in the dialog box to start a console in authoring mode. Select Console ➪ Add/Remove Snap-in, then choose Add to open a dialog box with a list of available snap-ins. Choose Local Users and Groups from that list and add it as a snap-in. Close all dialog boxes to return to the console.

The Local Users and Groups console enables you to perform many activities, including the following:

✦ Creating, editing, and deleting users and groups

✦ Setting passwords and password policies

✦ Disabling accounts

✦ Changing descriptions

✦ Assigning a user profile, logon script, and home directory

✦ Exporting user and group lists

Many of these functions are not available through the Users and Passwords dialog box.

Managing users

At the heart of advanced user and group management is not only having the ability to create new users and groups but also control certain settings like whether or not they can change their password, disabling their account, creating new groups, and assigning user storage directories.

1. Select the Users folder in the left pane of the Local User Manager console, right-click inside the right pane, and choose Create User from the pop-up menu.

2. The New User dialog box shown in Figure 27-49 appears, and it has more options than the Users and Passwords dialog box. Enter the user name, full name, and description as usual, set the password, and select whether or not to force the user to change his or her password at the next login, prevent the user from ever changing the password, and even create the account in a disabled state. Notice that you do not assign a group at this time.

3. Click the Create button. The new user will appear in the MMC but the New User dialog box will remain open (with all data cleared), allowing you to create more new users. You can either create more new users at this time or close the dialog box.

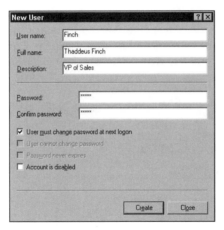

Figure 27-49: Creating a new user with the Local User Manager.

4. To edit a user and assign group membership, select the user by double-clicking the name in the right pane of the Local User Manager to open the user's Properties dialog box.

5. Use the General tab to change the name, description, and password settings for the user.

6. Click the Member Of tab to see the screen in Figure 27-50. By definition, new users are assigned to the users group. This is a local, computer-specific group. To change or add group membership (users can be in multiple groups), select the group name and click Remove or click the Add button and assign more groups to the user.

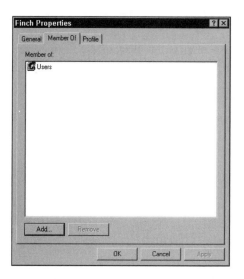

Figure 27-50: New users are automatically assigned to the users group.

7. Click the Profile tab, shown in Figure 27-51, to set the path to the user profile, a logon script to be run when the user logs on, and the path to the user's home directory.

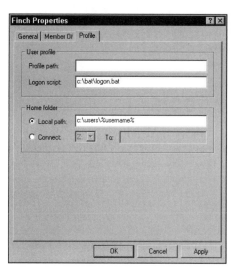

Figure 27-51: Assign a logon batch file and user directory through the Profile tab. Note the user name in the dialog box title.

Managing groups

The Local Users and Groups console also provides powerful group management tools. You can create new groups by selecting the Groups folder, right-clicking in the right pane window, and choosing New ➪ Group from the pop-up menu. Figure

27-52 shows the Create Group dialog box. Although Windows 2000 provides a number of predefined groups such as Users, Power Users, and Administrator, you can choose to create your own custom groups to organize your user population.

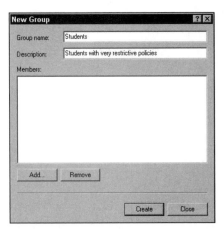

Figure 27-52: Creating a customized group.

Enter the name of the group and a description, assign members if you like, and click the Create button. When you are finished, click Close, and the new group appears in the details pane of the Local User Manager console.

To edit a group name or description, or to assign or remove members from the group, double-click the group name (or right-click and choose properties) and enter your new values in the group properties dialog box.

Other Administrative Tools

Several other administrative tools come with Window 2000 Professional that allow you to manage your computer more efficiently, view and edit security policies, administer COM applications, configure database sources, and more.

Computer Management

Computer Management provides a central point for administering your computer and includes several other management tools or resources all located in one convenient interface. To open the Computer Management console, follow these steps:

1. Click Start ➪ Settings ➪ Control Panel.

2. Choose Administrative Tools.

3. Select Computer Management to open the Local Computer Management console as shown in Figure 27-53.

Figure 27-53: The Computer Management interface.

The Computer Management tool has three main categories of functionality:

✦ **System Tools:** Tools that manage the local computer, such as the Performance Monitor and Event Viewer.

✦ **Storage:** Tools that manage hard disks and removable storage.

✦ **Services and Applications:** Tools that manage services and applications.

Do you see anything familiar here? You should, because most of the system tools are the same components found elsewhere in Windows 2000 Professional.

To use a tool, select it in the left window pane. This will update the right window pane and enable the functions specific to the tool you have selected. In some cases you may need to expand the tree in the left window to reveal sub-tree items.

Group Policy

Group policy is an amalgamation of settings that define a user's working environment — what they can and cannot do — while using their computer as well as policies for the computer itself. This includes such things as what programs appear on the Start menu, managing access to offline files, configuring Windows Explorer settings, and so on. Inherent in this concept is your ability to manage and secure computers and therefore your network.

Group policy has two components: users and computers. You manage groups of users by modifying User Configuration and computers by modifying Computer Configuration. Each time a computer boots it obtains computer policy settings, and when a user logs in they will obtain the user settings applicable to their group regardless of the computer they log on to.

To create a Group Policy console, follow these steps:

1. Select Start ⇨ Run.

2. Enter mmc /a to launch the Microsoft Management Console in author mode.

3. Select Console ⇨ Add/Remove Snap-in.

4. Choose Add to open a dialog box with a list of available snap-ins.

5. Choose Group Policy from that list and add it as a snap-in. Close all dialog boxes to return to the console.

Component Services

Component Services enables you to administer COM applications. This primarily involves deploying COM-based applications and monitoring performance and security for the deployed applications. Major tasks include the following:

✦ Configuring your system for Component Services

✦ Making initial services settings

✦ Installing and configuring applications

✦ Monitoring and tuning component services

To launch Component Services, follow these steps:

1. Click Start ⇨ Settings ⇨ Control Panel.

2. Choose Administrative Tools.

3. Select Component Services.

Figure 27-54 shows the Component Services tool.

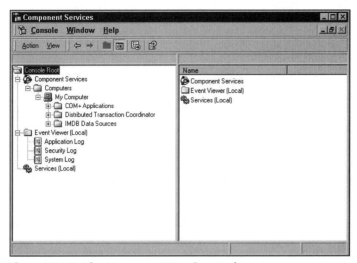

Figure 27-54: The Component Services tool.

Data Sources (ODBC)

Data Sources (ODBC) is an Open Database Connectivity tool that provides an interface between programs and database management systems. This enables applications to access the data through Structured Query Language (SQL), a database access standard. Figure 27-55 shows the Data Sources (ODBC) dialog box.

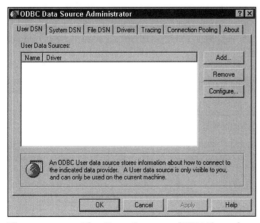

Figure 27-55: The Data Sources (ODBC) tool.

To use this tool, you need to add and configure user, system, or file data sources with data source names. You can view the current ODBC drivers installed on your system, configure trace calls, alter connection properties, and view information about the ODBC core components.

Internet Services Manager and Personal Web Manager

The Internet Services Manager is an administrative tool for Internet Information Services 5.0. You can create and host an FTP or Web site on your computer as well as create a virtual mail server. The Internet Services Manager is an optional Windows component that may not already be installed.

Please refer to Chapter 22 for more detailed information about the Internet Services Manager and Personal Web Manager.

Server Extensions Administrator

The Server Extensions Administrator administers FrontPage Server Extensions, which are necessary to install if you use and want to get the full benefits of Microsoft FrontPage as a Web page creation and site administration tool. Please refer to Chapter 22 for more information.

Summary

This chapter has been eventful! You've seen the administration tools provided with Windows 2000 Professional. Experiment with different ones to see which tool best suits your needs and then play with it to really learn it. The tools are supposed to make your life easier, but getting the most out of them can take time and patience. To sum up, here's what you learned in this chapter:

✦ Use the Performance Monitor to look at performance objects and counters and analyze the effects of running the tasks you want to perform with the machine.

✦ Create performance logs to gather data and analyze it later.

✦ Alerts inform you if your performance drops below a certain threshold.

✦ The Event Viewer shows system events that have occurred. They can be informational, warn you of impending doom, or document errors and security events.

✦ The advanced User and Group Manager gives you more power in creating and managing users and groups.

✦ Other administration tools include Computer Management, Group Policy, Component Services, Data Sources (ODBC), Internet Services Manager, Personal Web Manager, and Server Extensions Administrator.

✦ Most of these tools are housed in a Microsoft Management Console that you can customize to suit your needs.

✦ The Windows 2000 Resource Kit is packed with more tools and information for you to use as you administer your computer and others.

This chapter concludes *Windows 2000 Professional Bible*! Whether you've chosen to read the book from cover to cover or have browsed and read topics of interest in the order you desired, you've got the information to install, configure, maintain, troubleshoot, and enhance Windows 2000 Professional.

✦   ✦   ✦

Introducing Intellimirror

✦ ✦ ✦ ✦

In This Chapter

Document availability

Settings availability

Application availability

✦ ✦ ✦ ✦

Intellimirror is a set of management tools that enable your personal documents and settings to be available on any computer in the domain, as well as making any software you may require to be available as well. Intellimirror uses group policies set up in the active directory to make this happen. Intellimirror can be used for many things, including the management of users' settings and data and the installation and maintenance of application software. The main goal of Intellimirror is to make users completely mobile. For users to be fully mobile, their data and any required applications must be available at any point on the network. An optional goal is to make their personal settings available as well. User data management and software management are discussed in this appendix.

Document Availability

Intellimirror can make life easier for both the users and system administrators. One advantage of Intellimirror is seen at the first logon to a system. On your first day at a new job, you sit down at your desk and log on to the Windows 2000 Professional computer provided for you. As you log in, the Windows 2000 Domain Controller references the active directory and sees that you are in the Marketing group. It then applies the group policy for this group to you. The group policy states that your My Documents folder is redirected to a share on the server containing the documents (company policies, for example) required by the Marketing group. To make this happen, a network administrator has already created a logon user name for you, placed you in the appropriate groups, and configured the group policies for those groups.

The following series of procedures redirects users' My Documents folders to a network location and makes them available for offline use. These steps must be performed by the system administrator. First, you must create a shared folder for the user documents and set the caching settings:

1. Log on to the file server on which you want the user documents stored. You must log on with administrative privileges.

2. Open My Computer by double-clicking the icon on the desktop.

3. Open the local disk on which you are going to store the document folders by double-clicking the icon.

4. Create a new folder on this disk and call it Documents.

5. Right-click the Documents folder you just created and click Properties from the pop-up menu.

6. Click the Sharing tab.

7. Select the Share this folder radio button as shown in Figure A-1.

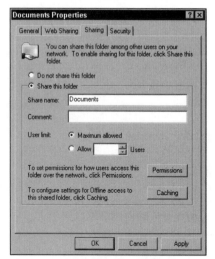

Figure A-1: The Sharing tab of the Document Properties window.

8. Click the Caching button to open the Caching Settings window.

9. Make sure the Allow caching of files in this shared folder checkbox is selected and select Automatic Caching for Documents from the Setting drop-down box as shown in Figure A-2.

Figure A-2: The Caching Settings window.

10. Click OK to close the Caching Settings window.

11. Click OK to close the Documents Properties window.

You must now configure the group policy to redirect users' My Documents folders to the network.

1. Click Start ➪ Programs ➪ Administrative Tools and select Active Directory Users and Computers.

2. Double-click the domain to administer (win2k.performance.net in this case), then open the organizational unit on which to set the policy. Organizational units are discussed in more detail in Appendix B. In this example, I set the group policy for the OU called Marketing, which resides in another OU called User Accounts. I double-click User Accounts, then right-click Marketing, and click Properties from the pop-up menu. This example is shown in Figure A-3. It is also possible to set a Group Policy for the entire domain. To do so, you right-click the domain instead of the OU and select Properties from the pop-up menu.

3. In the Properties window, click the Group Policy tab.

4. Click the New button to create a new group policy object (GPO).

5. Name the new GPO (Redirect My Documents, in this example) and press Enter. The Group Policies tab with the new policy is shown in Figure A-4.

6. Click the Edit button to edit the Redirect My Documents policy.

7. The group policy administration tool opens as shown in Figure A-5. Double-click User Configuration to display the tree structure and then double-click Windows Settings, followed by Folder Redirection.

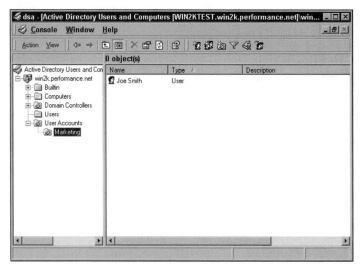

Figure A-3: The Active Directory Users and Computers administration tool showing the organizational units User Accounts and Marketing.

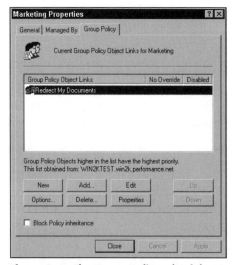

Figure A-4: The Group Policy tab of the Marketing Properties window showing the newly created Redirect My Documents group policy object.

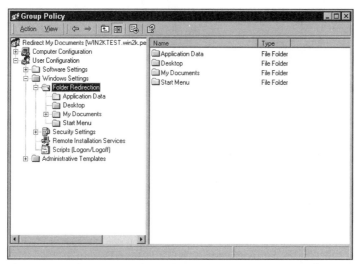

Figure A-5: The Group Policy administration tool showing the Folder Redirection option.

8. Right-click My Documents under Folder Redirection and select Properties from the pop-up menu.

9. To redirect all user folders to the newly created Documents folder on the server, choose Basic from the Setting drop-down box on the properties dialog box. Enter the target folder location as shown in Figure A-6. The server name in this example is WIN2KTEST, so the path for the folder redirection is \\WIN2KTEST\Documents\%username%. This creates a folder for each user in the group to which this policy applies as needed. In addition, an Advanced option specifies the redirection location based on the user groups (not the OUs) to which the user belongs. This is useful when setting the group policy for the entire domain, but in most cases, group policies are set for each OU and the Advanced setting is unnecessary.

10. Click the Settings tab, shown in Figure A-7, to set the folder redirection settings.

You should grant the user exclusive rights to My Documents seeing as you are using %username% as the directory name. This ensures that only the user who owns the folder can access it.

You can choose to move the current contents of My Documents to the new location.

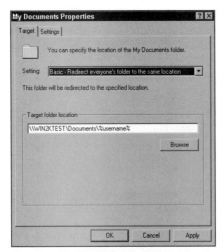

Figure A-6: The folder redirection basic property showing a redirection of the My Documents folder to \\WIN2KTEST\ Documents\%username%.

You can choose whether to move the new My Documents folder back to the original location when the policy is removed. If the folder redirection is removed and the Leave the folder in the new location when the policy is removed checkbox is checked, the contents of My Documents remain in the redirected location, and the user can't access them without knowing that location.

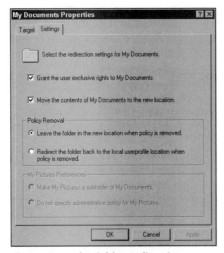

Figure A-7: The folder redirection properties Settings tab.

11. Click OK to close the My Documents Properties window.

12. Close the Group Policy administration tool.

13. Click Close to close the Marketing Properties window.

14. Close the Active Directory Users and Computers administration tool.

The My Documents folder should now be redirected to the specified network drive. Any users to whom the GPO applies must log off and log on again for the changes to their policies to take effect. You can test the redirection by logging in as a user to whom the policy applies and doing the following:

1. Log on to the domain as a user in the OU on which the GPO is set (jsmith, in this example).

2. Create a document. For this example, we use WordPad to create a test text document.

3. Save the document (Using Save As from the File menu) in the My Documents folder.

4. Open \\WIN2KTEST\Documents and locate the jsmith directory.

5. Verify that the file you saved in Step 3 is in this directory. If so, the folder redirection was successful.

6. Right-click the My Documents folder on the desktop.

7. Click Properties from the pop-up menu.

8. Ensure that the Target Folder Location shows the redirection folder assigned earlier in Step 9 (in the procedure preceding this one). It is \\WIN2KTEST\ Documents\%username% in this example. The user logged in is Joe Smith. An example of the My Documents Properties showing the Target Folder Location is shown in Figure A-8.

9. Click OK to close the My Documents Properties window.

Having the My Documents folder available offline is useful for mobile users. They can still work on any of their documents, even while disconnected from the network.

We can now make the folder available offline. You need to log on to the domain as a user contained in the OU on which you set the GPO. In this case, we log on to a workstation in the domain as Joe Smith from the Marketing OU on which we set the Redirect My Documents GPO.

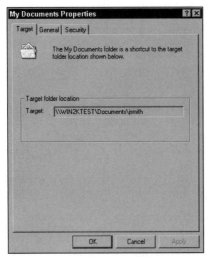

Figure A-8: The My Documents Properties window showing the Target folder location.

To enable My Documents to be available offline:

1. Log on to the workstation on which you want the folder available offline as the regular user (jsmith, in this example).

2. Double-click My Documents on the desktop.

3. Click Folder Options from the Tools menu.

4. The Folder Options window appears. Click the Offline Files tab.

5. Ensure the Enable Offline Files box is checked. This setting only has to be set once; it takes effect for the entire workstation and not just the current folder.

6. Click OK to close the Folder Options window and close the My Documents window.

7. Right-click the My Documents folder on the desktop and click Make Available Offline on the pop-up menu.

8. This causes the Offline Files Wizard to appear. Click Next to continue.

9. Check the Automatically synchronize the Offline Files when I log on and off my computer checkbox.

10. Make sure the Enable Reminders box is checked. This causes a message to appear periodically when you are working offline. You also have an option to create a shortcut on the desktop to the Offline Files folder. The Offline Files folder is a central point where all folders that are set to work offline can be accessed.

11. Click Finish. The Offline Folders Wizard appears only once to initially set the configuration. The next time you click the Make Available Offline option from a folder's pop-up menu, it happens automatically using the settings configured in Steps 9 and 10. If the folder contains subfolders, you are prompted to select whether to make the subfolders available offline as well as the base folder.

The folder is now cached on the local workstations to enable offline use. This capability is especially useful for laptop users. If a file is updated by a user offline and also updated online, when the synchronization occurs (usually at logon and logoff), the user is prompted to save either the new online version, the new offline version, or both. If you choose to save both, you are prompted for a name for the new offline version. You must have security permissions on the new online version if you wish to overwrite it with the new offline version.

Settings Availability

You can use folder redirection to do much more than just redirect the My Documents folder. You can also redirect the Application Data, Desktop, and Start Menu folders to network locations using the same method previously shown for My Documents. This enables a complete implementation of roaming profiles. Roaming profiles enable a user to be able to log on to any workstation in the domain and be faced with the same user interface, including all programs, documents, and desktop settings. Intellimirror enables the implementation of roaming profiles using group policies stored in the Active Directory. The following is an example of how to implement roaming profiles. The following procedure must be performed by a system administrator.

1. Log on to an Active Directory server as an administrator.

2. Open My Computer by double-clicking the icon on the desktop.

3. Open the Local Disk on which you are going to store the document folders by double-clicking the icon.

4. Create a new folder on this disk and call it Profiles.

5. Right click the Profiles folder you just created and click Properties from the pop-up menu.

6. Click the Sharing tab.

7. Select the Share this folder radio button.

8. Click OK to close the Profiles Properties window.

9. Click Start ⇨ Programs ⇨ Administrative Tools and select Active Directory Users and Computers.

10. Locate the user for whom to implement a roaming profile. In this case, I make Joe Smith in the Marketing OU use a roaming profile. Right click the user and click Properties from the pop-up menu.

11. Click the Profile tab.

12. Enter the user profile path in the User Profile box. In this example, the path is \\WIN2KTEST\Profiles\%username%. %username% creates a directory within the profiles directory named after the user name. The profile for Joe Smith is stored in \\WIN2KTEST\Profiles\jsmith.

13. Click OK to close the Joe Smith properties window.

14. Close the Active Directory Users and Computers administration tool.

Joe Smith can now log into any computer on the network and see the same wallpaper, desktop layout, favorites, and other personalized settings as specified on that computer.

Application Availability

Intellimirror can use the Windows Installer service to give you access to the software you require anywhere on the network, on demand. The Windows Installer service is an integral part of Windows 2000 and many applications written for Windows 2000. In the first example, you were given access to the company policies in the shared folder. The company policies are a Microsoft Word document, but because this workstation is new, it does not have Word installed. If you double-click the company policies document, Windows Installer looks for the Microsoft Word application and checks to see that all files are present. Because the application is not installed, Windows Installer automatically installs the software in the background, completely transparent to you, as long as the server can be contacted. The document then opens.

Applications can be either assigned or published to you based on the group policy. If an application is assigned to you, a shortcut appears in your Start menu, and the file associations are made (for example, .DOC with Microsoft Word files), but the application is not fully installed. When you click the document or the shortcut, the Windows Installer service checks for the application, and if it is not present or if files are missing or corrupt, it installs the software. When an application is published to you, it appears in the Add/Remove Programs box in the Control Panel, and it is up to you to decide whether or not to install the software. It does not automatically show up in the Start menu, and file associations are not made automatically.

When assigning an application, it must contain a Windows Installer (.MSI) file. Many new applications written for Windows 2000 use the Windows Installer and contain a .MSI file. SETUP.EXE-based applications can be published but not assigned. SETUP.EXE-based applications are older programs written for versions of Windows prior to Windows 2000. They do not use the Windows Installer but use a Setup Wizard and a file called SETUP.EXE on their distribution media. It is preferential to publish applications based on the Windows Installer service and not traditional SETUP.EXE files, although it is possible to publish both.

Here's how to assign an appliction. This procedure must be done by a system administrator logged on to the server:

1. Open the Active Directory Users and Computers administration tool (click Start ⇨ Programs ⇨ Administrative Tools).

2. Double-click the domain to administer (win2k.performance.net, in this case), then open the organizational unit on which to set the policy. Right-click the OU on which to set the policy and click Properties on the pop-up menu. Organizational units are discussed in more detail in Appendix B. It is also possible to set a group policy for the entire domain. To do so, you right-click the domain instead of the OU and select Properties from the pop-up menu.

3. Click the Group Policy tab on the Properties window.

4. Click the New button to create a new group policy object (GPO).

5. Name the new GPO (Redirect My Documents, in this example) and press Enter.

6. Click Edit to configure the new GPO.

7. Select Computer Configuration ⇨ Software Settings as shown in Figure A-9. Then right-click Software installation and select New ⇨ Package to access the Open window shown in Figure A-10.

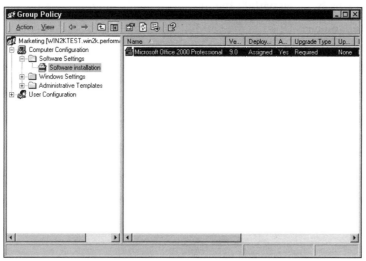

Figure A-9: The Group Policy administration tool showing the Software Installation option.

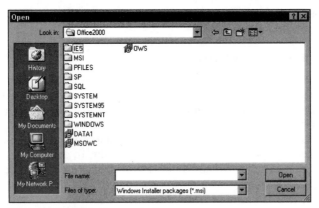

Figure A-10: The Open window.

8. Select the windows installer package (.MSI) file to assign and click Open. The default file for Microsoft Office 2000 is DATA1.MSI. Instructions for creating custom Windows installer (.MSI) files for packages are included with the applications. The package should be in a shared network directory. In this case, the entire Microsoft Office 2000 CD must be copied to a shared folder on the server. In this example, it is stored at \\WIN2KTEST\Packages\Office2000. If it is not, you get a dialog box warning you that the system cannot verify the availability of the path to the network.

9. After you click Open in the previous step, the Deploy Software dialog box appears. Choose Assign to assign the package. You can also choose Advanced published or assigned if you wish to apply modifications to a package. Modifications are updates made to a package after it is installed.

10. The assigned package now shows up in the right window,. assigned to all users who fall under this group policy. You can right-click the package in the right window of the Group Policy administration tool and select Properties to modify the settings for this assignment. From the Properties dialog box, you can set security options, rename the package, set deployment options, set modifications to the package, select packages upgraded by this package, and categorize this package in the Add/Remove Programs dialog box on the workstations. The package properties window is shown in Figure A-11.

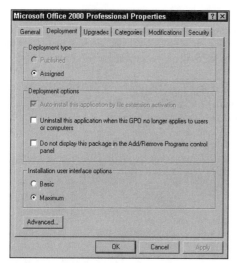

Figure A-11: The assigned package properties dialog box showing the Deployment tab.

From the package properties window, you can configure a number of options. From the General tab, you can change the name of the package. The Deployment tab enables you to select whether the package is Assigned or Published, uninstall the application when the GPO no longer applies to any users or computers, choose not to display the package in the Add/Remove Programs Control Panel, and choose the installation user interface options. The installation user interface options are the screens presented to the user when the package is installed. The basic option provides a more automated installation, while the maximum option provides more options to the user. The Advanced Deployment Options, reached by clicking the Advanced button on the Deployment tab, enable you to ignore language when deploying this package, which installs the package on workstations regardless of the language configured on those workstations. Normally a package installs only on a workstation with a matching language. You can also select to install this x86 package on Alpha computers. Normally an x86 package cannot be installed on an Alpha processor workstation.

The Upgrades tab enables you to select other packages to be upgraded by the current package. To select a package to upgrade, click the Add button and select the package to be upgraded. Then you can select whether the upgraded package must first be uninstalled or if the new package can upgrade over the existing package.

The Categories tab enables you to select the categories under the Add/Remove Programs Control Panel in which the package is listed. Available categories are listed on the left, selected categories on the right. Select a category from the Available categories section and click the Select button to add it to selected categories.

The Modifications tab enables you to add modifications or transforms to a package after installation in order to customize the package. They are applied in the order shown in the list. You can add and remove modifications if you have any and change the order in which they are applied.

The Security tab enables you to set permissions on the package. This enables you to configure who can change the package properties.

Summary

Intellimirror is a group of features that make the system administrator's job easier and makes the user's environment more convenient. In this chapter you learned

- ✦ How to configure folder redirection
- ✦ How to configure offline folders
- ✦ How to configure roaming profiles
- ✦ How to configure application packages and assignments

✦   ✦   ✦

Introducing Active Directory

Active Directory is a structured method of organizing all of the administration objects in a domain, such as computers, groups, and users. Active Directory is a directory service. A directory service combines a listing of all objects in the network with the services needed to make them accessible to the end users and administrators. Active Directory enables a directory of all resources on the network to be available to users, which enables users to find an object based on some information about that object. They may be looking for the closest printer or a certain file or database. Active Directory enables the listing and categorizing of literally millions of objects on the network.

Active Directory requires the Windows 2000 Server to be installed on an NTFS disk partition due to its use of permissions. It also requires the TCP/IP protocol and a fully established Domain Name Service (DNS) on the network. If a DNS server is not already on the network, Active Directory installs DNS on the server.

Windows Domain security (the overall security structure for the entire network) has traditionally relied on three levels of security: computer security, user security, and application security. These levels of security are addressed in separate administration tools in Windows NT 4.0. Server Manager enables control of computer security—that is, which computers are allowed to log on to the domain. User Manager controls user security, including rights and password policies. Application Security has traditionally been addressed within the administration program for the application in question, an example being Microsoft Exchange Administrator to set user rights for Microsoft Exchange.

Active Directory is a single point of administration for all of the security settings. It can be scaled from a small, single-domain local area network to a large wide area network with multiple domains. Active Directory contains objects and containers. Objects are items such as printers, files, and users. Objects have attributes associated with them, such as names, e-mail addresses, and network addresses. Containers also have attributes associated with them but are logical collections of objects and other containers. A container is simply a group and can contain both objects and other containers.

Active Directory enables increased security and a central point of administration for the entire enterprise including multiple domains. With Active Directory, permissions can apply across all domains so users do not need separate accounts for each. For example, a large organization may have multiple domains for separate locations. Permissions can be assigned to objects in one domain for users in another domain. If a user is in one domain, they can be assigned permissions to access a file in another domain. With Active Directory, a more granular level of security permissions enables minimum required access for users. The permissions granted to users go beyond the traditional read, write, list permissions and enable the configuration of permissions for file attributes and permissions to create files
or folders.

When objects are moved in the Active Directory, they do not necessarily keep the same security settings assigned to them. They take on the security settings of whatever container they are in (usually an organizational unit). They do, however, keep the settings assigned directly to them.

Active Directory stores definitions of all permissions on all objects on the network. Object permissions are governed by rules of inheritance. Any child objects created automatically inherit the permissions set on their parent objects unless specified otherwise.

Security

All objects and containers in Active Directory have an associated access control list (ACL) that contains access control entities (ACEs). An ACE contains a security identifier naming the user or group to whom the ACE applies and the access right that is granted or denied. An ACL is just a listing of the ACEs associated with an object, and ACEs are simply the permissions for the object. Active Directory security also enables delegation and inheritance. Delegation enables administrative rights to be assigned to other users or groups by a higher level administrator, which helps to distribute administrative load. Inheritance enables ACEs to automatically apply to objects and containers within the container to which the ACE applies.

Replication

Active Directory provides services for replication. Replication is necessary when multiple Active Directory servers are on the network. The Active Directory can be replicated across multiple servers to enable fault tolerance and faster access. Fault tolerance enables the domain to continue functioning when one Active Directory server goes down.

Active directory replication is transparent. Whenever a change to a property is made by a system administrator, the Active Directory server increments an Update Sequence Number (USN). Every Active Directory server in the organization keeps a record of the USNs from their replication partners. When a partner notifies that replication is required, the server checks the USNs in the record with the USNs on the replication partner (the server with which it is replicating). Only changes with USNs that are not matching are made, to avoid replication of information that is already in the directory. The USN system also avoids problems associated with time stamps, such as time synchronization, by enabling a server to request all updates with a USN greater than a certain value instead of updates after a certain time. With USNs, time synchronization is unnecessary. USNs also enable recovery from server and replication failures. When the replication is restarted, the server checks its USN table with the replication partner, and all lost changes are replicated.

Forests, Trees, Domains, and Namespaces

Active Directory supports several levels of domains organized into forests and trees. Definitions of these terms is in order. First of all, a *domain* is a group of computers that share a common security configuration. Domains contain one or more domain controllers, which are the systems that authenticate users and computers and give them access to resources on the network. Domain structure should be familiar to you if you are familiar with Windows NT. With Windows 2000, the Active Directory servers are the domain controllers. There are no longer a dedicated primary domain controller and backup domain controllers; all domain controllers in Windows 2000 are peers. Domain names in Windows 2000 are fully qualified domain names (FQDNs), meaning they have a proper Internet domain name. An example of a domain name is `win2k.performance.net`. The namespace of the domain is `performance.net`. Domains with contiguous namespaces are all those that are suffixed with the same Internet domain — `performance.net` in this case.

Trees are groups of domains that are in a contiguous namespace. The domains `win2k.performance.net`, `marketing.performance.net`, and `accounting.performance.net` can all be contained in a tree. Domains in a tree must, by definition, share trust relationships and common schema and configurations. Trust relationships are relationships set up between domains to enable users from one domain to access resources in another.

The *schema* of the Active Directory is essentially a list of the object classes and their attributes that can be stored in the directory. Object classes are simply definitions of types of objects. The schema is stored in the directory itself. It defines what can be created in the directory and where it can be located. The locations of new objects are limited by definitions of legal parents of the object classes; thus, an object can be created only under a legal parent, such as a user under the users container.

Forests are groups of trees that do not share a contiguous namespace. The tree `performance.net` could be in a forest with the domain `newdomain.com`. Forests also share trusts between the trees (and therefore domains) contained within. Trees in a forest also share a common configuration and global catalog (GC). A GC is a catalog of all objects in the forest but is not a complete directory in that it contains only the most commonly used attributes in search operations. A GC enables users to locate resources within the forest without knowing which tree or domain they are contained in. Figure B-1 shows examples of forests, trees, and domains.

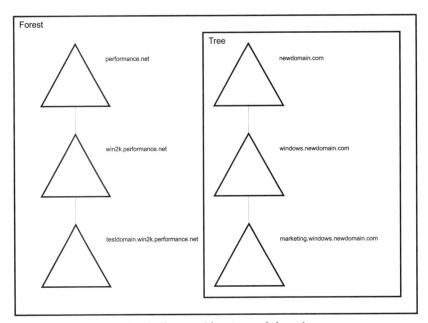

Figure B-1: An example of a forest with trees and domains.

Sites

Sites are sections of the physical network with good connectivity, generally high bandwidth. Sites usually contain complete IP subnets assuming that the IP subnets do not span slow connections. Sites are used to define the Active Directory server to which a specified workstation connects. When a workstation is first connected to the network (that is, when it is powered up), the Windows 2000 Domain Controller Locator attempts to find an Active Directory server on the same subnet as the workstation, which enables faster access and lower network traffic.

Organizational Units

Organizational units (OUs) are objects within the Active Directory used for group policies or administrative delegation. Delegation is discussed in the section "Security," earlier in this appendix, and group policies are discussed in the section "Group Policies," later in this appendix. An OU is a container that can contain users, groups, computers, and other OUs. In other words, OUs can be nested within each other. OUs function only within the domain they are in and cannot be used beyond that boundary. Using OUs, one can structure security and personalization settings for specific groups of users. Group policies cannot be specified for users, groups, or computers within a domain, so those users or groups must be contained within an OU. Once the users, groups, and computers are moved to the OU, you can specify group policies for them as well as delegate administrative tasks to them. OUs are a requirement for using group policies, administrative delegation, and Intellimirror unless you wish to apply those policies to the entire domain. Intellimirror is discussed at length in Appendix A. OUs are created from the Active Directory Users and Computers administrative tool, discussed later in this appendix.

Installing Active Directory

Active Directory is best installed when you log in to a new installation of Windows 2000 Server for the first time. The first time you start Windows 2000 Server, you are presented with the Configure Your Server Wizard. To configure a new Active Directory server, you must be a system administrator.

1. Log in to your new server with the user name Administrator and the password assigned during the setup process.

2. You are presented with the Windows 2000 Configure Your Server Wizard as shown in Figure B-2. The first step is to decide whether this is the only (or first) server in the network or whether other Active Directory servers are in the network. If you select the option that other servers are in the network, you must manually configure the required options for your network. For this example, this is the first server on the network, and thus I select the option This is the only server in my network and click Next to continue. From this screen, you can also choose to configure the server at a later time. To restart the Windows 2000 Configure Your Server wizard, select Configure Your Server from the Start ⇨ Programs ⇨ Administrative Tools menu.

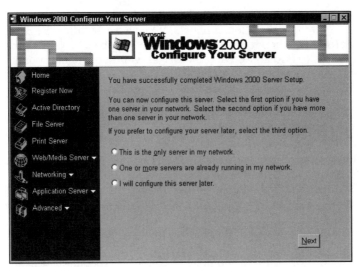

Figure B-2: The Windows 2000 Configure Your Server Wizard opening screen.

3. The next window informs you that the wizard is automatically going to configure the server as a domain controller and set up Active Directory, DHCP, and DNS. You have the options to see more details about the installation and to learn more about Active Directory, DHCP, and DNS. Click Next to continue.

4. In the next screen, you must assign a name to your domain. This name should have some meaning such as Marketing. I name the test domain I am going to create "win2k." You must also enter the name of the domain you have registered on the Internet. In my case, it is `performance.net`. If you do not have an Internet domain name registered, enter **local:**. You see a preview of what your domain name looks like to Active Directory clients (Windows 2000) and downlevel clients (Windows NT 3.51/4.0, Windows 9x). An example of this completed screen is shown in Figure B-3. Click Next to continue.

5. The next screen informs you that the setup process takes several minutes and your system will restart. Click Next to continue.

6. The Windows Components Wizard may appear to install any components required that were not installed during setup. At this point, you will be prompted to select the default permissions for user and group objects (see figure B-4). Of the two choices, pick Permissions compatible with pre-Windows 2000 servers if your domain contains domain controllers or servers which use domain permissions (such as remote access servers) which use an earlier version of Windows NT. Only choose Permissions compatible only with Windows 2000 servers if you are sure that all domain controllers and other servers are Windows 2000. Click next to continue.

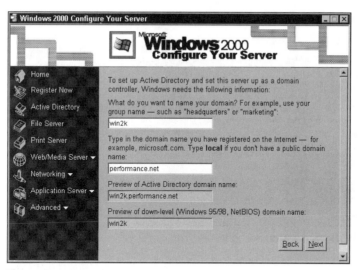

Figure B-3: The Configure Your Server Wizard domain name configuration page.

7. Next, the Active Directory Installation Wizard prompts you to enter an administrator password in order to allow the computer to be started in Directory Services Restore Mode. This mode is used if there is a problem with the Active Directory database at a later date and it needs to be repaired. Click next to continue.

8. The Active Directory Installation Wizard presents you with a summary of the options you have chosen. Click next to continue if you are satisfied with these selections.

9. Active Directory is also configured, and a status window appears on the screen (see Figure B-5).

10. When the installation of active directory is complete, you will be presented with a window showing the status of the installation. Click finish to close the wizard. You will be prompted to reboot the system.

11. Once the system restarts, the Configure Your Server Wizard appears again. Active Directory is now fully installed. You can use the icons on the left side of the screen to customize your server setup. You can also choose not to show this screen at startup again.

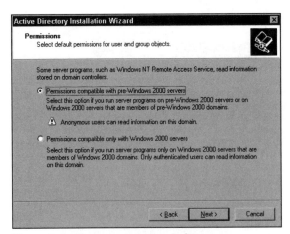

Figure B-4: The permissions window

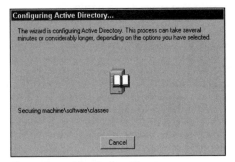

Figure B-5: The Active Directory
configuration status window.

Administering Active Directory

You administer Active Directory through a series of tools, all based around
the Microsoft Management Console. The difference between Windows NT 4.0
administration and Active Directory administration is that any trusting domains
can be administered from the Active Directory tools. A trusting domain is one
that has been configured to enable your domain access.

The three main components for active directory administration are found in the
Start menu under Programs ⇨ Administrative Tools:

- ✦ Active Directory Domains and Trusts
- ✦ Active Directory Sites and Services
- ✦ Active Directory Users and Computers

Active Directory Domains and Trusts enables you to configure relationships among domains, including downlevel domains such as Windows NT 4.0 and 3.51. Right-click the domain you wish to administer and click Properties to see the Domain Properties dialog box. Trusts are configured under the Trusts tab, much the same way as they are in Windows NT 4.0 User Manager. Figure B-6 shows a Windows 2000 domain in a two-way trust with a Windows NT 4.0 domain.

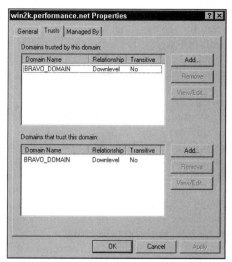

Figure B-6: The Trusts tab of the Windows 2000 Active Directory Domains and Trusts tool Domain Properties page showing a two-way trust with the Windows NT 4.0 domain Bravo_Domain.

Active Directory Sites and Services enables the configuration of Active Directory replication and Active Directory sites. Sites are logical groupings of computers on the same local network (or fast wide area network connection). If a network contains several distant locations, each location can become a site. Active Directory replication is configured between each site, but the workstations within a site always connect to a domain controller within their site for authentication. This enables lower network traffic and faster logons. Replication within a site is usually set to a shorter interval than replication between sites, to cut down wide area network traffic.

For example, suppose you had a domain that contained a head office and a branch office connected by an ISDN data link. You would want to make each office a site to cut down traffic over the ISDN connection. Replication between the two sites (that is, traffic over the ISDN connection) could be configured to occur less frequently than replication within the sites over the LAN connection, which is faster. The workstations in each office can connect to domain controllers within that office to further reduce traffic over the slower ISDN link.

Service publishing is also configured from the Sites and Services tool. Services are published to the Active Directory when they are needed by many users across the domain. Directory services are commonly published in the Active Directory. Directory services are used when the network consists of operating systems other than Windows 2000. A directory service enables Windows 2000 users to access resources on non-Windows 2000 systems. You can also publish configuration settings for applications commonly used in the domain. This enables a more consistent desktop across the domain as well as easier installation by the users.

The Active Directory Users and Computers tool is the most familiar to Windows NT 4.0 users and administrators. This tool combines the functionality of User Manager for Domains and Server Manager. It enables the system administrator to administer user accounts, groups, computer accounts, and organizational units.

Figure B-7 shows the Active Directory Users and Computers administration tool with the users container open. The users container includes all domain users as well as domain local and global groups. Right-clicking a user and selecting Properties brings up the User Properties dialog box. The General tab contains the personal information of the user, such as name and description. The Address tab holds the user's address information. The Profile tab contains the user's profile path, logon script, and home directory. The Telephones tab contains space for the user's telephone numbers. The Organization tab contains the user's corporate organization information, such as their manager and title. The Dial-in tab configures the user to allow or deny dial-up access, as well as setting their dial-up configuration. The Remote control, Environment, Sessions, and Terminal Services Profile tabs allow configuration of Windows 2000 Terminal Services for the user, if it is installed. The Terminal Services Profile tab is used to set user profile and home directory information for when the user is logging in using Terminal Services, as well as a check box to allow or deny the use of Terminal Services for this user. The Remote control tab contains information about how the Terminal Services remote control feature functions when controlling this user. The Environment tab sets the behavior of the Terminal Services client when the user logs in. The Sessions tab configures the session timeout settings and limits for the user when using Terminal Services. The Account and Member Of tabs are of the most interest. The other tabs contain basic descriptive information.

Use the Account tab to set the user's logon name, which can be different than the display name. You can also set the user's downlevel logon name for logging on to Windows NT 4.0 and 3.51 workstations. You can set a list of workstations to which the user can log on, as well as the hours when the user is allowed logon access. You can also set account options such as password expiration on this tab. The Account tab is shown in Figure B-8.

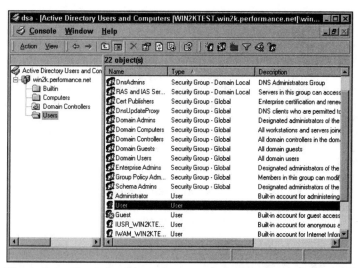

Figure B-7: The Active Directory Users and Computers administration tool with the users container open.

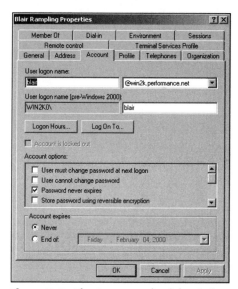

Figure B-8: The Account tab of the Active Directory Users and Computers User Properties dialog box.

Use the Member Of tab to specify the groups to which the user belongs. You can also set the primary group for the user. Active Directory includes three types of user groups: the domain local group, the global group, and the universal group. A domain local group can contain users only from within a domain but can be used to set permissions only within that domain. Global groups can contain users only from within a domain but can be used to grant access in any domain in the forest to which the domain belongs. Universal groups are available only when the domain is in native mode. Native mode is enabled by the system administrator once all domain controllers in the domain are running Windows 2000. Universal groups can contain members from any domain in the forest and can be used to grant permissions anywhere in the forest. With Active Directory in native mode, groups can also be nested. Nesting enables groups to contain other groups, a feature not available in earlier versions of Windows NT. To ease administration, groups can be members of other groups, which saves having to add users to groups multiple times. The Create New Object – (Group) window is shown in Figure B-9.

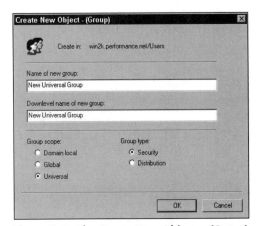

Figure B-9: The Create New Object – (Group) dialog box showing the group type selections.

OUs are another type of group. OUs are not used for setting security permissions but are used for setting group policies and delegating administrative tasks. Unlike user groups, OUs cannot be used outside the domain. OUs are containers within the Active Directory that can contain users, groups, computers, and other OUs. In the following process, I create two OUs for use later in the section "Group Policies." To create an OU:

1. Open the Active Directory Users and Computers administration tool.

2. Right-click the domain in which to add the OU (win2k.performance.net in this case).

3. Select New ⇨ Organizational Unit from the pop-up menu.

4. Name this first OU "User Accounts."

5. Right-click the newly created User Accounts OU.

6. Select New ⇨ Organizational Unit from the pop-up menu.

7. Name this OU "Marketing."

You have now created two new OUs to which you can apply group policies. You can now move users, groups, and computers into these OUs. To move an object into an OU:

1. Find the object you wish to move in the Active Directory. In this example, I move a user, Joe Smith, from the Users container to the Marketing OU. Right-click the object.

2. Select Move from the pop-up menu.

3. Double-click the domain (`win2k` in this example), and then double-click the User Accounts OU.

4. Click the Marketing OU to highlight it.

5. Click OK to move the object.

The user Joe Smith now exists in the Marketing OU. Any group policies applied to the domain (`win2k.performance.net`), the User Accounts OU, or the Marketing OU are applied to Joe Smith.

 Tip

Group Policies are applied as follows:

If two policies are compatible (that is, they do not specify conflicting options), then both are applied.

If two policies are incompatible, the one highest in the tree is applied. In the example used here, if a policy applied to the User Accounts OU conflicts with a policy applied to the Marketing OU, the policy for User Accounts is applied.

Migrating Domains to Active Directory

Migrating a Windows NT 4.0 domain to a Windows 2000 Server Active Directory model is a relatively straightforward process. A Windows NT 3.51 and 4.0 domain model contains one primary domain controller (PDC) and several backup domain controllers (BDCs) in each domain. When changes are made on a BDC, the changes are replicated to the PDC before they are replicated to the other BDCs. The Windows 2000 Active Directory model does away with separate types of domain controllers. All domain controllers in a Windows 2000 directory can make changes to the directory and propagate it to the others.

Migration of a Windows NT 3.51 or 4.0 domain begins with upgrading the primary domain controller. Upgrading the primary and backup domain controllers involves running the Windows 2000 Server setup program from the CD. When this server is upgraded to Windows 2000, you must choose where this domain fits in the overall enterprise. It can be the root of a new tree in a new forest of domains, it can be the root of a new tree in an existing forest of domains, or it can be a child of an existing domain tree. If it is the only domain on the network, or the first domain to be converted to Windows 2000, it must be the root of a new domain tree in a new forest. The forest and trees of domains are a group who share common configurations and global catalogs, and have trust relationships.

Once the primary domain controller has been migrated to Windows 2000, the domain is what is known as a *mixed domain*. It has a combination of Windows 2000 domain controllers and Windows NT domain controllers. When the domain is mixed, nested groups are not supported, but the Active Directory administration tools are fully functional. The next step is to upgrade all backup domain controllers to Windows 2000. When a BDC is upgraded, the Active Directory automatically sets it up as a Windows 2000 domain controller and sets up the Active Directory replication. Once all domain controllers have been migrated, the domain can be changed to native mode. Once the domain is in native mode, it supports universal groups and nested groups. Here's how to change the domain to native mode:

1. Click Start ⇨ Programs ⇨ Administrative Tools ⇨ Active Directory Users and Computers.

2. Right-click the domain you want to change and then click Properties on the pop-up menu.

3. The domain Properties window shows the domain name, the downlevel domain name (the name seen by non-Windows 2000 clients), and the current domain operation mode. Click the Change Mode button on the domain Properties page. The domain Properties page is shown in Figure B-10.

4. A Properties dialog box verifies that you want to change to native mode. Once in native mode, a domain cannot be changed to mixed mode. You must be sure no more Windows NT domain controllers will be on the domain. Click Yes to continue.

The domain is now a native mode Windows 2000 domain. Universal groups and nested groups are now supported.

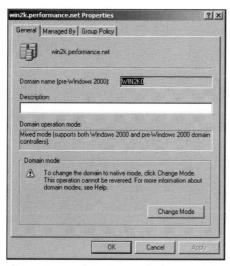

Figure B-10: Changing a Windows 2000 domain to native mode.

Group Policies

Group policies are the equivalent to policies generated by the Windows NT 4.0 policy editor but enable more granularity. They enable the administrator to set up items such as login and logout scripts, folder redirections, and desktop settings. The entire Windows 2000 user interface can be controlled and customized using group policies.

Here's how to access the Group Policy administration window:

1. Open the Active Directory Users and Groups Administration tool.

2. Right-click the organizational unit or domain for which you want to view group policies and select Properties from the pop-up menu. In this example, I apply a group policy to the Marketing OU.

3. Select the Group Policy tab.

From this screen, shown in Figure B-11, you can view the existing group policies, create and delete group policies, and edit properties.

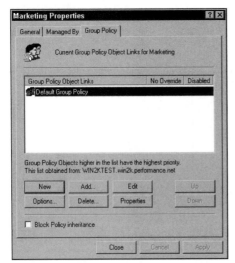

Figure B-11: The Active Directory Users and Groups tool domain Properties Group Policy tab.

To create a new group policy:

1. Click the New button from the Group Policy tab of the Properties window.

2. Give the new policy a name and press Enter ("Default Group Policy" is the name in the example).

3. Click the Edit button to begin configuring the policy.

The Group Policy configuration console opens as shown in Figure B-12. You can set a wide variety of configuration options for users and computers.

As shown in Figure B-13, each policy option has an Explain tab that describes the results of the policy. The options range from scripts that run at system startup and shutdown to enabling and disabling the addition and deletion of printers.

To limit the Marketing group so its users cannot see the Run command on the Start menu:

1. You should already be in the Group Policy administration tool after following the last two procedures. Double-click User Configuration, and then double-click Administrative Templates in the left window.

2. Click Start Menu & Taskbar. The available options appear in the Policy window on the right side.

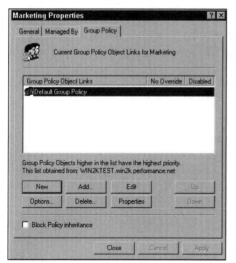

Figure B-12: The Group Policy configuration console with the User Configuration ⇨ Administrative Templates ⇨ Start Menu & Taskbar container open.

3. Right-click Remove Run menu from Start Menu and click Properties from the pop-up menu.

4. Click the Remove Run menu from Start Menu on the Policy tab of the Properties window.

5. Click OK to finish the procedure.

The Marketing group no longer sees the Run command in the Start menu.

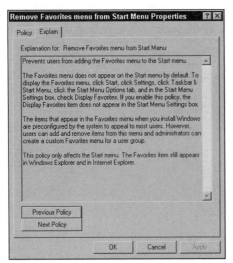

Figure B-13: The Explain tab of the Remove Favorites menu from Start Menu policy.

Summary

Active Directory is a highly scalable and configurable directory for cataloging all objects in a Windows 2000–based network. In this appendix, you learned:

✦ What is Active Directory?

✦ How do I install Active Directory?

✦ How do I administer the Active Directory?

✦ How do I migrate Windows NT 4.0 and 3.51 servers to Active Directory?

✦ What are group policies and how are they used?

✦   ✦   ✦

Windows 2000 Resource Guide

When it comes to computing technology and operating systems, a reference book such as *Windows 2000 Professional Bible* can only do so much. Anyone who has used Windows NT 4.0 has witnessed the parade of bug fixes, system patches, and service packs that accompanied that operating system. Network administrators wrung their hands as they faced the choice between a time-consuming and potentially dangerous service pack update and leaving their networks exposed to a known bug or deficiency.

Of course, the Internet is partly to blame for all this. (Judging from reports in the mainstream media, you'd think it was to blame for everything!) The ease with which an operating system can be updated and patched via freely available downloads tempts a lot of post-ship tinkering. Gone are those disciplined and well-paced product updates, replaced by weekend bug fixes.

Part of the issue is security. Ubiquitous, always-on Internet connections mean that the operating system must provide unprecedented levels of security. Your system — whether a corporate server or a home PC linked to the Internet via a cable modem — can fall under sustained and determined attack at any time. The high-profile coverage of products such as Back Orifice from the Cult of the Dead Cow (CDC) virtually ensures ongoing activity aimed at cracking open Microsoft's latest operating system.

Unfortunately, it falls to you to monitor, understand, and react to these issues and others. The Windows 2000 Resource Guide offers a quick-glance index of publications, Web sites, services, and users groups that you can access to stay abreast of Windows 2000-related issues. Among the areas this appendix addresses are the following.

- ✦ **Web site resources:** News, updates, file downloads, and advice
- ✦ **Print publications:** Newsletters and magazines
- ✦ **User groups:** Great for face-to-face interaction in your local area
- ✦ **Conference:** Where the industry meets and puts the latest on display

Web Sites

No surprise, the Web has become a critical resource for administrators and end users alike. You can find a vast amount of focused and timely content about Windows 2000 on the Internet, and that store of content is growing every day. Among the resources listed here are general-purpose industry news and information sites, in-depth Windows 2000 sites, user groups, and Internet newsgroups.

General purpose

PC Magazine Online: www.pcmag.com

The world's largest computing magazine extends its terrific coverage to the Web. Find the contents of every issue on this terrific site.

News.com: www.news.com

Day in and day out, News.com delivers broad, deep, and well-organized coverage of the computing and technology industries. From short-breaking news stories to in-depth feature series, News.com offers plenty to come back to. Links to hot stories on other Web sites add value.

ZDNet: www.zdnet.com/windows/

It could be the definitive technical portal site. I find ZDNet lacking a bit in structure and organization, but a little digging pays off handsomely. What would you expect when the content hails from such industry stalwarts as *PC Magazine* and *PC Week*?

TechWeb: www.techweb.com

Like ZDNet, another strong umbrella Web site, TechWeb aggregates the content from the many technical publications owned by technology publisher CMP Media, from *Computer Reseller News* to *Information Week*. A great portal for the technically minded.

Network World Fusion: www.nwfusion.com

The Web arm of IDG's *Network World*, Network World Fusion appeals to administrators and others looking for help maintaining large corporate networks.

In-depth sites

Windows Magazine: www.winmag.com/win2000

Windows Magazine's Windows 2000 SuperSite offers a well-organized store of tips, reviews, community feedback, and resources. Useful for the breadth of its content.

Sys Internals: www.sysinternals.com

Terrific Web-based source of cutting-edge utilities, technical information, and source code. A must-visit site on the Web for any advanced Windows 2000 user or administrator.

WUGNET: www.wugnet.com/wininfo/win2000/

The Web site of the Windows Users Group Network includes a specific area covering Windows 2000. Exhaustive, hands-on reviews, useful FAQs, and frequently updated news make this site a great general-purpose resource. Sign up for the WinInfo e-mail newsletter to get updates sent directly to your e-mail inbox.

Planet IT: Windows 2000: www.planetit.com/techcenters/windows_2000

From the folks who brought you TechWeb, this Windows 2000-specific site offers focused news story links, opinion pieces, file downloads, and more. The Ask the Experts area is a terrific place to dig around for solutions to what you suspect is a common problem.

BetaOS: www.betaos.com/

Good place to be if you're working with an OS-in-progress, the way many network administrators did with Windows 2000. Includes timely news, links to drivers and utilities, a message forum, and other information.

CNET Topic Center: Windows NT: www.cnet.com/Content/Reports/Special/NT/

Find links to all of CNET's coverage of Windows NT and Windows 2000 at this aggregate site.

NTBugTraq: ntbugtraq.ntadvice.com/

If you are tasked with keeping your network safe and secure, NT BugTraq is *the* place to be. Visit it early and often for real-time bug alerts and download the latest solutions in the NTFixes section. Subscribe to the BugTraq newsletter to get alerts sent to you daily.

WinPlanet: www.winplanet.com

Software, news, reports, and reviews.

WinStuff: www.winstuff.com

Find Registry tweaks, hands-on tips, software, and links to other Windows-related sites.

The All Windows Information Page: www.plazaone.com/allwindows/

Services all versions of Windows, but includes a dedicated Windows 2000 resource page at `www.plazaone/allwindows/winnt.htm`. This page includes links to press articles on Windows 2000, as well as information on Web pages and newsgroup locations.

Frank Condron's World O'Windows: www.conitech.com/windows/nt5.html

News updates, feature information, and Internet newsgroups specifically tailored to Windows 2000.

Windows 2000 at About.com: windowsnt.about.com

About.com is a large network of individually managed sites covering a specific area of interest. The Windows NT site for About.com is a good starting place to find useful links, weekly features, and helpful insights.

Microsoft Web resources

There is no lack of Microsoft-supplied resources. After all, Microsoft has a greater interest in helping companies move to Windows 2000 than anybody. Here is a list of helpful Web URLs addressing everything from basic overview information to in-depth migration advice and techniques.

Information regarding Microsoft operating systems

✦ Microsoft Windows Family home page: `www.microsoft.com/windows`

✦ Hardware Compatibility List: `www.microsoft.com/hcl`

General Windows 2000 information

✦ Windows 2000 Professional: `www.microsoft.com/windows/professional`

✦ Windows 2000 Server family: `www.microsoft.com/windows/server`

Directory of tested applications

✦ Windows 2000 Professional:
www.microsoft.com/windows/professional/deploy/compatible/

✦ Windows 2000 Server family:
www.microsoft.com/windows/server/deploy/compatible/

Deployment guides

✦ Windows 2000 Professional:
www.microsoft.com/windows/professional/Deploy/

✦ Windows 2000 Server family:
www.microsoft.com/windows/server/Deploy/

Technical resources

The Windows 2000 Professional site is broken into two sections, White Papers and Step-by-Step Guides, while the Server site offers much deeper discussions. Topics such as Active Directory, File and Print Services, and Security Services are all addressed in the Server section.

✦ Windows 2000 Professional:
www.microsoft.com/windows/professional/technical/default.asp

✦ Windows 2000 Server family:
www.microsoft.com/windows/server/technical/default.asp

Other important sites

✦ Microsoft TechNet: www.microsoft.com/technet/

This Web site and CD-ROM subscription program offers all sorts of in-depth Windows 2000 information for IT professionals.

✦ Windows 2000 Developer Center: msdn.microsoft.com/windows2000/

Get under the hood to solve problems or anticipate issues. This resource includes technical articles, specifications, compatibility requirements, and more.

✦ Microsoft Developer Network: msdn.microsoft.com/

Another terrific developer resource. Technical documentation and articles, tools, and information about upcoming tech events help you stay ahead of the learning curve.

✦ BackOffice: backoffice.microsoft.com/

If you're installing Windows 2000 Server edition operating systems, you may well be wrestling with Microsoft's server application products. This site offers detailed information about BackOffice applications and server suites, as well as useful downloads.

User Groups

User groups are a great way to do some face-to-face networking. The following list presents all the Windows NT-specific user groups listed under Yahoo's directory. In addition, thousands of general-purpose user groups address a broader range of issues, including Windows 2000. You can typically seek out these organizations by conducting a Web search based on your local area or by checking the local phone listings.

+ Albuquerque Windows NT User Group: www.lobo.net/~jheald/ntuser/ntuser.html

+ Anchorage Windows NT Users Group (AWNTUG): rmm.com/awntug/

+ Big Island NT Users Group: bintug.org/

+ Birmingham Windows NT User Group: www.bwntug.org/

+ BUGME—the Baltimore area Windows NT users group: www.techarchitects.com/BUGME/

+ French Windows NT User Group (FWNTUG): www.fwntug.org/

+ Interior Alaska Windows NT Users Group: www.iawntug.org/

+ Iowa NT User Group: nt-resources.idesignworks.com/

+ Japan Windows NT Users Group (JWNTUG): www.jwntug.or.jp/

+ Los Angeles Windows NT/Microsoft Networking User Group: www.lantug.org/

+ NT Engineering Association of Silicon Valley: www.ntea.net/

+ NT*Pro—association of Windows NT systems professionals: www.ntpro.org/

+ NTique—Windows NT networking support group in the Portland area: www.ntique.org/

+ Orange County NT Users Group: www.ocntug.org/

+ Orlando NT Professional Association: www.orlandont.org/

+ Plano BackOffice User Group: www.pbug.org/

+ Rocky Mountain Windows NT Users Group: www.rmwntug.org/

+ San Diego Windows NT User Group: www.sdwntug.org/

+ South Florida Windows NT Users Group—NeaT: www.pc-depot.com/neat/

+ Vancouver Windows NT User Group: www.vantug.com/

+ Wichita, Kansas NT Users Group: www.wichita.org/wntug/

✦ Windows NT Special Interest Group of CCS: `billslater.com/ntsig.htm`

✦ Windows NT Users Group of Indianapolis: `www.wintugi.org/`

Print Publications

One problem with the Web is that you can't take it with you (usually). Below is a list of top computing publications in print, along with the URL for subscription information.

✦ *PC Magazine:* `www.zdnet.com/zdsubs/pcmag/home.html`

✦ *PC World* Magazine: `www.pcworld.com/resource/subscribe/`

✦ *Dr. Dobbs Journal:* `www.ddj.com`

✦ *PC Computing:* `www.zdnet.com/zdsubs/pcc/shome.html`

✦ *Windows NT Magazine:* `www.winntmag.com`

✦ *Infoworld:* `www.iwsubscribe.com/`

✦ *PC Week:* `www.pub-serv.com/sf/zp/`

✦ *Computerworld:* `www.computerworld.com`

✦ *Network World:* `www.nwfusion.com/nw/subscribe.html`

Newsgroups

At press time, Windows 2000 was still in beta testing. Expect the number of Windows 2000 newsgroups to rise dramatically once the operating system is available on store shelves. To find new newsgroups, type the word **windows** in the filter text box of your e-mail client's newsgroup finder dialog box. You can then browse through the list of all Windows-related newsgroups, including those dedicated to Windows 2000.

Among the newsgroups you will find:

✦ `comp.os.ms-windows.networking.misc`: Addresses all sorts of network related issues.

✦ `comp.os.ms-windows.nt.setup`: Installing or upgrading with Windows 2000? The setup newsgroup is the place to start.

✦ `comp.os.ms-windows.nt.software`: The newsgroup to check out if you're worried about compatibility or wondering which applications to match with your new operating system.

Summary

There is no lack of online information regarding Windows 2000 and that's a good thing indeed. By touring some of these resources, you can access sites that address general industry news, focused technical content, and useful support services. Automatic e-mail updates and interactive forums and newsgroups fill out these valuable information sources.

Among the valuable resources you can draw on are the following:

✦ General-interest technical Web sites

✦ Focused Windows 2000 Web sites

✦ Microsoft's family of Windows 2000 Web sites

✦ Print publications

✦ Internet newsgroups and Web forums

✦ Windows NT and 2000 newsgroups

✦   ✦   ✦

What's on the CD-ROM

The CD-ROM in this book contains a raft of useful, entertaining, and valuable software that you can use to get the most out of your Windows 2000 PC. The disc contains a mix of *shareware* (software you can use on a trial basis before purchasing) and *freeware* (software you can use at no cost). Read the license agreements that come with each application to make sure you know if you need to pay for the software.

For those who run an operating system other than Windows 2000, you'll also find applications that imbue Windows 95 and NT 4.0 PCs with features found under Windows 2000.

A Word About Shareware

Before you install and use any of these applications, you should be aware that shareware and freeware are very different things. Freeware is software that you can install and run for as long as you like, without every paying a cent. Shareware, on the other hand, typically requires purchase after a certain trial period. Typically, the license agreement and readme file will spell out the approved trial usage, after which time you are required to purchase the software.

Why pay for software that's already installed and running on your PC? After all, in many cases, shareware authors rely on the honor system to ensure payment. In other cases, the software will either stop working after the trial period or will employ reminders that make using the software more difficult after the trial period is over. All that said, users should make a point to pay for the software they use. Shareware authors rely on honest use of their products to pay for future enhancements, bug fixes, and new product development. By paying for shareware, you help promote better, affordable solutions, while ensuring that you get full and convenient use of the product.

Applications on the CD-ROM

Company: JerMar Software
URL: www.jermar.com
Product(s): Tweaki, Profiler 2000

ProFILER 2000 allows you to save custom operating system settings. ProFILER 2000 will also save customizations and setup information made within Microsoft Office 97 and many popular e-mail and Web browser packages. Settings you spent hours getting just right can now be saved to a "profile" for safekeeping. ProFILER 2000 is also great for IT people who support multiple workstations. Now you can save a profile of a user's system so that when that call comes to fix a problem, you only need to restore the profile saved when the system was running smoothly.

Company: CoffeeCup
URL: www.coffeecup.com
Product(s): CoffeeCup HTML Editor, CoffeeCup Image Mapper++, CoffeeCup Direct FTP, CoffeeCup HTML Express, CoffeeCup StyleSheet Maker++, CoffeeCup GIF Animator, Applet Button Factory, Applet Headline Factory, Applet Marquee Wizard, Applet Navigation Factory, Applet Password Wizard, Applet Effects Factory

The Award Winning CoffeeCup HTML Editor++ is a full-featured HTML editor that includes Expresso FTP for uploading and downloading, an image gallery with quick-linking images, highlighted tags, and automatic image sizing. It comes with 30 background images, more than 175 animated GIFs, upwards of 140 Web icon graphics, 60 JavaScripts, a frame designer, and DHTML snippets. You can work on and test multiple pages at once. Other features include an image-previewing utility, a sound gallery, online help, and a step-by-step Web design guide and references for HTML 4.0 tags. During the installation process, you may receive the following warnings: "OLE2.DLL not valid" and "Unable to find LFFAX9ON.DLL." The installation, however, will continue and the program will work correctly.

Image Mapper++ includes a fully functional image map wizard, and enables users to attach links to different parts of an image. Image Mapper++ can map any noninterlaced GIF, interlaced GIF, standard JPEG, and progressive JPEG, as well as the first frame of an animated GIF. Users can choose from three different shape methods and use mouseover pop-up tags as well.

Do you have a Web page? Need to make a quick change? Get Direct FTP, the perfect drag and drop FTP program for all your Web maintenance needs. It will make your on-the-fly editing a breeze. Direct FTP can edit HTML on the server, preview images on the server, and zip your entire site all in one convenient easy-to-use program. It can keep commonly used code in a built-in Snippets Editor, and more! This handy utility is a must for any Webmaster who wants to make updating their Web site easy.

For any beginning Webmaster, creating your first Web Page can be frustrating. Not with CoffeeCup HTML Express. This streamlined Web Page Wizard walks you through the creation process. No experience necessary. With HTML Express adding images, links, text paragraphs, and bullet lists is a snap. Simply drag and drop the components into your Web Page. With CoffeeCup HTML Express, you can make a great looking page and have it online in minutes!

The CoffeeCup StyleSheet Maker++ allows you to easily create Cascading Style Sheets for your Web page to add Style, Alignment, and DHTML effects. You'll be able to achieve effects you can't get any other way, like overlap text, create links that aren't underlined, place image backgrounds in tables, and even create your own tags with custom functions you assign. This program will work for Windows NT 4.0 but not for Windows 2000. The installer looks for service pack 3 or above, which is not part of Windows 2000 at this date.

CoffeeCup GIF Animator allows you to easily create animated GIFs for your Web pages. Browse for images by previewing thumbnails, and then drag and drop images into your animation. CoffeeCup GIF Animator can convert JPEG and BMP graphics to GIF automatically, as well as import and export AVI files. HTML source is generated for easy insertion into Web pages.

Make cool Java buttons, easy scrolling headlines, banners, and Java navigation menus. Protect your pages, and create neat image effects. Do it all with the powerful tools provided by CoffeeCup.

Company: Windmill Point Software
URL: www.windmillpoint.com
Product(s): Resource Assistant, Dependency Assistant, Version Assistant, File Date Assistant

Company: Polybytes
URL: www.polybytes.com
Product(s): Polyview

PolyView is a fast and powerful image viewer, conversion, and printing utility for 32-bit Windows (95/98/NT). PolyView is designed to be easy and intuitive to use for beginners, but has the advanced image manipulation, printing, and management features needed for dealing with large image collections.

Company: XLink Technology, Inc.
URL: www.xlink.com
Product(s): Omni-NFS Enterprise, Omni-NFS Gateway/Dual Gateway

These products are compatible with Windows 2000 servers only and will not install on Windows 2000 Professional workstations. They are placed in a separtate For Servers folder.

Omni-NFS Enterprise is a comprehensive network solution for integrating Windows 2000/NT/98/95 PCs and UNIX (NFS) files and printers. It delivers the full power of NFS straight to your Windows/UNIX desktop for bidirectional connectivity.

The Omni-NFS Gateway allows a Windows 2000 or NT Server to act as a gateway between Windows-based workstations and NFS files/resources that utilize industry-standard NFS protocol. It achieves this by attaching itself to the NFS files/resources then shares the devices to the workstations as if the devices were its own. The gateway actually becomes a translator, translating NFS protocol to standard Microsoft Windows networking server message block (SMB) protocol. By doing so, system administrators have more control, users can gain access to UNIX files without having to learn anything new, Windows and UNIX users have transparent access to files without having to duplicate the files into their own stations, and security measures are easier to enforce since all individual workstation identities (UIDs) are mapped to NFS accounts. The Dual Gateway product creates a two-way street, allowing transparent, secure, and user-friendly access for Windows users to NFS/UNIX resources and vice versa.

Company: Extensis
URL: www.extensis.com
Product(s): Extensis Intellihance Pro 4.0 — Demo Version

Intellihance Pro 4.0 streamlines image enhancement and color correction to make it easy to make your images look their best. Split or repeat the fully customizable preview to compare up to 25 setting combinations at once. Intellihance Pro is perfect for enhancing images from any source, including digital cameras, flatbed and drum scanners, and original digital artwork.

Company: Blue Squirrel
URL: www.bluesquirrel.com
Product(s): WebSeeker, LegalSeeker, TechSeeker, WebWhacker, LinkSync

WebWhacker is the ultimate off-line browser! Put Web pages directly onto your hard drive, so you can view them offline at highly accelerated speeds when you want to view them.

In a single search, you can combine the knowledge base of over a hundred Internet search engines pinpointing the exact info you need with WebSeeker.

With LegalSeeker, in a single search you can tap into 40 legal search engines for the ultimate legal resource — case closed!

With TechSeeker, find drivers, software, technical solutions, & product info using 75+ online technical resources in one step!

Company: SmartDraw
URL: www.smartdraw.com
Product(s): SmartDraw Trial Edition

SmartDraw is the ideal choice for people who need to create professional-quality drawings quickly and simply, without having to learn a complex program. SmartDraw is an inexpensive and easy-to-use Windows program for drawing flowcharts, organizational charts, technical drawings, Web graphics, diagrams, and business presentations.

Company: Archgrove House
URL: www.archgrove.co.uk
Product(s): TransIT

Microsoft added an intriguing new feature to windows and menus under Windows 2000: translucency. TransIT is a freeware program that lets you set the translucency level of a Windows 2000 application window.

Company: Radient Software, Inc.
URL: www.radient.com
Product(s): Commnet

CommNet seamlessly integrates Internet Telnet client/server and modem dial-up capabilities into a fast, full-featured, easy-to-use application. New features in this Internet Telnet/data communications software application include SCO ANSI terminal emulation, scripting support, keyboard remapping, and a unique Telnet Host Mode Server feature that allows two end-users to communicate and transfer files directly over the Internet.

✦ ✦ ✦

Glossary

ACPI Industry specification that defines power-management capabilities and is supported by Windows 2000.

Active Directory The integrated directory service within Windows 2000 Server, Advanced Server, and Data Center that enables centralized management of user, group, and device properties.

ActiveX A set of technologies that enables software components to interact in a networked environment. ActiveX is frequently used to enable programmatic interaction over the Internet.

administrator The person responsible for assigning and managing network access, user accounts, passwords, and other areas of network operation. Administrator rights are frequently required to access key features under Windows 2000 Professional.

alignment Positioning of text relative to the left or right margin.

anchor position The beginning of the object or selection.

animated cursor A mouse pointer that includes movement.

argument A piece of additional information controlling how a program runs. Also known as a parameter.

attach To include a file with a message.

Audio Visual Interleave (AVI) Windows 98 video files in which the audio and video portions are both included, or interleaved, in the same file.

authentication The process of comparing a user's input with the name and password stored in an authorized list. Authentication is used to determine what resources a user may access.

Basic Input/Output System (BIOS) The lowest-level code that starts the system during boot time and manages transactions among devices. The BIOS is stored in read only memory (ROM) on the motherboard.

bitmap An image file in which all objects are part of a single object.

blind carbon copy (Bcc) A copy that the other recipients don't know about.

boot disk A disk you can use to start Windows 98.

boot partition The disk partition that contains Windows 2000 and its system files.

Boss key The key that quickly hides 3D Pinball, the Esc key.

bounding box An imaginary rectangular box as wide and as high as the object being drawn.

bullets Markers often seen at the left of a list of summary points.

cascading menu A menu that appears and offers additional choices when a menu item that has an arrow is selected.

certificate Used to authenticate and secure information exchange over the Internet, a certificate verifies the sender's identity. An issuing certificate authority distributes digitally signed certificates, which securely bind a public encryption key to the entity that holds the corresponding private encryption key.

client A computer or application that connects to or requests services from another computer or application. Web browsers, for example, are client applications that request information from servers over the Internet.

Clipboard A Windows 98 tool you can use to cut, copy, and paste objects.

color management A system used to produce consistent color output from a variety of input and output devices, such as printers, monitors, and scanners. A color management system (CMS) maps colors between different devices and translates between different color space definitions (such as RGB to CMYK) to enable accurate representations of color on different devices.

color profile Windows 2000 uses color profiles to translate the values of a color gamut for a specific device, such as a display or printer.

combo box A box that includes a list box and a text box.

command-line interface The MS-DOS window where you type commands. Also known as the prompt.

compound documents Documents containing data from a number of sources.

Compressed Volume File (CVF) A special file used by DriveSpace to create additional space on a disk by storing everything in a single, compressed file.

cookie A text file that contains information about a Web surfer's visits to Web sites.

cover page An extra sheet sent at the beginning of a fax.

cross-linked Multiple files that seem to be using the same disk space. At least one of each pair of cross-linked files will probably be unusable.

defragmentation The process of combining files on the hard disk that have been split up due to lack of contiguous disk space. Defragmentation helps speed file access and system responsiveness.

desktop theme A special collection of color schemes, wallpaper, animated cursors, and sounds in Plus!

destination disk The target disk.

device driver Software that allows the operating system and a hardware device to talk to each other. Hardware makers often release updated device drivers to add functionality, improve performance, or fix bugs.

Device Manager A useful administrative tool under Windows 2000 that allows the user to view and change device properties.

Digital Subscriber Line (DSL) Also known as ADSL (for Asynchronous DSL), xDSL, and other variants, DSL is a telephone system–based networking service that enables fast, digital online connections over existing copper wire.

Domain Name System (DNS) A name service for TCP/IP hosts that translates numeric IP addresses into user-friendly URLs and host names. The network administrator configures the DNS with the list of host names and IP addresses. A DNS Server contains the information for this service.

Distribution Media Format (DMF) Diskettes specially formatted to prevent them from being copied.

downloading Receiving files.

dragging Holding down the left mouse button while moving a selected object.

draw program A program that creates objects that can be stretched or moved independently of any other objects in the image.

dropping Releasing an object by letting up on the mouse button.

dual boot Describes a computer that contains two operating systems, either of which may be selected when the computer is first started. Windows 2000 is able to dual boot with a variety of different operating systems.

Dynamic Host Configuration Protocol (DHCP) A TCP/IP service protocol that automates the distribution of IP addresses to clients on the network. A DHCP server manages IP addresses, which client systems request when they log on. Useful for managing large pools of systems, where managing static IP addresses can become unwieldy.

ellipsis Three periods that follow a menu command indicating that a dialog box will appear when the command is selected.

embedding Placing an OLE object in a document.

emergency repair disk (ERD) A disk that contains information about current Windows 2000 system settings and enables recovery from a failed state. Emergency repair disks are created in the Windows 2000 Backup application.

encryption A means of protected data from unauthorized access by encoding the contents.

error-correcting file transfer protocol A method of breaking up files into relatively small pieces and verifying that each of those pieces is received properly to ensure that files are transferred properly.

event Something that can be assigned a sound, such as starting Windows 98, opening a menu, or closing a program.

extended partition A portion of a basic disk that can contain logical drives. Extended partitions must be used if you want to have more than four volumes on a basic disk.

File Allocation Table (FAT) The basic file system used by DOS and older versions of Windows to track the location of files on the hard disk. Windows 98, new versions of Windows 95, and Windows 2000 employ an advanced form of FAT, called FAT-32.

file system The scheme used by the operating system to read, write, and find files on the hard disk. FAT, FAT-32, and NTFS are all file systems available to Windows 2000.

file transfer protocol A method ensuring that files are transferred properly.

focus The dotted outline showing which dialog box element is currently active.

formatting The process of creating the electronic marks that allow your disk drives to write in the right places on a disk.

fragmented Stored in several noncontiguous pieces on a disk.

Graphics Device Interface (GDI) The basic graphics engine of Windows 2000, graphics cards interact with GDI to accelerate basic 2D graphics such as application windows, drop-down menus, and on-screen fonts.

Graphical User Interface or GUI ("gooey") The Windows 98 visual-style interface. In contrast, MS-DOS uses a command line interface or prompt.

Hardware Compatibility List (HCL) A list of systems and devices that are compatible with various Microsoft operating systems. Microsoft publishes a constantly updated HCL at www.microsoft.com/hcl.

hive A section of the Windows 2000 Registry that incorporates a discrete body of keys, subkeys, and values.

host drive The drive letter used to access the physical drive rather than the compressed drive.

hotkey Alt + the underlined character, which activates a menu command.

Hypertext Markup Language (HTML) The standard text-based language used to create Web pages. HTML tags are embedded into documents to signify formatting and other visual properties.

icon A small picture that represents a program or document.

indent Extra distance between the document margin and the paragraph margin.

in-place editing A temporary appearance change that allows use of a source application's toolbars so an object can edited without leaving the document.

insertion pointer The slowly blinking vertical line where new text will appear.

integrated drive electronics (IDE) A standard interface for disk-based storage devices on PCs. Most PC motherboards provide up to four available IDE device connections.

Infrared Data Association (IrDA) The organization that established an industry standard method for devices to connect over an infrared link. IrDA-compliant notebooks, printers, and other devices can trade data at up to 4 Mbps.

Integrated Services Digital Network (ISDN) An established circuit-switched connection service that provides digital dial-up connections. Typical ISDN service — called basic rate interface, or BRI — provides 128 Kbps of bandwidth. Faster primary rate interface (PRI) ISDN delivers up to 1.55 Mbps.

Internet Protocol (IP) The messenger protocol of TCP/IP. IP enables addressing and sending of IP packets over the Internet using a best-effort, connectionless delivery system.

IPX/SPX The transport protocols used in Novell NetWare networks.

Internet Service Provider (ISP) A company that provides access to the Internet.

invert A special effect in which each color is replaced by its complement.

junction point A physical point on the hard disk that points to data located at another location. Junction points are created when you create a mounted drive.

link A connection to another Web page.

linking Placing a reference to an OLE in a document.

local area network (LAN)' A group of computers or other devices located in relative proximity to each other (typically in the same building or perhaps a campus). Larger networks are called wide area networks (WAN) or metropolitan area networks (MAN).

log file Typically a text file that is created by Windows 2000, a device, or an application to provide a detailed list of activities for later review. Log files are a useful tool in ferreting out device conflicts and other problems.

lost file fragments Leftover pieces of files that are taking up space even though the file was deleted.

margin The distance printing begins from the edge of the paper.

master boot record The first sector on any hard disk, the MBR contains a small amount of executable code and the partition table. This table stores information about the disk's primary and extended partitions.

memory address The portion of system memory used by a device or application. Users can view memory address assignments for many devices from the Windows Device Manager.

mirror A copy of a disk volume used to provide redundancy for disk subsystems. If one mirror fails, another stored on a different disk can immediately step in.

mounted drive A drive that is attached to an empty folder on an NTFS volume. Mounted drives are assigned a label or name instead of a drive letter, enabling administrators to assign drive letters beyond the available 26 on a Windows 2000 system.

MS-DOS mode The operating mode in which your entire system is dedicated to running an MS-DOS program.

MS-DOS prompt The MS-DOS command line you use to issue DOS commands.

Musical Instrument Digital Interface (MIDI) A method of generating music using a synthesizer.

NETBEUI The native network protocol for Microsoft Networking, it is a fast protocol best suited for small networks of 1 to 200 clients.

network interface card (NIC) Also called a network adapter, the NIC is the hardware that connects the PC to the network.

NT file system (NTFS) The advanced file system native to Windows NT and Windows 2000; it supports file system recovery, file level compression and encryption, activity logging, and extremely large storage media.

Null modem cable A special cable that enables two PCs to talk directly to each other.

Object Linking and Embedding (OLE) A way to share data that allows you to create compound documents.

OLE client A program that can receive drag-and-drop information.

OLE server A program that can send drag-and-drop data.

packet An Open Systems Interconnection (OSI) network layer transmission unit. A packet contains both data and a header that includes an identification number, source and destination addresses, and error-control data.

paging file A hidden file on the hard disk that is used to store data and code that does not fit in main system memory. Also called virtual memory, the paging file is used to swap out and in data as it is needed.

paint program A graphics program that creates bitmap images.

parameter A piece of additional information that controls how a program runs. Also known as an argument.

partition The portion of a physical disk that functions like a physically separate disk, with its own drive letter.

password A secret word that allows access to a resource such as a folder.

pica A typographic measurement approximately one twelfth of an inch.

pixel A unit of measure of screen resolution. Short for picture element.

point A typographic measurement. There are approximately 72 points in an inch.

Point-to-Point protocol (PPP) A set of industry-standard framing and authentication protocols that enable connections to remote servers. PPP negotiates configuration parameters for networking protocols such as TCP/IP, IPX, and AppleTalk. PPP is the standard method for linking to Internet service providers.

Point-to-Point Tunneling Protocol (PPTP) Used for virtual private networks (VPNs), PPTP enables remote users to securely access networks over the Internet using a standard Internet connection. PPTP encapsulates different protocol-based traffic inside encrypted IP packets, preventing others from accessing the data. Encapsulated protocol traffic is revealed at the destination, enabling native access to networks over the IP-based Internet.

polygon A multisided object.

protocol A set of rules and conventions for sending information over a network. Protocols enable disparate systems and devices to interoperate over the Internet and other networks.

public key encryption A method of encryption that uses two mathematically-related encryption keys — a private key and a public key, which is accessible to others. A sender uses the receiver's public key to encrypt a method, enabling the receiver to use its private key to decipher the message. Because no one else has this private key, the message is incomprehensible to other parties.

recovery console A command-line interface that makes it possible to repair a Windows 2000 computer that is otherwise inoperative. The Recovery Console can start and stop services, read and write data on a local drive, repair a master boot record (MBR), and format drives.

redundant array of independent disks (RAID) A series of methods for enabling fault-tolerant disk subsystems. There are six RAID levels, of which Windows 2000 supports three: Level 0 (striping), Level 1 (mirroring), and Level 5 (RAID-5).

refresh rate The frequency with which a CRT monitor repaints the image onscreen. At refresh rates of less than 70 times per second (or 70 hertz), the fading of pixels between refreshes becomes perceptible, yielding an annoying flicker. Note that flat panel displays do not require this refresh operation.

Registry A special database Windows 98 uses to keep track of a lot of important information about your system. If the Registry is damaged, you may not be able to use your computer.

restore The process of making backed-up files available for use.

root directory The ultimate parent of all the folders on a disk.

Ruler The measurement line just above the text window in a word processor.

sampling rate The number of times per second sound is recorded.

scrap A piece of a document saved on the desktop.

search engine A service that indexes Web pages.

serial line Internet protocol (SLIP) An older protocol that was once widely used for remote access to the Internet. Today, SLIP is often used for remote access to UNIX servers.

server A system that provides services and data to other computers.

shortcut A copy of an icon used to access a program or document.

skewing Leaning a selection at an angle.

source disk The original disk used in a copy operation.

stretching Making a selection grow or shrink by a percentage.

tabs Fixed points used to specify precise text positioning.

taskbar The gray bar along the bottom of the Windows 2000 display. The taskbar contains the Start button as well as buttons that indicate open programs or documents.

telephony API (TAPI) Application programming interface (API) that enables access to telephony and network services. Programs use TAPI to dial, answer, and route telephone calls on PBXs, modems, fax machines, and other telephony devices. TAPI 3.0 adds support for Internet Protocol (IP) telephony, which other programs use to transmit, route, and control real-time audio and video signals over the Internet.

terminal program A program that makes your PC into a communications terminal so you can upload and download files.

title bar The horizontal bar along the top of a window that contains the window name. Often, the program icon and the Maximize, Minimize, and Close buttons can be found on the title bar.

toggle A command that changes states from selected to deselected, or deselected to selected, each time the command is selected.

Tooltips Hints that appear when the mouse pointer is you held over toolbar buttons.

Transmission Control Protocol/Internet Protocol (TCP/IP) The standard set of protocols used to enable communication over the Internet.

TrueType fonts Scalable fonts.

uploading Sending files.

Uniform Resource Locator (URL) The address for a Web page.

Universal Serial Bus (USB) The Plug-and-Play connector used for external devices such as mice, keyboards, scanners, and monitor-top cameras.

virtual desktop An area larger than the actual monitor display provided by some display adapters.

virtual memory Space on the hard disk used to hold open data or programs that cannot fit in main system memory. Windows 2000 creates a file for virtual memory—called a paging file—on the hard disk.

virtual private network Secure form of point-to-point communication over the Internet, typically used for remote network access. Encryption is used to scramble the contents of data packets and form secure "tunnels" that prevent third parties from seeing connections.

wave files Windows 98 sound files that are simply a digital recording of sounds.

Web browser A program that enables a Web surfer to view the contents of pages on the World Wide Web, the graphical portion of the Internet.

word wrap The action used to display lines longer than the width of the window.

World Wide Web The graphical portion of the Internet. Often simply called the Web.

write-protect slider A small plastic rectangle on the diskette that prevents your PC from writing anything on this diskette until you move the slider back to cover the hole.

Index

continued

IDG Books Worldwide, Inc.
End-User License Agreement

<u>READ THIS</u>. You should carefully read these terms and conditions before opening the software packet(s) included with this book ("Book"). This is a license agreement ("Agreement") between you and IDG Books Worldwide, Inc. ("IDGB"). By opening the accompanying software packet(s), you acknowledge that you have read and accept the following terms and conditions. If you do not agree and do not want to be bound by such terms and conditions, promptly return the Book and the unopened software packet(s) to the place you obtained them for a full refund.

1. **<u>License Grant</u>.** IDGB grants to you (either an individual or entity) a nonexclusive license to use one copy of the enclosed software program(s) (collectively, the "Software") solely for your own personal or business purposes on a single computer (whether a standard computer or a workstation component of a multiuser network). The Software is in use on a computer when it is loaded into temporary memory (RAM) or installed into permanent memory (hard disk, CD-ROM, or other storage device). IDGB reserves all rights not expressly granted herein.

2. **<u>Ownership</u>.** IDGB is the owner of all right, title, and interest, including copyright, in and to the compilation of the Software recorded on the disk(s) or CD-ROM ("Software Media"). Copyright to the individual programs recorded on the Software Media is owned by the author or other authorized copyright owner of each program. Ownership of the Software and all proprietary rights relating thereto remain with IDGB and its licensers.

3. **<u>Restrictions On Use and Transfer</u>.**

   (a) You may only (i) make one copy of the Software for backup or archival purposes, or (ii) transfer the Software to a single hard disk, provided that you keep the original for backup or archival purposes. You may not (i) rent or lease the Software, (ii) copy or reproduce the Software through a LAN or other network system or through any computer subscriber system or bulletin-board system, or (iii) modify, adapt, or create derivative works based on the Software.

   (b) You may not reverse engineer, decompile, or disassemble the Software. You may transfer the Software and user documentation on a permanent basis, provided that the transferee agrees to accept the terms and conditions of this Agreement and you retain no copies. If the Software is an update or has been updated, any transfer must include the most recent update and all prior versions.

4. **<u>Restrictions on Use of Individual Programs</u>.** You must follow the individual requirements and restrictions detailed for each individual program in Appendix D of this Book. These limitations are also contained in the

individual license agreements recorded on the Software Media. These limitations may include a requirement that after using the program for a specified period of time, the user must pay a registration fee or discontinue use. By opening the Software packet(s), you will be agreeing to abide by the licenses and restrictions for these individual programs that are detailed in Appendix D and on the Software Media. None of the material on this Software Media or listed in this Book may ever be redistributed, in original or modified form, for commercial purposes.

5. **Limited Warranty.**

(a) IDGB warrants that the Software and Software Media are free from defects in materials and workmanship under normal use for a period of sixty (60) days from the date of purchase of this Book. If IDGB receives notification within the warranty period of defects in materials or workmanship, IDGB will replace the defective Software Media.

(b) **IDGB AND THE AUTHORS OF THE BOOK DISCLAIM ALL OTHER WARRANTIES, EXPRESS OR IMPLIED, INCLUDING WITHOUT LIMITATION IMPLIED WARRANTIES OF MERCHANTABILITY AND FITNESS FOR A PARTICULAR PURPOSE, WITH RESPECT TO THE SOFTWARE, THE PROGRAMS, THE SOURCE CODE CONTAINED THEREIN, AND/OR THE TECHNIQUES DESCRIBED IN THIS BOOK. IDGB DOES NOT WARRANT THAT THE FUNCTIONS CONTAINED IN THE SOFTWARE WILL MEET YOUR REQUIREMENTS OR THAT THE OPERATION OF THE SOFTWARE WILL BE ERROR FREE.**

(c) This limited warranty gives you specific legal rights, and you may have other rights that vary from jurisdiction to jurisdiction.

6. **Remedies.**

(a) IDGB's entire liability and your exclusive remedy for defects in materials and workmanship shall be limited to replacement of the Software Media, which may be returned to IDGB with a copy of your receipt at the following address: Software Media Fulfillment Department, Attn.: *Windows 2000 Professional Bible*, IDG Books Worldwide, Inc., 7260 Shadeland Station, Ste. 100, Indianapolis, IN 46256, or call 1-800-762-2974. Please allow three to four weeks for delivery. This Limited Warranty is void if failure of the Software Media has resulted from accident, abuse, or misapplication. Any replacement Software Media will be warranted for the remainder of the original warranty period or thirty (30) days, whichever is longer.

(b) In no event shall IDGB or the authors be liable for any damages whatsoever (including without limitation damages for loss of business profits, business interruption, loss of business information, or any other pecuniary loss) arising from the use of or inability to use the Book or the Software, even if IDGB has been advised of the possibility of such damages.

(c) Because some jurisdictions do not allow the exclusion or limitation of liability for consequential or incidental damages, the above limitation or exclusion may not apply to you.

7. **U.S. Government Restricted Rights**. Use, duplication, or disclosure of the Software by the U.S. Government is subject to restrictions stated in paragraph (c)(1)(ii) of the Rights in Technical Data and Computer Software clause of DFARS 252.227-7013, and in subparagraphs (a) through (d) of the Commercial Computer—Restricted Rights clause at FAR 52.227-19, and in similar clauses in the NASA FAR supplement, when applicable.

8. **General**. This Agreement constitutes the entire understanding of the parties and revokes and supersedes all prior agreements, oral or written, between them and may not be modified or amended except in a writing signed by both parties hereto that specifically refers to this Agreement. This Agreement shall take precedence over any other documents that may be in conflict herewith. If any one or more provisions contained in this Agreement are held by any court or tribunal to be invalid, illegal, or otherwise unenforceable, each and every other provision shall remain in full force and effect.

my2cents.idgbooks.com

Register This Book — And Win!

Visit **http://my2cents.idgbooks.com** to register this book and we'll automatically enter you in our fantastic monthly prize giveaway. It's also your opportunity to give us feedback: let us know what you thought of this book and how you would like to see other topics covered.

Discover IDG Books Online!

The IDG Books Online Web site is your online resource for tackling technology — at home and at the office. Frequently updated, the IDG Books Online Web site features exclusive software, insider information, online books, and live events!

10 Productive & Career-Enhancing Things You Can Do at www.idgbooks.com

- Nab source code for your own programming projects.

- Download software.

- Read Web exclusives: special articles and book excerpts by IDG Books Worldwide authors.

- Take advantage of resources to help you advance your career as a Novell or Microsoft professional.

- Buy IDG Books Worldwide titles or find a convenient bookstore that carries them.

- Register your book and win a prize.

- Chat live online with authors.

- Sign up for regular e-mail updates about our latest books.

- Suggest a book you'd like to read or write.

- Give us your 2¢ about our books and about our Web site.

You say you're not on the Web yet? It's easy to get started with IDG Books' *Discover the Internet,* available at local retailers everywhere.

CD-ROM Installation Instructions

This CD-ROM includes all the installation files, documentation, and licensing information for the bundled applications. To install an application, simply launch the Shareware Installation Program. By default, Windows 2000, Windows 95/98, and Windows NT will automatically launch the applet when you insert the CD-ROM into the drive.

If the AutoRun feature is disabled, you can launch the applet by browsing the CD-ROM contents in a Windows Explorer or browser window. Double click the CDSETUP.EXE file. The application window will appear.

To install a program, select the desired program in the Choose a program list box. You will see the program name, the author or company name, and a complete description appear in the boxes at the bottom of the application window. To install the selected program, click the Install button. The selected application's installation routine will run. Follow the steps onscreen to setup the program.

In some cases, you can run programs directly from the CD-ROM, without updating the Windows Registry or going through a setup routine. For programs that allow this option, the Run from CD button will become active. Clicking the button will run the application from the CD-ROM.